Explicit quotations from the Jewish Scriptures play a vital role in several of the apostle Paul's letters to struggling Christian congregations. In most cases the wording of these quotations differs markedly from all known versions of the biblical text. Studies of Paul's use of Scripture routinely note the problem and suggest possible solutions, but none to date has made this phenomenon the primary object of investigation. The present study aims to remedy this deficiency with a careful examination of the way Paul and other ancient authors handled the wording of their explicit quotations. In drawing general conclusions, Dr. Stanley examines the broader social environment that made "interpretive renderings" a normal and accepted part of the literary landscape of antiquity.

SOCIETY FOR NEW TESTAMENT STUDIES

MONOGRAPH SERIES

General Editor: G. N. Stanton

69

PAUL AND THE LANGUAGE OF SCRIPTURE

Paul and the language of Scripture

Citation technique in the Pauline Epistles and contemporary literature

CHRISTOPHER D. STANLEY
Hastings College

CAMBRIDGE UNIVERSITY PRESS

Published by the Press Syndicate of the University of Cambridge
The Pitt Building, Trumpington Street, Cambridge CB2 1RP
40 West 20th Street, New York, NY 10011-4211, USA
10 Stamford Road, Oakleigh, Victoria 3166, Australia

© Cambridge University Press 1992

First published 1992

Printed and bound in Great Britain by
Woolnough Bookbinding, Irthlingborough, Northants

A catalogue record for this book is available from the British Library

Library of Congress cataloguing in publication data

Stanley, Christopher D.
Paul and the language of Scripture: citation technique in the
Pauline Epistles and contemporary literature / Christopher D. Stanley.
   p.   cm.
Revision of the author's thesis (Ph.D.) – Duke University, 1990.
Includes bibliographical references and index.
ISBN 0 521 41925 5
1. Bible. N.T. Epistles of Paul – Relation to the Old Testament.
2. Bible. O.T. – Quotations in the New Testament.
3. Bible. N.T. Epistles of Paul – Language, style.
4. Quotation.   5. Literature, Ancient – History and criticism.   I. Title.
BS2655.R32S73   1992   91-39844
227'.06–dc20   CIP

ISBN 0 521 41925 5 hardback

CE

CONTENTS

PREFACE

Ancient authors relied far more on the works of their predecessors than one would ever guess from a study of their explicit quotations. The same holds true for modern scholars who have the benefit of computerized reference systems and automatic footnotes to ease their task.

The present work is a slightly revised version of a Ph.D. dissertation submitted to Duke University in the summer of 1990. Many of those who have contributed the most to this project would never find mention in the footnotes. Special thanks are due to Dr. Moody Smith, my adviser, who allowed me to pursue my interests well beyond the usual limits of a Duke dissertation. His own studies in early Christian exegesis made him an invaluable resource at numerous points along the way. Dr. Melvin Peters, in a class on the Septuagint, was the first to suggest that I explore Paul's use of the Greek biblical text. His faith in my abilities has been a constant source of encouragement. Dr. Orval Wintermute shared the fruit of years of careful research as we examined the biblical exegesis of the Qumran community and the Jewish "pseudepigrapha." Discussions with friends and colleagues likewise helped to hone my thinking in a number of key areas.

Thanks are also due to Dr. Graham Stanton for accepting this volume for publication in the SNTS series, and to Alex Wright and his colleagues at Cambridge University Press for handling a difficult manuscript with skill and aplomb. An earlier version of the section on citation technique at Qumran (chapter 8) was presented at the Annual Meeting of the Society of Biblical Literature in Anaheim, California, in November 1989. A slightly longer version of chapter 7 appeared in *Novum Testamentum* 32 (1990), 48–78, and is used here with the kind permission of the publishers.

Two other people deserve special mention for their support in the years leading up to the completion of this study. To Dr. John

Nolland, now Vice Principal at Trinity College, Bristol, goes the credit for introducing me to the world of New Testament studies. His love for learning and patient attention to detail have been an inspiration and a model to me throughout my scholarly career. To my wife, Laurel, is due an immeasurable load of gratitude for the support and encouragement that she has given me through sixteen years of marriage. This book is dedicated to the two of them.

ABBREVIATIONS

Abbreviations follow the system set forth in the *Journal of Biblical Literature* 107 (1988), 583–96, with the following additions:

Brooke–McLean   Brooke, Alan England, Norman McLean, and Henry St. J. Thackeray (eds.), *The Old Testament in Greek* (Cambridge University Press, 1906–40)

Field   Field, Frederick (ed.), *Origenis Hexaplorum quae supersunt*, 2 vols. (Oxford: Clarendon, 1867, 1875; repr., Hildesheim: G. Olms, 1964)

Göttingen LXX   Academia Litterarum Gottingensis, *Septuaginta: Vetus Testamentum Graecum* (Göttingen: Vandenhoeck and Ruprecht, 1931–)

Hatch & Redpath   Hatch, Edwin, and Henry A. Redpath, *A Concordance to the Septuagint*, 3 vols. (Oxford: Clarendon, 1897–1906; repr., Grand Rapids: Baker, 1987)

Holmes–Parsons   Holmes, A. Roberto, and Jacobus Parsons (eds.), *Vetus Testamentum Graecum cum variis lectionibus*, 5 vols. (Oxford: Clarendon, 1798–1827)

Jastrow   Jastrow, Marcus, *A Dictionary of the Targumim, the Talmud Babli and Yerushalmi, and the Midrashic Literature*, 2 vols. (London: Luzac and Co., 1903; New York: G. P. Putnam's Sons, 1903; repr., New York: Judaica Press, 1971)

Strack–Billerbeck   Strack, Hermann L., and Paul Billerbeck, *Kommentar zum Neuen Testament aus Talmud und Midrasch*, 6 vols. (Munich: Beck, 1922–61)

Tischendorf   Tischendorf, Constantinus (ed.), *Novum Testamentum Graece*, 2 vols. (Leipzig: Giesecke and Devrient, 1869–72)

PART I

The issues

1

DEFINING THE ISSUES

1. Introduction

The practice of incorporating earlier materials into the body of a later composition is as old as literacy itself. Where the language of the earlier source text is used to advance the literary or rhetorical purposes of the later author, the technique is termed "quotation" or "citation."[1] Quotations can be used to provide authoritative grounding for a questionable assertion, to illustrate a point made elsewhere in more prosaic form, to embellish the style of an independent composition, or simply to impress potential readers with an author's literary knowledge. Western literature is replete with echoes of long-forgotten works whose language thus remains part of the living literary heritage of the culture.

As used in the present study, the term "citation technique" refers to a relatively narrow and technical aspect of this broader phenomenon of "quotation." The word "technique" is employed here in the sense of the Greek τέχνη, designating the practical means by which a particular project is carried out.[2] The issue here is not how faithfully a given citation adheres to the sense of its original context, nor how the older language functions in its new rhetorical setting, but rather the mechanics of the citation process itself. Included under this heading are such practical matters as whether an author quotes from memory or from some sort of written text, what cues

---

[1] Though differences in meaning can be established under certain circumstances, the terms "quotation" and "citation" have become practically synonymous in normal English usage (see *Webster's New Universal Unabridged Dictionary*, 2nd edn), and will be used interchangeably in the present study. The term "later author" refers to the person who reproduces the wording of an earlier source within a new composition.

[2] Cf. LSJ, s.v. τέχνη, III: "an art or craft, i.e. a set of rules, system or method of making or doing." Socrates (according to Plato) used the term to deride the practical pursuits of the Sophists over against his own concern for pure knowledge (γνῶσις).

the author uses to signal the presence of a citation, how quotations are ordered within the primary composition, and how the author handles the wording of his source text.[3] The latter question is especially important for the present study.

The term "citation" is also used in a more restricted sense here than in most other studies. The question of what constitutes a "citation" is one of the most controverted issues in the modern study of ancient quotations.[4] For now it will suffice to note that the term "citation" is limited here to those places where the author's appeal to an outside source is so blatant that any attentive reader would recognize the secondary character of the materials in question.[5] An inquiry into an author's "citation technique" will therefore focus on the mechanics by which the author attempts to integrate the language of his source text into an entirely new rhetorical and linguistic context, as seen in his explicit quotations.

2. A confusion of voices

Very little reading is required to discover what widely divergent explanations have been put forward by modern investigators to account for the seemingly cavalier way in which the apostle Paul handles the wording of his biblical quotations. This multiplication of theories can be traced in part to the vagaries of the materials themselves. While the bulk of Paul's quotations are marked by some sort of formal introductory expression ("as it is written," "Scripture says," etc.), there remain numerous places where Paul reproduces the wording of the Jewish Scriptures with little or no sign to his readers that a quotation was ever intended.[6] Investigators who take

---

[3] The use of the masculine gender when referring to ancient authors here and elsewhere is both intentional and unavoidable, since it appears that all of the documents examined here were composed by males.

[4] The whole issue will be examined more fully in chap. 2.

[5] In practical terms, this means passages that (a) are introduced by an explicit citation formula ("as it is written," etc.); (b) are accompanied by a clear interpretive gloss; or (c) stand in clear syntactical tension with their present linguistic environment. The justification for this narrow approach is set forth in chap. 2.

[6] The question of which of these unmarked texts represent genuine "quotations" has divided students of Paul to this day (cf. the divergent lists in the studies by Ellis, Longenecker, Smith, and Koch listed in the bibliography). Even the Nestle and UBS editions of the Greek New Testament differ over the presence of citations in such places as Rom 2.6, 4.9, 4.23, 9.20, 11.2, 1 Cor 9.10, 14.25, 15.25, 2 Cor 3.16, 9.7, 9.10, and Gal 2.16. The Nestle text is typically the more "liberal" of the two in such cases, accepting the citation character of all but Rom 4.9 and Gal 2.16. The problem of identifying Pauline citations is discussed at length in chap. 2.

these verses into account must then decide where to draw the line
between genuine "quotations" and other less immediate forms of
engagement with the biblical text such as "paraphrase," "allusion,"
and "reminiscence." Estimates range from less than a hundred to
several hundred "quotations" in Paul's letters, depending on how
the researcher resolves these matters of definition.[7]

Additional problems arise from the variety of situations in which
the materials are employed. All of the passages in question appear in
a series of letters addressed to Christian churches of diverse backgrounds and varying levels of maturity, each with its own special
relation to the apostle and each facing a unique set of problems. In
some instances a single verse is cited in isolation, while in other
places the texts are arrayed in clusters or as part of a composite unit.
The reasons behind Paul's appeals to Scripture likewise vary, from
offering authoritative grounding for a specific theological pronouncement, to illustrating a type of behavior that the readers are
encouraged to imitate or avoid, to emphasizing a key element in a
developing argument. Failure to take these differences into account
has led many a researcher to oversimplify the issues at stake.

Complicating the task still further are various unresolved questions concerning the status of the underlying biblical texts (both
Greek and Hebrew) in Paul's day. Here, too, the complexities of the
evidence have often been underestimated by students of Paul's
quotations. For those more familiar with the problems, on the other
hand, the temptation has been to despair of all efforts to distinguish
between a genuine authorial adaptation and the use of a deviant text
in those places where the language of Paul's quotations appears to
diverge from the "standard" wording of his ancestral Scriptures.[8]

Nevertheless, the diversity of opinions that investigators have
entertained concerning the way Paul handled the wording of his
quotations cannot be attributed entirely to the irregularity of the

---

[7] The most extensive lists appear in W. Dittmar, *Vetus Testamentum in Novo: Die
alttestamentlichen Paralleles des Neuen Testaments im Wortlaut der Urtexte und der
Septuaginta* (Göttingen: Vandenhoeck, 1903) and Eugen Hühn, *Die alttestamentlichen Citate und Reminiscenzen im Neuen Testamente*, 2 vols. (Freiburg: Mohr,
1899–1900).

[8] The use of the word "standard" in this connection is of course highly anachronistic, since the texts of both the Greek and Hebrew Bibles remained relatively fluid
throughout the period in question (see chap. 2). As used here (and throughout the
present study), the word "standard" refers to those editions of the biblical text that
eventually came to be regarded as normative within the Jewish synagogue and the
Christian church respectively – the Masoretic Hebrew text and the Greek "Septuagint" as it appears in the great uncials (ℵ, A, B) of the fourth and fifth centuries.

materials. Deeper issues have in fact set the tone and agenda for the debate in this area until fairly recent days. Many of the earlier modern studies were carried out with the express intention of either disparaging or defending the overall veracity of the New Testament authors by examining how faithfully they adhered to the wording and sense of their biblical quotations. Against those who sought to impugn the apostle's integrity on this score, the orthodox defenders of Paul repeatedly affirmed the fundamental reliability of his citations with regard to both the sense and the language of the biblical text. Typical of these earlier studies were numerous attempts to reconcile the wording of Paul's Greek citations with that of their presumed Hebrew *Vorlage*.[9] As further studies made it increasingly clear that Paul had drawn his quotations from the Greek "Septuagint" with little or no recourse to the Hebrew, the attention of the apologists turned to demonstrating the faithfulness of the Septuagint to the original sense of the Hebrew, at least in those passages cited by the apostle Paul.[10] With this shift in strategy came the call to explain a whole series of instances where Paul's quotations appeared to diverge from the language of both the Greek and Hebrew texts of Scripture. Out of this new round of activity arose a number of judgments that soon came to be regarded as axiomatic in the field, e.g. that Paul normally quoted loosely from memory, though without straying from the basic sense of the (Hebrew) biblical text; that he sometimes "corrected" the wording of his Greek *Vorlage* to accord with his own reading of the Hebrew original; and that he drew at least some of his quotations from Greek, Hebrew, or Aramaic biblical texts no longer extant.[11] Only in more recent times has it occurred to Paul's defenders to challenge the basic notion that the purposeful adaptation of a citation must

---

[9] Though lambasted by conservatives in his own day, William Whiston's attempts (*An Essay Toward Restoring the True Text of the Old Testament* (London: J. Senex, 1722)) to show that the New Testament authors always quoted correctly from a reliable Hebrew text that had been corrupted by Jewish leaders in the second century C.E. (see further below) only carried the conservative argument to its logical conclusion.

[10] Argued as early as 1650 by L. Capellus ("Quaestiones de locis parallelis Veteris et Novi Testamenti," in *Critica sacra* (Paris: S. et G. Cramoisy, 1650), 443–557), the idea that Paul quoted primarily from the Septuagint was finally established as one of the "assured results" of nineteenth-century biblical scholarship through the careful studies of G. Roepe (*De Veteris Testamenti locrum in apostolorum libris allegatione* (n.p., 1827) and especially Emil Kautzsch, *De Veteris Testamenti locis a Paulo Apostolo allegatis* (Leipzig: Metzger und Wittig, 1869).

[11] Each of these explanations is discussed further below.

somehow reflect a measure of dishonesty or even moral turpitude on the part of the apostle.[12]

With these debates in the background, it becomes easier to understand how certain explanations of Paul's use of Scripture have come to be hallowed over the years through frequent repetition. But these earlier conflicts cannot begin to account for the differing judgments of more recent investigators for whom apologetic concerns have been removed (for the most part) to a decidedly secondary position. At this point one must begin to ask more fundamental questions about the way researchers have typically envisioned their task in this area. Although it has become common for broader treatments of Paul's use of Scripture to offer at least passing remarks on the subject of how Paul handled the wording of his quotations, it seems that no monograph has ever been published that deals exclusively with this issue.[13] Equally hard to come by are any systematic examinations of how Paul's citation technique compares with the practices of other writers in the ancient world. What one sees instead is a series of theologically motivated studies whose focus

[12] An early exception was the German Johann Carpzov (*A Defense of the Hebrew Bible*, trans. Moses Marcus (London: Bernard Lintot, 1729)), whose forward-looking views deserve extended quotation: "Sometimes the Strength of the Argument, as taken rather from the Sense than from the Words, obliged them [the New Testament authors] to recede from the strict Tenor of the Words in the Original: Sometimes Brevity required it, when Things were to be summarily mentioned, just as much as would serve the Purpose: Sometimes a fuller Illustration that was to be added to the Words of the Old Testament by way of Explication, required it ... Sometimes the Application of a Testimony to the present Purpose, which might be properly made by changing the Words of the Prophecy a little: Sometimes a synonymous Expression wanted to be unfolded and explain'd ... Finally, at other times we need look no farther than the absolute Freedom and good Pleasure of the Holy Ghost, according to which he thought proper to substitute one Word in place of another; which ought so much the less to be wondered at or blamed, as it is a very common Thing in Quotations of this Kind, whether sacred or prophane [sic], sometimes only to give the Sense in different and fewer Words; sometimes to repeat the very same Words, but turn'd a little to our Design and Purpose, and accommodated to the Connexion, yet without incurring the Charge of Corruption ..." (111–12).

[13] The closest to a monograph treatment is probably Emil Kautzsch's 1869 Leipzig dissertation (see note 10), though Kautzsch's primary concern is to establish the nature of Paul's *Vorlage* and not to examine the way he handled the wording of his quotations. The roughly contemporary study by James Scott (*Principles of New Testament Quotation*, 2nd edn (Edinburgh: T. and T. Clark, 1877)) includes a number of useful comments on the citation technique of the New Testament authors as a whole, but none specifically on Paul. Joseph Bonsirven's *Exégèse rabbinique et exégèse paulinienne* (Paris: Beauchesne, 1939), though primarily a comparison of exegetical methods, includes a brief discussion of how Paul and the rabbis handled the wording of their quotations (327–45). The recent discussion by Dietrich-Alex Koch (*Die Schrift als Zeuge des Evangeliums* (Tübingen: Mohr, 1986), 102–98), while not a separate monograph, is by far the best treatment to date.

remains fixed on such ideological questions as how Paul the Christian viewed his ancestral Scriptures and what broader principles guided his application of the biblical text to the concerns of his churches. Comparisons with contemporary literature abound at this level, including the usual remarks about how Paul's exegetical methods relate to the seven rules of Hillel, the "contemporizing" hermeneutic of Qumran, and the allegorical interpretations of Philo. Only rarely, however, does one find even a brief discussion of such technical questions as: what differentiates a "citation" from other levels of engagement with the biblical text; what sorts of evidence might indicate whether an author is quoting from memory or from some sort of written text; how an authorial adaptation might be distinguished from the use of a non-"standard" textual *Vorlage*; what types of adaptations occur more or less frequently in the writings of a given author; and what typically takes place in the construction of a combined or conflated citation. The present study has been designed to fill this gap.

3. Proposed solutions

This does not mean, of course, that proposals are lacking to account for the evident discrepancies between the wording of Paul's quotations and the language of his presumed *Vorlage*. At least five different approaches can be identified in existing studies of Paul's use of Scripture.[14]

(1) *The problem does not exist.* The most radical and consistent proponent of this position was the Englishman William Whiston,

---

[14] A number of good surveys of scholarship on the broad question of Paul's use of Scripture (and the related issue of "the use of the Old Testament in the New") can be found already in the literature, and need not be repeated here. See (in order of appearance) F. A. G. Tholuck, "The Old Testament in the New," trans. Charles A. Aiken, *BSac* 11 (1854), 569–76; C. H. Toy, *Quotations in the New Testament* (New York: Scribner, 1884), xxxvii–xliii; August Clemen, *Der Gebrauch des Alten Testaments in den neutestamentlichen Schriften* (Gütersloh: C. Bertelsmann, 1895), 1–11; Hans Vollmer, *Die alttestamentlichen Citate bei Paulus* (Freiburg: Mohr, 1895), 6–9; Otto Michel, *Paulus und seine Bibel* (Gütersloh: C. Bertelsmann, 1929; repr., Darmstadt: Wissenschaftliche Buchgesellschaft, 1972), 1–7; E. Earle Ellis, *Paul's Use of the Old Testament* (Edinburgh: Oliver and Boyd, 1957; repr., Grand Rapids: Baker, 1981), 2–5; Merrill Miller, "Targum, Midrash, and the Use of the Old Testament in the New Testament," *JSJ* 2 (1971), 64–78; I. Howard Marshall, "An Assessment of Recent Developments," in *It is Written: Scripture Citing Scripture: Essays in Honour of Barnabas Lindars*, ed. D. A. Carson and H. G. M. Williamson (Cambridge University Press, 1988), 1–21; and Richard B. Hays, *Echoes of Scripture in the Letters of Paul* (New Haven, London: Yale University Press, 1989), 5–14.

who argued in 1722 that the disparities between the wording of the New Testament citations and present Greek and Hebrew biblical texts should be attributed, not to a supposed "loose" citation technique on the part of the apostolic writers, but rather to a willful corruption of the Hebrew Bible by Jewish leaders under the guidance of Rabbi Akiba in the second century C.E. This corrupted tradition was introduced into Christian circles by Origen and Jerome, both of whom received their Hebrew texts directly from Jewish rabbis.[15] As Whiston sees it, the reliability of the New Testament quotations is confirmed by their overall closeness to the language of the Septuagint and the Samaritan Pentateuch ("the greatest treasure relating to those times now extant in the whole Christian world"),[16] the absence of objections from either the apostles or their Jewish opponents (who of course would have checked their references), the unanimous testimony of the early church fathers, and the universal religious duty to offer accurate transcriptions of any sacred text.[17] Minor adaptations and possibly even slips of memory may indeed have occurred on occasion,[18] but the bulk of the passages adduced by the New Testament authors were rendered correctly in accordance with the common Greek and Hebrew texts of their day. Only through the painstaking process of textual criticism, for which the Samaritan Pentateuch, the Gallican Psalter of Jerome, and the New Testament quotations are especially valuable witnesses, can the present Greek and Hebrew texts be restored to their original purity.[19]

The provocative nature of Whiston's proposal raised firestorms of controversy in the church of his day. Rebuttals were published almost immediately. On the one side, the esteemed Hebrew scholar Johann Carpzov decried Whiston's reconstruction of history as

---

[15] *Essay*, 99, 133, 149–62, 220–81 (on Jewish corruption of the text); 17–18, 112, 133, 253–4, 264–5 (on Origen and the LXX); 102, 284 (on Jerome, "the grand Introducer and Supporter of the present Hebrew among Christians" (102)).

[16] Whiston regarded the Samaritan Pentateuch as (for the most part) a faithful and uncorrupt copy of the original Hebrew Pentateuch (164–9, 329), even going so far as to declare it "doubtful whether the Samaritans ever admitted any one voluntary Corruption into their whole Pentateuch" (168). Even the original designation of Mt. Gerizim as the proper place for sacrifice has been corrupted by the Jews, not the Samaritans (168–9).

[17] *Ibid.*, 3–17, 287–328.

[18] *Ibid.*, 129–33, 300–17.

[19] Whiston also allows for the use of the Syriac version, the Targumim, and the quotations of Josephus in reconstructing the Hebrew text and the Old Latin, the early Jewish revisions, and the quotations of Philo and the early church fathers for correcting the LXX (329–33).

thoroughly implausible and argued for the primacy and integrity of the Hebrew text over against the Samaritan Pentateuch and the other versions.[20] At the same time, Anthony Collins pointed out that the bulk of the differences between the present Greek and Hebrew manuscripts and the New Testament citations show no anti-Christian bias, but rather reflect the kinds of errors that occur naturally in the course of transmission.[21] More recently, the discovery at Qumran of Hebrew biblical manuscripts that date from before the Common Era has rendered Whiston's position not only untenable but actually obsolete for modern scholars. The continuing importance of Whiston's study lies not in its positive contributions to scholarship, but rather in its demonstration of the absurdities that inevitably result from any serious attempt to defend the verbal accuracy of the New Testament quotations.

More notable are the labors of a steady stream of investigators whose studies echo Whiston's concern, if not his method, for minimizing the apparent discrepancies between the language of the New Testament quotations and modern printed editions of the Greek and Hebrew Bibles. Common to these researchers is the notion that Paul remained faithful at all times to the original sense of the verses he cited, even if he did diverge on occasion (for whatever reasons) from their precise wording. Here it is not so much the presence of authorial adaptations that is being contested as their significance. Investigators who approach Paul's quotations from this perspective normally work from one of two convictions: (a) that Paul was fundamentally a creative biblical theologian whose appeals to Scripture can be understood (if not approved) by anyone sensitive enough to view the original context of his quotations through the eyes of a first-century Jewish–Christian interpreter, or (b) that free adaptation of the biblical text is in some way inconsistent with fundamental theological notions concerning the inspiration and inerrancy of Scripture. For writers in the first category (e.g. C. H. Dodd and A. T. Hanson),[22] the primary concern seems to be to

[20] On Carpzov's views, see note 12.

[21] *A Discourse on the Grounds and Reasons of the Christian Religion* (London, n. p., 1724). The tone of the rebuttals was actually more heated than the summaries would indicate: Carpzov calls Whiston an "Enemy to the Scriptures" whose work displays a "mortal hatred to the Word of God" (ii), while Collins observes (correctly) that "the design of Mr. Whiston is to vindicate the citations made from the Old in the New Testament" (215).

[22] C. H. Dodd, *According to the Scriptures* (London: Nisbet, 1952) and *The Old Testament in the New* (London: University of London Press, Athlone Press, 1952); A. T. Hanson, *Jesus Christ in the Old Testament* (London: SPCK, 1965); *Studies in*

defend the apostle against charges that he was typically "loose" and even arbitrary in the way he applied the language of Scripture to the needs of his congregations. For those in the second group, whose long lineage includes such authors as Thomas Randolph, F. A. G. Tholuck, David M. Turpie, Joseph Bonsirven, Roger Nicole, and Walter C. Kaiser,[23] it is the theological implications of these same accusations that arouses concern.

When it comes to the question of how Paul handled the wording of his quotations, however, both groups of authors stand in virtual agreement: any adaptation that might conceivably be traced back to Paul must be regarded as purely incidental to his purpose in adducing the passage. To think that Paul might have actively manipulated the language of Scripture to bring it into line with his own literary and/or rhetorical purposes is anathema to these investigators.[24] While most of the authors surveyed seem willing to accept a measure of Pauline intervention into the wording of the text, the whole issue is typically shunted to the side (if it is addressed at all) in favor of the more urgent task of defending Paul's method of interpreting the biblical text. Attempts to explain why Paul handled the text in such

---

Paul's Technique and Theology (Grand Rapids: Eerdmans, 1974; London: SPCK, 1974); *The New Testament Interpretation of Scripture* (London: SPCK, 1980); *The Living Utterances of God* (London: Darton, Longman, and Todd, 1983).

[23] T. Randolph, *The Prophecies and Other Texts Cited in the New Testament* (Oxford: J. and J. Fletcher, 1782); F. A. G. Tholuck, *Das Alte Testament im Neuen Testament*, 6th edn (Gotha: F. A. Perthes, 1877) (see note 14); David M. Turpie, *The Old Testament in the New* (London: Williams and Norgate, 1868) and *The New Testament View of the Old* (London: Hodder and Stoughton, 1872); Joseph Bonsirven (see note 13); Roger Nicole, "The New Testament Use of the Old Testament," in *Revelation and the Bible*, ed. Carl F. H. Henry (Grand Rapids: Baker, 1958), 137–51; Walter C. Kaiser, *The Uses of the Old Testament in the New* (Chicago: Moody, 1985). See also the introductory comments in Gleason L. Archer and G. C. Chirichigno, *Old Testament Quotations in the New Testament: A Complete Survey* (Chicago: Moody, 1983), ix–xxxii.

[24] A representative statement from each camp will demonstrate the common attitude. According to A. T. Hanson (*Studies*, 147), "Paul never consciously 'moulded' texts. When we do find him following this or that tradition of interpretation it usually proves to be an accepted tradition, not Paul's own invention. If the present work has shown anything, it has shown that Paul often regarded his Scripture citations as proofs. Proof texts that have been arbitrarily tampered with are ineffective as proofs." Walter C. Kaiser, while allowing for the possibility of paraphrastic renderings in the New Testament, insists that "the text cited [must] be totally authentic, according to the high views of Scripture fostered by the Reformers and their doctrinal heirs today ... where that word or limited word-set *on which the argument hinges* in those passages when the appeal to the OT is for the purpose of authoritatively supporting the doctrine, practice, or view being presented in the NT" (5; italics his). See further the article by Darrell L. Bock, "Evangelicals and the Use of the Old Testament in the New," *BSac* 142 (1985), 209–23, 306–19.

a "loose" fashion, where they appear at all, are typically brief and superficial. As a result, there is little to be learned from any of these authors about the way Paul handled the wording of his biblical quotations.

(2) *Divergent wording shows the use of a different text.* Questions concerning the nature of the biblical text used by Paul and the other New Testament authors go back at least as far as Origen and Jerome. But it was only after the Reformation that the issue became a subject of intense debate, as study of the Bible in the original languages once again became common in scholarly circles.[25] The question of whether Paul drew his texts from a Greek or a Hebrew source (or both) was settled by the mid-nineteenth century in favor of a Greek *Vorlage* for the bulk of Paul's quotations.[26] Since then, a variety of attempts have been made to trace Paul's various deviations from the Septuagint (as exemplified in the great uncials A, B, and ℵ) to the use or influence of some other (= non-"LXX") form of the biblical text.

The simplest and most obvious explanation is to assume that Paul corrected the wording of the Septuagint to bring it into closer alignment with the Hebrew in places where the Greek version diverged too far from the "original text." This solution was offered already by Jerome, and has found countless adherents over the centuries. But while the thesis does have an air of plausibility about it, careful studies have shown it to be untenable.[27] Objections have been raised on at least three counts: (1) Paul often follows the wording of the Septuagint where the latter diverges sharply from the Masoretic Hebrew text; (2) Paul fails to correct his text from the Hebrew in certain places where it would actually have aided his argument to do so; and (3) only a handful of Paul's deviations actually bring the wording of the Septuagint closer to a known Hebrew text, and all of these can be explained equally well by other means.[28] While most would agree that at least a few of Paul's quotations have been influenced by a Semitic text at some level, it seems that in this case the simplest explanation is not the correct one.

---

[25] Among the earliest studies are Franciscus Junius, *Sacrorum parallelorum libri tres* (London: G. Bishop, 1590) and Joannes Drusius, *Parallela sacra* (Frankfurt: Aegidium Radacum, 1594).

[26] See note 10 and the discussion in chap. 3.

[27] Kautzsch's study is typically cited as the most compelling argument for the use of a Greek *Vorlage* and against any resort to the Hebrew. For others who have taken a similar position, see the historical surveys listed in note 14.

[28] See chap. 2 for examples.

A second solution would posit an Aramaic *Vorlage* for at least some of Paul's biblical quotations. The most sweeping proposal of this type was put forward toward the end of the nineteenth century by Eduard Böhl,[29] who argued that Paul (along with the other New Testament writers) used a written Aramaic Targum alongside the Septuagint for several of his citations. Though recent developments in Targum studies have made the idea less incredible than it once appeared,[30] Böhl's hypothesis has found few adherents over the years, mainly because there is next to no evidence that the Semitic base presupposed in several of Paul's deviant quotations was Aramaic and not Hebrew.[31] Furthermore, the discoveries at Qumran have laid to rest all notions that Hebrew was a dead language at the time of Paul and the early church, an assumption that Böhl shared with many of his contemporaries. Even the narrower thesis of C. H. Toy, who argued that quotations that stand closer to the Hebrew should be traced to the influence of oral Aramaic renderings known through the synagogue, has found little favor among subsequent investigators.[32] While there is nothing inherently implausible about such a notion, the evidence is once again weak, and open to other explanations.

A novel approach to the textual question can be seen in the work of Alexander Sperber, whose analysis formed one of the keystones of Paul Kahle's multiple-translation theory of Septuagint origins.[33] In Sperber's view, the problem of divergent readings in the New

---

[29] E. Böhl, *Forschungen nach einer Volksbibel zur Zeit Jesu, und deren Zusammenhang mit der Septuaginta Übersetzung* (Vienna: W. Braumüller, 1873) and *Die alttestamentlichen Citaten im Neuen Testament* (Vienna: W. Braumüller, 1878). The roots of Böhl's thesis are evident in his fundamental assumption that "unsere neutestamentlichen Schriftsteller citieren wirklich; das Citat wird nicht erst in ihrem Kopfe, wie es bisher an vielen Stellen den Anschein hatte, sondern es ist schon da, in einem textus receptus oder einer lectio tunc usitata" (viii).

[30] See Martin McNamara, *The New Testament and the Palestinian Targum to the Pentateuch* (Rome: Pontifical Biblical Institute, 1966) and *Targum and Testament* (Shannon, New York: Irish University Press, 1972); Miller, "Targum"; R. Le Déaut, "Targumic Literature and New Testament Interpretation," *BTB* 4 (1974), 243–89.

[31] Even in the few cases where a Pauline reading finds support in the later Targumim (e.g. Rom 12.19, 1 Cor 15.54, Eph 4.8), it remains uncertain whether the readings in question reflect an Aramaic substratum or merely the common Hebrew background of the two sources. For further comments on Böhl's thesis, see Vollmer, 8, 26, 43; Ellis, *Use*, 15–16.

[32] Toy, ix, xv–xviii, xxxvi. Recent developments in Targum studies could well bring about a reevaluation of Toy's thesis: see the works cited in note 30.

[33] See A. Sperber, "The New Testament and the Septuagint," *Tarbiz* 6 (1934), 1–29 [Heb.], and "New Testament and Septuagint," *JBL* 59 (1940), 193–293; P. Kahle, *The Cairo Genizah*, 2nd edn (Oxford: Basil Blackwell, 1959), 249–52.

Testament quotations is more apparent than real, the result of a mistaken approach to the evidence on the part of modern investigators. According to Sperber, New Testament scholars have always assumed that the text of Codex B gives the best readings for both the New Testament quotations and their Greek *Vorlage*, while Codex A was viewed as at best a corrupted version of the same basic Greek tradition. Over against this traditional position, Sperber erects an elaborate argument to show that the tradition preserved in part in Codex A and more fully in the Vetus Latina, the citations of Theodoret, and the asterisk readings of Origen's *Hexapla* reflects an independent translation of the Hebrew whose language can be seen also in a number of New Testament quotations.[34] But while none would deny that the New Testament authors have preserved a variety of textual traditions in their quotations from the Greek Bible, few have accepted Sperber's contention that these divergent traditions represent unique translations and not simply differing forms of the same basic text.[35] Indeed, Sperber's insistence that the tradition underlying Codex A witnesses to "an independent translation, based upon a Hebrew original, and not a mere stylistic revision of an already existent Greek translation" sounds naïve in the bright light of the post-Qumran era.[36] In the final analysis, Sperber's "Bible of the Apostles" (his name for the Codex A tradition) sheds little light on those places where the New Testament authors diverge from the present wording of the Septuagint text.

More promising are those explanations that see the New Testament writers drawing at least some of their quotations from a version of the Greek Bible that had already been revised to bring it into closer conformity with a later Hebrew text. Among modern writers, the credit normally goes to Hans Vollmer for being the first to underscore the close verbal agreement between several of Paul's quotations and the later Greek versions of Aquila, Symmachus, and

---

[34] Among the Pauline readings cited by Sperber are Rom 3.17 (ἔγνωσαν), 9.17 (δύναμιν), 9.33 (ἐπ' αὐτῷ), 11.4 (ἔκαμψαν), and 1 Cor 5.13 (ἐξάρατε).

[35] The true picture is probably not so simple as either side has traditionally thought – see the discussion in chap. 2. Paul may in fact have relied on a non-"LXX" translation for at least two of his quotations: see the discussions of 1 Cor 3.19 and 14.21 in chap. 5.

[36] Discoveries at Qumran have confirmed the existence of Jewish revisions of the LXX in the pre-Christian era – see the discussion in chap. 2. Sperber himself recognized that a "Hebraizing" revision of the LXX could account for much of the data that he used to argue for two independent translations, though he quickly glossed over the possibility: see *JBL*, 211.

Theodotion.[37] For Vollmer, these agreements proved the existence of independent, pre-Christian translations of individual books of Scripture that circulated alongside the Septuagint in Jewish and Christian circles during the New Testament era.[38] Subsequent discoveries in the Judean desert have confirmed Vollmer's views of a link between the New Testament quotations and the early versions of Aquila, Symmachus, and Theodotion, though not in the way that Vollmer expected. Fragmentary Greek biblical manuscripts from Qumran and especially a partially preserved Minor Prophets scroll found further south at Naḥal Ḥever have shown that the text of the Septuagint had experienced significant revisions already in the pre-Christian period. In most cases the revisions are of a "Hebraizing" nature, but examples of improving the style of the Greek are also known.[39] Only now is the significance of these discoveries for the New Testament quotations beginning to be analyzed.[40]

One final explanation that should be considered here asserts that at least some of the New Testament quotations came from indirect sources where the wording of the text had been adapted for an earlier use. The simplest form of this thesis assumes that certain verses had taken on the status of oral maxims or proverbs in Jewish or early Christian usage. In these cases the New Testament author simply quoted the verse in the form in which he knew it. A certain amount of rounding and smoothing is to be expected in the case of oral transmission.[41] A more complex scenario is outlined by Barnabas Lindars, who scrutinizes the wording of the New Testament quotations for evidence that some of them might have been used as apologetic prooftexts before being fixed in their present literary

[37] Vollmer, 23–35.

[38] *Ibid.*, 35, 48.

[39] The texts and their significance are discussed at length in chap. 2. Frank Moore Cross's argument for a pre-Christian "proto-Lucianic" revision of the LXX (see chap. 2) draws its Greek support from materials that were available prior to Qumran.

[40] The first systematic examination of the Pauline quotations in light of these discoveries appears in Koch, *Schrift*, 57–83. The value of Koch's study will be noted throughout the present work. Part of the delay in applying these discoveries to the New Testament citations can be attributed to the fact that the *editio princeps* of the Minor Prophets scroll did not appear until 1963, when Dominique Barthélemy published his monumental work, *Les devanciers d'Aquila* (VTSup 10 (Leiden: Brill, 1963)). The Greek fragments from Qumran, on the other hand, have been published sporadically since the 1950s (see chap. 2 for references). Why it should have taken over twenty years for a study such as Koch's to appear is difficult to comprehend unless one posits a tremendous gulf between New Testament and Septuagint studies.

[41] Dietrich-Alex Koch (*Schrift*, 95) posits an oral tradition behind the adapted quotations in Rom 12.19, 13.9a, 1 Cor 1.31 (= 2 Cor 10.17), 2.9, 9.10, and 2 Cor 13.1.

settings.[42] Lindars' method involves looking for places where an otherwise unattested deviation in wording coincides with an apparent shift in the way a verse was used within the early Christian community. Unlike Rendel Harris, who argued that the early Christians compiled written "testimony books" for use against their Jewish opponents, Lindars traces the revised wording to a common oral tradition that was disseminated by Christian missionaries and catechists.[43] On the whole, Lindars makes a solid case that at least some of the deviant language in the New Testament quotations goes back to an earlier oral stage of Christian biblical interpretation. At the same time, the level of confidence with which Lindars' specific conclusions can be affirmed varies from citation to citation. The problem is especially acute in the case of Paul, whom even Lindars concedes has left his own creative stamp on the bulk of his quotations.[44] Still, Lindars' warning against assigning a divergent reading too quickly to the author who penned the quotation is *apropos*, and accords well with the conservative methodology of the present study.[45]

(3) *Variations are the result of memory quotation.* Perhaps the most common explanation for Paul's numerous deviations from the language of the Septuagint is to assert that he had a habit of quoting the biblical text rather loosely from memory.[46] Supporters of this position typically point to three lines of evidence in support of their contention: (a) the practical difficulties associated with looking up specific verses in multiple scrolls that contained none of the chapter and verse references present in modern Bibles; (b) the central role of rote memorization in the educational systems of antiquity (both Greco–Roman and Jewish), including examples of rabbis who could quote the entire Hebrew Bible from memory;[47] and (c) the language

---

[42] Barnabas Lindars, *New Testament Apologetic* (Philadelphia: Westminster, 1961).

[43] *Ibid.*, 16, 259. For more on Rendel Harris's "testimony book" hypothesis, see chap. 3.

[44] *Apologetic*, 222, 247. Lindars judges that all but one or two of the quotations adduced in Romans 9–11, the most intensive collection in the Pauline corpus, are original with Paul (242).

[45] On the question of methodology, see chap. 2

[46] Among the long line of researchers supporting this position are G. Roepe (per Ellis, *Use*, 4; Roepe's work was unavailable for the present study); Kautzsch, 108–10; Toy, xv, xx; Franklin Johnson, *The Quotations in the New Testament From the Old* (London: Baptist Tract and Book Society, 1895), 1, 29; Michel, 8, 10, 73, 80–2, 86–90; Ellis, *Use*, 14–15; Lindars, *Apologetic*, 26; and Hanson, *Studies*, 148.

[47] On the importance of rote memorization in the educational systems of antiquity, see H. I. Marrou, *History of Education in Antiquity*, trans. George Lamb, 3rd

of the citations themselves, where deviations from the precise wording of the biblical text seem to be the rule rather than the exception, and where combined and conflated citations indicate a degree of confusion as to the exact phrasing of the original text.[48] As can readily be seen, however, the last two arguments effectively cancel one another out: if the ancients were so capable of quoting the basic texts of their culture from memory, why does Paul (along with the other New Testament writers) find it so difficult to give a precise rendition of the wording of his ancestral Scriptures? The observation that even well-known biblical passages are often quoted "inaccurately" while more obscure texts are cited nearly verbatim only adds to the problems of this explanation.[49] At the same time, the difficulties associated with looking up specific verses in a bulky scroll while composing a letter are real, and present a severe obstacle for those who would maintain that Paul consulted written texts for the bulk of his quotations.[50] More will be said on this subject in a later chapter.[51]

(4) *Paul adapts the wording of the biblical text for his own purposes.* Most of the investigators cited thus far have worked with

edn (New York: Sheed and Ward, 1956). Numerous examples of ancient memory feats are cited (and critically examined) by William Harris, *Ancient Literacy* (Cambridge: Harvard University Press. 1989), 30–3, 301. Birger Gerhardsson (*Memory and Manuscript*, trans. Eric J. Sharpe (Lund: Gleerup, 1961; Copenhagen: Munksgaard, 1961), chaps. 9–11) offers a fine discussion of the role of memorization in the rabbinic educational system, but his retrojection of this system into the Second Temple period remains problematic.

[48] Otto Michel in particular appeals to the combined and mixed citations in support of his contention that Paul quoted the biblical text entirely from memory (10, 80–2, 86–7, 217). The inherent difficulties of this approach can be seen in Michel's own musings regarding which text Paul really had in mind when he incorporated these rather jumbled clusters of biblical recollections into his own letters (10, 80–1).

[49] Compare Paul''s "loose" quotations of Gen 2.7 (1 Cor 15.45), Gen 12.3 (Gal 3.8), Lev 18.5 (Rom 10.5/Gal 3.12), Isa 52.7 (Rom 10.15), etc., with his close reproduction of Ps 68.10 (Rom 15.3), Deut 32.43 (Rom 15.10), Ps 5.10 (Rom 3.13), Ps 18.5 (Rom 10.18), etc. A similar pattern can be seen in other New Testament writers. E. E. Ellis, while accepting the view that Paul quoted from memory, finds it necessary to qualify his position in the face of such clear textual evidence. As Ellis puts it, "'Memory quotation' should be understood as a free rendering in accordance with literary custom or for an exegetical purpose, rather than as a result of 'memory lapse'. The importance of scriptural memorization for the Jew, Paul's rabbinic training, and the verbal exactness of many of his quotations, militate against the latter explanation" (*Use*, 14).

[50] Not to mention the fact that such a wide range of manuscripts would most likely have been available only in the local synagogue – an unlikely setting for the composition of Paul's letters in view of his strained relations with the Jewish community as a whole.

[51] See the discussion of Paul's *Vorlage* in chap. 3.

the assumption that Paul rarely if ever molded the wording of the biblical text to coincide with his own use of a particular passage. Some would allow that Paul occasionally altered grammatical details and made other minor changes to conform a verse to its new linguistic setting, but most would quail at the thought that Paul actively shaped the wording of his quotations to insure that they conveyed precisely what he had in mind when he appealed to the passage in question. But this is precisely what the authors to be considered next are at pains to affirm. Significant differences emerge, however, when the question is posed as to why Paul handles his quotations in this manner. These divergent responses can be traced in turn to three different ways of viewing the problem: the theological approach, the sociological approach, and the literary approach.

(a) *Theological explanations.* Common to every explanation included under this heading is the notion that Paul's evident freedom with the biblical text is rooted in certain convictions that he received for the first time as a Christian. Parallels from non-Christian sources are considered useful only as indicators of the extent to which the beliefs and practices of Paul and other early Christian interpreters stand in continuity with their broader environment.

Perhaps the oldest theological explanation argues that Paul was obliged to reshape the wording of the biblical text as he felt led by the Spirit into an awareness of the true, "Christian" meaning of the passages he cited.[52] The most influential proponent of this position in the present century has been Otto Michel, who coined the term "charismatic exegesis" to describe the phenomenon.[53] According to Michel, Paul the Christian came to regard his ancestral Scriptures as in essence a closed book, open only to those who possessed a certain χάρισμα that enabled them to interpret it aright. By this "gifting" the Spirit opened up to believers the divinely intended meaning of the Scriptures as pertaining to the lives of Christ and his followers. This view in turn shaped the way Paul approached the wording of his biblical citations. "According to him," says Michel, "it is no longer individual verses but rather the whole of the Old Testament

[52] This position can be seen already in the quotation from Johann Carpzov (1729) reproduced in note 12, and he no doubt had his predecessors.

[53] Michel, 115, 128–9, 132–4, 138, 156, 178. In this he had been anticipated to some degree by Vollmer, who spoke of a "Charisma der Schriftdeutung" behind Paul's citation technique (69).

that must be understood from a Christian perspective. For this reason the apostle remains oblivious to any notion that he might be doing violence to the text or somehow jeopardizing his Christian salvation."[54] The adaptations, in other words, were required to bring to light the underlying truths that the Spirit had already made known to the charismatic interpreter, i.e. Paul.[55]

A different though related explanation would downplay the "charismatic" dimensions of Paul's exegesis, stressing instead the new view of Scripture that came to Paul along with his new Christian understanding of existence. In this approach, Paul is regarded more as a traditional Jewish scholar, spending hours poring over his ancestral Scriptures with the aim of reconciling the finality of the Christ-event with the absolute authority of the holy Torah. His motive throughout this process is intensely personal – as Hans Vollmer puts it, "The Old Testament is for him an authority whose testimony he requires to give certainty to his own faith."[56] Paul's solution to this dilemma is summed up in the formula that the Jewish Scriptures serve in God's plan as a "witness to the gospel," a veiled testimony to the final revelatory act of God in Jesus Christ. Conversely, the "gospel concerning Jesus Christ" is now the *sine qua non* for a proper understanding of the words of Scripture.[57] This fundamental unity between Scripture and gospel means that each can and indeed must be used to unfold the significance of the other. Citations thus become a constitutive part of the apostle's argumentation, so much so that the precise wording of the biblical text sometimes has to be reshaped to underline its new significance "in

[54] Michel, 138 (translation mine).
[55] A more recent exposition of the same basic viewpoint can be seen in J. Christiaan Beker, *Paul the Apostle* (Philadelphia: Fortress, 1980), 112–16, 122. Beker offers an extended discussion of what he calls "the *prophetic–pneumatic* character of [Paul's] apostolate and hermeneutic" (113; italics his), arguing along the way that "Paul's freedom with the written Old Testament text signifies an apocalyptic–pneumatic claim of immediate access to its meaning" (122).
[56] Vollmer, 49 (translation mine).
[57] This is the central thesis of Dietrich-Alex Koch's recent study, as the title (*Die Schrift als Zeuge des Evangeliums*) indicates (see especially pp. 338–40, 347–50). But this view of Paul's activities is by no means new with Koch. Almost a century earlier, Hans Vollmer summed up Paul's view of Scripture with the words, "Das Alte Testament ist dem Apostel in der That ein latentes Evangelium" (78). Vollmer for his part cites Henri Monnet, *Les citations de l'Ancien Testament dans les épîtres de S. Paul* (Lausanne: n. p., 1874) as holding a similar view (8). Where Vollmer and Koch differ is in Vollmer's desire to affirm this thesis in conjunction with an emphasis on the "pneumatic" character of Paul's exegesis. Joseph Bonsirven (337–8, 348–50) stands closer to Koch at this point.

Christ."[58] The result is a quotation whose true "Christian" meaning is plain for all to see.

One final explanation that can stand either on its own or alongside one of the other theological proposals would trace Paul's freedom with the biblical text to his keen awareness of living in the eschaton, the era when all the individual pronouncements of Scripture would be fulfilled. This solution has become increasingly popular in recent years due to the discovery of a similar phenomenon in the materials from Qumran. There the words of Scripture are applied with varying degrees of freedom to the past or present circumstances of the community, in the belief that the final days foretold by the prophets were now being realized in their midst.[59] Behind this approach lies the conviction that the prophets had spoken more than they knew: the true meaning of their words had been locked up until the "last days," at which time their full significance would at last become clear.[60] Supporters of this explanation discover a similar attitude in the way the New Testament authors handle the Jewish Scriptures. Applying these observations to his analysis of Paul's quotations, E. E. Ellis describes Paul's approach to the biblical text as "a 'quotation-exposition,' a *Midrash pesher*, which drew from the text the meaning originally implanted there by the Holy Spirit and expressed that meaning in the most appropriate words and phrases known to him."[61] Where expound-

---

[58] Vollmer, 78; Koch, *Schrift*, 196–7, 284–5, 295, 339, 346–7. Cf. Lindars, *Apologetic*, 28: "There was nothing morally reprehensible about such treatment of the text, because it was felt that the real meaning of the Scriptures was being clarified by it. This is because the Church's interpretation is based on the rule that what God has done in Christ is the key to the understanding of all the Scriptures."

[59] Krister Stendahl (*The School of St. Matthew*, ASNU 20 (Lund: Gleerup, 1954; Copenhagen: Munksgaard, 1954), 194–201) was probably the first to argue that "eschatological conviction explains the remarkable 'freedom' in relation to the text" in both the Qumran *pesharim* and the New Testament. Stendahl's analysis was quickly picked up by E. E. Ellis (*Use*, 139–47), who applied the same idea to his study of Paul's approach to Scripture. From Stendahl (184) Ellis appropriated the term *midrash pesher* to describe this technique, which he defined as "an interpretive moulding of the text within an apocalyptic framework" (147). Ellis's approach was endorsed by Otto Michel in the Postscript to the 1972 reprint of his own classic work (215). Barnabas Lindars (*Apologetic*, 15–16) appeals to the studies of both Stendahl and Ellis to explain why the early Christians adapted the wording of their quotations to reflect their peculiar apologetic interests.

[60] The standard reference is *1QpHab* 7.1, where the interpreter declares, "And God told Habakkuk to write the things that would come upon the last generation; but he did not show him the final consummation." In 7.3, the Teacher of Righteousness is described as "the one to whom God showed all the mysteries of the words of his servants the prophets."

[61] Ellis, *Use*, 146.

ing this meaning required adapting the wording of the text, Paul obviously did not hesitate to do so. The important thing was to uncover the meaning of the passage for the "last days"; when this could not be done using the language of the verse in question, the latter was required to give way.

(b) *Sociological explanations.* Included here are a variety of approaches that seek to explain Paul's handling of the biblical text by pointing to similar practices among his contemporaries. For the most part the answers offered here are antithetical to the theological explanations considered above. The reasons for the rivalry are obvious. Where theological approaches assume an ideological basis for Paul's practice, sociological explanations look for broader cultural patterns; where theological solutions stress uniqueness, sociological interpretations emphasize agreement. In sum, if a certain procedure can be shown to be typical of both Paul and his non-Christian contemporaries, the need for a narrow theological explanation of Paul's activities is obviated.

Perhaps the earliest attempt to posit a social framework for Paul's approach to the biblical text appears in the massive work of Guilielmus Surenhusius (1713).[62] The backbone of Surenhusius' study is an extended comparison of the interpretational techniques found in the New Testament and rabbinic literature. Along the way he argues that the New Testament authors' rather "free" approach to the biblical text finds ample parallel in the rabbinic sources. Surenhusius' stance is thoroughly apologetic: the New Testament authors cannot be blamed for the way they handled the wording of their biblical quotations, since they were simply following the normal Jewish practice of the time. Surenhusius' examination of the subject was considered bedrock by most early modern investigators, as their frequent references to his work show.[63] An equally extensive collection of parallels was published by J. C. C. Döpke in 1829, sparking a fresh wave of comparisons with rabbinic practice.[64]

---

[62] ספר המשוה sive βιβλος καταλλαγης in quo secundum veterum Theologorum Hebraeorum (Amsterdam: Johannes Boom, 1713). Surenhusius's study was unavailable for the present study, but his method is summed up in some detail in Collins, 56–78.

[63] Carpzov and Collins in particular appeal to Surenhusius to counter Whiston's overly defensive attitude toward the New Testament citations.

[64] Döpke, *Hermeneutik der neutestamentlichen Schriftsteller* (Leipzig: Vogel, 1829), 70–87. Tholuck describes Döpke's study as "merely an uncritical compilation of passages, [which] needs very much to be sifted" ("Citations," 577). The characterization is apt: the bulk of the materials cited by Döpke are quite late, and examples of

More recent scholars, on the other hand, have adopted a more reticent attitude toward the relevance of the rabbinic literature at this point.[65] In fact, problems plague virtually every attempt to compare Paul's citation technique with that of the Jewish rabbis. The most pressing difficulty concerns the lack of a critical text for the bulk of the rabbinic materials. Without such a text, there is simply no way to be certain exactly how the rabbis themselves handled the wording of their biblical *Vorlage*. The possibility that later copyists may have assimilated the rabbis' quotations to the later Masoretic text creates further problems for this approach. Finally, the nagging question of how well the rabbinic materials reflect the practices of the Second Temple period becomes especially acute at this point, since the stabilization of the biblical text is itself a product of the early rabbinic period.[66] Dietrich-Alex Koch sums up the situation well: "The highly orthodox molding of the rabbinic literature and its reworked traditions, combined with the simultaneous movement toward a stable biblical text, makes it unlikely that one would ever find here even an approximation of that freedom with the wording of Scripture that one sees in the case of Paul."[67]

Another type of sociological comparison that has been put forward on occasion would relate Paul's handling of the biblical text to the targumizing procedures of the Jewish synagogue. The idea appears to have gained a measure of currency around the turn of the century, but its popularity has waned in recent years.[68] The luke-

rabbinic adaptations few. Döpke does, however, offer useful examples of composite quotations in the rabbinic literature.

[65] The standard modern study is the uncompleted work of Victor Aptowitzer, *Das Schriftwort in der rabbinischen Literatur* (Vienna: Kais. Akademie der Wissenschaften, 1906–15; reprinted with Prolegomenon by Samuel Loewinger in Library of Biblical Studies, ed. H. M. Orlinsky, New York: Ktav, 1970). Aptowitzer discovered a wealth of variant readings but almost no genuine adaptations of the biblical wording in rabbinic quotations from the books of Samuel and Joshua. The judgment of Joseph Bonsirven (336), that the rabbis almost never adapted the wording of their quotations, has been echoed by numerous later investigators (see Stendahl, 193; Ellis, *Use*, 45; Koch, *Schrift*, 192). A notable exception is Richard Longenecker (*Biblical Exegesis in the Apostolic Period* (Grand Rapids: Eerdmans, 1974)), who refers to parallels in the rabbinic *midrashim* to explain Paul's free approach to the biblical text (130), though he offers no evidence to support his claim.

[66] See chap. 2.

[67] *Schrift*, 192 (translation mine). As will be seen below, the fact that the same techniques appear in non-rabbinic and even pagan literature presents additional problems for this view – see Johnson, 372–6.

[68] Alfred Edersheim (*The Life and Times of Jesus the Messiah*, 8th rev. edn (New York: Longmans, Green and Co., 1896–8; repr., Grand Rapids: Eerdmans, 1971),

warm reception that the suggestion has received from subsequent investigators may be due as much to the lack of specificity with which the proposal has been put forward as to any problems inherent in the notion itself. Implicit in this explanation is the assumption that the New Testament authors were all familiar with the art of "targuming" the Scriptures from their own experience in the Jewish synagogue. As Alfred Edersheim puts it, "At that time each one *Targumed* for himself, and these *Targumim* (as our existing one on the prophets shows) were neither literal versions, nor yet paraphrases, but something between them, a sort of interpreting translation." With this experience behind them, says Edersheim, "it is needless to remark, that the New Testament writers would *Targum* as Christians."[69] But does this really follow? The technique of reproducing a biblical passage within a new literary setting is quite different from the process of rendering the same passage into a foreign language. Interpretation is a necessary part of every translation; not so with quotations. Whether literary citations were normally handled in a manner similar to translations (i.e. incorporating interpretive elements into the very wording of the text) in the ancient world is a matter to be investigated, not assumed. A second problem with this solution concerns the relative comparability of the evidence. It is simply not enough to say that both the Jewish Targumim and the New Testament citations render the biblical text in an interpretive fashion. The same observation would apply to that assortment of Jewish writings that modern scholars have labelled "rewritten Bible."[70] What is needed is a careful study of how closely the techniques used in rendering the Hebrew Bible into Aramaic resemble the types of adaptations encountered in the New Testament quotations. Without such data, it is simply impossible to judge whether the practice of "targumizing" the Scriptures in the Jewish synagogue might have affected the way Paul and the other

206) discovers here the chief reason behind the free renderings of the New Testament authors, while C. H. Toy (xv, xviii) suggests more narrowly that the New Testament writers may have been influenced in some cases by memories of Aramaic translations rendered orally in the synagogue. More recent references to the "targumic" quality of the New Testament citations (e.g. Stendahl, 115; Lindars, *Apologetic*, 28) reflect a growing tendency toward a more abstract use of the term – no concrete link with Jewish synagogal practice is actually proposed in any of these studies.

[69] Edersheim, 206 (italics his).

[70] Examples include the book of *Jubilees*, the so-called *Genesis Apocryphon*, and the *Biblical Antiquities* of Pseudo-Philo. See Daniel J. Harrington, "The Bible Rewritten (Narratives)," in *Early Judaism and Its Modern Interpreters*, ed. Robert A. Kraft and George W. E. Nickelsburg (Atlanta: Scholars, 1986), 239–46.

New Testament authors handled the wording of their biblical quotations.

Attempts to situate Paul's adaptive techniques within the apocalyptic thought-world exemplified by the Qumran community have already been noted. Though the parallel appears impressive at first glance, it too falls apart under careful examination. In the first place, it is not at all clear that the Qumran materials are being properly represented in the way the comparison is normally framed. Much that was originally described as interpretive molding of the biblical text in the Qumran *pesharim* is now commonly traced to a non-Masoretic Hebrew *Vorlage*.[71] Closer to Paul's handling of Scripture are the numerous quotations that appear in such non-*pesher* texts as the *Damascus Document (CD)* and *4QFlorilegium*. Here adaptations are common, even in passages where apocalyptic interests are nowhere in sight.[72] In other words, the link between eschatological expectation and adaptation of the biblical text is by no means asured even at Qumran. The picture is much the same on the Pauline side. As Richard Longenecker points out, the *pesher* mode of interpretation (i.e. the application of a contemporizing hermeneutic to a specific biblical passage) is actually quite rare in the Pauline epistles.[73] Adapted quotations, on the other hand, appear in virtually every type of context (theological, liturgical, parenetic, etc.) in association with a wide range of interpretive approaches (literal, typological, allegorical, etc.) throughout the Pauline corpus.[74] To say that these adaptations are all to be explained by the general eschatological orientation of the New Testament authors and then to point to the Qumran materials as evidence for a similar pattern in early Judaism is to misrepresent the evidence on both sides of the equation. Parallels to Paul's technique do indeed appear in the Qumran materials, but an adequate explanation for these similarities must be sought elsewhere.

[71] See especially Lou H. Silberman, "Unriddling the Riddle: A Study in the Structure and Language of the Habakkuk *Pesher*," *RevQ* 3 (1961–2), 323–64. Silberman explores the links between text and interpretation throughout the *pesharim* and shows how many of the instances that appear to reflect a modified text actually represent creative exegesis of a pre-existing *Vorlage*. Krister Stendahl likewise acknowledged in the second edition (1967) of *The School of St. Matthew* (ii–iii) that he had been less than cautious in attributing deviations from the Masoretic Hebrew text to the hand of the later interpreter.

[72] A thorough investigation of the Qumran evidence appears in chap. 8 of the present study.

[73] Longenecker, 130.

[74] See chaps. 4 through 6 of the present study.

One final approach that has yet to be mentioned would look more widely at the way Greco–Roman authors who operated outside the Judeo–Christian sphere of influence handled the wording of their quotations. If parallels to New Testament patterns can be found here, it is reasoned, every effort to clarify the techniques of the New Testament authors by reference to contemporary Jewish practice or the theological outlook of a particular author would be rendered superfluous. Though occasional references to the classical Greek writers can be found throughout the literature, it seems that only one modern investigator, Franklin Johnson, has made the Greco–Roman materials a key witness in his attempt to explain the citation technique of the New Testament writers.[75] Even here the question of how the two sets of authors handled the wording of their quotations is only one element in a broader study that includes lengthy discussions of several other topics that bear on "the use of the Old Testament in the New."[76] As a result, Johnson's study yields little more than a series of examples designed to show that this or that practice that occurs in the New Testament appears already in the literature of the Greco–Roman world. Among the practices cited are: omitting words for the sake of brevity; creating "exegetical paraphrases" to highlight the chief point of the original passage; and combining verses from more than one passage to produce a "composite quotation." Johnson's sources include Plato, Aristotle, Cicero, Seneca, Philo, Plutarch, Lucian, and various other authors from the classical period through the early Christian era.

Clearly Johnson is onto something when he looks to Greco–Roman literature for parallels to the citation techniques of the New Testament authors. His examples of systematic omissions and "composite quotations" in particular are sufficient to show that the New Testament writers adopted at least these particular practices from their broader cultural environment.[77] Nonetheless, Johnson's

[75] On Johnson's book, see note 46. James Scott (87–8, 94) included a handful of examples from classical literature in his 1875 study of the New Testament quotations, but only as part of a broader appeal to the history of literature. Johnson, writing in 1895, appears to have been unacquainted with Scott's earlier study. He writes: "So far as I am aware, this is the first attempt ever made to compare the quotations of the New Testament with those of general literature" (xvii).

[76] Other issues treated include memory quotation, the purpose of allegory, the function of the quotations in their present literary and rhetorical setting, the question of "double reference," and the presence of "illogical reasoning" in the argumentative use of quotations.

[77] It is interesting to note how E. E. Ellis can criticize J. C. C. Döpke for asserting a rabbinic background for such common techniques as exegetical paraphrase and

study leaves many questions unanswered. In the first place, Johnson shows no awareness of the textual problems that hinder every attempt to analyze the way Greco–Roman writers handled the wording of their citations. Broader phenomena such as omissions of lines and combinations of verses can be identified with relative confidence from a simple comparison of the standard printed editions of the texts involved. But when it comes to investigating such subtle practices as adding or omitting individual words or phrases, substituting one word for another, or changing the order of words in the text, the complexities of the textual evidence must be squarely faced. Secondly, Johnson offers no information as to how often the techniques that he discusses are employed by any of the authors cited. The argument would be strengthened considerably if it could be shown that the examples Johnson cites reflect the authors' normal citation techniques and not a tendentious selection designed to support a particular view of the New Testament authors' relation to their environment. Thirdly, Johnson offers no concrete analysis of the various ways the New Testament writers and their Greco–Roman contemporaries handled the wording of their quotations. Further study is needed to discover exactly where the two sets of authors agree and disagree on this key issue. Finally, Johnson gives no indication as to where contemporary Jewish practice fits into his schema. Apart from an occasional reference to Philo, Johnson draws his examples exclusively from pagan sources. Is this a sign that the New Testament authors followed pagan models in the way they handled their citations, or did contemporary Jewish writers employ the same techniques? Johnson is completely silent on this question. For a century-old study, Johnson's investigation still has much to say to modern researchers about the way the New Testament authors incorporated citations into their own compositions. But more analysis remains to be done before Johnson's seminal observations can be regarded as sufficiently grounded for use by modern investigators.[78]

(c). *Literary explanations.* The idea that Paul's citation technique might be explained by reference to the broader history of literature appears to have fallen out of favor with recent investigators. Among earlier researchers, on the other hand, the notion

composite quotations (Ellis describes them as "about as rabbinic as the use of papyrus" (*Use*, 45)), and then proceed to argue for a narrow comparison with the practices of the Qumran community.

[78] See chap. 7 of the present study.

appears with a fair degree of regularity. Both Johann Carpzov (1729) and Thomas Randolph (1782) appeal to common literary practice to justify the various additions, omissions, substitutions, and grammatical changes that characterize the New Testament quotations.[79] The fullest explication of this position can be found in the writings of James Scott (1875) and to a lesser degree Franklin Johnson (1895).[80] Scott's fundamental premise can be summed up in a few words: "We must accept and examine quotation in all its extent, as we find it in general literature as well as in the New Testament."[81] Where earlier investigators had been content to offer sweeping generalizations about the way good writers of every age have handled the wording of their quotations, Scott marshals a host of examples from classical writers to more recent literature to support his contention that "truthful representation, and not verbal accuracy, was all that was required or sought" from quotations in any era.[82] Turning to the phenomenon of adapted quotations in the New Testament, Scott notes that "we find such forms of citation actually employed by writers of different ages and of distant countries, writing in different languages, on various subjects and in various stages of civilization."[83] In such cases the authors clearly felt that their purposes "were more suitably accomplished by a transformation or verbal adaptation of the text, than by an application of it which left its form unaltered and its sense less perspicuous."[84] Accordingly, there is no cause for concern when the New Testament

[79] Carpzov's sentiments can be seen in the quotation reproduced in note 12. According to Randolph, "The writers of the *New Testament* took no other Liberties in their Citations from the *Old*, than other the best, and most impartial, Writers do. Some of these are not properly Citations, but References, or Allusions: Many others are not brought in Proof, but by way of Illustration of the Subject: in which Case some slight Alteration may be allowed to accommodate it to the Point in Hand. Farther it is not necessary in *Citations*, as it is in *Translations*, to keep to the precise Words of the *Original*: It is always allowable to abridge the Passage cited, and leave out some Part, provided nothing is omitted which affects the Sense. And again it is lawful to add something by way of Illustration, or Explication, if we add nothing which alters the Sense" (47; italics his).

[80] Franklin Johnson (see above) offers examples from more recent literature to demonstrate the commonness of what he calls "exegetical paraphrase" (85–8), "quotation by sound" (168–73), and "double reference" (198–209). The bulk of his comparative materials, however, come from the ancient world.

[81] Scott, 97.

[82] *Ibid.*, 84–100. Scott's examples from the history of literature include passages from Thomas à Kempis, John Calvin, Samuel Rutherford, John Owen, Francis Bacon, Hugo Grotius, and Joseph Butler, among others.

[83] *Ibid.*, 97.

[84] *Ibid.*, 99.

authors show a similar degree of freedom in the way they handle the wording of the Jewish Scriptures.

The relevance of Scott's approach for the present study is obvious. By calling attention to the frequency of adapted citations throughout the broad history of (Western) literature, Scott effectively vitiates every explanation that would trace the practices of the New Testament authors to the influence of this or that community or current of thought within the ancient world. At the same time, Scott's method leaves ample room for distinguishing between proximate and more distant causes in investigating the wording of the New Testament citations. But something is still missing. While his study sounds almost modern in its attention to the broader literary parameters of the New Testament quotations, Scott has little to say about why any of the authors cited (writing both before and after the advent of the printing press) should have felt free to offer such a loose rendition of the language of an outside text.[85] What is needed to set Scott's findings on a firm footing is a sound theoretical discussion of the technique of quotation *per se*, including a review of the way various social, rhetorical, literary, and hermeneutical factors help to determine whether the wording of a text will be reshaped or reproduced verbatim in a given instance.[86] Until such a study becomes available, the usefulness of Scott's findings will remain limited.

4. Charting the course

The foregoing survey of the way various investigators have sought to explain Paul's use of Scripture has pointed up a number of areas where further study might help to move the discussion forward. Perhaps the most pressing need is for a careful examination of the

---

[85] Scott's few comments on the subject show a preoccupation with psychological speculation. Speaking of what he calls "analytic or eclectic quotation" (the practice labelled "limited selection" in the present study – see chap. 2), Scott describes how "in this case the cited text was mentally analysed, and the part of it most appropriate to the subject or object of the author was selected" (26). A similar explanation accompanies his treatment of "idealistic or paraphrastic quotation," which according to Scott involves a process of analyzing the text, abstracting the sense from the form, generalizing the underlying idea, and finally encasing this abstract notion in a new objective expression (29).

[86] Richard B. Hays' recent attempt (see note 14) to apply the categories of intertextuality to expound the meaning of Paul's explicit appeals to Scripture is a laudable first step in this direction, but more needs to be said about the way adaptive techniques fit into this broader hermeneutical matrix.

thorny methodological problems that confront any attempt to analyze the way Paul handled the wording of his biblical quotations. Included under this heading are such basic issues as what constitutes a "citation" in Paul's letters; what sources Paul might have used for his quotations; and what standards might be applied to determine where Paul has indeed adapted the wording of the biblical text. These and similar questions will be addressed in chapter 2.

The next step is to determine what techniques Paul actually used when quoting from the Jewish Scriptures. The only way to do this is to examine every one of Paul's citations with a view to cataloguing the way he handled the wording of his biblical *Vorlage* in each case. The method to be followed in the present investigation is outlined at the end of chapter 2. The details of the examination occupy chapters 3 through 5, with chapter 6 tallying up the findings.

Once Paul's normal citation technique has been identified, the question arises as to why Paul formulates his quotations in the way that he does. At issue here is whether Paul's freedom with the biblical text is somehow conditioned by his Christian presuppositions, or whether he is simply following the normal literary conventions of his day. Building on the sociological approaches outlined above, chapters 7 and 8 examine the writings of various Greco–Roman and Jewish authors to determine to what extent their way of handling citations coincides with the method found in the letters of Paul. Finally, chapter 9 explores the broader social factors that conspired to shape the way written texts were handled throughout the ancient world.

To anticipate the conclusions of the investigation, the present study aims to demonstrate two basic theses: (1) that Paul actively adapted the wording of his biblical quotations to communicate his own understanding of the passage in question and to obviate other possible readings of the same text, and (2) that, in offering such "interpretive renderings" of the biblical text, Paul was working consciously but unreflectively within the accepted literary conventions of his day. Every observation concerning the way Paul and his contemporaries handled this or that passage is offered in support of one or the other of these two fundamental theses. Though neither conclusion will evoke surprise from anyone familiar with the discussion, both points have been hotly debated over the years, as the foregoing survey of scholarship has made clear. This implies that neither finding has been established with the sort of thoroughness and methodological rigor that is required to put an end to the

debate on a particular issue.[87] It is for this reason that questions of
method will occupy a central place in the discussion that follows.

[87] Perhaps the best parallel is Emil Kautzsch's 1869 dissertation on the nature of
Paul's biblical *Vorlage*. Though Kautzsch was certainly not the first to argue that
Paul drew his quotations primarily from the Septuagint, with little if any recourse to
the Hebrew text, it was his careful and painstaking analysis that established this fact
beyond all doubt (see chap. 3). It is hoped that the present study will do the same for
the issues outlined above.

2

A QUESTION OF METHOD

1. The importance of methodology

Surely the most vexing problem that confronts any attempt to analyze the citation technique of the apostle Paul concerns how one can know where Paul has adapted the wording of the biblical text and where he has simply reproduced the wording of a non-"standard" *Vorlage*. It comes therefore as something of a surprise to discover how little attention has been paid to this key question in the standard examinations of Paul's use of Scripture. In fact, a careful review of available studies turns up not one significant discussion of the thorny methodological issues raised by this perennial *crux*. For the most part investigators have been content to compare the wording of the Pauline text with the standard editions of the Greek and Hebrew Bibles (the more astute include references to the critical apparatus) and then to offer a few perfunctory remarks as to why this or that reading should or should not be attributed to the apostle Paul.[1] Questions such as what constitutes reliable criteria for adjudicating such matters have been largely ignored. As a result, one finds almost no guidance in the literature on such vital subjects as: how to distinguish between intentional adaptations and other forms of textual variation, such as arise from memory quotation or the use of a different *Vorlage*; what types of modifications Paul typically introduces into the wording of his citations; how Paul's handling of the biblical text compares with the approaches of his contemporaries; and similar matters. Even the fundamental question of what constitutes a "citation" (as over against, say, a para-

---

[1] See for example the studies of Randolph, H. Gough (*The New Testament Quotations* (London: Walton and Maberly, 1855)), Kautzsch and Böhl, each of whom approaches the text with his own distinctive agenda. When it comes to determining where Paul has adapted the wording of his *Vorlage*, bald assertion is the rule, careful demonstration the exception.

phrase or an allusion) receives almost no theoretical examination in the standard studies on the subject.[2]

Something vital is missing here. With basic issues of method so ill-defined, it is no wonder that many scholars either dismiss the question of how Paul handled the biblical text as an insoluble riddle or else press Paul's citations into the service of this or that tendentious argument. The remainder of the present chapter is devoted to this question of methodology.

Since the ultimate aim of the present study is to compare Paul's citation technique with the practices of other ancient authors, a model is needed that will prove equally useful with non-biblical materials. The method to be outlined in the following pages is really quite simple: first, identify the assured citations; next, isolate those instances where it can be established with reasonable certainty (using the criteria set forth below) that the author has either followed the wording of his *Vorlage* or else adapted the text for his own use;[3] and finally, catalogue these instances in a way that yields a reliable portrait of an author's normal citation technique. In the same way, the criteria to be used for identifying authorial adaptations are by no means new, though their formalization into an explicit methodology might be viewed as a new departure in the study of Paul's citation technique. The aim throughout is to establish a minimum of "assured results," not to offer a definitive judgment on the origins of every problematic reading in the Pauline corpus. The effectiveness of such an investigation is clearly cumulative: conclusions are derived not from a few passages taken in isolation, nor even from an author's own statements about the materials he cites, but rather from a careful examination of every passage in which an author appeals to an outside text.[4] As a result, differences over the handling of a particular passage will rarely have any significant effect on the validity of the overall conclusions of the study.

---

[2] The usual practice is to present a list of those passages that the investigator considers to be "citations," with little or no attempt to justify the selections. The brief discussions offered by Michel (10) and Ellis (*Use*, 11) are merely the exceptions that prove the rule. Dietrich-Alex Koch finds no evident predecessors in his explicit attention to methodology at this point (*Schrift*, 11–23).

[3] Many examples will be seen to fit neither category.

[4] The sole exception is the material in chap. 7, where the study is limited to quotations from Homer in contemporary Greco–Roman literature, ignoring appeals to other authors.

2. Identifying the citations

In order to render an adequate description of Paul's or any other author's citation technique, it is necessary to define first what is meant by a "citation." The very fact that virtually every author who has set out to study Paul's use of Scripture has felt compelled to offer a new listing of Paul's quotations highlights the need for greater methodological clarity in this area. Though most recent investigators have recognized the need to distinguish between various levels of engagement with the biblical text in Paul's writings (citations, paraphrases, allusions, reminiscences, etc.), researchers have typically assumed that the meaning of each of these terms is self-evident, so that the only difficulty lay in deciding how to allocate the Pauline materials among a fixed set of clearly under-stood categories. Yet the proliferation of lists has continued, their very contradictions offering mute testimony to the diverse criteria used to determine what represents a "citation" in the writings of Paul.

The differences of opinion that have persisted in this area can be traced to two related problems, the first textual, the second methodological. On the one hand, the materials themselves offer no sure criteria for distinguishing between the various ways in which Paul appropriated the text of Scripture. Explicit quotations are normally indicated by the use of a formulaic expression such as "as it is written," "the Scripture says," or "as it says in Hosea."[5] Included under these headings, however, are materials that range from verbatim quotations from the Greek Septuagint (e.g. Rom 3.4, 8.36, 15.10) to texts that show clear signs of Pauline adaptation (e.g. Rom 9.25–6, 10.11, 11.8) to statements whose precise origin has baffled investigators to the present day (1 Cor 2.9, 9.10, 2 Cor 4.6, Eph 5.14).[6] In other places, Paul quotes biblical texts virtually word-perfect with no indication to his readers that a citation is even present (e.g. Rom 2.6, 1 Cor 5.13, 15.32, 2 Cor 13.1). Classification becomes increasingly difficult as such unmarked "citations" diverge further and further from the wording of their presumed *Vorlage*. In most of these cases only a familiarity with the text under consider-

---

[5] The various formulae that Paul uses to introduce his citations will receive only cursory treatment in the present study. See also chap. 3, note 5.

[6] See also 1 Tim 5.18b and 2 Tim 2.19b. The quotation from Menander (or Euripides) in 1 Cor 15.33 has no such introductory formula, though most would agree that Paul appropriated this saying from popular usage and not from a literary source anyway – see Koch, *Schrift*, 42–5.

ation would alert the reader to the presence of a "citation" of any sort.

This last observation points up the fundamental methodological difference that divides those who seek to determine what counts as a "citation" in Paul's writings. Though nowhere framed in these terms, the controversy seems to revolve around whether it is better to take a "reader-centered" or an "author-centered" approach to the problem at hand. In a reader-centered approach, the investigator classifies as "citations" only those passages that give the reader at least some indication that a quotation is indeed present. Indicators might include explicit introductory formulae, interpretive comments, or a literary style that differs markedly from the surrounding verses (e.g. a section of poetry in the midst of a prose discourse). In an author-centered approach, on the other hand, any verse that exhibits substantial verbal agreement with a known passage of Scripture, whether marked or not, would be counted in a listing of Pauline "citations." The strength of the first approach lies in its conservatism: investigation is limited to a body of texts whose status as citations is reasonably assured, thus minimizing the possibility that the results will be contaminated by the accidental inclusion of heterogeneous materials. The cost of this measure of security is the exclusion of a number of passages whose closeness to a particular biblical passage reveals a clear intent to reproduce the wording of that passage within the later Pauline context (e.g. Rom 2.6, 1 Cor 5.13, 15.32, 2 Cor 13.1). The second approach makes greater allowances for the manifold diversity that characterizes Paul's handling of his biblical citations. But an analysis conducted under such ill-defined parameters runs the risk of becoming so broad and diffuse as to render its findings suspect when applied to the narrower body of clearly identifiable citations.[7]

In reality, few scholars have followed either approach with wooden loyalty. But this practical flexibility should not be mistaken for agreement on a third position intermediate between the two approaches outlined above. What it reveals instead is a lack of definitional clarity on the part of all concerned. Not until the recent study of Dietrich-Alex Koch (1986) had any investigator set forth with methodological precision the criteria used in his own study for

---

[7] E.g. what does one do under this approach with such passages as Rom 11.2 (cf. Ps 93.14), 11.25/12.16 (cf. Prov 3.7), 12.16/2 Cor 8.21 (Prov 3.17), 1 Cor 10.5 (Num 14.16), 2 Cor 3.16 (Exod 34.34), and Phil 1.19 (Job 13.16), 2.10–11 (Isa 45.23), 2.15 (Deut 32.5)?

determining what constitutes a "citation."[8] Following what amounts to a reader-centered approach, Koch describes seven different conditions under which a given Pauline statement might legitimately be viewed as a quotation: (1) when accompanied by a clear citation formula (Rom 2.24, 3.4, 3.10–18, 4.3, etc.); (2) when the same words appear in another context where they are marked clearly as a citation (Rom 4.22/4.3, 2 Cor 10.17/1 Cor 1.31, Gal 3.11/Rom 1.17); (3) when followed by an interpretive gloss (1 Cor 15.27, 2 Cor 3.16); (4) when the words in question stand out syntactically from their Pauline context, showing that they were not first formulated for their present position (Rom 9.7, 10.18, Gal 3.12); (5) when the passage differs stylistically from the verses that surround it (Rom 11.34, 12.20, 1 Cor 10.26, 15.32, 15.33); (6) when introduced by a light particle of emphasis such as μενοῦνγε, ὅτι, ἀλλά, or an introductory γάρ or δέ (Rom 9.7, 10.13, 10.18, 2 Cor 8.21, 10.17, Gal 3.11); and (7) when the verse reproduces a tradition that the author clearly assumes will be familiar to his readers (Rom 13.9, Gal 5.14).[9]

As with any pioneering endeavor, Koch's analysis cannot be considered the last word on the subject. Though his concern to develop objective criteria for identifying the presence of a citation is laudable, Koch has left himself open to criticism regarding the level of literary competence required by his definition. Whether Paul's Gentile readers would have understood even some of his more explicit biblical quotations is at least open to question. To assume that these same people would have recognized the citation character of passages with only the lightest of markings (as in category 6 above) is surely to build hypothesis upon hypothesis.[10] Moreover, certain of Koch's criteria appear more credible when cast in the form of abstract principles than when applied to actual passages. For example, included in Koch's list of citations said to be recogniz-

---

[8] Discussed in *Schrift*, 11–23.

[9] Koch's list of citations, broken down according to these seven categories, can be examined in *Schrift*, 21–4. Note that Koch excludes from his study as "non-Pauline" not only Ephesians and the Pastorals but also 2 Cor 6.14–7.1 (*ibid.*, 24 n. 43).

[10] Koch does attempt to forestall this objection with his observation that "beim Fehlen einer eindeutigen Einleitungsformulierung wird man dann sicher von einem Zitat sprechen können, wenn hinreichend deutlich ist, daß der Verfasser hier bewust einen ihm vorgegebenen Wortlaut reproduziert, und wenn zugleich angenommen werden kann, daß der Leser den Wortlaut als übernommen erkennen könnte (*bzw. daß der Verfasser offenbar damit rechnete*)" (*Schrift*, 13; emphasis mine). Despite the apparent concession here to a more author-centered approach, the criteria Koch employs remain reader-centered throughout.

able by their stylistic distinctiveness from the surrounding verses are
1 Cor 15.33 and 2 Cor 9.10. In both places, however, the words in
question could well be mistaken for Pauline formulations by a
Gentile reader unacquainted with their original source. The same
could be said for many of the verses that Koch describes as "only
indirectly marked" with such introductory particles as ὅτι, ἀλλά,
and γάρ (see Rom 10.13, 1 Cor 2.16, and 2 Cor 8.21, 9.7).[11] Finally,
what is one to make of Koch's inclusion of four passages (Rom 2.6,
9.20, 1 Cor 5.13, and 2 Cor 13.1) that he describes as "wholly
unmarked citations"? It seems difficult to avoid the conclusion that
Koch has in reality departed very little from the common pattern of
comparing the Pauline materials with the Jewish Scriptures to
identify possible Pauline citations, then eliminating those that
would appear wholly unrecognizable to the uninformed reader.
Such a mixed approach to defining what is meant by the term
"citation" serves no one well. The result is a conglomeration of texts
that the modern investigator feels the original readers could or
should have recognized as quotations, regardless of whether they
ever actually did so. Deftly sidestepped by this approach are all
questions concerning the actual literary competence of the original
readers, as well as the question of whether Paul's predominantly
Gentile congregations would have recognized the source of the
quotations (i.e. the Jewish Scriptures) even when their citation
character was apparent.

Clearly some better method is needed for deciding what does and
does not count as a "citation." The crucial question remains where
to draw the line that would distinguish "citations" from other less
direct methods of appropriating the language of Scripture. To
attempt to establish any hard and fast guidelines would be to
misrepresent the broad diversity that characterizes Paul's repeated
appeals to the biblical text. One approach would be to classify as a
"citation" any series of several words that reproduces with a reasonable degree of faithfulness the general word order and at least some
of the actual language (whether original or in translation) of an
identifiable passage from an outside text. The opposite view would
be to accept as "citations" only those passages whose citation
character is clearly marked within the text itself, on the grounds that

[11] The citation character of 2 Cor 8.21 and 9.7 is disputed even by modern
commentators: the second is rejected by the UBS Greek New Testament (Nestle
includes it) as well as by Ellis and Longenecker, while Koch stands virtually alone in
accepting the first as a citation (neither UBS nor Nestle treats it as such).

only in these cases can one be certain of attributing the correct motive to the author who adduced the text. An ideal study would utilize both approaches in tandem, relying on the narrower group of texts to set the parameters for understanding Paul's normal citation technique and then analyzing the broader corpus in the light of these findings. For now, however, attention will be restricted to the first set of texts, those that offer a clear indication to the reader that a quotation is indeed present.[12] Three criteria will be used to determine which verses count as "citations" under this narrower definition: (1) those introduced by an explicit quotation formula ("as it is written," etc. – the bulk of the texts); (2) those accompanied by a clear interpretive gloss (e.g. 1 Cor 15.27); and (3) those that stand in demonstrable syntactical tension with their present Pauline surroundings (e.g. Rom 9.7, 10.18, Gal 3.12).[13] The rigid application of such narrow criteria means that a number of texts normally regarded as Pauline citations (Rom 10.13, 11.34–5, 12.20, 1 Cor 2.16, 5.13, 10.26, 15.32, 2 Cor 9.7, 10.17, 13.1, Gal 3.11) will not be addressed in the pages that follow, on the grounds that the uninformed reader could readily take any or all of them as Pauline formulations.[14] At the same time, restricting the study to this narrower body of texts should make it possible to establish a homogeneous data base from which to derive reliable conclusions about the normal citation technique of the apostle Paul.

3. Establishing the text

The status of the Greek and Hebrew texts of the Jewish Scriptures around the turn of the era has long been a subject of debate.[15] No

[12] The second part of the study, an examination of various passages that might qualify as "citations" under the broadest "author-centered" definition set forth above, will follow at a later date.

[13] These will be recognized as categories 1, 3, and 4 in Koch's list of criteria. Michael V. Fox argues for a similar approach in his article, "The Identification of Quotations in Biblical Literature," *ZAW* 92 (1980), 416–31. The same criteria will be applied to the non-Pauline materials to be examined later in this study.

[14] As Fox puts it (427), "If there is no marking at all, we must start with the assumption that there is no quotation, or at least that the quotation is an expression of the speaker's viewpoint and sentiments." Verses excluded from the present study that will be examined at a later date include Rom 2.6, 3.20, 4.9, 9.20, 10.13, 11.2, 11.25, 11.34, 11.35, 12.16, 12.17, 12.20, 1 Cor 2.16, 5.13, 10.5, 10.26, 14.25, 15.25, 15.32, 2 Cor 3.16, 8.21, 9.7, 9.10, 10.17, 13.1, Gal 2.16, 3.11, Phil 1.19, 2.10–11, 2.15, and all of the quotations in Ephesians (1.22, 4.8, 4.25, 4.26, 5.14, 5.18, 5.31, 6.2–3) and the Pastorals (1 Tim 5.18, 5.19, 2 Tim 2.19).

[15] Questions concerning the nature of the Homeric text available to the Greco-Roman authors examined in chap. 7 will be reserved for that chapter.

development has had a more profound impact on studies in this area than the discovery around mid-century of numerous biblical manuscripts from this precise time period in the caves around Khirbet Qumran, Wadi Muraba'at, and Naḥal Ḥever in the Judean desert.[16] Almost overnight, every previous theory concerning the text history of the Jewish Scriptures was rendered obsolete. The result was a whole new round of investigations aimed at discovering which aspects of the earlier views might be salvaged and which would have to be thoroughly revamped in light of the data now available. The ensuing discussion has produced a wealth of new insights concerning the history of the biblical text, resolving lingering controversies in certain areas while intensifying the conflict in others.

The importance of these discussions for the present study can hardly be overstated. If the text of the Jewish Scriptures had assumed a reasonably fixed form by around the turn of the era, one could presumably arrive at a reliable portrait of the way an author handled the wording of his quotations by simply comparing the text of his quotations with that of their presumed *Vorlage*. If, on the other hand, the biblical text remained relatively fluid until well after this time, one would have to develop some other means of distinguishing between apparent authorial adaptations and the use of a deviant text before proceeding to an analysis of the citation technique of a given Jewish or Christian author.

Not surprisingly, most studies in this area until very recent times proceeded on the assumption that the wording of the Hebrew Bible had attained fixed form at a relatively early date. From this fixed text had arisen, with varying degrees of faithfulness to the original, the old Alexandrian Greek translation known as the "Septuagint." The original text of this unified Greek translation, though corrupted somewhat through centuries of transmission, could still (it was supposed) be recovered with reasonable confidence through a critical sifting of the readings of the three great uncial manuscripts from the fourth and fifth centuries C.E., the codices Vaticanus (B), Alexandrinus (A), and Sinaiticus (ℵ). The present Masoretic text of the Hebrew Scriptures and the published editions of the Greek uncials were thus all the tools that the scholar needed to determine

[16] For a concise history of developments in this area before and after the Qumran discoveries, see Shemaryahu Talmon, "The Old Testament Text," in *The Cambridge History of the Bible*, vol. I: *From the Beginnings to Jerome*, ed. P. R. Ackroyd and C. F. Evans (Cambridge University Press, 1970), 159–99; reprinted in *Qumran and the History of the Biblical Text*, ed. Frank M. Cross and Shemaryahu Talmon (Cambridge: Harvard University Press, 1975), 1–41.

what texts might have been available to Jewish and Christian writers around the turn of the era when they quoted from the Jewish Scriptures. Investigation could then be directed toward ascertaining why certain authors appeared to deviate at times from these "standard" texts, with "loose citation from memory" and "correction toward the Hebrew" (in the case of Greek writers) the most common explanations.[17]

More recently, however, careful study of the scrolls from the Judean desert has made it clear that the history of the biblical text was far more complex than these earlier scholars could have imagined. On the one hand, the sheer diversity of the Hebrew manuscripts found at Qumran has shown that the Hebrew text of the Jewish Scriptures was by no means fixed during the period when biblical manuscripts were being copied for the Qumran library. As Shemaryahu Talmon puts it, "The coexistence of diverse text-types in the numerically, geographically, and temporally restricted Covenanters' community, the fact that (some or most of) the conflicting MSS had very probably been copied in the Qumrân scriptorium, and that no obvious attempts at the suppression of divergent MSS or of individual variants can be discovered in that voluminous literature, proves beyond doubt that the very notion of an exclusive *textus receptus* had not yet taken hold at Qumrân."[18] Conditions outside the restricted Qumran community would appear to have been essentially the same, though opinion is divided as to the contemporary attitude toward this state of affairs. Talmon for his part continues, "We have no reason to doubt that this 'liberal' attitude towards divergent textual traditions of the Old Testament prevailed also in 'normative' Jewish circles of the second and first centuries B.C."[19]

---

[17] This does not mean that other evidence was ignored entirely, but rather that investigation normally proceeded as though these basic sources were sufficient except in the most difficult of circumstances. Only when these materials proved inadequate, as in Rom 12.19, 1 Cor 15.54, etc., were parallels sought in such outside materials as the Targumim and the later translations of Aquila, Symmachus, and Theodotion. Kautzsch's study goes further than most toward considering the full range of the evidence, but he too rests his judgments almost exclusively on the testimony of the three great uncials (see his programmatic statement on pp. 6–7).

[18] "Text," 185. Similar statements can be found in Frank M. Cross, "The History of the Biblical Text in the Light of Discoveries in the Judaean Desert," *HTR* 57 (1964), 286; "The Contribution of the Qumrân Discoveries to the Study of the Biblical Text," *IEJ* 16 (1966), 91; and Dominique Barthélemy, "Text, Hebrew, History of," in *Interpreter's Dictionary of the Bible: Supplementary Volume*, ed. Keith Crim (Nashville: Abingdon, 1976), 879.

[19] "Text," 185. Over against the "local texts" theory of Frank M. Cross (see next note), Talmon adheres to a sociological approach that stresses the necessity of

Frank Moore Cross, on the other hand, describes what he calls a "textual crisis" that arose in late Hellenistic and early Roman Palestine as diverse textual traditions imported from the Jewish communities of Egypt and Babylon came into contact with the native tradition of Palestine. The roots of this "crisis" Cross traces to an increase in immigration from the Diaspora following the establishment of the Hasmonean monarchy, coupled with the Parthian expulsion of the Jews in the second century B.C.E.[20] A mediating approach can be seen in the work of Saul Lieberman, who traces the three known Hebrew text-families to three distinct spheres of usage in pre–70 Palestinian Judaism.[21] Whether one

"acceptance by a sociologically definable integrated body" as a precondition to the preservation of a textual tradition ("The Textual Study of the Bible – A New Outlook," in Cross and Talmon (eds.), *Qumran*, 325). According to Talmon, the three surviving biblical text-types represent not independent local traditions (as per Cross), but "the remains of a yet more variegated transmission of the Bible text in the preceding centuries" (325), in which "other constituted deviant Jewish communities may have embraced one specific text-type in their time" (326). Talmon concludes that "with the disappearance of these groups also their respective literary heritages disappeared or were suppressed, and with them their particular biblical textual traditions" (326).

[20] Cross's well-known "local texts" theory has been set forth in a number of influential articles, three of which have been collected in Cross and Talmon (eds.), *Qumran*. His reconstruction of the events that led to the fixing of a standard Jewish biblical text is set forth most fully in "The Text Behind the Text of the Bible," *Bible Review* 1 (Summer 1985), 13–25. Criticisms of Cross's position can be found in Talmon, "Text," 39–40; Barthélemy, "Text," 879; Robert Hanhart, "Zum gegenwärtigen Stand der Septuagintaforschung," in *De Septuaginta: Studies in Honour of John William Wevers on his Sixty-Fifth Birthday*, ed. Albert Pietersma and Claude Cox (Mississauga, Ont.: Benben Publications, 1984), 10–11; and especially George Howard, "Frank Cross and Recensional Criticism," *VT* 21 (1971), 440–50.

[21] Lieberman ("The Texts of Scripture in the Early Rabbinic Period," in *Hellenism in Jewish Palestine* (New York: Jewish Theological Seminary, 1950), 20–7) classifies the families using the terms of classical text-criticism: (a) "base" (φαυλότερα) (= "expansive") manuscripts that circulated primarily among uneducated villagers; (b) "popular" (κοινά) texts that served as the basis for serious study in the cities, including the rabbinical schools; and (c) "excellent" (ἠκριβομένα) copies that were meticulously transmitted by the sages in Jerusalem for use in rendering legal decisions. Frank M. Cross criticizes this explanation: "Distinct textual families take centuries to develop but are exceedingly fragile creations. When manuscripts stemming from different traditions come into contact, the result is their dissolution into a mixed text, or the precipitation of a textual crisis which results in recensional activity, and often in the fixing of a uniform or standard text" ("The Evolution of a Theory of Local Texts," in *[1972] Proceedings of IOSCS: Pseudepigrapha Seminar*, ed. Robert A. Kraft, SBLSCS 2 (Missoula, Mont.: Scholars, 1972), 111–12 (reprinted in Cross and Talmon (eds.), Qumran, 309); cf. "Contribution," 91–2). Observations of this sort offer little problem for Lieberman's approach, however, since in Lieberman's scenario there would have been no motive for recensional standardization on the part of the Jewish authorities so long as the final jurisdiction of the meticulously guarded "excellent" texts was acknowledged by all. The fundamental problem with Lieber-

discerns in it a "liberal attitude," a "textual crisis," or the effects of broader social divisions, however, the textual situation remains the same: a limited diversity of Hebrew text-types (three, according to present knowledge) circulating side-by-side within Palestinian Judaism throughout the late Second Temple period.[22] By the time of the Second Revolt (132–5 C.E.), on the other hand, conditions had changed. The archetype of the later Masoretic text now reigned supreme as the official *textus receptus* of Palestinian Judaism, as witnessed by the remarkable proximity of the Wadi Muraba'at finds (Second Revolt) to the medieval Masoretic textual tradition.[23]

The picture is much the same when one turns to the Greek text. Apart from the Qumran materials and the rabbinic corpus, nearly all of the biblical quotations adduced by Jewish and Christian authors during the Hellenistic and early Roman periods show signs of having been taken from some sort of Greek translation, and not directly from the Hebrew. Extensive comparisons of language, word order, and translation technique have demonstrated further that the great majority of these citations stand quite close to that collection of Greek biblical texts known today as the "Septuagint."[24] These

man's approach lies rather in its inability to explain how a distinct textual family could have arisen among those manuscripts that Lieberman classifies as "base," as opposed to a gradual diffusion into a myriad of individual text-forms.

[22] Almost nothing is known about the status of the Hebrew text outside Palestine during this period, a point often raised against Frank M. Cross's association of one of his three "local text" families with the Jewish community of Babylon.

[23] This is not to deny the existence of a "proto-Masoretic" text-form as early as the turn of the era, when it served as the basis for the so-called *kaige* or "proto-Theodotionic" revision of the common Old Greek translation (see further below). On the Wadi Muraba'at discoveries and their significance for the rabbinic fixing of the "Masoretic" *textus receptus*, see Cross, "History," 287–92; Barthélemy, "History," 880–1; and B. J. Roberts, "Text, Old Testament," *Interpreter's Dictionary of the Bible* (1962), 4:583.

[24] The ambiguity surrounding the term "Septuagint" (and its abbreviated form "LXX") in modern scholarship has led many investigators to adopt the designation "Old Greek" to refer to the (theoretical) original translation of a given biblical book. The label "Septuagint" is then reserved either for the Greek Pentateuch (so Leonard Greenspoon, "The Use and Misuse of the Term 'LXX' and Related Terminology in Recent Scholarship," *BIOSCS* 20 (1987), 21–9) or else for that collection of translations represented in the great codices of the fourth and fifth centuries C.E. (so Emanuel Tov, "The Septuagint," in *Mikra: Text, Translation, Reading and Interpretation of the Hebrew Bible in Ancient Judaism and Early Christianity*, ed. Martin Jan Mulder, Compendia Rerum Iudaicarum II/1 (Assen, Maastricht: Van Gorcum, 1988; Philadelphia: Fortress, 1988), 161). While restricting "Septuagint" to the Greek Pentateuch would no doubt preserve the etymology of the term, the weight of tradition lies on the side of the broader designation. Accordingly, the term "Septuagint" will be applied in the present study to the collection of Greek biblical texts

common observations, however, conceal as much as they reveal. There remains in fact a great deal of uncertainty concerning the precise form in which the Greek text of the Jewish Scriptures would have been available to authors of the late Hellenistic and early Roman periods. In the first place, the very existence of the "Septuagint" as a recognized and accepted translation of the entire Hebrew Bible (with certain additions) at this early date is contested by many. The standard view of Paul de Lagarde, who argued for a single original translation from a non-Masoretic Hebrew original, has been forcefully challenged in recent years by Paul Kahle, who sees in the "Septuagint" a late (Christian) attempt to impose unity upon a highly diffuse earlier translation history.[25] Supporters of both views have claimed to find support for their positions in the various biblical texts recovered in the Judean desert.[26]

A second problem concerns the tendency of investigators to speak of the "Septuagint" as though it were a fixed entity whose wording remained consistent at all times and in all places (apart from the usual corruptions in transmission) throughout the ancient world. Two difficulties stand in the way of such a facile assumption. In the first place, very little is actually known about the translation histories of the individual books of the Jewish canon prior to their incorporation in the standard collection represented by the great uncial manuscripts of the fourth and fifth centuries C.E. The internal evidence of the documents themselves points toward a gradual and decentralized process in which individual books (or parts of books) were rendered into Greek by different translators over several generations.[27] Investigators have documented the distinctive

found in the later codices, whatever their individual origins and text-histories, while "Old Greek" will be used for the (theoretical) earliest translation of each book.

[25] The basic texts are Paul de Lagarde, *Ankündigung einer neuen Ausgabe der griechischen Übersetzung des Alten Testaments* (Göttingen: Dieterischen Univ.-Buchdruckerei, 1882) and Paul Kahle, *Genizah*.

[26] Cross, "History," 283, speaks of a "qualified victory" for the Lagarde school, while Kahle presents his own interpretation of the data in "Der gegenwartige Stand der Erforschung der in Palästina neu gefundenen hebräischen Handschriften: 27. Die in August 1952 entdeckte Lederrolle mit dem griechischen Text der kleinen Propheten und das Problem der Septuaginta," *TLZ* 79 (1954), 81–94. In the view of John William Wevers, the Minor Prophets scroll discovered at Naḥal Ḥever (see below) is decisive: "Hier ist ein Text, die offensichtlich jüdisch ist und der ebenso offensichtlich zeigt, daß eine Revision des sogenannten 'christlichen' LXX-Textes ist" ("Septuaginta: Forschungen seit 1954," *TRu* 33 (1968), 68).

[27] Most investigators date the authoritative translation of the Pentateuch to the late third century B.C.E. on the basis of early quotations combined with a critical reading of the *Letter of Aristeas*. Scholars remain divided, however, over whether this translation was carried out under Ptolemaic sponsorship or at the instigation of the

translational character of nearly every book of the Jewish Scriptures,[28] while multiple recensions are normally printed for the books of Judges and Daniel to reflect the complex textual histories of these books.[29] Recent studies have shown further that all or parts of several other books of the "Septuagint" contain not the original Old Greek translation, but rather a revised form "corrected" to bring it into line with a later Hebrew *Vorlage*.[30] Emanuel Tov sums up the current state of affairs: "As a result of recent finds and studies in early recensions, the heterogeneity of the canon of the LXX has become increasingly evident. It has been recognized that 'the LXX' contains translations of different types, early and late, relatively original and significantly revised, official and private, literal and free."[31] The very fact that the various books of the Jewish canon were transmitted for the most part in individual scrolls prior to the emergence of the codex in the second century C.E. makes such a diverse translation history all the more understandable.[32] How the

Alexandrian Jewish community. At the other end of the spectrum, the colophon to the Greek book of Esther gives a date of 114 B.C.E. (or possibly 78 B.C.E.) for its translation. Whether the non-Pentateuchal books were rendered into Greek under some sort of "official" auspices or as private translations (so Elias Bickermann, "Some Notes on the Transmission of the Septuagint," in *Studies in Jewish and Christian History* (Leiden: Brill, 1976), 1:148, 166) remains unclear. The evidence used to date the various translations is summed up in Gilles Dorival, Marguerite Harl, and Olivier Munnich, *La Bible grecque des Septante* (Paris: Cerf, 1988), 84–98, 110–11. For a helpful summary of the current state of the debate on LXX origins, see Robert Hanhart, "Septuagintaforschung," 3–8.

[28] See the list of studies cited in Tov, "Jewish Greek Scriptures," in Kraft and Nickelsburg (eds.), *Early Judaism*, 227. Other relevant works include E. J. Bickermann, "The Septuagint as a Translation," *PAAJR* 28 (1959), 1–39; Homer Heater, *A Septuagint Translation Technique in the Book of Job* (Washington, DC: Catholic Biblical Association, 1982); Jan de Waard, "Translation Techniques Used by the Greek Translators of Amos," *Bib* 59 (1978), 39–50, and "Translation Techniques Used by the Greek Translators of Ruth," *Bib* 54 (1973), 499–515.

[29] Recently Natalio Fernández Marcos has suggested that the same should be done for the Greek books of Kingdoms (= 1–2 Samuel and 1–2 Kings) to allow for separate consideration of the "Lucianic" recension of those books ("The Lucianic Text in the Books of Kingdoms: From Lagarde to the Textual Pluralism," in Pietersma and Cox (eds.), *De Septuaginta*, 173). Shemaryahu Talmon makes a similar recommendation for the books of Esther (since followed in the Göttingen edition) and Jeremiah in "Textual Study," 327.

[30] See below for the evidence regarding early revisions of the Old Greek.

[31] "Jewish Greek Scriptures," 225.

[32] According to Emanuel Tov, "This mixture [of original translations and revisions in the 'LXX'] probably originated in the time when scribes started to compose large scale codices copied from scrolls of apparently variegated character" ("Septuagint," 169). So also Elias Bickermann, "Notes," 147: "Behind the one volume of the fourth century which Jerome had in mind we must visualize not another volume which is their common source ... but a confused plurality of

various scrolls that were eventually incorporated into the "Septuagint" circulated and when they were first collected into a unified corpus remains shrouded in mystery.

Of greater importance for the present study is the growing awareness in the post-Qumran era of the variety of forms in which the same book of the Jewish Greek Scriptures might have been available to different contemporary users. Recent textual discoveries have pushed the issue far beyond the traditional question of whether an author's biblical citations stand closer to the textual tradition represented by LXX$_A$ or LXX$_B$. Investigators now speak of multiple revisions to the original Old Greek translation intended to bring it into closer alignment with differing versions of the Hebrew biblical text. In the famous words of Frank Moore Cross, "We see, then, a series of attempts to bring the Greek Bible into conformity with a *changing* Hebrew textual tradition."[33]

The roots of this new consensus can be traced to the publication in 1963 of Dominique Barthélemy's landmark studies in a fragmentary biblical scroll discovered a decade earlier at Naḥal Ḥever, due south of Qumran.[34] This scroll, dubbed *8ḤevXIIgr*, originally contained a Greek translation of the Hebrew minor prophets. Though it was found in a cache of materials linked to the Bar Kochba revolt, paleographic studies have dated the manuscript to the middle of the first century C.E.[35] Careful comparison with the existing "Septuagint" translation of the minor prophets shows the version in the scroll to be a thorough reworking of the Old Greek version designed to bring it into closer agreement with a forerunner of the Masoretic

divergent papyrus rolls." On the nature and use of books in the ancient world (including the rise of the codex in the early Christian era), see C. H. Roberts and T. C. Skeat, *The Birth of the Codex* (Oxford University Press for the British Academy, 1983); E. G. Turner, *Greek Manuscripts of the Ancient World* (Princeton University Press, 1971); *The Typology of the Early Codex* (Philadelphia: University of Pennsylvania Press, 1977); and the various entries under "Buch" in *Reallexicon für Antike und Christentum* (1954).

[33] "History," 283 (emphasis his).

[34] See Barthélemy, *Devanciers*. A lengthy preview of Barthélemy's later work appeared ten years earlier in an article entitled "Redécouverte d'un chaînon manquant de l'histoire de la Septante," *RB* 60 (1953), 18–29.

[35] Barthélemy ("Redécouverte," 19, and *Devanciers*, 167–8) argued for a mid-first-century C.E. date, a position confirmed by Frank M. Cross ("History," 282). A more recent study by Peter J. Parsons ("The Scripts and Their Date," in Emanuel Tov (ed.), *The Greek Minor Prophets Scroll from Naḥal Ḥever (8ḤevXIIgr)*, DJD VIII (Oxford: Clarendon, 1990), 19–26) would move the date back to the late first century B.C.E.

Hebrew text.[36] Characteristic features of this early revision have since been identified in the "Theodotionic" version of Daniel; the B version of LXX Judges; the standard "Septuagint" texts of Lamentations, Ruth, Song of Songs, and most of the books of Kingdoms (2 Sam 11.1–1Kgs 2.11 and 1 Kgs 22.1–2 Kgs 25.30 MT); certain additions in the "Septuagint" versions of Job and Jeremiah; the Quinta column of Origen's *Hexapla*; the biblical quotations of Justin Martyr; portions of the Sahidic Coptic translation of the Jewish Scriptures; and the later versions of Aquila, Symmachus, and Theodotion.[37] The existence of such a "proto-Theodotionic" revision of the Old Greek in the early first century C.E. (the commonly accepted date for such a project) would go far toward explaining the agreement of certain New Testament passages with readings found in the later (second-century) text of Theodotion, who now appears as a reviser of this earlier revision and not as an independent translator. The same holds true for Aquila, who apparently adopted and systematized many of the translation techniques already present in this earlier revision, and possibly also for Symmachus, though the evidence is less clear in his case.[38] Further evidence for the existence of early "Hebraizing" revisions of the Old Greek comes from fragmentary papyrus finds in Egypt and at Qumran.[39]

[36] An exhaustive comparison of the various textual traditions is now available in Tov (ed.), *Minor Prophets Scroll*, 99–158. Though he offers little in the way of synthesis, Tov is clear in his judgment that "the Hebrew *Vorlage* of R [= *8HevXIIgr*] [was] much closer to MT than to that of the LXX, so that R's revisional labour must have included the approximating of the 'LXX' to a forerunner of MT, which however was not identical with it" (145).

[37] In addition to the works of Barthélemy and Cross cited above, see Kevin G. O'Connell, "Greek Versions (Minor)," in Crim (ed.), *IDB Supplement*, 377–81. Barthélemy's conclusions concerning the "proto-Theodotionic" nature of portions of Kingdoms had been anticipated by Henry St. J. Thackeray: see "The Greek Translators of the Four Books of Kings," *JTS* 8 (1907), 262–78, and *The Septuagint and Jewish Worship*, 2nd edn (London: H. Milford, 1923).

[38] On Symmachus, note the contrasting opinions in Barthélemy, "Redécouverte," 135–6 (dependent), and O'Connell, "Versions," 378–9 (uncertain).

[39] Fragments of three different Egyptian Greek scrolls from the first century B.C.E. (P. Fouad 266), one with parts of Genesis and two others from Deuteronomy, show clear signs of sporadic correction toward the Hebrew text, according to the editors of the recent photographic edition (Z. Aly and L. Koenen, *Three Rolls of the Early Septuagint: Genesis and Deuteronomy* (Bonn: R. Habelt, 1980), 1, 9, 16–20). See also John William Wevers, *Text History of the Greek Deuteronomy*, MSU 13 (Göttingen: Vandenhoeck und Ruprecht, 1978), 69–71. Patrick Skehan had already noted similar tendencies in three fragmentary Greek Pentateuchal texts from Qumran (*4QLXXNum*, *4QLXXLev*[a], and *7QLXXExod*) in separate articles in 1957 and 1965, where he also discussed a similar phenomenon in the secondary recension of the Greek *Sirach*, the reworked form of the first nine chapters of Proverbs, and P. 967 of Ezekiel. See "The Qumran Manuscripts and Textual Criticism," in *Volume de*

Building on Barthélemy's conclusions, Frank Moore Cross has argued for an even earlier "proto-Lucianic" revision (first century B.C.E.) that he believes was used by the church father Lucian (third century C.E.) as the basis for his own edition of the Old Greek text. This revision, evidence for which can be seen in the "Septuagint" manuscripts b o c_2 e_2, certain parts of the Old Latin tradition, the sixth column of Origen's *Hexapla* (for a portion of the book of Kingdoms), and the Greek biblical quotations of Josephus, was carried out (according to Cross) to bring the Old Greek translation into closer alignment with a Hebrew text of the type contained in the Qumran fragment *4QSam^a*, the oldest biblical fragment unearthed at Qumran (from the third century B.C.E.).[40] Cross' reading of the evidence has been subjected to intense scrutiny; the latest restatement of his position appears to represent a partial retreat in the face of repeated criticism.[41]

Of equal interest are a number of cases where the Old Greek has experienced modifications of a type unrelated to any concern to bring it closer to the Hebrew text. In most such instances, the aim appears to have been to create a smoother reading to replace a

[IOSOT 2nd] Congrès, Strasbourg, 1956, ed. G. W. Anderson, VTSup 4 (Leiden: Brill, 1957), 148–58, and "The Biblical Scrolls from Qumran and the Text of the Old Testament," *BA* 28 (1965), 87–100. A similar position is argued by John William Wevers in "Forschungen seit 1954," 47–51. Eugene Ulrich lists the textual variants (a total of 57) in all the Qumran LXX fragments published to date in "The Greek Manuscripts of the Pentateuch From Qumran, Including Newly-Identified Fragments of Deuteronomy (*4QLXXDeut*)," in Pietersma and Cox (eds.), *De Septuaginta*, 77–81.

[40] The evidence is discussed in "History," 292–6, and repeated in "Contribution," 88–9. The designations b o c_2 e_2 are those of Brooke–McLean (= Göttingen MSS 19, 82, 127, 93), which have become something of a technical shorthand for the "Lucianic" tradition in certain books of the LXX. The Göttingen edition of Kingdoms is not yet available.

[41] The restated position can be found in "Evolution," 116 ("a light sprinkling of readings derived from the Palestinian text family ... to which the Old Greek was sporadically corrected") and especially 126 n. 30 ("At most the proto-Lucianic text is a light revision of the Old Greek, consisting of occasional corrections to the closely allied Palestinian [Hebrew] text"). Criticisms and alternative readings of the evidence are offered by George Howard, "Cross," 443–9, and Emanuel Tov, "Lucian and Proto-Lucian," *RB* 79 (1972), 101–13. Cross responds to both in "Evolution," 120–1 (Tov) and 126 n. 30 (Howard). On the whole question of "Lucian" and "proto-Lucian," see also Sebastian Brock, "Lucian *redivivus*: Some Reflections on Barthélemy's *Les devanciers d'Aquila*," in *Studia Evangelica 5*, ed. F. L. Cross, TU 103 (Berlin: Akademie Verlag, 1968), 176–81; Emanuel Tov, "The State of the Question: Problems and Proposed Solutions," in Kraft (ed.), *[1972] Proceedings*, 3–15; Dominique Barthélemy, "A Reexamination of the Textual Problems in 2 Sam 11.2–1 Kings 2.11 in the Light of Certain Criticisms of *Les devanciers d'Aquila*," in Kraft (ed.), *[1972] Proceedings*, 16–89; and Fernández Marcos, "Lucianic Text."

somewhat awkward Greek original. The evidence for such revisions
is scattered and diverse. In his discussion of the Greek Minor
Prophets scroll from Naḥal Ḥever, Dominique Barthélemy remarks
that "one also finds a certain number [of variants] where our text
seems to distance itself from both the LXX and the MT."[42] In a
recent discussion of the Qumran fragment *4QLXXNum*, the eminent
LXX scholar John William Wevers concluded that its language
"tend[s] rather to a clearer and more exact Greek than that of [LXX]
Num."[43] A similar analysis of *4QLXXLev^a* by Patrick Skehan
revealed ten unique readings in the space of fifteen verses, of which
nine "are farther from a mechanical reading of the Masoretic text
than what is contained in the codices."[44] Emanuel Tov sums up the
present consensus with his observation that "the purpose of some
revisions was the clarification and stylistic improvement of the
Greek wording without any connection to the Hebrew *Vorlage*."[45]
Apparently the inevitable attempts to bring the Old Greek into
conformity with a diverse Hebrew textual tradition were accompanied by a parallel movement to improve on what was thought to
be an awkward Greek style in the original translation.

This emerging understanding of the history of the biblical text
must be given full weight by anyone who seeks to analyze the
citation techniques of Jewish and Christian writers in the late
Hellenistic and early Roman periods. At the very least it points up
the fallacy of assuming that every divergence from the Masoretic

[42] "Redécouverte," 22 (translation mine). Barthélemy suggests the possibility of a
different Hebrew *Vorlage* in such cases, but adduces only two examples. If Frank M.
Cross is correct in viewing this scroll as an attempt to bring the Old Greek into line
with a proto-Masoretic ("Babylonian") form of the Hebrew text ("History," 282, 292,
296; "Evolution," 117) and in equating this "Babylonian" text with the so-called
"Palestinian" (expansionist) text in the minor prophets ("Evolution," 110), the
possibility that a deviant Hebrew text might lie behind such divergent readings in the
Minor Prophets scroll would be substantially reduced.

[43] Wevers's analysis ("An Early Revision of the Septuagint of Numbers," *Eretz
Israel* 16 (1982), 235*–9*) essentially confirmed Patrick Skehan's earlier judgments
concerning the revisionary nature of *4QLXXNum* ("*4QLXXNum*: A Pre-Christian
Reworking of the Septuagint," *HTR* 70 (1977), 39–50), while rejecting his characterization of the manuscript as "Hebraizing" in character.

[44] "Manuscripts," 158.

[45] "Jewish Greek Scriptures," 230. In an unpublished Ph. D. dissertation ("The
Recensions of the Septuagint Version of 1 Samuel" (Oxford, 1966), 265–6), Sebastian
Brock discusses two types of recensional activity that he finds in the so-called
"Lucianic" revision of the LXX: one aiming to improve the Greek style by eliminat-
ing certain Hellenistic terms and grammatical forms, the other adapting the text to
the requirements of public reading (described by Natalio Fernández Marcos in
"Lucianic Text," 167–8). The revision of Symmachus appears to reflect a similar
procedure.

Hebrew text or the printed editions of the Septuagint reflects a modification introduced into the passage (whether consciously or unconsciously) by the author who cites the text. Studies in the post-Qumran era have shown that both the Hebrew and the Greek texts of the Jewish Scriptures remained unsettled throughout the Second Temple period, a fact that is easy to overlook in the face of printed editions that reflect the relatively unified traditions of a later time.

On the other hand, the biblical text was by no means so fluid that one has to suspend all judgment concerning its specific content. Frank Moore Cross sums up his studies in the Hebrew biblical scrolls from the Judean desert with the observation that "their diversity is not fluid or chaotic but conforms to a clear and simple pattern [consisting of] distinct families limited in number."[46] The situation is less clear in the case of the Greek text, but the evidence seems to suggest the existence of a primary version that enjoyed wide circulation and use throughout the late Second Temple period,[47] together with one or more (perhaps partial) "Hebraizing" revisions whose influence remained more limited. Alongside these major versions circulated an indeterminate number of manuscripts characterized by more sporadic "corrections" designed either to bring the text into closer agreement with a particular Hebrew *Vorlage* or to smooth out perceived irregularities in its Greek style.[48]

Such a picture of what might be called the "limited diversity" of the biblical text around the turn of the era carries several practical implications for research on the biblical quotations of Jewish and Christian authors. In the first place, it means that the investigator cannot presume to know in advance what type of biblical text might have been used by a given author as the basis for his citations. In the case of quotations from the Hebrew Bible, it will be necessary to

---

[46] "Contribution," 84.

[47] In arguing that the "Septuagint" is a uniquely Christian creation, Paul Kahle (Genizah, 158–79) overlooks the countless citations by both Jews and Jewish Christians (e.g. the apostle Paul: see chap. 3), drawn from virtually every book of the Bible, that agree verbatim with the present text of the Septuagint.

[48] Whether the mix of texts in circulation might have included independent translations of certain books remains a difficult question. Though he clearly outran his evidence at certain points, the arguments marshaled by Kahle in favor of multiple early translations (the divided textual traditions of such books as Ezra/*Esdras*, Judges, Esther, and *Tobit*; fragmentary texts that appear to reflect independent renderings of the same Hebrew *Vorlage*; parallels with other translations; etc.) have not always received the attention they deserve. See the discussions of 1 Cor 3.19 (cf. Rom 11.35) and 1 Cor 14.21 in chap. 5.

consult not only the printed editions of the Masoretic text, but also the readings of the various Qumran biblical manuscripts (where available), the Samaritan Pentateuch, the full range of Septuagintal traditions, and the evidence of the other early versions.[49] For citations taken from the Greek, every piece of evidence listed in the critical apparatus to the printed editions will have to be taken into consideration. In both cases, the researcher will have to develop criteria for judging whether a given reading that lacks support in the manuscript tradition might nevertheless reflect the original *Vorlage* of a particular citation. In the absence of a highly consistent pattern of citation, there is simply no basis for assuming that an author's agreement with one strand of the manuscript tradition in certain instances can be used to resolve a difficult textual problem in an entirely separate location.

A second result of this view of the biblical text is to urge caution in appealing to the translation practice of "the Septuagint" to settle difficult questions concerning a problematic reading in a later quotation. The Greek version known today as "the Septuagint" is best regarded not as a single translation, but rather as a collection of translations prepared over the course of perhaps two and a half centuries, whose language, style, and mode of translation vary widely from book to book. Appeals to the practice of "the Septuagint" can be quite useful when the aim is to define the linguistic possibilities open to a given translator in rendering a particular word or phrase from Hebrew into Greek. But such generalized evidence must not be allowed to substitute for an understanding of a specific translator's normal translation practice as revealed elsewhere in the same book.[50] A reading in a later quotation that coincides with a translator's normal translation technique might well be original despite very limited support in the LXX manuscript tradition; conversely, a reading that runs counter to the same translator's usual practice should be considered suspect no matter how closely it coincides with "Septuagintal" usages elsewhere.

[49] The discovery at Qumran of a number of Hebrew texts that stand closer to the Septuagint than to the Masoretic text, especially the "short" version of Jeremiah witnessed in *4QJer^b*, have convinced most scholars that "the Septuagint faithfully reflects a conservative Hebrew textual family" (Cross, "Contribution," 82). Whether this text can be localized in Egypt as Cross argues remains a subject of debate: see Barthélemy, "Reexamination," 72 (with response by Cross in "Evolution," 122 n. 11); "Text," 879; and especially Howard, "Cross," 442–3.

[50] As Tov puts it, "The maximal entity which can be considered as separate translation unit is a single book and at times only part of a book" ("Septuagint," 169).

A third implication concerns the need to be alert to the possibility that a questionable reading might reflect the use of a biblical *Vorlage* that has experienced a greater or lesser amount of revision. This is true even where manuscript support for the proposed revision is entirely lacking: the fragmentary finds in the Judean desert have revealed nothing if not the woeful inadequacy of modern evidence for the rich diversity of readings available to ancient users of the biblical text. Still, the options are not unlimited. The evidence uncovered thus far shows two basic patterns of revision: (1) to bring a manuscript into closer conformity with a particular Hebrew *Vorlage*,[51] or (2) to clarify or improve upon a rendering perceived to be especially awkward by later readers.[52] For every questionable reading, then, the intrinsic probability that an author might have adapted the biblical text for his own use must be weighed against the possibility that the words in question were derived from a manuscript that had already been revised according to one of these two patterns.

One final consequence of this post-Qumran understanding of the history of the biblical text can only be mentioned in passing at this point. Modern investigators are fond of noting that the Septuagint is as much an interpretation as a translation. Behind this remark lies the recognition that the translation of the biblical text into a new language entailed countless exegetical decisions whereby the translators' (or their contemporaries') judgments as to the meaning of the text were enshrined in the language of the resulting translation. With the discovery of the Hebrew biblical manuscripts from Qumran, scholars have now been able to observe a similar process at work within the scribal tradition of the Hebrew text itself.[53] Such

---

[51] This applies equally to citations from the Hebrew Bible – several of the biblical manuscripts from Qumran contain supralineal "corrections" intended to bring their wording into line with that of other text-families. Shemaryahu Talmon ("Aspects of the Textual Transmission of the Bible in the Light of the Qumran Manuscripts," *Textus* 4 (1964), 97) points especially to *1QIs^a*, where the superscribed readings come from a proto-Masoretic text-type, and to a roughly contemporaneous manuscript of Deuteronomy from Cave 5 (*5QDeut*: see DJD III, 169–71), where corrections tend toward a Septuagintal text-type. A lengthy discussion in the same article shows how easily such "corrections" could become embedded in the text itself through subsequent copying errors (101–6).

[52] This sort of "correction," too, is not limited to Greek texts. Talmon (*ibid.*, 101) discusses the possibility of similar alterations being introduced into a Hebrew text to conform its language to a copyist's own Aramaic background.

[53] Detailed investigation has focused primarily on the two great Isaiah manuscripts from Qumran, especially *1QIs^a*. See for example Joseph Ziegler, "Die Vorlage der Isaias-Septuaginta (LXX) und die erste Isaias-Rolle von Qumran (*1QIs^a*)," *JBL*

visible testimony to what Shemaryahu Talmon calls a "controlled freedom of textual variation"[54] raises intriguing questions about whether this same scribal ethos might have influenced the way contemporary authors viewed the language of Scripture in framing explicit quotations. More will be said about this possibility in a later chapter.[55]

4. Isolating the adaptations

As was noted in chapter 1, modern research into the use of the Jewish Scriptures in antiquity has been dominated for the most part by Christian attempts to account for the unusual (by modern standards) character of many of the biblical quotations found in the canonical books of the New Testament. The question of how a particular author handled the wording of his *Vorlage*, where addressed at all, has received only cursory attention in such studies, usually as part of a more technical inquiry into the nature of the author's biblical text. For this reason the recent attempt by Dietrich-Alex Koch to analyze the wording of Paul's quotations deserves special consideration.[56]

Unlike most earlier investigators, Koch is keenly aware of recent developments in Septuagintal studies, and argues convincingly that Paul has quoted from non-"standard" Greek texts on a number of occasions.[57] Some of these are places where Paul has (unknowingly) followed one strand of the extant Septuagintal tradition over another.[58] Others reveal Paul's familiarity with revised editions of the Old Greek text.[59] Still other passages show signs of having been

---

78 (1959), 34–59; Talmon, "Aspects" and "*DSIa* as a Witness to Ancient Exegesis of the Book of Isaiah," *Annual of the Swedish Theological Institute* 1 (1962), 62–72. Frank M. Cross comments frequently on the "expansionist" tendencies of the so-called "Palestinian" text-type, especially in the Pentateuch – see "Contribution," 86, 88, and "Evolution," 112–13.

54 "Textual Study," 326. Talmon clarifies what he means with the observation that "the limited flux of the textual transmission of the Bible appears to be a legitimate and accepted phenomenon of ancient scribal tradition and not a matter which resulted from sheer incompetence or professional laxity" (*ibid.*).

55 See the discussion in chap. 9.

56 *Schrift*, 102–90.

57 In his *Vorwort*, Koch thanks Dr. Robert Hanhart, head of the Göttingen Septuagint project, for his assistance in the sections where Septuagintal matters are discussed.

58 Examples include Rom 9.27 (omitting αὐτῶν with A Q), Rom 9.33/10.11 (including ἐπ'αὐτῷ with B V), and Rom 14.11 (reading ἐξομολογήσεται instead of ὀμεῖται, following A Q Sᶜ ᵐᵍ). Other instances are listed in *Schrift*, 49, 52, 54–7.

59 E.g. Rom 9.27–8, 10.15, 11.3–4, 11.35, 1 Cor 3.19, 14.21, 15.54.

adapted for use in the oral tradition of synagogue or church.[60] Places where the Pauline tradition might have influenced the Septuagint manuscripts and vice versa are also noted on several occasions.[61]

Still, there remain dozens of places where the wording of Paul's quotations resists every attempt at a manuscript-based explanation. Rather than pursuing an inductive analysis in which each of these passages is examined individually, Koch catalogues his findings under seven headings that reflect the types of adaptations that he sees occurring routinely in Paul's quotations: (1) reversing the order of words (primarily for accentuation);[62] (2) changing person, number, gender, tense, and mood of various words (to suit a new context or to draw out a new meaning from a given verse);[63] (3) omitting words from the text (to make it more concise, to accentuate, or to offer a new interpretation);[64] (4) adding words to the text (relatively infrequent, usually to clarify the sense);[65] (5) replacing words or phrases by new formulations (to adapt a passage to Pauline patterns of speech, to accentuate, or to express a new

[60] E.g. Rom 9.33, 11.26–7, 12.19, 13.9a.

[61] *Schrift*, 54, and frequently in the examination of individual texts, 102–90. These and other textual matters are discussed at length in *ibid.*, 48–83. On the whole question, see chap. 3 of the present study.

[62] Included among Koch's examples are the reversal of clauses in Paul's (highly adapted) citation of Hos 2.25 in Rom 9.25, which brings "not my people" into a place of prominence to accord with his application of the verse to Gentile Christians, and 2 Cor 8.15, where a transposition of subject and verb in the first clause creates a neat formal parallelism. Additional examples are noted in Rom 2.25 (citing Isa 52.5) and 1 Cor 15.55 (citing Hos 13.14).

[63] Typical examples of conforming the text to its new grammatical context include Rom 3.18 (αὐτοῦ from Ps 35.2 changed to αὐτῶν); Rom 10.19 (αὐτούς from Deut 32.21 modified to ὑμᾶς); and 1 Cor 15.27 (ὑπέταξας from Ps 8.7 replaced by ὑπέταξεν). More theologically motivated changes appear in Rom 9.17, where the reversion to the MT's first-person address (ἐξήγειρα in place of the διετηρήθης of Exod 9.16_LXX) suits Paul's emphasis on the absolute sovereignty of God, and Rom 10.15, where the shift from the singular εὐαγγελιζομένου of Isa 52.7 to the plural τῶν εὐαγγελιζομένων is required by Paul's re-application of the verse to Christian missionaries. Further examples include Rom 10.11 (citing Isa 28.16), 1 Cor 14.21 (Isa 28.11–12), and 1 Cor 15.54–5 (combining Isa 25.8 with Hos 13.14).

[64] Instances of omissions that affect the meaning of the text include Rom. 1.17 (the μου in Hab 2.4_LXX clearly refers to the πίστις of God, not humanity); Gal 3.13 (reflecting Paul's Christian sensitivity to speaking of Christ as "cursed ὑπὸ θεοῦ," as in Deut 21.23); and Gal 4.30 (adapting a narrative declaration by Sarah into a divine injunction by omitting the words ταύτην, ταύτης, and μου Ἰσαακ from Gen 21.10). Other omissions of various types can be seen in Rom 3.15–17 (Isa 59.7–8), Rom 9.28 (Isa 10.22–3), Rom 10.6–8 (Deut 30.12–14), and 1 Cor 2.16 (Isa 40.13; cf. Rom 11.34).

[65] For instance, the twofold addition of οὐκ to Ps 13.2 in Rom 3.11, used to maintain the sense of the original in a new context, and the emphatic addition of ἐγώ to Deut 32.35 in Rom 12.19.

interpretation);[66] (6) merging a portion of one verse into the text of another (the so-called "mixed" or "conflated" citations);[67] and (7) combining different texts back-to-back under a single introductory formula (labelled "combined citations").[68] According to Koch's calculations, adaptations can be seen in fully 56 percent of Paul's quotations (52 out of a total of 93), with over half the affected texts experiencing multiple alterations. Up to three-fourths of these adaptations effect a basic change in the meaning of the verse so treated. Most of these changes relate directly to the way the verse functions in its new context. Taken together, says Koch, all the evidence seems to indicate that Paul was aware of the precise wording of the biblical text in every instance, and chose either to retain or alter that wording depending on his reasons for adducing a particular verse.[69]

On the whole, there is much to applaud about Koch's findings in this portion of his study.[70] What is missing, however, is a comprehensive statement of method that would allow the reader to evaluate whether Koch has made his case in regard to any individual citation. The difficulty is heightened by the fact that Koch rarely considers alternatives to his own analysis of a particular reading. Enough is said, however, to allow the reader to infer with reasonable confidence the principles that guided Koch's analysis of the Pauline materials as a whole. These principles can be framed as a

[66] From the numerous examples adduced by Koch may be noted the substitution of ἐλεύσομαι for ἀναστρέψω in Rom 9.9 (the original reference to the angel's "return" in Gen 18.14 would have made no sense in the new context); the use of ἀθετήσω in place of κρύψω in 1 Cor 1.19 (strengthening the depiction of the divine action in Isa 29.14 and creating a better parallel with ἀπολῶ); and the substitution of σοφῶν for the more general ἀνθρώπων in 1 Cor 3.20, quoting Ps 93.11 (linking the verse more explicitly to the theme of the vanity of human wisdom that dominates 1 Cor 1–3).

[67] E.g. Rom 9.25–7, where the καλέσω that introduces v. 25 (citing Hos 2.25) is derived from the κληθήσονται of v. 26 (citing Hos 2.1); Rom 9.33, which merges a phrase from Isa 8.14 into Isa 28.16; and Gal 3.8, where Gen 12.3 and 18.18 are conflated.

[68] The classic example is Rom 3.10–18, which combines into a single "quotation" verses from Ps 13.1–3, Ps 5.10, Ps 139.4, Ps 9.28, Isa 59.7–8, and Ps 35.2. Other instances cited by Koch include Rom 11.26–7, which brings together Isa 59.20–1 and Isa 27.9; Rom 11.33–6, combining Isa 40.13 and Job 41.3; and 1 Cor 15.54–5, juxtaposing Isa 25.8 with Hos 13.14.

[69] Koch's conclusions are summarized in *Schrift*, 186–90. On the question of whether Paul drew his citations from a written text whose wording he consciously molded or simply quoted loosely from memory, see chap. 3. Koch's analysis of Paul's adaptive techniques is little affected by such judgments.

[70] Comments on Koch's handling of specific texts will be reserved for chaps. 4 and 5.

series of questions that seem to have been put to every problematic reading to determine its likely origin:

(1)   Does the reading in question coincide with (or diverge from) the normal linguistic usage (vocabulary, syntax, style, etc.) of either Paul or his presumed *Vorlage*?

(2)   Does the present wording of the quotation show the influence of (or run counter to) Paul's own characteristic theology?

(3)   Does the questionable wording diverge from normal Greek usage in such a way as to make editorial intrusion likely?

(4)   Is the questionable reading integral to Paul's use of the quotation in its present context? Was the passage unusable to Paul in its original wording?

(5)   Is the Pauline form of the text markedly incongruent (either grammatically or conceptually) with its original Greek context?

(6)   Does a reading of questionable origin appear in conjunction with other more secure alterations? Does it fit with Paul's normal pattern of adapting the biblical text as seen in other passages?

When reduced in this way to a series of heuristic principles, the value of Koch's decision-making criteria becomes readily apparent. The generally convincing nature of much of Koch's analysis can be traced to the use of a reasonable set of guidelines for judging what does and does not constitute a Pauline adaptation. Still, Koch's method has its faults. At times Koch is too quick to infer a Pauline origin for a deviant reading on the basis of a perceived correspondence with normal Pauline practice (numbers 1, 2, and 6b above), without seriously considering whether that same usage might be typical of Septuagintal or early Christian practice as well.[71] Many of the rules of Greek grammar to which Koch appeals (number 3 above) are likewise too variable or uncertain to produce reliable conclusions as to the origins of an otherwise questionable reading.[72]

[71] As when he points to Rom 13.6 and 2 Cor 5.5 to explain the shift from ἕνεκεν τούτου to εἰς αὐτὸ τοῦτο in Rom 9.17 (= Exod 9.16) (*Schrift*, 141), or when he appeals to the infrequency of the expression οὐ μή in Paul (it actually occurs five times) to argue that Paul himself dropped the word μή from his quotation of Isa 28.16 in Rom 9.33 (115), or when he attributes the addition of κύριε in Rom 11.3 to the influence of the quotation from Isa 53.1 in Rom 11.1 (87, 139).

[72] Examples include his argument that Paul has replaced ἵνα with ὅπως in Rom 9.16 in order to strengthen the "final" sense of the clause (*Schrift*, 151); his assump-

Additional controls are also needed to insure the integrity of Koch's favorite criterion, the relative "usability" of the original text in its new Pauline context (number 4 above). Only when the wording of a quotation is clearly incompatible with its original biblical context (number 5 above) can the investigator be reasonably certain that a given reading has been introduced into the text to suit the later Pauline context rather than the Pauline argument arising out of an unusual rendering in Paul's Greek *Vorlage*.[73] Similarly, the fact that a questionable reading appears in a verse that contains other more assuredly Pauline adaptations (number 6a above) says little about the origins of the uncertain reading in the absence of further evidence in one direction or the other.[74] Textual evidence that might support a manuscript-based explanation is also minimized on a number of occasions.[75]

One final weakness remains to be addressed before considering whether Koch's criteria can be restructured into a more useful system. No matter how carefully he weighs the alternatives, Koch inevitably pronounces a verdict of "Pauline" or "pre-Pauline" on virtually every reading that he investigates. Explicit declarations of uncertainty are uncommon, despite the cautious tone created by the frequent appearance of the word "probably" (*wahrscheinlich*) in Koch's presentation of his conclusions. To be sure, he does allow in a few instances that the origin of a particular reading might finally be indeterminable, i.e. that it could reflect either a Pauline adaptation or the use of a deviant or previously modified text.[76] In the

tion that the slight advancement of καὶ εἰς σκάνδαλον ahead of καὶ εἰς ἀνταπόδομα in Rom 11.9 would communicate emphasis to the ordinary reader (137–8); and his explanation of the changed position of πάντα τὰ ἔθνη in Rom 15.11 as due to a Pauline reversion to the normal Greek position for the Vocative (109).

[73] Examples abound in the analysis that follows. Noteworthy are the shift to first-person singular speech (λαλήσω) in 1 Cor 14.21 (*Schrift*, 65, 111–12); the addition of Ἀδαμ in 1 Cor 15.45 (134–7); and the substitution of ὀλίγον for ἔλαττον in 2 Cor 8.15 (142), all of which Koch attributes to Paul.

[74] In most cases Koch restricts this argument to a subsidiary role, as with the substitution of δύναμιν for ἰσχύν in Rom 9.17 (*Schrift*, 141) and the shift from ᾅδη to θάνατε in 1 Cor 15.55 (170), but it becomes primary in his explanation of the shift from αὐτούς to αὐτά in Gal 3.10 (111).

[75] E.g. the shift from οἴδασιν to ἔγνωσαν in Rom 3.17 (found also in A Q^mg and a number of minuscules and citations) (*Schrift*, 143); the insertion of δέ in Rom 4.3 (see James, Philo and the minuscule group b) (132–3); the shift from the passive διετηρήθης to the active ἐξήγειρα in Rom 9.16 (in agreement with the Masoretic Hebrew text) (112, 150–1); and the substitution of δύναμιν for ἰσχύν in the same verse (with A M* and a wide range of minuscules)(151).

[76] Examples include the omission of σφόδρα in Rom 10.8; the substitution of κημώσεις for φιμώσεις in 1 Cor 9.9; the use of ὑπόλειμμα in place of κατάλειμμα in

overwhelming majority of cases, however, Koch does not hesitate to offer a definitive judgment concerning the origin of the reading in question.[77] Such an "all-or-nothing" approach, however nuanced the language in which it is presented, simply cannot do justice to the inherent ambiguities of the data with which the investigator has to work.

What is needed to insure the integrity of such a study is not the insertion of an occasional qualifier to indicate uncertainty about a handful of questionable readings, but rather some formal means of ranking the evidence to show the degree of probability with which the origins of each individual reading can be established. Generalizations about the citation technique of a given author could then be grounded on cases where authorial adaptation of the text (whether conscious or unconscious) could be demonstrated beyond a reasonable doubt. Of course, even the best of studies could never claim absolute reliability, since the very ambiguity of the data requires a measure of subjective judgment on the part of any investigator. Nonetheless, there appears to be no reason why a carefully constructed study that included a set of reasonably verifiable criteria along with a system for assigning probabilities to its conclusions could not produce a reliable (though perhaps minimalistic) portrait of the citation technique of a given author.

The following four-step procedure seeks to incorporate the most useful elements of Koch's approach into a structured method that remains broad enough to handle a wide range of materials.

(1) Identifying the citations.   The first step in establishing what can be known with relative certainty about the citation technique of a given author is to settle on a clear and verifiable definition of the word "citation." As discussed earlier, the present study will adhere to a narrow "reader-centered" definition in order to minimize the possibility of contaminating the data (and thus the conclusions) with heterogeneous materials. Three criteria will be used to determine which verses qualify for inclusion in this narrower group of texts: (1) those introduced by an explicit quotation formula ("as it is written," "therefore it says," etc.); (2) those accompanied by a clear interpretive gloss (e.g. 1 Cor 15.27); and (3) those that stand in

Rom 9.27; the addition of καὶ εἰς θήραν in Rom 11.9; and the addition of ἐμαυτῷ in Rom 11.4.

[77] Exceptions include the substitution of σήμερον ἡμέρας for ἡμέρας ταύτης in Rom 11.8 (140); the use of ὑπό in place of ὑποκάτω in 1 Cor 15.27 (140 n. 1); and the advancing of πᾶσα γλῶσσα to primary position in Rom 14.11 (108).

demonstrable syntactical tension with their new literary environment (e.g. Rom 9.7, 10.18, Gal 3.12). These verses will serve as a control group within which to observe the author's citation technique at work under the most rigid of conditions.

(2) Establishing the text.   Before anything can be said about the way an author handled the wording of his citations, something must be known about the text that the author had in front of him (or in his mind, as the case may be) while writing. The approach to be followed in the present study could be described as both pragmatic and eclectic: "pragmatic," in that the standard printed text of the author's primary *Vorlage* will serve as the initial touchstone for identifying questionable readings in his citations; "eclectic," in that every explanation that would trace such a reading to the use of a non-"standard" text will receive due consideration before the possibility of authorial adaptation will be entertained.[78] In the case of quotations from the Hebrew Bible, this will mean consulting not only the printed editions of the Masoretic text, but also the various Qumran biblical manuscripts (where available), the Samaritan Pentateuch, the full range of Septuagintal traditions, and the evidence of the other early versions. In the case of citations from the Greek, the evidence will include not only the variants listed in the critical apparatus for the various printed editions of the Septuagint (Holmes–Parsons, Brooke–McLean, and the Göttingen series), but also the possibilities opened up by the discovery of early Jewish revisions and corrections to the Old Greek text. Conjectures regarding the likelihood of transcriptional errors must also be pursued within reasonable limits, and the possibility that a text might have been modified prior to its appropriation by the present author can never be overlooked. Only after every reasonable possibility of a manuscript-based explanation has been effectively eliminated will deviation from a presumed *Vorlage* be counted as evidence in favor of a possible authorial adaptation.

In cases where a questionable reading can be traced with reasonable likelihood to a particular *Vorlage*, the following set of notations will be used to characterize the relationship between the quotation and its source text:

---

[78] Evidence concerning the nature of the Homeric text available to Greco–Roman writers around the turn of the era will be examined in chap. 7.

U^+ = Full agreement with the standard printed edition of the author's normal *Vorlage*, with no significant variations in either text

U^- = Agreement with the standard printed edition of the author's normal *Vorlage*, but with significant variant readings in one or both manuscript traditions

V = Agreement with a variant reading known from the manuscript tradition of the author's normal *Vorlage*

T = Apparently drawn from a text that finds little or no support in the manuscript tradition of the author's normal *Vorlage* (includes early Jewish revisions of the Old Greek)

O = Apparently drawn from oral tradition, though lacking direct testimony to that effect

(3) Isolating the adaptations. As the foregoing review of Dietrich-Alex Koch's study has shown, it is far easier to bring forward arguments that suggest the possibility of an authorial adaptation than to develop criteria for determining when such an adaptation has in fact occurred. A solid first step in this direction lies in the simple recognition that the origins of certain readings can be identified with a greater degree of precision than others. Instead of straining to render a positive judgment on every uncertain reading, the investigator needs to develop a system for indicating the level of confidence with which the origins of each reading can be established using the best available evidence. Additional study would then be restricted to those readings that received the highest probability ratings, leaving out the rest. Assuming that the various probabilities were assigned according to a system of consistent and reasonably verifiable criteria (see below), it could be expected that such a study would yield a trustworthy (though not unassailable) portrait of the normal citation practice of a given author.

In contrast to Koch's approach, where a single piece of evidence was often considered sufficient to support the designation of a reading as an intentional modification, the present study will require a confluence of positive indicators along with a general lack of negative testimony before a reading can be adjudged an authorial adaptation with the highest degree of probability. The presence of any hard evidence that might support an alternative explanation will result in a correspondingly lower probability rating. Probabilities will be assigned to each variant reading according to the following scale:[79]

A = Beyond reasonable doubt (agreement of multiple indicators coupled with a general lack of reasonable alternatives)

B = Reasonably assured (agreement of multiple indicators or other strong evidence with no direct testimony to the contrary)

C = Likely (arguable predominance of favorable evidence over possible alternative explanations)

D = Possible (strong evidence for more than one explanation, with reasonable support for the possibility of authorial adaptation)

E = Open (countervailing evidence for more than one explanation, with no apparent basis for deciding between them)

Of course, such a system of probabilities is only as good as the criteria used to fix the origins of the various readings involved. The present study has identified four sets of criteria that can be used to establish the presence of an adapted citation on a more reliable footing.

(a) *Relation to context.* As noted above, the fact that an author frames an argument around precisely those parts of a citation that diverge from his presumed *Vorlage* is no sure proof that the wording in question was introduced into the verse by the author himself. The same holds true for instances where a questionable reading accords well with the broader ideological concerns of the author who cited the text. In both cases it could be argued that the author's ideas arose out of an unusual rendering in his *Vorlage* rather than the author shaping the wording of the text to suit its new context. Only when the divergent wording can be shown to be awkward or even impossible in its original context can one conclude with reasonable assurance that an editorial hand has indeed intruded into the text. Conversely, the fact that a questionable reading bears no evident

[79] Probability indicators have been noted in the text only for the Pauline materials examined in chaps. 4 and 5. The same system has been followed for the comparative materials in chaps. 7 and 8, but space limitations have made it necessary to summarize the evidence in those cases. Victor Aptowitzer (28, 146) uses a similar set of designations in his study of rabbinic quotations (*Sicher/Höchstwahrscheinliche/Wahrscheinliche/Mögliche + /Mögliche*), but his rankings indicate the likelihood that a particular reading represents a genuine textual variant, not an adaptation.

relation to the later author's use of the text can be taken as an indication that the author may have relied on a non-"standard" *Vorlage* or oral tradition at this point, regardless of whether textual evidence is available to support this judgment.

(b) *Typical linguistic usages.* As with the issue of context, the fact that an otherwise unattested reading agrees well with the normal linguistic usages (vocabulary, syntax, style, etc.) of the author who adduces the citation says nothing definitive about the origins of that reading. Such agreements might signify nothing more than the use of a common literary style by the later author and his *Vorlage*.[80] To count as evidence in favor of a particular origin, the usage in question must occur commonly in the work of the later author and not in his *Vorlage* (or vice versa), or else be so characteristic of a particular author (or translator, in the case of the Jewish Greek Scriptures) that one could hardly expect any other rendering than the one that appears in the passage cited. In the absence of such conditions, the most that can be said about this sort of evidence is that it is suggestive.

(c) *Abnormal expressions.* Though clearly a secondary indicator, account must be taken of those instances where the wording of a quotation diverges from the normal rules of an author's language in such a way as to suggest the influence of an editorial hand on the wording of the citation. Included under this heading are unusual arrangements of words (common in Greek to express emphasis), impossible renderings of Hebrew words or expressions (where a Greek version of the Scriptures is in view), grammatical inconsistencies, and similar phenomena. As with the previous indicators, the presence of such abnormal expressions can be adduced as independent testimony for the origins of a given reading only when the abnormality affords some vital point of contact with the later author's use of the text and not with the original, or vice versa.

(d) *Correlation with practice elsewhere.* Another secondary indicator that will occasionally prove helpful asks how closely a proposed authorial adaptation coincides with an author's normal citation practice as revealed elsewhere in his writings. The fact that a particular reading does or does not correspond to an author's usual way of handling texts can offer additional support for an explanation developed independently from other sources.

---

[80] The influence of Septuagintal style on the literary products of Diaspora Judaism and the early Christian community is well-known, while the Hebrew compositions of the Qumran community are replete with biblical language.

(4) <u>Compiling the evidence.</u> The ultimate aim of this sort of painstaking analysis is to construct a reliable portrait of the way an author ordinarily handles outside texts in order to compare his technique with the normal citation practice of other contemporary authors. The hope is that certain common patterns might emerge in the course of such a study that would allow one to speak about a "normal citation technique" that prevailed among Greco–Roman authors in the late Hellenistic and early Roman eras.

As the present chapter has indicated, reliable conclusions about such matters can be developed only by applying a clear and consistent method of analysis to a broad range of texts in a way that minimizes the distortions that might arise from the inclusion of misidentified materials. It follows from this that the investigation must be limited to verses whose character as citations is immediately evident. It also follows that generalizations about the normal citation technique of an individual author must be limited to those materials whose origins can be pinned down with a reasonable degree of certainty. In practical terms, this means that only those deviant readings that can qualify for an A or B rating on the above probability scale will count as authorial adaptations for the present study. Such a restrictive standard will inevitably result in many uncertain readings being excluded from the discussion of an author's normal citation technique. This does not mean that the origins of these neglected readings must now be relegated to obscurity, but rather that the evidence for their background is too uncertain to allow them to influence the conclusions of the broader study.

Only a practical demonstration can show whether the method outlined in the present chapter will produce the results it promises. The biblical citations of the apostle Paul would appear to offer an excellent arena in which to put the proposed method to the test.

PART II

Citation technique in the letters of Paul

3

SOURCES

1. Identifying the citations

Modern studies of Paul's use of Scripture have been unanimous in finding just under a hundred quotations in the various letters that make up the Pauline corpus. Almost all of these passages appear in the four *Hauptbriefe*, so research in this area has been little affected by questions concerning the authorship of several of the letters that circulated under the apostle's name. Of the disputed letters, only Ephesians and the two letters to Timothy contain any citations at all, and even here the number is quite small.[1] Debates over the integrity of 2 Cor 6.14–7.1 have recently added the citation unit in 2 Cor 6.16–18 to the "questionable" list.[2] Arguments against the Pauline origin of the latter passage have been ably answered by a number of scholars, and need not affect the inclusion of 2 Cor 6.16–18 in the present study.[3] Questions concerning the authorship of Ephesians and the Pastorals have proven more intractable. A concern for methodological purity has dictated their exclusion from the present investigation.

Despite general agreement on the basic number of citations, consensus on the precise identity of those citations has been slow in coming. Almost all the disagreements in this area can be traced to differing notions as to what constitutes a "citation."[4] Fortunately,

---

[1] Only Eph 4.8, 5.31, 6.2–3, 1 Tim 5.18 (*bis*), and 2 Tim 2.19 (*bis*) are universally regarded as citations, while many investigators would add Eph 4.25, 4.26, and 5.18 to the list. Eph 1.22 and 1 Tim 5.19 are the only other texts that might qualify under the broadest "author-centered" definition considered in chap. 2.

[2] Koch (*Schrift*, 24 n. 43) was apparently the first to omit the citation unit 2 Cor 6.16–18 from his study entirely.

[3] See W. G. Kümmel, *Introduction to the New Testament*, trans. Howard C. Kee, rev. Eng. edn (Nashville: Abingdon, 1975), 288–93, and C. K. Barrett, *The Second Epistle to the Corinthians*, Harper's NT Commentaries (New York: Harper and Row, 1973), 193–204.

[4] See the discussion of "reader-centered" versus "author-centered" approaches to identifying citations in chap. 2.

Paul has made his intentions quite clear in the great majority of cases. At least seventy-six times Paul introduces (or concludes) a quotation with a phrase or clause that specifically identifies the accompanying text as having come from an outside source.[5] In three other places, interpretive comments in the surrounding verses make it clear that a citation is being offered.[6] On four occasions, the presence of a citation is obvious from a lack of grammatical concord between the citation and its new context.[7] Omitting the materials in Ephesians and the Pastorals, this means that nearly 90 percent of the passages normally regarded as citations are marked in such a way that their presence (if not their significance) is clear to any attentive reader.[8] It is these texts that form the core of the present study.

[5] To call these markers "formulae" (as in "introductory formulae" or "citation formulae") is somewhat misleading in Paul's case, as Paul can be quite creative in the way he incorporates citations into his own literary compositions. Alongside the usual stereotyped expressions ("as it is written," "as Scripture says," etc.), one finds such transitional statements as "for this is the word of promise" (Rom 9.9); "but Isaiah cries out concerning Israel" (Rom 9.27); "but what does the (divine) decree say?" (Rom 11.4); "if (there be) any other commandment, it is summed up in this word" (Rom 13.9b); "but Scripture ... announced beforehand to Abraham" (Gal 3.8); etc. Only passing comments concerning these formulae are offered in the present study, since there appears to be no correlation between the way Paul introduces a citation and the degree to which he adheres to the wording of his *Vorlage*. For further information on Paul's use of introductory formulae, see Michel, 68–71; Ellis, *Use*, 22–5, 48–9; and Koch, *Schrift*, 25–32.

[6] In Rom 4.22 (the passage has already been cited several times in the preceding verses); Rom 13.9a (the subsequent reference to "any other commandment"); and 1 Cor 15.27 (the follow-up comment, "but when he said ..."). The interpretive comments that accompany Rom 10. 6, 7, 8 (note the repeated τοῦτ' ἔστιν) are not counted here, since the passage both begins (v. 5) and ends (v. 8) with a relatively explicit citation formula.

[7] In Rom 9.7 (shift to second-person singular); Rom 10.18 (different antecedent for "their"); Gal 3.8 (shift to second-person singular); and Gal 3.12 (changed subject). See chap. 6.

[8] The precise identity of the remaining 10 percent varies widely from investigator to investigator. Texts in this category divide naturally into two groups. On the one side is a handful of passages that almost all researchers have accepted as quotations on the basis of their closeness to the wording of the biblical text (Rom 10.13, 11.34, 11.35, 1 Cor 2.16, 10.26, 15.32, 2 Cor 10.17, 13.1, Gal 3.6, 3.11). Unlike the passages included above, none of these verses offers any indication that a quotation is being offered – in fact, an uninformed reader might mistake any of them for a Pauline formulation. On the other side is a collection of diverse texts whose status as quotations has always been subject to debate. Most offer no hint that a biblical text is being adduced (but note 1 Cor 9.10 and 2 Cor 4.6), and the wording of a few diverges far enough from that of their presumed *Vorlagen* to raise questions about where one draws the line between "citations" and such categories as "paraphrase" or "allusion" (Rom 9.20, 11.2, 1 Cor 14.25, 15.25, 2 Cor 3.16, Phil 2.10–11, 2.15). Others stand close to the wording of the biblical text, but are rejected by many as being indis-

2. Establishing the text

All modern investigators are agreed in viewing the Greek Septuagint as the primary *Vorlage* for Paul's citations from the Jewish Scriptures. The reasons for this consensus are not far to seek. Of the roughly eighty-three biblical texts adduced by Paul in his undisputed quotations, thirty-four come from places where the Septuagint is closely allied with the Masoretic text. These texts offer no evidence one way or the other as to the nature of Paul's *Vorlage*. Of the remaining forty-nine texts, however, fully forty-four follow the Septuagint at points where it diverges from the Masoretic text.[9] Included here are passages that agree verbatim with the Septuagint as well as verses that show signs of significant editorial activity. The results are the same across every book of Scripture, and extend to the questionably Pauline materials as well.[10] Only five Pauline quotations show a measure of agreement with the Masoretic text over against the Septuagint tradition, and even these five are accompanied by deviations from the Masoretic tradition that make direct resort to the Hebrew unlikely. Support is growing for the view that Paul relied on a Hebraizing revision of the Old Greek, or even a different translation altogether, in these cases.[11]

Alongside these textual data stands the linguistic evidence. The pervasive influence of Septuagintal vocabulary, diction, idioms, and thought-forms on Paul's manner of expression has been noted by numerous scholars. From this it has been concluded that Paul's use of the Septuagint in his letters is no mere concession to the ignorance of his Greek-speaking Gentile readers, but reflects his own

tinguishable from Pauline formulations in their present contexts (Rom 2.6, 3.20, 4.9, 1 Cor 5.13, 10.5, 2 Cor 9.7, 9.10, Gal 2.16). In a few cases the question has been raised as to whether the phrase or clause in question might already have evolved into a common Jewish idiom, such that no explicit citation is to be posited (Rom 11.25/ 12.16, Rom 12.17/2 Cor 8.21, Phil 1.19).

[9] Otto Michel (68) points out how this loyalty to the Greek text extends even to places where the LXX is manifestly inaccurate as compared with the MT (cf. Gal 3.17 = Exod 12.40, 1 Cor 10.8 = Num 25.9), and includes places where the Hebrew text would have been more congenial to Paul's argument (as in 1 Cor 2.16 = Isa 40.13).

[10] The one possible exception is the book of Job, cited twice in forms closer to the Hebrew than the Greek text (Rom 11.35, 1 Cor 3.19). Divergences from the Masoretic text in both instances make it likely that Paul relied on a different translation of Job for these two quotations, as already proposed by Kautzsch (69–70). See the treatment of 1 Cor 3.19 in chap. 5.

[11] The five texts are Rom 10.15, 11.4, 12.19, 1 Cor 3.19, and 15.54. Other texts that show only tenuous links with either tradition include Rom 11.3, 11.35 (not included in the main body of texts), and 1 Cor 14.21. The same is true for Eph 4.8 among the questionably Pauline texts.

pattern of study in the standard Greek version of his day.[12] The same pattern can be seen in the use of the Septuagint by virtually every Diaspora Jew whose writings have survived from that period.[13] In the face of such overwhelming evidence, the normal presumption that Paul drew his quotations from the Greek Septuagint can hardly be disputed. Such at any rate will be the working assumption of the present study except where specific evidence to the contrary is forthcoming.

The next question that arises is whether Paul's biblical text can be defined more narrowly as belonging to any particular strand in the extant Septuagint manuscript tradition. Here the results are decidedly mixed. In his recent re-examination of the relevant data, Dietrich-Alex Koch essentially confirmed the century-old findings of Hans Vollmer regarding the diversity of text-types that one encounters in Paul's quotations.[14] Though certain tendencies can be identified on occasion, a study of the textual affinities of Paul's citations reveals no consistent preference for one text-family over another, with the possible exception of quotations from Isaiah.[15] A similar lack of consistency is evident within the individual letters: repeated quotations from a particular book of Scripture show divergent textual affiliations even within the same letter.[16] This last observation causes serious problems for what might otherwise be considered the most obvious explanation for the extreme textual

[12] A helpful listing of numerous parallels can be found in Vollmer, 10–13. Decisive for Vollmer is the frequency with which even Paul's allusions to the biblical narrative reproduce the language of the Septuagint: he notes Rom 4.4, 5, 13, 19, 7.8, 10, 11, 8.32, 1 Cor 10.6, 9, 10, 2 Cor 3.3, 7–11, 13, 16, 18, 4.4, 6, Gal 4.22–3, 24 (*ibid.*, 13). Otto Michel (59–60) points out echoes of the Septuagint version of the Psalms in such passages as Rom 1.23, 3.4, 5.5, 10.6–7, 11.1, 1 Cor 10.1, etc. Koch in particular stresses the significance of such data as evidence for Paul's intensive labors in the Septuagint: "Je stärker Paulus sich veranlaßt sieht, seine eigene Position theologisch zu klären, desto intensiver wird zugleich auch die Beschäftigung mit der Schrift und ihre Verwendung in seinen Briefen" (*Schrift*, 101; cf. 98–9).

[13] As will become apparent from an examination of a number of these writings in chap. 8.

[14] Koch, *Schrift*, 48–57; cf. Vollmer, 20–1.

[15] Like Vollmer before him, Koch finds significant agreements with the tradition represented by A and Q over against that of B and V in Paul's citations from Isaiah, along with a similar favoring of F (and less commonly of A) over B in citations from the Pentateuch. The pattern of usage is noteworthy in the case of Isaiah, but the textual picture is more complicated in the case of the Pentateuch, as Koch himself acknowledges.

[16] As when Paul agrees with B V over against A Q (or A F) in his quotations from Isaiah and the Pentateuch in Rom 9.28, 13.9a, and Gal 3.8, 3.10, contrary to his practice in Rom 9.20, 9.27, 9.33/10.11, 11.34, 14.11, and Gal 3.10, 3.12. Extracted from Koch, *Schrift*, 49, 52.

diversity of the Pauline citations, i.e. the fact that all individual manuscripts are ultimately eclectic, so that no single manuscript reflects in full the characteristics of the textual family with which it is associated. When one encounters within one letter (Romans) a pattern of quotations from a single biblical book (Isaiah) that includes not only unique agreements with each of the major text-families of the Septuagint but also extracts from a pre-Christian Hebraizing revision of the Old Greek text,[17] it becomes impossible to maintain that all of these quotations were derived from a single highly eclectic manuscript. If nothing else, such evidence highlights the precarious nature of every attempt to define Paul's biblical text more closely on the basis of his "usual" agreement with this or that tradition within the diverse text-history of the Septuagint.

This leads directly to one of the most vexing and controversial questions in the study of Paul's biblical citations: did Paul draw his citations entirely from memory, or did he have recourse to written sources in certain cases? The usual arguments in favor of memory quotation have already been considered and for the most part rejected in chapter 1.[18] The only point that was found to have merit concerned the immense difficulties associated with looking up individual references in multiple unmarked scrolls in the process of composing a letter. On the other hand, the evidence runs wide and deep that Paul did indeed draw many of his quotations from some sort of written text. Dietrich-Alex Koch sums up the traditional arguments for this position and adds a few of his own along the way:[19]

[17] See the discussion of individual passages in chaps. 4 and 5 and the examples in chap. 6, notes 12 and 15.

[18] See pages 16–17.

[19] Discussed in less orderly fashion in *Schrift*, 93–9. Several other arguments put forward by Koch have been omitted here because they seemed less than convincing. (1) In two places Paul repeats a quotation that appears elsewhere in one of his letters (Lev 18.5 in Rom 10.5/Gal 3.11 and Isa 28.16 in Rom 9.33/10.11). On each occasion one site reproduces the wording of the Septuagint nearly verbatim, while the other diverges from it. From this Koch argues that Paul was capable of reproducing the precise wording in both instances had he wished to do so, implying that he chose to deviate from a text that lay open before him (*ibid.*, 93–4). The verses themselves, however, offer little support for Koch's position. On the one hand, the textual problems associated with Paul's quotations in Rom 10.5 and Gal 3.11 make it difficult to draw reliable conclusions about Paul's handling of the Leviticus text in either instance. Koch's observation that Paul follows the Septuagint in including the word ἄνθρωπος in the Romans citation and not in Galatians, if textually sound, could at best support recourse to a written text between the writing of Galatians and Romans, and need not indicate even that. As for the Isaiah passage, while it is true that Paul adds a contextually determined πᾶς to his second quotation in Rom 10.11,

(1) The great bulk of Paul's quotations follow the wording of the Septuagint either precisely or with only minor changes that can be traced with confidence to the editorial work of the apostle himself.

(2) The use of the divine names ὁ θεός and κύριος, an easy matter to confuse in memory quotation, normally agrees with the form found in the underlying Septuagintal text.

(3) Deviations from the Septuagint are by no means random, as one might expect in the case of errors of memory, but correspond closely to the function of the quotation in Paul's own developing argument.

(4) The distinctive literary and rhetorical artistry of Paul's combined and conflated citations shows that these texts at least were selected and shaped in advance for a particular argumentative purpose.[20]

(5) Several of Paul's citations show a reliance on earlier "Hebraizing" or "Graecizing" revisions of the common Old Greek text, a phenomenon that seems to require recourse to a written *Vorlage* in at least these instances.[21]

it is simply incorrect to say (with Koch) that the first citation in Rom 9.33 reproduces the Septuagint text "unverändert" (*ibid.*, 93 n. 10). The most that can be shown from a comparison of these two parallel texts is that Paul clearly added the πᾶς at the beginning of the second occurrence in Rom 10.11. (2) Koch points to the lack of citations in the so-called "prison epistles" as further evidence that Paul normally preferred to quote from written texts, since such texts would presumably have been unavailable to Paul in prison (*ibid.*, 96). Apart from its complete unverifiability, such an assumption flies in the face of Koch's own contention (to be discussed below) that Paul relied on a collection of written excerpts from the biblical text and not the biblical scrolls themselves when adducing a biblical quotation for one of his letters (*ibid.*, 99, 253, 284). (3) From Paul's apparent use of revised texts of the Old Greek for certain of his quotations in 1 Corinthians and Romans, Koch concludes that Paul must have had access to written texts of Isaiah and Job when composing 1 Corinthians and these two books plus 3 Kingdoms when writing Romans (*ibid.*, 96). The fact that none of the other quotations from Isaiah in either book contains similar "revised" readings, however, seems fatal to this view – not to mention the fact that this, too, runs counter to Koch's thesis that Paul relied primarily on written excerpts from Scripture in the composition of his letters. (4) Finally, Koch points to the often-noted shift in Paul's handling of the Abraham narrative between Galatians 3 and Romans 4 as evidence for Paul's continued exegetical labors in the text of Scripture (*ibid.*, 97–8, 101). While the basic observation is no doubt true, it is difficult to see what bearing it has on the question of whether Paul relied on written texts for his citations from the Abraham narrative in either letter.

[20] For further details, see *Schrift*, 94–5, plus the discussions of the individual passages in Koch and in chaps. 4 and 5 of the present study.

[21] The texts that Koch cites in this connection are Rom 9.33, 10.15, 11.3, 11.4, 11.35, 1 Cor 3.19b, 14.21, and 15.54. See the extended discussion in *Schrift*, 57–81, along with the comments in chap. 2 (on the likelihood of such revisions) and chaps.

(6) On two separate occasions (Rom 9.28 and 10.15), Paul appears to have taken his quotation from a manuscript that had suffered the effects of haplography.[22]

All in all, the evidence seems strong that the great majority of Paul's biblical quotations were taken directly from written texts of some sort. But the practical difficulties that stand in the way of such an explanation would appear to be insuperable. How can such conflicting data be resolved? Clearly the answer is not to be found in casting Paul as a modern biblical scholar, scrambling through a mountain of unwieldy scrolls (in a Jewish synagogue, no less) in search of the precise wording of a verse that he has decided to include in a letter that he is in the midst of dictating to an increasingly impatient amanuensis. But what is the alternative? Is there any other social model that might help to explain the data currently under review?

One possible explanation is that Paul drew his quotations from some sort of pre-existing collection of biblical "prooftexts," a Christian "testimony-book," as argued earlier in this century by J. Rendel Harris.[23] The evidence for the existence of such a collection is of course entirely circumstantial. Harris' own argument sought to combine certain observations about the wording of various citations that appear in both the New Testament and various church fathers (especially Justin) with accounts of later Christian "testimony-books" (no earlier than Cyprian) compiled for use in apologetic

4 and 5 (on individual texts) of the present study. While it is always possible that Paul had learned these particular passages from non-"standard" manuscripts in the first place, it seems unlikely that he would have continued to adhere to such idiosyncratic traditions in view of his constant exposure to the standard language of the Septuagint. The fact that he quotes other passages from the same books in full agreement with the Septuagint makes such an explanation all the more unlikely (see the examples in chap. 6, notes 12 and 15). The fact that Paul's quotations often agree with one strand of the Septuagint tradition over against others cannot be counted as evidence for the use of written texts without further clarification.

[22] From συντέμνων (Isa 10.22) to συντετμημένον (Isa 10.23) in the first passage (Rom 9.28), and from the first to the second occurrence of εὐαγγελιζομένου (Isa 52.7) in the second (Rom 10.15). The argument is more convincing for the second passage than for the first: the homoioteleuton in Rom 9.28 is rough at best. See the full discussion in *Schrift*, 81–3.

[23] *Testimonies*, 2 vols. (Cambridge University Press, 1916–20). The idea that the New Testament authors drew on pre-existing collections of biblical excerpts goes back at least as far as Hans Vollmer (35–43), who argued that a number of the quotations in the New Testament were taken from Hebrew anthologies compiled for use in the Jewish community. Harris, by contrast, argued that such collections were normally employed in anti-Jewish polemic, which meant that they must have originated in Christian circles.

debates with representatives of Judaism. The discovery of a collection of biblical excerpts at Qumran (*4QTestimonia*) was hailed by
many as exactly the sort of hard evidence needed to ground Harris'
"testimony-book" hypothesis in the firm soil of first-century
realia.[24]

Though it created quite a stir when first introduced, due in no
small part to the obvious erudition of its author, the popularity of
Harris' thesis has waned significantly over the years. Part of this
decline can be attributed to the faddish treatment accorded all new
ideas, but the bulk of the retrenchment would appear to reflect a
more sober evaluation of the data adduced by Harris in support of
his thesis. Several studies have demonstrated the tenuous nature of
much of Harris' theorizing concerning the duplicate citations that
occur in the New Testament and the early church fathers.[25] The fact
that only a handful of Paul's citations might be traced to such a
collection in any event also bodes ill for its relevance to the present
discussion. In fact, everything that can be observed about Paul's use
of the biblical materials – the obvious care with which the quotations were selected and extracted from their original contexts,
their close integration into the apostle's arguments, even the sheer
obscurity of many of the passages adduced by Paul in support of his
own positions – argues against reliance on any pre-existing collection and in favor of some sort of direct recourse to the biblical text
on the part of the apostle.

[24] Robert Kraft takes a more sober view of the Qumran evidence ("Barnabas'
Isaiah-Text and the 'Testimony Book' Hypothesis," *JBL* 79 (1960), 336–50):
4QTestimonia supports at most the use of a variety of localized "testimony note-
sheets" in early Judaism and Christianity, not the relatively standardized collection
posited by Harris.

[25] The criticisms put forward by C. H. Dodd (*Scriptures*, 23–7) have been
especially influential with later scholars. Dodd's own explanation, that the early
Christians had developed what amounted to a "canon within the canon" of important biblical passages that were used as a source-book for missionary preaching, has
its own problems, among them Dodd's baseless assumption of broad access to
biblical scrolls within the early Christian community and his unrealistically high
assessment of early Christian sensitivity to the original context of biblical citations.
For a trenchant critique, see A. C. Sundberg, "On Testimonies," *NovT* 3 (1959),
268–81. Koch's observation that only a very small percentage of Paul's citations (15
out of 93, by Koch's count) comes from those passages that Dodd designates "the
Bible of the early church" is also damaging. As Koch puts it, "Also hat entweder
Dodd die 'Bibel der frühen Kirche' selbst falsch bestimmt, oder Paulus hat sie
ignoriert – oder sie ist überhaupt eine Fiktion" (*Schrift*, 254). Koch's evaluation of
Harris' thesis is noteworthy for its clarity and perception: see *Schrift*, 247–55. More
recent proponents reject Harris' idea of a single written collection, arguing instead
for a common oral tradition of interpretation that was eventually reduced to writing
(e.g. Robert Hodgson, "The Testimony Hypothesis," *JBL* 98 (1979), 361–78).

How then is this "direct recourse" to be understood? Once again Dietrich-Alex Koch appears to have pointed the way toward a more adequate solution.[26] As Koch points out, Paul's primary interaction with the biblical text would have taken place not in the moment of dictation, when he was deciding whether to include a particular verse in a letter to one of his churches, but in his own private study in his ancestral Scriptures.[27] The letters offer clear evidence that Paul engaged in a regular and persistent study of Scripture throughout his missionary travels. Such an ongoing program of study was clearly vital to the former Pharisee's efforts to clarify his own understanding of Christian existence over against various opposing views that in his judgment threatened the very existence of the churches that he had labored so intently to establish throughout the eastern Mediterranean world. With these opposing views in mind, Paul searched the authoritative Scriptures for arguments that he could use in dealing with the various problems that kept recurring in his local congregations. As a good pastor, he no doubt remained mindful as well of texts that would support (or at least

[26] *Schrift*, 99–101, 253, 284. Koch's own view, developed at greater length in the present study, is best summed up in his statement that "Paulus im Zuge seiner eigenen Beschäftigung mit der Schrift auch dazu übergangen ist, planmäßig geeignet erscheinende Schriftworte zu sammeln, auf die er dann bei Abfassung seiner Briefe zurückgreifen konnte" (*ibid.*, 99). Otto Michel (8, 170–1) pointed likewise to Paul's personal study of Scripture as the proper background for understanding his frequent resort to biblical citations in his letters, though he still assumed that Paul drew his actual citations from memory. Personal study of Scripture plays an equally important role in Krister Stendahl's explanation of the text-form of the "formula quotations" in Matthew (115, 163, 194, 196–8, 201–2).

[27] Whether the scrolls in question were owned by the Jewish synagogue, local Christian leaders, or even Paul himself remains unclear. Both Otto Michel (123) and E. E. Ellis (*Use*, 19 n. 5) conclude on the basis of 2 Tim 4.13 that Paul probably carried copies of biblical scrolls with him during his missionary travels. Dietrich-Alex Koch examines the evidence for personal ownership of books in the ancient world (*Schrift*, 99–100), but comes to no firm conclusions (though he inclines toward the position of Michel and Ellis). On the textual side, only the quotations from Isaiah come close to the kind of consistency that one would expect from the regular use of a single roll of Scripture. The fact that several quotations from this book appear to have come from a revised edition of the Old Greek while others follow the Septuagint precisely (and both in the same letter, that to the Romans) seems to argue against even this possibility. The likelihood that local Christian leaders might have owned biblical scrolls for use by their own congregations, a possibility normally overlooked by investigators, is increased by recent sociological studies that highlight the patronal role of local house-church leaders in the Pauline congregations. See Gerd Theissen, *The Social Setting of Pauline Christianity*, ed. and trans. John H. Schütz (Philadelphia: Fortress, 1982); Wayne Meeks, *The First Urban Christians* (New Haven: Yale University Press, 1983); Abraham Malherbe, *Social Aspects of Early Christianity* , 2nd edn (Philadelphia: Fortress, 1983).

illustrate) the kinds of conduct that he sought to inculcate in his churches everywhere. As he came across passages that promised to be useful later on, he presumably copied them down onto his handy wax tablet, or perhaps even directly onto a loose sheet of parchment. At times he may even have included brief annotations to remind himself of how certain verses might be integrated into a later sermon or letter. This growing collection of biblical excerpts would then have become his primary resource for meditation and study in those times when he was traveling or staying in a private residence and had no immediate access to physical rolls of Scripture. When the time came to compose a letter to one of his churches, many of the points that he wished to make would have been framed already around one of the excerpts contained in this by now well-worn and highly familiar anthology. While other verses not included in this collection may occasionally have found a place in one of his letters in the moment of composition, the great majority of Paul's quotations would have come directly from this Pauline biblical anthology.

If such a picture of the apostle's activities sounds all too modern, perhaps a brief survey of some of the evidence for the common ancient practice of compiling excerpts from written texts for later use might help to dispel that notion.[28] In Greek literature, Xenophon's *Memorabilia* (1.6.14) presents Socrates as saying, "The treasures that the wise men of old have left us in their writings I open and explore with my friends. If we come on any good thing, we extract it (ἐκλεγόμεθα)."[29] Aristotle (*Topics* 1.14), describing various ways of securing propositions for use in constructing an argument, encourages his readers to "make extracts also from written works (ἐκλέγειν ... ἐκ τῶν γεγραμμένων λόγων)."[30] From a later period, one of the guests in Athenaeus's fictional *Deipno-*

---

[28] Koch describes it as "eine in der Antike geläufige Arbeitstechnik" (*Schrift*, 99 n. 40), but offers as evidence only the passage from Pliny the Younger cited below. Additional references can be found in the wide-ranging article by Henry Chadwick, "Florilegium," in *Reallexicon für Antike und Christentum*, 7:1131–60.

[29] English translation by E. C. Marchant in the Loeb Classical Library series (Cambridge: Harvard University Press, 1938; London: William Heinemann, 1938). This and the next two references were taken from a useful article by B. M. W. Knox and P. E. Easterling, "Books and Readers in the Ancient World," in *Cambridge History of Ancient Literature*, ed. B. M. W. Knox and P. E. Easterling, 2 vols. (Cambridge University Press, 1985), 1:11, 13, 16, 25. The authors also note in passing the phenomenon of the Homeric scholia, which are little more than a series of excerpts from various Alexandrian commentators on the Homeric text (*ibid.*, 34).

[30] B. M. W. Knox (*ibid.*, 13) points to the wide-ranging use of citations in Aristotle's own writings as evidence that the philosopher practiced what he preached.

sophists (8.336d) claims to have "read more than eight hundred plays from the so-called Middle Comedy and ... made excerpts from them (ἐκλογὰς ποιησάμενος)."[31] Plutarch (*Peri Euthumias* 464F) likewise refers to collections of notes (ὑπομνήματα) that he compiled in the course of his own reading.[32] On the institutional side, selections from classical authors were often used in reading and writing exercises in schools of the Hellenistic period,[33] while anthologies of classical citations arranged according to topic were common fare in the second-century rhetorical schools of the Second Sophistic.[34] The various examples of "sublime" style quoted by the late first-century author of the treatise *On the Sublime* appear to have been taken from just such a collection of texts compiled by the writer for use in his own rhetorical school.[35]

Similar practices can be seen in the Latin-speaking world. Cicero (*De Inventione* 2.4) explains to his reader that "when the inclination arose to write a text-book of rhetoric, I did not set before myself some one model ... but after collecting all the works on the subject, I excerpted [*excerpsimus*] what seemed the most suitable precepts from each, and so culled the flower of many minds."[36] Pliny the Younger (*Epistles* 3.5) describes how his uncle Pliny the Elder, a contemporary of Paul, was able to compile more than 160 volumes of excerpts and notes gleaned from his personal reading. Every afternoon while he rested in the sun, and again in the evening, "some author was read to him, from whence he made extracts and observations [*adnotabat excerpebatque*], as indeed this was his con-

---

[31] English translation by Charles Burton Glick in the Loeb Classical Library series. The whole treatise is framed around the author's own extensive collection of excerpts from the whole of Greek literature on the proper preparation, eating, and enjoyment of food.

[32] Noted in William C. Helmbold and Edward O'Neill, eds., *Plutarch's Quotations*, American Philological Association Monographs 19 (Oxford: B. H. Blackwell, 1959), ix. Plutarch's precise language is both interesting and pertinent: ἀνελεξάμην περὶ εὐθυμίας ἐκ τῶν ὑπομνημάτων ὧν ἐμαυτῷ πεποιημένος ἐτύγχανον ("I gathered together from my note-books those observations on tranquility of mind which I happened to have made for my own use"). Translation by W. C. Helmbold from the Loeb Classical Library version of *Plutarch's Moralia*, 6:167.

[33] According to H. I. Marrou, *History*, 153–4. For the papyrological evidence, see E. G. Turner, *Greek Papyri: An Introduction* (Oxford: Clarendon, 1968), 91–2.

[34] See Jean Hani, *Consolation à Apollonius* (Paris: Editions Klincksieck, 1972), 30, 49–50. Hani makes this point as a backdrop to his argument that the author of the *Consolation* made use of a pre-existing collection of "consolation" texts in preparing a letter to his grieving friend. The letter is discussed in chap. 7 of the present study.

[35] See the discussion of this treatise in chap. 7.

[36] English translation by H. M. Hubbell in the Loeb Classical Library series.

stant method whatever book he read."[37] According to Pliny, the process continued even when his uncle went traveling in his chariot, though at such times he left the note-taking to a shorthand writer [*notarius*], who would write out the requisite passages onto wax tablets [*pugillares*] and presumably transfer them later to the primary collection. Of himself (*Epistles* 6.20.5), Pliny describes how, upon hearing of his uncle's death, "I called for a volume of Livy, and began to read, and even went on with the extracts I was making from it, as if nothing was the matter." From a later period, Aulus Gellius (*Attic Nights* 17.21.1) describes how "to guard against such errors in dates and periods of time [i.e. facts of history], I made notes [*excerpebamus*] from the books known as the *Chronicles* ..."[38]

On the Jewish side, the presence of a document like *4Q Testimonia* among the finds at Qumran provides ample evidence that at least some Palestinian Jews could and did prepare written anthologies of biblical texts arranged according to a common theme. A fragment of a similar collection is included in the conglomeration of materials from Qumran Cave 4 published by J. M. Allegro under the designation *4Q158*.[39] Three other fragments listed under the same heading show a similar combination of texts from different sources, though in these the interpretive element has become more explicit.[40] In addition, at least two of the fragments described by Allegro as "Catena" texts (*4Q177*) appear to have come from a similar type of biblical anthology in which passages from a variety of sources were written down one after the other, interspersed with occasional interpretive comments.[41]

Especially interesting are the fragmentary remains of a text

---

[37] The passage is referenced but not quoted in Koch, *Schrift*, 99 n. 40. The translation used here is by W. M. L. Hutchinson in the Loeb Classical Library series.

[38] English translation by John C. Rolfe in the Loeb Classical Library series.

[39] The reference is to fragments 6–12, published in DJD V, 3. Here excerpts from Exod 20.19–22, Deut 5.29, and Deut 18.18–22 have been ordered back-to-back to stress the importance of a proper response to the divine speech, the only interruption being the remains of a divine injunction ("...the sound of my words, say to them") that introduces the final citation (line 6; cf. the similar introductions in *4Q Testimonia* 1, 9, 21–2). For a brief discussion, see Michael Fishbane, "Use, Authority and Interpretation of Mikra at Qumran," in Mulder (ed.), *Mikra*, 352–3.

[40] In fragments 1–2 (Gen 32.25–32, Exod 4.27–8) and fragment 4 (Exod 3.12, Exod 24.4–6), lengthy excerpts from the Pentateuch have been supplemented by later expansions designed to fill in perceived gaps in the biblical narrative, in a manner similar to other "rewritten Bible" materials. In fragments 7–8, two verses from Deut 5 have replaced Exod 20.18–21 in a scribal attempt to harmonize the Exod and Deut accounts of the giving of the Torah at Sinai.

[41] The reference is to fragments 5 and 11. See DJD V, 68–71.

known commonly as *4QTanhumim* (*4Q176*).[42] Fragments one and two of this unusual document contain back-to-back excerpts from Isa 40.1–5 and 41.8–9 in one partially preserved column and Isa 49.7 and 49.13–17 in another. Fragments three and four continue the progression of the first column with a citation from Isa 43.1–6, while fragments six and seven line up readily under column two with a quote from Isa 51.22–3. Fragments eight to eleven round off the collection with a back-to-back rendering of Isa 52.1–3 and 54.4–10.[43] Every one of these verses appears to have been copied verbatim from the excerptor's biblical *Vorlage*, with little or no adaptation and no explicit comment. Though additional passages may have been lost, the presence of several back-to-back citations makes it clear that a conscious editorial purpose has guided the selection of these particular verses from the book of Isaiah and not others. In every case, the verses included accord well with the concern for the *tanhûmîm* ("comforts") of God that was announced in the fragmentary remarks that open and close the collection.[44] Apparently an anonymous reader interested in Yahweh's promises of "comfort" for his afflicted people compiled this anthology of biblical texts in the course of a progressive reading through the text of Isaiah 40–55.[45]

It thus appears that there is ample historical precedent for the idea that Paul in the course of his own study of Scripture drew up a written anthology of biblical texts that he thought might prove useful in a sermon or letter to one of his congregations at a later date. Besides accounting for the evidence that favors a written *Vorlage* for many of Paul's biblical citations, such a view of Paul's

[42] DJD V, 60–7. The title comes from the words that introduce this section in the original text: "And from the book of Isaiah, *tanhûmîm* . . ." (frag. 1, 1.4; cf. frag. 11, line 13). For more on this text, see the author's study, "The Importance of *4QTanhumim*," forthcoming in *RevQ*.

[43] In fragment one, the text of Isa 41.8–9 continues on the same line as the citation from Isa 40.1–5 after no more than the usual spacing between words. In fragment ten, the excerpt from Isa 52.1–3 ends some eight spaces before the end of the line, while the citation from Isa 54.4–10 (its first words now lost) appears to have commenced immediately on the following line. See DJD V, Plates XXXII–XXXIII.

[44] Allegro's labelling of these opening and closing comments as "*pesher*" is misleading: the initial remarks are in the nature of a prayer, not a commentary, while the words that follow the final citation show no apparent link to this or any other specific verse of Scripture.

[45] One could add here the evidence brought forward by Birger Gerhardsson (160–2) for the use of written notebooks in the later rabbinic schools, though it remains unclear whether the same practice can be presumed for the period studied here.

activities would explain several other features of Paul's citation technique that have often troubled modern investigators. The diversity of text-types that appear in Paul's quotations could now be traced to the fact that Paul copied his excerpts from a variety of manuscripts housed at sites all around the eastern Mediterranean world, where he was a constant traveler.[46] The close integration of the majority of Paul's quotations into their present argumentative contexts would likewise be more understandable if the verses in question had been selected and studied with a view to their use in just such a literary setting instead of being recalled *ad hoc* in the moment of composition.[47] The same can be said for the intrusion of interpretive elements into the wording of many of Paul's quotations: through continued meditation on the verses contained in his anthology, Paul would have arrived at certain convictions as to the true meaning of these texts, a situation that in Paul's day would have resulted in a molding of the wording of the passage to reflect those convictions.[48] Finally, the fact that a number of Paul's citations are used in a sense quite foreign to their original context is easily understood if Paul is pictured as copying his citations not directly from the pages of Scripture, but rather from a diverse collection of biblical texts in which the only link with the original context is the one that is preserved in the compiler's mind.

[46] Apart from the questionable 2 Tim 4.13 (μεμβράνα as a Latin loan-word can only refer to "parchment"), there is nothing in Paul's letters to indicate the physical form that such an anthology might have taken. Several techniques were available: to copy the texts directly onto a papyrus scroll, to use one of the sturdier parchment notebooks that were already becoming available by this time (Knox and Easterling, 18; Roberts and Skeat, *Codex*, 18–29; Frederic Kenyon, *Books and Readers in Ancient Greece and Rome* (Oxford: Clarendon, 1932), 91–2), or even to take notes onto a wax tablet and then transfer them later to a more permanent repository. (According to William Harris (194), codices of up to ten wax tablets were common, with each tablet holding fifty or more words per side.) Any of these explanations would suffice for the present study.

[47] The latter point is one of the primary arguments of Koch's study: see especially *Schrift*, 257–85, where he addresses the question of how the quotations functioned within the various Pauline letters. In Koch's view, the citations are "ein konstitutiver Bestandteil der Argumentation des Paulus, die gar nicht unter Absehung von den Zitaten erfaßt werden kann" (*ibid.*, 284). This is exactly the position of the present study.

[48] The demonstration of the latter point is of course the primary aim of the present study. Koch's concern to discover in this a uniquely Pauline phenomenon (as summed up, for example, in his assertion that "die hohe argumentative Bedeutung der Schriftzitate und der radikale Zugriff des Paulus auf Inhalt und oft auch Wortlaut der Schriftzitate bedingen einander gegenseitig" (*Schrift*, 285)) causes him to understate the evidence for similar adaptations throughout the whole of ancient literature.

From this it follows that the investigator should approach the Pauline materials with the working assumption that Paul drew his quotations directly from written sources (i.e. a collection of passages excerpted from biblical scrolls) and not from memory, unless the evidence indicates a different practice in a particular situation.[49] The original *Vorlage* for such texts will normally be the Greek "Septuagint," though here too the investigator must remain fundamentally open to other possibilities where the textual evidence seems to demand it. Clearly not every divergence from the Septuagintal tradition can be regarded as a sign of conscious adaptation on the part of the apostle. Nevertheless, the burden of proof will now lie squarely with those who would introduce the theory of "memory quotation" to explain a questionable reading in the text of a Pauline quotation.

3. Isolating the adaptations

The process of deciding which divergences from the Septuagintal tradition can be ascribed with confidence to the editorial activity of Paul himself contains few shortcuts. Only by a careful weighing of the evidence for every deviant reading can it be determined which ones might reflect the use of a non-Septuagintal *Vorlage*, which represent genuine Pauline adaptations, and which (perhaps the majority) offer insufficient evidence to support any reliable judgment. Accordingly, the following two chapters will be devoted to a verse-by-verse examination of exactly this sort of evidence for the entire Pauline corpus.[50]

First, however, a few comments about the structure of the presen-

---

[49] As in his quotations from such well-known passages as the Ten Commandments or from texts that show signs of earlier Christian adaptation. Whether Paul looked up the relevant excerpts in the moment of dictation or simply quoted from memory out of this highly familiar collection is impossible to say at this point, though the latter appears more likely.

[50] Similar verse-by-verse treatments can be seen in several of the older studies of Paul's citations (e.g. the works by Randolph, Gough, Kautzsch, and Böhl cited in the bibliography), but the focus is different in every case. Randolph and Gough are concerned to show that the New Testament writers have remained faithful to the sense of the original Old Testament passage; Kautzsch aims to discover the true nature of Paul's *Vorlage* (Greek or Hebrew); Böhl sets out to collect evidence for the New Testament writers' use of an early Aramaic targum (his *Volksbibel* hypothesis). All offer various comments to the effect that Paul has changed the wording of his *Vorlage* in this or that instance, but in almost every case the point is simply asserted without explanation. None of these authors offers the sort of sustained inquiry into the way Paul handled the wording of his citations that is offered here.

tation would appear to be in order. Quotations are arranged according to their order of appearance in the Pauline text. Where a citation agrees precisely with one or another of the primary Septuagintal traditions, the fact is simply noted with little additional comment. In places where the Pauline quotation diverges from the wording of the Septuagint, the relevant Greek texts are given first (from the standard printed editions), followed by a series of comments on each divergent reading.[51] In cases where it might prove useful, the Masoretic Hebrew is also included. A system of coded underlines and typefaces helps to highlight the various questionable readings in the Pauline passages and indicates certain judgments about the probable origins of each reading. These codes are explained at the end of the present chapter. The discussion of each divergent reading is accompanied by an alphabetic code that indicates either the probable origin of the reading (in cases where a non-Septuagintal *Vorlage* is to be posited) or the degree of confidence with which the deviation can be treated as a Pauline adaptation (in the case of adapted or uncertain texts). The purpose of this latter group of codes was discussed in chapter 2. They, too, are reproduced at the end of the present chapter.

Within the commentary section, the discussion is limited as nearly as possible to the narrow question of the origins of each deviation from the primary Septuagintal tradition. Exegetical questions are ignored except where they bear directly on the matter at hand, as when the Pauline wording shows vital contacts with the broader argumentative context. In most cases the individual readings are treated separately, the few exceptions being places where several deviations can be traced to the same source. The criteria to be applied in analyzing these readings (relation to context, typical linguistic usages, abnormal expressions, and relation to other passages) were discussed in chapter 2.

Broader conclusions are left for the most part to chapter 6, where the evidence relating to all of the passages is compiled and evaluated. Only after the entire process has been completed will a reliable portrait of the citation technique of the apostle Paul begin to emerge.

---

[51] The bulk of the manuscript evidence has been relegated to the footnotes to improve the readability of the presentation.

4. Identification codes

The following codes have been used to characterize the origins of the many questionable readings that can be identified in the Pauline citations.

(a) Within the printed text of the Pauline citations

ὁ δίκαιος = Agrees with undivided LXX tradition

ὁ δίκαιος = Agrees with one strand of a divided LXX tradition

ὁ δίκαιος = Follows a non-"standard" LXX text or oral tradition

<u>ὁ δίκαιος</u> = Highly probable Pauline adaptation (A/B readings)

<u>ὁ δίκαιος</u> = Possible Pauline adaptation (C/D readings)

<u>ὁ δίκαιος</u> = Origins uncertain (E readings)

[ ] = Words or phrases omitted[52]

* = Limited selection[53]

+ = Combined or conflated citations[54]

(b) Commentary section: status of text[55]

U[+] = Full agreement with the standard printed edition of the author's normal *Vorlage*, with no significant variations in either text

U = Agreement with the standard printed edition of the author's normal *Vorlage*, but with significant variant readings in one or both manuscript traditions

V = Agreement with a variant reading known from the manuscript tradition of the author's normal *Vorlage*

---

[52] All three of these signs will of course have to be accompanied by the appropriate code in the discussion section to indicate the likely origins of the present reading.

[53] This sign will be used to indicate places where the Pauline form of a citation has been achieved by omitting significant words at the beginning or end of the original text. The term "limited selection" is more apt than James Scott's "analytic or eclectic quotation" (26).

[54] "Combined citations" occur when two or more biblical texts are cited back-to-back under a single citation formula; "conflated citations" are created when a part of one biblical text is incorporated into the wording of another. The + code will be placed at the point of combination/conflation.

[55] See chap. 2 for further explanation of these codes.

        T   = Apparently drawn from a text that finds little or no support in the manuscript tradition of the author's normal *Vorlage* (includes early Jewish revisions of the Old Greek)

        O   = Apparently drawn from oral tradition, though lacking direct testimony to that effect

(c) Commentary section: probability of Pauline origin[56]

        A   = Beyond reasonable doubt (agreement of multiple indicators coupled with a general lack of reasonable alternatives)

        B   = Reasonably assured (agreement of multiple indicators or other strong evidence with no direct testimony to the contrary)

        C   = Likely (arguable predominance of favorable evidence over possible alternative explanations)

        D   = Possible (strong evidence for more than one explanation, with reasonable support for the possibility of authorial adaptation)

        E   = Open (countervailing evidence for more than one explanation, with no apparent basis for deciding between them)

---

[56] See chap. 2 for further explanation of these codes.

4

THE EVIDENCE OF ROMANS[1]

(1) **Rom 1.17** (= Hab 2.4b)

Paul: ὁ δὲ δίκαιος ἐκ πίστεως [ ] ζήσεται.

LXX: [ἐὰν ὑποστείληται, οὐκ εὐδοκεῖ ἡ ψυχή μου ἐν αὐτῷ·] ὁ δὲ δίκαιος ἐκ πίστεως μου ζήσεται.

B   Omission of μου. The question of the proper placement of the pronoun μου in the LXX of Hab 2.4b has long troubled interpreters of both Paul and Habakkuk. The problem hinges on the relation between three different readings in the LXX tradition (μου after πίστεως, μου after δίκαιος, or omit μου entirely) and the wording found in Rom 1.17/Gal 3.11 (omit μου) and Heb 10.38 (μου after δίκαιος).[2] In the most recent investigation of the textual data, Dietrich-Alex Koch concluded that the form in which μου followed πίστεως was clearly the original reading of the LXX, so that the other two readings should be viewed as assimilations to the language of Hebrews

---

[1] See the end of chap. 3 for an explanation of the format and symbols employed in this and the following chapter.

[2] The first reading (μου after πίστεως) appears in W* B S Q V and several manuscripts from the A L C traditions, as well as in a few manuscripts of Heb 10.38 (D* 1518 1611 it^{d.e} sy^{p.h} Eus) and Rom 1.17 (C* vg^{cdd} sy^p Or Hier). The word order of the Greek minor prophets scroll *8ḤevXIIgr* and the later versions of ᾽Α Σ Θ also supports the first reading, though here assimilation to the nascent Masoretic tradition is clearly in view. The second reading (μου after δίκαιος) rests primarily on the testimony of the uncial A (along with a few manuscripts from the A L C traditions), and is also the majority reading of Heb 10.38. (Koch's argument for the originality of this reading in Heb 10.38 ("Der Text von Hab 2.4b in der Septuaginta und im Neuen Testament," *ZNW* 76 (1985), 74–5), following 𝔓^{46} א A H* 33 1739 *pc* lat sa bo^{ms} Cl over against D* *pc* μ sy (μου after πίστεως), is thoroughly convincing.) The third reading (omit μου entirely) occurs in the LXX tradition only in the late minuscules 763* 106 130 311, the Bohairic, Ethiopic, and Armenian versions, and the church fathers Tert Chr Cyr Genn Phot. In addition, it is the nearly unanimous reading of Rom 1.17. The support of W^c for the third reading (as given by Ziegler in the Göttingen text) is highly questionable, as Koch has shown (*ibid.*, 79–80).

and Paul respectively.[3] Even if Koch should be wrong in his judgment that the second reading arose under the influence of the passage in Hebrews, his argument that either form with μου would have been incongruous with Paul's argument concerning the nature of "righteousness by faith" is surely correct.[4] Since the Pauline reading is not absolutely discordant with either the grammar or the sense of the original LXX context, however, it cannot be accorded the highest degree of probability within the parameters of the present study.

(2) **Rom 2.24** (= Isa 52.5)[5]

Paul: τὸ [γὰρ] ὄνομα τοῦ θεοῦ δι' ὑμᾶς [ ] βλασφημεῖται ἐν τοῖς ἔθνεσιν.

LXX: [καὶ νῦν τί ὧδέ ἐστε; τάδε λέγει κύριος. ὅτι ἐλήμφθη ὁ λαός μου δωρεάν, θαυμάζετε καὶ ὀλολύζετε· τάδε λέγει κύριος.] δι' ὑμᾶς διὰ παντὸς τὸ ὄνομά μου βλασφημεῖται ἐν τοῖς ἔθνεσιν.

B Advancing τὸ ὄνομα. Though by no means incongruous with the LXX of Isaiah 52, the Pauline word order finds no support in the LXX manuscript tradition, and the textual tradition of Rom 2.24 is equally secure.[6] In the Septuagint rendering, the emphasis lies on the δι' ὑμᾶς that has been inserted at the beginning of the divine pronouncement in v. 5: it was because of their unfaithfulness to Yahweh that he has brought upon his people this judgment for which his name is now being slandered among (or by) the nations (= "Gen-

---

[3] *Ibid.*, 68–85. In addition to the strong external support outlined above, Koch's explanation of how the first reading arose from the way the original translator read his Hebrew text is also convincing (*ibid.*, 72–4). The obvious conclusion is that the first reading "ist nicht nur am frühesten bezeugt und am weitesten verbreitet, sondern ist auch als der ursprüngliche LXX–Wortlaut anzusehen" (*ibid.*, 73).

[4] *Ibid.*, 83–4. The addition of μου after δίκαιος in certain manuscripts of Rom 1.17 (see note 2) should therefore be understood as a later assimilation either to the passage in Hebrews or to one strand of the LXX manuscript tradition.

[5] The apparent quotation from Ps 61.13/Prov 24.12 in Rom 2.6 is omitted from consideration here in accordance with the strict guidelines of the present study, which is confined to passages that offer explicit indication to the reader that a citation is being offered (introductory formula, interpretive comments, etc.).

[6] Assimilation to the Hebrew is unlikely: the LXX follows the word order of the MT at this point, while Paul's retention of the "extra" language found in the LXX version (see below) shows that he has relied on the standard Greek text for this quotation.

tiles").[7] The conversion of several verbs to second-person plural forms reinforces this theme by highlighting the difficulty that Yahweh's people have experienced in comprehending why he has scattered them in this way among the nations.[8] In Paul's use of the verse, on the other hand, the meaning is just the opposite: it is the hypocritical deeds of the Jews themselves (portrayed in overly vivid colors in 2.21–3) that have caused the Gentiles to cast aspersions on the name of the God they profess to serve. The last words of Paul's extended indictment (2.23) charge the Jews with "dishonoring God" by transgressing the very law they profess to uphold (2.23). Expressed in common Jewish parlance, it is God's "name" that has been called into question by such behavior. The advancing of τὸ ὄνομα to a position of emphasis in place of the equally relevant δι' ὑμᾶς of the presumed original coincides perfectly with this concern for the honor of God's "name" among the Gentiles.[9] The clear appropriateness of each reading (the Pauline and the Septuagintal) to its respective context, along with the unified textual tradition for each reading, makes a Pauline origin for this minor adaptation highly probable.

A   Substitution of τοῦ θεοῦ for μου.   For Yahweh to speak of himself in the third person, as would be the case if this reading were to be traced to Paul's *Vorlage*, would not in itself be unusual in the Jewish Scriptures. But the fact that the surrounding verses in the LXX are cast entirely in the first person (note μου in vv. 4, 5b, and 6), combined with the unified textual tradition behind both readings, shows the present reading to be

---

[7] Of course, the same idea is latent throughout the Hebrew passage, but only in the Greek does the idea come to clear expression – and in emphatic position no less.

[8] The Septuagint translator has done his best to make sense of a somewhat awkward Hebrew text here. The RSV renders the verse, "Now therefore what have I here, says the LORD, seeing that my people are taken away for nothing? Their rulers wail, says the LORD, and continually all the day my name is despised." A literal translation of the Septuagint translation, on the other hand, might run as follows: "And now why are you here? Thus says the Lord: Because my people were carried off for nothing, you marvel and cry out (to God). Thus says the Lord: On account of you my name is continually being slandered among the Gentiles." Note that the phrase ἐν τοῖς ἔθνεσιν has been added by the translator at the end of the verse. The point of view of later Diaspora Judaism is clearly reflected in this rendering.

[9] The appearance of the citation formula καθὼς γέγραπται at the end of the quotation rather than at the beginning, unique in the Pauline corpus, further reinforces the continuity between the citation and the words immediately preceding it, as Koch also notes (*Schrift*, 105).

a Pauline adaptation. The reason for the change is probably no more significant than to make the referent of the original μου clear in its new Pauline context.

D   Omission of διὰ παντός.   Though the evidence is admittedly limited, the fact that a handful of church fathers (Justin, Tertullian, Eusebius) omit these same words while adopting none of the other phrasing of Rom 2.24 raises the possibility that at least a few Greek manuscripts may already have omitted these words,[10] though none has survived to today. An omission by Paul himself, on the other hand, is difficult to justify. The phrase appears in Paul's letters only in the biblical quotation in Rom 11.10, where it seems more integral to the argument. Its complete absence elsewhere might suggest some Pauline antipathy to the phrase itself. Another possibility would assume that the temporal reference was felt to be redundant or simply irrelevant at this point, allowing for a measure of rhetorical compression at this point. The origin of the deviation remains uncertain in any case.[11]

V   Including the words ἐν τοῖς ἔθνεσιν.   Here Paul agrees with the majority Septuagint tradition (A Q S B L C) against a minority reading (V)[12] that would omit these final words.

(3)   **Rom 3.4** (= Ps 50.6)

Paul: * ὅπως ἂν δικαιωθῆς ἐν τοῖς λόγοις σου καὶ νικήσεις ἐν τῳ κρίνεσθαί σε.

LXX: [σοὶ μόνῳ ἥμαρτον καὶ τὸ πονερὸν ἐνώπιόν σου ἐποίησα,] ὅπως ἂν δικαιωθῆς ἐν τοῖς λόγοις σου καὶ νικήσῃς ἐν τῳ κρίνεσθαί σε.

A   Selecting only the last half of the verse.   In Ps 50 (Ps 51 MT), it is Yahweh's judgment against sin and not his faithfulness to his people (Rom 3.3) that stands in need of vindication. By select-

---

[10] By parablepsis with the preceding δι' ὑμᾶς?

[11] Koch apparently sees no such difficulties in attributing the deviation to Paul himself: the phrase is "überflüssig" to Paul's purpose in the present passage, and is therefore "entbehrlich" (*ibid.*, 116). This is the first of many such instances in which Koch's judgments appear to outrun the evidence.

[12] The text occurs under the obelus in B Q and part of the O tradition, coinciding with the absence of the words from the present Masoretic tradition.

ing only the latter half of the verse, whose link with the first half is already grammatically tenuous,[13] Paul eliminates entirely the self-abasement theme that figured so prominently in the original. In the process, he converts what was once a humble acknowledgment of Yahweh's rightness in punishing sin into a powerful affirmation of his inevitable victory over all who would seek to challenge him.

C Change from νικήσῃς to νικήσεις. Textual problems make it difficult to speak with confidence about the origins of this shift from Aorist Subjunctive to Future Indicative forms. The handful of Septuagint minuscules that show the Future form (against the united testimony of the majuscules) should presumably be traced either to Pauline influence or to the frequent confusion of Future and Aorist forms after ὅπως in the Greek manuscript tradition.[14] The evidence for the Pauline wording is more divided, but seems stronger for the Future.[15] A Future form would accord well with Paul's use of Ps 50.6 in the present passage, clarifying the Passive sense of κρίνεσθαι and emphasizing the absolute certainty of God's victory over those who would seek to question his ways.[16] The same reading would be awkward, though not impossible, in the LXX. In view of the uncertain textual situation and the commonness of this particular type of variant, however, the possibility cannot be ruled out that Paul found the Future form (if he used it at all) already in his *Vorlage*.

(4) **Rom 3.10–18** (= Ps 13.1–3, Ps 5.10, Ps 139.4, Ps 9.28, Isa 59.7–8, Ps 35.2; see below on individual verses)

[13] While the general sense is clear, the thought expressed in the ὅπως clause does not really follow from the verbs to which it is grammatically linked in the first half of the verse. The ambiguity is present in the Hebrew text as well.

[14] See BAGD, s.v. ὅπως; cf. BDF § 369. The Future is cited in Holmes–Parsons for MSS 106, 142, 144, 154, 165, 167, 170, 187, 193, 196, 208, 285, 289, and 290.

[15] Nestle cites ℵ A D K 81 2484 *pm* for the Future and B G L Ψ 365 1175 1739 1881 *pm* for the Aorist. Tischendorf includes K among his evidence for the Aorist, not the Future.

[16] With the Aorist form, the second verb stands in parallel with the first, completing the thought introduced by the preceding ὅπως: "that you might be vindicated in what you say, and come out victorious when you enter into judgment." (For the Middle form of the final verb, see BAGD, s.v. κρίνω, 4ab, and LSJ, s.v. κρίνω, II. 2b.) With the Future form, however, the last line becomes a ringing affirmation: "yes, you will come out victorious when you are judged." The asyndeton of the MT could be rendered the same way.

B   Combined citation. The presence of this entire section at the
end of Ps 13.3 (= Rom 3.12) in countless manuscripts of the
Septuagint is perhaps the clearest evidence (along with a similar
addition in Isa 40.13 from Rom 11.34–5) for the influence of the
New Testament citations on the textual tradition of the Septuagint.[17] The composite nature of the passage is clear from the
fact that all of its parts can be traced with confidence to various
other locations in the Old Greek text (see list above). The
question of when these verses were first brought together into
the present tightly-knit theological and rhetorical unit has
nonetheless been hotly debated. The issue is crucial for the
present study, since if the combination should prove to be
pre-Pauline, the passage would have nothing to say about the
way Paul handled the wording of his biblical quotations.
Nearly a century ago, Hans Vollmer argued forcefully for a
pre-Pauline origin on the basis of certain similarities and differences between Rom 3.10–18 and a similar citation in Justin's
Dialogue With Trypho (27.3) that he felt pointed to independent
use of the same tradition.[18] More recently, Dietrich-Alex Koch
re-examined the passage and concluded after a careful analysis
that Justin had simply shortened and modified the Pauline
citation to render it more suitable for his own purpose of
demonstrating the "hardness" of the Jews to the Christian
gospel.[19] Koch also rejects Otto Michel's suggestion[20] that
Rom 3.10–18 represents a common early Christian liturgical
formulation, pointing to the total absence of features normally
associated with liturgical texts. That Paul created the citation in
the moment of dictation is also highly unlikely, according to
Koch: the presence of "a conscious stylistic construction and a

[17] No comprehensive listing of the manuscript evidence is available, since the
Göttingen edition of the Psalms is still some time from completion. Rahlfs prints the
passage in brackets and lists only A' L' 55 as omitting it, in addition to the Gallican
Psalter which places it under the obelus. W. Dittmar (176) adds ℵ^{c a} to the list of
evidence. Holmes–Parsons prints the full text without brackets, but then cites 95
minuscules (some two-thirds of their evidence, according to Kautzsch, 2) plus A
Thdrt Slav Vindob as omitting the passage.

[18] Vollmer, 40–1. Koch (*Schrift*, 180 n. 52) cites Luz, Vielhauer, Käsemann,
Schlier, Wilckens, van der Minde, and Keck as agreeing with Vollmer here.

[19] *Schrift*, 180–3. Koch sums up his investigation with the words, "Weder die
Textform der einzelnen Schriftanführungen noch deren Umfang nötigen zu der
Annahme, daß Justin eine von Röm 3, 10–18 unabhängige Quelle verwendet hat"
(*ibid.*, 182).

[20] *Der Brief an der Römer* (Göttingen: Vandenhoeck und Ruprecht, 1955). Koch
cites Schenke and Wilckens as accepting Michel's view (*Schrift*, 183 n. 63).

definite arrangement of content" shows the passage to be "a planned composition."[21] Koch's own conclusion, that the passage was composed by Paul himself some time before its incorporation into the letter to the Romans, appears well-founded, and is the view that will be followed in the present study.[22]

(4a)   **Rom 3.10–12** (= Ps 13.1–3)[23]

Paul: * οὐκ ἔστιν δίκαιος οὐδὲ εἷς,
       * οὐκ ἔστιν ὁ συνίων,
       οὐκ ἔστιν ὁ ἐκζητῶν τὸν θεόν.
       πάντες ἐξέκλιναν, ἅμα ἠχρεώθησαν,
       οὐκ ἔστιν ὁ ποιῶν **χρηστότητα**, οὐκ ἔστιν ἕως ἑνός.

LXX: [Εἶπεν ἄφρων ἐν καρδίᾳ αὐτοῦ Οὐκ ἔστιν θεός·
       διέφθειραν καὶ ἐβδελύχθησαν ἐν ἐπιτηδεύμασιν,]
       οὐκ ἔστιν ποιῶν χρηστότητα, οὐκ ἔστιν ἕως ἑνός.
       [κύριος ἐκ τοῦ οὐρανοῦ διέκυψεν ἐπὶ τοὺς υἱοὺς τῶν
          ἀνθρώπων
       τοῦ ἰδεῖν εἰ] ἔστιν συνίων ἢ ἐκζητῶν τὸν θεόν.
       πάντες ἐξέκλιναν, ἅμα ἠχρεώθησαν,
       οὐκ ἔστιν ποιῶν χρηστότητα, οὐκ ἔστιν ἕως ἑνός.

A   Beginning citation with v. 1d (limited selection). The fact that Paul skips over the first three lines of Ps 13.1 before commencing his quotation is hardly coincidental. The depiction of the activities of the ἄφρων in v. 1a–c is clearly ill-suited for the generalized indictment of all humanity that forms the backbone of Rom 3.10–18.[24] The same holds true of Ps 13.2a, which Paul

[21] *Schrift*, 181, 183 (translation mine). Koch points to such structural features as the corresponding denials that open and close the passage in vv. 10 and 18; the fivefold repetition of οὐκ ἔστιν in the first three verses, reiterated in the closing summary in v. 18; and the concentration of all the references to concrete behaviors in vv. 13–16, so that vv. 13–14 focus on sins of "word" and vv. 15–16 on sins of "deed" (*ibid.*, 183.).

[22] As Koch puts it, "Löst man sich von der Annahme, daß die Briefe des Paulus insgesamt erst im Augenblick des Diktierens entstanden sind, und setzt man außerdem einen eigenständen Umgang des Paulus mit dem Text der Schrift voraus, dann ist auch eine derart umfangreiche Zitatkomposition – jedenfalls im Römerbrief – nicht mehr überraschend" (*ibid.*, 184).

[23] That Paul drew his citation here from Ps 13 and not from the very similar passage in Ps 52 is clear from his inclusion of the phrase οὐδὲ εἷς (= οὐκ ἔστιν ἕως ἑνός) at the end of v. 10 and his use of χρηστότητα rather than ἀγαθόν at the end of v. 12b.

[24] Note the introductory words of v. 9b, προῃτιασάμεθα ... πάντας ὑφ' ἁμαρτίαν εἶναι, and especially the thrice repeated πᾶς of vv. 19–20.

similarly omits (see below). Only those parts of the Psalm that speak in broad terms of the sinfulness of "all" (v. 3a) have been included in the present "quotation"; irrelevant materials have simply been set aside. The molding force of Paul's editorial purpose is evident before the citation even begins.

A   Substitution of δίκαιος for ποιῶν χρηστότητα. In addition to the unified textual evidence in both traditions, the introduction here of a word from the δικ- group could hardly be more Pauline. Moreover, the passage would have been of little use to Paul in its original wording. As the summary statement in 3.9 makes clear, Paul's point in Rom 1.18–2.29 is not that no one ever does anything that could be considered "good" (χρηστότης) according to human standards, but rather that all are equally "under sin" (ὑφ᾽ ἁμαρτίαν) and therefore lacking in true "righteousness" (δικαιοσύνη) before God (3.20; cf. 2.13). Since the argument of Rom 2 has left open the possibility that some might still attain to this "righteousness" by a full and faithful adherence to God's requirements (2.7, 10, 13–16, 26–7), the empirico–philosophical judgments of 1.18–2.29 must now be reinforced and absolutized by an appeal to Scripture, which (as Paul sees it) indicates clearly the failure of all humanity actually to live up to those standards. The sweeping affirmation of v. 10 (in its Pauline formulation) thus plays a crucial role in the passage as a summary introduction to the entire citation. Though the Pauline wording would not be out of place in the original (LXX) context, the convergence of these several lines of evidence renders the Pauline origin of the present reading quite secure.

B   Substitution of οὐδὲ εἷς for οὐκ ἔστιν ἕως ἑνός. A few LXX manuscripts follow the Masoretic Hebrew text in placing this last phrase under the obelus or omitting it entirely, but none shows the alternate wording encountered in Rom 3.10.[25] The Pauline wording is likewise secure, despite the textual problems associated with the second appearance of the Septua-

---

[25] Rahlfs cites only the Gallican Psalter of Jerome (under the obelus), the Lucianic manuscripts, and MS 55 as having any difficulties with the primary Septuagintal reading. Holmes–Parsons, on the other hand, cites 92 minuscules plus Thdrt Arm Slav Vindob as omitting the words in question, besides noting the presence of an obelus in A. Assimilation to the Hebrew is to be posited in every case.

gintal phrase in v. 12c. Since the entire citation (vv. 10–18) appears to have been constructed in advance (see above), the possibility of a memory error can probably be ruled out. Verse 12c shows further that Paul is capable of reproducing the proper wording had he desired to do so.[26] The observation that the entire passage shows a carefully balanced rhetorical structure supports the view that the phrasing of v. 10 has been altered for rhetorical purposes, both to create a more condensed formulation and to avoid redundancy with v. 12c, where the οὐκ ἔστιν is retained for structural reasons.[27] Since the Pauline form could fit equally well into the original LXX context, however, the method of the present study precludes assigning the highest probability rating to this substitution.

A   Omission of v. 2a (limited selection).   The shift in Ps 13.2a to a description of Yahweh's activities in heaven is clearly inappropriate to Paul's more limited program of offering a generalized indictment of all humanity as sinners. In a passage in which rhetorical compactness is an obvious concern, it is only to be expected that clearly extraneous elements would be left to one side, as has obviously happened here. No other explanation for this omission, textual or otherwise, is forthcoming.

A   Substitution of οὐκ for εἰ (v. 11a)/Addition of οὐκ ἔστιν
A   (v. 11b).   Since both of these changes can be traced with confidence to the same rhetorical motive, a single discussion can suffice for both. Not only is the textual evidence fully united on both sides of the question, but the repeated οὐκ ἔστιν of Rom 3.11 creates an almost impossible reading when transposed back into its original Septuagintal context.[28] In the Pauline context, on the other hand, the modification produces a five-membered anaphora in vv. 10–12 whose sheer repetitiveness serves to heighten the rhetorical effectiveness of the passage as a whole. Here again the Pauline origin of the present reading seems assured.

---

[26] This same verse militates against the possibility that Paul might have used a text that had already been revised to produce a smoother Greek reading at this point, since any revision that affected the wording of v. 10 would surely have touched v. 12 as well.

[27] So Koch, *Schrift*, 145 n. 18. See also note 21 above.

[28] Even reading the clauses as the combined object of τοῦ ἰδεῖν (i.e. "to see that there was no one . . .") would technically require the use of a ὅτι.

B   Addition of the definite article before συνίων and ἐκζητῶν in v. 11 and before ποιῶν in v. 12.   The Septuagint tradition is nearly unanimous in omitting the article before the two participles in Ps 13.2, but the evidence is more divided for v. 3.[29] This discrepancy opens up the possibility that Paul might have used a Greek text that contained the article in v. 3 and not in v. 2, a format that he subsequently standardized for the sake of rhetorical parallelism. Attractive as such an explanation might appear, it becomes highly questionable once it is observed that all of the manuscripts that contain the article in v. 3 also add the composite quotation Rom 3.13–18 to the end of Ps 13.3. Assimilation to the Pauline text is thus a more likely explanation for the preposited article in v. 3. Paul's *Vorlage* apparently contained only indefinite participial forms in all three locations, in accordance with the majority LXX reading. The somewhat divided testimony for the omission of the article in the Pauline passage is the result of scribal assimilations to this primary Septuagintal tradition.[30] The addition of the article in the Pauline context, on the other hand, further absolutizes the "not even one" of the Pauline indictment: not a single individual can be found who does the things set forth in vv. 10–12.[31] Since the definite forms would not be out of place in the original LXX context, however, the present study must retain at least a modicum of reserve in attributing the additions to Paul himself.

V   Reading χρηστότητα in v. 12.   The uncial R and the Gallican Psalter of Jerome read ἀγαθόν in Ps 13.3b in place of χρηστότητα, which appears in MSS B S U L A *et al.* A similar variability can be seen in the parallel passage Ps 52.1–4, where ἀγαθόν is the dominant reading. The Pauline tradition is quite

---

[29] Rahlfs cites only the seventh-century palimpsest MS 1221 in favor of the article in the first two instances, but adds the important testimony of S and U plus MS 2019 for v. 3. The Hebrew forms are indefinite throughout.

[30] According to Nestle, the uncials B and G are the only texts that omit the article in all three instances. Codex A omits the article before ποιῶν in v. 12b and apparently in v. 11a as well, but not in v. 11b. (Nestle lists A on both sides of the question in v. 11a, but Tischendorf is clear that A omits the article). The same course is followed by the manuscripts that Nestle cites as "*pc*" in v. 11a, presumably part of the 𝔐 (constant witnesses) cited in v. 12b. Other manuscripts omit only the first (81 1241 sa) or last (Ψ and remainder of 𝔐) article.

[31] The addition therefore goes beyond the merely "stilistisch" purpose assigned to it by Koch (*Schrift*, 132).

secure in reading χρηστότητα at this point, in accordance with the majority reading for Ps 13. The variation in the LXX text is the result of mutual influence between two parallel but different Psalms traditions.[32]

(4b)   **Rom 3.13ab** (= Ps 5.10)

U⁺ The Pauline quotation from Ps 5.10 agrees in full with a wholly unified LXX tradition. The verse that follows in the combined citation (Rom 3.13c) is added to the end of Ps 5.10 in the Sahidic version, but nowhere else.

(4c)   **Rom 3.13c** (= Ps 139.4)

U⁺ As in the first part of v. 13, the Pauline and LXX traditions are unanimous in their readings and stand in full agreement.

(4d)   **Rom 3.14** (= Ps 9.28)

Paul: ὧν τὸ στόμα [ ] ἀρᾶς καὶ πικρίας [ ] γέμει.
LXX: οὗ ἀρᾶς τὸ στόμα αὐτοῦ γέμει καὶ πικρίας καὶ δόλου, [ὑπὸ τὴν γλῶσσαν αὐτοῦ κόπος καὶ πόνος.]

A   Conversion of relative pronoun from singular to plural.   In one of the clearest examples of textual adaptation in the entire Pauline corpus, the plural pronoun that appears in the Pauline quotation of Ps 9.28 is wholly incongruous with the third-person singular framework of the original passage. The conversion, however, is entirely natural from the Pauline point of view: what the psalmist says about the generic "sinner" (ὁ ἁμαρτωλός, vv. 24, 25, 36) Paul applies to "all humanity" (πάντες, Rom 3.12a) on the normal Pauline assumption that all are equally ἁμαρτωλοί. The undivided textual tradition only adds to the confidence with which this modification can be attributed to the editorial activity of Paul.

---

[32] The omission of the initial οὐκ ἔστιν from part of the Pauline tradition for v. 12c would represent a deviation to be investigated here only if it proved to be original, which is highly doubtful. Not only is the textual evidence less than overwhelming (the combined evidence of the Nestle, UBS, and Tischendorf editions yields only B 6 67* 1739 syrᵖ ˢᶜʰ Or in favor of the omission), but the careful rhetorical structure of the passage fairly demands its inclusion if it stood in Paul's *Vorlage* – and there exists absolutely no evidence for the omission of the phrase from the LXX. The reading that includes these words is therefore quite secure, despite the C rating and brackets assigned to it by the UBS Committee.

A   Omitting αὐτοῦ. Whether he converted the pronoun to a plural form (with B 17 33 Cyp) or omitted it entirely (with the majority tradition), the adaptation here is clearly Pauline in origin, meant to remove the discrepancy between the already pleonastic singular pronoun found in the original and the plural pronoun (ὧν) that introduces the Pauline form of the text.

B   Shifting the position of ἀρᾶς. With a unified textual tradition on both sides of the question, one can only assume that Paul felt the awkwardness of the original reading (which separated ἀρᾶς from its natural correlatives πικρίας and δόλου) and consequently restored what appeared to be the natural order of the words in question.[33] The possibility that the change took place prior to Paul cannot be ruled out entirely, but the fact that it occurs in a verse and passage already marked by a number of clearly Pauline adaptations renders the Pauline explanation more likely.

C   Omission of καὶ δόλου. The fact that both traditions stand united behind their respective readings at this point presents an obstacle to any text-based explanation for the present omission. If a Pauline adaptation is in view, rhetorical foreshortening is the only feasible explanation, since nothing in the content of the words would appear to justify their omission. Perhaps Dietrich-Alex Koch is right in thinking that the words would have appeared redundant after the verb ἐδολιοῦσαν in v. 13b,[34] or else the desire for rhetorical compactness in the broader composition may have dictated the removal of one element of the tripartite object. The alternative, that the omission took place prior to Paul's appropriation of the text, is attractive in that the reduction from a triple to a dual object actually

---

[33] Interestingly, the result of this "improvement" is to create a text that stands even farther from the original Hebrew reading, if one takes the אָלָה that introduces Ps 10.7 as part of the preceding verse. The same process of smoothing out an awkward Greek rendering while unwittingly moving the text further from the Hebrew was noted in chap. 2 for certain LXX fragments from Qumran, and will be encountered again in the discussion of passages such as Rom 11.3–4, where similar revisions occur. The alternative, that the verse has been conformed to the Hebrew by dropping the initial ἀρᾶς and then translating וּמִרְמוֹת וָתֹךְ as ἀρᾶς καὶ πικρίας founders on the awkwardness of the translation equivalents required in both instances.

[34] *Schrift*, 116 n. 3.

improves the structural and semantic parallelism between the two cola in the LXX text. Without supporting textual evidence, however, such an explanation can be considered no more than an interesting possibility. The probability rating assigned to this deviation may well give this latter option more weight than it deserves.

B   Shifting the position of γέμει.   Not only is there no textual evidence to support a pre-Pauline origin for this minor change in word order, but moving the verb to the final position would also disrupt the clear structural parallelism of the original passage. The very same change, on the other hand, actually improves the rhetorical symmetry of the Pauline combined citation. Every other finite verb in Rom 3.10–18 (except for the emphatic οὐκ ἔστιν) appears as the final word in its clause (see vv. 12a, 13b, and 17). Shifting γέμει to the final position therefore lends greater structural uniformity to the passage as a whole. On a more limited scale, the move also sets the verb in structural parallelism with ἐδολιοῦσαν in v. 13b. Only the fact that the shift would not be completely out of place in the original passage hinders the unqualified acceptance of this deviation as a Pauline adaptation.

(4e)   **Rom 3.15–17** (= Isa 59.7–8)

Paul: ὀξεῖς οἱ [ ] πόδες αὐτῶν [ ] ἐκχέαι **αἷμα**,
        * σύντριμμα καὶ ταλαιπωρία ἐν ταῖς ὁδοῖς αὐτῶν,
        καὶ ὁδὸν εἰρήνης οὐκ ἔγνωσαν.
LXX: οἱ δὲ πόδες αὐτῶν ἐπὶ πονερίαν τρέξουσιν ταχινοὶ ἐκχέαι
        αἷμα· [καὶ οἱ διαλογισμοὶ αὐτων διαλογισμοὶ ἀφρόνων,]
        σύντριμμα καὶ ταλαιπωρία ἐν ταῖς ὁδοῖς αὐτῶν. καὶ ὁδὸν
        εἰρήνης οὐκ οἴδασιν, [καὶ οὐκ ἔστιν κρίσις ἐν ταῖς ὁδοῖς
        αὐτῶν.]

B   Omitting initial δέ.   Textual evidence for this minor omission is entirely lacking in the LXX tradition. Leaving off initial connectives, on the other hand, is standard fare in Paul's handling of the biblical text, as the present study will repeatedly attest. Including the conjunction at this point would only disrupt the flow and unity of this tightly woven Pauline composition. At the same time, the word would hardly be missed had it already dropped out of Paul's *Vorlage*, as such particles are prone to do. The latter observation means that absolute confidence in the Pauline origin of this omission must be withheld under the terms of the present study.

D   Substituting ὀξεῖς for ταχινοί.   The translational equivalence between members of the ταχ- family and the Hebrew root מהר is firmly entrenched throughout all quarters of the LXX.[35] This fact combined with the total lack of manuscript evidence to the contrary establishes ταχινοί as without doubt the original reading in the present passage. Though the ταχ- family is common throughout Greek literature, the adjective ταχινός is a rare form, with ταχύς the preferred expression for normal prose writing.[36] It should come as no surprise, then, to see a later writer introducing a more common word (ὀξύς) in place of this rather unusual expression. Why the cognate adjective ταχύς should have been passed over in favor of the equally common ὀξύς, however, remains a mystery. The subtleties of connotation and usage that distinguish near-synonyms are among the most difficult features for the non-native speaker to master. Given the lack of manuscript evidence for any other explanation and the likelihood of Pauline editorial activity in the rest of the quotation, it would be quite natural to attribute this change, too, to the apostle. Without firm evidence in either direction, however, the present study cannot embrace any solution with a high degree of confidence.

A   Advancing ὀξεῖς to primary position in v. 15.   Though the occasion for the change in wording remains unclear, the question of who first advanced ὀξεῖς to its present position can be answered with greater assurance. What was originally two parallel statements depicting the sinful practices of Yahweh's people ("their feet run to evil, they are swift to shed blood") has here been reduced to one ("their feet are swift to shed blood") by shifting the adjective from the second clause to the first and

[35] The adjective ταχινός occurs only 6 times in the LXX, translating forms of מהר in all 3 cases where the Hebrew original is known. The more common adjective ταχύς is found 26 times, of which 22 render forms of מהר. The same equivalence holds true for the noun τάχος (16 out of 19 times), the verb ταχύνω (all 16 instances), and the adverb ταχέως (9 out of 10 occurrences).

[36] LSJ labels ταχινός a poetic and late prose form of ταχύς. The adjective ταχινός appears in the New Testament only here and seven times in Revelation.

simultaneously suppressing the latter part of the first clause (see below). Nothing in the original context (or the subsequent textual tradition) can explain such a radical reworking of v. 7a. Within the Pauline context, on the other hand, these simple adaptations yield a compact statement that preserves the basic content of the original indictment without adding unnecessarily to the overall length of the Pauline composition. The shift of ὀξεῖς to primary position also serves to emphasize the "hastiness" of the actions described, thus subtly reinforcing the notion of the culpability of those who follow such a path. The effect on the sense is minor at best, but the resultant "quotation" works much better as part of a highly condensed Pauline formulation.

A   Omission of ἐπὶ πονηρίαν τρέχουσιν in v. 15.   The omission of the words ἐπὶ πονηρίαν τρέχουσιν at the end of the first colon of Isa 59.7 goes hand in hand with the shift of ὀξεῖς [= ταχινός] from the second colon to the first (see above). No other explanation for why the words might have dropped out of the original is forthcoming. Clearly the rhetorical interests of the later user (in this case, Paul) have produced a significant change in the wording of the original biblical passage.

V   Reading αἷμα without ἀναίτιον.   The addition of the adjective ἀναίτιον in a number of LXX manuscripts immediately after the noun αἷμα is best viewed as a later attempt to bring the Greek text into closer conformity with the wording of the Masoretic Hebrew.[37] Not only is there no evidence for the inclusion of the word in any Pauline manuscript, but it is difficult to see why Paul would have omitted from his *Vorlage* a word that would have added such force to his own indictment of human sin.

A   Omitting καὶ ... ἀφρόνων.   Here the editorial activity of Paul himself is clearly in view – no other explanation is either plausible or necessary. As Koch points out, the present omission parallels Paul's handling of Ps 13 in the same passage (vv. 10–12).[38] In both cases, a line that attributes the behavior of the people under discussion to their "foolishness" is left out (cf. Ps

---

[37] The addition is found in V L'' Q^mg 62 403' 407 449' 544 Thdrt Hier.
[38] *Schrift*, 119.

13.1a), presumably because it conflicts with Paul's emphasis on the moral culpability of those who act in the manner described. The problem for Paul's interpretation is that both of these passages were originally written to censure the conduct of a particular group of people, not that of humanity as a whole. Only by omitting their particularist elements could Paul use either passage to support his contention that all are equally "under sin" (v. 9).

D   Substituting ἔγνωσαν for οἴδασιν. According to the lexicographers, the difference between the verbs οἶδα and γινώσκω is somewhat akin to the English distinction between "to have knowledge of/be acquainted with" and "to comprehend/ understand." The latter can also bear the sense of "to come to know/learn about" something.[39] As with most synonyms, however, the overlap in meaning is at least as great as the distinction, as the regular interchange between the two in the Greek manuscript tradition testifies. In the present passage, the Pauline evidence is thoroughly unified, whereas the LXX tradition shows important support for both οἴδασιν and ἔγνωσαν.[40] It seems quite possible therefore that Paul has simply followed the wording of his *Vorlage* at this point. On the other hand, one could argue that a form of γινώσκω is actually better suited to Paul's purpose here than the reading οἴδασιν, on the view that γινώσκω carries a clearer sense of personal responsibility. The people in question are not simply unacquainted with "the way of peace"; they are unable to comprehend it even when it is set before them.[41] Even if this distinction be granted, however, it is hard to see why Paul would have been so troubled by the reading οἴδασιν that he would have felt any great desire to change it. The origin of the Pauline wording must remain in obscurity.

[39] See the listings in LSJ and BAGD for both words.
[40] The majority reading οἴδασιν has the support of the uncials Q S B V and the Lucianic and Catena traditions, while the alternate reading ἔγνωσαν is found in the uncials A and Q^mg, part of the Hexaplaric tradition (oI'), MSS 403', and the church fathers Clem Eus Hier.
[41] This is essentially Koch's argument: "Während bei εἰδέναι der Gesichtspunkt des inhaltlichen Wissens stärker im Vordergrund steht, enthält γινώσκειν darüber hinaus das Moment der Anerkenntnis und des Gehorsams" (*Schrift*, 143).

(4f)   **Rom 3.18** (= Ps 35.2)

Paul: * οὐκ ἔστιν φόβος θεοῦ ἀπέναντι τῶν ὀφθαλμῶν <u>αὐτῶν</u>
LXX: [Φησὶν ὁ παράνομος τοῦ ἁμαρτάνειν ἐν ἑαυτῷ,]
       οὐκ ἔστιν φόβος θεοῦ ἀπέναντι τῶν ὀφθαλμῶν αὐτοῦ.

A   Omitting v. 2a (limited selection).   As with the depiction of the
    ἄφρονων in Ps 13.1 (Rom 3.10), so here the specific reference to
    the παράνομος is wholly inappropriate to Paul's purpose in
    Rom 3.10–18. By dropping the initial line of the Psalm and
    adjusting the grammar of the second (see below), however, Paul
    is able to shift the focus of the verse from the person of the
    wrongdoer to the quality of his actions. In its new (Pauline)
    context, the verse serves as a fitting conclusion to all that has
    gone before, summing up the entire indictment in one poignant
    phrase: "there is no fear of God before their eyes." Only by
    eliminating the first line of Ps 35.2 could Paul have achieved so
    magnificent a rhetorical effect.

A   Changing αὐτοῦ to αὐτῶν.   Just as the repeated references to
    ὁ ἁμαρτωλός in Ps 9 drew Paul to the verse that he reproduced
    (in modified form) in v. 14 above, so the reference to ὁ παράνο-
    μος in Ps 35.2a allowed him to read the statement in Ps 35.2b as
    a description of humanity as a whole. As with the earlier
    passage, however, the shift to a generalizing application meant
    that the singular reference of the original had to be changed to
    a plural to bring it into line with the plurals that run
    throughout Rom 3.10–18.[42] Such a plural reading would of
    course be totally out of place in Ps 35, which makes the Pauline
    origin of the revised wording plain. The textual evidence fully
    supports this conclusion.

(5)   **Rom 4.3** (= Gen 15.6)[43]

Paul: ἐπίστευσεν δὲ Ἀβραὰμ τῷ θεῷ, καὶ ἐλογίσθη αὐτῷ εἰς
       δικαιοσύνη.

---

[42] So also Ellis, *Use*, 11 n. 6; Koch, *Schrift*, 112.
[43] Though often taken as a quotation due to its verbal closeness to Ps 143.2$_{LXX}$,
Rom 3.20 has been omitted from the present study in accordance with strict guidelines that limit the investigation to passages that offer explicit indication to the reader
that a citation is being offered (introductory formula, interpretive comments, etc.).

LXX: καὶ ἐπίστευσεν Ἀβραάμ τῷ θεῷ, καὶ ἐλογίσθη αὐτῷ εἰς δικαιοσύνη.

D   Substitution of δέ for καί. The awkwardness of the present Pauline wording was clearly felt by later copyists, who omitted the connective δέ from a number of the lesser manuscripts and most of the versions.[44] The LXX tradition, on the other hand, is all but united in reading καί at this point.[45] Still, the fact that both Philo and James (2.23) give the same reading as Paul opens up at least the possibility that the text may have varied more in antiquity than the present manuscript tradition would suggest. The absence of any connective whatsoever in the parallel passage in Gal 3.6 only adds to the problem. According to Koch, Paul added the δέ to Rom 4.3 to stress the contrast between this verse and v. 2, where the possibility was allowed that Abraham might conceivably have been justified ἐξ ἔργων (νόμου).[46] If this were the case, however, one would expect the δέ to appear as part of the introductory formula, where the γάρ now stands, and not in the citation itself. The truth is that the δέ is awkward and serves no useful purpose in its present location. This in turn lends support to the view that Paul has simply reproduced the wording of his *Vorlage* in Rom 4.3.[47] The connective δέ would then have been omitted in Gal 3.6, where the segue into Gen 15.6 made it superfluous.[48] In the final analysis, the difficulty of arguing with confidence on such a minor and variable point rules out firm conclusions in either direction.

---

[44] The evidence is primarily "Western": Tischendorf cites D* F G 61 108* b^scr* o^scr d e f g vg syr^sch arm aeth Chr Euthal Cyp Or in favor of the omission.

[45] The sole exception is the manuscript group b (δέ), which according to Koch (*Schrift*, 133 n. 5) conforms to the Pauline wording at other points as well (see the list in *Schrift*, 54).

[46] *Schrift*, 132–3. Kautzsch (25) voices a similar view. Both authors are required by their position to assert that Philo and James came up with the same reading independently of Paul, and that all of the church fathers who offer the same wording (Clem Or Aug Hier) are dependent on the New Testament. In the case of such a minor variation as the substitution of δέ for καί, such a reading of the evidence strains credulity.

[47] A memory error is less likely, since the same reading is found in Philo and James.

[48] Similar omissions of introductory δέ can be seen in Rom 3.15 and Gal 3.11, while the δέ is retained in Rom 1.17 and 2 Cor 3.16 in situations quite like the present.

(6)   **Rom 4.7–8** (= Ps 31.1–2)

U⁻ A number of manuscripts in both the Pauline and LXX traditions substitute the Dative ᾧ for the Genitive οὗ in the third
line of the present citation.[49] As the Dative is normal with
λογίζεσθαι,[50] the explanation that the Dative represents a
scribal correction lies ready at hand. The overall strength of the
external evidence also supports the view that both the LXX and
Paul originally read οὗ at this point.

A   Omitting the second colon of Ps 31.2.   The fact that Paul ends
his quotation after the first colon of Ps 31.2 is noteworthy.
Quite often Paul will simply pull a useful line or two out of a
longer passage in a way that says nothing about his attitude
toward the materials immediately before and after the excerpt.
Not uncommonly, however, a Pauline citation will begin or end
at precisely the point where the original passage turns in a
direction different from or even contrary to Paul's own application of the text.[51] In such cases it is legitimate to speak of
"limited selection" as an aspect of Paul's regular citation technique. The present passage supplies a helpful though innocuous
example of how this procedure works. Since Paul began his
citation with the first verse of Ps 31, it was obviously up to him
to decide how far he would go before bringing the citation to a
close. The first three lines of the Psalm fit well with Paul's stress
in Rom 4 on the mercy of Yahweh in forgiving human sin. But
with the fourth line (οὐδὲ ἔστιν ἐν τῷ στόματι αὐτοῦ δόλος),
the usefulness of the passage ends. Indeed, the parallel that it
presents between maintaining a pure mouth (v. 2b) and having
one's sin overlooked by the Lord (v. 2a) might have suggested
to some exactly the kind of "works-righteousness" that Paul is
at such pains to root out. The fact that Paul chooses to end his
citation at this point rather than at the natural break at the end
of v. 2 is no coincidence. Instead, it reflects a calculated decision by Paul as to the usefulness of the passage under consideration.

[49] For the LXX, Rahlfs cites L' 1219' in favor of the Dative reading and B' U R A
for the Genitive. For the Pauline text, Nestle gives ℵ² A Dᶜ F Ψ 𝔐 for the Dative,
over against ℵ* B C D* G 1506(*) 1739 *pc* for the Genitive reading. Tischendorf adds
a number of church fathers and versions, almost all "Western," to the evidence for
the Dative.

[50] See BAGD under this heading.

[51] As seen already in the case of Rom 3.4.

(7)   **Rom 4.17** (= Gen 17.5)

U⁺ Only one insignificant manuscript in each tradition mars the perfect agreement between Paul and the Septuagint at this point.[52]

(8)   **Rom 4.18** (= Gen 15.5)

U⁺ Here again Paul follows the Septuagint precisely, though a handful of witnesses conflate the present text with parts of Gen 22.17.[53]

(9)   **Rom 4.22** (= Gen 15.6)[54]

U⁺ The present citation stands in full agreement with a nearly unified LXX tradition whether or not the introductory καί is considered an integral part of the citation.[55] Though the introduction is highly unusual (a clearly elliptical διό or διὸ καί), the citation status of the verse is secure not only because it repeats a part of the explicit quotation offered in v. 3, but also because the next verse selects two words from the present verse for further comment.[56]

[52] LXX MS 46 omits ἐθνῶν, while Pauline MS 37 reverses the order of πατέρα πολλῶν.

[53] The conflation involves the addition of the phrase ὡς τοὺς ἀστέρας τοῦ οὐρανοῦ καὶ ὡς τὴν ἄμμον τῆς θαλάσσης or parts thereof to the end of the present citation. The evidence is primarily "Western": Nestle lists only F G a, while Tischendorf adds 106 108ᵐᵍ f demid floriac vgˢⁱˣ Thphyl Pelag for the full addition and g harl* fu marian tol Or for partial additions. Other minor variants in the LXX tradition show no contact with the Pauline use of the verse.

[54] A similar brief excerpt from Gen 15.6 in Rom 4.9 was omitted from consideration in accordance with the strict guidelines of the present study, which is confined to passages that offer explicit indication to the reader that a citation is being offered (introductory formula, interpretive comments, etc.).

[55] Despite the brackets in the UBS edition, the evidence for dropping the καί is only moderately strong, and the omission is easily explained by the awkward wording that results when the καί is included. The combined listings of the Nestle and UBS editions show only B D* F G 1984 *pc* b m it ᵉ,ᶠ,ᵍ syᵖ·ᵖᵃˡ co arm in favor of the omission, while the evidence for retaining καί includes the uncials ℵ A C Dᵇ·ᶜ K P Ψ, an extensive listing of minuscules, the remainder of the Latin evidence, the Syrohexapla, and numerous church fathers. The question of whether the καί was meant as part of the citation or the surrounding argument (in the sense of "also" or "indeed") is less easily resolved. The unusual nature of the introduction, a simple διό, only adds to the uncertainty. Fortunately, the resolution of the issue has no significance for the present study, since the καί is present in the LXX in any case.

[56] A similar treatment secures the citation status of Rom 10.6–8 and 1 Cor 15.27. Though one could conceivably count both Rom 4.23 (ἐλογίσθη αὐτῷ) and 1 Cor 15.27b (πάντα ὑποτέτεκται) as biblical citations, it is probably better to regard them

(10)   **Rom 7.7** (= Exod 20.17/Deut 5.21)

O   Leaving off the last part of the verse. Though formally an instance of "limited selection," the generalizing omission of the compound objects (τὴν γυναῖκα κτλ.) when citing this commandment is standard practice in Diaspora Judaism.[57] The foreshortening of the verse here is thus to be attributed to oral tradition, not to Paul's specific literary purpose.

(11)   **Rom 8.36** (= Ps 43.23)

V   Substitution of ἕνεκεν for ἕνεκα. Though Rahlfs prints the Attic form ἕνεκα following the testimony of B R L, the Ionic–Hellenistic ἕνεκεν has the strong backing of S A T L^pau 2013, and may indeed be original. Whatever the case, the availability of significant LXX evidence with the same reading as Paul coupled with the absence of a Pauline motive for the change makes it more than likely that Paul has simply followed the wording of his *Vorlage* here.[58]

(12)   **Rom 9.7** (= Gen 21.12)

U[+]   The idea of the divine election of Isaac's descendants has remained central to the self-definition of Judaism throughout its history. To this no doubt is to be traced the nearly unanimous testimony to this verse in the LXX manuscript tradition, with which Paul's citation fully agrees.

(13)   **Rom 9.9** (= Gen 18.14)

Paul: κατὰ τὸν καιρὸν τοῦτον ἐλεύσομαι [ ], καὶ ἔσται τῇ Σαρρᾳ υἱός.
LXX: εἰς τὸν καιρὸν τοῦτον ἀναστρέψω πρὸς σὲ εἰς ὥρας, καὶ ἔσται τῇ Σαρρᾳ υἱός.

as extracts from the previous quotation (with the tense modified in the second instance) and thus to omit them from the present study.

[57] Koch, *Schrift*, 117, citing K. Berger, *Die Gesetzesauslegung Jesu: Ihr historischer Hintergrund im Judentum und im Alten Testament. Teil I: Markus und Parallelen*, WMANT 40 (Neukirchen-Vluyn: Neukirchener Verlag, 1972), 346–7.

[58] It is interesting to note that the Attic form ἕνεκα never appears in any of Paul's letters, while ἕνεκεν occurs three times apart from the present context (Rom 14.20, 2 Cor 3.10, 7.12). Tischendorf cites C K *al plu* and several church fathers as reading ἕνεκα for Rom 8.36.

D   Substitution of κατά for εἰς. The common assertion that the present verse represents a conflation of Gen 18.10 and 18.14 founders on the observation that the Pauline quotation contains only one word found in verse 10 and not in verse 14, the preposition κατά.[59] The LXX witnesses are united in reading εἰς in verse 14, while the Pauline tradition stands equally secure behind κατά in Rom 9.9. No clear exegetical motive for the change can be identified, though the substitution of the more specific temporal designation κατά ("at")[60] is well suited to the dehistoricizing treatment accorded the Genesis passage in the rest of the verse (see below). Otherwise, an unattested manuscript variant or a memory slip (influenced by Gen 18.10?) afford equally plausible explanations.

B   Substitution of ἐλεύσομαι for ἀναστρέψω/Elimination of the
B   words πρὸς σὲ εἰς ὥρας. Two questionable readings from Rom 9.9 will be considered together here, as both seem to have arisen from the same exegetical concern. In neither case is there any evidence for a manuscript-based explanation.[61] While the Pauline ἐλεύσομαι would not be out of place in the LXX context, it is difficult to imagine what might have led a copyist to omit the temporal references that play so important a role in the story of the birth of Isaac. In the context of Romans 9, on the other hand, these same references become irrelevant and therefore dispensable. While the original story line remains vital to Paul's use of Gen 18.14 here, the importance of the verse for Paul lies specifically in its status as a "word of promise" (ἐπαγγελίας γὰρ ὁ λόγος οὗτος, v. 9a) to which Yahweh subsequently proved himself faithful. In other words, the promise of the angel to "return" (ἀναστρέψω) is less important to Paul than the assurance that God himself would indeed "come" (ἐλεύσομαι) to fulfill his promise. By eliminating the temporal elements from his citation (though not from the minds of his readers, who are expected to know how the story turns out), Paul calls attention to the central point that he wants his readers to grasp from this small slice of the Abraham-

---

[59] So also Koch, *Schrift*, 172.

[60] See BAGD, s. v. κατά, II.2a.

[61] The Pauline tradition is unanimous in both instances; the only deviations in the LXX tradition are in one minuscule that leaves out πρὸς σέ and another that omits εἰς ὥρας.

ic narrative. At the same time, the full effect of the change is heard only as the original and Pauline forms of this verse echo off one another in the minds of readers familiar with the original passage.

(14)   **Rom 9.12** (= Gen 25.23)

U$^+$ Apart from a few spelling variants on the final word in the LXX, both textual traditions are united and in full agreement concerning the reading of the present verse.

(15)   **Rom 9.13** (= Mal 1.2–3)

Paul: [ ] τὸν Ἰακωβ ἠγάπησα, τὸν δὲ Ἠσαυ ἐμίσησα.
LXX: καὶ ἠγάπησα τὸν Ἰακωβ, τὸν δὲ Ἠσαυ ἐμίσησα [καὶ ἔταξα τὰ ὅρια αὐτοῦ εἰς ἀφανισμὸν καὶ τὴν κληρονομίαν αὐτοῦ εἰς δόματα ἐρήμου].

B   Omission of initial καί.   Even in the LXX, the presence of a καί immediately after λέγει κύριος is awkward, as attested by the attempts of a handful of scribes to eliminate it from the text altogether.[62] The same awkwardness can be felt after the Pauline καθὼς γέγραπται. While it is always possible that the word had already dropped out of Paul's *Vorlage* (or the Hebrew text behind it), the frequency with which Paul eliminates introductory particles that conflict with his own syntax reveals his sensitivity to the manner in which a quotation fits into the flow of his argument.[63] The omission of initial καί here is wholly consistent with Paul's normal practice as seen in other passages.

B   Shifting τὸν Ἰακώβ to primary position.   Tracing the origins of a shift in word order is always difficult due to the infinite possibilities for transposition that arose in the process of copying ancient manuscripts. Nonetheless, the fact that the LXX and Pauline traditions stand united behind their respective readings offers *prima facie* evidence that the word order of Rom 9.13 goes back to Paul himself.[64] The effect of the

---

[62] The omission is limited to 763 91* Ach Aeth. The MT contains a ו at this point.
[63] For the evidence on Paul's omission of initial particles, see note 197.
[64] Only the Bohairic text (rendered into Latin as "et iacob μεν dilexi" in the Göttingen apparatus) appears to follow the Pauline reading, presumably under New Testament influence.

change is more rhetorical than substantial: shifting τὸν Ἰακώβ to primary position creates a verbal parallelism that heightens the contrast between Jacob and Esau in the present passage, while also creating a closer link with the immediately preceding citation (ὁ ἐλάσσων in v. 12 = τὸν Ἰακώβ in v. 13).[65] A subtle shift in emphasis is likewise evident: whereas in Malachi the focus is on the divine "hating" of Esau (as seen both in the emphatic position of τὸν Ἠσαυ and the content of the verse as a whole), the Pauline version sets both members on a (verbally) equal footing, in line with Paul's stress on the sovereign freedom of God in electing one brother and rejecting the other (vv. 10–12). Though the change is minor, its suitability for the Pauline use of Mal 1.2–3 is clear.

(16)   **Rom 9.15** (= Exod 33.19)

U[+]   In this important proclamation about the divine character, the Pauline text agrees precisely with a nearly unanimous LXX tradition.

(17)   **Rom 9.17** (= Exod 9.16)

Paul: [ ] εἰς αὐτὸ τοῦτο ἐξήγειρά σε, ὅπως ἐνδείξωμαι ἐν σοὶ τὴν δύναμίν μου, καὶ ὅπως διαγγελῇ τὸ ὄνομά μου ἐν πάσῃ τῇ γῇ.

LXX: καὶ ἕνεκεν τούτου διετηρήθης, ἵνα ἐνδείξωμαι ἐν σοὶ τὴν ἰσχύν μου, καὶ ὅπως διαγγελῇ τὸ ὄνομά μου ἐν πάσῃ τῇ γῇ.

MT: וְאוּלָם בַּעֲבוּר זֹאת הֶעֱמַדְתִּיךָ בַּעֲבוּר הַרְאֹתְךָ אֶת־כֹּחִי
וּלְמַעַן סַפֵּר שְׁמִי בְּכָל־הָאָרֶץ

A   <u>Omitting initial καί.</u>   The textual witnesses are wholly united in their respective readings at this point, while the omission of introductory particles is a common Pauline citation technique.[66] Even if the present citation should be traced to a non-"standard" Greek *Vorlage* (see below), there is nothing in either the Greek or Hebrew traditions to suggest that the present omission should be attributed to anyone but Paul.

C   <u>Substituting εἰς αὐτὸ τοῦτο for ἕνεκεν τούτου.</u>   The fact that neither the LXX nor the Pauline tradition shows any

---

[65] So also Koch, *Schrift*, 107–8. Kautzsch (10) and Vollmer (43 n. 1) also label this shift a Pauline alteration.
[66] See note 197.

variation in wording at this point is a strong argument in favor of the Pauline origin of the form found in Romans.[67] In this case, however, the difference in meaning between the two phrases is so negligible as to render conscious adaptation unlikely. Koch points out that ἕνεκεν τούτου appears nowhere in Paul's letters while εἰς αὐτὸ τοῦτο can be seen in Rom 13.6 and 2 Cor 5.5,[68] but the significance of such evidence is unclear. If a conscious alteration is to be posited, a more likely explanation might be sought in the ambiguity of ἕνεκεν τούτου, which could be read as pointing either backward or forward, whereas its replacement εἰς αὐτὸ τοῦτο is more clearly anticipatory.[69] In view of the insignificance of the change, however, the possibility that Paul might have used an unattested text in which the Hebrew was rendered somewhat idiomatically, or even a simple memory slip, cannot be ruled out.

D   Replacing the Passive διετηρήθης with the Active ἐξήγειρά σε. Though the first person Active form is clearly a better rendering of the Hebrew הֶעֱמַדְתִּיךָ than the Passive expression found in the LXX, the difficulties associated with the idea that Paul used the Hebrew to correct the LXX at this point would appear to be insuperable. The fact that Paul consistently follows the Greek version in his citations even where the Hebrew wording would have been more congenial to his argument (e.g. 1 Cor 2.16) shows that Paul was not in the habit of comparing readings and "correcting" the LXX by the Hebrew.[70] As for the even more remote possibility that Paul might have translated the present verse directly from the Hebrew, the substantial agreement of the rest of the quotation with the LXX, including its addition of the preposition ἐν and its rendering of the active סַפֵּר by the passive διαγγελῇ, shows that it was the standard Greek text that stands behind Paul's citation of Exod 9.16. This does not mean, however, that Paul could not have used a Greek text that had already been "corrected" toward the Hebrew by

[67] No additional evidence is provided by the upcoming Göttingen edition of Exodus, kindly made available by Dr. John William Wevers.

[68] *Schrift*, 141.

[69] For Koch's attempt to link this change to a supposed strengthening of the "final" sense of the next clause through an intentional substitution of ὅπως for ἵνα, see below.

[70] *Contra* Ellis on both the present passage (*Use*, 14 n. 6) and Paul in general (139–47).

an earlier reviser at this point.[71] The alternative, that Paul himself might have modified the text to highlight the active role of God in the hardening of Pharaoh, is certainly in line with Paul's use of Exod 9.16 here, but can hardly be proven.[72] The fact that the Pauline reading coincides with the Hebrew text at this point renders all suggestions of a Pauline origin dubious.

D   Substitution of ὅπως (1°) for ἵνα.   Though the manuscript tradition is nearly unanimous on both sides,[73] it remains difficult to comprehend why these two almost synonymous particles should have been exchanged intentionally. Koch's attempt to discover in this substitution a strengthening of the "final" sense of the clause falters on the observation that ἵνα-clauses are actually used more frequently than ὅπως-clauses to express purpose in the New Testament.[74] Exchanging ὅπως and ἵνα in successive clauses is likewise common in the literature, including several instances in Paul (1 Cor 1.28–9, 2 Cor 8.14, 2 Thess 1.11–12),[75] so that an attempt to improve the parallelism with the following clause is equally unlikely. In view of the evidence already accumulated for the use of a poorly attested divergent text for the present citation (see above), any explanation that would posit a Pauline adaptation should probably be regarded as suspect.

[71] Indeed, one can find minor LXX evidence that agrees with Paul in reading an Active verb at this point while showing none of the other variations that appear in Rom 9.17. According to the soon-to-be published Göttingen edition of Exodus (kindly supplied by Dr. John William Wevers), the form διετήρησα [*not* ἐξήγειρα] σε appears in the minuscules 135 85^mg–343–344^mg and in the Ethiopic and Arabic versions. The retention of the inappropriate διατηρεῖσθαι as a rendering of the Hebrew root עמד (a translation equivalent found nowhere else in the LXX) shows that it is only a minor "correction" of the LXX and not a thorough revision that is in view in these manuscripts. Kautzsch (74–5) argued that the Pauline form reflected acquaintance with just such an "ancient Alexandrian reading" that Paul had subsequently modified to ἐξήγειρα σε to accord with his emphasis on the divine sovereignty in the present passage. The question of why the supposed original διετήρησα should have required modification to suit Paul's point in Rom 9.17 is never addressed.

[72] Both Vollmer (43 n. 1) and Koch (*Schrift*, 112, 150–1) argue for a Pauline modification here.

[73] Holmes–Parsons lists one minuscule and quotations from Chrysostom and Origen as reading ὅπως here. The soon-to-be published Göttingen edition of Exodus cites only a small portion of the Hexaplaric evidence (oI^−64mg) as agreeing with the wording of Paul.

[74] *Schrift*, 151. On final clauses in the New Testament, see C. F. D. Moule, *An Idiom-Book of New Testament Greek* (Cambridge University Press, 1968), 138.

[75] See BDF §369 (4).

V   Substitution of δύναμιν for ἰσχύν. The New Testament manuscripts are agreed in reading δύναμιν here, but the LXX is strongly divided between δύναμιν and ἰσχύν.[76] The observation that ἰσχύς is never found in the undisputed letters of Paul (versus nearly three dozen instances of δύναμις) and is uncommon in Hellenistic Greek generally[77] makes a Pauline adaptation plausible, but it hardly proves the case. The evidence is simply inadequate to support a Pauline origin for the present reading in light of the highly divided testimony of the LXX.

(18)   **Rom 9.25–6** (= Hos 2.25, 2.1)[78]

A   Combined citation.   Few would doubt the Pauline origins of the combination and massive reworking of Hos 2.25 and Hos 2.1 that appears in Rom 9.25–6. The text of Hos 2.25 in particular has been so thoroughly adapted to suit its present application that few of its original words remain intact. What was once a promise of divine mercy toward wayward Israel has been transformed in Paul's hands into a prophecy of Yahweh's coming election of the Gentiles (those who once were "not my people") to share in the benefits of his covenant. Some of these same modifications serve to link Hos 2.25 into a continuous thematic whole with the subsequent quotation from Hos 2.1. The skill with which the two verses have been knit together and adapted for their present purpose shows that it is no careless lapse of memory but rather the conscious effort of a thoughtful editor that has produced this sophisticated piece of literary and rhetorical artistry.

(18a)   **Rom 9.25** (= Hos 2.25)

Paul: καλέσω τὸν οὐ λαόν μου λαόν μου [ ] καὶ [ ] τὴν οὐκ ἠγαπημένην ἠγαπημένην.

[76] Brooke–McLean lists A M* d e g j l p s t y z^mg a₂ b₂ c₂ as reading δύναμιν in Exod 9.16, versus B M^c and an equally wide range of minuscules in support of ἰσχύν. The evidence cited in the upcoming Göttingen edition of Exodus is substantially the same. The fact that ἰσχύς is the most common translation of כֹּחַ in the LXX (especially in the Pentateuch) and that δύναμις is almost never used in such situations (not at all in the Pentateuch) makes it likely that ἰσχύς is the original reading here. Still, Koch's ascription of all the δύναμιν readings in the LXX to Pauline influence (*Schrift*, 54) strains credulity.

[77] Noted in Koch, *Schrift*, 141.

[78] Though often treated as a quotation, the adapted form of Isa 29.16 reproduced in Rom 9.20 has been omitted from consideration here in accordance with the strict

LXX: [καὶ σπερῶ αὐτὴν ἐμαυτῷ ἐπὶ τῆς γῆς καὶ] ἐλεήσω τὴν
Οὐκ-ἠλεημένην καὶ ἐρῶ τῷ Οὐ-λαῷ-μου Λαός μου εἶ σύ,
[καὶ αὐτὸς ἐρεῖ Κύριος ὁ θεός μου εἶ σύ].

A Reversing order of clauses. Not only is there no textual evidence to support a pre-Pauline reversal of the two clauses in the
portion of Hos 2.25 cited by Paul, but the resulting
advancement of the "not my people" clause to primary position
creates a smooth link with the preceding affirmation that God
has called a people οὐ μόνον ἐξ Ἰουδαίων ἀλλὰ καὶ ἐξ
ἐθνῶν.[79] The effect on the sense is minimal, but as a rhetorical
device the reversal supplies a fitting introduction to the entire
citation, much as the statement οὐκ ἔστιν δίκαιος οὐδὲ εἷς
sums up all that follows in Rom 3.10–18.

A Substitution of καλέσω for ἐρῶ. Here again a lack of textual
evidence combined with a close link to the new context makes
the Pauline origin of the present wording clear. The resultant
verbal interplay with the preceding verse (οὓς καὶ ἐκάλεσεν
ἡμᾶς ...) is typically Pauline, designed to bring citation and
"interpretation" into closer verbal agreement.[80] The effect is to
impress upon the hearer the appropriateness of the citation for
its present use. The choice of καλέσω also highlights the thematic unity of the two citations as applied here to the Gentiles, as
the idea of "calling" both opens and closes the citation in its
new Pauline form.[81]

A Shifting from Dative τῷ ... λαῷ to Accusative τὸν ... λαόν/
A Omitting εἶ σύ/Converting λαός from Nominative to Accusa-
A tive. Taken together, these three adaptations show how even
a minor shift in emphasis (i.e. the substitution of καλέσω for
ἐρῶ – see above) can lead to far-reaching changes in the
wording of a quotation in the hands of Paul. In its original
form, the expression "I will say to 'Not my people' ..." antici-

guidelines of the present study, which is confined to passages that offer explicit
indication to the reader that a citation is being offered (introductory formula,
interpretive comments, etc.).

[79] The implicit identification of (τὰ) ἔθνη with οὐ λαὸν μου would be apparent
to anyone familiar with Jewish self-definition.

[80] Other places where Paul creates such verbal links between citations include
Rom 11.8, 10; 1 Cor 3.19, 20; 1 Cor 15.54, 55; and Gal 3.10, 13.

[81] A similar point is made by Michel (77) and Koch (*Schrift*, 105, 167, 173).

pates some form of direct or indirect speech to complete the thought of the verse. With the change to καλέσω, however, a different construction is required to express the same idea. The double accusative that results (literally, "I will call 'Not my people' my people") is little more than a condensed version of the original ("I will say to 'Not my people,' 'You are my people!'") with the direct speech removed. The effect on the sense is minimal – in fact, the same point could have been made using the original wording had Paul not been concerned to create a verbal link with his own earlier comments concerning the "calling" of the Gentiles. This leads to an important observation concerning Paul's handling of the biblical text: the extent to which the wording of a passage has undergone modification is no sure sign of how far Paul has deviated from the "original sense" in his application/interpretation of a given biblical verse.[82]

A   Adding καί.   After reversing the two clauses of Hos 2.25 (see above), Paul could simply have left the clauses in parallel alignment without a connector, as he does in Rom 10.20. In the present case, however, the added καί does more than connect the clauses. With the disappearance of the verb from the second clause, the καί now serves to link together the two elements of the compound object of the verb καλέσω. As the omission of the second verb is surely Pauline (see below), so also is the addition of this connector.

A   Omitting ἐλεήσω (or ἀγαπήσω).[83]   In addition to the complete lack of manuscript evidence for such an omission, it is only in its revised Pauline form that the verb of what was originally the first clause of Hos 2.25 could have been eliminated without making nonsense of the entire verse. At the same time, a

---

[82] This is not to say, of course, that Paul has remained faithful to the "original sense" in his use of the present verse: the divine promise of restoration for wayward Israel in Hos 2.25 says nothing about the future status of the Gentiles. The point is rather that Paul could have applied the same verse in the same way without altering its wording in the least, had he not had other reasons for making a change. As will be seen throughout the present study, Paul can alter the wording of a text considerably while remaining relatively true to its original context (as in Rom 3.14, 3.15, 1 Cor 15.55, 2 Cor 6.16), or he can quote a verse verbatim while applying it in a sense only tangentially related to the original (see Rom 10.16, 10.18, 15.3, 2 Cor 4.13).

[83] On the question of the wording of Paul's *Vorlage* at this point, see the following discussion of the substitution of ἠγαπημένην for ἠλεημένην.

Pauline motive for the omission is ready at hand: dropping the verb from the (now) second part of the verse allows its object to be subsumed under the "calling" theme that so dominates Paul's use of the present verse. What was once a two-part promise of the reversal of the divine judgment on Israel ("I will have mercy on/show love toward ... and I will say ...") is here concentrated into a single statement ("I will call ...") that is then offered as a prophecy of Yahweh's coming election of the Gentiles (i.e. those who were "not my people" and "not loved"). Though the violence of the reinterpretation is undeniable, the smoothness of the resultant "quotation" is a sure indicator of the remarkable literary artistry with which the Pauline interpretation has been incorporated into the very wording of the text itself.

V   Substitution of ἠγαπημένην for ἠλεημένην. Though the usual reading ἐλεήσω ... ἠλεημένην is well-attested (A Q O L C *et al.*), an alternate reading, ἀγαπήσω ... ἠγαπημένην, appears in several important witnesses to the LXX text (B V 407 Co Aeth[P] Cyr[P] Hil). That ἐλεήσω ... ἠλεημένην is the original text seems beyond dispute: the Hebrew רחם is translated by forms of ἐλεεῖν in all seven of its occurrences in Hosea and throughout most of the rest of the LXX, while ἀγαπᾶν appears only four times out of scores of references. At the same time, the composite nature of the quotation in Rom 9.25–6 makes it unlikely that the Pauline text (with ἀγαπήσω) has influenced the LXX here, as does the presence of similar variants in V 407 La[SW] at Hos 1.6, 1.8, and 2.3.[84] There is likewise no reason to think that Paul would have altered an original ἠλεημένην to ἠγαπημένην when he has already used forms of ἐλεεῖν three times in the same general context (Rom 9.15, 18, 23).[85] That Paul's text of Hos 2.25 read ἀγαπήσω ... ἠγαπημένην with B V *et al.* seems assured.

A   Adding ἠγαπημένην at end of verse.   As with the conversion of λαός from Nominative to Accusative in the first line of the verse, some sort of object was needed after οὐκ ἠγαπημένην to complete the double accusative construction introduced with the shift from ἐρῶ to καλέσω (see above). The obvious choice,

[84] Pointed out by Koch, *Schrift*, 55 n. 34.
[85] *Ibid.*

following the pattern of the first line (already present in the original), was ἠγαπημένην. As with the other adaptations in Rom 9.25, there is nothing to indicate that the present form of the verse should be attributed to anyone other than Paul himself.

(18b)   **Rom 9.26** (= Hos 2.1)

Paul: καὶ ἔσται ἐν τῷ τόπῳ οὗ ἐρρέθη αὐτοῖς[86] οὐ λαός μου ὑμεῖς, ἐκεῖ κληθήσονται [ ] υἱοὶ θεοῦ ζῶντος.

LXX: καὶ ἔσται ἐν τῷ τόπῳ, οὗ ἐρρέθη αὐτοῖς Οὐ λαός μου ὑμεῖς, κληθήσονται καὶ αὐτοὶ υἱοὶ θεοῦ ζῶντος.

E   <u>Adding ἐκεῖ/Omitting (καὶ) αὐτοί.</u>   The Pauline textual tradi-
E   tion is unanimous at this point, but the LXX manuscripts are divided. The uncials S B Q and most of the Alexandrian minuscules and Catena texts read κληθήσονται καὶ αὐτοὶ υἱοί (echoed by most of the Lucianic manuscripts, which drop καί and advance αὐτοί before κληθήσονται), while A V and a portion of the Lucianic tradition agree with the Pauline reading. The question is whether the latter group of manuscripts is dependent on the Pauline wording or represents an independent tradition that might have been available to Paul in the first century C.E. The arguments for a pre-Pauline origin are not entirely convincing,[87] but no clear Pauline interest in the change is evident either. For the purposes of the present study, the question is probably best left open.

(19)   **Rom 9.27–8** (= Hos 2.1a, Isa 10.22–3)

Paul: [ ] ἐὰν ᾖ ὁ ἀριθμὸς τῶν υἱῶν Ἰσραηλ + ὡς ἡ ἄμμος τῆς

---

[86] The reading of 𝔓[46] a b d* sy[p] (replacing ἐρρέθη αὐτοῖς with (ε)ἄν κληθήσονται and dropping the following ὑμεῖς) would accord well with Paul's emphasis on the "calling" of the Gentiles in the present passage, and is unattested in the LXX tradition. But the rarity of οὗ (ε)ἄν in Hellenistic Greek (see BAGD, οὗ) and the awkwardness of the Future Indicative that accompanies it (see BDF § 380 (3)) renders the entire substitution problematic.

[87] Koch (*Schrift*, 54, 174) thinks he can explain the latter reading as an inner-Greek development. In Koch's view, the awkwardness of καὶ αὐτοί led to its omission in part of the manuscript tradition, while the "local" sense of ἐν τῷ τόπῳ gave rise to the parallel ἐκεῖ in the latter half of the verse. Why these two distinct changes should have occurred in the same manuscripts (and only in those manuscripts) remains unanswered.

θαλάσσης, τὸ <u>ὑπόλειμμα</u> σωθήσεται· λόγον γὰρ συντελῶν καὶ συντέμνων [ ] ποιήσει **κύριος** <u>ἐπὶ τῆς γῆς</u>.

Isa 10.22–3ₗₓₓ: καὶ ἐὰν γένηται ὁ λαὸς Ἰσραηλ ὡς ἡ ἄμμος τῆς θαλάσσης, τὸ κατάλειμμα σωθήσεται· λόγον γὰρ συντελῶν καὶ συντέμνων ἐν δικαιοσύνῃ, ὅτι λόγον συντετμημένον ποιήσει ὁ θεὸς ἐν τῇ οἰκουμένῃ ὅλῃ.

Hos 2.1aₗₓₓ: καὶ ἦν ὁ ἀριθμὸς τῶν υἱῶν Ἰσραηλ ὡς ἡ ἄμμος τῆς θαλάσσης, [οὐκ ἐκμετρηθήσεται οὐδὲ ἐξαριθμηθήσεται].

B   Omitting initial καί.   The LXX witnesses are unanimous in reading καί as the first word of both Isa 10.22 and Hos 2.1, while the Pauline evidence is equally united behind the omission. As has already been noted (Rom 3.15, 9.13, 9.17), eliminating introductory particles to create a smoother transition from text to citation is characteristic of Paul's handling of the wording of his biblical quotations.[88] While it is always possible that the conjunction was simply overlooked in the formation of the conflated text witnessed in Rom 9.27 (see below), the fact that Paul does the same thing in numerous other places makes it far more likely that the present omission is part of the same broad pattern.

A   Conflated citation: replacing ὁ λαὸς Ἰσραηλ (Isa 10.22) with ὁ ἀριθμὸς τῶν υἱῶν Ἰσραηλ (Hos 2.1a).   Both the introductory reference to Ἡσαῖας (cf. ἐν τῷ Ὡσηέ in v. 25a) and the initial word of the citation itself (ἐάν, from Isa 10.22) suggest that Paul had the Isaiah passage clearly in view before he penned the first word of his quotation in v. 27.[89] Why then does he substitute the words of Hos 2.1a (ὁ ἀριθμὸς τῶν υἱῶν Ἰσραηλ) for the very similar language of Isa 10.22 (ὁ λαὸς Ἰσραηλ) in the first line of his citation? A memory lapse is always possible, if one assumes that the latter verse simply sprang to Paul's mind under the influence of Hos 2.1 and did not come from the same collection of written notes from which most of his other cit-

[88] For further evidence, see note 197.
[89] This is true regardless of whether it was the verbal resemblance of Isa 10.22 to Hos 2.1a that first suggested the present link. In addition to the closely parallel introductory words, note the identical ὡς ἡ ἄμμος τῆς θαλάσσης that follows in both verses.

ations appear to have been taken.[90] Nevertheless, the fact that Paul's other "mixed citations" all show signs of having been carefully molded to fit their present contexts[91] raises the question of whether the same procedure might have been followed here as well. An attractive explanation along these lines has been put forward by Dietrich-Alex Koch, who traces the modification to a conscious concern to avoid designating Israel as the λαός of God, a term applied explicitly to the Gentiles in verses 25–6.[92] Whether one attributes the commingling to an accidental oversight or a willful adaptation, the Pauline origin of the final product would appear to be quite secure.[93]

B   Substitution of ἦ for γένηται. While the easy interchangeability of certain forms of εἰμί and γίνομαι might suggest a textual origin for the present reading, neither the LXX nor the Pauline manuscript tradition supports any such explanation here. A conscious substitution of verbal forms is always possible, but hardly likely. Perhaps Paul wanted to eliminate the futuristic orientation of the ambiguous γένηται in order to bring the text into line with his own picture of a world rampant with physical "sons of Israel," of whom only a minute "remnant" will ultimately be "saved" (v. 27b) through their response to the Christian gospel. A more plausible explanation would see Paul making a necessary (and somewhat arbitrary) choice between two relatively synonymous verbs at the point where the Isaiah and Hosea passages merged together to form the present cit-

---

[90] The careful integration of the Isaiah citation into its present context (introduced as a counterpoise to the Hosea text applied here to the Gentiles) argues against such a spontaneous origin. Otto Michel, followed by countless others, finds in such "mixed citations" the primary evidence for his contention that Paul quoted entirely from memory (10, 80–2, 86–7, 217). For the view that Paul relied primarily on written sources, see chap. 3.

[91] See below on Rom 9.33, 11.8, and Gal 3.8, 3.10.

[92] *Schrift*, 167–8. As Koch puts it, "Λαός᾽ – und damit υἱοὶ θεοῦ ζῶντος – ist nicht mehr Israel in seiner Gesamtheit (vgl. Röm 9,6!), sondern, wie Paulus ja gerade durch dieses Zitat zeigen will, nur τὸ ὑπόλειμμα" (168).

[93] A contrary view is taken by Barnabas Lindars (*Apologetic*, 243), who finds in Rom 9.25–8 "the clustering of related scriptures characteristic of the living tradition of apologetic." From this he concludes, "It is thus unnecessary to suppose that the shaping of this little group of texts is Paul's work at all" (*ibid.*). Why Paul should be denied participation in the church's ongoing tradition of apologetic use of Scripture is left unanswered. The numerous points of contact between the citations in Rom 9.25–8 and their present Pauline context make it highly unlikely that Paul has adopted a previously conflated text here.

ation. The textual evidence makes a Pauline origin all but
assured, but the reason for the change remains unclear.

E   Substituting ὑπόλειμμα for κατάλειμμα. Though the reading
κατάλειμμα has significant support in the Pauline tradition (p⁴⁶
ℵ¹ D F G Ψ 𝔐 Eusᵖᵗ, per Nestle), the complete lack of
testimony for ὑπόλειμμα in the LXX and the strength of the
evidence for the same reading in Romans (ℵ* A B 81 1739ᵛ·ˡ·
Eusᵖᵗ) together show that the latter is the original Pauline
text.⁹⁴ The two words were already indistinguishable in secular
Greek usage as well as in the LXX,⁹⁵ so that an intentional
substitution is unlikely. If the present citation should be judged
an exception to Paul's normal reliance on a collection of
written excerpts (see above), then a memory slip is an obvious
possibility, though the use of a divergent but no longer extant
Greek text cannot be ruled out. In the final analysis, the source
of the present reading remains opaque to the modern reader.

V   Omitting αὐτῶν. A number of important LXX manuscripts
and quotations (the uncials S and Qᵐᵍ, the Hexaplaric minuscules, the majority of the Lucianic and Catena texts, and a
variety of mixed codices and Greek fathers) add αὐτῶν either
before or after σωθήσεται in Isa 10.22.⁹⁶ Paul, however, follows
the minority reading of A Q* *et al.* in omitting the word here, a
fact that might support the use of a written text for the present
citation (see above).

C   Omitting ἐν δικαιοσύνῃ ὅτι λόγον συντετμημένον. Though
a wide range of witnesses (predominantly Western) contain the
words omitted from the printed editions at this point,⁹⁷ there is
little doubt that the shorter reading is the original. Not only is

---

⁹⁴ The texts with κατάλειμμα are thus to be seen as assimilations to the LXX. So
also Koch, *Schrift*, 142.
⁹⁵ So Koch, *Schrift*, 142 n. 17, citing G. Schrenk, *TWNT*, 4:199–200 (= *TDNT*,
4:195–6).
⁹⁶ A minority tradition (though including Codex B) leaves out the γάρ that
appears at the beginning of Paul's quotation in v. 28. Here Paul follows the majority
reading.
⁹⁷ Nestle lists ℵ² D F G Ψ 𝔐 lat syʰ as agreeing with the LXX here, while the UBS
Greek text adds the uncials K P, a variety of minuscules, the bulk of the Byzantine
lectionaries, the Vulgate, Gothic, and Armenian versions, and citations from Eus
Ambst Chr Euth Ps-Oec Theoph. The LXX tradition stands united behind the longer
text.

the evidence stronger for the omission,[98] but the explanation of an intentional assimilation to the LXX in the longer reading is ready at hand. Uncovering the reason for the original omission, however, is a more troublesome task. Dietrich-Alex Koch, following an earlier suggestion by E. Kühl,[99] believes that the words were already missing from Paul's *Vorlage* as a result of haplography by an earlier scribe (a skip of the eye from συντέμνων to συντετμημένον). Against the possibility that the omission should be traced to Paul himself, Koch offers two arguments: (a) that an accidental omission is more likely to occur in the copying of an entire manuscript than in the excision of a small segment from it, and (b) that whereas the ὅτι clause might be viewed as dispensable in the present context, no rationale can be posited for the omission of the typically Pauline phrase ἐν δικαιοσύνῃ that precedes it. Though clearly attractive, the haplography argument is weakened by two observations: (a) that the two words involved are only loosely similar in appearance, i.e. it is not a pure case of parablepsis or homoioteleuton (though homoioarchon remains a possibility), and (b) that the retention of the phrase ἐν δικαιοσύνῃ here would give to the word δικαιοσύνη a sense inconsistent with Paul's normal use of the δικ- terminology.[100] The fact that the LXX grammar is extremely awkward at precisely the point of the omission is also noteworthy.[101] This observation combined

---

[98] Nestle cites 𝔭[46] ℵ* A B 6 1506 1739 1881 *pc* m* sy[p] co, while UBS adds eth and citations from Or Eus Aug (Theod) JnDam. The opposite possibility, that an early omission came to be replicated throughout the majority of the non-Western textual tradition, is too remote to be considered. The UBS text assigns the shorter version its highest level of certainty (A).

[99] E. Kühl, *Der Brief des Paulus an die Römer* (Leipzig: Quelle und Meyer, 1913), 338; noted in Koch, *Schrift*, 83 n. 11. Unlike Koch, Kühl attributes the haplography to Paul himself.

[100] Though the grammar is highly uncertain in both texts, the sense of the LXX clearly differs from the Hebrew at this point. Whereas the Hebrew text speaks of the absolutely finality of Yahweh's decree to "cut off" rebellious Israel, the translator apparently read these same words as a promise that the coming judgment would be "cut short" so that a "remnant" of Israel might be saved. In this context, the phrase ἐν δικαιοσύνῃ refers to Yahweh's act of extending mercy to his covenant people, which places it quite close to the normal Pauline usage. In Rom 9.28, on the other hand, Paul cites Isa 10.22–3 as a declaration of God's judgment on unbelieving Israel, an interpretation that brings him closer to the original Hebrew sense. To use the phrase ἐν δικαιοσύνῃ to describe the execution of the divine verdict against a rebellious people would be highly uncharacteristic of Paul.

[101] The problems are several: the syntax of the Nominative participles, the sense of ὅτι here (and its relation to the γάρ that precedes it), the meaning of the repeated

with the potentially troublesome sense of δικαιοσύνη might in fact offer sufficient motive for a Pauline omission of the words in question. Whether this is what actually happened, or whether Paul simply relied on a defective *Vorlage* at this point, cannot ultimately be determined with certainty.

V   <u>Substituting κύριος for ὁ θεός</u>. Support for the Pauline reading within the LXX tradition is somewhat narrow, but significant: the uncials B V, the marginal reading of the uncial Q, the bulk of the Hexaplaric materials, the Syriac version, and quotations from Eusebius, Basil, and Tertullian. A survey of Pauline usage offers further reason for thinking that these scattered manuscripts and citations have preserved the reading of Paul's *Vorlage* at this point. The anarthrous κύριος is almost never used by Paul as the subject of a sentence,[102] whereas the word appears without the article in all but two of the biblical quotations in the Pauline corpus (Rom 15.11 and 1 Cor 10.26, both following the LXX). Support for the arthrous form ὁ κύριος in Rom 9.28 is quite weak (only the uncial B), while evidence for ὁ θεός is nowhere to be found. Unless he is consciously imitating the dominant LXX usage in supplying an anarthrous form here, a Pauline origin for the shift from ὁ θεός to κύριος would appear to be highly unlikely.[103]

B   <u>Substituting ἐπὶ τῆς γῆς for ἐν τῇ οἰκουμένῃ ὅλῃ</u>. Though the Pauline wording would certainly offer no problems in the LXX context, there is no manuscript evidence to suggest that such a reading ever existed outside Rom 9.28.[104] The Pauline tradition is equally united in its testimony. Koch attributes the change to a shift in focus that appears in the Pauline appropriation of the

---

λόγον, the relation of the perfect participle συντετμημένον to the present participles of the previous clause, etc. See the discussion in Koch, *Schrift*, 146–8.

[102] In 1 Thess 4.6, the omission of the article occurs under the influence of traditional language; in 1 Cor 4.4, the form is really a predicate Nominative; in 1 Tim 6.15, the noun is governed by the article preceding the compound subject. Otherwise the anarthrous form appears only in the oblique cases (especially the Genitive) and in prepositional phrases.

[103] Koch also traces the divergence here to a different text: see *Schrift*, 50, 86.

[104] The phrase כָּל־הָאָרֶץ occurs eleven times in the MT, of which five are translated by forms of ἡ οἰκουμένη ὅλη (as here) and six by πᾶσα ἡ γῆ. In every case the word כָּל receives an independent translation, unlike here, where it is omitted. The closest approximation to the Pauline reading is found in Symmachus and Theodotion, where ἐν μέσῳ πάσης τῆς γῆς is an obvious assimilation to the Hebrew בְּקֶרֶב כָּל־הָאָרֶץ.

verse. Whereas the LXX translator, looking from the perspective of the Diaspora, emphasizes the worldwide extent of Yahweh's anticipated deliverance, Paul foresees the reduction of Israel to a mere shadow of its former self as a result of the coming judgment. As a result, Paul feels compelled to tone down the language of Isaiah by removing the universalizing ὅλη and replacing the broader οἰκουμένη with the more neutral γῆ.[105] Another possibility, dismissed without argument by Koch,[106] would have Paul adapting the present passage under the influence of Isa 28.22, where much the same wording occurs (διότι <u>συντετελεσμένα</u> καὶ <u>συντετμημένα</u> πράγματα [cf. λόγον in Rom 9.28] ἤκουσα παρὰ κυρίου σαβαωθ, ἃ <u>ποιήσει ἐπὶ</u> πᾶσαν <u>τὴν γῆν</u>). In either case, the fact that Paul never uses the word οἰκουμένη (except in the quotation from Ps 18.5 in Rom 10.18) could be adduced as additional support for a Pauline modification.[107] Either explanation is clearly possible, though neither can finally be proven. What matters for the present study is the fact that both internal and external evidence points to the likelihood of a Pauline origin for the present reading.

(20) **Rom 9.29** (= Isa 1.9)

U[+] As in other instances where a unified Pauline tradition follows the unanimous testimony of the LXX, no further comment is necessary.

(21) **Rom 9.33** (= Isa 28.16, 8.14)

Paul: *Ἰδοὺ τίθημι ἐν Σιων* [ ] + * *λίθον προσκόμματος καὶ πέτραν σκανδάλου* * +, *καὶ ὁ πιστεύων ἐπ᾽* **αὐτῷ** <u>οὐ</u> <u>καταισ-</u> <u>χυνθήσεται.</u>

Isa 28.16_{LXX}: [διὰ τοῦτο οὕτως λέγει κύριος] Ἰδοὺ ἐγὼ ἐμβαλῶ εἰς τὰ θεμέλια Σιων λίθον πολυτελῆ ἐκλεκτὸν ἀκρογωνιαῖον ἔντιμον εἰς τὰ θεμέλια αὐτῆς, καὶ ὁ πιστεύων ἐπ᾽ αὐτῷ οὐ μὴ καταισχυνθῇ.

Isa 8.14_{LXX}: [καὶ ἐὰν ἐπ᾽ αὐτῷ πεποιθὼς ᾖς, ἔσται σοι εἰς ἁγίασμα, καὶ οὐχ ὡς] λίθου προσκόμματι [συναντήσεσθε αὐτῷ οὐδὲ ὡς] πέτρας πτώματι.

---

[105] See the discussion in *Schrift*, 145–50.
[106] *Schrift*, 149 n. 46.
[107] *Ibid.*

A   Conflation of Isa 28.16 with Isa 8.14.   The question of how to account for the common wording of the citations from Isa 28.16 in Rom 9.33 and 1 Pet 2.6 (over against both the Masoretic text and the LXX) has provoked endless rounds of debate and given rise to a number of important theories concerning early Christian use of the Bible during the last century of New Testament scholarship. When it comes to explaining how this verse came to be conflated with an excerpt from Isa 8.14 in Rom 9.33, on the other hand, investigators have found much broader grounds for agreement. There is simply no evidence, textual or otherwise, to indicate that the verses in question had been merged together in this fashion in either Jewish or Christian tradition prior to their amalgamation in the present context by Paul himself. Though the framework and primary content of the citation are drawn from Isa 28.16, a short selection from Isa 8.14 has taken the place of the central portion of the verse. The reason for this substitution is obvious: whereas the original passage spoke of the "cornerstone" in positive, glowing terms, the context of Rom 9.33 demanded that the negative consequences of the divine action for those who refused to "believe" be spelled out as well. Rather than extending the quotation several more lines to include the negative pronouncements already present in Isa 28, Paul chose to introduce words from a similar "stone" passage in Isa 8 that would make the same point in clearer and more concise terms.[108] The two passages were already being used together in the pre-Pauline community (cf. 1 Pet 2.6–8), so the combination would have been a natural one.[109] Whether this earlier associ-

---

[108] If the form of Isa 28.16 used by Paul was derived from Christian tradition and not directly from the biblical text, as will be argued below, the judgment language of Isa 28 would not necessarily have been ready at hand to be included with the present citation. Introducing another passage with similar wording to reinforce or develop a point (the rabbinic *gezera shawa*) is certainly more typical of early Jewish citation practice than appeals to the broader context of a passage.

[109] Dietrich-Alex Koch strains mightily to show that Paul and the author of 1 Peter have brought these two passages together in complete independence of one another (*Schrift*, 59–60, 69–71, 161–2, 250). In Koch's view, such a conclusion is warranted by the differing text-histories behind the two quotations: the form of Isa 28.16 presupposed in both passages betrays the Christological concerns of the early Christian community (with 1 Peter standing closer to the fountainhead of this tradition – see pp. 69–71), while the language of the excerpt from Isa 8.14 comes from a pre-Christian Jewish revision of the LXX (59–60). Koch is surely correct (69, 162) in rejecting the possibility that 1 Peter has disentangled (and only partially restored) the two constituent parts of Paul's combined citation, as also the idea that Paul

ation of Isa 28.16 with Isa 8.14 was mediated to Paul through oral or written channels reaches beyond present knowledge.[110] The conflation of the two verses in Rom 9.33, however, can be attributed to no-one else.

O? Substitution of ἰδοὺ τίθημι ἐν Σιων for ἰδοὺ ἐγὼ ἐμβαλῶ εἰς τὰ θεμέλια Σιών. Though the several differences between the Pauline version and the LXX text could be studied separately according to the types of deviations they represent (adding ἐγώ, replacing the verb, converting the verb from Present to Future, and substituting ἐν for εἰς τὰ θεμέλια), the complete verbal agreement between Rom 9.33 and 1 Pet 2.6 at this point calls for an explanation that goes beyond a simple analysis of the individual variants. In theory, the options are simple: either 1 Peter drew on Paul, or Paul used 1 Peter, or both derived their citations from some unknown third source.[111] Only in the first instance could the wording in question be attributed to the apostle Paul. Though common wisdom holds 1 Peter to be dependent on the writings of Paul,[112] there is nothing in this first part of the verse to suggest that it was shaped to fit the context of either writing. The words "in Zion" have of course proven useful to both writers, but the very diversity of their uses of the term (a cipher for physical Israel in Paul, a symbolic reference to the church in 1 Peter) makes reliance on a third source a more likely option. With the observation that both authors presuppose an existing Christological interpretation of the present verse (understanding Christ as the "stone"), that

derived his quotation directly from 1 Peter (so also Kraft, "Barnabas," 344–5). At the same time, Koch appears to miss the significance of the fact that the wording of the extract from Isa 8.14 in 1 Pet 2.8 is identical to that found in Rom 9.33, where it was traced to a Hebraizing revision of the LXX. The odds against both authors extracting precisely the same words from the same non-LXX text-form of Isa 8.14 and then placing this excerpt alongside a similar "Christianized" form of Isa 28.16 in total independence of one another defy calculation. While the present conflation clearly originated with Paul, the use of the two verses together in a relatively fixed wording is earlier than either Paul or 1 Peter.

[110] The relatively fixed wording of the tradition is no argument for the use of a written source, as Dietrich-Alex Koch demonstrates clearly in his analysis of the parallel forms of Isa 28.16 in Rom 9.33 and 1 Pet 2.6. See *Schrift*, 69–71.

[111] The LXX shows no trace of the NT wording at this point, nor can it be explained as an assimilation to the Hebrew (בְּצִיּוֹן [1QIs$_a$ = מיסד, 1QIs$_b$ = יוסד] הִנְנִי יִסַּד). The latter reading is clearly behind the rendering of ʼΑ Σ Θ, all of whom read θεμέλιων in place of εἰς τὰ θεμέλια.

[112] See the summary discussion in Kümmel, *Introduction*, 423–4.

possibility becomes a virtual certainty.[113] Whether the authors made use of a written source (as in the so-called "testimony-book" hypothesis) or merely echoed the oral tradition of early Christian biblical interpretation (so Koch) is beyond the interests of the present study.[114] All that matters here is the observation that the common wording of Rom 9.33 and 1 Pet 2.6 is not a Pauline creation, but reflects the dependence of both authors on an earlier Christian source.

A   Omission of λίθον ... αὐτῆς. With this omission, the polar contrast between the uses of Isa 28.16 in Rom 9.33 and 1 Pet 2.6 becomes readily apparent. Whereas 1 Peter simply appropriates (in abbreviated form) the positive associations of the original passage and applies them to Christ, Paul's concern centers on the paradoxical role of Christ as a source of both hope (for believers) and judgment (for non-believers). As a result, the Christological orientation that dominated early Christian appeals to Isa 28.16 (as exemplified in 1 Peter)[115] gives way in Romans 9 to a focus on the divergent responses of Jew and Gentile to the gospel about Christ. The very profusion of "Christological" epithets that made Isa 28.16 so attractive to early Christian interpreters (cf. 1 Peter) becomes superfluous in this context, and can therefore be eliminated. The resultant "citation" offers vivid testimony to the creativity and skill with which Paul could shape the wording of the biblical text to suit his own use of a particular passage.

A   Limited selection (Isa 8.14). Though it hardly needs to be stated, the fact that Paul extracted only certain key words from Isa 8.14 means that he also chose to bypass other elements of the verse that failed to suit his purpose. In the way he applies the words he selected, Paul actually stands closer to the Masoretic Hebrew text, where it is promised that Yahweh

---

[113] The same point is made by Koch, *Schrift*, 71, 161–2.

[114] Jan de Waard (*Study*, 58) points out that the church fathers follow the wording of the LXX exclusively when quoting from Isa 28.16. This observation raises problems for every attempt to trace the common wording of Rom 9.33 and 1 Pet 2.6 to the use of a well-known early Christian "testimony book."

[115] Dietrich-Alex Koch (*Schrift*, 69) believes that 1 Peter preserves intact the original wording of the citation as it was applied to Christ in the early church. For a more extensive discussion of the relation of the two texts, see Koch, "Beobachtungen zum christologischen Schriftgebrauch in den vorpaulinischen Gemeinden," *ZNW* 71 (1980), 178–84.

himself will become a "stone of striking and a rock of stumbling" for wayward Israel, than to the LXX, where a conditional element has been introduced.[116] This closeness to the sense of the Hebrew is entirely understandable if Paul has drawn his quotation from an edition of the LXX that has been revised toward a "proto-Masoretic" Hebrew text, as will be argued below. Even so, the selectivity of Paul's appropriation of Isa 8.14 can hardly be denied.

T   Reading λίθον προσκόμματος καὶ πέτραν σκανδάλου in place of the fuller expression (καὶ οὐχ ... πτώματι) of the LXX. While it is always possible that Paul could have (1) extracted the phrases λίθου προσκόμματι and πέτρας πτώματι from their separate locations in Isa 8.14, and then (2) replaced the unusual πτῶμα (found nowhere in Paul) with the typically Pauline σκάνδαλον (cf. Rom 11.9, 14.13, 16.17, 1 Cor 1.23, Gal 5.11), (3) modified the cases of every word to fit the new context, and (4) inserted a connective καὶ to complete the new construction, a much simpler explanation for Paul's divergence from the LXX lies ready at hand. The closeness of the Pauline wording to the Masoretic Hebrew text at the precise point where the LXX offers a significantly divergent reading has already been noted.[117] A comparison with the later editions of Aquila, Symmachus, and Theodotion is equally instructive. With only the most minor of variations among them, all three offer word-for-word renderings of what would later be called the Masoretic Hebrew text.[118] For the specific phrases adduced in Rom 9.33, all three employ the same sort of Genitive + Accusative construction found in the Pauline text, including a

[116] Neither the introductory clause καὶ ἐὰν ἐπ' αὐτῷ πεποιθὼς ᾖς nor the negative construction καὶ οὐχ ὡς in the third clause has any counterpart in the MT. What is presented as the inevitable fate of "many" (רַבִּים, v. 15) in the MT becomes in the LXX an outcome to be avoided ("If you trust in him, he will become a sanctuary for you, and you will not encounter him as a stone that causes you to stumble or as a rock that makes you fall"). Except for the introductory ל that links both nouns to their context, the Pauline wording follows the MT precisely.

[117] See the previous note.

[118] Apart from the omission of the first εἰς and the substitution of δέ for the second καί in Symmachus, the three agree fully on all but the last two words of Isa 8.14a. The rendering of Theodotion can fairly represent all three in a comparison with the Masoretic Hebrew:

MT: וְהָיָה לְמִקְדָּשׁ וּלְאֶבֶן נֶגֶף וּלְצוּר מִכְשׁוֹל
Θ: καὶ ἔσται εἰς ἁγίασμα καὶ εἰς λίθον προσκόμματος καὶ εἰς πέτραν πτώματος

unanimous reading of λίθον προσκόμματος for the first phrase. For the second phrase, the witnesses are divided between στερεὸν σκανδάλου (Aquila), πέτραν πτώματος (Theodotion and Symmachus according to Procopius), and πέτραν σκανδάλου (Symmachus according to Eusebius). The latter reading, it should be noted, agrees precisely with Rom 9.33, though it is always possible that the Christian Eusebius has confused the readings of Paul and Symmachus.[119] From these remarkable similarities, Dietrich-Alex Koch draws the inevitable conclusion that Paul derived his citation from an edition of the LXX that had already been revised to bring it into closer alignment with a "proto-Masoretic" Hebrew text.[120] If this is accepted, only the omission of the preposition εἰς before the two nouns might conceivably go back to Paul himself, and even this cannot be viewed as certain.[121]

V   Including ἐπ' αὐτῷ as part of the citation.[122]   The words in question are absent from the important uncials B V, the editions of Aquila, Theodotion, and Symmachus, the Syro-hexapla, and the citations of Origen and Jerome. Whatever the origin of this shorter reading, the Pauline wording is well-grounded in the testimony of the uncials A Q S, the Lucianic and Catena texts, and a variety of other witnesses.

E   Substitution of οὐ καταισχυνθήσεται (Future Indicative) for οὐ μή καταισχυνθῇ (Aorist Subjunctive).   The fact that Paul offers exactly the same reading in a somewhat different setting in Rom 10.11[123] argues against any attempt to uncover a

[119] Koch, following Ziegler, relegates Eusebius's testimony to secondary status (*Schrift*, 60 n. 12).

[120] See the excellent discussion in *Schrift*, 58–60. For a survey of the evidence for such pre-Christian Jewish revisions of the LXX, see chap. 2.

[121] Note the omission of the same word before ἁγίασμα in the text of Symmachus. Though the prominence of the notion of the gospel as a σκάνδαλον in the letters of Paul raises the possibility of a Pauline origin for at least the final word of the text, the use of the same word in Aquila reveals the uncertainty of any such presumption. So also Koch, *Schrift*, 60.

[122] A number of Pauline manuscripts add πᾶς before ὁ πιστεύων in the last line of Rom 9.33. The UBS text gives a fuller listing than Nestle at this point, but even here the evidence is limited to the uncials K P Ψ, a long list of minuscules, the Latin, Syriac, and Armenian versions, and citations in Did Chr Hier Theod Euth Thdrt. The reading is easily explained as an assimilation to Rom 10.11, where not a single witness omits πᾶς. In the LXX tradition, only the minuscule 407 reads πᾶς in Isa 28.16.

[123] In Rom 10.11, the word μή appears only in the uncials D E F G (per Tischendorf), while the Future form is unanimously attested.

contextual motive for the present substitution. In fact, the inclusion of an emphatic double negative would actually have added force to Paul's argument had it been present in his *Vorlage*. The shift to a Future form of the verb might technically have occurred independently of the change in the negative, since the introduction of a Future Indicative would have required no modification of an emphatic οὐ μή.[124] But the fact that none of the textual witnesses contains such a reading is clear proof that the two changes occurred together.[125] Dietrich-Alex Koch traces the change in the form of the verb to Paul himself, describing the adaptation as "purely stylistic in character."[126] To explain why Paul altered the text at all, Koch points out that Paul uses οὐ μή only infrequently (outside of citations, only in 1 Cor 8.13, Gal 5.16, 1 Thess 4.15, 5.3), while also implying that Paul wanted to remove the emphatic element from the present context.[127] But Koch's appeal to Pauline usage is weakened by the observation that Paul allows the same construction to stand in a quotation from Ps 31.2 in Rom 4.8, where any emphatic quality would appear to be superfluous, and seems to have done the same in his quotation from Gen 21.10 in Gal 4.30.[128] Moreover, there is nothing to indicate that Paul had any reason to tone down the emphatic nature of the LXX wording in Rom 9:33, as the present form surely does.[129] This leaves the same pre-Pauline Christian source from which the first part of the citation was drawn as the most likely background for the present reading. In the absence of concrete evidence, however, this origin cannot be established with certainty.

[124] See BDF § 365; Moule, *Idiom-Book*, 156–7. Of the various Pauline manuscripts, only the uncials D F G (Tischendorf adds E) diverge in reading οὐ μή καταισχυνθῇ here along with 1 Pet 2.6 and the unified testimony of the LXX.

[125] The unusual rendering of יֵחִישׁ by a form of καταισχύνειν and the inclusion of ἐπ' αὐτῷ in both texts make it clear that the base text is the standard LXX and not a version that has been revised toward the Hebrew (cf. Koch, *Schrift*, 70–1). The question of whether the present form of the text should be traced to Paul or to the same pre-Pauline version that yielded the initial ἰδοὺ τίθημι ἐν Σιών remains to be discussed.

[126] *Schrift*, 115 (translation mine).

[127] *Ibid.*, 115 n. 6. No explanation is offered for the latter assumption.

[128] See below on Gal 4.30.

[129] BDF § 365 calls the use of οὐ μή with either the Aorist Subjunctive or the Future Indicative "the most definite form of negation regarding the future."

(22)   **Rom 10.5** (= Lev 18.5)

Paul: [Μωῦσῆς γὰρ γράφει τὴν δικαιοσύνην τὴν ἐκ τοῦ νόμου ὅτι]
ὁ ποιήσας **αὐτὰ** ἄνθρωπος ζήσεται ἐν **αὐτῇ**.[130]
LXX: [καὶ φυλάξεσθε πάντα τὰ προστάγματά μου καὶ πάντα τὰ
κρίματά μου καὶ ποιήσετε αὐτά,] ἃ ποιήσας ἄνθρωπος
ζήσεται ἐν αὐτοῖς.

B   Converting the relative pronoun ἃ (neuter plural) to the article
ὁ (masculine singular).   Textual problems plague almost every
word of the LXX and Pauline forms of the present verse. The
first problem concerns the starting point of the citation itself.
The reasons adduced by Bruce Metzger for locating the ὅτι
(and thus the beginning of the citation) after νόμου rather than
after γράφει would appear to be well-founded, and will be
accepted for the purposes of the present study.[131] This leaves
the form of the relative pronoun as the first real textual
problem to be addressed within the citation proper. While the
Pauline reading is secure, a number of LXX manuscripts agree
with Paul in reading a masculine singular article in Lev 18.5.[132]
Though the article is by no means impossible in the LXX, the
weight of the external evidence together with the resultant
awkwardness in the LXX supports the notion that the LXX
wording has been assimilated to the well-known Pauline
passage in these instances. In the Pauline context, on the other
hand, the reverse is true: the original neuter plural pronoun
would have found no referent whatsoever in Rom 10.5. The
Pauline origin of the masculine singular form would thus
appear to be reasonably secure.

V   Including αὐτά in the text.   Both the LXX and Pauline witnesses are highly divided at this point. On the LXX side, the
pronoun αὐτά is omitted in A B V 381′ y⁻³⁹² 55 Arm, while the
same word is absent from the Pauline manuscripts ℵ* A (D*)
(33*) 81 630 1506 1739 (1881) *pc* vg cop.[133] Among the many

---

[130] On reading αὐτῇ rather than αὐτοῖς here, see the discussion below.

[131] *A Textual Commentary on the Greek New Testament* (London, New York:
United Bible Societies, 1975), 524–5.

[132] The Göttingen LXX lists the evidence as Fᶜ ᵖʳ ᵐ O–15–72′ 16ᶜ–46–413–417–
529ᶜ–550ᶜ–552–739ᶜ b d f(⁻¹²⁹ᵗˣᵗ) 767 t 392 407 18 59 319 799 Phil Ath Chr. Presumably these manuscripts assumed a partial stop after the preceding αὐτά in order
to make sense of the passage.

[133] Combining the evidence of Nestle and UBS.

LXX witnesses that contain the reading are the uncials F M, the versions of Aquila and Theodotion, and a quotation from Philo. The Pauline evidence includes 𝔭⁴⁶, the uncials ℵᶜ B D² G K P Ψ, numerous minuscules, much of the Old Latin and Syriac evidence, and several church fathers.[134] The most plausible explanation for this diversity of evidence is to suppose that an earlier Greek text without αὐτά was "corrected" at some point toward the Hebrew by the addition of an equivalent for the Hebrew אֹתָם, and that Paul then drew his citation from a manuscript that reflected this later tradition.[135] The omissions within the Pauline tradition could then be explained as attempts to bring the Pauline text into line with a different (earlier) LXX tradition. Lending support to a text-based explanation is the fact that neither here nor in Gal 3.12 does the form of the pronoun agree with its grammatical antecedent.[136] While certainty is impossible in the face of such a divided textual tradition, the evidence that Paul drew his quotation from a manuscript that already included αὐτά appears strong.[137]

C <u>Substituting αὐτῇ for αὐτοῖς.</u> The Pauline evidence is deeply divided at this point, as witnessed in the recent shift from the former to the latter reading in the standard Nestle Greek text.[138] The discovery of 𝔭⁴⁶ would appear to be the primary reason for the revised assessment of the manuscript evidence. In favor of the reading αὐτῇ stand the important uncials ℵ* A B, a number of minuscules, and the Vulgate, Coptic, Gothic, and

[134] Note also that all the witnesses for the parallel citation in Gal 3.12 include the pronoun.

[135] This interpretation is preferable to that of Metzger (*Commentary*, 525), who overlooks the divided LXX evidence in favor of the explanation that "the context contains no antecedent to which the plural may refer." This is the only point at which the LXX differs significantly from the MT. Note also that אֹתָם is missing from a citation of Lev 18.5 in *CD* 3.15: does the mixed LXX testimony go back to a divided Hebrew tradition?

[136] If an intentional adaptation were in view, one would have expected αὐτήν in Rom 10.5 (to conform to the antecedent δικαιοσύνην) and αὐτόν in Gal 3.12 (to agree with νόμος). Noted already by Kautzsch, 44, and Koch, *Schrift*, 52 n. 20.

[137] The same can be said for the inclusion of ἄνθρωπος, which is found in all the LXX witnesses except for the minuscules 53′ and citations by Philo and Chrysostom. The word is omitted from Rom 10.5 in F G a syᵖ, in obvious assimilation to the wording of Gal 3.12 (q. v.).

[138] Tischendorf accepted αὐτῇ as the original reading in his Greek text, and was followed by all subsequent editors (Westcott and Hort, von Soden, Vogels, Merk, Bover, and Nestle) until the recent adoption of the alternative reading in the combined Nestle 26th/UBS 3rd edn Greek text.

Armenian versions. For αὐτοῖς, the evidence includes ℘⁴⁶, the uncials ℵ² D F G Ψ, an equally large number of minuscules, and a large portion of the Old Latin and Syriac manuscripts. In his report on the decision of the Nestle/UBS editorial committee, Bruce Metzger classes the substitution of αὐτῇ with the omission of αὐτά earlier in the verse and traces both to "scribal emendations, prompted because the context contains no antecedent to which the plural may refer."[139] Overlooked in this assessment is not only the strength of the external evidence in favor of αὐτοῖς, but also the fact that none of these same scribes saw fit to make the same emendation in Gal 3.12, where the link to the grammar of the context is equally tenuous.[140] While the conjunction of the singular αὐτῇ with the preceding αὐτά is certainly discordant to the modern ear, this is precisely the reading that appears in the LXX manuscripts B (33* ταῦτα) 33ᶜ 436 1881 itˣ, presumably as a result of assimilation to the Pauline text.[141] If this is indeed the original reading, then Paul has adapted the text to present an understanding of τὴν δικαιο-σύνην τὴν ἐκ [τοῦ] νόμου similar to that expressed in Gal 3.21: "For if a law had been given which was able to impart life, then surely righteousness would have been based on law." Still, the possibility of a scribal alteration along the lines suggested by Metzger cannot be ruled out, which means that the likelihood of a Pauline alteration can be rated no more than probable for the purposes of the present study.

(23)   **Rom 10.6–8** (= Deut 9.4, 30.12–14)

Paul: [ἡ δὲ ἐκ πίστεως δικαιοσύνη οὕτως λέγει·] μή εἴπης ἐν τῇ καρδίᾳ σου· + * τίς ἀναβήσεται [ ] εἰς τὸν οὐρανὸν *, τοῦτ᾽ ἔστιν Χριστὸν καταγαγεῖν ἤ] * <u>τίς καταβήσεται</u> [ ] <u>εἰς τὴν</u> ἄβυσσον *, [τοῦτ᾽ ἔστιν Χριστὸν ἐκ νεκρῶν ἀναγαγεῖν. ἀλλὰ τί λέγει;] ἐγγύς σου <u>τὸ ῥῆμα</u> [ ] ἔστιν, ἐν τῷ στόματί σου καὶ ἐν τῇ καρδίᾳ σου *, [τοῦτ᾽ ἔστιν τὸ ῥῆμα τῆς πίστεως ὃ κηρύσσομεν].

Deut 9.4ₗₓₓ: μή εἴπης ἐν τῇ καρδίᾳ σου [ἐν τῷ ἐξαναλῶσαι κύριον τὸν θεόν σου τὰ ἔθνη ταῦτα πρὸ προσώπου σου λέγων Διὰ

---

139 *Commentary*, 525.
140 The corresponding change to αὐτῷ is found only in Fᵍʳ G g, according to Tischendorf.
141 The phrase ἐν αὐτῇ would make no sense in the LXX of Lev 18.5.

τὴν δικαιοσύνην μου εἰσήγαγεν με κύριος κληρονομῆσαι τὴν γῆν ἀγαθὴν ταύτην.]

Deut 30.11–14ₗₓₓ: [ὅτι ἡ ἐντολὴ αὕτη, ἣν ἐγὼ ἐντέλλομαί σοι σήμερον, οὐχ ὑπέρογκός ἐστιν οὐδὲ μακραν ἀπὸ σοῦ. οὐκ ἐν τῷ οὐρανῷ ἄνω ἐστὶν λέγων] Τίς ἀναβήσεται ἡμῖν εἰς τὸν οὐρανὸν [καὶ λήμψεται αὐτὴν ἡμῖν; καὶ ἀκούσαντες αὐτὴν ποιήσομεν. οὐδὲ πέραν τῆς θαλάσσης ἐστιν λέγων] Τίς δια-περάσει ἡμῖν εἰς τὸ πέραν τῆς θαλάσσης [καὶ λήμψεται ἡμῖν αὐτὴν; καὶ ἀκουστὴν ἡμῖν ποιήσει αὐτήν, καὶ ποιήσομεν.] ἔστιν σου ἐγγὺς τὸ ῥῆμα σφόδρα ἐν τῷ στόματί σου καὶ ἐν τῇ καρδίᾳ σου [καὶ ἐν ταῖς χερσίν σου αὐτὸ ποιεῖν].

A   Conflated citation: substituting the first line of Deut 9.4 for Deut 30.11.[142] Some interpreters have sought to deny the citation character of this unit altogether on account of its lack of a proper introductory formula and its obvious freedom with the biblical text.[143] But the thrice-repeated τοῦτ' ἔστιν (vv. 6, 7, 8), along with the ἀλλὰ τί λέγει which introduces the climactic statement of v. 8 (cf. λέγει in v. 6), makes it clear that Paul understood himself to be offering his own interpretation/ application of a specific biblical passage.[144] Though Deut 30.11–14 was often adduced by the rabbis when they wanted to stress the nearness of the divine word to Yahweh's covenant people,[145] there is absolutely no evidence to indicate that the passage had been united with Deut 9.4 to create a composite quotation prior to Paul. Of course, Paul could just as easily have used his own words to integrate the questions of Deut 30.11–14 into their new argumentative context, so his appeal to Deut 9.4 is surely significant. The reason for the association is not hard to find: the words cited come from a passage in which the people of Israel are warned against viewing Yahweh's mighty acts of deliverance as an affirmation of their own righteous conduct. The same idea is implicit in Paul's negative

[142] The wording of Paul's excerpt from Deut 9.4 agrees precisely with the unified LXX tradition.
[143] See the references in Ellis, *Use*, 123 n. 1, and Ernst Käsemann, *Commentary on Romans*, trans. Geoffrey W. Bromiley (Grand Rapids: Eerdmans, 1980), 284.
[144] So also Ellis and Käsemann (see previous note), Koch (*Schrift*, 130), and most recent commentators. C. K. Barrett discusses the similarities to Qumran *pesher* exegesis in "The Interpretation of the Old Testament in the New," in *Cambridge History of the Bible*, ed. P. R. Ackroyd and C. F. Evans, 3 vols. (Cambridge University Press, 1963–70), 1:392.
[145] Noted by Käsemann, 288, who cites Strack–Billerbeck.

pronouncements regarding those who seek to establish their own righteousness by obedience to Torah apart from faith in Christ (vv. 3–5). Whether or not his readers appreciated the subtlety of the reference, the parallel was certainly not lost on Paul, who appears to have found here exactly the sort of "biblical"-sounding introduction that he needed to replace the problematic language of Deut 30.11 (see below). Both the substitution and the combination are typically Pauline.

A   Limited selection: omitting vv. 11, 12a, 12c (καὶ to the end), 13a, 13c (καὶ to the end), and 14b (second καὶ to the end).   By beginning his citation with v. 12, a verse whose meaning becomes entirely obscure when divorced from its antecedent in v. 11, Paul serves notice that his interpretation of the present passage might deviate somewhat from the obvious sense of the original.[146] When a similar pattern of omissions appears in the following verses, the activity of an editorial hand can hardly be doubted. Koch speaks of it as "dissociating the citation from the theme of the law";[147] Käsemann observes that "everything that refers to commandment and work is left out."[148] In essence, Paul has eliminated everything that pertains to the original subject of the passage, the Mosaic law. On one level, the reason for the omissions is obvious: the idea voiced in the original passage – that the law can and should be fulfilled – is clearly at odds with Paul's own efforts to wean his Gentile converts from the notion that they need to accept the yoke of Torah in order to assure their participation in the covenant of Yahweh. On another level, the changes give voice to a far-reaching hermeneutical judgment: the same "word" (τὸ ῥῆμα, Rom 10.8 = Deut 30.14) that Moses described as being "near" in the law has now come to full expression and become available to all in Christ. The numerous omissions that mark Paul's handling of Deut 30.11–14 are thus firmly grounded in his own Christian theology.

---

[146] Of course, this indication is apparent only to the modern investigator who can compare the Pauline quotation to its LXX antecedent. Whether any of Paul's original hearers would have recognized how Paul had adapted the biblical text is entirely unknown.

[147] *Schrift*, 131.

[148] *Romans*, 284.

B   Omission of ἡμῖν from v. 12 and v. 13. The textual evidence
B   for omitting ἡμῖν from Deut 30.12$_{LXX}$ is quite meager, and can
probably be traced to Christian copyists.[149] The fact that none
of these witnesses (except for the Arabic version) follows Paul
in omitting the same word in v. 13 is no argument to the
contrary, since the thoroughly reworked form of v. 13 that
appears in Rom 10.7 has left no evident traces in the LXX
manuscript tradition. Koch attributes both omissions to stylistic concerns that dictated the elimination of elements deemed
unnecessary in the new context.[150] A simpler solution would
recognize the need to overcome the discrepancy between the
singular form of the introductory words from Deut 9.4 (εἴπῃς,
σου) and the plural constructions of Deut 30.12–13 (the
repeated ἡμῖν). Whatever the reason, the Pauline origin of both
omissions seems assured. Only the fact that the same omissions
could have occurred in the original passage with little effect on
the sense stands in the way of assigning the highest probability
rating to this adaptation.

A   Substitution of τίς ἀναβήσεται εἰς τὸν οὐρανόν for τίς δια-
περάσει ἡμῖν εἰς τὸ πέραν τῆς θαλάσσης. Few would doubt
the Pauline origin of the radically reworked version of Deut
30.13 that appears in Rom 10.7a. Not only is there no evidence
that such a reading ever existed in any text of Deut 30.13, but
the Pauline wording could hardly fit better with the "interpretation" put forward in v. 7b. Further evidence for a Pauline
origin can be seen in the close verbal parallels with v. 6. The
text of the "quotation" portion of the verse is identical in both
cases except for the prefix of the verb (κατα- vs. ἀνα-) and the
object of the preposition εἰς (ἄβυσσον instead of οὐρανόν),
while the wording of the "interpretation" sections differs only
in the verbal prefix used (κατα- vs. ἀνα- again) and the addition
of the words ἐκ νεκρῶν to v. 7b. Clearly the wording of v. 7
was modeled on that of v. 6 (= Deut 30.12), presumably
because the original image of "crossing the sea" could not be
made to fit the Christological "facts" that Paul presupposes in

---

[149] Outside of Christian authors, the omission occurs only in the minuscules 246
767 55 and the Arabic and Bohairic versions for v. 12, and in the minuscule family b
and the Arabic and Armenian texts for v. 13.
[150] *Schrift*, 132.

the present context. Whatever the background of the various Christological motifs employed here,[151] the Pauline origin of the present form of v. 7b seems assured.

C   Advancing τὸ ῥῆμα to emphatic position. Though the evidence is divided, the reading of the Pauline text in Rom 10.8a is relatively secure, with only the uncials D E F G, a portion of the Latin evidence (including the Vulgate), and the Gothic and Armenian versions diverging from the primary tradition in placing τὸ ῥῆμα after ἔστιν. Within the LXX tradition, on the other hand, almost every conceivable permutation is attested for the first six words of Deut 30.14. In spite of this diversity, the weight of the external evidence is clearly on the side of ἐγγύς σου ἔστιν τὸ ῥῆμα σφόδρα as the original reading.[152] Agreement with the Pauline wording appears only in the minuscules 29 320–552 55 and in quotations from Chrysostom and Origen. Though the conclusion is not beyond dispute, the evidence of both manuscript traditions seems to indicate that the Pauline reading represents an intentional adaptation of the LXX text, and not the use of a divergent *Vorlage*. Nevertheless, the reason for such a modification remains far from clear. If the aim was to lay stress on the subject τὸ ῥῆμα, the point could have been made less ambiguously by advancing these words to primary position in the sentence, rather than to their present position ahead of the verb. Dietrich-Alex Koch suggests that the present wording serves rather to emphasize the predicate by creating an artificial separation between its two primary elements (cf. 1 Cor 15.55).[153] In the absence of a clear rationale for the modification, reservations must attend any argument that would affirm a Pauline origin for the present reading.

[151] Dietrich-Alex Koch devotes several pages to an examination of the tradition-history behind this passage, concluding that the combination of Christological motifs encountered here is a distinctly Pauline creation. References to additional literature on the subject are scattered throughout. See *Schrift*, 153–60.

[152] This is the order found in the uncials A F M, the bulk of the Hexaplaric and Catena texts, and the minuscule families b d f s t y z *et al.* The wording ἔστιν σου ἐγγύς is found in the uncial B and the minuscules 707 18–120 509, while the reading ἔστιν ἐγγὺς σου appears in W′–54–458.

[153] *Schrift*, 107. According to BDF § 473, "Poetic language and that rhetorically stylized in any way frequently pulls them [closely related elements in the sentence] apart in order to give greater effect to the separated elements by their isolation."

E   Omission of σφόδρα.   The LXX evidence for the elimination
    of σφόδρα in Deut 30.14 is quite limited (the uncial F and the
    minuscules 53 and 664). In this case, however, the quantity of
    the evidence may prove less significant than its quality. Accord-
    ing to Koch's calculations, the text of Paul's quotations from
    the Pentateuch stands closer to the uncial F (which omits
    σφόδρα here) than to any of the other major manuscripts.[154]
    This means that a pre-Pauline origin for the present reading
    cannot be ruled out on the basis of limited textual support.
    Moreover, had the word σφόδρα been present in Paul's
    Vorlage, it is difficult to see what could have caused him to omit
    it, since its inclusion would surely have strengthened the point
    that he wishes to make in Rom 10.8. Still, the strength of the
    external evidence cannot be set aside so easily, and the possi-
    bility that Paul might have omitted the word as superfluous
    cannot be denied.[155] In the end, the origin of the present
    Pauline wording is probably best left undetermined.

(24)   **Rom 10.11** (= Isa 28.16)

Paul: [ ] πᾶς ὁ πιστεύων ἐπ᾽ αὐτῷ οὐ καταισχυνθήσεται.
LXX: καὶ ὁ πιστεύων ἐπ᾽ αὐτῷ οὐ μὴ καταισχυνθῇ.

A   Omission of initial καί.   The inclusion of the article in the
    identical quotation only twelve verses earlier (Rom 9:33) shows
    that Paul was quite aware of the proper wording of the present
    text. Its omission here is wholly in line with Paul's regular
    practice of omitting introductory particles that would impede a
    smooth transition from text to quotation.[156]

A   Addition of πᾶς.   Both the Pauline and LXX textual tradi-
    tions offer unanimous support for their disparate readings at
    this point. The fact that Paul could cite the same verse without
    πᾶς in Rom 9.33 shows further that he is quite aware of the
    correct wording of the LXX text. When these observations are
    correlated with the emphasis on the universality of salvation in
    Rom 10.9–13, including a threefold repetition of the word πᾶς
    in the two verses immediately following the present citation, the

---

[154] *Schrift*, 53. The Pauline tradition is wholly united in its reading at this point.
[155] So also Koch, *Schrift*, 117 n. 10.
[156] See note 197 for additional references.

conclusion becomes inescapable that Paul has adapted the wording of Isa 28.16 for its present use.[157] Moreover, the fact that he can quote the same verse in different forms within a span of only twelve verses shows how little Paul was concerned to hide from his readers the freedom with which he could handle the wording of the biblical text.[158]

V   Including ἐπ᾽ αὐτῷ as part of the quotation. See the discussion at Rom 9.33.

E   Substitution of οὐ καταισχυνθήσεται (Future Indicative) for οὐ μή καταισχυνθῇ (Aorist Subjunctive). See under Rom 9.33.

(25)   **Rom 10.15** (= Isa 52.7)[159]

Paul: ὡς ὡραῖοι [ ] [ ] οἱ πόδες τῶν εὐαγγελιζομένων [ ] τὰ ἀγαθά.

LXX: ὡς ὥρα ἐπὶ τῶν ὀρέων, ὡς πόδες εὐαγγελιζομένου ἀκοὴν εἰρήνης, ὡς εὐαγγελιζόμενος ἀγαθά, [ὅτι ἀκουστὴν ποιήσω τὴν σωτηρίαν σου λέγων Σιων Βασιλεύσει σου ὁ θεός].

MT: מַה־נָּאווּ עַל־הֶהָרִים רַגְלֵי מְבַשֵּׂר מַשְׁמִיעַ שָׁלוֹם מְבַשֵּׂר
       טוֹב מַשְׁמִיעַ יְשׁוּעָה אֹמֵר לְצִיּוֹן מָלַךְ אֱלֹהָיִךְ

T   Substitution of ὡραῖοι for ὥρα. The fact that Paul's quotation of Isa 52.7 in Rom 10.15 stands closer to the Masoretic Hebrew text than to the LXX has been noted by numerous investigators. Some have supposed that Paul had direct resort to the Hebrew at this point;[160] others have posited reliance on an early Aramaic targum;[161] still others have argued that the

---

[157] The addition of the universalizing πᾶς to v. 11 is clearly intended to create a verbal link with the quotation from Joel 3.5 in v. 13, as most commentators have noted.

[158] So Koch, *Schrift*, 133: "Paulus kennt also nicht nur den Text des Schriftwortes und ändert ihn bewußt ab, sondern er bemüht sich auch nicht, die Abänderung vor dem Leser zu verschleiern."

[159] Though there is little doubt that Paul intended it as a citation, the quotation from Joel 3.5 in Rom 10.13 has been omitted from consideration here in accordance with the strict guidelines of the present study, which is confined to passages that offer explicit indication to the reader that a citation is being offered (introductory formula, interpretive comments, etc.).

[160] Among more recent investigators, Ellis (*Use*, 14 n. 5) affirms this position.

[161] E.g. Toy, 150.

LXX text is itself corrupt, and originally agreed with the reading of Paul.[162] The fact that Paul appears to have adapted the wording of the biblical text at several points to reflect his own interpretation of the verse makes it even harder to establish the nature of his *Vorlage*.[163] After a careful comparison with the readings of Aquila, Symmachus, and Theodotion, Dietrich-Alex Koch concluded that Paul drew his citation from the same sort of Hebraizing revision of the LXX already encountered in the quotation from Isa 8.14 in Rom 9.33.[164] In this case, however, the Pauline citation is simply too brief and worked over to allow for a direct comparison with either the Masoretic Hebrew or the later Jewish revisers of the LXX.[165]

Firmer grounds for supposing that Paul drew his quotation from some sort of non-"standard" Greek text can be found among the witnesses to the LXX itself. In a number of extant manuscripts, most of them from the "Lucianic" family, there appears a form of Isa 52.7 that agrees for the most part with the reading of Rom 10.15, diverging at precisely those points where Pauline editorial activity appears most likely.[166] The close relationship between the two texts becomes evident when they are viewed side by side (underlines indicate differences):

---

[162] Clearly the dominant explanation in the older studies: see Gough, 322; Kautzsch, 95–6; Vollmer, 30.

[163] Likely adaptations include omitting the words ἐπὶ τῶν ὀρέων, converting εὐαγγελιζομένου from singular to plural (and adding the definite article τῶν), and possibly inserting the definite article τὰ. See the discussion below.

[164] *Schrift*, 66–9. For information on pre-Christian Jewish revisions of the LXX, see chap. 2 of the present study.

[165] Koch can offer only the retention of ὡς and the verbal proximity of ὡραῖοι to ὥρα to support his argument that the text used by Paul represents a revision of the LXX and not an independent translation. Neither of these points carries weight: ὡραῖος is the most common translation of נָאוּ throughout the LXX, as Koch himself acknowledges (*Schrift*, 68 n. 45), and ὡς would be an altogether natural rendering of מָה under the present circumstances (see BDB, s. v. מָה, 2b). There is simply no reason to think that an independent translator could not have arrived at exactly the same rendering of these two Hebrew words as appears in the text of Rom 10.15. Though Koch is ultimately correct in supposing that Paul has drawn his quotation from a revised form of the LXX text (see below), the evidence of the later versions is inadequate to support this conclusion.

[166] The texts at issue are the minuscules 88 22ᶜ–62-*l* II [= 90–130–311]–93–86ᶜ–456 403′ [= 403–613] and a quotation from Theodoret. MSS 88 22ᶜ–93 differ from the others in including οἱ before πόδες, while MS 88 diverges further by omitting ἐπὶ τῶν ὀρέων after ὡραῖοι (cf. Rom 10.15). The manuscripts agree fully in the remainder of their readings, however, including the crucial Genitive singular form εὐαγγελιζομένου (see below).

Rom 10.15: ὡς ὡραῖοι [ ] οἱ πόδες [ ] τῶν εὐαγγελιζομένων [τὰ]¹⁶⁷ ἀγαθά
Isa 52.7₍ₗᵤ꜀₎: ὡς ὡραῖοι ἐπὶ τῶν ὀρέων [οἱ] πόδες
εὐαγγελιζομένου ἀκοὴν εἰρήνης εὐαγγελιζομένου
ἀγαθά

As will appear below, practically every deviation from the "Lucianic" text in Rom 10.15 can be explained as a Pauline adaptation intended to bring the language of the source text into closer alignment with its present application.¹⁶⁸ The opposite possibility, that this "Lucianic" text arose under the influence of Rom 10.15, is foreclosed by the observation that the "Lucianic" version omits practically every distinctive feature of the Pauline form of the text.¹⁶⁹ A more likely explanation would see in these manuscripts the remains of an early attempt to "correct" the reading of the LXX to bring it into closer conformity with the Masoretic Hebrew text.¹⁷⁰ The use of such

---

¹⁶⁷ A number of important manuscripts omit the definite article here – see the discussion below.

¹⁶⁸ The sole exception is the omission of the phrase εὐαγγελιζομένου ἀκοὴν εἰρήνης, which Dietrich-Alex Koch rightly attributes to an earlier instance of haplography within Paul's own *Vorlage*. See the discussion in the appropriate section below.

¹⁶⁹ Such as the excision of ἐπὶ τῶν ὀρέων (found only in MS 88), the addition of the definite article τῶν, the pluralizing of the Genitive εὐαγγελιζομένου, and possibly the addition of the definite article τά. How Koch can set the influence of Rom 10.15 on a par with the MT as a possible explanation for this "Lucianic" version is utterly baffling. In his sole reference to these "Lucianic" manuscripts (*Schrift*, 69 n. 53), Koch can say only that "doch ist fraglich, ob hier eine vorpln Texttradition wieder auftaucht. Eher dürfte es sich um eine Korrektur der LXX in Kenntnis sowohl von Röm 10,15 als auch des MT handeln." Koch's ambivalent position becomes all the more puzzling when it is observed that these "Lucianic" texts agree precisely with Koch's own reconstruction of the wording of Paul's *Vorlage* (*ibid.*, 69).

¹⁷⁰ That this "Lucianic" version represents a revision of the LXX and not a new translation is apparent from the retention of ἀκοήν as a rendering of the Hiphil participle מַשְׁמִיעַ (only here in the LXX) and the use of the plural ἀγαφά to represent the singular טוֹב. Hebraizing "corrections" are apparent in the shift from ὥρα ("spring") to ὡραῖοι ("timely, seasonable"), the most common LXX rendering of the Hebrew נָאווּ; the elimination of the second and third instances of ὡς, neither of which has any equivalent in the MT; and the shift from the Nominative εὐαγγελι-ζομένος to the Genitive εὐαγγελιζομένου, produced by reading the second מְבַשֵּׂר as a *nomen rectum* as in the first appearance of the same word. Koch offers an excellent account of how the LXX translator derived his version of v. 7 from a mistaken combination of the first clause of v. 7 with v. 6 instead of what follows (*Schrift*, 66–8). The opposite possibility, that this "Lucianic" text represents the original reading of the LXX that was later corrupted into its present form, is unlikely in light of the types of "corruptions" that would be required to satisfy such a theory: see Koch, *Schrift*, 68 n. 47.

a text by Paul in the first century C.E. shows that this particular "Lucianic" reading is in fact much older than the fourth-century Christian editor to whom it has traditionally been attributed.[171] That Paul has relied on a revised Greek text for his quotation in Rom 10.15, including the initial substitution of ὡραῖοι for ὥρα, seems assured.

A Omission of ἐπὶ τῶν ὀρέων. As was noted above, only one manuscript in the entire LXX tradition omits the phrase ἐπὶ τῶν ὀρέων, while the Pauline tradition is unanimous in its rejection of the same words. The suitability of the omission to the Pauline context is readily apparent: a localized geographical reference ("upon the mountains") is hardly appropriate in a passage that emphasizes the necessity of a universal proclamation of the Christian gospel.[172] In the original context, on the other hand, the same words lend an element of local color to the depiction of the divine herald approaching Mt. Zion with the message of salvation, and would hardly be dropped in a later revision.[173] The Pauline origin of the present omission would appear to be assured.

T Omission of the second ὡς. The elimination of this word, which has no parallel in the Masoretic Hebrew text, was one of the primary results of the Hebraizing "proto-Lucianic" revision of Isa 52.7 discussed above. Its absence from the text of Rom 10.15 can be traced with fair confidence to the wording of Paul's own biblical *Vorlage*.

E Addition of οἱ before πόδες. The definite article is weakly attested in those manuscripts that witness to Paul's "proto-Lucianic" *Vorlage* here, appearing in only three of eleven instances.[174] At the same time, a suitable motive for a Pauline adaptation is hard to find. Perhaps Koch is right in linking it with a presumed Pauline insertion of τῶν before εὐαγγελι-ζομένων,[175] in which case the present reading would go back to

[171] For further arguments in favor of an early "proto-Lucianic" revision of the LXX, see the evidence cited in chap. 2, note 41.
[172] So also Koch, *Schrift*, 120.
[173] The LXX agrees with the MT at this point.
[174] The MSS are 88 22ᶜ–93. MS 36ᶜ, which follows the "Lucianic" version only in substituting ὡραῖοι for ὥρα, contains a correction that adds the definite article here.
[175] *Schrift*, 68.

Paul himself. But since the article also represents a faithful rendering of the Masoretic text at this point, it remains possible that the insertion had already occurred in the "Hebraizing" revision of the LXX text that served as Paul's *Vorlage* here. In view of the ambivalent nature of the evidence, the origin of this element of the Pauline wording is best left open for the purposes of the present study.

T   Omission of εὐαγγελιζομένου ἀκοὴν εἰρήνης [ὡς].[176] A number of Pauline manuscripts include the phrase τῶν εὐαγ-γελιζομένων εἰρήνην after the word πόδες and before τῶν εὐαγγελιζομένων in Rom 10.15. The extra words are normally regarded as a scribal insertion meant to fill a perceived gap in the text over against the LXX of Isa 52.7.[177] Still, the language of the insertion is problematic. While a measure of adaptation was clearly necessary to conform the omitted phrase to its new Pauline context (adding τῶν, pluralizing εὐαγγελιζομένου, omitting ὡς), it is not at all clear why a later scribe should have substituted the simple εἰρήνην for the ἀκοὴν εἰρήνης of the LXX.[178] The difficulty is by no means avoided if one accepts the extra words as part of the original Pauline text, since the question would still remain as to why Paul (or anyone else) should have effected so benign a substitution. A comparison with the readings of the later versions suggests another possible explanation. In place of the ἀκοὴν εἰρήνης of the LXX, both Aquila and Symmachus use the simple εἰρήνην in their renderings of Isa 52.7, though in neither case is the word preceded as here by a form of εὐαγγελιζομένος.[179] This raises the possibility that a similar substitution might already have found its way into the Greek text used by Paul or a later scribe, whether through an intentional revision (as in the "Lucianic" version of Isa 52.7 used by Paul for the present citation)[180] or an accidental conflation with the reading of Aquila or Symma-

---

[176] As noted above, this last word had already fallen out of Paul's *Vorlage*.

[177] The addition appears in the uncials ℵ² D F G K P Ψ, a number of minuscules, most of the Latin and Syriac evidence, the Armenian and Gothic versions, and the quotations of a number of primarily Western fathers. The reading is omitted in 𝔓⁴⁶, the uncials ℵ* A B C, an equal number of minuscules, the Coptic and Ethiopic versions, and a number of mostly Eastern fathers.

[178] The substitution finds no support in the LXX manuscripts.

[179] Aquila has ἀκουστὴν ποιοῦντος εἰρήνην, while Symmachus reads ἀκουτί-ζοντος εἰρήνην.

[180] The shorter reading is clearly a more accurate rendering of the MT's שָׁלוֹם.

chus (or a text that lay behind both of them). The fact that none of the "Lucianic" manuscripts used to reconstruct Paul's text of Isa 52.7 shows a similar substitution speaks against the first explanation, as does the fact that the phrase τῶν εὐαγγε-λιζομένων εἰρήνην contains no equivalent for the Masoretic Hebrew מַשְׁמִיעַ. If the second explanation is accepted, then the insertion will be the work of a later scribe who adapted his Greek *Vorlage* as needed to suit the Pauline context.[181] Still, the insertion must be quite old (second century C.E.), as witnessed by its presence in both the Old Latin and Syriac versions.[182]

Thus the question of why the words εὐαγγελιζομένου ἀκοὴν εἰρήνης might have been omitted from the Pauline quotation of Isa 52.7 remains. The manuscript tradition offers no support for a pre-Pauline omission, and nothing in the meaning of the phrase would appear to justify its elimination. The suggestion that Paul himself might have dropped the words either for rhetorical effect or because he considered the phrase redundant or irrelevant is voided by the importance of the "hearing" theme in Rom 10.14–18.[183] The only workable solution would appear to be that put forward by Dietrich-Alex Koch, who argues that the words were already missing from Paul's *Vorlage* as a result of haplography from one occurrence of εὐαγγελιζομένου to the next.[184] As Koch notes, such an oversight is more likely to occur in the reproduction of a lengthy manuscript than in the copying of a small excerpt from the same text.[185] This is all the more true when the omitted portion is highly pertinent to the extractor's own understanding of the text, as is the case here. Though the evidence remains entirely circumstantial, the idea of a pre-Pauline haplography would appear to be the most plausible explanation for the omission of the phrase εὐαγγελιζομένου ἀκοὴν εἰρήνης from Paul's quotation of Isa 52.7 in Rom 10.15.

[181] So also Metzger, *Commentary*, 525.

[182] As noted by Kautzsch, 95.

[183] As pointed out by Koch, *Schrift*, 81–2. Note especially the uses of ἀκοή in vv. 16 and 17, to which the omitted phrase would have provided an excellent link.

[184] As noted above, the second participle had already been revised to a Genitive in Paul's *Vorlage*. The alternate possibility, that the words might have dropped out of the Pauline text in the course of transmission, is negated by the breadth of the evidence for the omission, as noted by Kautzsch (95).

[185] *Ibid.*, 83.

B   Insertion of τῶν before εὐαγγελιζομένων. Though its Genitive plural form is clearly related to the Pauline pluralizing of
the following word,[186] the question of how the article entered
Paul's text at all is a separate issue. In theory, one could always
maintain that a translator has mistakenly rendered the indefinite Hebrew *nomen regens* by a definite expression here. But
since none of the LXX witnesses shows any evidence of such a
rendering, such a position could hardly be defended. The text is
almost as united on the Pauline side, with only the uncials F
and G omitting the article here.[187] Indeed, the inclusion of an
article is almost demanded to make sense of the passage once
the following word has been converted into a plural (see
below). Only the frequency of variants involving the definite
article in the ancient manuscript tradition as a whole prevents
this reading from being assigned the highest probability rating
as a Pauline adaptation.

T   Converting εὐαγγελιζομένων from Nominative singular to
B   Genitive plural. Though presented here as a single modification, the shift to the Genitive plural in Rom 10.15 actually
involves two steps. The shift from the Nominative εὐαγγελιζόμενος to the Genitive εὐαγγελιζομένου has already been
traced to a pre-Christian Jewish revision of the LXX that
sought to align its wording with a "proto-Masoretic" Hebrew
text.[188] The shift to the plural, on the other hand, finds no
support in either the manuscript tradition or the original context.[189] The same form makes perfect sense, however, in the
context of Rom 10.15, where it is interpreted as a reference to
the work of Christian evangelists.[190] The plural form of the

---

[186] See further below.

[187] Even here the omission occurs in conjunction with another textual variant
found in these and several other manuscripts, the addition of τῶν εὐαγγελιζομένων
εἰρήνην after πόδες (cf. LXX).

[188] See the first entry above. Alternatively, one could think of the haplography as
eliminating the second εὐαγγελιζομένου and retaining the first, which appears as a
Genitive already in the LXX. The result is the same in either case.

[189] The sole testimony to the presence of a plural here is in Eusebius's account of
the reading of Theodotion, which Koch rightly challenges as a memory slip by this
Christian author under the influence of Rom 10.15 (*Schrift*, 66 n. 41). Otherwise the
entire verse might have been converted to the plural in some aberrant Greek
manuscript, but no evidence for such a change is forthcoming.

[190] So most commentators. Note especially the plural κηρύξωσιν that immediately
precedes the quotation. As Koch puts it, "Da Paulus also das Zitat als Aussage über

participle is thus best regarded as an editorial adaptation introduced by Paul himself.

C   Addition of τά. Though the evidence is highly divided,[191] most
commentators have accepted the article as part of the original
Pauline text on the strength of the internal evidence: its omission is understandable as an assimilation to the LXX, while no
plausible reason can be suggested as to why it should have been
added in the course of transmission.[192] Since the article finds no
support in either the LXX or Hebrew traditions, one can
presume that the insertion goes back to Paul himself. Even so,
its significance remains obscure. The explanation offered by C.
E. B. Cranfield, that "its presence would have the effect of
underlining the identification of the message of the εὐαγγελι-
ζόμενοι with the gospel of Christ," is probably as good as
any.[193] In the absence of a clear motive for the addition,
however, the highly divided external evidence casts a veil of
suspicion over every judgment concerning the origin of this
reading.

(26)   **Rom 10.16** (= Isa 53.1)

U[+] Apart from two minuscules and the Coptic version that add the
second line of Isa 53.1 to the text of Rom 10.16, the wording of
this Pauline quotation agrees precisely with the undivided testimony of the LXX.

(27)   **Rom 10.18** (= Ps 18.5)

U[+] Here again the undivided Pauline textual tradition follows the
unanimous reading of the LXX. The only question concerns
the inclusion of this passage in the category of recognizable
citations, as it contains neither an explicit introductory formula
nor an interpretive comment that would signify to the reader

die heutige Verkündigung und ihre Träger verwendet, war er gezwungen, den
vorgegebenen Singular in den Plural abzuändern" (*Schrift*, 113–14).
[191] The definite article appears in 𝔓[46], the uncials ℵ* and Ψ, the bulk of the
minuscule tradition, and quotations of a number of church fathers. Supporting the
omission are the uncials ℵ[2] A B C D F G P, a few minuscules, and several other
fathers.
[192] So Kautzsch, 95, and Koch, *Schrift*, 67 n. 44.
[193] C. E. B. Cranfield, *A Critical and Exegetical Commentary on the Epistle to the
Romans*, ICC Series (Edinburgh: T. and T. Clark, 1979), 2:535 n. 1.

that a citation was intended. In this case, it is the obvious incongruity between the citation and its context that makes the citation character of Rom 10.18b plain: the antecedent of the twofold αὐτῶν cannot possibly be the same as the indefinite "they" (i.e. the hearers of the gospel) mentioned in v. 18a.[194] Though the shift is subtle, an attentive hearer would have had no trouble noting this aural cue that v. 18b had been drawn from an outside source.

(28)   **Rom 10.19** (= Deut 32.21)

Paul: [ ] ἐγὼ παραζηλώσω ὑμᾶς ἐπ᾽ οὐκ ἔθνει,
ἐπ᾽ ἔθνει ἀσυνέτῳ παροργιῶ ὑμᾶς.
LXX: κἀγὼ παραζηλώσω αὐτοὺς ἐπ᾽ οὐκ ἔθνει,[195]
ἐπ᾽ ἔθνει ἀσυνέτῳ παροργιῶ αὐτούς.

A   Substituting ἐγώ for κἀγώ. Though a number of LXX minuscules read καὶ ἐγώ here in place of the composite form κἀγώ,[196] only a portion of the Ethiopic evidence and two Christian citations follow Paul in omitting the conjunction entirely. The Pauline tradition, on the other hand, is unanimous in its reading. If this were an isolated instance, it would be natural to attribute such a simple omission to the vagaries of the transmission process. A careful examination of the entire Pauline corpus, however, shows that Paul regularly drops introductory particles from his biblical quotations in order to create a smoother transition from introduction to citation.[197] Though the effect on the sense is minimal, the consistency of the pattern helps to identify this as a typically Pauline adaptation.

[194] In the original passage, the reference is to the "heavens" that continually declare the glory of their Creator; in Rom 10.18, by contrast, most commentators see an allusion to the work of the Christian evangelists mentioned in vv. 14–15. See further Cranfield, *Romans*, 2.537–8; Käsemann, *Romans*, 295–6.

[195] The confusion in the LXX tradition between ἔθνει (so Paul and the majority tradition) and ἔθνη (found in M V in the first instance, M b d in the second) represents an aural error and not a true variant, as the constant testimony to the Dative singular ἀσυνέτῳ makes clear.

[196] The witnesses are 426 54' 30'–130 59 and a citation from Origen.

[197] In fully a quarter of his citations Paul omits an initial καί, while other particles (mostly δέ and ὅτι) are dropped in another 10 percent of the cases. Introductory particles are retained in only a handful of instances (Rom 4.17, 8.36, 9.26, 11.35, 2 Cor 6.17, Gal 3.16), and in half of these the conjunction plays a vital role in linking the two parts of a composite quotation.

B   Conversion of both occurrences of αὐτούς to ὑμᾶς. Though
it would no doubt sound awkward to modern ears, a momen-
tary shift to second-person plural would not be entirely out of
place in Deut 32, where both the Masoretic Hebrew text and
the LXX offer several unusual variations in person and number
in the course of the divine address to Israel.[198] Apart from
Christian sources, however, evidence for a second-person form
in v. 21 is entirely lacking, and in these cases the influence of
Rom 10.19 must be presumed.[199] At the same time, the Pauline
context offers no clear rationale for the shift from αὐτούς to
ὑμᾶς. All the verses surrounding the quotation, including
several other biblical quotations, are framed in third-person
speech, and there is no obvious reason why this one should
have been treated any differently.[200] The explanation offered
by Dietrich-Alex Koch, that such a shift was necessary to
distinguish the subject of the present citation from the αὐτῶν of
the preceding verse,[201] falters on the opening words of v. 19
(ἀλλὰ λέγω, μή Ἰσραὴλ οὐκ ἔγνω;), where the shift in subject
is made quite clear. If the change of persons is to be attributed
to Paul himself, as the textual evidence suggests, then some
other explanation must be found. Otto Michel may well be on
the right track in describing the change as stylistic in nature,
meant to sharpen the point by setting the verse apart from its
immediate context.[202] In verse 19, the focus of Paul's argument
shifts from the universal availability of the message of salvation
(10.5–18) to the contrasting response of Jews and Gentiles to
the gospel message (10.19–11.36). The quotation in Rom
10.19b thus occupies a key place in the structure of Rom 10–11.
Beyond supplying a biblical justification for the statement in v.
19a (which it does in only the most elliptical fashion), the

[198] Though the pronouncements concerning Israel are framed primarily in third-
person speech (using both singular and plural forms), sudden shifts to the second-
person are apparent at several points in the first half of the discourse (see vv. 6, 7, 14,
15, 17, 18). In most of these places the LXX stays agrees with the MT, even when the
latter shifts inexplicably from second-person plural to second singular forms in the
same verse (as in vv. 6 and 7). In two instances the LXX gives a third-person form
where the MT reads second-person (vv. 14e, 15b), but nowhere does the opposite
occur.

[199] The Pauline wording is followed only in quotes by Chrysostom, Theodoret,
and Hippolytus.

[200] This is no doubt the reason behind the restoration of the third-person form in
ℵ^c C* eth.

[201] *Schrift*, 110.

[202] Michel, 78.

quotation from Deut 32.21 actually foreshadows the position that Paul will develop in fuller terms throughout the whole of chapter 11.[203] The element of rhetorical intensification that results from framing the citation as an apostrophe to Israel highlights for the hearer the important place of this verse in the following discussion.[204] In this instance, the subtle artistry with which Paul can adapt the wording of a citation to suit its present application is clearly on display.

(29)   **Rom 10.20** (= Isa 65.1)

Paul: εὑρέθην ἐν τοῖς ἐμὲ μὴ ζητοῦσιν,
          ἐμφανὴς ἐγενόμην τοῖς ἐμὲ μὴ ἐπερωτῶσιν.
LXX: ἐμφανὴς ἐγενόμην τοῖς ἐμὲ μὴ ζητοῦσιν,
          εὑρέθην τοῖς ἐμὲ μὴ ἐπερωτῶσιν.

E   Reversing εὑρέθην and ἐμφανὴς ἐγενόμην (or ζητοῦσιν and ἐπερωτῶσιν). The relation between the various forms in which this verse occurs in the LXX and Pauline traditions is exceedingly complex, and no great confidence can attach to any the several reconstructions that have been proposed. Even to describe how Paul might have adapted the wording of the text requires certain assumptions about the nature of Paul's *Vorlage* that can in no way be verified. In addition to the LXX text printed above, significant evidence exists for a reading that agrees with the Masoretic text (reversing ζητοῦσιν and ἐπερωτῶσιν while leaving the initial verbs as above),[205] as well as a lesser tradition that reproduces the wording found in the Pauline text.[206] The simplest explanation would trace the latter two readings to the influence of the Masoretic and Pauline texts respectively, then explain the Pauline wording as a conscious adaptation of the LXX designed to bring the "seeking/finding"

---

[203] Note especially 11.11–15, where Paul explicitly takes up the "jealousy" theme.

[204] Paul Achtemeier ("*Omne verbum sonat*: The New Testament and the Oral Environment of Late Western Antiquity," *JBL* 109 (1990), 17–25) calls attention to the importance of such verbal cues in signaling transition points in a text composed for use in a predominantly oral society.

[205] This is the reading of the uncials B V, the entire Hexaplaric tradition, most of the Lucianic materials, a handful of additional minuscules, and quotations by Eusebius and Theodoret. In the Pauline tradition, a small portion of the Old Latin evidence and quotations by Hilary and Ambrosiaster contain the same reading.

[206] Limited to a portion of the Lucianic tradition (62-*l* II), the minuscule 403, and quotations by Origen and Clement.

theme into greater prominence.[207] The problem with this view is that it is difficult to see why the original LXX text could not have served Paul's purpose equally well in Rom 10.20, especially since the "seeking/finding" theme is not even developed there.[208] The same objection applies if Paul is viewed as starting with a text that had already been revised to accord with the Masoretic Hebrew and then reversing the two clauses to achieve the same effect. A more likely explanation is offered by Dietrich-Alex Koch, who argues that Paul may have simply reproduced the wording of his *Vorlage* at this point. According to Koch, the form of Isa 65.1 found in Rom 10.20 can be understood as a wholly inner-Greek development, in which the natural relation between "seeking" and "finding" that had been disrupted (for whatever reason) in the original LXX text was restored by a later scribe without resort to the Masoretic text.[209] This explanation, too, remains rather speculative, but at least it is free from the kinds of problems that accompany the various attempts to attribute the present wording to Paul himself. Without further evidence, however, the origin of the Pauline wording must remain open.

E   Adding ἐν before the first τοῖς. The somewhat awkward ἐν that appears in the first line of Rom 10.20 finds no support in the LXX manuscripts of Isa 65.1. Taken together with the inherent difficulty of the reading, such a lack of support would normally argue for a Pauline origin for the present wording. In this case, however, the picture is complicated by the difficulty of establishing the wording of Paul's own biblical text.[210] As a Pauline insertion, the preposition would presumably bear the sense "among," intended perhaps to underline the real presence of God/Christ in the preached word by which the Gentiles came to faith (cf. the literal sense of the parallel ἐμφανὴς ἐγενόμην in the second colon). But if the reversal of the initial

---

[207] So apparently Kautzsch, 46; Vollmer, 43 n. 1; Michel, 77.

[208] The argument would carry more weight had the quotation occurred in connection with Rom 9.30–10.4.

[209] *Schrift*, 50–1. The latter qualification is required to account for the reversed order of the clauses in the Pauline text. Koch actually allows for either a Pauline or pre-Pauline origin for the latter reading, but he gives no reason for thinking that Paul might have modified the text in a manner that has no apparent bearing on his argument.

[210] The preposition is read by 𝔭[46] B D* F G 1506[vid] (it vg[cl]) sah go Ambst, while it is omitted in ℵ A C D[1] Ψ 𝔐 vg[st] sy Clem Chr Euthal Thdrt Dam Hil.

verbs should be traced to a pre-Pauline scribal "correction" (see above), then it is always possible that the same scribe might have thought to improve the grammar of the first clause by inserting an instrumental ἐν after the passive verb εὑρέθην.[211] Given the difficulty of knowing exactly what sort of text Paul might have used as the basis for his citation here, the origin of the present reading cannot be ascertained with any measure of confidence.

V   Reading ἐγενόμην in place of ἐγενήθην.   Here Paul follows the reading of A S* and the Lucianic manuscripts against S^c Q and the Hexaplaric and Catena texts. The meaning is the same in either case.

(30)   **Rom 10.21** (= Isa 65.2)[212]

Paul: ὅλην τὴν ἡμέραν ἐξεπέτασα τὰς χεῖράς μου **πρὸς** λαὸν ἀπειθοῦντα **καὶ ἀντιλέγοντα**.

LXX: ἐξεπέτασα τὰς χεῖράς μου ὅλην τὴν ἡμέραν πρὸς λαὸν ἀπειθοῦντα καὶ ἀντιλέγοντα ...

B   Advancing ὅλην τὴν ἡμέραν to primary position.   Though the wording of Rom 10.21 could be transposed into the LXX of Isa 65.1 without difficulty, both the Pauline and LXX traditions stand firmly united behind their respective readings. The natural presumption is that the present word order goes back to Paul himself. Though nothing in the Pauline context would require such a change, the shift accords well with Paul's evident purpose in adducing the text, emphasizing as it does the persistence with which Yahweh has reached out to his stubborn people.[213] The high pathos of the Pauline word order supplies a

---

[211] Normally the simple Dative cannot be used with the Passive to signify the personal agent (BDF § 195, 219(1)). In the case of εὑρίσκειν, however, the use of ἐν for this purpose would actually be incorrect, since the Passive of this word retains its deponent meaning (BDF § 191(3), 313). The same is true for the insertion of ἐν before the second τοῖς in B D* 1506^vid (*ibid.*).

[212] The omission of Isa 65.1b between Rom 10.20 and 10.21 might be labelled an instance of "limited selection," though the reason for the omission is far from clear. Perhaps the simple desire to avoid unnecessary repetition affords an adequate explanation.

[213] Cf. *Schrift*, 106 n. 12. Koch also calls attention to the resultant verbal parallel – which he describes as "sicher nicht zufällig" – with the quotation from Ps 18.5 in Rom 10.18. The physical distance between the two texts, however, makes intentional assimilation unlikely.

fitting conclusion to a catena of biblical texts (vv. 19–21) designed to answer the plaintive question of v. 19, ἀλλὰ λέγω, μὴ Ἰσραὴλ οὐκ ἔγνω. Though certainty will always be elusive where shifts in word order are concerned, the combination of external and internal evidence seems adequate to support a Pauline origin for the present wording.

V   Reading πρός instead of ἐπί.   A number of LXX manuscripts, mostly from the Lucianic tradition, read ἐπὶ λαόν rather than πρὸς λαόν in Isa 65.2. On the Pauline side, the uncial D and citations from Clement and Justin offer the same reading in Rom 10.21. In both cases, the strength of the external evidence makes it clear that Paul has followed the primary LXX tradition in reading πρός here.

V   Including καὶ ἀντιλέγοντα as part of the citation.   Following the Masoretic Hebrew text, the uncials B Q and a portion of the Hexaplaric evidence place the words καὶ ἀντιλέγοντα in Isa 65.2 under the obelus. Within the Pauline tradition, the uncials F G, a small portion of the Old Latin witnesses, and quotes by Hilary and Ambrosiaster omit the same phrase. Joseph Ziegler traces the LXX wording to a conflation of the readings found in the Masoretic text (סוֹרֵר) and *1QIs*^{a} (מוֹרֶה), which in his view appeared already in the Hebrew *Vorlage* of the LXX.[214] As with the previous reading, the external evidence makes it quite clear that Paul has followed the majority LXX tradition at this point.

(31)   **Rom 11.3**[215] (= 3 Kgdms 19.10)[216]

Paul: κύριε, τοὺς προφήτας σου ἀπέκτειναν [ ], [ ] τὰ θυσιαστήριά σου κατέσκαψαν, κἀγὼ ὑπελείφθην μόνος καὶ ζητοῦσιν τὴν ψυχήν μου [ ].

[214] "Vorlage," 113. Kautzsch (47) points to a number of other places where סוֹרֵר occurs together with מוֹרֶה (Deut 21.18, 20, Jer 5.23, Ps 78.8), though in none of these places is the Hebrew translated as here.

[215] Though some would regard it as a quotation, the adapted form of Ps 93.14/1 Kgdms 12.22 that appears in Rom 11.2 has been omitted from consideration here in accordance with the strict guidelines of the present study, which is confined to passages that offer explicit indication to the reader that a citation is being offered (introductory formula, interpretive comments, etc.).

[216] The wording is identical in 3 Kgdms 19.14 except for the substitution of τὴν διαθήκην σου for σε and καθεῖλαν for κατέσκαψαν.

LXX: [καὶ εἶπεν Ἡλιου Ζηλῶν ἐζήλωκα τῷ κυρίῳ παντοκρά-
τορι, ὅτι ἐγκατέλιπόν σε οἱ υἱοὶ Ἰσραηλ·] τὰ θυσιαστήριά
σου κατέσκαψαν καὶ τοὺς προφήτας σου ἀπέκτειναν ἐν
ῥομφαίᾳ, καὶ ὑπολέλειμμαι ἐγὼ μονώτατος, καὶ ζητοῦσι
τὴν ψυχήν μου λαβεῖν αὐτήν.

LXX$_L$: τὰ θυσιαστήριά σου κατέσκαψαν καὶ τοὺς προφήτας σου
ἀπέκτειναν ἐν ῥομφαίᾳ, καὶ ὑπελείφθην ἐγὼ μονώτατος,
καὶ ζητοῦσι τὴν ψυχήν μου λαβεῖν αὐτήν.

MT: [וַיֹּאמֶר קַנֹּא קִנֵּאתִי לַיהוָה אֱלֹהֵי צְבָאוֹת כִּי־עָזְבוּ
בְרִיתְךָ בְּנֵי יִשְׂרָאֵל] אֶת־מִזְבְּחֹתֶיךָ הָרָסוּ וְאֶת־נְבִיאֶיךָ
הָרְגוּ בֶחָרֶב וָאִוָּתֵר אֲנִי לְבַדִּי וַיְבַקְשׁוּ אֶת־נַפְשִׁי
לְקַחְתָּהּ

C   Addition of κύριε. With no support from the LXX manuscripts and a unified Pauline tradition,[217] the *prima facie*
assumption is that the present wording is original with Paul.
Whether any rationale for the addition can be demonstrated,
however, remains open to question. Koch supposes that Paul
has consciously modelled the text after Isa 53.1, quoted only a
few verses earlier in Rom 10.16.[218] Why the one citation should
have served as a pattern for the other, however, is never
explained. A simpler solution would see here the sort of pious
addition that could easily creep into any prayer text, whether
accidentally or by design. Yet another possibility arises from
the fact that this is the only place in the LXX account (apart
from the repetition in v. 14) where Elijah addresses Yahweh
without the vocative κύριε (cf. 3 Kgdms 17.20, 21, 18.36, 37,
19.4).[219] If Paul derived his quotation from a Greek text that
diverged somewhat from the primary LXX tradition, as
appears likely (see below), then the possibility that a harmoniz-
ing insertion might have found its way already into Paul's
Vorlage cannot be entirely discounted.

B   Reversing the order of the first two clauses. Here again the
Pauline and LXX traditions stand united behind their
respective readings, but the reason for the change remains far

---

[217] The addition is found only in quotations from Justin and Origen. As these are
also the only witnesses to agree with Rom 11.3 in reversing the order of the first two
clauses, the influence of the Pauline wording is unmistakable.

[218] *Schrift*, 87, 139.

[219] The LXX agrees with the MT in every instance.

from clear. Koch, citing a study by Odil Steck, traces the reversal to Paul's desire to emphasize that part of the prophetic indictment that could be seen as pertaining to Israel in his own day, viz., the "killing of the prophets" (cf. 1 Thess 2.15).[220] The appearance of similar accusations in the Synoptic tradition (Matt 23.29–39 (cf. Matt 10.17–21), Luke 11.47–51, 13.34–5) demonstrates the currency of the notion that Christian preachers were "prophets" whose harsh treatment by the synagogue echoed biblical Israel's rejection of the divine message-bearers. On the other hand, there is nothing to indicate that either a translator or a reviser would have felt any need to modify the wording of the LXX at this point. The case is far from proven, but the likelihood that any better explanation will come forward appears slight.

B   Omission of καί.   The fact that several Pauline witnesses insert a καί to link the first two clauses of Rom 11.3 reveals a measure of discomfort among certain scribes with the asyndetic construction that characterizes the majority tradition.[221] As the same conjunction is absent from Codex A of the LXX tradition, a textual basis for the Pauline reading cannot be entirely ruled out.[222] Though the sense is unaffected by the change, the asyndetic parallelism of Rom 11.3 is clearly more effective from a rhetorical standpoint than the simple coordination found in the original.[223] In the absence of a more viable explanation, one can only presume that it was the high degree of rhetorical stylization in the original passage that prompted Paul to expand the effect still further in his own version of 3 Kgdms 19.10.

---

[220]   *Schrift*, 74 n. 83. Cf. p. 104: "Paulus stellt den als Anklage wesentlich wirkungs-volleren Vorwurf des Prophetenmordes voran, während der Vorwurf der Zerstörung der Altäre, der z. Zt. des Paulus nur noch eine historische Reminiszenz darstellt, erst an zweiter Stelle folgt." The work by Steck is *Israel und das gewaltsame Geschick der Propheten*, WMANT 23 (Neukirchen-Vluyn: Neukirchener Verlag, 1967), 62–3, 274–8.

[221]   Tischendorf lists D E L *al pler* syr[utr] arm aeth Just Chr Thdrt Euthal Dam as adding καί.

[222]   The same manuscript shows no further links with the Pauline wording. The only other witnesses cited in the older editions are Origen, who follows Paul throughout, and Priscilian (both noted by Brooke–McLean). The Göttingen edition for 3 Kingdoms is not yet available.

[223]   Cf. the similar omission in Rom 11.26, though the origin of that change is less than certain.

B   Omission of ἐν ῥομφαίᾳ. Here again, rhetorical stylization offers the most likely explanation for the divergence of the Pauline wording from the unified testimony of the LXX. Not only is the phrase ἐν ῥομφαίᾳ unnecessary in the Pauline context, but it may well have been viewed as overly specific (not to mention inaccurate) if a reference to Jewish persecution of Christian "prophets" is intended (see above). Eliminating the phrase also produces a neat verbal parallelism between the first two clauses of Rom 11.3, a result that Paul would not be slow to notice (cf. Rom 9.13, 1 Cor 15.55, 2 Cor 8.15). When taken together with the other rhetorically motivated adaptations in the same verse, the Pauline origin of the present omission would appear to be secure.

T   Substituting κἀγὼ ὑπελείφθην μόνος for καὶ ὑπολέλειμμαι ἐγὼ μονώτατος. As none of the variations in wording has any noticeable effect on either the meaning or the rhetorical effectiveness of the passage, the possibility that Paul might have drawn his quotation from a divergent *Vorlage* must be counted likely from the start. The only part of the Pauline wording that finds any support in the LXX manuscript tradition is the substitution of the Aorist ὑπελείφθην for the Perfect ὑπολέλειμμαι. This piece of evidence, however, turns out to be crucial to understanding the background of the Pauline wording in Rom 11.3. The witnesses that contain this reading are precisely those "Lucianic" manuscripts (b o c_2 e_2) that Frank Moore Cross has linked to the Qumran Hebrew text *4QSam^a*.[224] Questions remain, however, over exactly how the relationship between these texts is to be understood. Where Cross finds evidence for an early "proto-Lucianic" revision of the Old Greek intended to bring it into line with a "Palestinian" Hebrew text of the type reflected in *4QSam^a*, Emanuel Tov discovers traces of the original Old Greek text that was subsequently revised toward a "proto-Masoretic" Hebrew text to yield the present "LXX" version of Samuel and Kings.[225] Koch stakes out a position close to that of Cross in arguing that the

---

[224] See Cross, "History," 292–6; "Evolution," 115–19. The MSS b c_2 e_2 give the same reading in the parallel passage in v. 14. The designations are those of Brooke–McLean (MSS 19, 82, 127, 93 in the Göttingen system), which have become something of a technical shorthand for the "Lucianic" tradition in these books. The Göttingen edition of Kingdoms is not yet available.

[225] See Tov, "Proto-Lucian," 293–305.

Pauline form of the text reflects the efforts of an early Jewish reviser to improve the grammar of the standard "LXX" translation.[226] In the present case, however, it would be just as easy to argue with Tov that the Pauline/"Lucianic" wording actually antedates the present "LXX" version of the text.[227] The wording of Rom 11.4 offers further support for this interpretation of the evidence (see below). Whichever explanation is finally adopted, the evidence seems clear that Paul has followed the wording of his *Vorlage* for at least this part of his citation, despite the lack of textual support for some of his language.[228]

B   Omission of λαβεῖν αὐτήν.   Once again, the textual evidence is wholly united in both traditions, yielding the presumption that the present wording should be traced to Paul himself.[229] As previous examples have established a pattern of omitting irrelevant words from the biblical text for the sake of rhetorical conciseness (e.g. Rom 3.10, 3.14, 3.15, 9.25), the elimination of one more phrase that adds nothing to the (Pauline) sense of the verse should come as no surprise. At the same time, lingering uncertainty concerning the wording of Paul's biblical text in this latter part of the verse (see above) urges caution in drawing any firm conclusions about the way Paul treated the biblical text in this section. The similarity of the omission to other rhetorically motivated changes in the same verse, however, makes a Pauline origin likely.

---

[226] *Schrift*, 74–7. Interestingly, Koch never cites either Cross or the "Lucianic" evidence.

[227] If anything, the evidence might lean more in the direction of Tov's theory. Koch's reasons for thinking that the Pauline text represents a "sprachliche Verbesserung" are weak: the superlative μονώτατος is "unsinnigen" in the LXX text, the Aorist ὑπελείφθην is "geläüfiger" than the Perfect ὑπολέλειμμαι, and the Pauline placement of ἐγώ is more grammatically correct. If on the other hand the Pauline reading (or a similar text) were the more original of the two, it would be easy to see why a subsequent editor might have wanted to "correct" this part of the verse to bring it into closer alignment with his own "proto-Masoretic" Hebrew text (לְבַדִּי וָאִוָּתֵר אָנִי). Both the placement of the first-person pronoun and the substitution of the Aorist for the Perfect can be explained along these lines. The word μονώτατος is limited almost exclusively to the books of Kingdoms in the LXX (8x), where it alternates with the simple μόνος (13x) as a translation for the Hebrew לְבַד from 2 Kgdms 13.22 through 4 Kgdms (sections βγ/γγ/γδ).

[228] I.e. the crasis of καί ... ἐγώ into κἀγώ and the use of the positive μόνος rather than the superlative μονώτατος.

[229] The words are missing only in the Sahidic and Ethiopic versions and a citation by Justin.

(32)   **Rom 11.4** (= 3 Kgdms 19.18)

Paul: [ ] κατέλιπον ἐμαυτῷ [ ] ἑπτακισχιλίους ἄνδρας οἵτινες
οὐκ ἔκαμψαν γόνυ τῇ Βάαλ.

LXX: καὶ καταλείψεις ἐν Ἰσραηλ ἑπτὰ χιλιάδας ἀνδρῶν, πάντα
γόνατα, ἃ οὐκ ὤκλασαν γόνυ τῷ Βάαλ, [καὶ πᾶν στόμα, ὃ
οὐ προσεκύνησεν αὐτῷ].

LXX_L: καὶ καταλείψω²³⁰ ἐξ Ἰσραηλ ἑπτὰ χιλιάδας ἀνδρῶν,
πάντα τὰ γόνατα, ἃ οὐκ ἔκαμψαν γόνυ τῇ Βάαλ.²³¹

MT: וְהִשְׁאַרְתִּי בְיִשְׂרָאֵל שִׁבְעַת אֲלָפִים כָּל־הַבִּרְכַּיִם אֲשֶׁר
לֹא־כָרְעוּ לַבַּעַל וְכָל־ חַפֶּה אֲשֶׁר לֹא־נָשַׁק לוֹ

E   Omission of initial καί.   Leaving off initial particles, especially
καί, is common fare in the Pauline citations.²³² In the present
case, however, questions concerning the nature of Paul's biblical text preclude any sure answers as to how Paul has handled
the wording of his *Vorlage*. In particular, the fact that Paul
gives the Aorist κατέλιπον rather than the Future form found
in the LXX and the Masoretic Hebrew raises questions as to
whether an initial ו might have fallen out of the Hebrew
manuscript that lay behind Paul's Greek biblical text here. In
this environment it becomes impossible to determine with any
measure of certainty where the present omission may have
originated.

T   Substituting κατέλιπον for καταλείψεις.²³³   Continuing his
focus on the Elijah narrative, Paul now quotes that portion of

²³⁰ Only MS i, closely allied with the Lucianic texts, follows Paul in reading
κατέλιπον here (and omitting the initial καί). For the remainder of the verse it
follows the majority tradition except for the final verb, where it reads ἐκλίναν in
place of ὤκλασαν. The same manuscript follows the majority tradition in v. 10 except
for advancing μου ahead of τὴν ψυχήν (with codex B).

²³¹ The text cited is the reading of MSS b c₂ e₂, the only deviation being the
spelling ἔκαψαν in MS e₂. MS o follows an independent course in v. 18: while it agrees
with the majority tradition in reading ἐν and ὤκλασαν and omitting τά, it also has
καταλείψει for the initial verb and Ιλημ (= Ἰερουσαλημ) for Ἰσραηλ, the former a
unique reading and the latter supported only by MS h (so far as the evidence of
Brooke–McLean goes).

²³² See note 197 for references.

²³³ The Aorist κατέλιπον is read by ℵ B D Ψ 𝔐 Did, while the Imperfect
κατέλειπον is found in 𝔭⁴⁶ A C F G L P 104 1175 1739 2464 *al*. In addition, a few
manuscripts read the First Aorist form κατέλειψα (81 1506 *pc*). A firm basis for
deciding between the various readings is hard to find, especially in view of the
uncertainties surrounding the wording of Paul's *Vorlage* at this point (see below).
The sense is little different in either case.

the divine response that bears directly on the complaint of Elijah cited in the previous verse. In view of the close proximity of the two verses in both the LXX and Pauline contexts, it is only natural to presume that Paul drew both citations from the same manuscript.[234] This assumption finds textual support in multiple agreements with three of the same "Lucianic" texts (b c_2 e_2) that yielded evidence for the use of a variant text in the previous citation.[235] Still, defining the precise relationship between these three texts (Rom 11.4, the "Lucianic" manuscripts, and the "LXX") is no easy task. (1) The "Lucianic" manuscripts diverge in numerous places from the wording of Rom 11.4, making it unlikely that the Pauline version of 3 Kgdms 19.18 has influenced the LXX tradition at this point. The possibility that both might have modified the "LXX" text in the same manner is also remote.[236] It must be presumed therefore that the Pauline and "Lucianic" texts offer independent testimony to a common earlier tradition, at least at the points in question. (2) Furthermore, the "Lucianic" manuscripts in their present form show a clear link with the LXX, as attested by their identical wording apart from the agreements with Rom 11.4. Which tradition is dependent on the other, however, remains to be clarified. (3) As for the link between Rom 11.4 and the majority reading of the LXX, it could be argued that the Pauline wording reflects a "Graecizing" revision of the awkward Semitic idiom of the "LXX," but the possibility that the "LXX" represents a "Hebraizing" revision of a Greek text of Kingdoms similar to Paul's *Vorlage* has perhaps more to be said for it.[237] The "Lucianic" texts b o c_2 e_2

[234] Cf. Rom 10.20–1, where a similar format appears.

[235] The agreements include the presence of a first-person singular verb at the beginning of the citation, the substitution of ἔκαμψαν [ἔκαψαν in e_2] for the LXX's ὤκλασαν, and the use of the feminine definite article rather than the masculine with the name Βάαλ (see below).

[236] Only in the case of the shift to a first-person verb could it be argued that both might have "corrected" the LXX toward the MT independently of one another. A common shift in the form of the article is unlikely, and nothing in the LXX or the Hebrew could have given rise to a simultaneous substitution of ἔκαμψαν for ὤκλασαν.

[237] Some sort of link between the two is required by their simultaneous addition of the words ἀνδρῶν/ἄνδρας and γόνυ to the Hebrew text. Koch (*Schrift*, 75–77) argues for a "Graecizing" revision, but the reasons he gives for why an editor might have introduced certain changes (e.g. the substitution of ἑπτακισχιλίους for ἑπτὰ χιλιά-δας and the shift from the masculine to the feminine form of the article with Βάαλ) seem forced. As a later assimilation to the Hebrew text, on the other hand, the LXX

would then represent the remnants of an earlier revision of this same Greek text intended to bring it into conformity with a "proto-Masoretic" Hebrew text, while the majority LXX reading would represent a minor revision of this "Lucianic" text.[238]

However the textual issue is resolved, it seems clear that deviations from the majority reading of the LXX in Rom 11.4 should be attributed to Paul only when there is reason to believe that the wording in question cannot be traced to the use of a minority tradition. This is clearly not the case with the substitution of κατέλιπον for καταλείψεις in the first line of the citation. Since the "Lucianic" manuscripts b c₂ e₂ show the same first-person singular reading as Rom 11.4,[239] this much at least should be attributed to the developing manuscript tradition. The use of the Aorist form of the verb, on the other hand, has no such textual support. But if the omission of καί at the beginning of the citation should reflect the absence of a ׳ in the Hebrew *Vorlage* of Paul's Greek text, Paul's own *Vorlage* may well have contained an Aorist form here.[240] As Paul's point in adducing the verse (implied in v. 5) could have been made just as well with the Future as with the Aorist, some such textual explanation is to be assumed.

D   Addition of ἐμαυτῷ.   The only piece of textual evidence that might pertain to the origin of this reading is the Vulgate's addition of *mihi* to the wording of 3 Kgdms 19.18. In the absence of further testimony, the influence of Rom 11.4 is to be

performs admirably: even the addition of the word ἀνδρῶν, only implied in the MT, is fairly required by the context. (For further details, see the discussions of the specific readings.) The shift from ἔκαμψαν to ὤκλασαν is more difficult: the Hebrew כרע is translated by κάμπτειν in 2 Kgdms 22.40, 4 Kgdms 1.13, 9.24, and five other places in the LXX while ὀκλάζειν occurs only here and in 3 Kgdms 8.54 in the entire LXX. At the same time, the fact that both Symmachus (8x) and Aquila (once) employ ὀκλάζειν in other contexts shows that the word is not so uncommon as Koch supposes, so that its use here could reflect a later idiom. The LXX καταλείψεις, which represents a Hebrew *Vorlage* in which the final ׳ has dropped off (or been overlooked) from the verb והשארתי, could have entered the tradition as easily in a later revision toward a divergent Hebrew manuscript as in an original translation.

[238] On the substitution of καταλείψεις for κατέλιπον/κατέλειπον and ὤκλασαν for ἔκαμψαν in the "LXX," see the previous note. The shift to the masculine article with Βάαλ in the LXX is only natural once the original reason for the feminine usage had been forgotten (see below).

[239] MS o diverges from the others in reading a third-person singular at this point.

[240] I.e. as a translation of the Hebrew Perfect that would remain after the omission. On the frequent omission of initial καί in Paul's citations, see note 197.

presumed. This does not mean, however, that the addition is to
be traced without further ado to Paul himself. Though it certainly accords well with the emphasis on the grace of God in
vv. 5–6, the close link between ἐμαυτῷ and the preceding verb
raises the possibility that the two words might have appeared
together in Paul's *Vorlage* as a translation of the Hebrew verb
הִשְׁאַרְתִּי. Though the addition has no basis in the Hebrew,[241]
the relatively free translation technique encountered throughout the present quotation renders that objection meaningless.
Though the external evidence certainly favors a Pauline origin,
continuing uncertainty regarding the wording of Paul's
Vorlage renders any firm conclusion suspect.

B   Omission of ἐν Ἰσραηλ.   Within the LXX tradition, only the
Ethiopic version follows Paul in omitting the words ἐν Ἰσραηλ
from 3 Kgdms 19.18. The Pauline tradition is wholly united in
its reading. A comparison of the respective contexts of the two
verses offers further reason for thinking that the omission is to
be traced to the apostle Paul. On the one hand, the reference to
"Israel" is clearly problematic in the context of Romans, where
the incorporation of the Gentiles into historic "Israel" as part
of the divine plan is constantly presupposed (9.24–6, 11.7,
17–24). In the LXX, on the other hand, the phrase ἐν Ἰσραηλ
plays a vital role in specifying the geographical setting in which
the actions described are to take place. Though certainty is
impossible in view of the questions surrounding the wording of
Paul's *Vorlage* here, a Pauline origin for the present omission
appears likely.

T   Substituting ἑπτακισχιλίους ἄνδρας for ἑπτὰ χιλιάδας
ἀνδρῶν.   Since Paul simply follows the wording of the biblical text in his only other use of either χιλιάς or χίλιοι
(χιλιάδες in 1 Cor 10.8), there is no reason to think that he
would have changed ἑπτὰ χιλιάδας to ἑπτακισχιλίους in
Rom 11.4. On the other hand, the total absence of scribal
substitutions for ἑπτὰ χιλιάδας in 3 Kgdms 19.18 argues
against Dietrich-Alex Koch's contention that an original ἑπτὰ
χιλιάδας was adapted to ἑπτακισχιλίους in an early "Graecizing" revision designed to conform the text to common

---

[241] Neither the Hiphil nor the Niphal of שאר carries any such "Middle" sense.

Greek usage.²⁴² The clear preference for χιλιάς (60x) over χίλιοι (11x) throughout the books of Kingdoms, coupled with the fact that χιλιάς is regularly accompanied by a numeral whereas χίλιοι occurs most often in generalized descriptions, creates a strong impression that the reading of the "LXX" text arose only in the final redaction of the book of Kingdoms.²⁴³ This in turn supports the contention of the present study that the language of Rom 11.4 reflects an earlier stage in the text history of the Greek book of Kingdoms than the version that appears in the present "LXX." All in all, the evidence seems conclusive that Paul drew the phrase ἑπτακισχιλίους ἄνδρας from the Greek text of Kingdoms from which he copied his citation.

T   Substituting οἵτινες οὐκ ἔκαμψαν for πάντα γόνατα ἃ οὐκ ὤκλασαν. When viewed as a revision of the LXX, the wording of Rom 11.4 actually reflects three changes from 3 Kgdms 19.18: the elimination of the intrusive πάντα γόνατα; the conversion of the relative pronoun from neuter plural ἃ (modifying γόνατα) to masculine plural οἵτινες (modifying ἄνδρας); and the substitution of ἔκαμψαν for ὤκλασαν. While the syntax of the LXX is awkward by any standard ("seven thousand men, every knee that has not bowed the knee ..."), a compelling reason for changing the verb from ὤκλασαν to ἔκαμψαν is harder to find.²⁴⁴ When the process is viewed in

---

²⁴² *Schrift*, 75–6. If the latter phrasing truly reflected "gewöhnlichen griechischen Sprachgebrauch," one would expect it to appear in more than just this one text.

²⁴³ The pattern is consistent across all sections of this composite work. Only 6 times (out of 60 occurrences) does χιλιάς appear without a numeral, and 3 of these are repetitions of the famous taunt about Saul having slain his "thousands." Χίλιοι, on the other hand, bears this generalized sense in 8 of its 11 occurrences. (The exceptions are 1 Kgdms 13.2, 25.2, and 4 Kgdms 24.16.) Moreover, χιλιάς is almost always followed by a Genitive in the LXX text (as in 3 Kgdms 19.18), while χίλιοι normally agrees with the case of the noun it modifies (as in Rom 11.4).

²⁴⁴ Koch (*Schrift*, 75 n. 89) traces the change to a concern for verbal precision, noting that κάμπτειν ("bend") is much more common with γόνυ than ὀκλάζειν ("slacken, abate"), which usually refers to "squatting." Though ὀκλάζειν is indeed rare in the LXX (only here and 3 Kgdms 8.54), its frequent use by Symmachus (8 times, including twice more in Kingdoms) shows that it was not a rare word *per se* in Jewish circles. In fact, fully half of Symmachus's uses of ὀκλάζειν occur in contexts involving physical obeisance, though none includes the word γόνυ as here. Κάμπτειν is indeed the most common rendering of כרע in the LXX (8x), but the association is by no means fixed: fully 18 different words are used to translate the Qal alone, including κλίνειν (3x), κατακλίνειν (3x), ὀκλάζειν (2x), πίπτειν (3x), προπίπτειν (2x), and συμποδίζειν (3x). In phrases describing the "bending" or "bowing" of the

reverse, on the other hand, it becomes quite clear why a "Hebraizing" reviser would have been troubled by the relatively "free" rendering of the Hebrew reflected in the Greek *Vorlage* of Rom 11.4. Here again the reason for replacing the verb is by no means clear, but the reading ἔκαμψαν has the support of the important "Lucianic" manuscripts b c₂ e₂ as well as the minuscules x and y.[245] The closeness of the "LXX" text to the Masoretic Hebrew can hardly be denied. In the final analysis, the best that can be said is that the data could support either view. In view of mounting evidence that the form of 3 Kgdms 19.18 preserved in Rom 11.4 is older than the version found in the "LXX," all that is required of the Pauline wording here is that it be amenable to such an explanation. In either interpretation, nothing can be found to link the wording in this part of the citation to Paul himself.[246]

T   Converting the definite article from τῇ (feminine) to τῷ (masculine) before Βάαλ.   The use of the feminine form of the article with the masculine noun Βάαλ goes back to the common Jewish practice of substituting the feminine בֹּשֶׁת ("object of shame": cf. Greek ἡ αἰσχύνη) or עֲבוֹדָה זָרָה ("loathsome worship") for the masculine בַּעַל in order to preclude the possibility of pronouncing the divine name while reading the biblical text.[247] The origins of the practice are obscure, but it

knees (γόνατα), forms of κάμπτειν are again the most common (7 out of 14 occurrences), but here too it would be incorrect to speak of any "established" usage. Both words were in common use in the patristic period. See G. W. H. Lampe, *A Patristic Greek Lexicon* (Oxford: Clarendon, 1961–8).

[245] MS o apparently follows the majority tradition at this point.

[246] Κάμπτειν appears in Paul's letters only in citations (with the possible exception of Eph 3.14), while ὀκλάζειν is foreign to the entire New Testament.

[247] So Koch, *Schrift*, 75 n. 87, citing an article by A. Dillmann, "Über Baal mit dem weiblichen Artikel (ἡ Βάαλ)," in *Monatsberichte der königlich preussischen Akademie der Wissenschaften zu Berlin [1881]* (Berlin: Verlag der königlich Akademie der Wissenschaften, 1882), 601–20. After examining and rejecting several different "history-of-religions" explanations, Dillmann brings forward a wealth of evidence to show how the practice of introducing a substitute for בַּעַל in the public reading of Scripture came to be normative in post-biblical Judaism, even influencing the transmission of the Hebrew text. The frequent occurrence of the feminine article with Βάαλ in the LXX (= ἡ αἰσχύνη) reflects the same process. Dillmann traces the substitution to an increasing veneration of the divine name, which led to an avoidance of the generic term Βάαλ even as the names of other deities continued to be pronounced. The same practice can be seen in Ἀ Σ Θ and the Targumim [examples from rabbinic literature in Strack-Billerbeck, 3:288]. Dillmann points to Lev 24.16 and Hos 2.16–17 as important passages for understanding the development of this

appears already in the LXX, and the wording of Rom 11.4 shows that it was still current in some form in the Christian era.[248] The fact that the important "Lucianic" manuscripts b o c₂ e₂ contain the feminine article in 3 Kgdms 19.18 also testifies to its antiquity.[249] On the hypothesis that the text underlying Paul's quotation of 3 Kgdms 19.18 represents a "Graecizing" revision of the present LXX text, it becomes nearly impossible to explain the shift from the grammatically "correct" masculine article to the technically incongruous feminine form. It requires little imagination, on the other hand, to see how a Christian scribe unacquainted with Jewish practice could have thought that he was improving his Greek text by substituting the "proper" masculine article to go with the masculine noun Βάαλ.[250] In either case, there is nothing that would point to Paul as the originator of the present reading.

(33)   **Rom 11.8** (= Deut 29.3, Isa 29.10)

Paul: [_] ἔδωκεν [_] αὐτοῖς [_] ὁ θεὸς + πνεύματι κατανύξεως + [_] ὀφθαλμοὺς τοῦ μὴ βλέπειν καὶ ὦτα τοῦ μὴ ἀκούειν ἕως τῆς σήμερον ἡμέρας.

Deut 29.3ₗₓₓ: καὶ οὐκ ἔδωκεν κύριος ὁ θεὸς ὑμῖν καρδίαν εἰδέναι καὶ ὀφθαλμοὺς βλέπειν καὶ ὦτα ἀκούειν ἕως τῆς ἡμέρας ταύτης.

Isa 29.10ₗₓₓ: [ὅτι πεπότικεν ὑμᾶς κύριος] πνεύματι κατανύξεως [καὶ καμμύσει τοὺς ὀφθαλμοὺς αὐτῶν καὶ τῶν προφητῶν αὐτῶν καὶ τῶν ἀρχόντων αὐτῶν, οἱ ὁρῶντες τὰ κρυπτά].

A   <u>Omitting initial καί.</u>   As in numerous other places, the omission of initial particles is thoroughly typical of Paul.[251]

---

attitude. Its influence is apparent in such Hebrew texts as Hos 9.10 and Jer 3.24, 11.13, as well as the LXX of 3 Kgdms 18.19, 25.

[248] For ἡ Βάαλ in the LXX, see Judg 2.13, 4 Kgdms 1.2, 3, 6, 16, 21.3, 23.4–5 (A), 2 Chr 23.17, Hos 2.10, 13.1, Zeph 1.4, and all ten occurrences in Jeremiah. Within the Pauline manuscript tradition, only the uncials F and G replace the feminine τῇ with the grammatically "correct" form τῷ.

[249] On the antiquity of the readings found in b o c₂ e₂, see the discussion at the beginning of this section. The feminine article is also found in the minuscules f* i j m n p q s t u w z.

[250] Of course, the possibility of two independent traditions concerning the form of the article in 3 Kgdms 19.18 cannot be ruled out.

[251] See note 197.

B   Shifting the negative from the main clause (οὐκ) to the subordinate clauses (μή ... μή). Nothing in the manuscript tradition supports the notion that Paul might have simply reproduced the wording of his *Vorlage* in shifting the position of the
negative in Deut 29.3. Though the change itself is minor, its
effect on the sense of the verse is substantial. Whereas the original passage ascribed Israel's incomprehension in the desert to
Yahweh's unwillingness to override their spiritual blindness,
the wording of Rom 11.8 interprets the present "hardness" of
Israel to the Christian gospel as part of the divine plan: God
has actually "hardened" his people for a time in order to give
the Gentiles a chance to turn to him through faith in Christ (v.
11). The verses that follow expound the full significance of this
view: despite its present "hardness," Paul is certain that the day
will come when Israel, too, will respond to the gospel and be
"saved" (11.25–7; cf. vv. 12, 14–15). The quotation in Rom
11.8 (in its Pauline wording) is wholly consistent with this
understanding of God's activity in history. Still, the idea that
Israel's rejection of the gospel represents a divine "hardening"
is by no means original with Paul,[252] so that it is at least conceivable that Paul is quoting a version of Deut 29.3 that had
already been adapted for use in early Christian apologetics.
Evidence for earlier use of this particular passage, however, is
entirely lacking.[253] All in all, the close integration of the
present wording with its Pauline context seems to indicate that
the shift in the position of the negative goes back to Paul
himself.

A   Converting the personal pronoun from second-person plural
(ὑμῖν) to third-person plural (αὐτοῖς). While the third-person
form would be entirely out of place in the original passage, it is
all but required in the Pauline context, where the references to

[252] The theme appears to have been widespread in early Christianity, to judge
from the number of biblical passages adduced to support it. Note the different ways
in which Isa 6.9–10 is used in Mark 4.12/Luke 8.10/Matt 13.13–15, John 12.40, and
Acts 28.26, as well as the citations from Jer 5.21 in Mark 8.18 and Hab 1.5 in Acts
13.40–1. Though quoted nowhere in the New Testament, Ezek 12.2 offers another
useful parallel.
[253] In his study of the use of Scripture in early Christian apologetics, Barnabas
Lindars concludes that this and all of the texts adduced in Rom 9–11 to explain
Israel's rejection of the gospel (with the possible exception of the appeal to Isa
10.22–3 in Rom 9.27–8) are original with Paul. See *Apologetic*, 164–7, 242.

Israel are all cast in third-person speech.[254] As the textual evidence is equally united in both passages, one can be virtually certain that Paul has adapted the wording of Deut 29.3 in the present instance.

C   Reversing the order of αὐτοῖς and ὁ θεός. Though the textual evidence is unanimous in both traditions, the precise nuance of the shift in word order is for the most part lost on the modern reader. Even the basic question of whether the advancing of αὐτοῖς conveys emphasis (referring back to οἱ λοιποί in v. 7) cannot be settled with any measure of certainty.[255] The best that can be said is that the shift in word order appears to go back to Paul, but the reason for the change remains shrouded in mystery.

B   Omitting κύριος. Though the omission of κύριος has little effect on the sense of the passage (note the retention of ὁ θεός), the textual evidence for both its presence in the LXX (in Deut 29.3 as well as Isa 29.10) and its absence from Rom 11.8 is quite secure. Assimilation to the Hebrew is an unlikely solution, as the Masoretic text reads only the Tetragrammaton here. Koch views the present passage as part of a larger pattern whereby Paul refers all texts that contain the word κύριος to the exalted Jesus, so that he has to omit the title from the text when a reference to "God" is intended.[256] The weakness of this explanation is apparent from the only other example that Koch cites (Rom 15.9), as the designation κύριος is retained in a parallel quotation only two verses later (Rom 15.11).[257] Nevertheless, there may be a germ of truth in Koch's solution: Paul nowhere uses the expression κύριος ὁ θεός that appears in Deut 29.3, while κύριος Ἰησοῦς Χριστός is perhaps his most common designation for the exalted Jesus. Whatever the explanation, the Pauline origin of the omission seems clear.

[254] Koch notes that Paul has reserved the second-person form for the "Gentiles" to whom he turns to speak in v. 13 (*Schrift*, 111).

[255] While advancement normally communicates stress in Hellenistic Greek, BDF § 472 indicates that unemphatic pronouns typically follow directly after the verb, as here. Koch (*Schrift*, 106 n. 14) offers the opinion that Paul has followed the word order of Isa 29.10 at this point (ὑμᾶς precedes κύριος in that passage), but the parallel with the Pauline wording of Deut 29.3 is not close.

[256] *Schrift*, 87, 121.

[257] Whether all the κύριος texts can be applied to Christ is also debatable: see Rom 4.8 (note θεός in v. 6), 9.29 (κύριος σαβαώθ), and 11.3 (note θεός in v. 2).

B   Conflated citation: replacing καρδίαν εἰδέναι καί with πνεῦμα
     κατανύξεως from Isa 29.10.[258]   The origin of this substitution
     is clearly related to the changed position of the negative in Deut
     29.3. Perhaps the idea that God might have blinded not only
     the sense organs but even the inmost faculties (καρδία) of his
     people to the truth of the gospel was too much even for the
     apostle Paul (cf. the omission of ὑπὸ θεοῦ in Gal 3.13). In place
     of the anticipated καρδίαν τοῦ μή εἰδέναι, he substitutes the
     similar but less definite phrase πνεῦμα κατανύξεως from Isa
     29.10.[259] Instead of being consigned to eternal ignorance, Israel
     is now portrayed as "stunned," a condition from which they
     may be already starting to recover (note ἕως τῆς σήμερον
     ἡμέρας). Such a portrait of Israel is entirely in line with Paul's
     explicit statements throughout Rom 11 on the present "harden-
     ing" and coming restoration of the Jewish nation. Though the
     possibility of a pre-Pauline Christian combination cannot be
     entirely ruled out,[260] the absence of any textual evidence that
     would support such an explanation and the close integration of
     the citation into its present context make a Pauline origin much
     more likely.

A   Omitting καί.   In view of the total absence of textual support
     in either tradition and its evident links with the preceding
     conflation, the elimination of καί before ὀφθαλμούς can hardly
     be traced to anyone but Paul.

---

[258] The actual wording in most texts of Isa 29.10 (A Q B V *et al.*) is πνεύματι
κατανύξεως, which Paul presumably adapted to the present context by converting
the Dative to an Accusative form. In several LXX manuscripts, however, the
Accusative is already present (the important uncial S, plus 93 309 301 538 Or Wirc
Spec), and the later versions of ᾽Α Σ Θ all seem to read the same way (see the note in
the Göttingen text of Isaiah). As Koch points out, the Accusative is clearly a
grammatical improvement over the reading of the LXX (see BAGD, s.v. ποτίζω),
and need not reflect reliance on the Pauline text (*Schrift*, 170 n. 48). Though Koch is
inclined to accept πνεύματι as Paul's *Vorlage* on the basis of his general closeness to
the uncials A and Q in his quotations from Isaiah, the testimony of the later versions
in particular makes it equally possible that the Accusative πνεῦμα had already
found its way into Paul's biblical text. The uncertainty surrounding the origin of this
reading makes it impossible to consider it a Pauline adaptation for the purposes of
the present study.

[259] No doubt the similar content (i.e. their emphasis on the divine "hardening" of
Israel) and sentence structure (the wording is quite close as far as ὀφθαλμούς in both
verses) suggested this particular verse to Paul. So also Koch, *Schrift*, 171.

[260] See the discussion above on the reversal of the negatives in Deut 29.3.

B   Inserting τοῦ before both infinitives. Only in the uncial A
does the LXX show any articular infinitives in Deut 29.3, and
there only with βλέπειν. The Pauline tradition, on the other
hand, uniformly includes τοῦ before both βλέπειν and
ἀκούειν. Already in classical Greek the Genitive of the articular infinitive was being used to express purpose, a construction
that appears quite often in Paul. The use of the negative τοῦ μή
with verbs of hindering, ceasing, etc., in the sense of "so that ...
not" was also common practice by Paul's time.[261] While it is
always possible that the insertions are wholly pleonastic,[262] an
added stress on the "purpose" aspect of the infinitives would be
quite consistent with the other changes noted in the verse.
Given the stability of both textual traditions at this point, it
seems reasonable to conclude that this pattern of related adaptations is not accidental. The presence of an identical construction in the very next citation (τοῦ μή βλέπειν in Rom 11.10)
offers a likely source for the present addition.[263] The fact that
the earlier text appears to have been molded in light of the later
one implies further that the links between the two citations
were not forged for the first time in the moment of dictation.

D   Substituting σήμερον for ταύτης (and advancing its position).[264] Though both textual traditions are united in their
readings here, a suitable rationale for a Pauline adaptation is
hard to find. The expression ἕως τῆς σήμερον ἡμέρας is
common in the LXX, and the tradition varies between σήμερον
ἡμέρας and ἡμέρας ταύτης on at least three occasions.[265] The
word σήμερον occurs only twice more in the Pauline corpus,
and nowhere in the precise formulation found here.[266] Of the

[261] On both points, see BDF § 400.

[262] The construction has lost much of its force in parts of the New Testament: see
BDF § 400(7).

[263] The influence could in fact be mutual: the substitution of αὐτοῖς for ἐνώπιον
αὐτῶν in v. 9 may well be patterned on the αὐτοῖς of v. 8 (see below). Other places
where Paul creates such verbal links between verses include Rom 9.25–6, 1 Cor
3.19–20, 1 Cor 15.54–5, and Gal 3.10, 13 (q.v.).

[264] The stereotyped nature of the formula ἕως τῆς σήμερον ἡμέρας (see next note)
precludes any special Pauline emphasis in the advancing of σήμερον here.

[265] For examples of ἕως τῆς σήμερον ἡμέρας in the LXX, see Gen 19.37–8, 26.33,
35.20, Num 22.30, Deut 11.4, Josh 4.9, 6.25, 9.27, 10.27, 13.13, 14.14 (A), 22.3, 1
Kgdms 29.6, 2 Kgdms 6.8 (A), Ezek 2.3, 20.29, 31, 24.2. The three passages in which
the readings alternate are Num 22.30, Josh 14.14, and 2 Kgdms 6.8.

[266] The closest is in 2 Cor 3.14, where the reading is ἄχρι τῆς σήμερον ἡμέρας.
The simple phrase ἕως σήμερον appears in 2 Cor 3.15.

various LXX passages where the expression appears, only Ezek 2.3 in any way resembles the present passage, and even here the similarity is too slight to support any direct influence. If the change should be attributed to Paul, then perhaps a note of emphasis might be detected in the expression "to this very day," i.e. until the coming of the gospel of Christ (cf. v. 14). In the absence of further evidence, however, the origin and significance of the present reading will remain obscure.

(34) **Rom 11.9–10** (= Ps 68.23–4)

Paul: γενηθήτω ἡ τράπεζα αὐτῶν [ ] εἰς παγίδα καὶ εἰς θήραν
      καὶ εἰς σκάνδαλον καὶ εἰς ἀνταπόδομα αὐτοῖς,
      σκοτισθήτωσαν οἱ ὀφθαλμοὶ αὐτῶν τοῦ μὴ βλέπειν καὶ τὸν
      νῶτον αὐτῶν διὰ παντὸς σύγκαμψον.

LXX: γενηθήτω ἡ τράπεζα αὐτῶν ἐνώπιον αὐτῶν εἰς παγίδα
      καὶ εἰς ἀνταπόδοσιν καὶ εἰς σκάνδαλον·
      σκοτισθήτωσαν οἱ ὀφθαλμοὶ αὐτῶν τοῦ μὴ βλέπειν, καὶ
      τὸν νῶτον αὐτῶν διὰ παντὸς σύγκαμψον.

D Omission of ἐνώπιον αὐτῶν and replacement by αὐτοῖς at the end of the line.[267] The link between these two changes is obvious, but not the reason for the substitution. The united LXX testimony limits the possibilities for a textual explanation, though the presence of other apparently "meaningless" variations within the same verse (the addition of καὶ εἰς θήραν and the substitution of ἀνταπόδομα for ἀνταπόδοσιν) could be read as evidence for a divergent text or even faulty citation from memory.[268] Any suggestion of a pre-Pauline Christian origin would be entirely speculative. As a Pauline adaptation, the shift in word order might be interpreted as an attempt to shift the emphasis from ἐνώπιον αὐτῶν to εἰς παγίδα κτλ. to coincide with Paul's own use of the verse, while the change to αὐτοῖς could be linked to the use of the same word in the

---

[267] While the words ἐνώπιον αὐτῶν can be found in scattered parts of the Pauline evidence, the influence of the unified LXX tradition is clearly to be seen in these instances. Tischendorf lists the witnesses as 4 k[scr] syr[scr] ar[e] aeth vg[six] et [cdd pauc] Thdrt Pelag.

[268] Koch (*Schrift*, 117 n. 11) thinks that the omission of ἐνώπιον αὐτῶν could well antedate Paul on the basis of a supposed link with the subsequent addition of καὶ εἰς θήραν, which he regards as pre-Pauline. Why one should assume a connection between the two changes is nowhere stated.

previous citation (Rom 11.8).[269] But even this explanation leads to no firm conclusions. In sum, the textual evidence makes a Pauline origin likely, but the reason for the change remains entirely unclear.

E   Adding καὶ εἰς θήραν. Though the manuscript evidence is quite secure,[270] the source of the addition of καὶ εἰς θήραν in Rom 11.9 is difficult to determine. The influence of LXX idiom is likely: παγίς and θήρα occur as a pair in Ps 34.8, 123.6–7, Prov 11.8–9, and Hos 5.1–2, though never in the precise combination found in Rom 11.9.[271] At the same time, none of these examples is close enough to the present passage to suggest direct influence. Assimilation to the Hebrew is also unlikely.[272] Apart from a possible intensifying effect, no clear reason for a Pauline addition can be discerned. In fact, the text would appear to have been quite serviceable to Paul in its original form.[273] Whether the addition of καὶ εἰς θήραν reflects an intentional alteration, a variant text, or a faulty citation from memory[274] simply cannot be determined from current evidence.

[269] Koch (*Schrift*, 138) compares the shift to αὐτοῖς with what he sees as a similar use of the Dative with σκάνδαλον in 1 Cor 1.23 (Ἰουδαίοις μὲν σκάνδαλον). The usefulness of this observation is muted, however, by the way in which καὶ εἰς σκάνδαλον is arrayed alongside three other prepositional phrases in the present context. As for the suggestion that the Dative form arose under the influence of v. 8, see the comments above on the possibility of a reverse influence in the insertion of τοῦ before the infinitives in the prior verse. Other places where Paul appears to have created such verbal links between his citations include Rom 9.25–6, 1 Cor 3.19–20, 1 Cor 15.54–5, and Gal 3.10, 13.

[270] Within the Pauline tradition, the additional phrase is absent only in 73 syr^sch aeth. Assimilation to the LXX is assured in these cases: the same manuscripts also reverse καὶ εἰς ἀνταπόδομα and καὶ εἰς σκάνδαλον. The possibility that the Pauline wording reflects an earlier reading from which καὶ εἰς θήραν later dropped out in the course of transmission (by parablepsis?) is belied by the unified nature of the LXX evidence.

[271] It is interesting to note that whereas παγίς and σκάνδαλον can be found together in the LXX as here (see Josh 23.13, Ps 139.5, 140.9, Wis 14.11, 1 Macc 5.4), θήρα and σκάνδαλον never appear in the same context.

[272] Only the translation of וּלְשִׁלּוּמִים by ἀνταπόδοσιν (reading וּלְשִׁלּוּמִים instead of וְלִשְׁלוֹמִים) is at all unusual. The Greek words παγίς and σκάνδαλον are regularly used to render the Hebrew פַּח and מוֹקֵשׁ, respectively, while θήρα never translates either of these words in the LXX.

[273] Noted by Koch, *Schrift*, 138.

[274] As argued by Kautzsch, 50, who sees the influence of Ps 34.8 here.

C Reversing the order of καὶ εἰς σκάνδαλον and καὶ εἰς ἀνταπόδομα.[275] Here again a textually secure Pauline reading offers
little clue as to its own background or purpose. The importance
of the σκάνδαλ- word-group to Paul's analysis of the Jewish
response to the Christian gospel (see Rom 9.33 in the present
discussion) has caused some to see here an attempt to lend a
measure of emphasis to the phrase καὶ εἰς σκάνδαλον.[276] To
communicate this sort of stress, however, the normal procedure
would be to move καὶ εἰς σκάνδαλον to the head of the list.
Only a reader familiar with the LXX wording of Ps 68.23 would
see any stress at all in the placement of καὶ εἰς σκάνδαλον
ahead of καὶ εἰς ἀνταπόδομα. A more likely solution would see
in the reversal an attempt to create a more natural rhetorical
transition to the next part of the citation. In this view, placing
καὶ εἰς ἀνταπόδομα at the end of the list in v. 9 gives the hearer
a subtle cue that the description of the blinding and sub-
jugation of Israel in v. 10 is to be understood in terms of divine
retribution, much as the previous citation attributed the spiritual blindness of Israel to the activity of God himself.[277] If this is
the meaning of the reversal, then the present word order clearly
goes back to Paul himself. The proposal remains speculative,
however, and the possibility of a variant text or a faulty
memory cannot be ruled out.

E Substitution of ἀνταπόδομα for ἀνταπόδοσιν. Somewhat surprisingly, both the LXX and Pauline traditions stand solidly
behind their divergent readings at this point. Any difference in
sense between the two words is minimal: the original distinction
between verbal action/abstraction (-σις suffix) and result (-μα
suffix) is regularly obscured in Hellenistic Greek. But the
distinction has not disappeared entirely, and the Pauline
ἀνταπόδομα is certainly a better parallel for the concrete nouns
in v. 9 than the verbal/abstract form ἀνταπόδοσις. Whether
this reading reflects an intentional stylistic improvement, an
independent translation, or a memory slip is impossible to say.
Nothing in the choice of words offers any guidance as to

---

[275] Here again a very small part of the Pauline evidence restores the order of the
LXX text. Tischendorf gives the evidence as F G 73 116 n^scr syr^sch aeth Dam.
[276] So Koch, *Schrift*, 106, 137–8.
[277] On the importance of such cues in an oral society, see Achtemeier, 17–25.

whether the use of ἀνταπόδομα might go back to Paul himself.[278]

(35)   **Rom 11.26–7** (= Isa 59.20–1, Isa 27.9)

Paul: [ ] ἥξει ἐκ Σιων ὁ ῥυόμενος, [ ] ἀποστρέψει ἀσεβείας ἀπὸ
        Ἰακωβ. καὶ αὕτη αὐτοῖς ἡ παρ᾽ ἐμοῦ διαθήκη, + ὅταν
        ἀφέλωμαι <u>τὰς ἁμαρτίας αὐτῶν</u>.

Isa 59.20–1$_{LXX}$: καὶ ἥξει ἕνεκεν Σιων ὁ ῥυόμενος καὶ ἀποστρέψει
        ἀσεβείας ἀπὸ Ἰακωβ. καὶ αὕτη αὐτοῖς ἡ παρ᾽ ἐμοῦ διαθήκη,
        [εἶπεν κύριος· τὸ πνεῦμα τὸ ἐμόν, ὅ ἐστιν ἐπὶ σοί, καὶ τὰ
        ῥήματα, ἃ ἔδωκα εἰς τὸ στόμα σου.]

Isa 27.9$_{LXX}$: [διὰ τοῦτο ἀφαιρεθήσεται ἡ ἀνομία Ἰακωβ, καὶ
        τοῦτο ἐστιν ἡ εὐλογία αὐτοῦ,] ὅταν ἀφέλωμαι αὐτοῦ τὴν
        ἁμαρτίαν, [ὅταν θῶσιν πάντας τοὺς λίθους τῶν βωμῶν
        κατακεκομμένους ὡς κονίαν λεπτήν.]

B   <u>Omission of initial καί</u>.   Unlike most other instances, the
    omission of καί at the beginning of Rom 11.26 has a measure of
    support in the LXX tradition (A*? and the Lucianic manu-
    scripts 90-130-311). Still, the evidence is weak and open to
    question, and might reflect the influence of Rom 11.26. In view
    of Paul's usual practice of dropping initial particles,[279] it seems
    likely that the omission of καί in Rom 11.26 goes back to Paul
    himself.

T   <u>Substitution of ἐκ for ἕνεκεν</u>.   Commentators have often
    noted that there is nothing in the present context to indicate
    that Paul attributed any significance to the preposition ἐκ in his
    quotation from Isa 59.20.[280] The total absence of any "Zion"

---

[278] The only other occurrence of either word in the Pauline corpus is in Col 3.24,
where the form ἀνταπόδοσις appears.

[279] On the regular omission of initial particles in Pauline citations, see note 197.

[280] In fact, the preposition ἕνεκεν would appear to be better suited to Paul's point
here. As Berndt Schaller puts it, "Dem Apostel geht es doch um den Nachweis, dass
Israel, dass Gottesvolk, vom eschatologicalischen Heil nicht ausgeschlossen ist. Dass
das Heil vom Zion kommt, spielt in diesem Zusammenhang keine Rolle" ("ΗΞΕΙ ΕΚ
ΣΙΩΝ Ο ΡΥΟΜΕΝΟΣ: Zur Textgestalt von Jes 59.20f. in Rom 11.26f.," in Pietersma
and Cox (eds.), *De Septuaginta*, 203. Still, a variety of interpreters have sought to
uncover a Pauline motive for the shift from ἕνεκεν to ἐκ. Typical is E. E. Ellis (*Use*,
123 n. 5), who finds here a contrast between "Zion" (= "true Israel") and "Jacob" (=
"national Israel") in which the church is viewed as the locus from which "the
Redeemer" goes forth. Dietrich-Alex Koch offers a similar solution, though he traces
the concept and the change in wording to the pre-Pauline Christian community
(*Schrift*, 176). Both authors overlook the substantial evidence for Jewish expectation
of a coming deliverance of God's people ἐκ Σιων (see below).

theme in Paul's theology (the word occurs only here and in Rom 9.33, both in citations) points in the same direction.[281] Establishing the origin of this ἐκ, on the other hand, is more difficult. Within the LXX tradition, the Pauline wording finds support in a handful of minuscules, the Bohairic Coptic version, and quotes by Epiphanius, Hilary, and Jerome.[282] Though assimilation to Rom 11.26 is the most obvious explanation, the possibility that these manuscripts might preserve valuable evidence for the reading of Paul's biblical text cannot be overlooked. The LXX rendering of the Hebrew in Isa 59.20 (ἕνεκεν for לְ) is unique unless its *Vorlage* differed from the Masoretic text,[283] and an early "correction" of this unusual LXX reading toward a Hebrew text that read מִצִּיּוֹן (instead of the Masoretic לְצִיּוֹן) is not out of the question.[284] The expectation that Yahweh would bring salvation to his people and establish his rule ἐκ Σιων is expressed in a variety of LXX contexts.[285] This same expectation is clearly presupposed in the ἐκ Σιων of Rom 11.26. Whether the variant entered the tradition at the level of the Hebrew text (rendering an underlying מִצִּיּוֹן)[286]

---

[281] Noted by de Waard, *Study*, 12 n. 1.

[282] The minuscules are 22ᶜ–93 564* 407 534. Koch (*Schrift*, 176 n. 23) points out a number of places where one or another of these manuscripts seems to show the influence of the Pauline citations. The agreements are all minor and quite scattered, however, and there is nothing to indicate that the same has occurred here.

[283] The preposition ἕνεκεν translates several Hebrew words in the LXX of Isaiah (eight times לְמַעַן, but also בְּ, בְּלִי, יַעַן, עֵקֶב, and לְבִלְתִּי one time each), but never לְ. The sole occurrence of לְמַעַן צִיּוֹן (Isa 62.1) is rendered διὰ Σιων. The phrase ἕνεκεν Σιων appears nowhere else in the LXX. The explanation put forward by Berndt Schaller (see note 280), that an original εἰς (itself a Hebraizing "correction" of the LXX's ἕνεκεν) was corrupted to ἐκ in the course of transmission (in uncial characters, EIC → EK), founders on the observation that לְצִיּוֹן is never translated by εἰς Σιων in the entire LXX. In the three other places where it appears in Isaiah (41.27, 51.16, 52.7), לְצִיּוֹן is rendered simply by Σιων, without any preposition or article. Aquila and Symmachus show a similar practice in translating the phrase as τῇ Σιών in Isa 59.20.

[284] For every occurrence of ἐκ Σιων in the LXX, the MT reads מִצִּיּוֹן (Ps 13.7, 49.2, 109.2, 127.5, 133.3, Amos 1.2, Mic 4.2, Joel 4.16, Isa 2.3, 52.7). In a similar way, Symmachus "corrects" the LXX rendering of מִצִּיּוֹן in Jer 9.19 from ἐν to ἐκ to accord with the Masoretic reading. Kittel offered a similar conjecture in his *Biblia Hebraica*, as did B. Duhm in *Das Buch Jesaia* (Göttingen: Vandenhoeck und Ruprecht, 1892), 417–18 (cf. 5th edition (1968), 446). Schaller ("Textgestalt," 202 n. 1) dismisses Duhm's suggestion with the simple assertion that it "trifft allerdings kaum zu."

[285] See Ps 13.7, 49.2 (where ἥξει is used as here), 52.7, 109.2, Mic 4.2/Isa 2.3, Joel 4.16 (cf. Amos 1.2). The same idea is conveyed in the expression ἐξ ὄρους Σιων in 4 Kgdms 19.31/Isa 37.32, Obad 21.

[286] This explanation is surely preferable to that of de Waard (11–12), who suggests that the reading אֶל צִיּוֹן (found in 1QIsᵃ) lies behind both Greek renderings. Accord-

or as an inner-Greek "correction" meant to reflect contemporary eschatological expectation can no longer be determined. In either case, it appears that the substitution of ἐκ for ἕνεκεν in Rom 11.26 had already taken place in Paul's Greek *Vorlage*.

D   Omission of second καί. Though a number of witnesses add καί before ἀποστρέψει in Rom 11.26, the strength of the evidence for the omission suggests that the Pauline text has been assimilated to the wording of the LXX in these instances.[287] The effect on the sense is minimal in either case, and a textual explanation cannot be wholly excluded. Still, it is worth noting that eliminating the καί creates a more nearly parallel relationship between the first two clauses, foreclosing the possibility that the second clause might be understood as following temporally or logically after the first.[288] This view of the relation between the two clauses is consistent with a Christian interpretation that would see the divine promise to "turn away ungodly deeds from Jacob" as being fulfilled in the very "coming" of the "Redeemer," Jesus Christ (cf. Rom 1.18, 4.5, 5.6).[289] Whether this was the actual reason for the omission, however, can no longer be determined. If the omission of the introductory καί is to be traced to Paul, then this secondary omission might well go back to him, too. In the absence of further evidence, however, the origin of the present reading must remain uncertain.

D   Conflated citation: substituting ὅταν ... αὐτῶν for εἶπεν κύριος κτλ. Though the description of the divine διαθήκη as

---

ing to de Waard, both the LXX translator and Paul's *Vorlage* interpreted this אֶל in the sense of עַל, "on account of, because of," echoing the common confusion between אֶל and עַל in the Hebrew tradition. What one translator sought to express by ἕνεκεν, the other rendered by ἐκ. Apart from the unnecessary complexity of this explanation, it is difficult to imagine why any translator would have rendered an original אֶל in a sense other than the obvious "to" (εἰς, πρός, etc.) in the context of Isa 59.20. It is also worth noting that neither אֶל nor עַל appears with צִיּוֹן anywhere else in Isaiah, and that nowhere in the entire LXX does ἐκ Σιων translate the Hebrew אֶל/עַל צִיּוֹן.

[287] Tischendorf cites D^b et ^c E L *al pler* syr^utr cop arm d e f g vg Or Chr Thdrt Hil Ambst etc. as adding καί here, over against ℵ A B C D* 39 47 80 aeth Euthal Dam which omit it. Kautzsch (82) traces both this reading and the infinitive ἀποστρέψαι (found in F G go) to a desire to avoid the asyndeton of the majority reading. The LXX tradition is united in reading καί ἀποστρέψει in Isa 59.20.

[288] A similar omission of καί for the sake of rhetorical parallelism can be seen in Rom 11.3.

[289] So Koch, *Schrift*, 175–7.

a "taking away of sins" echoes Christian soteriological formulations, the presence of similar language in Jer 38 (31).31–4 and
Ezek 37.23–6 counsels caution in assuming a Christian background for the conflation of Isa 27.9 with Isa 59.21 in Rom
11.27. The primary hindrance to a Pauline origin lies in the
stress placed here on the word διαθήκη, which plays a surprisingly limited role in Paul's theology.[290] The plural ἁμαρτίαι is
also uncommon in Paul, while the idea of "taking away sins"
appears almost exclusively in quotations (Rom 4.7–8) and
traditional formulae (1 Cor 15.3, Gal 1.4, Col 1.14).[291] The
evidence of the context is inconclusive. The basic "problem" of
Israel is described in various ways in Rom 9–11 – "hardness"
(11.7, 25), "unbelief" (10.16, 11.20, 23, 30–2), reliance on
"works of law" (9.32, 10.2–3), "transgression" (11.11–12), etc. –
but never as one of "sins" that need to be "taken away." On the
other hand, it might be inferred from the verses immediately
following the citation (11.30–2) that Paul viewed the "unbelief"
of Israel as its fundamental "sin" that would at last be set aside
in the demonstration of God's abundant mercy. In view of the
eschatological context of Isa 27, it is easy to see why Isa 27.9
would have seemed an attractive choice to depict this "spiritual" aspect of the final restoration of Israel anticipated in
11.26. But the verbal similarities between Isa 59.20–1 and Isa
27.9 could easily have led another interpreter (whether Jewish
or Christian) to the same combination.[292] The fact that not one
of the deviations from the LXX in Rom 11.27 can be attributed
with confidence to Paul lends support to the latter explanation,
as do a number of tensions between the wording of the citation
and its use in Rom 11.[293] Though it remains possible that the

---

[290] The notion of a "new" covenant in Christ comes to expression in Paul's letters
only in 1 Cor 11.25 (where it reflects traditional language), 2 Cor 3.6, 14 (where the
idea is presupposed rather than developed), and Gal 4.24 (again presupposed). The
legal analogy in Gal 3.15, 17 does not enter into account here, and the plurals in Rom
9.4 and Eph 2.12 refer to the biblical covenants with Israel.

[291] The idea is implied but not stated in 1 Cor 15.17 and Eph 2.1. In other places,
the plural is used to describe the condition of those outside the faith, with no direct
mention of "forgiveness" (Rom 7.5, 1 Thess 2.16; cf. 1 Tim 5.22, 24, 2 Tim 3.6). So
also Berndt Schaller, "Textgestalt," 206.

[292] Isa 59.20–21: ἀποστρέψει ἀσεβείας ἀπὸ Ἰακωβ. καὶ αὕτη αὐτοῖς ἡ παρ' ἐμοῦ
διαθήκη ...
Isa 27.9: ἀφαιρεθήσεται ἡ ἀνομία Ἰακωβ. καὶ τοῦτό ἐστιν ἡ εὐλογία αὐτοῦ ...

[293] In addition to the retention of the apparently irrelevant ἐκ Σιων, Koch points
out an apparent discrepancy as to when the "coming" is viewed as taking place (in the

combination of Isa 59.20–1 and Isa 27.9 was original with Paul, it seems more likely that Paul has appropriated a traditional prooftext from either the Jewish synagogue (reflecting common "Messianic" expectations) or Jewish Christian apologetics (depicting Jesus as the promised "Redeemer" of Israel), which he then used to express his own expectation that Israel would be fully restored at the future return of Jesus Christ, the "Redeemer."[294]

D   Conversion of τὴν ἁμαρτίαν from singular to plural. As noted above, the use of the plural form of ἁμαρτία is uncommon in Paul, and the idea of "taking away sins" finds little place in his theology. The fact that both traditions stand united behind their respective readings suggests that the wording of Isa 27.9 has been adapted here, but the origin of the adaptation is presumably to be sought in pre-Pauline Jewish or Christian usage (see above).

D   Converting pronoun from αὐτοῦ to αὐτῶν. The united testimony of the various textual traditions and the obvious conflict with the singular αὐτοῦ in Isa 27.9a make it clear that shift to the plural αὐτῶν in Rom 11.27 represents an adaptation of the biblical text. The reason for the change is equally obvious: the plural pronoun was needed to produce a smooth reading alongside the αὐτοῖς of Isa 59.20–1. In other words, the adaptation was required to knit the two biblical passages together into one. Unfortunately, the question of who first combined Isa 27.9 with Isa 59.20–1 to create the present "citation" remains enveloped in mystery (see above). Consequently, the same reservations must be voiced regarding the possible Pauline origin of this reading as for the combination as a whole.

E   Shifting αὐτοῦ/αὐτῶν to final position. A handful of LXX witnesses agree with Paul in placing the pronoun at the end of

Christ-event or at some future date), plus the fact that Paul nowhere speaks (as in Isa 59.21) of a "new covenant" with Israel *per se* (*Schrift*, 177–8).

[294] Koch's view (*Schrift*, 177), that Paul has taken a traditional form of Isa 59.20–1 and joined it himself with Isa 27.9 in Rom 11.26–7, fails on two counts: his belief that the shift from ἕνεκεν to ἐκ in Rom 11.26 represents a pre-Pauline Christian adaptation, and his failure to recognize the inconsistencies between Isa 27.9 and Paul's chosen modes of expression.

the present clause in Isa 27.9.[295] Assimilation to the wording of either Rom 11.27 or the Hebrew is unlikely: none of the texts contains any of the plural forms introduced in Rom 11.27, and all of them follow the LXX for the remainder of the verse despite its significant deviations from the Masoretic Hebrew. The same word order appears in Symmachus and Theodotion, but here a major revision of the entire verse toward the Masoretic text is in view.[296] Whether a scribe or interpreter has simply returned αὐτοῦ to its proper position in the sentence, as Koch suggests,[297] or whether the reading should be traced to a memory slip or a copying error in the author's Greek *Vorlage* remains entirely unclear.

(36)   **Rom 12.19** (= Deut 32.35)[298]

Paul: ἐμοὶ ἐκδίκησις, ἐγὼ ἀνταποδώσω, λέγει κύριος.
LXX: ἐν ἡμέρᾳ ἐκδικήσεως ἀνταποδώσω,
         [ἐν καιρῷ, ὅταν σφαλῇ ὁ ποὺς αὐτῶν.]
MT: לִי נָקָם וְשִׁלֵּם

T   Substitution of ἐμοὶ ἐκδίκησις ἐγὼ ἀνταποδώσω for ἐν ἡμέρᾳ ἐκδικήσεως ἀνταποδώσω.[299]   The wording of Rom 12.19 has been cited by many as evidence that Paul resorted at least occasionally to the Hebrew original to "correct" particularly egregious errors in the LXX rendering of the biblical text.[300]

[295] The witnesses are the Hexaplaric MS 88, the Syrohexapla, and the marginal reading of Catena MS 377.

[296] See the readings in the Göttingen volume on *Isaias*.

[297] *Schrift*, 109, appealing to BDF § 284. Koch attributes the change to Paul himself, on the assumption that Paul would have felt free to shift the placement of the word once he had already intruded into the text (in Koch's view) to alter its number. The questionable nature of such an assumption is obvious.

[298] Though there is no doubt that the words of Rom 11.34–5 were taken directly from the biblical text (= Isa 40.13 + Job 41.3), this combined citation has been omitted from the present study in accordance with strict guidelines that limit the investigation to passages that offer explicit indication to the reader that a citation is being offered (introductory formula, interpretive comments, etc.). The same is true for Rom 12.16 (= Prov 3.7) and 12.17 (= Prov 3.4).

[299] The plural ἐκδικήσεις is read in Rom 12.19 by the uncials A F G and a citation from Origen, according to Tischendorf. Though somewhat unusual, the plural is not without parallel in the LXX (see 2 Kgdms 22.48, Ps 17.48, 93.1, Ezek 14.21, 16.41, 23.10, 25.17), where it usually refers to specific "acts" of vengeance. As nothing in the Pauline context would require the plural and the reading has no foundation in the LXX, an aural error in the course of transmission offers perhaps the best explanation for this very limited evidence.

[300] E.g. Ellis, *Use*, 14 n. 6.

The weighty arguments against this interpretation of the evidence were considered and rejected in chapter 3. More helpful in the present situation are the often-noted similarities between the wording of Rom 12.19 and the texts of Symmachus and the Aramaic Targumim to Deut 32.35.[301] All three appear to presuppose a Hebrew text on the order of וְאֲשַׁלֵּם לִי נָקָם, which differs from the Masoretic text in reading a first-person rather than a third-person form (שִׁלֵּם) for the final word. The same first-person form is presupposed in the wording of the LXX (note ἀνταποδώσω), which seems to have read לְיוֹם instead of לִי at the beginning of the verse.[302] Prior to the discoveries at Qumran, it was common to trace these scattered agreements to a common oral tradition in which the wording of Deut 32.35 had taken on something of a proverbial usage.[303] With the discovery that the Old Greek text went through a number of revisions intended to bring it closer to this or that Hebrew text, however, a clearer picture has emerged. Now the Pauline wording can be understood as a literal reproduction of a Greek text that had been revised to bring it into line with a Hebrew text that contained the same first person singular form of שׁלם that appears in Symmachus and the Targumim.[304] The question of whether Paul might have added the emphatic ἐγώ himself or dropped out a medial καί for rhetorical effect (cf. Symmachus and the Targumim) cannot be answered without more precise information as to the wording of Paul's *Vorlage*.[305] For the bulk of its deviations from the LXX and the

[301] Symmachus[Syh] = *mihi ultio et retribuam*

Targum Onkelos = קדמי פורענותא ואנא אשלים

Targum Fragment = דידי היא נקמתא ואנא הוא די משלים

[302] Unless, as has sometimes been suggested, the LXX translator somehow read the לִי of his *Vorlage* as an abbreviation for לְיוֹם. The LXX tradition shows no trace of any reading corresponding to the לִי of the MT. The Samaritan version supplies the only other evidence for the LXX reading.

[303] See Kautzsch, 77; Toy, 162; and surprisingly Koch, *Schrift*, 77–8, 95. Koch offers little evidence for his contention that Paul quoted from memory a form of Deut 32.35 that circulated orally (having "die Form eines kurzen und sehr prägnanten Logions") in early Christian circles.

[304] Hans Vollmer (30–2) had already reached the same conclusion nearly a century ago by a more circuitous route. Accepting the common identification of "Onkelos" with Aquila, Vollmer argued that Paul's reading reflected the wording of Aquila's Greek text (as preserved in the Targum Onkelos), which was itself dependent on an earlier Greek revision of the LXX. The actual reading of Aquila's text at this point is unknown.

[305] The LXX tradition shows no trace of the ἐγώ that appears in all of the manuscripts of Rom 12.19. Some of the versions (primarily the Coptic and Arme-

Masoretic Hebrew traditions, however, the quotation in Rom 12.19 would appear to have a solid textual basis.

B   Adding λέγει κύριος. The origin and significance of this insertion are difficult to unravel, and may well lie beyond the reach of modern scholarship. The phrase λέγει κύριος appears five times in the Pauline corpus, each time as an addition to the wording of a biblical quotation. In Rom 14.11 and 2 Cor 6.18, the addition appears as part of a brief excerpt from a specific verse in the LXX; in Rom 12.19, 1 Cor 14.21, and 2 Cor 6.17, the insertion is entirely gratuitous. Similar additions can be seen in Acts 7.49 and sixteen times in the Apostolic Fathers, most of them in Epistle of Barnabas.[306] A reliable explanation for the insertions is hard to find. On the textual side, the Pauline passages all diverge substantially from the wording of the LXX, but only Rom 12.19 and 1 Cor 14.21 show signs of having been drawn from any but the "standard" LXX version of the Greek text. The themes and contexts of the citations are likewise quite diverse.[307] The phrase appears often in the LXX version of the prophetic literature, though the witnesses are often divided as to its proper placement.[308] The words are wholly absent from the LXX of Deuteronomy, however, which makes a textual explanation rather unlikely in the case of Rom 12.19. One approach that might explain both the fluctuating LXX evidence and the occasional Christian uses would be to

nian, plus small portions of the Old Latin and Syriac) add a connective καί to Rom 12.19, but none of the Greek manuscripts contains it. The fact that the identical wording appears in Heb 10.30 (with ἐγώ and without καί) is of no help in the present instance, as the citation there could reflect familiarity with the Epistle to the Romans or the use of an identical *Vorlage*.

[306] The instances in the Apostolic Fathers are noted by David Aune in *Prophecy in Early Christianity and the Ancient Mediterranean World* (Grand Rapids: Eerdmans, 1983), 343. In Aune's view, "The *legei kurios* formula is simply a useful way of identifying God as speaker when that is not obvious" (344). Though such a simple solution has an obvious appeal, Aune offers no explanation as to why the phrase should have been appended to these particular first-person quotations and not to others where the identity of the speaker might be in doubt (e.g. Rom 4.17, 4.18, 9.12, 9.13, 9.15, etc.). The occurrences in Acts 15.17 and Heb 8.8–12 (three times), 10.16, 10.30 (?) (cf. λέγει ὁ θεός in Acts 2.17) all follow the wording of the LXX, except that the Hebrews passages have λέγει where the LXX reads φησίν.

[307] Contra Ellis, *Use*, 107–10, who seeks to unite the texts under the thematic umbrella of the "testimony-book" hypothesis.

[308] The primary witnesses are divided over the inclusion of the words in Amos 3.15, 5.25, 6.15, 8.3, Hag 1.6, Zech 1.3, Mal 1.2, Isa 39.6, 66.1, Jer 2.9, 3.2, 5.11, 9.24, 23.16, 23.23, 23.29, Ezek 12.28, 24.20, 25.14, 28.10, 33.20, 36.23, 36.32, 37.28.

assume that the frequency of the phrase in the prophetic literature had given rise to a practice of adding λέγει κύριος to oral
renderings of "prophetic" passages of Scripture in order to
emphasize the divine authority inherent in the original pronouncement, a practice that eventually left its mark on the
textual tradition of the LXX.[309] Such a reading of the evidence
would be highly speculative at this point, however, and thus
beyond the rather strict parameters of the present study. In the
final analysis, it seems safe to say that the insertion in Rom
12.19 probably goes back to Paul himself, while leaving open
the question of its historical background and significance.

(37)   **Rom 13.9a** (= Deut 5.17–21)[310]

Paul: **οὐ μοιχεύσεις, οὐ φονεύσεις, οὐ κλέψεις,** [ ] οὐκ ἐπιθυμήσεις / /.

LXX: οὐ μοιχεύσεις. οὐ φονεύσεις. οὐ κλέψεις. οὐ ψευδομαρτυρήσεις κατὰ τοῦ πλησίον σου μαρτυρίαν ψευδῆ. οὐκ
ἐπιθυμήσεις τὴν γυναῖκα τοῦ πλησίον σου. οὐκ ἐπιθυμήσεις τὴν οἰκίαν τοῦ πλησίον σου οὔτε τὸν παῖδα αὐτοῦ
οὔτε ...

V   Reading <u>οὐ μοιχεύσεις, οὐ φονεύσεις, οὐ κλέψεις</u> in place of
<u>various other possible arrangements.</u>[311]   The textual con-
fusion surrounding the order of the prohibitions in the LXX
text of Exod 20.13–15 and Deut 5.17–19 is well-known, and

[309] Though its significance is unclear, it is interesting to note that the only instance
of an added λέγει κύριος in the NT outside the orally dictated letters of Paul occurs
in a speech attributed to the martyr Stephen in Acts 7.49 (cf. λέγει ὁ θεός in the
speech of Peter in Acts 2.17). The approach suggested here differs from that of E. E.
Ellis (*Use*, 109–12), who sees in such passages the influence of early Christian
prophets who sometimes added the phrase λέγει κύριος to their own biblical
paraphrases. In place of purely hypothetical appeals to early Christian prophets and
"testimony-books," the present explanation stresses the known influence of the
written biblical text on both the Jewish and Christian communities. Ellis's explanation is roundly criticized by David Aune in *Prophecy*, 339–46.
[310] The apparently verbatim citation of Prov 25.21–2 in Rom 12.20 has been
omitted from the present study in accordance with strict guidelines that limit the
investigation to passages that offer explicit indication to the reader that a citation is
being offered (introductory formula, interpretive comments, etc.). The intrusion of
ἀλλά at the beginning of the verse and the shift to third-person combine to give the
appearance of a return to direct speech, while the same factors make it impossible to
regard v. 20 as a continuation of the citation in v. 19.
[311] Apart from several manuscripts that add οὐ ψευδομαρτυρήσεις after οὐ
κλέψεις (see below), the word order in Rom 13.9a is textually secure.

need not be rehearsed here. All that matters for the present study is to note that Paul in Rom 13.9a follows one traditional order, apparently that of Deuteronomy, over various other possible arrangements.[312] In view of the likelihood that these variant phrasings go back to divergent local customs and not simple scribal error, the chances seem good that Rom 13.9a preserves the order in which Paul himself originally learned the Decalogue.

A Omission of οὐ ψευδομαρτυρήσεις κτλ.. Despite the diversity of the LXX tradition at this point (see above), nothing in the LXX manuscripts offers any support for the idea that the omission of the eighth commandment in Rom 13.9a might be textually based.[313] As Dietrich-Alex Koch observes, Paul himself makes it clear that he is offering only a selection from the Decalogue with his subsequent comment καὶ εἴ τις ἑτέρα ἐντολή,[314] though it remains unclear why he should have omitted this commandment and included the next. The fact that the omission goes back to Paul remains clear in any case.

O Omission of τήν γυναῖκα κτλ. after οὐκ ἐπιθυμήσεις. Here again LXX support for the Pauline omission is entirely lacking, but this time an explanation is ready at hand. Citing a study by Klaus Berger on the use of the Decalogue in early Judaism,

[312] Even in Deuteronomy the textual evidence is divided, with B V 963 b d n⁻¹²⁷ t 407′ Chr Hipp ᴸᵃᵗAmbst Ruf Aeth Arm Sa supporting the Pauline order and A F M O C f s y z placing οὐ φονεύσεις ahead of οὐ μοιχεύσεις. As the latter reading would appear to reflect assimilation to the MT, the former is most likely original. A small part of the evidence for Exod 20.13–15 follows the Deuteronomy order (the upcoming Göttingen edition of Exodus, kindly supplied by Dr. John William Wevers, lists C′-422 125 n⁻¹²⁷ 30′ x and a quotation from Philo), but assimilation appears likely here as well. A thorough study of the order of these three commandments in various literary traditions is Richard Freund, "Murder, Adultery, or Theft?" *SJOT* 2 (1989), 72–80.

[313] A number of Pauline manuscripts and some of the versions (the uncials ℵ Ψ 048, the minuscules 81 88 104 326 330 365 436 451 629 1506 1962 1984ᶜ 2127, a sizeable part of the Old Latin evidence, the Syrohexapla, and the Bohairic, Armenian, and Ethiopic versions) add the shortened form οὐ ψευδομαρτυρήσεις here (as in Matt 19.18; Mark 10.19 and Luke 18.20 read μή ψευδομαρτυρήσῃς, as does the uncial P in Rom 13.9), but this is surely a later insertion intended to fill a perceived gap in the Pauline text. The evidence for the omission includes 𝔭⁴⁶, the uncials A B D F G L, a variety of minuscules, a significant portion of the Old Latin evidence, the Syriac Peshitta, and the Sahidic and Gothic versions.

[314] *Schrift*, 116–17. It is this comment also that allows the text to be included in the present study, as as the verse offers no other indication that the words were intended as a citation.

Dietrich-Alex Koch argues that "when he abbreviates Deut 5.21 by summing up the last two commandments under a general injunction against covetousness, Paul is accommodating himself to a Hellenistic Jewish tradition of interpretation."[315] Since the Pauline context offers no other reason for the omission, it seems best to follow Koch in tracing this aspect of Paul's language to the influence of a common Jewish oral tradition.

(38)   **Rom 13.9b** (= Lev 19.18)

U⁻   Apart from the fact that both traditions show a measure of fluctuation between σεαυτόν and ἑαυτόν,[316] the Pauline text appears to represent a precise rendering of the standard LXX wording.

(39)   **Rom 14.11** (= Isa 45.23)

Paul: <u>ζῶ ἐγώ λέγει κύριος</u>, ὅτι ἐμοὶ κάμψει πᾶν γόνυ καὶ <u>πᾶσα γλῶσσα</u> ἐξομολογήσεται τῷ θεῷ.

LXX: κατ' ἐμαυτοῦ ὀμνύω Ἦ μὴν ἐξελεύσεται ἐκ τοῦ στόματός μου δικαιοσύνη, οἱ λόγοι μου οὐκ ἀποστραφήσονται ὅτι ἐμοὶ κάμψει πᾶν γόνυ καὶ ἐξομολογήσεται πᾶσα γλῶσσα τῷ θεῷ.

A   <u>Substitution of ζῶ ἐγώ λέγει κύριος for κατ' ἐμαυτοῦ ὀμνύω ... ἀποστραφήσονται.</u> The unanimous readings of both textual traditions make it highly unlikely that the words ζῶ ἐγώ λέγει κύριος found in Rom 14.11 ever appeared in any written text of Isa 45.23. Evidence for a pre-Pauline Christian origin is also lacking.[317] The phrase ζῶ ἐγώ occurs some twenty-two times in the LXX, fifteen times with the words λέγει κύριος, while the third-person form ζῇ κύριος appears

---

[315] *Schrift*, 117. On Berger's study, see note 57 on Rom 7.7.

[316] In the LXX tradition, ἑαυτόν is found only in minuscules, including the majority of the Catena texts, a minority of the Hexaplaric evidence, the entire b family, samplings from the d f n s t x y z groups, and a handful of mixed codices. On the Pauline side, the same reading appears in the uncials F G L N* P, a number of minuscules, and citations from Chr Thphyl Oec. In both cases the external evidence is weighted heavily in favor of σεαυτόν.

[317] The reformulation of Isa 45.23 in Phil 2.6–11 contains no hint of such an oath formula.

an additional forty-three times.[318] Had Paul wanted to substitute a shorter expression for the more cumbersome κατ' ἐμαυτοῦ ὀμνύω κτλ. of Isa 45.23, it is easy to understand how this one might have come to mind. Questions remain, however, as to why he did not simply omit the middle portion of the verse and retain the initial κατ' ἐμαυτοῦ ὀμνύω, a move that would have made exactly the same point as the wording that appears in Rom 14.11. Perhaps he meant to replace an unusual expression with a more common one,[319] or to call forth echoes of a specific passage in which the new expression occurred.[320] Otherwise, the substitution might reflect the influence of biblical language on the oral reproduction of Scripture in the synagogue,[321] or even a simple memory error.[322] Whatever his purpose, there is little reason to think that the change goes back to anyone but Paul himself. Whether the substitution occurred intentionally or by accident, however, can no longer be determined.

B Advancing πᾶσα γλῶσσα ahead of ἐξομολογήσεται. The LXX tradition is united in placing πᾶσα γλῶσσα after the verb, and a number of Pauline manuscripts and versions follow this LXX reading.[323] Still, inherent probability favors the non-LXX order as original in Rom 14.11, and the strength of

---

[318] The occurrences of ζῶ ἐγώ are concentrated in the book of Ezekiel (16 of 22 instances), with additional instances in Num 14.21, 28, Zeph 2.9, Isa 49.18, Jer 22.24, 26.18. The more common ζῇ κύριος is found primarily in the books of Kingdoms (30 of 43 instances), with occurrences also in 2 Chr 18.13, Job 27.1, Ps 17.46, Amos 8.14 (*bis*), and Jer 4.2, 5.2, 12.16, 16.14, 16.15, 23.7, 23.8, 51.26.

[319] First-person uses of ὀμνύω by Yahweh are common in the LXX, but the expression κατ' ἐμαυτοῦ ὀμνύω is not (Gen 22.16, Jer 22.5, 29.13; cf. Jer 51.26). Second- and third-person forms are equally rare, appearing only in Deut 9.27 and Amos 6.8 (cf. Amos 4.2, 8.7, Isa 62.8, Jer 28.14, 51.26, where a different object follows after κατά). The phrase appears to be used in the same kinds of situations and with the same degree of solemnity and force as the more common ζῶ ἐγώ.

[320] Koch (*Schrift*, 184–5) agrees with others in seeing Isa 49.18 as the immediate background for the use of the phrase in Rom 14.11. His evidence is limited to the observation that only here and in Jer 26.18 is the phrase followed by a ὅτι. Besides the fact that Isa 49.18 has almost nothing in common with the present passage, the commonness of the phrase ζῶ ἐγώ λέγει κύριος in the LXX makes it unlikely that even the most informed reader would have seen anything more than a general appropriation of biblical language in the use of the phrase in Rom 14.11.

[321] See above on the addition of λέγει κύριος in Rom 12.19.

[322] So Kautzsch, 85–6; Michel, 74.

[323] Tischendorf lists the evidence as B D* et ᶜ E F G d e f g guelph go syrˢᶜʰ aethᵘᵗʳ Or Ambst *al.*

the external evidence confirms this judgment.[324] As there is no reason to believe that the text had been altered prior to Paul, the question arises as to why Paul himself might have wanted to make such a subtle change in the wording of his citation. The possibility that he was influenced by the traditional language of Phil 2.10 cannot be excluded,[325] but the fact that the parallel phrase κάμψει πᾶν γόνυ follows the order of the LXX rather than the Philippians passage speaks against this explanation. The interpretational comment that follows in Rom 14.12 (ἕκαστος ... λόγον δώσει τῷ θεῷ) offers a better clue: the advancing of πᾶσα γλῶσσα serves to highlight both the universality of the coming judgment and the requirement of verbal "confession" before God, which is exactly why Paul introduces the citation in the first place (cf. πάντες in v. 10). Though the effect is subtle, the same kind of creative interplay between text and citation is found throughout the letters of Paul. While the wording of Rom 14.11 would certainly not be out of place in Isa 45.23, the Pauline origin of the present reading seems assured.

E   Substituting ἐξομολογήσεται τῷ θεῷ for ὀμεῖται τὸν θεόν (?).   The Pauline witnesses are unanimous in their wording at this point, but the LXX textual tradition is thoroughly divided. For the verb, forms of ὀμνύω (in most cases, the Future ὀμεῖται) are found in the uncials S B V, the bulk of the Lucianic and Catena texts, a number of mixed codices, the Coptic version, and a portion of the Old Latin evidence. The Pauline ἐξομολογήσεται occurs in the margin of the uncial S, all but one of the Alexandrian group of texts (including the uncials A Q), the Hexaplaric minuscules, the Syrohexapla, and the majority of the mixed codices. Most of the manuscripts that contain forms of ὀμνύω read τὸν θεόν as the object, while those with ἐξομολογήσεται usually have τῷ θεῷ, in accordance with the normal usages for each verb. The dual sense of ἐξομολογεῖν ("confess" with an Accusative object, "praise" with the Dative)[326] is apparent in a handful of witnesses that combine the verb ἐξομολογήσεται with the object τὸν θεόν (88 233 Syl).

---

[324] Kautzsch (85) cites ℵ A C D** L al vg copt syr Just Chr Thdrt Theoph *al* in support of the altered word order. The variant is not listed in the Nestle or UBS Greek texts.

[325] So Kautzsch, 85; Koch, *Schrift*, 108.

[326] See BAGD, s. v. ἐξομολογέω.

The fact that ὀμεῖται is a closer translation of the Hebrew תִּשָּׁבַע is normally taken as evidence that ἐξομολογήσεται is the earlier reading. The weakness of this explanation is that a proper assimilation to the Masoretic Hebrew would have required dropping the final τὸν θεόν as well.[327] Alternatively, one could always argue that the texts with ἐξομολογήσεται τῷ θεῷ have been influenced by the Pauline tradition, but the fact that none of these witnesses follows Paul in reversing πᾶσα γλῶσσα and ἐξομολογήσεται (see above) causes problems for this explanation as well. A reading of ἐξομολογήσεται τὸν θεόν would accord well with the emphasis on giving glory to God in Isa 45.24, but the evidence for this reading is weak. In the final analysis, the uncertainties surrounding the LXX evidence make it impossible to say whether Paul has adapted the language of the biblical text or merely followed the wording of his *Vorlage* at this point.

(40)   **Rom 15.3** (= Ps 68.10)

Paul: [ ] οἱ ὀνειδισμοὶ τῶν ὀνειδιζόντων σε ἐπέπεσαν ἐπ᾽ ἐμέ.
LXX: [ὅτι ὁ ζῆλος τοῦ οἴκου σου κατέφαγέν με,]
       καὶ οἱ ὀνειδισμοὶ τῶν ὀνειδιζόντων σε ἐπέπεσαν ἐπ᾽ ἐμέ.

A   Omitting initial καί. As in numerous other cases,[328] Paul has left off the initial conjunction in order to create a smoother transition from his own language to that of the biblical citation. Otherwise he reproduces exactly the wording of a unified LXX tradition.

(41)   **Rom 15.9** (= Ps 17.50)[329]

Paul: διὰ τοῦτο ἐξομολογήσομαί σοι ἐν ἔθνεσιν, [ ] καὶ τῷ ὀνόματί σου ψαλῶ.
LXX: διὰ τοῦτο ἐξομολογήσομαί σοι ἐν ἔθνεσιν, κύριε, καὶ τῷ ὀνόματί σου ψαλῶ.

B   Omission of κύριε. A few manuscripts in the Pauline tradition contain the Vocative left out by the bulk of the wit-

---

[327] None of the Hebrew manuscripts contains an object for תִּשָּׁבַע.
[328] See note 197.
[329] Though the wording is nearly identical in 2 Kgdms 22.50, the presence of an extra τοῖς and ἐν in the latter text leaves no doubt that Ps 17.50 is the proper source for Paul's quotation here.

nesses,[330] but the breadth of the evidence for the omission and
the unity of the LXX tradition leave no doubt that the addition
reflects assimilation to the LXX text. The purpose of the
omission, on the other hand, is far from clear. Despite the lack
of manuscript evidence, a textual explanation cannot be
entirely ruled out. The uncertainty of both the Hebrew and
Greek traditions (supported by the Syriac) concerning the
placement of יהוה/κύριε in the parallel passage in 2 Kgdms
22.50 could be taken as evidence that the addition of the
Tetragrammaton was a later development.[331] Since the alternative placement is the same as in Ps 17.50, however, assimilation to the better-known language of the Psalms is a more likely
explanation. On the Pauline side, Dietrich-Alex Koch has
pointed to this text as evidence for his contention that Paul
occasionally adapted the wording of his *Vorlage* to foreclose
the possibility that the term κύριος might be improperly referred to the exalted Christ (note τὸν θεόν in the introductory
phrase).[332] Against this theory stands the observation that Paul
has retained τὸν κύριον in a parallel quotation in the same
catena (Rom 15.11) where the referent is clearly the same as in
v. 9. Another approach would see Christ himself as the speaker
here, echoing a similar reading of Ps 68.10 only a few verses
earlier (Rom 15.3) in which the first-person speech of the
Psalms was also attributed to Christ.[333] In this case the omission would presumably reflect the apostle's discomfort at
having the exalted Christ address God by his own usual designation, "Lord." In the end, the reason for the modification will
probably remain obscure, but the strength of the textual evidence makes a Pauline origin likely.

(42)   **Rom 15.10** (= Deut 32.43)

U⁺ The Pauline and LXX traditions stand unanimously behind the
wording of Deut 32.43 reproduced in Rom 15.10. Incidentally,

---

[330] The witnesses include the corrector of the uncial ℵ, a handful of minuscules,
portions of the Old Latin and Syriac evidence, the Coptic and Gothic versions, and a
few citations.

[331] The vocative κύριε is found after σοι in all of the uncials of 2 Kgdms 22.50, but
almost all of the minuscules cited by Brooke–McLean locate it after ἔθνεσιν (b–f l m
o-t z c₂ e₂ Arm).

[332] *Schrift*, 87–8, 121.

[333] See A. T. Hanson, *Jesus Christ*, 153–60, and *Studies*, 155. Hanson argues that
Paul viewed such texts as "prophetic utterances by Christ" (*Studies*, 155). According

the fact that Paul selected this brief excerpt out of a longer passage on the basis of its reference to "Gentiles" praising God lends support to the notion that Paul regularly made notes of potentially useful verses in the course of his own personal study of Scripture.

(43) **Rom 15.11** (= Ps 116.1)

Paul: αἰνεῖτε, <u>πάντα τὰ ἔθνη</u>, τὸν κύριον,
       καὶ ἐπαινεσάτωσαν αὐτὸν πάντες οἱ λαοί.
LXX: αἰνεῖτε τὸν κύριον, πάντα τὰ ἔθνη,
       ἐπαινέσατε αὐτόν, πάντες οἱ λαοί.

B   Advancing πάντα τὰ ἔθνη. The LXX evidence is united in placing πάντα τὰ ἔθνη after τὸν κύριον, which is exactly where one would expect it in view of the close verbal parallel between the first and second cola of Ps 116.1. A number of manuscripts in the Pauline tradition agree with the LXX reading,[334] but the importance and breadth of the evidence for the reverse order shows these texts to be assimilations to the wording of the LXX. Though Koch could be right in finding here no more than a reversion to the normal Greek placement of the vocative, it would be quite unlike Paul to alter the wording of the biblical text with no more aim than to bring it into conformity with the uncertain norms of Greek grammar.[335] At the same time, the obviousness of the departure from an original parallel structure (πάντα τὰ ἔθνη ‖ πάντες οἱ λαοί) could hardly fail to communicate stress to the average Greek reader.[336] Moreover, it is surely no accident that the very words affected by the change are the ones that secure the link with the rest of the "Gentile" catena in Rom 15.8–12. In sum, the altered word order would appear to be a Pauline creation designed to call his readers' attention to what was for him the most important part

to Hanson, "Paul sees Christ personally speaking in the Psalms, describing his passion" (*Jesus Christ*, 156).

[334] Tischendorf lists C F G L *al pler* f g syr[sch] arm[cdd] aeth Or Thphyl Oec.

[335] *Schrift*, 109, citing BDF § 474 (6). Koch cites only two other examples (ἀρᾶς in Rom 3.14, αὐτῶν in Rom 11.27), both of which are highly questionable (see above on each). In this case, the "standard" to which Paul is supposed to be conforming is no standard at all: BDF § 474 (6) cites four "normal" positions for the vocative in Hellenistic Greek.

[336] See BDF § 473.

of the citation, its reference to the Gentiles offering praise to the true God (τὸν κύριον).

V   Adding καί. Apart from a handful of minor texts that omit the word,[337] the Pauline tradition is secure in reading καί before ἐπαινεσάτωσαν in Rom 15.11. Within the LXX tradition, various witnesses insert the same καί with both second- and third-person forms of the verb (see below),[338] which implies that the mixed evidence concerning the conjunction is fundamentally unrelated to the variations in the form of the verb. Assimilation to the Pauline text is unlikely, as none of the witnesses with καί reproduces the Pauline wording of the first colon of Ps 116.1. In the case of such a minor variant, the possibility of an independent addition in both the Pauline and LXX traditions cannot be ruled out. But the lack of an apparent motive for the insertion in Rom 15.11 makes it more likely that a common textual explanation underlies all the various readings with καί.

V   Substitution of ἐπαινεσάτωσαν for ἐπαινέσατε. Both the Pauline and LXX traditions are highly divided in their readings at this point. On the Pauline side, the originality of the third-person plural form seems relatively assured. Testifying in its favor are 𝔭[46], the uncials ℵ A B C D Ψ, and a number of important minuscules, over against the witness of the uncials F G, the entire Latin and Syriac traditions, and the bulk of the minuscule evidence. On the LXX side, however, the picture is more uncertain. Rahlfs lists S La[R] A' 55 as reading ἐπαινεσάτωσαν, versus B Sa R' Aug Ga L'' 2019 which favor ἐπαινέσατε.[339] What matters for the present study is the fact that the Pauline wording has strong and diverse support throughout the LXX tradition, whereas none of the manuscripts with ἐπαινεσάτωσαν reproduces the Pauline word order in the first colon of Ps 116.1. On this basis, it seems reasonable to conclude that Paul has simply followed the wording of his *Vorlage* in reading ἐπαινεσάτωσαν in Rom 15.11.

---

[337] Tischendorf cites 17 42 63 109 a[scr] c[scr] al fere[10] syr[sch] Chr as omitting καί.

[338] The combined evidence of Holmes–Parsons and the Göttingen edition indicates that the conjunction occurs with ἐπαινέσατε in R La[G] Or and the Old Latin, while the same καί appears with ἐπαινεσάτωσαν in A'' Did Eus.

[339] The lack of a full critical text for the book of Psalms limits the evidence that can be cited.

(44) **Rom 15.12** (= Isa 11.10)

Paul: [ ] ἔσται [ ] ἡ ῥίζα τοῦ Ἰεσσαὶ καὶ ὁ ἀνιστάμενος ἄρχειν ἐθνῶν, ἐπ᾽ αὐτῷ ἔθνη ἐλπιοῦσιν.

LXX: καὶ ἔσται ἐν τῇ ἡμέρᾳ ἐκείνῃ ἡ ῥίζα τοῦ Ἰεσσαι καὶ ὁ ἀνιστάμενος ἄρχειν ἐθνῶν, ἐπ᾽ αὐτῷ ἔθνη ἐλπιοῦσιν, [καὶ ἔσται ἡ ἀνάπαυσις αὐτοῦ τιμή].

A Omission of initial καί. As usual, Paul omits the initial conjunction to create a smoother flow from text to citation.[340]

D Omission of ἐν τῇ ἡμέρᾳ ἐκείνῃ. In view of the united testimony of both the Pauline and LXX traditions, the likelihood of a textual explanation for the present omission is quite low. The question remains, however, as to whether a Pauline motive for the change can be identified. Dietrich-Alex Koch maintains that the change is pre-Pauline, as the temporal reference was felt to be superfluous in early Christological applications of Isa 11.10.[341] In support of a pre-Pauline origin is the fact that the Davidic sonship of Jesus plays no part in Paul's own Christology outside the traditional context of Rom 1.3–4.[342] The fact remains, however, that the only references to this verse in the entire New Testament appear in the clearly post-Pauline book of Revelation (5.5, 22.16). Moreover, while it is clear that the quotation in Rom 15.12 presupposes a Christological interpretation, it is difficult to see why anyone in the early Christian community would have viewed the eschatologically-charged phrase ἐν τῇ ἡμέρᾳ ἐκείνῃ as "superfluous" to an application of this verse to Christ. One could just as easily argue that Paul himself felt the temporal reference to be inappropriate in a passage that emphasized the present access of the Gentiles to the one true God through faith in Jesus Christ. In the absence of further information, it will remain difficult to fix the origin of the present omission with any degree of certainty.

(45) **Rom 15.21** (= Isa 52.15)

Paul: [ ] οἷς οὐκ ἀναγγέλη περὶ αὐτοῦ ὄψονται, καὶ οἳ οὐκ ἀκηκόασιν συνήσουσιν.

---

[340] See note 197.
[341] *Schrift*, 117, 185, 241–2.
[342] Expressed more clearly in "Beobachtungen," 185–6.

LXX: [οὕτως θαυμάσονται ἔθνη πολλὰ ἐπ᾽ αὐτῷ, καὶ συνέξουσιν
βασιλεῖς τὸ στόμα αὐτῶν·] ὅτι οἷς οὐκ ἀναγγέλη περὶ
αὐτοῦ, ὄψονται, καὶ οἳ οὐκ ἀκηκόασιν, συνήσουσιν.

A   Omission of initial ὅτι.   Here again Paul has omitted an initial
particle that would have interrupted the transition from his
own argument to the language of his quotation.[343] Otherwise
Paul quotes the unified LXX tradition verbatim.[344]

---

[343] See note 197.

[344] One minor variant in the Pauline tradition is sure to have arisen in the course of
transmission. In the important uncial B, supported by a handful of minuscules, the
Coptic version, and a quote from Ambrosiaster, the verb ὄψονται appears at the
beginning of the sentence. The obvious reason for the change is to smooth out the
awkward grammar that results from beginning the verse with a relative pronoun (=
"those to whom . . .").

5

THE EVIDENCE OF 1 AND 2 CORINTHIANS AND GALATIANS[1]

(46)   **1 Cor 1.19** (= Isa 29.14)[2]

Paul: ἀπολῶ τὴν σοφίαν τῶν σοφῶν καὶ τὴν σύνεσιν τῶν συνετῶν ἀθετήσω.

LXX: [διὰ τοῦτο ἰδοὺ προσθήσω τοῦ μεταθεῖναι τὸν λαὸν τοῦτον καὶ μεταθήσω αὐτοὺς καὶ] ἀπολῶ τὴν σοφίαν τῶν σοφῶν[3] καὶ τὴν σύνεσιν τῶν συνετῶν κρύψω.

B   Substitution of ἀθετήσω for κρύψω. With the textual tradition all but united on both sides,[4] the natural presumption is
that the present substitution represents an adaptation of the
text by the apostle Paul. The only other possibility, that Paul's
Vorlage had already used a form of ἀθετέω to render the
Hebrew תְּסַתָּר (in accordance with the later sense of "upset,
tear down" (Hith. "be undone"),[5] is rendered unlikely by the
commonness of the verb סתר and the fact that the Pauline text
uses a first-person Active verb in place of the third-person
Passive form found in the Masoretic text.[6] Though the Pauline

[1] See the end of chap. 3 for an explanation of the format and symbols employed in
this and the following chapter.
[2] Hans Vollmer (33), following Surenhusius, wants to see v. 20 as a continuation of
the Pauline quotation (cf. Isa 33.18 MT) in which Paul has again followed a Greek
text that has been revised to bring it into closer conformity with a "proto-Masoretic"
textual tradition. Though the resemblance is indeed striking, the shift to third-person
speech (maintained in the verses that follow) makes it unlikely that Paul's readers
would have recognized v. 20 as a citation, hence its exclusion from the present study
(cf. Rom 12.20).
[3] A number of LXX manuscripts from the Lucianic tradition add αὐτοῦ after
both σοφῶν and συνετῶν (V 93 Eus read αὐτῶν), but this is clearly an assimilation to
the MT and not an early tradition that might have been available to Paul.
[4] The only LXX evidence for the Pauline reading is found in the minuscules 564[txt]
301 and a citation from Eusebius, all of which are surely assimilations to the united
Pauline tradition.
[5] See Jastrow, s. v. סתר II.
[6] Though the equivalence is far from rigid, κρύπτειν (along with its derivatives) is
by far the most common translation of סתר in the LXX, while ἀθετέω is never used

wording would not be out of place in the LXX, it is clearly more appropriate in 1 Cor 1.19, where the quotation serves to ground the proposition statement (v. 18) for the ensuing argument.[7] Paul's point in 1 Cor 1.18–29 is not that God has simply "hidden" understanding from the "wise," but rather that he has done a work in the death of Jesus that defies all purely rational understanding. By substituting the stronger ἀθετήσω, Paul creates a chiastic parallel with the preceding ἀπολῶ that serves to drive this point home to his hearers.[8] Kautzsch may be right in tracing the choice of this particular word to the influence of Ps 32.10, where a similar theme appears, but he is surely wrong in seeing a memory error as the reason for its appearance in 1 Cor 1.19.[9] The close links between the Pauline form of the citation and its immediate context make it almost certain that the wording of the biblical text has been altered by the apostle at this point.

(47)   **1 Cor 1.31** (= Jer 9.23)

Paul: [ ] ὁ καυχώμενος ἐν κυρίῳ καυχάσθω.

LXX: ἀλλ᾽ ἢ ἐν τούτῳ καυχάσθω ὁ καυχώμενος, [συνίειν καὶ γινώσκειν ὅτι ἐγώ εἰμι κύριος ποιῶν ἔλεος καὶ κρίμα καὶ δικαιοσύνη ἐπὶ τῆς γῆς, ὅτι ἐν τούτοις τὸ θέλημά μου, λέγει κύριος].

A   Omitting initial ἀλλ᾽ ἢ.   In addition to coinciding with Paul's usual practice of overlooking initial conjunctions,[10] the present omission eliminates a transitional link to the original context ("but rather ...") that would have cried out for some sort of explanation in the new Pauline setting.

B   Advancing ὁ καυχώμενος.   With the textual tradition wholly secure in both passages, the only real question is whether this

in such instances. The fact that both Paul and the LXX omit the third-person singular suffixes from the Hebrew nouns is further proof that Paul has followed the LXX and not a revised text here.

[7] A similar situation has already been encountered in Rom 10.19, where an adapted citation also served to ground the (implied) thesis of an argument.

[8] So also Kautzsch, 55, and Koch, *Schrift*, 152–3. The verb ἀθετεῖν is used elsewhere by Paul in Gal 2.21, 3.15, and 1 Thess 4.8 (cf. 1 Tim 5.12).

[9] *Ibid.* On the other hand, as Koch points out (*Schrift*, 153 n. 20), the word is not an unusual one for Paul (see previous note), so that the resemblance could be entirely coincidental.

[10] See chap. 4, note 197.

well-rounded maxim is original with Paul or goes back to Jewish or early Christian usage. Koch argues for a pre-Pauline (Jewish or Christian) origin on the grounds that Paul could not possibly have overlooked the opportunity to quote the initial words of the same passage (μὴ καυχάσθω ὁ σοφὸς ἐν τῇ σοφίᾳ αὐτοῦ, Jer 9.22) in the present context had he selected the text from Jeremiah himself.[11] In making this observation, however, Koch overlooks the striking echoes of Jer 9.22 that appear already in 1 Cor 1.27–8, where the categories τοὺς σοφούς . . . τὰ ἰσχυρά . . . τὰ ὄντα seem to have been modelled directly on the ὁ σοφός . . . ὁ ἰσχυρός . . . ὁ πλούσιος of the Jeremiah passage.[12] If this observation is correct, then the likelihood that the quotation in v. 31 was coined by Paul himself increases accordingly.[13] The fact that the saying never occurs in the same wording anywhere else in Jewish or Christian literature, while certainly not decisive, at least offers a measure of balance to Koch's unfounded insistence that Paul drew the verse in its present form from contemporary (Jewish or Christian) parenesis.[14]

While the possibility of a pre-Pauline origin cannot be ruled out, the available evidence seems to suggest that the present wording of 1 Cor 1.31 goes back to Paul himself. The prominence of the καυχ- stem in Pauline polemics and parenesis would certainly help to explain why this particular verse would have been so attractive to Paul. The shifting of ὁ καυχώμενος to primary position might then be understood as an attempt to heighten the contrast (after the interruption in v. 30) with the somber conclusion of v. 29, ὅπως μὴ καυχήσηται πᾶσα σάρξ ἐνώπιον τοῦ θεοῦ. The resultant antithesis shows the full extent of Paul's indebtedness to Jer 9.23–4 in the present passage.

B Substitution of κυρίῳ for τούτῳ. The phrase ἐν κυρίῳ has lost some of the stress of the original ἐν τούτῳ as a result of the shift

---

[11] *Schrift*, 36.

[12] W. Dittmar (206–7) notes the parallel with the σοφοί and ἰσχυρά of vv. 26–7, but not the closer parallelism of vv. 27–8.

[13] The fact that Paul can quote the same verse in an entirely different context in 2 Cor 10.17 could be taken to support either position, as the verse in its Pauline wording is clear enough to be employed with or without reference to the original context.

[14] *Schrift*, 36.

of ὁ καυχώμενος to the head of the sentence. At the same time, its position ahead of the verb insures that its emphatic character will not be entirely overlooked. The substitution of κυρίῳ for τούτῳ does not appreciably change the meaning of the verse,[15] but it does create a concise and generalized expression that could be adapted to a variety of contexts (cf. 2 Cor 10.17). The frequent appearance of the phrase ἐν κυρίῳ in the Pauline epistles would certainly help to explain how Paul arrived at this particular choice of words, even if the sense here is somewhat different from Paul's "formulaic" use of the phrase in other passages (but note Rom 14.14, 16.2, Eph 4.17, 6.1, Phil 1.14, 2.19, 3.1, 1 Thess 4.1, 2 Thess 3.4, 3.12). This last piece of evidence offers one more reason for thinking that the present wording of 1 Cor 1.31 represents a generalized appropriation of an attractive phrase from Jer 9.23$_{LXX}$ by Paul himself.

(48)   **1 Cor 2.9** (= Isa 64.3?)

Paul: ἃ ὀφθαλμὸς οὐκ εἶδεν καὶ οὓς οὐκ ἤκουσεν καὶ ἐπὶ καρδίαν ἀνθρώπου οὐκ ἀνέβη, ἃ ἡτοίμασεν ὁ θεὸς τοῖς ἀγαπῶσιν αὐτόν.

LXX: ἀπὸ τοῦ αἰῶνος οὐκ ἠκούσαμεν οὐδὲ οἱ ὀφθαλμοὶ ἡμῶν εἶδον θεὸν πλὴν σοῦ καὶ τὰ ἔργα σου, ἃ ποιήσεις τοῖς ὑπομένουσιν ἔλεον.

E   Wording of the entire verse.   The difficulties associated with this verse are well-documented, beginning with the problem of the source of Paul's citation. The presence of the standard Pauline introductory formula καθὼς γέγραπται tells the reader that a citation is intended, but the wording that follows agrees with no known verse in the Greek or Hebrew Bibles. The closest would appear to be Isa 64.3, but even here the resemblance is quite loose, and extends only to the first line of the quotation.[16] Other sources have been suggested for the remainder of the verse, on the assumption that it contains a mixed citation as in Rom 9.27, 9.33, 11.8, Gal 3.10, etc., but

---

[15] The person or object that supplies the basis for "boasting" is commonly rendered by an ἐν phrase in both the NT and the LXX.

[16] Vollmer (44–8), Michel (34–6), and Koch (*Schrift*, 37–8) all list numerous places where similar phrasing can be seen in both Jewish and Christian writers. The full evidence is cited in Michael E. Stone and John Strugnell, *The Books of Elijah, Parts 1–2* (Missoula, MT: Scholars, 1979), 42–73.

none of these suggestions has met with widespread approval.[17] Origen's statement that he found the same text "in secretis Eliae prophetae" has been variously interpreted.[18] Other solutions would trace the wording of 1 Cor 2.9 to early Jewish or Christian tradition,[19] or even declare the present Hebrew text of Isa 64.3 to be corrupt.[20] In view of the difficulty of determining what text Paul had in mind in adducing this quotation, it would be presumptuous to offer any analysis of the way Paul handles the wording of his *Vorlage* in 1 Cor 2.9.

(49)   **1 Cor 3.19** (= Job 5.13)[21]

Paul: ὁ *δρασσόμενος* τοὺς σοφοὺς ἐν τῇ *πανουργίᾳ αὐτῶν*.
LXX: ὁ καταλαμβάνων σοφοὺς ἐν τῇ φρονήσει,
        [βουλὴν δὲ πολυπλόκων ἐξέστησεν].
MT: לֹכֵד חֲכָמִים בְּעָרְמָם [וַעֲצַת נִפְתָּלִים נִמְהָרָה]

T   Substitution of ὁ δρασσόμενος for ὁ καταλαμβάνων. With the textual tradition wholly united on both sides, the usual presumption would be that the present reading goes back to Paul himself. In view of the difficulty of identifying a Pauline motive for the change, however, this presumption has rightly been called into question. Neither the broader context of 1 Cor 3 nor Pauline usage in general offers any reason for thinking that Paul would have replaced a common word with an unfamiliar synonym in his quotation from Job 5.13.[22] The same

---

[17] The most common candidates are Isa 65.16, Jer 3.16, and *Sir* 1.10. See especially Dittmar, 207, and Vollmer, 44–8.

[18] E.g. Michel (36) accepts the explanation that Paul drew his citation from some such apocryphal text, while Koch (*Schrift*, 37) rejects it.

[19] Vollmer (44–8) posits a pre-Pauline Jewish (Gnostic?) anthology as the source for Paul's quotation, while Koch (*Schrift*, 41) points to the oral tradition of the early Christian community. Supporters of the various views are listed in Koch, *Schrift*, 36 n. 9. See further K. Berger, "Zur Diskussion über die Herkunft von 1 Kor 2, 9," *NTS* 24 (1978), 270–83.

[20] So Gough, 323.

[21] The quotation from Isa 40.13 in 1 Cor 2.16 has been omitted here as in Rom 11.34 in accordance with strict guidelines that limit the investigation to passages that offer explicit indication to the reader that a citation is being offered (introductory formula, interpretive comments, etc.).

[22] Both καταλαμβάνω ("seize, lay hold of") and δράσσομαι ("grasp, lay hold of") represent fair renderings of the Hebrew לכד, but only the former appears in the LXX as a translation for this common Hebrew word. In fact, δράσσομαι is an uncommon word in biblical literature generally, occurring only eight times in the LXX and never in the NT. Καταλαμβάνω, on the other hand, is quite common in both texts, occurring some 128 times in the LXX and another 15 times in the NT,

applies *mutatis mutandis* to the early Christian community. Only a text-based explanation can do justice to the divergence encountered here between the LXX and the Pauline text.

Still, the precise relation between these two texts remains far from clear. In what has quickly become the standard treatment of the subject, Berndt Schaller argues that the Pauline text represents a Hebraizing revision of the present LXX text.[23] But whether it is fair to affirm with Schaller that "the rendering of the Masoretic text in 1 Cor 3.19b is actually closer than in the LXX"[24] is not at all certain. Only the addition of the possessive pronoun αὐτῶν clearly reflects the wording of the Masoretic Hebrew, while the presence of the plural article before σοφούς actually moves 1 Cor 3.19 farther away from that text.[25] The evidence of the other words is mixed: καταλαμβάνω (LXX) is one of the more common translations of לכד in the LXX, while the Greek πανουργ- stem (1 Cor 3.19) renders almost every occurrence of the Hebrew root ערם.[26] On the other side, both δράσσομαι (1 Cor 3.19) and φρονήσει (LXX) represent unusual renderings when compared to normal LXX practice, though the basic appropriateness of both translations is beyond question.[27] All in all, it is difficult to see why any of these words should have required modification in the course of a truly "Hebraizing" revision of an earlier translation of Job.[28] The

including six instances in the Pauline corpus (Rom 9.30, 1 Cor 9.24, Eph 3.18, Phil 3.12, 3.13, 1 Thess 5.4). Moreover, as Koch points out (*Schrift*, 72 n. 71), it is a form of λαμβάνω, not δράσσομαι, that Paul uses in a similar context in 2 Cor 12.16 (ἀλλὰ ὑπάρχων πανοῦργος δόλῳ ὑμᾶς ἔλαβον).

[23] "Zum Textcharakter der Hiobzitate im paulinischen Schrifttum," *ZNW* 71 (1980), 21–6. The high regard that has accrued to Schaller's study is seen in the fact that the Göttingen edition of Job cites only this article (alongside its listing of the Pauline evidence) in its apparatus for Job 5.13 and 41.3 (= Rom 11.35). Koch (*Schrift*, 71 n. 67) describes Schaller's analysis as "überzeugend," and adopts its conclusions as his own.

[24] Koch, *Schrift*, 72, summarizing the position of Schaller (translation mine).

[25] Schaller totally ignores the latter point.

[26] Twenty times the Hebrew לכד is rendered by the Greek καταλαμβάνειν in the LXX (out of some 73 instances where the Hebrew base can be identified), while forms of the πανουργ- stem are used to translate all three assured instances of the noun ערמה, all four occurrences of the verb ערם, and nine of the thirteen appearances of the adjective ערום.

[27] Δράσσεσθαι is never used for לכד in the LXX, while φρόνησις renders ערמה only here. Both are quite common, however, in normal Greek usage. On the suitability of the translation equivalencies, see the respective listings in BDB and LSJ.

[28] Schaller's attempt to explain the puzzling substitution of δράσσεσθαι for καταλαμβάνειν ("mit ihm [καταλαμβάνειν] gewöhnlich Akte kriegerischer Gewalt, z. B. die Einnahme und Zerstörung von Städten, beschrieben werden"; see "Hiobtexte,"

only piece of evidence that might indicate some sort of genetic
link between the two texts is the insertion of the definite article
before the initial participle in both renderings, an insertion that
is almost required to render the series of divine epithets found
in Job 5.9–13.[29]

This means that the question must be raised again as to
whether Job 5.13_{LXX} and 1 Cor 3.19b might represent wholly
independent translations of the Hebrew text of Job.[30] In addition to explaining why the two texts appear to use equally valid
synonyms to translate the Hebrew words לֹכֵד and עׇרְמָה, this
solution might also account for the discrepancies between the
two texts concerning the inclusion of τούς and αὐτῶν, as it
requires little imagination to see how each could have arisen
from a different Hebrew *Vorlage*.[31] The non-"LXX" wording
of Job 41.3 in Rom 11.35 could be explained on the same
basis.[32] Whichever solution is finally adopted, it should be clear

24–5) is quite artificial, as a quick perusal of the listings in Hatch and Redpath or LSJ
will show.

[29] Job 5.13 stands in the middle of a hymnic unit in which Job recounts the deeds
and character of Yahweh. Included in this section is a series of five parallel verses (vv.
9–13) in which a divine epithet is introduced by a participial phrase. (Verse 11
actually begins with an infinitive in the Hebrew and a participle in the Greek.) Only
one of these participles (v. 10) is accompanied by an article in the MT. The LXX, on
the other hand, inserts an article before every one of the participles except v. 12,
which the translator no doubt read as a continuation of v. 11 (cf. v. 10b). While a
different Hebrew *Vorlage* cannot be ruled out, the added articles would have been
virtually required to preserve the epithet quality of the participles as they were
rendered into Greek, whether in the LXX or in the text underlying 1 Cor 3.19. The
omission of the article in the LXX minuscules 637 and 797 and the NT uncials F and
G is clearly an assimilation to the MT, and not the detritus of an earlier rendering.

[30] As suggested by Kautzsch, 67–8. Schaller ("Hiobzitate," 22 n. 5) lists Vollmer,
Heinrici, Lietzmann, Cerfaux, Héring, Conzelmann, and Orr/Walter as holding the
same view. The earliest manuscript evidence for the standard "LXX" translation of
Job is P. Oxyr. 3522 (= Job 42.11–12), which dates from the first century C.E. (so
Gilles Dorival in Dorival, Harl, and Munnich, *Septante*, 91). But since Aristeas the
Exegete (writing before 50 B.C.E.) shows a definite familiarity with the traditions and
language of LXX Job, the present translation must have originated no later than the
early first century B.C.E. (per R. Doran in Charlesworth, *OT Pseudepigrapha*,
2:855–7). Still, the fact that the LXX of Job differs so markedly from the emerging
"proto-Masoretic" Hebrew tradition seems adequate motivation for a new translation, unless Paul's *Vorlage* reflects an older or simply an independent rendering of
the same text.

[31] Though concrete manuscript evidence is lacking, it is easy to see how a ם could
have dropped off the end of בְּעׇרְמָם in the *Vorlage* of the LXX as a result of
dittography. A similar omission of ה before חֲכׇמִים is not beyond the realm of
possibility, though the addition of τούς is probably better viewed as a translational
clarification or a Pauline addition (see below).

[32] Though the passage was excluded from the present study because it lacked the
special markers that would identify it as a quotation to Paul's readers, a few

by now that the change from ὁ καταλαμβάνων to ὁ δρασσόμενος in 1 Cor 3.19 should not be attributed to Paul, but goes
back to his Greek biblical *Vorlage*.

D   Addition of τούς.[33]   As noted above, it is at least conceivable
that an initial ה has fallen out before חֲכָמִים in the *Vorlage*
of the LXX, though the parallel with the anarthrous נִפְתָּלִים in
the second colon of Job 5.13 diminishes the likelihood of this
explanation. Even if it were absent from the translator's
Vorlage, however, the insertion of an article before the plural
noun to create a smoother Greek rendering would be quite
understandable, though the presence of such a purpose can be
neither verified nor denied. At the same time, reasons can be
adduced for a Pauline insertion at this point, including a desire
to establish an explicit verbal link with the quotations in 1.19
and 3.20 (τῶν σοφῶν; note also τοὺς σοφούς in 1.27).[34] Though
the resultant link is certainly fortuitous, there is no way to be
certain that Paul did not find it already in his biblical text. For
this reason the origin of this reading must remain open.

T   Substitution of πανουργίᾳ for φρονήσει.   As noted above,
there is no basis for thinking that one of these readings repre-

comments about the wording of Rom 11.35 as it relates to Job 41.3_{LXX} would be
helpful at this point. Overlooking the clearly Pauline conversion of μοι to αὐτῷ, the
picture is the same here as in 1 Cor 3.19: the Pauline text stands closer to the MT in
rendering the first verb by an Aorist, but is still far from a literal rendering of the MT
in the case of the second verb (if indeed the Passive here is a so-called "divine Passive"
and not the product of a different text). As for the different verbs used in the two
texts, neither can be said to offer a "better" rendering of the MT. Instead, each text
offers a different interpretation of the same two ambivalent Hebrew verbs: the Hiphil
of קדם can mean both "meet (with hostility), confront" (= LXX) or "anticipate,
precede" (= Rom 11.35), while the Piel of שלם can mean either "complete, finish" (=
LXX) or "reward, requite" (= Rom 11.35). If anything, the LXX rendering might
stand closer to the usual sense of the word in the first instance, and the Pauline
wording in the second (see the respective listings in BDB and LSJ). The discrepancy
concerning the form of the second verb could easily reflect the use of a different text
(the א being absent from the *Vorlage* of the LXX), or else the LXX translator may
have read אשלם through Aramaic eyes as an Aphel form of שלם (see Jastrow). Only
the initial ἤ remains to connect Rom 11.35 with Job 41.3_{LXX}, and a textual or
stylistic basis for this agreement is equally plausible (see Job 36.23, 38.12, 14, 24, 32,
33, 39.9, 10, 19, 40.9 (*bis*), 29, etc., and BAGD, ἤ, 1d). As in 1 Cor 3.19, it appears
that to assume a relationship of dependence between the Pauline text and the LXX
is to outstrip the evidence.

[33]   Only the uncials F and G omit the word, again in assimilation to the MT.
[34]   Cf. Koch, *Schrift*, 132 n. 2. The presence of σοφῶν in 3.20 is a Pauline insertion
(see below), but the definite article is original in both texts.

sents a more faithful rendering of the Hebrew than the other. The Hebrew root עֲרַם can carry either a positive ("prudence") or a negative ("craftiness") sense, depending on the nature of the context.[35] Though πανουργία is without doubt the preferred translation for עָרְמָה in the LXX,[36] there is no reason why the common Greek word φρόνησις (in the sense of "practical wisdom, prudence") should be viewed as an unusual translation of the same word in one of its more "positive" occurrences. In fact, the translator of LXX Job shows his sensitivity to exactly this point when he renders the cognate word עָרוּם by πανοῦργος in the clearly negative context of v. 12. While it is always possible that a scribe might have changed an original φρόνησις to πανουργία to reflect his displeasure with the use of the more "positive" term for the opponents of Yahweh, it would be wholly inaccurate to describe such a revision as "Hebraizing." If anything, the term "Graecizing" might better characterize this sort of change, as it was only in extrabiblical Greek that πανουργία bore a consistently negative connotation.[37] It should be noted again, however, that nothing requires that one text be dependent on the other at this point: the same results could equally well stem from two independent translations. In either case, there is little reason to think that the modification goes back to Paul himself.[38]

T   Addition of αὐτῶν. Though the bulk of the Lucianic manuscripts and a few of the versions add αὐτῶν to their LXX texts here,[39] the fact that none of these witnesses contains any of the

---

[35] For the positive sense, see Prov 1.4, 8.5, 12.23, 15.5, 22.3, etc.; for the negative usage, see Gen 3.1, Exod 21.14, Job 15.5, Ps 83.4. The positive use is actually more common than the negative in biblical usage: see the listings in BDB.

[36] See note 25. It is worth noting, however, that nearly all these passages are found in the book of Proverbs, so that the close association could reflect a single author's translation technique.

[37] For the negative sense of πανουργία in classical Greek, see the appropriate entry in LSJ. For the predominantly positive sense of the same word in the LXX, see the listings for πανουργία/πανοῦργος in Hatch and Redpath. The fact that none of the manuscripts that adds αὐτῶν to v. 13 in conformity with the Masoretic tradition (see below) saw any need to "correct" the reading of the LXX at this point is powerful testimony to the general acceptability of this translation.

[38] The πανουργ- stem is by no means foreign to Paul, appearing in 2 Cor 4.2, 11.3 (based on Gen 3.1$_{LXX}$), 12.16, and Eph 4.14. Koch (*Schrift*, 72) is surely right, however, in thinking that a rendering with φρόνησις (= σοφία) would actually have suited the Pauline context better than πανουργία had it been present in Paul's *Vorlage*.

[39] The addition is found in L''-534'-644^c-728 Co Aeth Syn.

other divergent language of 1 Cor 3.19 shows that it is an independent assimilation to the Masoretic tradition that is in view. The LXX rendering is admittedly awkward without the pronoun, but there is nothing in the Pauline context that would require the addition. One can only presume that the suffix had fallen out of the Hebrew *Vorlage* of the LXX through dittography, while the manuscript behind Paul's Greek text still preserved the original reading. In any event, it seems safe to say that the addition of the pronoun was not original with Paul.

(50)   **1 Cor 3.20** (= Ps 93.11)

Paul: κύριος γινώσκει τοὺς διαλογισμοὺς τῶν <u>σοφῶν</u> ὅτι εἰσὶν μάταιοι.

LXX: κύριος γινώσκει τοὺς διαλογισμοὺς τῶν ἀνθρώπων ὅτι εἰσὶν μάταιοι.

A   <u>Substitution of σοφῶν for ἀνθρώπων</u>.   A number of lesser Pauline manuscripts agree with the united LXX tradition in reading ἀνθρώπων instead of σοφῶν in 1 Cor 3.20.[40] Nonetheless, the strength of the external evidence makes it clear that σοφῶν is the original reading. The possibility that a deviant textual tradition might lie behind the Pauline reading cannot be denied outright, but there is nothing in either the Hebrew or LXX evidence to support such a possibility. In Ps 93, it is not the "wise" who are chided for their inability to understand the divine plan of recompense, but the "foolish" (note ἄφρονες and μωροί in v. 8). In 1 Cor 1–3, on the other hand, the futility of human σοφία is one of the central themes (1.19–27a, 2.4–6, 3.18–19). This focus has left its marks on the wording of every other biblical passage adduced in this section,[41] and it is quite reasonable to assume that the same has happened here. The verbal link that such a substitution creates between vv. 19 and 20 (τοὺς σοφούς/τῶν σοφῶν) is thoroughly typical of con-

----

[40] Nestle cites 33 630 1506 *pc* a vg^mss bo^mss Epiph^pt. Tischendorf includes a few additional texts in his listing (3 17 38 39 46 55 76 238 k^scr am harl*^vid arm^cdd Mcion Chr Euthal Hier).

[41] In addition to the passages discussed above, note 1 Cor 2.16, where an "irrelevant" clause has dropped out of Paul's quotation from Isa 40.13 (cf. Rom 11.34). The loose wording of 1 Cor 2.9 is probably also to be explained on this basis.

temporary Jewish exegesis.[42] All in all, there is little reason to doubt that the present modification goes back to Paul himself.[43]

(51)   **1 Cor 6.16** (= Gen 2.24)[44]

U⁺ Apart from the intrusion of the introductory formula γάρ φησίν into the middle of the citation, which occurs only here in the Pauline corpus,[45] the quotation in 1 Cor 6.16 follows the unanimous wording of the LXX tradition for Gen 2.24.

(52)   **1 Cor 9.9** (= Deut 25.4)

Paul: οὐ κημώσεις βοῦν ἀλοῶντα.
LXX: οὐ φιμώσεις βοῦν ἀλοῶντα.

E   <u>Substitution of κημώσεις for φιμώσεις.</u>   The LXX tradition is unanimous in reading φιμώσεις in Deut 25.4, to which the quotation in 1 Tim 5.18 also testifies. In 1 Cor 9.9, on the other hand, the textual evidence is thoroughly divided. Though κημώσεις is the reading normally printed, the external evidence is actually stronger for φιμώσεις.[46] The argument for the originality of κημώσεις is based primarily on transcriptional probability, the assumption being that a copyist would be more likely to assimilate the unliterary word κημώσεις to the reading

---

[42] The technique later called *gezera shawa*. Other places where Paul creates new verbal links between related citations include Rom 9.25–6, 11.8, 10, 1 Cor 15.54–5, and Gal 3.10, 13.

[43] Practically every investigator has found a Pauline adaptation here: see Randolph, 40; Kautzsch, 56; Vollmer, 40; Michel, 78–9; Ellis, *Use*, 15; Koch, *Schrift*, 152–3.

[44] The nearly verbatim quotation (adapted to suit its second-person plural context) of Deut 17.7/ 19.19/21.21/22.21/22.24/24.7 in 1 Cor 5.13 has been omitted from the present study in accordance with strict guidelines that limit the investigation to passages that offer explicit indication to the reader that a citation is being offered (introductory formula, interpretive comments, etc.).

[45] Interpretive comments intrude into the wording of the text in Rom 10.6–8 and Eph 6.2, and an introductory γάρ becomes part of the text in Rom 2.24 and 1 Cor 15.27 (cf. also Rom 10.13, 1 Cor 2.16, 10.26, not included in the present study). The additions of λέγει κύριος in Rom 12.19, 1 Cor 14.21, and 2 Cor 6.17 are not really comparable, as each of these verses is accompanied by a separate introductory formula.

[46] Nestle lists 𝔭⁴⁶ ℵ A B² C D¹ Ψ 𝔐 Or Epip as reading φιμώσεις, versus B* D* F G 1739 for κημώσεις. Tischendorf adds citations from Chr Euthal Cyr Thdrt Dam to the former list and Chr Thdrt to the latter.

of the LXX than vice versa.[47] Φιμοῦν is clearly the word of
choice in the few biblical passages where the idea of "muzzling"
comes into view: in addition to Deut 25.4, *Sus* 61, and *4 Macc*
1.35 (S R) in the LXX, the word is found in the later versions in
Prov 17.28 (*Quinta*), Prov 25.17 (Symmachus), and Prov 26.10
(Theodotion), and in the New Testament at Matt 22.12, 34,
Mark 1.25, 4.39, Luke 4.35, 1 Tim 5.18, and 1 Pet 2.15.
Κημοῦν, on the other hand, appears nowhere in any of these
materials.[48] In secular Greek literature, φιμοῦν is by far the
more common word.[49] Nonetheless, the argument from transcriptional probability has its problems: clearly someone somewhere felt that κημώσεις would be the more suitable term in the
present context, so that one cannot simply assume that φιμώσεις represents an "improved" reading.[50] Whether the substitution originated with Paul (whether intentionally or by memory
error) or with an editor or copyist before or after him is
impossible to say at this point.

(53)   **1 Cor 9.10** (= ?)

Paul: [ἢ δι᾽ ἡμᾶς πάντως λέγει; δι᾽ ἡμᾶς γὰρ ἐγράφη ὅτι] ὀφείλει
        ἐπ᾽ ἐλπίδι ὁ ἀροτριᾶν καὶ ὁ ἀλοῶν ἐπ᾽ ἐλπίδι τοῦ μετέχειν.
LXX: ???

E   <u>Wording of the entire verse.</u>   Though its citation character is
    disputed by some, it is difficult to see how an early reader could
    have taken 1 Cor 9.10b as anything but an intentional quo-
    tation.[51] The alternative, which involves viewing ἐγράφη as
    looking back to the citation in v. 9 instead of forward to v. 10b,
    has difficulty accounting for both the introductory γάρ and the
    ὅτι. Whether the latter word is rendered "because" or as the

---

[47] See Metzger, *Commentary*, 558.

[48] The cognate noun κημός is found in Ps 31.9 and Ezek 19.4, 9 in the LXX, Prov
26.3 in Aquila and Theodotion, and Ps 31.9 in Symmachus.

[49] See the respective listings in LSJ along with the summary in Koch, *Schrift*, 142
n. 20.

[50] Kautzsch (57–8) offers the interesting suggestion that κημώσεις might have
originated as an ancient gloss intended to explain the meaning of φιμώσεις for a less
literate audience.

[51] In the printed editions, Nestle lists the verse as a quotation, while the UBS text
does not. Among significant treatments of the Pauline citations, D. Moody Smith
("The Pauline Literature," in Carson and Williamson (eds.), *It is Written*, 270) and
Koch (*Schrift*, 22) treat 1 Cor 9.10 as a quotation, while Kautzsch, Dittmar, Michel,
Ellis, and Longenecker omit it from their investigations.

mark of a quotation, the statement that follows is clearly meant to offer some sort of grounding for the assertion in v. 10a. Its poetic structure and content likewise show it to be an independent, pre-formed unit of tradition.[52] Whether that tradition circulated in oral or written form is impossible to say at this point, as the wording of v. 10b is not appreciably close to any single passage in the Jewish Scriptures.[53] So long as the base text remains uncertain, it is obvious that nothing can be said about the way Paul handled the wording of his citation in 1 Cor 9.10b.

(54)   **1 Cor 10.7** (= Exod 32.6)

U[+]   With only the most minor of differences within the respective traditions over whether ὁ λαός should be followed by a singular or plural verb,[54] the wording of 1 Cor 10.7 reproduces the LXX text of Exod 32.6 verbatim.

(55)   **1 Cor 14.21** (= Isa 28.11–12)[55]

Paul: ἐν ἑτερογλώσσοις καὶ ἐν χείλεσιν ἑτέρων <u>λαλήσω</u> τῷ λαῷ
τούτῳ [ ] <u>+</u> καὶ <u>οὐδ' οὕτως</u> <u>εἰσακούσονταί</u> μου, λέγει
<u>κύριος</u>.

LXX: διὰ φαυλισμὸν χειλέων διὰ γλώσσης ἑτέρας, ὅτι λαλήσουσιν τῷ λαῷ τούτῳ λέγοντες αὐτῷ Τοῦτο τὸ ἀνάπαυμα τῷ πεινῶντι καὶ τοῦτο τὸ σύντριμμα, καὶ οὐκ ἠθέλησαν ἀκούειν.

---

[52]   As Koch points out (*Schrift*, 41), not only do the two lines of v. 10b form a neat verbal parallelism, but the first line is actually extraneous to the point being made in vv. 9–10a. Also notable is the fact that Paul replaces both verbs with his own language when he applies the statement in v. 10b to his own situation in v. 11. Neither ἀροτριᾶν nor ἀλοῶν occurs anywhere else in the Pauline corpus, while σπείρειν appears a full dozen times and θερίζειν four times.

[53]   Koch (*Schrift*, 42 n. 33) believes that he can demonstrate its oral basis by pointing to a number of passages in the Greek Bible where similar language appears, such as Isa 28.24, 28.28 (Σ and Θ), and 45.9. *Sir* 6.19 has also been suggested by some as a possible source. In neither case is there any reason to exclude the possibility that the same biblical passages helped to shape the language of a pre-Pauline written source, whether Jewish or Christian.

[54]   Within the LXX tradition, singular forms are substituted in citations by John of Damascus (ἀνέστησεν) and Justin (ἀνέστη). On the Pauline side, the Greek text of the uncials F and G reads ἀνέστη.

[55]   The verbatim quotation from Ps 23.1 in 1 Cor 10.26 has been omitted from the present study in accordance with strict guidelines that limit the investigation to passages that offer explicit indication to the reader that a citation is being offered (introductory formula, interpretive comments, etc.).

MT: כִּי בְּלַעֲגֵי שָׂפָה וּבְלָשׁוֹן אַחֶרֶת יְדַבֵּר אֶל־הָעָם הַזֶּה
אֲשֶׁר אָמַר אֲלֵיהֶם זֹאת הַמְּנוּחָה הָנִיחוּ לֶעָיֵף וְזֹאת
הַמַּרְגֵּעָה וְלֹא אָבוּא שְׁמוֹעַ

T   Substituting ἐν ἑτερογλώσσοις καὶ ἐν χείλεσιν ἑτέρων for διὰ
φαυλισμὸν χειλέων διὰ γλώσσης ἑτέρας.[56]   Determining the
precise relationship between the wording of 1 Cor 14.21 and the
text of the LXX is one of the greatest challenges in the entire
corpus of Pauline citations. Unlike such passages as 1 Cor 2.9
and 9.10, the base text is clearly identifiable here. The problem
with 1 Cor 14.21 lies rather in the distance of the Pauline
wording from both the LXX and Masoretic Hebrew textual
traditions.[57] On the one hand, the present wording is clearly
more appropriate than the LXX for the point Paul wants to
make concerning the function of *glossolalia* in the Corinthian
church, so much so that a Pauline origin might very well be
suspected. On the other hand, the fact that the Pauline wording
stands somewhat closer to the Masoretic Hebrew tradition, and
could in fact be understood as a somewhat loose "correction"
of the manifestly "inaccurate" rendering of the LXX, has given
rise to the suggestion that Paul is working here with a previously revised text of the LXX that just happened to suit his
purpose better than the original wording. The problem here lies
in the "somewhat loose" nature of this rendering of Isa
28.11–12. If the Pauline wording does indeed reflect an earlier
Jewish revision of the original LXX, it was carried out by
someone whose philosophy of translation was far from
wooden.

The evidence in this first part of the verse is quite conflicting.
Over against the obvious suitability of the present wording to
the context of 1 Cor 14 stands the observation that Paul

---

[56] Apart from a minor variant in which the uncials F and G substitute ἑτέραις
γλώσσαις (cf. Acts 2.4) for ἑτερογλώσσοις, the only significant deviation in the
Pauline tradition concerns whether the final word should be placed in the Genitive
(ἑτέρων) or Dative (ἑτέροις) case. The Genitive has the strong external support of ℵ
A B Ψ 0201 0243 6 33 81 104 326 1241ˢ 1739 2464 *pc*, while the Dative reading is
preferred by 𝔭⁴⁶ Dˢ F G 𝔐 lat syᵖ co Epiph. A shift from the somewhat awkward
Genitive toward a supposed grammatical concord with χείλεσιν in the course of
transmission would be quite understandable, though Kautzsch (97) accepts ἑτέροις
as original due to the strength of the external evidence and what he perceives as the
greater difficulty of the reading.

[57] The LXX tradition offers no parallels to any of the variant language found in 1
Cor 14.21.

nowhere uses the phrase "other tongues" (found only in Acts 2.4, ἑτέραις γλώσσαις) to describe the phenomenon of *glosso-lalia*, and certainly not the rare compound ἑτερογλώσσοι. Moreover, Paul would have had nothing to gain from reversing χεῖλος and γλῶσσα while leaving ἑτέρας/ἑτέρων in its original position. While it is always possible that the two near-synonyms stood in opposite positions in the Hebrew *Vorlage* of Paul's Greek text of Isaiah, textual evidence for such a reversal is entirely lacking. Further support for a non-Pauline origin is found in the words of Origen, who testifies that he found "the equivalent expression" (τὰ ἰσοδυναμοῦντα) to 1 Cor 14.21 in the version of Aquila.[58] Jerome remarks that Symmachus and Theodotion also diverge from the LXX here, though he fails to give their readings.[59] Perhaps the most important piece of evidence, however, is the fact that Aquila uses the adjective ἑτερογλώσσος in Ps 113.1 to render the rare Hebrew word לֹעֵז ("speak unintelligibly," found only here in the Hebrew Bible – cf. לעג in Isa 28.11), while Theodotion uses the same word in Isa 33.19 to render a Hebrew expression almost identical to the one cited here (נִלְעַג לָשׁוֹן).[60] Taken together, these two examples help to explain how 1 Cor 14.21 might be traced to "Hebraizing" revision of the LXX despite the fact that it reverses the Hebrew words שָׂפָה and לָשׁוֹן and contains no equivalent for the Masoretic לַעֲנִי. According to one pos-sible scenario, the Hebrew לעג became confused with לעז at some point in the tradition (whether in the manuscript tradition or in the eye of the translator/reviser), with the result that the initial phrase בְּלַעֲנֵי שָׂפָה came to be rendered as ἐν ἑτερο-

---

[58] The full sentence (from *Philocalia* 9.2) reads εὗρον γὰρ τὰ ἰσοδυναμοῦντα τῇ λέξει ταύτῃ ἐν τῇ τοῦ Ἀκύλου ἑρμενείᾳ κείμενα. As Kautzsch observes (99), it is highly unlikely that such a literalist as Aquila would have diverged from the "Masoretic" tradition as far as the present text would require, so that Origen's τὰ ἰσοδυναμοῦντα is probably best understood in the sense of "similar to" or "agreed in part."

[59] In his *Commentariorum in Esaias*, Book 9, commenting on Isa 28.9–13 (noted in Koch, *Schrift*, 65 n. 32). From a marginal note in MS 86 it is known that Symmachus substituted ἀλλοίας for ἑτέρας, but nothing more is known concerning his or Theodotion's readings.

[60] Nearly a century ago, Hans Vollmer (28) made this observation one of the foundation-stones for his argument that Paul relied on deviant Greek texts for a number of his citations, including this one in 1 Cor 14.21. Interestingly, the LXX uses the same Greek word in Isa 33.19 as here (πεφαυλισμένος).

γλώσσοις (cf. Isa 33.19 Θ).[61] Having selected what seemed to be an apt rendering of the first clause, however, the style-conscious translator/reviser could not simply repeat γλῶσσα in the parallel phrase, so that the virtually synonymous χείλεσιν was used instead.[62] Though the final shift from ἑτέρας ("another") to ἑτέρων ("of other men") has no basis in the Masoretic tradition and might therefore reflect a Pauline adaptation, the change does serve to bring the second clause into conceptual if not linguistic parallel with the first (= "by men of foreign tongues"), and could well go back to the same process that produced Paul's *Vorlage*.[63]

This leads to one final question: what sort of process was it that produced the Greek text presupposed by Paul in 1 Cor 14.21? Was it a revision of the standard LXX text of Isaiah, or does such a widely differing text presuppose an independent translation? The fact that the translator/reviser of Paul's *Vorlage* has relied on the Hebrew text is clear. But how sure is his dependence on the LXX? Only two similarities link the wording of 1 Cor 14.21 to the LXX of Isa 28.11–12, the omission of the initial כִּי and the use of a Genitive form to render the Hebrew אַחֶרֶת. The former could easily be attributed to Paul's common practice of omitting initial particles from his citations, while the latter rests on a Pauline reading that is at least open to question.[64] Dietrich-Alex Koch offers a plausible account of why a reviser might have wanted to correct

---

[61] The same confusion presumably also lies behind Symmachus's translation of Isa 33.19, since the various renderings of לָעֵג throughout the LXX show that its meaning was clearly understood by the translators. That the phrase ἐν ἑτερογλώσσοις implicitly renders the Hebrew שָׂפָה by γλῶσσα rather than χεῖλος is no problem, as the two words are virtually synonymous when referring to "language." The LXX itself offers the same translation in Gen 11.7, Ps 80.5, and Isa 19.18. The use of a form of γλῶσσα here is dictated by the translator's desire to use an existing compound that seemed to offer a suitable rendering of the entire phrase. The translation technique is obviously far from a wooden literalism.

[62] Rightly perceived by Koch, *Schrift*, 64. The shift to the plural is purely idiomatic, as the LXX rendering of the singular שָׂפָה by the plural χειλέων in Isa 28.11 shows. The addition of καί reflects the influence of the Masoretic tradition.

[63] As Koch notes (*Schrift*, 65 n. 31), the form ἑτέροις, found in many Pauline manuscripts (see note 56 for the evidence), would actually have suited Paul's purpose better here.

[64] On Paul's practice of omitting initial particles, see chap. 4, note 197. The textual problem associated with reading ἑτέρων instead of ἑτέροις is discussed in note 56. Even the similarity between the Genitives is only superficial: in the LXX, the Genitive ἑτέρας functions adjectivally, modifying the noun γλώσσης, while in 1 Cor 14 the same word has been nominalized.

the LXX's rendering of the Hebrew at this point. In the LXX text, vv. 10–12 are mistakenly read as continuing the description of the disgraceful deeds of the "priest and prophet" that begins in v. 7 (note especially ὅτι λαλήλουσιν in v. 11b). In the text-form found in 1 Cor 14.21, on the other hand, "the syntactical independence and unity of v. 11 has been restored, and v. 11 is understood – as in the Hebrew text – as a statement about God's (reproachful) manner of addressing his people."[65] Nowhere in this account, however, does Koch explain why this later reviser should have so radically modified the first several words of v. 11, when a simple shift from the Accusative to the Genitive of φαυλισμός (or some similar word) would have produced an even closer alignment with the Masoretic Hebrew text.[66] In the final analysis, the evidence of the present passage is simply inadequate to determine whether the text used by Paul in 1 Cor 14.21 represents a revision of the Greek text known through the LXX tradition or a different translation entirely. Whichever is the case, it seems clear that Paul has relied on an existing Greek text for at least the first several words of his quotation from Isa 28.11–12.

D   Shift to first-person singular λαλήσω.   Whether the text of 1 Cor 14.21 stems from the LXX or directly from the Hebrew (see above), the first-person singular form of the verb is unique to Paul in the manuscript tradition. Such a form would be entirely out of place in the LXX, where the "priest and prophet" of v. 7 are construed as the speakers, while evidence for a first-person reading is totally absent from the Hebrew tradition. Even so, a text-based explanation cannot be entirely ruled out. The ambiguous form אבוא in Isa 28.12b is properly a first-person singular form of בוא, and even if the reading אָבוּ (found in *1QIs*[a] and several other Hebrew manuscripts[67]) is correct, it is not difficult to see how the Masoretic אבוא (along with the equally ambiguous אמר of v. 12a) could have given rise to

---

[65] *Schrift*, 64–5. A similar "misreading" can be see in the LXX text of Rom 10.15 (q.v.).

[66] Koch's explanation does, however, effectively rule out the opposite possibility, that the LXX itself might be a later version of the Greek text presupposed in 1 Cor 14.21. It is difficult to see why any post-NT reviser would have "corrected" an earlier text in such a way as to leave it further from the Masoretic textual tradition while also producing no notable improvement in the Greek style of the original.

[67] See the note in BHS.

either a deviant reading or an exegetical tradition that would convert v. 11b to first-person speech as well.[68] The alternative, that Paul himself cast the verse into first-person form to add force to the prophetic indictment,[69] can be neither verified nor refuted. Even the fact that λαλήσω agrees well with the adjectival μου added to the end of the citation says nothing about the origin of the first-person expression here,[70] since it is just as likely that Paul has allowed the form of the verb to dictate the pronoun to be inserted later in the verse. While tracing the adaptation to Paul remains a live option, the possibility of a text-based explanation must be left open as well.

A   <u>Omission of λέγοντες … σύντριμμα.</u> Not only is the LXX tradition totally united in including λέγοντες … σύντριμμα as part of the text here, but the LXX phrasing would make little sense without these intervening words.[71] The Hebrew text could conceivably stand without them, but there is absolutely no textual evidence to support such an omission, and nothing in the text that would explain how it might have come about. For Paul's use of the verse, however, the excluded words would have been totally irrelevant, so that it comes as no surprise to see them eliminated from his quotation. A Pauline origin for this omission would seem to be assured.[72]

B   <u>Substitution of οὐδ' οὕτως for οὐκ.</u> Regardless of the textual background of the remainder of the clause (see below), there is little reason to think that the present substitution goes back to anyone but Paul. While nothing in either the Hebrew or Greek texts would preclude such a reading, οὐδ' οὕτως would represent a notably free rendering of the simple לֹא of the Masoretic Hebrew text, with absolutely no justification from the context.

---

[68] Unless of course the first-person form is original in all three places, in which case the MT preserves a corrupted text in v. 11b. De Waard (*Study*, 65) notes that the first-person form is actually found in the Syriac, though the possibility of Christian influence cannot be ruled out in that case. In the first-person, the passage would read, "For with mocking speech and another language I will speak (אֲדַבֵּר) to this people. (This is) what I will say (אֹמַר) to them … and I will not come (אָבוֹא) to listen."

[69] So Koch, *Schrift*, 65, 111–12, who cites Lietzmann and Conzelmann in agreement.

[70] Contrary to the assertion of Koch, *Schrift*, 112 n. 4.

[71] Note especially the shift from Future λαλήσουσιν (v. 11b) to Aorist ἠθέλησαν (v. 12b).

[72] So also Koch, *Schrift*, 123.

In 1 Cor 14.21, on the other hand, the words play a vital role in bridging the gap created by the elimination of Isa 28.12a from the citation.[73] As a reference to the unintelligibility of *glossolalia*, the expression is particularly apt: not even (οὐδέ) when the voice of Yahweh takes this unusual form of speech (οὕτως) will "this people" hearken to his words (cf. vv. 22–3). Though the possibility of a textual origin cannot be entirely ruled out,[74] the present reading shows every sign of having been introduced into the text by Paul himself.

C   Conflated citation (καὶ οὐκ εἰσακούσονται μου). Explanations for the divergent wording of 1 Cor 14.21b typically assume that Paul has either quoted the LXX of Isa 28.12b rather loosely from memory or else significantly adapted the wording of the text for his own use.[75] Each of these approaches, however, has its problems. If Paul has reproduced the wording of a non-"standard" Greek text of Isaiah nearly verbatim in the first part of his citation (see above), it is difficult to see why he would have shifted to quoting loosely from memory for the second part. A satisfactory motive for a Pauline adaptation, on the other hand, is hard to come by. Koch thinks that he can explain Paul's extensive reworking of v. 12b by noting Paul's emphasis in 1 Cor 14 on the absolute unintelligibility of *glossolalia* as practiced in the Corinthian congregation. As Koch sees it, the problem in Corinth is not that the hearers have somehow closed themselves off from receiving the divine message (as in Isa 28), but rather that the phenomenon itself is thoroughly incomprehensible. As a result, the stress in the original passage on the "unwillingness" of the hearers (οὐκ ἠθέλησαν) could not be allowed to stand.[76] Once ἠθέλησαν had been removed, however, the citation appeared somewhat unbalanced, so Paul resorted to the compound εἰσακούειν to add weight to the latter part of the verse. As a final touch, the pronoun μου was

---

[73] So Koch, *Schrift*, 151.

[74] The closest thing to a textual witness in the LXX tradition is probably the addition of οὐδέ before καὶ οὐκ in a few Lucianic manuscripts of Zech 1.4 (62–147 46–86–711), one of the passages from which the latter part of 1 Cor 14.21 might have been drawn (see below).

[75] Kautzsch (98) argues for the first approach, Koch (*Schrift*, 123, 151) for the second.

[76] Koch, *Schrift*, 123. As Koch puts it, "Paulus macht auch in Bezug auf die Außenstehenden nicht geltend, daß sie glossolalisches Reden nicht verstehen wollen, sondern daß sie es nicht verstehen können."

inserted at the end of the clause to tighten the verbal link with the first part of the citation (cf. λαλήσω in v. 21a).[77]

Apart from the purely speculative nature of the bulk of Koch's proposal (a point that he freely acknowledges),[78] the exegetical basis of Koch's explanation requires a measure of correction. While it is true that Paul says much about the unintelligibility of *glossolalia* in 1 Cor 14, his focus is somewhat different in vv. 20–5. As the Pauline οὐδ' οὕτως (v. 21b) makes clear, Paul has no intention of absolving from responsibility those ἰδιῶται ἢ ἄπιστοι who fail to discern the voice of God in the *glossolalia* of the Corinthian congregation. "Speaking in tongues" remains a sign of the divine presence to those who have ears to hear (v. 22), even if its content remains wholly unintelligible to them. Nothing in these verses indicates that Paul would have felt the slightest hesitation in saying of those who declare μαίνεσφε (v. 23b) in the presence of the divine speech that οὐκ ἠθέλησαν ἀκούειν (Isa 28.12b$_{LXX}$).

If Koch's explanation is to be rejected, however, what is to be put in its place? One solution would be to consider whether 1 Cor 14.21 might represent a conflated citation of the same type encountered in Rom 9.27, 9.33, 10.6–8, 11.8, etc. At six different points in the prophetic literature (Mic 5.5 (A text), Jer 7.24 (A Q C), 7.26 (A C), 13.11 (B V Q), 25.7 (A), Zech 1.4 (B S V L C)), the LXX uses exactly the same wording to summarize Yahweh's case against wayward Israel as is presupposed in 1 Cor 14.21b (οὐκ εἰσήκουσαν μου).[79] The same phrase slightly modified (person, tense, etc.) occurs dozens more times in similar contexts throughout the Deuteronomic and prophetic

---

[77] *Ibid.*, 151.

[78] *Ibid.*, 65 n. 33. The supposed insertion of εἰσακούειν presents additional problems, as the compound form appears nowhere else in Paul's letters.

[79] The evidence wavers between ἤκουσαν and εἰσήκουσαν throughout, but the evidence is diverse enough to preclude any systematic revision. In Mic 5.5, the full phrase οὐκ εἰσήκουσαν μου appears only in A'' (= A–26–106) La^{CS} Co Aeth. In Jer 7.24, the phrase is read by the entire A and Q families and the Catena group; in Jer 7.26, by the A family, the Catena group, and a smattering of manuscripts from the Q, Hexaplaric, and Lucianic families. In Jer 13.11, εἰσήκουσαν is the majority reading, appearing in all but S*–239 A–166' L'–86^{mg}–198–588 Thdrt. The same phrase appears in Jer 25.7 only in the uncial A, while several other texts (S 410 Q^{mg} 534 538 613) use the second-person plural form εἰσηκούσατε. The reading in Zech 1.4 is probably the best attested of all, appearing in B-V-S L''–613–770^c C–68 Syh Arm Th Thdrt, though a few of the Lucianic manuscripts (62–147–86) omit μου. The phrase οὐδ' οὕτως and the Future tense in 1 Cor 14.21b are Pauline adaptations – see the discussions in the appropriate sections.

literature.[80] As for why Paul should have substituted this familiar prophetic indictment for the equally useful wording of the LXX, it should be remembered that Paul was working not with the LXX itself, but with a "Hebraizing" Greek text that may have read the Hebrew אבוא as a first-person Imperfect form of בוא.[81] If this is the case, then the last clause of Isa 28.12b as it stood in Paul's *Vorlage* would have been totally useless in the present context. Whether Paul had one of these passages in mind more than the others, or whether he intended merely to raise echoes of this well-known prophetic refrain in the minds of his readers, is impossible to say at this point. Still, the likelihood that Paul meant to introduce an outside text in 1 Cor 14.21b is high enough to render any comparisons with Isa 28.12b highly suspect.

B   Shift to Future tense of εἰσακούειν.[82]   Regardless of what one sees as the textual basis of Paul's citation in 1 Cor 14.21b (see above), the Future tense of the verb is clearly a Pauline innovation. Though the use of a Future form would not be out of place in the LXX of Isa 28.12b, there is nothing in the textual tradition to indicate that such a reading ever existed, and as a translation of the Masoretic Hebrew the wording of 1 Cor 14.21b would be clearly impossible.[83] In addition, no trace of a Future form can be found in any of the prophetic passages noted above as possible alternative *Vorlagen* for the present citation. In the Pauline context, on the other hand, the Future verb is virtually required by the presence of a Future form in the first line of the same citation.[84] Though the use of an unknown LXX text cannot be entirely ruled out, all the evidence points to the apostle Paul as the likely originator of the present reading.

A   Addition of λέγει κύριος.   See the discussion at Rom 12.19.

---

[80] See the listings in Hatch and Redpath.

[81] See above on λαλήσω.

[82] The substitution of a third-person singular form (εἰσακούσεται) for the plural in F^gr G 43 g is clearly a grammatical "improvement" intended to bring the verb into line with the properly singular noun λαός.

[83] This holds true even if the Hebrew אבא were to be read as an Imperfect form, as the distance from אבא שמוע to εἰσακούσονται (μου) is simply too great.

[84] So also Koch, *Schrift*, 65.

(56)   **1 Cor 15.27** (= Ps 8.6)[85]

Paul: πάντα [γὰρ] <u>ὑπέταξεν</u> <u>ὑπὸ τοὺς πόδας</u> αὐτοῦ.

LXX: [καὶ κατέστησας αὐτὸν ἐπὶ τὰ ἔργα τῶν χειρῶν σου,]
        πάντα ὑπέταξας ὑποκάτω τῶν ποδῶν αὐτοῦ.

B   <u>Converting verb from second-person to third-person form.</u>
    Not only are both textual traditions wholly united behind their
    respective readings, but the third-person form ὑπέταξεν would
    be totally out of place among the series of second-person verbs
    that runs throughout the Greek and Hebrew texts of Ps 8. The
    same form is virtually required, on the other hand, by the
    third-person verbs that surround the quotation in 1 Cor 15.[86]
    The only question is whether the third-person form might have
    arisen already in the Christological use of this Psalm within the
    pre-Pauline Christian community.[87] While such a possibility
    could never be denied outright, the third-person verb appears
    only in Eph 1.22 among the several New Testament passages
    where Ps 8.6 is in view, and here dependence on 1 Cor 15.25–7
    is virtually assured.[88] All in all, there seems little reason to
    doubt that the third-person form ὑπέταξεν arose out of Paul's
    desire to conform the wording of his citation to the grammati-
    cal constraints of its new context in 1 Cor 15.

B   <u>Substituting ὑπὸ τοὺς πόδας for ὑποκάτω τῶν ποδῶν.</u>
    Though the shift is quite minor and has no effect on the sense,

[85] Possible quotations in 1 Cor 14.25 (Isa 45.14) and 15.25 (Ps 109.1) have been
omitted from the present study in accordance with strict guidelines that limit the
investigation to passages that offer explicit indication to the reader that a citation is
being offered (introductory formula, interpretive comments, etc.). The present verse
qualifies for inclusion on the basis of the interpretive comment that follows in v. 27b.
The freedom that Paul feels in adapting the wording of his quotations to suit his own
needs is nowhere more apparent than here, where he adjusts the tense of the verb
(from Aorist ὑπέταξεν to Perfect ὑποτέτακται) in full view of his readers. The
identical procedure can be seen in *1QpHab* 12.6–7.

[86] Of course, Paul could have retained the second-person form (as a sort of
apostrophe) had he been inclined to do so, as he does in Rom 3.4 and 9.7. Similar
discordances between citation and context can be seen in Rom 10.18, 10.19 (apparently a Pauline creation), and Gal 3.12. See also Koch, *Schrift*, 111 n. 1.

[87] See Lindars, *Apologetic*, 168–9, though he never takes up the question at issue
here.

[88] Otto Michel (193) calls attention to the close parallel between the two passages,
in which Eph 1.20 = 1 Cor 15.25 and Eph 1.22 = 1 Cor 15.27. The other NT passages
where quotations or allusions to Ps 8.6 appear are Phil 3.21, Heb 2.6–8, and 1 Pet
3.22.

both the Pauline and LXX traditions are unanimous in their readings at this point. The only real question is whether the change might reflect the traditional wording of this verse as it was employed in pre-Pauline Christianity. Here again the evidence to support such a conclusion is entirely lacking: the only other place where ὑπό appears in a reference to Ps 8.6 is Eph 1.22, whose dependence on the present passage has already been noted.[89] A comparison with the handling of Ps 109.1 in the New Testament is instructive. Despite the obvious importance of this verse in early Christological speculation, the wording of its last line was by no means fixed in early Christian usage. Whereas Luke 20.43, Acts 2.35, and Heb 1.13 follow the exact wording of the LXX (ὑποπόδιον τῶν ποδῶν σου),[90] the quotations in Matt 22.44 and Mark 12.36 replace ὑποπόδιον with ὑποκάτω,[91] while Paul alone uses the simple ὑπό in his loose rendering in 1 Cor 15.25. Regardless of the form in which Paul knew either verse, it seems that ὑπό was his word of choice in such situations. The fact that ὑποκάτω appears nowhere in any of Paul's letters while ὑπό is quite common reinforces the impression that Paul has intentionally preferred ὑπό in both 1 Cor 15.25 and 15.27.[92] Though a pre-Pauline origin cannot be ruled out, all the evidence seems to favor the view that Paul has (perhaps unconsciously) adapted the wording of this common quotation to conform to his own linguistic usage.

(57)   **1 Cor 15.45 (= Gen 2.7)[93]**

Paul: [ ] ἐγένετο ὁ πρῶτος ἄνθρωπος Ἀδὰμ εἰς ψυχὴν ζῶσαν.
LXX: [καὶ ἔπλασεν ὁ θεὸς τὸν ἄνθρωπον χοῦν ἀπὸ τῆς γῆς καὶ

---

89 See the previous note. The LXX wording is retained in the citation in Hebrews 2.6–8.

90 The LXX textual tradition is unanimous in its reading here.

91 According to the editors of the Nestle and UBS Greek texts. Transcriptional probability appears to have weighed heavily in the editors' decisions in both cases: the external evidence is actually stronger for ὑποπόδιον in Mark 12.36 (ℵ A L Θ Ψ 092 b *f*[1.13] 𝔐 lat sy[p.h] versus B D W 28 sy[s] co). See Metzger, *Commentary*, 111. The evidence is stronger in the Matthew passage: ὑποπόδιον is found only in W 0138 0161 *f*[1] 𝔐 lat mae, while ὑποκάτω appears in ℵ B D L Z G *f*[13] 892 *al* it sa bo.

92 Noted by Koch, *Schrift*, 140. The Pauline manuscripts are unanimous in reading ὑπό in 1 Cor 15.25, 15.27, and Eph 1.22.

93 The verbatim quotation from Isa 22.13 in 1 Cor 15.32 has been omitted from the present study in accordance with strict guidelines that limit the investigation to passages that offer explicit indication to the reader that a citation is being offered (introductory formula, interpretive comments, etc.).

ἐνεφύσησεν εἰς τὸ πρόσωπον αὐτοῦ πνοὴν ζωῆς,] καὶ ἐγένετο ὁ ἄνθρωπος εἰς ψυχὴν ζῶσαν.

A   Omission of initial καί. Though it appears this time in the middle of a verse, the link between the καί in v. 7b and the clause it introduces is clear, and the textual evidence is secure. The omission is typically Pauline.[94]

A   Addition of πρῶτος. Nothing in either the Greek or Hebrew textual traditions offers any reason to think that Paul might have found the word πρῶτος in his *Vorlage* of Gen 2.7. In the context of 1 Cor 15, on the other hand, the addition brings to formal expression the fundamental contrast between Adam and Christ as the πρῶτος and ἔσχατος Adam (v. 45b) that forms the backbone of the ensuing argument.[95] Though the insertion would not be out of place in the original text, all the evidence would trace the addition of πρῶτος here to the argumentative interests of the apostle Paul.

D   Addition of Ἀδάμ.[96] Though it might be supposed that the addition of Ἀδάμ would go hand in hand with the insertion of πρῶτος in the same verse, there are reasons to think that the two additions should be traced to different sources. Chief among them is the textual evidence: though none of the LXX manuscripts shows any of the Pauline wording in Gen 2.7, both Theodotion and Symmachus have ὁ Ἀδάμ ἄνθρωπος at this point in their texts.[97] Though the word order is the reverse of Paul's, it seems clear that the ambiguous sense of the Hebrew אדם (either a generic term or a proper name) lies behind the dual rendering in both texts. Whether the Pauline wording

[94] See chap. 4, note 197.

[95] For a thorough discussion of the background of the "πρῶτος/ἔσχατος man" conception and its function within the argument of 1 Cor 15, see Koch, *Schrift*, 134–7.

[96] The omission of ἄνθρωπος in B K 326 365 *pc* Ir Or Did Ambst Aug can be attributed both to its apparent redundancy (with the nominalized πρῶτος) and a desire to make the contrast between ὁ πρῶτος Ἀδάμ and ὁ ἔσχατος Ἀδάμ even more explicit. The inclusion of ἄνθρωπος is supported by ℵ A C D E F G L P *al pler* d e f g m vg syr^{utr} cop arm aeth and numerous citations (Tischendorf), and is surely original.

[97] Apart from the reversal of ὁ Ἀδάμ and ἄνθρωπος, the wording of both texts is identical to that presupposed by Paul in 1 Cor 15.45. (For full citations, see the Göttingen volume on Genesis). Koch (*Schrift*, 135 n. 13) mistakenly attributes this reading to Aquila.

testifies to an earlier written text or merely reflects a common exegetical tradition is impossible to say at this point.[98] What matters is that significant evidence exists to indicate that Paul may not have added the proper name Ἀδάμ to his text of Gen 2.7. This means that the insertion cannot properly be credited to Paul for the purposes of the present study.[99]

(58) **1 Cor 15.54–5** (= Isa 25.8, Hos 13.14)

A Combined citation. Though questions exist concerning Paul's treatment of the individual verses, there is no evidence to suggest that anyone had combined these two passages from Isaiah and Hosea into a single citation prior to Paul. As with his other combined citations (e.g. Rom 9.25–6, 11.26–7, 2 Cor 6.16–18), Paul gives his reader no indication that vv. 54b–55 might represent anything other than a continuous quotation from a single biblical passage. Equally typical of Paul is the way the two verses have been knit together through a series of thoughtful adaptations to form a coherent, well-rounded rhetorical unit with a single, transparent theme (see below). Here again the evidence supports the view that the various combined citations that appear in Paul's epistles are the carefully culti-

---

[98] Koch (*ibid.*) is surely wrong in thinking that Paul's development of the πρῶτος Ἀδάμ/ἔσχατος Ἀδάμ contrast somehow requires him to have added Ἀδάμ to Gen 2.7 apart from its presence in the texts of Symmachus and Theodotion. There is simply no reason why Paul could not have found the words ὁ Ἀδάμ ἄνθρωπος (or its converse) in his *Vorlage* or tradition and then shaped the ἔσχατος Ἀδάμ figure around it.

[99] Ever since John Calvin, various commentators have argued that the second half of 1 Cor 15.45, which reads ὁ ἔσχατος Ἀδάμ εἰς πνεῦμα ζωοποιοῦν, should be regarded as part of the Pauline citation. The argument is based on three facts: (1) the second half of the verse offers a perfect verbal parallel to the first; (2) a single verb (ἐγένετο) governs both cola of the resultant parallel structure; and (3) the interpretation of the combined expression only begins in v. 46. See Vollmer, 54–5 (who cites Calvin, Bengel and Kautzsch as holding the same view) and Koch, *Schrift*, 134–7. Even when these points are acknowledged, however, there seems to be little reason to think that either Paul or his readers would have regarded the citation as extending to the end of v. 45. The very explicitness of the Christological reference in the latter half of the verse (ὁ ἔσχατος Ἀδάμ) would have made it clear to Paul's readers that an interpretive element had been added to the end of what was most likely a well-known verse of Scripture. While Paul has no difficulty finding Christ either present or mentioned at numerous points in the biblical text (e.g. Rom 11.26–7, 15.3, 1 Cor 10.4, 2 Cor 3.16), in no other place does he actually incorporate a Christological reference into the body of a citation (though see Eph 5.14). To insist that v. 45b constitutes anything more than an (antithetical) interpretive parallel to the actual quotation in v. 45a is surely to tax the ignorance of both Paul and his readers.

vated fruit of a sophisticated literary artistry and not the unfortunate by-product of a rather careless citation technique.

(58a)   **1 Cor 15.54** (= Isa 25.8)

Paul: κατεπόθη ὁ θάνατος εἰς νῖκος.

LXX: κατέπιεν ὁ θάνατος ἰσχύσας, [καὶ πάλιν ἀφεῖλεν ὁ θεὸς πᾶν δάκρυον ἀπὸ παντὸς προσώπου].

MT: בִּלַּע הַמָּוֶת לָנֶצַח

T Substituting κατεπόθη for κατέπιεν and εἰς νῖκος for ἰσχύσας.[100] Both deviations from the LXX will be treated together here, as both would appear to go back to the same source. Taken on its own, the manuscript evidence would seem to favor a Pauline origin for the present wording, as both traditions stand united behind their respective readings. When the later Jewish versions are taken into account, however, the picture changes considerably:

Ἀ = καταποντίσει τὸν θάνατον εἰς νῖκος
Θ = κατεπόθη ὁ θάνατος εἰς νῖκος
Σ = καταποθῆναι ποιήσει τὸν θάνατον εἰς τέλος

Two facts stand out from this listing of the evidence: (1) the marked divergence of all three renderings from the wording of the LXX, and (2) the verbatim agreement between the translation attributed to Theodotion and the text of Paul's quotation in 1 Cor 15.54. The reason for the common shift away from the LXX is not far to seek: all three revisers were attempting to correct what to them was a faulty rendering of the Hebrew on the part of the LXX translator.[101] The matter of

---

[100] A number of important witnesses (𝔭⁴⁶ B D* 088 *pc* Tert Cyp Hil Hier) read νεῖκος ("strife, contention") rather than νῖκος here. An aural error is clearly at the base of the confusion, though where it arose is impossible to say. The formal nature of the idiom and the agreement of Aquila and Theodotion leave no doubt as to the originality of νῖκος.

[101] The problem is twofold: the LXX makes הַמָּוֶת the subject, in clear contradiction to the surrounding verses (cf. vv. 6a, 8b), and renders לָנֶצַח in the sense of the Aramaic נצח, "surpass, overcome" (as also several times in the LXX) rather than the Hebrew idiom meaning "forever." Moreover, legitimate differences remain over whether the Hebrew verb should be read as an Active (Piel) or Passive (Pual) construction and whether the sense is better rendered by an Aorist (following the grammar) or Future (following the sense) form. On the whole question, see Koch, *Schrift*, 61–3. Similar "corrections" of mistaken LXX readings in the later versions have already been noted in Isa 52.7 (= Rom 10.15) and Isa 28.11–12 (= 1 Cor 14.21).

Paul's agreement with Theodotion, on the other hand, is not so simple. The problem is that the evidence is divided concerning the wording of Theodotion's text at this point. Whereas the uncial Q (in a marginal gloss) gives the Passive κατεπόθη as the reading of Theodotion, the Syrohexapla seems to presuppose an Active form of the verb (κατέπιεν) in its rendering.[102] Since the Hebrew בלע could support either witness, it is difficult to find an objective basis on which to judge the reliability of the two accounts.[103] The possibility that the Q reading could have arisen through assimilation to the text of 1 Cor 15.54 cannot be ruled out.[104] Nonetheless, the Pauline wording is not without support in the other versions: a Passive form of the same verb (καταποθῆναι) appears in the otherwise distinctive rendering of Symmachus, while Aquila joins with Paul in offering the unusual translation εἰς νῖκος for the Hebrew לנצח.[105] Clearly some sort of common tradition lies behind all three texts. Whether the marginal entry of Q has rightly preserved the wording of Theodotion is thus finally irrelevant to the present study. The agreements between Paul and the other two versions are sufficient to show that Paul has most likely followed a pre-existing Greek text at this point, one that may have exercised at least a measure of influence over the subsequent translations of Aquila, Symmachus, and (possibly) Theodotion.

(58b)   **1 Cor 15.55** (= Hos 13.14)

Paul: ποῦ σου, θάνατε, τὸ νῖκος;
        ποῦ σου, θάνατε, τὸ κέντρον;
LXX: [ἐκ χειρὸς ᾅδου ῥύσομαι αὐτοὺς καὶ ἐκ θανάτου λυτρώ-

---

[102] Pointed out by Koch, *Schrift*, 62 n. 22.

[103] Koch (*ibid.*) notes that Rahlfs ("Über Theodotion–Lesarten in Neuen Testament und Aquila–Lesarten bei Justin," *ZNW* 20 (1921), 182–99) argues for the originality of Syh, while Ziegler (in the Göttingen volume on Isaiah) cites Q as the original.

[104] Kautzsch (104 n. 1) suggests that the reading attested in Q arose when a marginal gloss containing the wording of 1 Cor 15.54 displaced Theodotion's reading from the text of the Hexapla as a result of a copyist's error. In attempting to deny all contacts between Theodotion and the New Testament, Kautzsch obviously did not have the benefit of more recent studies that would date many "Theodotionic" readings to the first century C.E. or before (see chap. 2).

[105] Pointed out already by Vollmer (27), who used this passage as the springboard for his prescient theory that Paul followed various unknown Greek texts for a number of his citations. It goes without saying that a translation that rendered לנצח in its temporal sense would have been quite useful to Paul here had he known one (note ἄφθαρτος and ἀθανασία in vv. 52–4).

σομαι αὐτούς·] ποῦ δίκη σου, θάνατε; ποῦ τὸ κέντρον σου,
ᾅδη;

MT: אֱהִי דְבָרֶיךָ מָוֶת אֱהִי קָטָבְךָ שְׁאוֹל

B   Advancing σου plus the Vocative in both lines. Though the
Pauline wording would not be impossible in the LXX, there is
no evidence to indicate that this word order ever appeared in
any text outside 1 Cor 15.55. The reason for the altered order is
purely rhetorical: separating two elements that would otherwise belong together (here the noun and its attributive) is a
common way of indicating emphasis in both classical and
Hellenistic Greek.[106] As Koch notes, the emphatic word order
is highly appropriate for a verse that serves to close out the
entire discussion of death and resurrection in 1 Cor 15.[107] The
Pauline origin of this minor adaptation seems assured.

B   Substitution of τὸ νῖκος for ἡ δίκη [?].[108] Though a handful
of LXX witnesses read ἡ νίκη ("victory") rather than ἡ δίκη
("lawsuit, judgment") in Hos 13.14,[109] none uses the later
Greek form τὸ νῖκος ("victory") that appears in 1 Cor 15.55.
Still, the LXX translation of דֶּבֶר ("plague, pestilence") by
δίκη is problematic,[110] and the possibility of a non-Masoretic
Vorlage for the primary LXX reading cannot be ruled out. The

106 See BDF § 473.
107 Schrift, 107.
108 As in v. 54, a handful of important witnesses read νεῖκος rather than νῖκος
here; in fact, the witnesses are almost identical in the two cases (here, 𝔭⁴⁶ B D* 088 pc
itᵃʳ Tert Cyp Hil). Once again an aural error is the most likely cause of the confusion
(see below in text). In addition, a sizeable part of the tradition reverses νῖκος/νεῖκος
and κέντρον in v. 55, including the uncials ℵ² Aᶜ D⁽ᶜ⁾ F G K P Ψ 075, the bulk of the
minuscules, portions of all the versions, and a wide range of quotations. In favor of
the LXX order are 𝔭⁴⁶, the uncials ℵ* B C 088 121a 0243, a number of minuscules, the
Vulgate, the entire Coptic tradition, and significant witnesses from the other versions,
plus numerous citations. The case is difficult to judge on its own merits (cf. Kautzsch,
106): the external evidence favors the word order cited above, but the same reading
could also be explained as an assimilation to the LXX. Two factors help to tip the
scales in favor of the order νῖκος/κέντρον: (1) the immediate mention of τὸ κέντρον
at the beginning of v. 56 implies that it appeared at the end of the previous citation
(noted by Koch, Schrift, 169 n. 39), and (2) the bulk of the evidence favoring the
reverse order concurs in the clearly secondary reading ᾅδης in v. 55b (so Kautzsch,
106). In either case, the evidence is so divided as to render it impossible to determine
whether Paul has indeed reversed the order of νῖκος/νεῖκος and κέντρον in the
present citation.
109 Found only in the minuscules 22ᶜ 130′–534, the Armenian version, and quotations by Cyr Thph.
110 דֶּבֶר is rendered by θάνατος in all of its 33 appearances in the LXX.

usual explanation assumes that the translator derived דבריך
from דְּבָר rather than דֶּבֶר, which he then rendered rather
loosely according to the sense of the context.[111] But the
required link between דְּבָר and δίκη is tenuous at best,[112] and
the proposed translation equivalent appears nowhere in the
LXX. Another approach would be to take the variant νεῖκος
("strife, contention"), found in a small but important part of
the Pauline tradition, to be the original reading of 1 Cor 15.55,
on the assumption that a similar Hebrew *Vorlage* (such as רִיב
or מָדוֹן) lay behind the wording of both the Pauline text and the
LXX here.[113] But the fact that the same variant occurs also in v.
54 (in most of the same texts) while the LXX tradition contains
no evidence for such a reading in either Isa 25.8 (= 1 Cor 15.54)
or Hos 13.14 (= 1 Cor 15.55) reveals the secondary nature of
νεῖκος in 1 Cor 15.54–5. One final possibility, that Paul found
τὸ νῖκος already in his Greek *Vorlage*, could be considered
only if it is assumed that the Hebrew behind Paul's Greek text
differed from both the Masoretic text and the *Vorlage* of the

---

[111] The commentaries offer little help here beyond the rather obvious observation
that Paul has replaced the LXX's δίκη with νῖκος from Isa 25.8. The comment by
Hans Walter Woolf on the subject (*Hosea*, trans. Gary Stansell, Hermeneia Series
(Philadelphia: Fortress, 1974), 221 n. gg) is typical of this tendency to assert rather
than to explain: "G [LXX] (ἡ δίκη σου) need not be a corrected spelling of νίκη made
within the Greek text's transmission (Nyberg, p. 104; he supposes that the Hebrew
text used by G contained an infinitive construct of גבר = 'to conquer'; cf. 1 Cor
15.55); rather, it is a translation of דְּבָר (Quell, *TDNT* 2, 174; cf. Ziegler, *Duodecim
prophetae*); accordingly, α' translates ῥήματα; θ' has δίκη." The solution put forward
by H. S. Nyberg (*Studien zum Hoseabuch*, Uppsala Universitets Årsskrift (Uppsala:
Almqvist & Wiksell, 1935)), to which Woolf refers above, would moreover require an
unattested reading of דרבנך (or possibly דרבך) in place of the MT's קטב to explain
the translation τὸ κέντρον in the second clause of the LXX (*ibid.*, 105). Nyberg's
explanation also fails to shed light on the move from νίκη (Paul's supposed *Vorlage*)
to νῖκος in 1 Cor 15.55.

[112] The closest approximation to an overlap in meaning between דְּבָר and δίκη
appears in the nuance of "way, custom, manner" that both nouns can bear (see BDB,
s.v. דְּבָר, IV.7, and LSJ, s.v. δίκη, I.1). Such a translation would be awkward at
best in the present context. Though דְּבָר can at times be used in a legal context (see
BDB, s.v. דְּבָר, I.1.g–h), the word itself carries none of the judicial overtones
associated with δίκη. Aquila likewise assumes a derivation from דְּבָר, but renders the
Hebrew by ῥήματα.

[113] See note 108 for the evidence on νῖκος/νεῖκος. The Greek δίκη translates רִיב
in nine of the seventeen places where the Hebrew text is known, while νεῖκος renders
מָדוֹן in three out of four instances. Though their meanings overlap in Greek, the two
words are clearly distinguished in the LXX: δίκη is never used to translate מָדוֹן, nor
does νεῖκος render רִיב.

LXX at this point. In view of the highly diverse textual data, this possibility cannot be dismissed lightly.[114]

At this point there is simply no way to determine whether Paul's biblical text contained either of the readings found in the LXX tradition. The reading ἡ δίκη is by far the better attested of the two, but an original ἡ νίκη would go far toward explaining both the combination with Isa 25.8 (a rather loose instance of *gezera shawa* with the preceding τὸ νῖκος) and the substitution of the neuter for the feminine form in 1 Cor 15.55 (to make the link between the two passages more explicit).[115] In either case, it seems clear that Paul has introduced the words τὸ νῖκος into the text to create a closer verbal and rhetorical link with the excerpt from Isa 25.8 in v. 54, where the notion of "victory" plays an equally prominent role.[116] The importance of this "victory" motif to Paul's use of both verses is apparent from the way he picks up the theme again in his closing benediction in v. 57 (τῷ δὲ θεῷ χάρις τῷ διδόντι ἡμῖν τὸ νῖκος διὰ τοῦ κυρίου ἡμῶν Ἰησοῦ Χριστοῦ). Though the textual backdrop is far from clear, the bulk of the evidence seems to favor a Pauline adaptation in the present instance.

A   Substitution of θάνατε (2°) for ᾅδη.[117]   Though it might be assumed that this was the sort of substitution that any pious Jew might make to avoid the use of a pagan religious term, the fact is that the word ᾅδης enjoyed wide currency in both Jewish

---

[114] Such a reading could also help to explain how Paul came to combine Isa 25.8 and Hos 13.14 in 1 Cor 15.54–5, as the *Stichwort* νῖκος would have provided a natural link via *gezera shawa*. Still, the linkage could just as easily have taken place through their common use of θάνατος, so the point cannot be pushed.

[115] Other places where Paul appears to have created new verbal links between related citations include Rom 9.25–6, 11.8, 10, 1 Cor 3.19, 20, and Gal 3.10, 12.

[116] So also Michel, 79, and Koch, *Schrift*, 169. Note again the total lack of LXX manuscript support for τὸ νῖκος in Hos 13.14.

[117] The LXX tradition stands united behind its reading, but the Pauline evidence is divided. The various printed editions of the Greek NT (Nestle, UBS, Tischendorf) list numerous witnesses that follow the ᾅδη of the LXX, including the uncials ℵ² Aᶜ K P Ψ 075 0121a 0243, the bulk of the minuscules, a number of the versions (syᵖ arm go aethᵖᵖ), and a wide range of citations from both East and West. In favor of θάνατε are 𝔭⁴⁶, the uncials ℵ* B C D F G 088, a number of minuscules, the entire Latin tradition, the Coptic and Ethiopic versions, and citations by an equally wide range of Fathers. Both the weight of the external evidence and the argument from transcriptional probability favor the view that the readings of the first group have been assimilated to the LXX.

and Christian circles throughout Antiquity.[118] The reason behind the change here is not religious, but rhetorical: the resultant parallelism between the two cola heightens the rhetorical effectiveness of the verse as a whole, while the threefold repetition of θάνατος (including the occurrence in v. 54) hammers home the fundamental conviction (Christ's final victory over death) that lay at the heart of the entire preceding discussion. The effect of this and other modifications to vv. 54–5, as Koch points out,[119] is to produce a tightly knit, three-membered "word of Scripture" structured around a threefold repetition of the word θάνατος, in which the first two lines are further united by the repetition of the key-word νῖκος and the last two by a thoroughgoing verbal parallelism. In this form, the verse serves as a rhetorical flourish to notify the hearers that the discussion is fast coming to an end.[120] The fundamentally Pauline origin of this carefully structured rhetorical unit can hardly be doubted.

(59)   **2 Cor 4.6** (= Gen 1.3?)

Paul: [ὅτι ὁ θεὸς ὁ εἰπών·] <u>ἐκ σκότους φῶς λάμψει</u>, [ὃς ἔλαμψεν ἐν ταῖς καρδίαις ἡμῶν ...]
LXX: καὶ εἶπεν ὁ θεός   Γενηθήτω φῶς. καὶ ἐγένετο φῶς.

E   <u>Wording of the entire verse.</u>   Here as in 1 Cor 2.9 and 9.10 (cf. Eph 5.14, 2 Tim 2.19) a saying is introduced with a normal citation formula which has no specific grounding in either the Hebrew or Greek Scriptures.[121] In content it echoes Gen 1.3, to which it surely refers, but its language stands so far from this or any other passage that most researchers have labelled it a "paraphrase" and excluded it from their investigations.[122] On

[118] See the article by J. Jeremias in *TDNT*, 1:146–9, and the listings in Hatch and Redpath.
[119] *Schrift*, 169–70.
[120] On the importance of such verbal cues in an oral society, see Achtemeier, 17–25.
[121] The fact that the formula is unusual for Paul (cf. 2 Cor 6.16) is no objection to labelling the saying as a quotation, since the important issue is how Paul's hearers would have understood the phrase. On this there appears to be unanimity: the phrase clearly anticipates a citation.
[122] In addition to the obvious parallels in content, note how the introductory formula employed here (almost unique in the Pauline corpus – cf. 2 Cor 6.16) echoes the wording of Gen 1.3$_{LXX}$ (see above). Victor Paul Furnish discusses the options in his recent Anchor Bible commentary, *II Corinthians* (Garden City, NY: Doubleday,

the other hand, the fact that the words in question are introduced with what any reader would take to be a quotation formula suggests caution in using such modern distinctions to describe the citation practice of the apostle Paul. The difference between this verse and such reworked citations as Rom 3.10–12 (= Ps 13.1–3) and 9.25–6 (= Hos 2.25, 2.1) is only one of degree. The very fact that Paul can use an explicit citation formula to introduce what modern readers would call a "paraphrase" may yet prove helpful in understanding the literary milieu that would allow Paul to adapt the wording of numerous other quotations to a somewhat lesser degree.[123]

(60)   **2 Cor 4.13** (= Ps 115.1)[124]

U⁺ A number of witnesses in the Pauline tradition add καί after διό against the united testimony of the LXX.[125] While it is always possible that the insertion is original, a more likely explanation would see here a scribal assimilation to the interpretive comment that follows in 2 Cor 4.13b (καὶ ἡμεῖς πιστεύομεν, διὸ καὶ λαλοῦμεν), where the second καί properly means "also," i.e. "just as the Psalmist did." The strength of the external evidence gives additional reason to think that Paul has faithfully reproduced the wording of the LXX in the present instance.

(61)   **2 Cor 6.2** (= Isa 49.8)

U⁺ Apart from a few very minor attempts to improve the parallelism between the two clauses by assimilating σου to σοι or vice

1984), 223–4. In addition to Gen 1.3, W. Dittmar lists Job 37.15, Isa 9.1, and 2 Kgdms 22.29/Ps 18.29 as possible sources for Paul's language here. For additional views on the subject, see Koch, *Schrift*, 16 n. 23.

[123] The various adaptations to Gen 1.3 implied in the acceptance of this verse as a quotation have not been treated separately here due to lingering uncertainties concerning the origin of the phrase. While it is always possible that the present loose rendering occurred to Paul in the moment of dictation, the repetition of the verb λάμπω in the application comment (ὃς ἔλαμψεν ἐν ταῖς καρδίαις) suggests that Paul may have been familiar with a form of the verse (from oral tradition?) that already contained this word. The question is best left open for now.

[124] Possible quotations in 2 Cor 3.13 and 3.16 have been omitted from the present study in accordance with strict guidelines that limit the investigation to passages that offer explicit indication to the reader that a citation is being offered (introductory formula, interpretive comments, etc.).

[125] The addition is found in ℵ F G 0186 1175 sy arm go (Eus) Epiph Aug, while the text without καί is witnessed by 𝔭⁴⁶ B Cᵛⁱᵈ D Ψ 𝔐 latt (cop aeth) Chr Thdrt Dam Ambst.

versa,[126] both textual traditions are united in declaring that Paul has followed the wording of his LXX *Vorlage* in 2 Cor 6.2.

(62) **2 Cor 6.16–18** (= Lev 26.11–12, Isa 52.11, Ezek 20.34, 2 Kgdms 7.14, 7.8)

A   Combined citation. As with the other combined citations encountered thus far (Rom 3.10–18, 9.25–6, 10.6–8, 11.26–7, 1 Cor 15.54–5), the present passage gives sure signs of having been knit together ahead of time into a tightly woven rhetorical unit rather than being thrown together haphazardly in the moment of dictation. Certainly nothing in the manuscript tradition would support the view that the combination might be pre-Pauline, while the close integration of the whole unit into its present context, where it virtually takes the place of direct Pauline speech, renders an earlier Christian origin unlikely.[127] The only real question is whether the whole of vv. 16–18 should be counted as a single combined citation, or whether v. 16 should be treated as an independent quote (see below on διό, v. 17). However the latter issue is resolved, the Pauline origin of the present combination seems assured.

(62a)   **2 Cor 6.16** (= Lev 26.11–12)[128]

Paul: [ ] ἐνοικήσω ἐν αὐτοῖς [ ] καὶ ἐμπεριπατήσω [ ] καὶ ἔσομαι αὐτῶν θεός, καὶ αὐτοὶ ἔσονταί μου λαός.

Lev 26.11–12$_{LXX}$: καὶ θήσω τὴν σκήνην μου ἐν ὑμῖν, καὶ οὐ βδελύξεται ἡ ψυχή μου ὑμᾶς· καὶ ἐμπεριπατήσω ἐν ὑμῖν καὶ ἔσομαι ὑμῶν θεός, καὶ ὑμεῖς ἔσεσθέ μου λαός.

Ezek 37.27$_{LXX}$: καὶ ἔσται ἡ κατασκήνωσις μου ἐν αὐτοῖς, καὶ ἔσομαι αὐτοῖς θεός, καὶ αὐτοὶ ἔσονταί μοι λαός.

---

[126] In the LXX tradition, the important uncial S* (standing on its own) reads σοι in place of σου in the first clause, while in the Pauline tradition the uncial F (again with no further support) offers the reverse assimilation (σοι to σου) in the second clause.

[127] The quotation in v. 16b supplies a biblical foundation for the assertion in v. 16a (ἡμεῖς γὰρ ναὸς θεοῦ ἐσμεν ζῶντος), while the thought of vv. 17–18 is picked up and applied in 7.1 (ταύτας οὖν ἔχοντες τὰς ἐπαγγελίας, ἀγαπητοί, καθαρίσωμεν ἑαυτούς).

[128] Koch omits all of 2 Cor 6.16–18 from his study on the assumption that the material in 6.14–7.1 is a non-Pauline insertion (*Schrift*, 24 n. 43). For arguments in favor of viewing the section as a typical Pauline digression, see the references in chap. 3, note 3.

A   Omission of initial καί. The omission of introductory particles is typically Pauline.[129]

A   Substitution of ἐνοικήσω for θήσω τὴν σκήνην. Immediately
the question arises as to what verse Paul had in mind when he
set down these words from Scripture (καθὼς εἶπεν ὁ θεός) in v.
16. The last half of the quotation echoes several passages from
the Hebrew Bible, but its language stands closest to the LXX of
Lev 26.12 and Ezek 37.27. In either case a Pauline adaptation is
in view, the only question being whether the apostle has
changed the second-person plural ἔσεσθε to a third-person
form (so Lev 26.12) or converted the Dative pronouns to
Genitives (so Ezek 37.27) (see below). The first half of the verse
offers little help in identifying the citation, as it follows neither
passage very closely. The Ezekiel passage has proven attractive
to many interpreters due to the fact that it uses a cognate of the
verb in 2 Cor 6.16 to express a similar expectation that Yahweh
would one day re-establish his earthly tabernacle in the midst of
his people (ἔσται ἡ κατασκήνωσις μου ‖ ἐνοικήσω). Against the
Ezekiel reference stands the absence of quotations from Ezekiel
in the rest of the Pauline literature and the difficulty of
explaining why Paul would have modified the Dative pronouns
to Genitives in the latter part of the verse.[130] The presence of
the verb ἐμπεριπατήσω in 2 Cor 6.16 (cf. Lev 26.12), uncommon in the LXX and a *hapax legomenon* in the New Testament,
has likewise indicated to most interpreters that Lev 26.12 must
somehow be taken into consideration.

The way out of this textual morass was already pointed out
by several scholars around the turn of the century.[131] Though
many printed editions (including Rahlfs) read καὶ θήσω τὴν

[129] See chap. 4, note 197 for references.
[130] A textual explanation for the latter problem is possible, though unlikely.
Αὐτῶν appears in place of αὐτοῖς in the Lucianic MSS of Ezek 37.27, while μου
replaces μοι in a number of the same MSS plus a sizeable portion of the Hexaplaric
evidence (excluding the Syrohexapla). The LXX text of Lev 26.12 contains similar
variations. A reverse assimilation (replacing Genitives with Dative forms) can be seen
in a portion of the Pauline evidence: αὐτοῖς stands in place of αὐτῶν in F^gr G P g Or
Eus Chr, while μοι replaces μου in D F G Ψ 0209 𝔐 latt sy co Tert Or Eus Ath Cyr
Epiph (Chr) Euthal Thdrt. The Genitive forms in 2 Cor 6.16 are nonetheless secure,
with firm support from ℵ B C I^vid P 0243 33 81 1175 1739 arm Clem Or Eus Dam.
[131] The suggestion was voiced already by Hans Vollmer (20 n. 1) in 1895, while W.
Dittmar (221) included the same observation in his compilation of data on the NT
quotations in 1903. A similar explanation was put forward by Kautzsch (90) as early
as 1869.

διαθήκην μου as the opening words of Lev 26.11 (following the uncials A B and a smattering of minuscule and versional evidence), the Göttingen LXX replaces διαθήκην with σκήνην, preferring the broader testimony of F M V O''⁻²⁹ C'' b d f s t⁻⁸⁴ z⁻⁶⁸ and a variety of mixed codices. Regardless of which is the original text, the breadth of support for the second reading makes it highly probable that the latter text could have been available to Paul in the first century C.E. The substitution of ἐνοικήσω for καὶ θήσω τὴν σκήνην μου would follow naturally for one who understood the establishment of Yahweh's "tabernacle" (σκήνη) not as the restoration of an earthly edifice, but rather as his spiritual presence among those who acknowledge his eschatological work of salvation in Christ.[132] The unusual placement of ἐμπεριπατήσω also becomes clear in this understanding of the passage, as καὶ ἐμπεριπατήσω is exactly what would follow after the pronoun αὐτοῖς (adapted from ὑμῖν in 2 Cor 6.16) once the irrelevant second clause of Lev 26.11 (καὶ οὐ βδελύξεται ἡ ψυχή μου ὑμᾶς) had been omitted (see below). The Pauline form of the passage is thus the product of a careful reshaping of Lev 26.11–12 to suit a particular argumentative context (note v. 16b, ἡμεῖς γὰρ ναὸς θεοῦ ἐσμεν ζῶντος) under the influence of a thoroughly Christian view of existence, and not a loose conflation of Lev 26.11–12 with Ezek 37.27.[133] Here again the consummate artistry with which Paul molds the wording of the biblical text to reflect his own understanding and use of Scripture comes clearly into view.

A   Shift from ὑμῖν to αὐτοῖς.   As with the other third-person plural pronouns in 2 Cor 6.16, the Pauline αὐτοῖς would be entirely out of place in the second-person context of Lev 26.11.[134] Once it is accepted that it is this passage and not Ezek 37.27 that lies behind the present citation, the Pauline origin of the third-person plural forms in 2 Cor 6.16 follows as a matter

---

[132] The fact that every occurrence of ἐνοικήσω in the New Testament is found in the Pauline corpus (Rom 7.17, 8.11, Col 3.16, 2 Tim 1.5, 14) offers further support for the Pauline origin of the present reading.

[133] As argued for example by Michel, 81, and de Waard, *Study*, 16.

[134] Though the evidence wavers somewhat between the Genitive and Dative forms of the pronouns in Lev 26.11–12ₗₓₓ, none of the witnesses offers a third-person plural form for any of the pronouns in either verse.

of course.¹³⁵ Explaining why this change should have been introduced, however, is no easy matter. If anything, the second-person plurals of Lev 26.11–12 would appear preferable in the present context, since the following verses are framed entirely in second-person address. At the same time, the fact that v. 16 functions quite differently than vv. 17–18 in the present context should not be overlooked. Whereas the citation in v. 16b is introduced to supply a biblical foundation for the assertion in v. 16a (note καθὼς εἶπεν ὁ θεός ὅτι), the succeeding quotations function as a sort of substitute for direct speech, which obviously requires the use of second-person forms. By converting the first quotation to the rather impersonal tones of third-person speech, Paul creates a verbal transition that signals to his hearers that a shift in application has begun between v. 16 and v. 17.¹³⁶ Whether or not this is the proper explanation for the change, however, the present third-person form clearly goes back to the apostle Paul.

A   Omission of καὶ οὐ βδελύξεται ἡ ψυχή μου ὑμᾶς.   From the standpoint of Paul's use of Lev 26.11–12 in 2 Cor 6.16, Lev 26.11b represents an unnecessary and irrelevant intrusion of the type that Paul shows no reticence in excising elsewhere (cf. Rom 10.6–8, 15.12, 1 Cor 2.16, 14.21). Standing as it does between the immediately useful references to Yahweh's immanent presence with his people in vv. 11a and 12, the antithetical expression of v. 11b would have seriously disrupted the flow of thought had v. 11 been incorporated *in toto* into the new Pauline context. The obvious solution was to drop the offending clause from the verse in the process of reproduction, a course that Paul was quick to follow. The resultant citation, though still rather awkward in its placement of καὶ ἐμπερι-πατήσω, is clearly better suited to the point that Paul wants to make. The entire procedure is typically Pauline.

B   Omission of ἐν αὐτοῖς (v. 12).   Nothing in the present passage required the elimination of ἐν αὐτοῖς in v. 12 – in fact, including the phrase would actually have improved the symmetry of

---

¹³⁵ Of course, the possibility cannot be ruled out that the Ezekiel passage might have influenced the casting of the present citation into third-person speech.
¹³⁶ On the importance of such verbal cues in an oral society, see Achtemeier, 17–25.

the Pauline text (Future + ἐν αὐτοῖς in both cola of line one). Nevertheless, the textual evidence is quite secure in both traditions. Rhetorical foreshortening is the most likely explanation for the omission, though it appears that Paul has allowed his concern for brevity to overcome his sense of esthetics in this instance. With no other explanation in sight, a Pauline origin must be presumed.

B   Converting pronouns and verb from second-person (ὑμῶν ... ὑμεῖς ἔσεσθε) to third-person (αὐτῶν ... αὐτοὶ ἔσονται) forms. While it remains possible that the third-person forms arose under the influence of the parallel passage in Ezek 37.27, the rhetorical solution outlined in the discussion of αὐτοῖς (see above) should be considered at least equally possible. In any event, there is absolutely no evidence to indicate that the Leviticus passage was ever framed in third-person terms outside of its appearance here in 2 Cor 6.16. Whatever the explanation for the change, the Pauline origin of the present wording appears secure.

(62b)   **2 Cor 6.17** (= Isa 52.11, Ezek 20.34)

Paul: διὸ [ ] ἐξέλθατε ἐκ μέσου αὐτῶν καὶ ἀφορίσθητε, λέγει κύριος, καὶ ἀκαθάρτου μὴ ἅπτεσθε [ ]· + κἀγὼ εἰσδέξομαι ὑμᾶς.
Isa 52.11ₗₓₓ: ἀποστήτε ἀποστήτε ἐξέλθατε ἐκεῖθεν καὶ ἀκαθάρτου μὴ ἅπτεσθε, ἐξέλθατε ἐκ μέσου αὐτῆς ἀφορίσθητε, [οἱ φέροντες τὰ σκεύη κυρίου.]
Ezek 20.34ₗₓₓ: [καὶ ἐξάξω ὑμᾶς ἐκ τῶν λαῶν] καὶ εἰσδέξομαι ὑμᾶς [ἐκ τῶν χωρῶν, οὗ διεσκορπίσθητε ἐν αὐταῖς.]

C   Addition of διό. The reason behind the shift to Isa 52.11 in 2 Cor 6.17 is not hard to comprehend: the picture of Yahweh's imminent restoration of his people in Isa 52.1–10 (cf. vv. 4, 10, 12) recalls the same "exodus" theme that is adduced in Lev 26.13 to ground the divine promises of Lev 26.11–12 (= 2 Cor 6.16). The transitional particle διό is well suited to the original context of Isa 52.11,[137] but there is nothing to indicate that either the Hebrew or the Greek text of Isaiah ever contained

---

[137] The imperatives in Isa 52.11 are grounded directly in the promises of deliverance found in vv. 1–10.

such a reading. In the Pauline context, on the other hand, the word plays a vital role, forging an interpretive link between the Imperatives of v. 17 and the Indicatives of v. 16 that stands at the heart of the combined citation. The same Indicative/Imperative association is restated in more general terms in the summary statement in 7.1. The only question concerns the role of the added διό in the passage as a whole: does it serve to create a single "quotation" that extends from v. 16b through v. 18, or does it act as a sort of abbreviated introduction to vv. 17–18, inserted to clarify the relationship between these verses and the previous citation? A similar uncertainty surrounds the insertion of the phrase λέγει κύριος at the end of v. 17b (see below). Though on first inspection the passage gives every appearance of offering a continuous quotation, the intrusion of a logical particle like διό in v. 17a at the exact point where the text shifts from third-person to second-person speech could well signify to the attentive reader that a transition had occurred at precisely that point.[138] Whether this was what Paul intended will probably never be known for sure. As a result, this clearly Pauline insertion cannot be counted as an adaptation for the purposes of the present study.

B   Advancing ἐξέλθατε ἐκ μέσου αὐτ[ῶν] [καὶ] ἀφορίσθητε to primary position in place of ἀπόστητε ἀπόστητε ἐξέλθατε ἐκεῖθεν.   Why Paul should have replaced the words ἀπόστητε ἀπόστητε ἐξέλθατε ἐκεῖθεν with the very similar phrase ἐξέλθατε ἐκ μέσου αὐτῆς ἀφορίσθητε (so the LXX) from later in the verse is not easy to understand. The textual evidence is quite secure in both traditions, and no rationale for a later "correction" can be identified. It seems reasonable therefore to assume that the present word order goes back to Paul himself. One way of understanding the change would be to assume that Paul has simply confounded the two occurrences of ἐξέλθατε in Isa 52.11 as a result of a memory slip. If this were true, however, one would expect to see a certain amount of confusion in the wording of the two clauses, and not (as here) the latter clause replacing the first clause in its entirety. In the same way, nothing is to be gained from positing an improvement in the content as a reason for the substitution, since the two clauses

---

[138] See the discussion of the shift to αὐτοῖς in v. 16.

are virtually synonymous in meaning. The final possibility, that the change was introduced to improve the rhetorical effectiveness of the entire citation unit 2 Cor 6.16–18, finds numerous parallels in the combined citations studied thus far (Rom 3.10–18, 9.25–6, 10.6–8, 11.26–7, 1 Cor 15.54–5). No doubt the doubled ἀπόστητε of Isa 52.11a was felt to be redundant and perhaps overly dramatic in the present context, while including ἐκεῖθεν without clarifying its intended referent would only have confused Paul's hearers.[139] By the simple expedient of converting αὐτῆς from singular to plural (if indeed he did even this – see below), Paul is able to construct out of the second clause of Isa 52.11 an Imperative that flows smoothly from the Indicative of v. 16, while preserving the basic sense of the clause that he thus replaces.[140] The care with which these diverse passages from Leviticus and Isaiah are woven together into a coherent whole is thoroughly typical of Paul's combined citations.

C   Converting αὐτῆς to αὐτῶν. A significant portion of the Lucianic evidence agrees with Paul in reading αὐτῶν instead of αὐτῆς in Isa 52.11.[141] Though assimilation to the text of 2 Cor 6.17 cannot be ruled out, such an influence from one small element of a combined citation would be highly unusual.[142] The fact that none of these texts contains any of the other divergent language of 2 Cor 6.17 makes the supposition all the more unlikely. A more plausible explanation would see in the Lucianic texts an interpretive rendering in which the antecedent

[139] The Pauline αὐτῶν, on the other hand, would be read as a reference to the ἄπιστοι *et al.* of vv. 14–16, which is exactly what Paul wants.

[140] This is not to say, of course, that Paul uses the verse itself in a manner consistent with its original sense. In Isaiah, the injunction is meant literally, referring to the coming departure from Babylon; in Paul, the verse is given an allegorical and ethical turn.

[141] Found in 11 of the 17 MSS listed in the Göttingen edition, plus the mixed codex 534 and a citation from Cyprian. Notably missing from this list are the minuscules 62 and 147, which form what Ziegler calls "die erste und wichtigste lukianische Unter-gruppe" (75).

[142] See the discussions of the combined citations at Rom 3.10–18, 9.25–6, 10.6–8, 11.26–7, and 1 Cor 15.54–5. Influence from the combined citations is limited almost exclusively to an occasional interpolation of an entire verse (or more) into a LXX manuscript to bring it into line with a Pauline "quotation," as in Isa 40.13 (where many manuscripts add the text of Job 41.3 following the combined citation in Rom 11.34–5) and especially Ps 13.3 (where the great majority of witnesses insert the whole of Rom 3.13–18).

of the Greek pronoun was understood to be the πάντα τὰ ἔθνη of Isa 52.10.[143] In this case it could be argued that it is the primary LXX text (which agrees with the Masoretic Hebrew מְתוֹכָהּ) and not the Lucianic tradition that reflects a later "correction" toward the Hebrew text. The Masoretic feminine singular form is unquestionably awkward, and it requires no great imagination to see why either an original translator or a later reviser would have felt that the plural pronoun made better sense of the passage. Whether such a reading would have been available to Paul in the first century C.E., however, remains uncertain. The same change could be explained equally well as a Pauline adaptation designed to create a meaningful antecedent (i.e. the ἀπίστοις of v. 14a) for the otherwise irrelevant pronoun αὐτῆς. The strength of the external evidence likewise favors a Pauline origin. In the final analysis, the possibility of a textual basis for the plural pronoun remains just strong enough to preclude identifying this alteration as a confirmed Pauline adaptation for the purposes of the present study.

C   Addition of καί.   Here again the external evidence in the LXX tradition is sufficiently divided to allow for the possibility that Paul was working with a form of the Greek text that included a καί before ἀφορίσθητε.[144] As noted above, it would be highly unusual to see the text of the LXX being influenced by such a minor deviation in a Pauline combined citation. At the same time, additions and omissions of καί are a notorious source of difficulty within the LXX tradition.[145] Such an addition would have come quite naturally to a scribe or editor who wanted to improve the verbal parallelism between the two cola of Isa 52.11 (ἐξέλθατε + καί + verb in both clauses), and need not reflect Pauline influence. Whether such a text would have been

---

[143] The Hebrew tradition is united behind the singular pronoun at this point.

[144] The evidence for the added καί is quite diverse: the uncial Q from the A family, two important witnesses from the Hexaplaric tradition (MS 88 and the Syrohexapla), a handful of Lucianic manuscripts (22ᶜ-93-456), one of the Catena texts (564), and two mixed codices (393 544), in addition to a citation from Eusebius. The scattered nature of the evidence suggests the possibility that an earlier reading has been refracted through a variety of textual traditions. Only the Lucianic manuscripts 22-93-456 contain both the plural pronoun and the added καί.

[145] Cf. the addition of καί before ἀκαθάρτου in the LXX of Isa 52.11, contrary to the MT. Does the insertion reflect translational freedom, or a different Hebrew *Vorlage*?

available to Paul in the first century C.E., on the other hand, is entirely unknown. The possibility of a textual base is nonetheless strong enough to render the Pauline origin of the present reading highly suspect.

C Addition of λέγει κύριος.[146] As with διό at the beginning of the verse, the Pauline origin of the words λέγει κύριος is clear (cf. Rom 12.19, 1 Cor 14.21), but their intended function in the verse is not. Though a superficial reader would likely have regarded them as an integral part of the extended "quotation" that runs from v. 16b through v. 18, the interpretive weight carried by the added διό (see above) suggests the possibility that Paul himself viewed the insertion as part of a fragmented introductory formula (διό ... λέγει κύριος), and not part of the citation proper. Similar intrusions of part of the introductory formula into the wording of the quotation can be seen in Rom 2.24 (γάρ ... καθὼς γέγραπται), 1 Cor 6.16 (γὰρ φησίν), 1 Cor 15.27 (γάρ), and Eph. 6.2 (ἥτις ἐστὶν ἐντολὴ πρώτη ἐν ἐπαγγελίᾳ). In this interpretation, the combined citation would comprise only vv. 17 and 18, with v. 16 representing an independent citation. Whether this was Paul's intention, or whether he meant the added words to be read as part of the citation proper, is beyond the reach of the modern investigator.[147] As a result, this clearly Pauline addition cannot be counted as an adaptation for the purposes of the present study.

A Conflated citation (with Ezek 20.34). As with the transition from v. 16b to v. 17, it requires little imagination to understand why this particular passage from Ezekiel came to Paul's mind as a complement to the excerpt from Isa 52.11 that he has just cited in v. 17a–c. Both passages refer to a coming restoration of Yahweh's people to the land of Israel, and both use the deliverance from Egypt as a paradigm to depict the events to come. The language of the two verses combined here, on the other hand, is so distinctive as to preclude the possibility that Paul has somehow conflated them by accident in the process of quoting Isa 52.11 from memory. In fact, the choice of words from the Ezekiel passage is itself rather curious – one might

---

[146] The words are omitted in K 4* Tert, presumably in assimilation to the LXX.
[147] For other possible explanations, see the discussion of the similar addition at Rom 12.19.

have expected προσδέξομαι ὑμᾶς from v. 41, where language reminiscent of the "dwelling" theme of 2 Cor 6.16 appears, instead of a phrase from v. 34, which anticipates the return of Israel from the Diaspora. On the thematic level, however, the link is quite understandable: it is in precisely these two verses (Isa 52.11 and Ezek 20.34) that the subject of the departure of Yahweh's people from their place of captivity is first broached in each passage. Perhaps Paul had even heard the two verses used together in the synagogue to support the common Jewish expectation of the ultimate return of Yahweh's people to their ancestral home. To argue that the actual combination had already occurred in the pre-Pauline synagogue, however, would be to outstrip the evidence.

From a formal standpoint, advancing ἐξέλθατε κτλ. to a position ahead of καὶ ἀκαθάρτου μὴ ἅπτεσθε[148] in v. 17a-b (see above) allowed Paul the freedom to end his citation after ἅπτεσθε rather than continuing with the useless and irrelevant phrase οἱ φέροντες τὰ σκεύη κυρίου, a freedom that he readily employs in 2 Cor 6.17. By replacing those parts of Isa 52.11 that diverge from his own rhetorical purposes with a more useful phrase from another passage, Paul is able to craft a new "quotation" in which every element speaks directly to the circumstances of his Corinthian hearers. The smoothness of the resultant literary product reinforces the (false) impression given by the introductory formula in v. 16 that vv. 16–18 (or at least vv. 17–18) represent a unified selection from a single passage of Scripture.

C   Substitution of κἀγώ for καί. A Pauline origin for the present substitution appears likely, but can hardly be confirmed. The LXX tradition shows no trace of the Pauline reading in Ezek 20.34, while the word κἀγώ appears more often in Paul's writings than in any other New Testament author except John.[149] In its emphatic sense of "I for my part, I in turn,"[150] the substitution is well suited to the Pauline context,

---

[148] A number of LXX manuscripts read the Aorist ἅψησθε in place of the Present ἅπτεσθε here (B-V–88 C 87 456 538 544 Eus), but the change is easily explained as an assimilation to the other Aorists that appear in Isa 52.11$_{LXX}$. No Pauline adaptation is in view here.

[149] The word occurs twenty-seven times in the Pauline epistles. The frequency of κἀγώ in the LXX of Ezekiel cannot be determined from Hatch and Redpath.

[150] See BAGD, s. v. κἀγώ, 3b.

calling the hearers' attention to the shift in subject matter (from divine imperative to divine response) that occurs at precisely this point in the citation. Nevertheless, the shift in wording is quite modest, and the Pauline form is by no means inappropriate in the LXX context. Though manuscript support is lacking, the possibility of a textual explanation for such a minor change cannot be dismissed out of hand. Prudence would dictate caution in assessing the origins of what could well be a simple stylistic improvement.

(62d)   **2 Cor 6.18** (= 2 Kgdms 7.14, 7.8)

Paul: καὶ ἐγὼ ἔσομαι <u>ὑμῖν</u> εἰς πατέρα, καὶ <u>ὑμεῖς ἔσεσθέ</u> μοι εἰς <u>υἱοὺς καὶ θυγατέρας,</u> + λέγει κύριος παντοκράτωρ.

2 Kgdms 7.14$_{LXX}$: ἐγὼ ἔσομαι αὐτῷ εἰς πατέρα, καὶ αὐτὸς ἔσται μοι εἰς υἱόν.

2 Kgdms 7.8$_{LXX}$: [καὶ νῦν τάδε ἐρεῖς τῷ δούλῳ μου Δαυιδ Τάδε] λέγει κύριος παντοκράτωρ [Ἔλαβόν σε ἐκ τῆς μάνδρας τῶν προβάτων ...]

C   Addition of καί.   Given Paul's proclivity for omitting initial particles like καί from his citations,[151] the apparent addition of such a particle here calls for an explanation. Had the word been absent from his *Vorlage*, an insertion would have been almost required to maintain the kind of verbal continuity and structural parallelism that Paul seems at great pains to establish in the present citation.[152] Nevertheless, it is by no means certain that the καί that opens 2 Cor 6.18a was absent from Paul's Greek text. The conjunction is found in several minuscules of 2 Kgdms,[153] the Sahidic Coptic, Ethiopic, and Georgian versions, and quotations by Cyril, Theodoret, and Cyprian. Since none of these witnesses shows any of the other modifications that characterize the Pauline form of the verse, the possibility of influence from 2 Cor 6.18 is largely excluded. Whether a text that contained a καί at the beginning of 2 Kgdms 7.14

---

[151] See chap. 4, note 197.

[152] In addition to the points noted throughout the preceding discussion, note the tripartite structure of both the injunction (v. 17a–c) and promise (v. 17d–18b) sections of the combined citation, where the last two lines of each section are introduced by a καί.

[153] Holmes–Parsons lists 55 93 108 119 123 158 246, while Brooke–McLean cites b g h n e$_2$. The absence of a true critical edition of 2 Kgdms presents a major obstacle to further research on this point.

would have been available to Paul in the first century C.E. can of course no longer be determined. The evidence that Paul might have drawn his citation from just such a text is nevertheless sufficient to preclude counting the addition of καί in v. 18 as a Pauline adaptation for the purposes of the present study.

A   Converting third-person singular forms (αὐτῷ ... αὐτὸς ἔσται) to second-person plurals (ὑμῖν ... ὑμεῖς ἔσεσθε).   The form in which Paul quotes 2 Kgdms 7.14 in 2 Cor 6.18 has been adapted to such a degree that some interpreters have refused to consider it a citation at all.[154] Nevertheless, the fact that Paul closes the verse with the same λέγει κύριος παντοκράτωρ that introduces the divine promise in 2 Kgdms 7.8–16 is enough to prove that Paul was aware of the broader context of the verse that he quotes here, as Kautzsch pointed out long ago.[155] As there is no evidence to indicate that the combination witnessed in 2 Cor 6.16–18 took place prior to Paul, it should be presumed that Paul drew the present quotation directly from the biblical text, and not from some intermediate source.[156]

Since the combined citation in vv. 17–18 has taken the place of a direct exhortation to Paul's Corinthian hearers, the shift to second-person plural forms in the Pauline form of 2 Kgdms 7.14 offers little difficulty. Behind this simple adaptation, however, lies a shift in perception that sets Paul apart from every contemporary interpretation of this important passage. In its Pauline form, the divine promise of 2 Kgdms 7.14 is applied not to the royal descendants of David, nor even to Jesus as the divinely appointed "Son of David," but to the Christian church. A similar hermeneutical move can be seen in Gal 3, where first Christ alone (v. 16) and then those who are

---

[154] According to Kautzsch (91), both Grotius and Ewald thought that Paul had drawn his words here from a common Jewish hymn. Ellis (*Use*, 109–12) sees in the addition of the phrase λέγει κύριος παντοκράτωρ a sign that the verse had already been paraphrased by pre-Pauline Christian prophets. Against Ellis's interpretation of the λέγει κύριος sayings, see Aune, 339–46.

[155] Kautzsch, 92.

[156] 2 Kgdms 7 was no doubt a familiar passage in early Christianity (see Heb 1.5, Rev 21.7) as in Judaism (note *4QFlor* 1.10–11), though the evidence for its use is slim. According to Donald Juel (*Messianic Exegesis: Christological Interpretation of the Old Testament in Early Christianity* (Philadelphia: Fortress, 1988), 61–2), the passage is cited nowhere in Second Temple Jewish literature outside the quotation in *4QFlor*, and rabbinic references are equally scarce. Against the possibility that Paul framed the closing phrase himself without reference to 2 Kgdms 7.8 stands the observation that Paul nowhere else refers to God as παντοκράτωρ.

"in Christ" (v. 29) are identified as the "seed" of Abraham. Whether the same thought process lies behind the present application can no longer be ascertained, but the idea certainly would not have been foreign to Paul.[157] Instead of offering a lengthy exposition to justify his reading of 2 Kgdms 7.14, Paul simply incorporates his own interpretation into the wording of the quotation in 2 Cor 6.18. In this way those who were familiar with the original passage could ruminate over the hermeneutical move implied in the revised wording if they wished, while even the most ignorant of listeners could comprehend Paul's basic message that Christians are now the "sons and daughters" of God. All in all, this passage offers one of the clearest examples of how Paul could adapt the wording of a biblical passage to communicate the precise sense in which he intended a particular verse to be understood.

A   Shift from singular υἱόν to plural υἱούς.   Since he meant to apply 2 Kgdms 7.14 to the Christian church and not to the royal line of David (see above), Paul could not allow the singular υἱόν of the LXX to stand. Accordingly, he converted it to a plural to coincide with the second-person plural forms that he had already introduced in the first part of the verse. Such an adaptation makes sense only in the context of the present Pauline interpretation of 2 Kgdms 7.14.

A   Addition of καὶ θυγατέρας.   The fact that Paul could have made his point quite effectively without this final addition has often been overlooked by modern commentators.[158] For some reason Paul felt compelled to make explicit his conviction that women and men stand on an equal footing as children of God. While it is quite possible that the addition should be read as a generalized theological pronouncement of the sort encountered in Gal 3.28, the fact that Paul can use the masculine υἱοὶ Θεοῦ

---

[157] Note especially the use of the word σπέρμα in 2 Kgdms 7.12. Similarly Barrett, *2 Corinthians*, 201: "The promise of 2 Sam. [2 Kgdms] vii. 14 was originally addressed to the king; the king is Jesus, and in him men and women participate in his status before God."

[158] No specific biblical antecedent for the phrase υἱοὺς καὶ θυγατέρας is apparent. Barrett (*2 Corinthians*, 201) follows Schlatter and Bonsirven in suggesting Isa 43.6, but the proposed link is tenuous at best. Dittmar (223) points to *Wis* 9.7, where the people of Israel are referred to as the "sons and daughters" of God, but here too the similarity is purely verbal.

elsewhere to include all Christians, both male and female, raises questions about the specific language employed here.[159] In Paul's earlier letter to the church at Corinth, statements affirming the basic equality of the sexes (e.g. 1 Cor 7.3–4, 12–16, 11.5, 11–12) stand alongside more traditional hierarchical assertions about the roles of women and men in the Christian church (e.g. 1 Cor 11.3–9, 14.34–5). This in turn implies that both sorts of statements were required (in Paul's mind) to address specific disagreements that had arisen with regard to the activities of women in the Corinthian church. The same concerns no doubt lie behind the addition of καὶ θυγατέρας to the quotation in 2 Cor 6.18, though the precise reason for the insertion lies beyond the reach of the present study.

A   Conflated citation: addition of λέγει κύριος παντοκράτωρ (2 Kgdms 7.8) at the end of v. 18. Nothing in the original context or subsequent history of the text gives any reason to think that the phrase λέγει κύριος παντοκράτωρ ever appeared in any LXX manuscript in the middle of 2 Kgdms 7.14. Though the ultimate purpose of this addition is as opaque as similar insertions of λέγει κύριος in Rom 12.19, 1 Cor 14.21, and 2 Cor 6.17,[160] the reason for the choice of a different expression here is not far to seek. The same words appear at the beginning of the divine pronouncement in 2 Kgdms 7.8–16, of which the verse quoted in 2 Cor 6.18 forms a vital part.[161] As the form of 2 Kgdms 7.14 quoted there shows clear signs of Pauline adaptation (see above), there is no reason to think that the present addition should be traced to any other source.[162] Whatever his intention in inserting these words at precisely this point, it seems clear that the resulting conflation is a Pauline construction.

---

[159] On the use of υἱοὶ Θεοῦ to refer to all Christians regardless of gender, see Rom 8.14, 19, Gal 3.26, 4.6–7, Col 1.13, 1 Thess 5.5, and especially the quotation in Rom 9.26.

[160] See the discussion at Rom 12.19.

[161] The phrase is common only in late prophetic literature. Outside of abundant references in the prophets Haggai, Zechariah, and Malachi, the phrase (τάδε) λέγει κύριος παντοκράτωρ is found only in 2 Kgdms 7.8, 1 Chr 17.7 (a parallel passage), and Jer 5.14, 23.16 in the entire LXX.

[162] See note 154.

(63)   **2 Cor 8.15** (= Exod 16.18)

Paul: ὁ τὸ πολύ οὐκ ἐπλεόνασεν, καὶ ὁ τὸ ὀλίγον οὐκ ἠλαττόνησεν.

LXX: [καὶ μετρήσαντες τῷ γομορ] οὐκ ἐπλεόνασεν ὁ τὸ πολύ, καὶ ὁ τὸ ἔλαττον οὐκ ἠλαττόνησεν.

A   Omission of καὶ μετρήσαντες τῷ γομορ (limited selection). Though technically dependent on the οἱ υἱοὶ Ἰσραηλ of Exod 16.17, the clause καὶ μετρήσαντες τῷ γομορ forms an integral part of Exod 16.18 in the original narrative context. The same phrase becomes an irrelevant and intrusive detail, however, in the framework of 2 Cor 8.15. Though he clearly presupposes a certain familiarity with the story of the manna in the wilderness – indeed, the highly allusive reference would make little sense without it – Paul leaves the task of supplying the details entirely to the hearers. By paring down the narrative to its essential point, the equality of Yahweh's provision for his people, Paul is able to highlight that element of the story that applies most directly to his Corinthian hearers. The practice is typically Pauline.

B   Advancing ὁ τὸ πολύ.   As it now stands, the LXX rendering agrees exactly with the word order of the Masoretic Hebrew text. The reversal of subject and verb in 2 Cor 8.15 is quite natural, designed to improve the structural parallelism between the two clauses of Exod 16.18b, and so might conceivably have arisen independentlc of Pauline influence. As Kautzsch noted long ago, however, the participle that precedes the portion of Exod 16.18 cited by Paul (μετρήσαντες) virtually requires that the primary verb stand ahead of ὁ τὸ πολύ,[163] so that the handful of LXX witnesses that agree with Paul most likely reflect assimilation to 2 Cor 8.15.[164] If this is so, then the possibility is small indeed that Paul might have derived the word order of 2 Cor 8.15 from his own Greek *Vorlage*. A more likely explanation would see Paul himself reversing the order of the words to create a better parallel with his own more natural

---

[163] Kautzsch, 20.
[164] Brooke–McLean could cite only one minuscule (n) and the Armenian and Bohairic Coptic versions in support of the Pauline word order. The soon-to-be-published Göttingen edition, graciously made available by Dr. John William Wevers, adds only two minuscules (318 799) and a quote from Cyril to this list.

expression of the same point in v. 14.[165] The resultant
heightening of the antithesis between the two halves of the
quotation serves to reinforce Paul's own contrast (v. 14)
between the present and (possible) future conditions of the
Corinthian donors. Though the change is minor and its effect
subtle to the modern ear,[166] all the evidence would seem to
point to Paul as the originator of the present reading.

E   Substitution of ὀλίγον for ἔλαττον. Possible explanations
for the Pauline reading abound, though none can claim any
measure of certainty. On the textual side, the only LXX witnesses with ὀλίγον are the first corrector of the uncial A, a
quotation in Philo, and two related minuscules.[167] All could be
explained as assimilations to the wording of 2 Cor 8.15, though
the agreement with Philo should cause at least a moment's
hesitation. The possibility that both Paul and Philo (and
perhaps also the corrector of A) relied on a biblical text that
contained ὀλίγον instead of ἔλαττον cannot be entirely ruled
out.[168] The Masoretic Hebrew does not support the cognate
construction found in the LXX (הַמַּמְעִיט לֹא הֶחְסִיר ≠ ὁ τὸ
ἔλαττον οὐκ ἠλαττόνησεν), and it is not difficult to see how a
literal-minded translator/reviser might have rendered הַמַּמְעִיט
by ὁ τὸ ὀλίγον to reflect the presence of different roots in the
underlying Hebrew (cf. Aquila).[169] A scribal modification

---

[165] So Koch, Schrift, 108, citing the similar reversal in Rom 9.12.
[166] Ancient audiences were much more attuned to such subtle verbal cues: see
Achtemeier, 17–25.
[167] The minuscule evidence (126–413) comes from the soon-to-be-published Göttingen edition of Exodus.
[168] The text of Philo's writings was preserved in Christian circles, so that assimilation of his biblical quotations to those of the New Testament is not unknown.
Kautzsch (20) is probably right, however, in rejecting the possibility that both writers
independently modified the biblical text to avoid cacophony with the following verb,
since both would have been quite familiar with such cognate constructions from the
LXX.
[169] One might have expected the verb to be changed in this case, since ἔλαττον has
just been used in the previous verse to translate the same Hebrew word as here. But
the association between forms of ἐλαττ- and חסר is strong in the LXX Pentateuch,
and indeed throughout most of the Bible (see the listings in Hatch and Redpath).
Both ὀλίγος and ἐλάττων are used regularly in the LXX to translate forms of מעט,
though the only place that employs ὀλίγος to translate the Hiphil participle (Jer
10.24) joins it with the verb ποιεῖν rather than ἐλαττονεῖν as here. The cognate
construction ἐλαττονεῖν/-νοῦν ἔλαττον appears in four other places in the Pentateuch (and nowhere else), but in all those cases (Lev 25.16, Num 26.54, 33.54, 35.8) it
follows a similar cognate construction in the Hebrew.

designed to balance out the inequity between the absolute form of the first clause (πολύ = "much," not "more") and the comparative employed in the second (ἔλαττον = "less," ὀλίγον = "little") is also not out of the question. On the Pauline side, on the other hand, it is difficult to see what might have been gained by such a substitution, except perhaps a more absolute depiction of the poverty of the Jerusalem Christians, i.e. they have "little," not just "less."[170] The general lack of evidence on both sides renders firm conclusions impossible.

(64)   **2 Cor 9.9** (= Ps 112.9)[171]

Paul: ἐσκόρπισεν, ἔδωκεν τοῖς πένησιν,
       ἡ δικαιοσύνη αὐτοῦ μένει εἰς τὸν αἰῶνα [_].
LXX: ἐσκόρπισεν, ἔδωκεν τοῖς πένησιν,
       ἡ δικαιοσύνη αὐτοῦ μένει εἰς τὸν αἰῶνα του αἰῶνος.

D   Omission of τοῦ αἰῶνος.   Though a number of lesser manuscripts include the phrase τοῦ αἰῶνος at the end of 2 Cor 9.9, the weight of the external evidence is clearly on the side of the omission.[172] The LXX tradition, on the other hand, is unanimous in reading εἰς τὸν αἰῶνα τοῦ αἰῶνος in Ps 112.9. It is worth noting, however, that even the major LXX witnesses vary between these and other forms of the same expression elsewhere in the Psalms, so that it would come as no surprise to discover that Paul had used a text that omitted the final phrase of Ps 112.9.[173] Moreover, the LXX of the Psalms is relatively consistent (though by no means uniform) in using the simple εἰς τὸν αἰῶνα to render the Hebrew עוֹלָם, while reserving the longer form εἰς (τὸν) αἰῶνα (τοῦ) αἰῶνος for the Hebrew לָעַד as here.[174] This raises the possibility that Paul might have

---

[170] Koch (*Schrift*, 142) attributes this "stilistische" change to Paul, his only explanation being that it "verstärkt ... die Parallelität der beiden Zitatglieder." The possibility that an earlier scribe might have shared the same concern is never addressed.

[171] The loose quotations/allusions in 2 Cor 8.21 (= Prov 3.4) and 9.7 (= Prov 22.8a) have been omitted from the present study in accordance with strict guidelines that limit the investigation to passages that offer explicit indication to the reader that a citation is being offered (introductory formula, interpretive comments, etc.).

[172] The phrase is included in F G K 0243 6 326 629 630 1241 1739 1881 *al* a vg^cl bo^mss aeth, while all the major witnesses (א A B *et al.*) omit it.

[173] See the variations listed in Hatch and Redpath on Ps 9.18, 20.4, 20.6, 24.2, 36.27, 40.12, 44.6, 47.14, 60.8, 84.5, 103.31, and 144.2.

[174] See the listings in Hatch and Redpath.

drawn his citation from a Greek text that presupposed a Hebrew *Vorlage* of עוֹלָם rather than לְעַד. But linguistic data can be adduced in favor of a Pauline omission as well. As Koch points out, the longer form of the expression (with τοῦ αἰῶνος) is never used by Paul, and the parallel form with τῶν αἰώνων is rare.[175] Though the evidence is skimpy, it should also be noted that, of the two shorter expressions employed by Paul (εἰς τοὺς αἰῶνας and εἰς τὸν αἰῶνα), only the latter appears in a non-liturgical context as here.[176] In sum, while the textual evidence favors a Pauline origin, substantial linguistic evidence can be adduced to support either explanation. No firm conclusions can be erected on such a shaky foundation.

(65)   **2 Cor 10.17** (= Jer 9.23)[177]

See under 1 Cor 1.31.[178]

(66)   **Gal 3.6** (= Gen 15.6)[179]

Paul: [καθὼς] [ ] Ἀβραὰμ ἐπίστευσεν τῷ θεῷ, καὶ ἐλογίσθη αὐτῷ εἰς δικαιοσύνην.

LXX: καὶ ἐπίστευσεν Ἀβραάμ τῷ θεῷ, καὶ ἐλογίσθη αὐτῷ εἰς δικαιοσύνην.

A   Omitting initial καί.[180] The present syntax, designed to connect the citation with the preceding argument (καθώς),

---

[175] *Schrift*, 116 n. 7. The longer expression εἰς τὸν αἰῶνα τῶν αἰώνων appears only in the liturgical contexts of Rom 16.27, Gal 1.5, and Phil 4.20 (so also 1 Tim 1.17 and 2 Tim 4.18).

[176] The form with the plural object (εἰς τοὺς αἰῶνας) appears in Rom 1.25, 9.5, 11.36, and 2 Cor 11.31, while the singular form (εἰς τὸν αἰῶνα) is found only in 1 Cor 8.13 and the present passage.

[177] The brief quotation/allusion in 2 Cor 9.10 has been omitted from the present study in accordance with strict guidelines that limit the investigation to passages that offer explicit indication to the reader that a citation is being offered (introductory formula, interpretive comments, etc.).

[178] This citation is included in the present study despite the absence of a formal introductory statement or explicit interpretive comment on the assumption that the Corinthians would recall its use in Paul's earlier letter (1 Cor 1.31), where it was introduced by καθὼς γέγραπται.

[179] The apparent quotations from Deut 19.15 in 2 Cor 13.1 and Ps 143.2 in Gal 2.16 (cf. Rom 3.20) have been omitted from the present study in accordance with strict guidelines that limit the investigation to passages that offer explicit indication to the reader that a citation is being offered (introductory formula, interpretive comments, etc.).

[180] Or possibly δέ, depending on how one views the origins of the latter particle in Rom 4.3 (q. v.).

leaves no room for an initial conjunction, while the omission of such particles is typically Pauline.[181]

B   Advancing Ἀβραάμ. That the present placement of Ἀβραάμ is to be traced to Paul himself is clear from a simple comparison with Rom 4.3, where Paul replicates the LXX word order precisely.[182] The LXX tradition contains no evidence for such a reversal of Ἀβραάμ and ἐπίστευσεν. Questions remain, however, as to whether Paul meant the proper name to function as part of the citation or the introduction in Gal 3.6. In favor of linking the name with the citation is the observation that the resultant stress on the figure of Abraham (the result of shifting Ἀβραάμ to primary position) accords well with the discussion that follows in vv. 7–9. Against this explanation stands the fact that nowhere else in Paul (or in the rest of the New Testament, for that matter) is an unaccompanied καθώς used to introduce a biblical quotation. The obvious alternative would be to take the phrase καθὼς Ἀβραάμ as a transitional statement designed to set up an actual comparison between the faith of Abraham and that of the Galatian believers (cf. v. 9). In this case, the present word order becomes explicable, if still elliptic: "(It is with you) just as (it was with) Abraham: he believed God ...."[183] Here too a minor adaptation of the biblical wording is required, this time an omission of the word Ἀβραάμ after ἐπίστευσεν so as to avoid redundancy with the preceding Ἀβραάμ. In truth, such distinctions are probably too fine for the present situation – this would certainly not be the first instance of a Pauline ellipsis placing an intolerable strain on the conventions of the Greek language. But whether one labels it an emphatic shift in the biblical word order or an omission meant to avoid redundancy, some sort of adaptation of the biblical text must clearly be assumed in Gal 3.6.

---

[181] On the omission of initial particles, see chap. 4, note 197. On the function of καθώς here, see the discussion of Ἀβραάμ in the section that follows.

[182] Tischendorf cites a handful of Pauline manuscripts and versions (F G f g fu al[lachm] syr[sch] arm Ambst) that reverse the order of Ἀβραάμ and ἐπίστευσεν in Gal 3.6, but this is clearly an assimilation to the LXX.

[183] Similarly Koch, *Schrift*, 106: "Paulus mit καθώς zunächst zu einem echten Vergleich ansetzt, dessen Fortsetzung (etwa durch οὕτως οἱ ἐκ πίστεως κτλ.) er jedoch durch die schlußfolgernde Zitatinterpretation von V 7 (γινώσκετε ἄρα ὅτι κτλ.) ersetzt."

(67) **Gal 3.8** (= Gen 12.3)[184]

Paul: [προϊδοῦσα δὲ ἡ γραφὴ ὅτι ἐκ πίστεως δικαιοῖ τὰ ἔθνη ὁ
θεός, προευαγγελίσατο τῷ Ἀβραὰμ ὅτι] [ ] **ἐνευλογηθήσονται** ἐν σοὶ πᾶσαι **πάντα τὰ ἔθνη** [ ].

LXX: [καὶ εὐλογήσω τοὺς εὐλογοῦντάς σε, καὶ τοὺς καταρω-
μένους σε καταράσομαι·] καὶ ἐνευλογηθήσονται ἐν σοὶ
πᾶσαι αἱ φυλαὶ τῆς γῆς.

A Omission of initial καί. Though the clause selected here
begins in the middle of a verse, the elimination of the καί that
introduces it in the original passage should not be overlooked.
As in numerous other instances,[185] retaining the conjunction
would have seriously impaired the transition from text to
quotation in the Pauline application of the verse. The omission
is typically Pauline.

V Reading ἐνευλογηθήσονται rather than εὐλογηθήσονται.
The wording of the Pauline text here is quite secure, despite
minor evidence in favor of the shorter εὐλογηθήσονται.[186] On
the LXX side, the evidence is more divided, with the uncial A,
the papyrus fragment 833, and several minuscules reading the
shorter form in Gen 12.3.[187] The wording of the Pauline citation agrees with the majority LXX tradition at this point. The
shift to εὐλογηθήσονται in both traditions is probably to be
understood as a scribal "correction" designed to replace an
unusual word with its more common equivalent.[188]

[184] Identical language is found in Gen 28.14 (with the phrase καὶ ἐν τῷ σπέρματί
σου appended to the end), and similar expressions appear in Gen 18.18 and 22.18.
But the context of Gal 3 makes it clear that the Gen 12 episode is the one Paul has in
mind here. Barnabas Lindars's comment is *apropos*: "The passage referred to must be
12.3, because the argument turns on the fact that the promise has already been made
before 15.6. In the other passages it could be argued that Abraham has works to his
credit, hospitality to strangers (Gen. 18), and the sacrifice of Isaac (Gen. 22)"
(*Apologetic*, 225).

[185] See chap. 4, note 197.

[186] Tischendorf cites F G 76 115 *al vix mu* Chr Theoph as containing the shorter
form of the verb.

[187] The minuscules come from a variety of families, comprising MSS 72–707 569
343 59. A quotation from Clement of Rome gives the same form. A handful of
Christian sources and Philo give the shorter reading in the parallel passage, Gen
28.14.

[188] LSJ, BAGD, and TDNT cite no evidence for the longer form outside the LXX
and the NT.

A Substituting πάντα τὰ ἔθνη for πᾶσαι αἱ φυλαί. Evidence for this substitution is almost non-existent in the textual tradition of the LXX, and is clearly to be traced to the influence of Gal 3.8 where it occurs.[189] The evidence on the Pauline side is equally united. The language of Gen 12.3 is so close to that of Gen 18.18 (where πάντα τὰ ἔθνη occurs) that the possibility of an accidental conflation in the course of quoting the text from memory cannot be ruled out.[190] But the familiarity of the passage makes such a slip less than likely, while the substitution clearly renders the wording of the text better suited to its present environment.[191] In its present wording, the quotation in v. 8b is fundamental to Paul's argument that the divine promise to Abraham has now been fulfilled in the presence of Gentile believers in the Christian church. As Paul sees it, Gen 12.3 shows that God had already declared long ago (προϊ-δοῦσα ... προευαγγελίσατο, v. 8a) that τὰ ἔθνη would share in the "blessing" of Abraham (= "justification," v. 8a) as they imitate the "faith" of Abraham (v. 9).[192] However one explains the change, the wording of the citation in Gal 3.8 is clearly Pauline.[193]

A Omission of τῆς γῆς at the end of the verse. Here again evidence for an earlier omission is almost entirely lacking in the LXX tradition,[194] while the same motive adduced for the pre-

[189] In Gen 12.3, none of the manuscripts supports this reading. In the parallel statement in Gen 28.14, only two texts from the f family (53 664) read πάντα τὰ ἔθνη in place of πᾶσαι αἱ φυλαί. Assimilation to Gen 12.3 is behind the reverse substitution of πᾶσαι αἱ φυλαί for πάντα τὰ ἔθνη in MSS 25–646 at Gen 18.18. No such assimilation can be seen in Gen 22.18.

[190] So *inter alia* Kautzsch, 60, and Michel, 75. Against the possibility that Gen 18.18 is the primary text in Gal 3.8 stands the fact that it is much easier to understand why Paul would have changed πᾶσαι αἱ φυλαί (Gen 12.3) to πάντα τὰ ἔθνη (Gen 18.18) than to explain the opposite shift from ἐν αὐτῷ (Gen 18.18) to ἐν σοί (Gen 12.3).

[191] Though the evidence is slim (Rom 11.1, Phil 3.5), Barnabas Lindars may be right in his further observation that "φυλαί in Paul's vocabulary always refers to the tribes of Israel, whereas here he is bound to use the technical term for the Gentiles" (*Apologetic*, 225).

[192] On this understanding of Gal 3.6–9, see the author's article, "'Under a Curse': A Fresh Reading of Gal 3.10–14," *NTS* 36 (1990), 481–511.

[193] Interestingly, a similar substitution occurs in Acts 3.25 (the word πατριαί replacing the ἔθνη of Gen 22.18₍LXX₎), the only other place in the NT where one of these "blessing of the nations" passages from Genesis appears.

[194] None of the manuscripts omits the phrase in Gen 12.3, but a shortened form can be found in MSS 53–664 at Gen 28.14 and in A Sa[20] at Gen 22.18. The first is clearly an assimilation to Gal 3.8 (πᾶσαι αἱ φυλαὶ τῆς γῆς replaced by a simple πάντα

vious adaptation could explain the present omission as well. Throughout his epistle, Paul assumes that his Galatian hearers will understand that he is using the expression τὰ ἔθνη in its religio–cultural sense, viz. "the Gentiles," the term commonly used by Jews to designate anyone outside their particular ethnic and religious heritage (1.16, 2.2, 8, 9, 12, 14, 15, 3.14). In Gen 12.3, on the other hand, the presence of the phrase τῆς γῆς has a broadening effect: a simple reading would see in the original wording a reference to a variety of ethnic and/or national entities who would benefit from the divine promise. To insure that the words τὰ ἔθνη would be understood in the same technical religious sense as in the rest of his letter (and indeed in the present argument – see 3.8a, 3.14), Paul simply leaves off the final phrase of the biblical text. Here again the close hermeneutical interplay between text and context has exercised a decisive influence on the wording of a Pauline biblical quotation.

(68)   **Gal 3.10** (= Deut 27.26, 28.58?)

Paul: ἐπικατάρατος πᾶς [ ] ὃς οὐκ ἐμμενεῖ [ ] πᾶσιν + τοῖς γεγραμμένοις ἐν τῷ βιβλίῳ + τοῦ νόμου [ ] τοῦ ποιῆσαι αὐτά.

Deut 27.26ₗₓₓ: ἐπικατάρατος πᾶς ἄνφρωπος, ὅστις ὀυκ ἐμμενεῖ ἐν πᾶσιν τοῖς λόγοις τοῦ νόμου τούτου ποιῆσαι αὐτούς.

Deut 28.58ₗₓₓ: [ἐὰν μὴ εἰσακούσητε ποιεῖν πάντα τὰ ῥήματα τοῦ νόμου τούτου] τὰ γεγραμμένα ἐν τῷ βιβλίῳ τούτῳ [φοβεῖσθαι τὸ ὄνομα τὸ ἔντιμον καὶ τὸ θαυμαστὸν τοῦτο ...]

Deut 30.10ₗₓₓ: [ἐὰν εἰσακούσῃς τῆς φωνῆς κυρίου τοῦ θεοῦ σου φυλάσσεσθαι καὶ ποιεῖν πάσας τὰς ἐντολὰς αὐτοῦ καὶ τὰ δικαιώματα αὐτοῦ καὶ τὰς κρίσεις αὐτοῦ] τὰς γεγραμμένας ἐν τῷ βιβλίῳ τοῦ νόμου τούτου, [ἐὰν ἐπιστραφῇς ἐπὶ κύριον τὸν θεόν σου ἐξ ὅλης τῆς καρδίας σου καὶ ὅλης τῆς ψυχῆς σου.]

B   Omission of ἄνθρωπος. Though the LXX tradition testifies to several variations in the wording of Deut 27.26 at this point,

---

τὰ ἔθνη), while the second can probably be explained in the same way (leaving πάντα τὰ ἔθνη as in Gal 3.8).

a simple omission of ἄνθρωπος is not among them.[195] The Pauline tradition is likewise unanimous in its reading. A pre-Pauline assimilation to a different Hebrew *Vorlage* is unlikely, as there is nothing to indicate that the Hebrew text ever contained a written equivalent to the πᾶς that appears in both the LXX and Gal 3.10.[196] A Pauline origin for the omission of ἄνθρωπος in Gal 3.10 can therefore be presumed. This presumption finds additional support in the observation that Paul omits the same word from the subsequent quotation in Gal 3.12b (= Lev 18.5), which he reproduces elsewhere (Rom 10.5) in full agreement with the LXX wording.[197] Clearly some sort of editorial purpose has dictated the removal of the word ἄνθρωπος in both instances. Just what that purpose was, however, remains somewhat obscure. One result of the change is to improve the rhetorical parallelism between the two sets of citations in Gal 3.10–13 (note πᾶς ὅς and πᾶς ὁ in vv. 10 and 13, along with ὁ ποιήσας and ὁ κρεμάμενος in vv. 11 and 12), an effect that subtly reinforces the chiastic structure of the passage as a whole.[198] Such an outcome is surely no accident, though the value of such constructions in leading the hearer through a complex and closely reasoned argument is often underappreciated by modern readers. Whether it is correct to say that the omissions serve the further purpose of strengthening the dichotomy between πίστις/εὐλογία and ἔργα νόμου/κατάρα in vv. 10–13 (so Koch) is more uncertain.[199] An attempt to generalize Deut 27.26 beyond traditional gender roles (cf. οὐκ ἔνι ἄρσεν καὶ θῆλυ in Gal 3.28 and the addition of καὶ θυγατέρας in 2 Cor 6.18) is not out of the question, but concrete evidence to support such a reading is lacking. The Pauline origin of the present wording appears secure by any account.

---

[195] A number of minuscules and citations omit either the entire phrase πᾶς ἄνθρωπος (so also Ἀ Σ Θ) or the word πᾶς alone, in clear assimilation to the MT. A wider range of witnesses (including the uncials A F M) adds a definite article before ἄνθρωπος. The omission of the single word ἄνθρωπος occurs only in Christian writers, where the influence of Gal 3.10 may be presumed.

[196] Noted by Koch, *Schrift*, 120 n. 6. At the same time, a few Hebrew manuscripts do contain a כֹּל at the site of the second "all" (πᾶσιν) of Deut 27.26_LXX (see BHS).

[197] *Ibid.*, 120.

[198] *Ibid.*

[199] *Ibid.* For an alternative reading of the present passage, see the article cited in note 192.

V   Reading ὅς instead of ὅστις. While the Pauline reading is secure, the LXX evidence is thoroughly divided between ὅς and ὅστις in Deut 27.26.[200] Paul himself uses both forms quite freely, so no Pauline rationale for the change can be discerned. Evidently Paul drew his citation of Deut 27.26 from a text that contained the shorter reading.

E   Omission of ἐν. The evidence for omitting ἐν after ἐμμένει in the LXX tradition is not strong, but cannot be wholly discounted.[201] On the Pauline side, the witnesses are strongly divided, with a number of important manuscripts including the preposition in Gal 3.10.[202] The presence or absence of the preposition has no effect on the meaning of the verb ἐμμένει, so that a Pauline adaptation is improbable.[203] In view of the weak external evidence for a pre-Pauline omission, however, the matter is probably best left undecided.

B   Conflated citation: replacing the words τοῖς λόγοις with τὰ γεγραμμένα ἐν τῷ βιβλίῳ from Deut 28.58. Variations on the phrase τοῖς γεγραμμένοις ἐν τῷ βιβλίῳ τοῦ νόμου (τούτου)[204] appear at several points in the recitation of the divine blessings and curses in Deut 28–30 (28.58, 61, 29.19, 20, 26, 30.10). In most places, however, it is the "curses" that are said to be "written in this book of the law," not the requirements of the law itself. Only in Deut 28.58 and 30.10 is the phrase used in a sense similar to Gal 3.10.[205] The latter passage stands closest to

---

[200] The relative ὅστις, which Wevers adopts in the Göttingen LXX, is supported by the uncials A F M and the bulk of the minuscules in the d f n t y z families. The shorter form ὅς is read by the uncials B F V, the Catena texts, and the b and s families. The Hexaplaric evidence and the mixed codices are divided. Koch (*Schrift*, 51–3) observes that Paul's citations from the Pentateuch stand especially close to the text of the uncial F, which contains the shorter form here.

[201] The omission occurs in MSS 15–64 (Hexaplaric), 528 (Catena), and 18-128-83-630-669 (z family), plus the Bohairic Coptic version and quotations by Chr Cyr Epiph Eus Thdrt. Assimilation to Gal 3.10 is evident only in the handful of Christian citations that also omit ἄνθρωπος; the remainder of the texts diverge from Paul here. Betz (144 n. 60) omits the article in Gal 3.10, calling the addition a probable assimilation to Deut 27.26.

[202] The preposition ἐν is found in ℵ² A C D F G 𝔐 latt Or Chr Cyr Thdrt, while p⁴⁶ ℵ* B Ψ 6 33 81 104 365 1175 1241ˢ 1739 1881 2464 (2494) Euthal Cyr Dam omit it.

[203] Koch, *Schrift*, 164 n. 19, citing Hauck, *TWNT* 4:581 [= *TDNT* 4:576–7].

[204] The tradition stands firmly behind this final word as part of the traditional formula in every instance – see further below.

[205] In settling on Deut 29.19 as the base text for Paul's conflation here, Koch (*Schrift*, 164) appears to overlook this difference in the way the phrase is used in

the wording of Gal 3.10 (Deut 28.58 omits τοῦ νόμου), but the fact that it appears in the midst of a list of "blessings" makes it an unlikely candidate for combination with Deut 27.26 in Gal 3.10. Deut 28.58, on the other hand, stands at the head of a section that recapitulates the list of "curses" set out in more detail in Deut 28.15–57. More to the point, the linkage in Deut 28.58 between the divine "curse" and the Israelites' failure to "do all the words of this law which are written in this book" accords well with the interpretation of Deut 27.26 presupposed in Paul's appeal to the latter text in Gal 3.10. If a single passage is to be sought as the background for Paul's use of the phrase τοῖς γεγραμμένοις ἐν τῷ βιβλίῳ τοῦ νόμου in Gal 3.10, then the correspondence with Deut 28.58 is surely the closest.[206] At the same time, the fact that the phrase recurs as a formula throughout Deut 28–30 makes it hazardous to rule out the possibility that the words might have crept into Paul's *Vorlage* as a result of scribal harmonization, despite the lack of manuscript support for such a reading.

A   Converting τὰ γεγραμμένα to Dative.   Whatever one concludes about the *Vorlage* of the present citation (see above), the Dative form of the participle and accompanying article clearly originated with Paul. None of the relevant verses in Deut 28–30 casts the words in the Dative case, while the same case is required to conform the excerpt to its new grammatical context as an addition to Deut 27.26. Such grammatical adaptations are typical of the way Paul conforms the wording of his quotations to their new epistolary context.

B   Omission of τούτου.   In every place where the formula τὰ γεγραμμένα ἐν τῷ βιβλίῳ τοῦ νόμου appears in Deut 28–30, the demonstrative τούτου occurs as the final word of the phrase.[207] No more than four minor manuscripts omit the word

Deuteronomy. What is needed to make sense of Paul's resort to this phrase is a context in which the words refer to the actual content of the law, as in Deut 28.58 and 30.10. Neither of these verses finds a place in Koch's analysis, the first presumably because it omits the words τοῦ νόμου, the second because it appears in a context of "blessing," not "cursing."

[206] In this reading of the passage, Paul will have replaced τούτου with τοῦ νόμου (or simply retained the latter phrase from Deut 27.26) to clarify the original referent of ἐν τῷ βιβλίῳ (= "the words of this law") in the context of Gal 3.10.

[207] The only exception is Deut 28.58, where the phrase τοῦ νόμου is also missing.

in any one passage.²⁰⁸ In the context of Gal 3.10, on the other hand, the word is left without an antecedent, and thus becomes superfluous. Without the demonstrative, the phrase τοῦ νόμου takes on an absolute sense ("the law") that accords well with Paul's repeated use of the same term throughout the present passage (3.2, 5, 11, 12, 13, etc.), and especially with his reference to ἔργα νόμου in the first part of the verse (3.10a). The evidence for a Pauline omission is thus quite strong. Nevertheless, the diversity of the external support for eliminating the word leaves open the possibility, however faint, that the omission might already have occurred in Paul's Greek *Vorlage*. As a result, full confidence in the Pauline origin of the present reading must be withheld in accordance with the guidelines of the present study.

V   Inserting τοῦ before ποιῆσαι.   The LXX tradition is strongly divided over the presence of the article before the infinitive in Deut 27.26.²⁰⁹ The Pauline tradition, on the other hand, is unanimous in including the article. With such strong attestation for the article in the LXX tradition, it would be vain to search for a possible Pauline motive behind its appearance in Gal 3.10. The natural presumption is that Paul has simply reproduced the wording of his Greek *Vorlage* at this point.²¹⁰

C   Converting the pronoun from masculine αὐτούς to neuter αὐτά.   The presence of a neuter pronoun in the minuscule family b (five manuscripts) and the two mixed codices 407 and 509 is remarkable in light of the masculine form of the antecedent λόγοις in Deut 27.26. Assimilation to Gal 3.10 is highly

---

²⁰⁸ In Deut 27.26, only three minuscules omit τούτου (16 127 799*); in 28.61, only one Sahidic MS (Sa¹⁶); in 29.19, four Catena texts (46–313 52–615); in 30.10, one Ethiopic MS (Aethᴹ). The witnesses are wholly united in Deut 29.20 (τούτου) and 29.26 (τούτῳ). The omissions can probably be explained as independent scribal responses to the evident anachronism of such references to "this [which one?] book of the law" within the narrative context of the Mosaic period.

²⁰⁹ Wevers follows the uncials B V, the papyrus manuscript 848, the bulk of the Catena texts, the t and z families, and a variety of other minuscules in omitting the article in his Göttingen edition of Deuteronomy. The article is found in the uncials A F M, the majority of the Hexaplaric manuscripts, and the bulk of the texts from the minuscule families b d f n s y.

²¹⁰ The same goes for Paul's use of the Aorist ποιῆσαι, the majority reading, instead of the Present ποιεῖν, found only in minuscule group b.

improbable: the same b family stands alone in reading ποιεῖν instead of ποιῆσαι (so Gal 3.10) in Deut 27.26, while none of the manuscripts in question contains any of the other adaptations (including the omission of ἄνθρωπος) encountered in Gal 3.10. Unconscious assimilation to one of the several passages in Deuteronomy where the phrase ποιεῖν αὐτά occurs as part of a general injunction to obedience (4.14, 5.1, 7.12, 26.16, etc. – the usual antecedents are δικαιώματα and κρίματα) is a more likely explanation, though when such a change might have occurred is impossible to say. On the other hand, the shift to a neuter form in Gal 3.10 is perfectly understandable as a Pauline adaptation, as both the original antecedent of τοῖς γεγραμμέ-νοις in Deut 28.58 (τὰ ῥήματα) and the implied reference in Gal 3.10 ("all the things that are written ...") involve neuter entities.[211] But whether one can say that such a change was actually required by the preceding adaptations is open to question.[212] An astute reader could easily have supplied λόγοις as the implied antecedent of τοῖς γεγραμμένοις in the presence of a masculine pronoun (cf. Deut 12.28, 27.3, 29.1, 29.9, 31.12, 32.46), while nothing else in the context would offer any diffi-culties for the masculine form. The observation that Paul adds the same pronoun to his quotation of Lev 18.5 in Gal 3.12 is less helpful than it appears, since Paul probably quotes that text in the form in which he knew it (cf. Rom 10.5).[213] On the other hand, it is not difficult to see how the close link between these two citations in the Pauline context could have produced a corresponding shift in the gender of the pronoun in v. 10 in anticipation of the quotation in v. 12. When all of the evidence is taken into account, a Pauline origin for the neuter pronoun remains probable, but the possibility of a textual basis for the change should not be discounted.

---

[211] Paul may in fact have had in mind the same δικαιώματα and κρίματα referred to above.

[212] Koch (*Schrift*, 111) thinks he can simply affirm this without discussion.

[213] See further below.

(69)   **Gal 3.12** (= Lev 18.5)[214]

Paul: [ὁ δὲ νόμος οὐκ ἔστιν ἐκ πίστεως, ἀλλ᾽] ὁ ποιήσας αὐτὰ [ ]
        ζήσεται ἐν αὐτοῖς.

LXX: [καὶ φυλάξεσθε πάντα τὰ προστάγματά μου καὶ πάντα τὰ
        κρίματά μου καὶ ποιήσετε αὐτά,] ἃ ποιήσας ἄνθρωπος
        ζήσεται ἐν αὐτοῖς.

B   Converting the relative pronoun ἃ (neuter plural) to the article
    ὁ (masculine singular).   See the discussion at Rom 10.5.

V   Including αὐτά in text.   See the discussion at Rom 10.5.

B   Omission of ἄνθρωπος.   The fact that Paul includes ἄνθρω-
    πος in his quotation of the same verse in Rom 10.5 offers *prima
    facie* evidence that Paul knew the verse in its LXX wording and
    consciously departed from that text in Gal 3.12. Supporting
    this presumption is the overwhelming testimony of the LXX
    tradition in favor of including the word.[215] The primary
    obstacle to declaring the omission a Pauline adaptation is the
    divided evidence for the Pauline text here. Though the earliest
    and best witnesses omit ἄνθρωπος, the bulk of the minuscules
    retain the word in agreement with the LXX.[216] Such late and
    weak evidence would present no problem if a clear Pauline
    rationale for the omission could be discovered. As with the
    similar deletion in Gal 3.10, however, the reason for such a
    change is far from transparent. Once again the rhetorical expla-
    nation seems most likely: by eliminating the superfluous word
    ἄνθρωπος, Paul is able to create a near-perfect verbal parallel

---

[214] The quotation from Hab 2.4 in Gal 3.11 has been omitted from the present
study in accordance with strict guidelines that limit the investigation to passages that
offer explicit indication to the reader that a citation is being offered (introductory
formula, interpretive comments, etc.). Though the second part of the verse is clearly
offered as a ground for the statement in the first part, there is nothing in the context
to indicate to the reader that the authority to which Paul appeals here is that of
Scripture and not his own apostolic pronouncement. For a discussion of the form of
Hab 2.4 found here, see above on Rom 1.17.

[215] Only two related minuscules from the f family (53–664) and a quotation in
Philo agree with Gal 3.12 in omitting the word. The passage from Philo appears to
have been assimilated to Gal 3.12 by a Christian copyist: it includes not only the
neuter pronoun αὐτά, which probably goes back to Paul's *Vorlage* (see above), but
also the clearly Pauline masculine article ὁ.

[216] In favor of the omission, Nestle lists p⁴⁶) Aᵛⁱᵈ B C D* F G P Ψ 6 33 81* 104 365
629 1175 1241ˢ 1739 pc b r vg syʰ co; retaining the word are D¹ 𝔐 [= the constant
witnesses not named above, including the bulk of the minuscules] a vgˢ syʰᵐᵍ.

between this verse and the quotation from Hab 2.4 in v. 11, thus throwing into sharp relief the inherent contradiction (in Paul's way of thinking) between their respective contents.[217] Such verbal cues to meaning carried substantially more weight in the oral culture of Antiquity than in the modern world of printed texts.[218] Taken together, the internal and external evidence would seem to support a Pauline origin for the present omission, but the result cannot be affirmed with absolute certainty.[219]

(70) **Gal 3.13** (= Deut 21.23)

Paul: [ ] ἐπικατάρατος [ ] πᾶς ὁ κρέμαμενος ἐπὶ ξύλου.
LXX: [οὐκ ἐπικοιμηθήσεται τὸ σῶμα αὐτοῦ ἐπὶ τοῦ ξύλου, ἀλλὰ ταφῇ θάψετε αὐτὸν ἐν τῇ ἡμέρᾳ ἐκείνῃ,] ὅτι κεκατηρα-μένος ὑπὸ θεοῦ πᾶς κρέμαμενος ἐπὶ ξύλου.

A Omission of ὅτι. The fact that the ὅτι in Deut 21.23 appears in the middle of the verse should not be allowed to obscure the fact that it serves as an integral part of the clause selected for quotation in Gal 3.13 (cf. καὶ in Gal 3.8). In the Pauline context, on the other hand, the same conjunction becomes meaningless and even somewhat intrusive. Following normal Pauline practice,[220] the ὅτι is omitted.

B Substitution of ἐπικατάρατος for κεκατηραμένος. The fact that both traditions stand united behind their divergent readings at this point creates the rebuttable presumption that the present wording of Gal 3.13 goes back to Paul himself.[221]

---

[217] The resultant parallelism becomes more apparent when the two verses are arranged side by side:
  v. 11: ὁ δίκαιος ἐκ πίστεως   ζήσεται   [ἐν αὐτῇ]
  v. 12: ὁ ποιήσας αὐτὰ   ζήσεται   ἐν αὐτοῖς
[218] See again the article by Paul Achtemeier, 17–25.
[219] In this case, the evidence cited in favor of retaining the word would represent a broad assimilation to the LXX in the later Pauline tradition, as one might expect. In a separate development, a handful of manuscripts replaces the final αὐτοῖς in Gal 3.12 with αὐτῷ (F^{gr} G g, per Tischendorf) in a "correction" designed to bring the pronoun into accord with its natural antecedent ὁ νόμος in v. 12a. A similar shift (to αὐτῇ) appears in certain texts of Rom 10.5.
[220] On Paul's common practice of omitting initial particles, see chap. 4, note 197.
[221] At the same time, the Pauline wording would not be grammatically impossible in the context of Deut 21.23, a fact that bars this change from receiving the highest probability rating under the guidelines of the present study. The adjective ἐπικατά-

Lending support to this presumption is the ease with which a Pauline motivation for the change can be identified. Despite being stripped from its original context, the Perfect participle κεκατηραμένος continues to imply that the "curse" of Deut 21.23 had already fallen upon the victim prior to his being "hung on a tree."[222] This implication was clearly unacceptable to Paul, who adduced the verse to support his contention that "Christ redeemed us from the curse of the law by becoming a curse for us" (v. 13a), presumably through his death on the cross (cf. 1 Cor 15.3). To eliminate the possibility of misunderstanding, Paul replaced the Perfect κεκατηραμένος with the neutral adjective ἐπικατάρατος, which was ready at hand from his previous citation of Deut 27.26 in Gal 3.10.[223] The resultant verbal link between vv. 10 and 13 highlights the connection (in the Pauline context) between the curse that Christ bore on the cross "for us" (v. 13) and the curse pronounced by the law on those who fail to live up to its demands (v. 10).[224] Once again a Pauline adaptation seems designed to increase the rhetorical effectiveness of a citation in the ears of an audience attuned to such interpretive cues.

A   Omission of ὑπὸ θεοῦ. Here again both traditions stand united behind their respective readings, while a Pauline motive

---

ρατος is common in the LXX (44x), almost always rendering the Hebrew participle אָרוּר (as in Deut 27.26/Gal 3.10). Only once does it translate a form of קלל (Isa 65.20), and never the noun קְלָלָה as here. The suggestion that the shift to ἐπικατάρατος might reflect anti-Christian polemic (e.g. Lindars, *Apologetic*, 232–3) remains entirely speculative (see note 227).

[222] As was indeed the case in the original passage: see the commentaries on Gal 3.13.

[223] Similar Pauline adaptations designed to create a closer verbal link between related citations have already been encountered in Rom 9.25–6, Rom 11.8, 10, 1 Cor 3.19–20, and 1 Cor 15.54–5. Hans Vollmer (29) offers the interesting suggestion that Paul's *Vorlage* might have contained not κεκατηραμένος ὑπὸ θεοῦ, as in the LXX, but κατάρα θεοῦ, the reading of Aquila and Theodotion. Paul's troublesome affirmation in v. 13a that Christ "became a κατάρα for us" could then be understood as arising directly out of the biblical text. From here Vollmer follows the usual explanation in saying that Paul modified the wording of Deut 21.23 to emphasize the link between this "curse" and the "curse" pronounced by the law in Deut 27.26. The suggestion is certainly worthy of more attention than it has received from subsequent commentators. Implicit in Vollmer's thesis is the presumption that Paul was more concerned to highlight the link with the "curse" in v. 10 (thus the modification) than to make clear to his readers why he took the unusual step of referring to Christ himself as a "curse" (as would be the case if an original κατάρα had been retained).

[224] So also Koch, *Schrift*, 166, and numerous other commentators.

for the omission is not far to seek. The idea that God's "curse" rests on those who have sinned is common in the Deuteronomic literature, especially Deut 28–30 (see Deut 28.15, 20, 45; 29.20, 27), and would have presented no problem for the typical Jewish reader of Paul's day.[225] In Paul's application of Deut 21.23, on the other hand, it is not a "sinner," but rather one who "knew no sin" (2 Cor 5.21) who is said to have "become a curse for us" (Gal 3.13a). While Paul would probably have agreed that the "curse of the law" (v. 10) is in fact the curse of God himself,[226] either his own Christian sensitivities or more likely his concern to avoid misunderstanding on the part of his audience has led him to eliminate the words ὑπὸ θεοῦ from his quotation of Deut 21.23. Evidence for a pre-Pauline omission is entirely lacking.[227]

D   Adding the definite article ὁ before the participle κρεμάμενος. Though the individual witnesses are not especially strong, the addition of the article finds significant support in virtually all the textual families that make up the LXX manuscript tradition.[228] The Pauline tradition, on the other hand, shows no

---

[225] The closest approximation to the actual language of Deut 21.23 appears in *Sir* 3.16, which reads κεκατηραμένος ὑπὸ κυρίου ὁ παροργίζων μητέρα αὐτοῦ. For a parallel to the reading found in Aquila and Theodotion, cf. Prov 3.33$_{LXX}$: κατάρα θεοῦ ἐν οἴκοις ἀσεβῶν.

[226] Contra Ernest deWitt Burton, *A Critical and Exegetical Commentary on the Epistle to the Galatians*, ICC Series (Edinburgh: T. and T. Clark, 1921), 164–5, 169–70, who attempts to drive a wedge between these two concepts by describing the "curse of the law" as the subjective "curse" felt by all who attempt to fulfill the law with a legalistic attitude. According to Burton, "The assumption of the legalist that the law is the basis of the divine judgment involves the conclusion that all men are accursed, and must be false" (165). The tenets of classic liberalism could hardly be expressed better.

[227] This is true even if one concludes that the verse itself was first used by Jewish opponents of the nascent church to challenge Christian claims about the Messianic dignity of the crucified Jesus, a view argued as far back as George S. Duncan (*The Epistle of Paul to the Galatians*, Moffatt NT Commentaries (London: Hodder and Stoughton, 1934), 97) and as recently as Heikki Räisänen (*Paul and the Law* (Tübingen: Mohr, 1983), 249–50). Jewish opponents of Christianity would surely have seized on this ὑπὸ θεοῦ rather than eliminating it from the text. On the fruitlessness of comparisons with contemporary Jewish interpretations of Deut 21.23, see Koch, *Schrift*, 125–6.

[228] The article is found in the uncial V, the entire d, n, and t families, and the following scattered minuscules: 15-72-82-376 [Hexaplaric manuscripts] 246 [f family] 30′-343 [s family] 318 [y family] 18′-120-630*-669 [z family] 646 [mixed]. Only the Catena texts and the b family are entirely devoid of manuscripts with the definite article.

such division. A Pauline assimilation to Deut 27.26 (cited in Gal 3.10), intended to create a more explicit verbal parallel between the two verses (as with the shift to ἐπικατάρατος), is a distinct possibility, though the effect would be the same had the word been present already in Paul's *Vorlage*. Certainly it would be hazardous to think that this argument is strong enough to negate the broad evidence for the addition of the article within the LXX manuscript tradition.[229] While a Pauline origin remains possible, the likelihood that Paul has simply reproduced the wording of his *Vorlage* at this point cannot be discounted.

(71)   **Gal 3.16** (= Gen 13.15)[230]

Ú⁺ This brief excerpt from the Genesis passage describing Yahweh's promise of the land to Abraham follows the wording of the united LXX tradition without deviation.

(72)   **Gal 4.27** (= Isa 54.1)

U⁻ With only minor variations in each tradition, the wording of Paul's biblical quotation in Gal 4.27 agrees precisely with the LXX text of Isa 54.1.[231]

(73)   **Gal 4.30** (= Gen 21.10)

Paul: ἔκβαλε τὴν παιδίσκην [ ] καὶ τὸν υἱὸν αὐτῆς οὐ γὰρ **μὴ κληρονομήσει** ὁ υἱὸς τῆς παιδίσκης [ ] μετὰ τοῦ υἱοῦ τῆς ἐλευθέρας.

LXX: [καὶ εἶπεν τῷ Ἀβραάμ]Ἔκβαλε τὴν παιδίσκην ταύτην καὶ τὸν υἱὸν αὐτῆς· οὐ γὰρ κληρονομήσει ὁ υἱὸς τῆς παιδίσκης ταύτης μετὰ τοῦ υἱοῦ μου Ἰσαακ.

---

[229] Such an extensive penetration of a Pauline reading into the LXX tradition would not be unprecedented, but appears highly unlikely in the case of such a minor deviation, especially when not one of the texts involved follows Paul in inserting ἐπικατάρατος or omitting ὑπὸ θεοῦ.

[230] The same language appears in Gen 24.7, but the statement in Gal 3.16 appears to be concerned with the initial promise of the land in Gen 13.15, and not the later recapitulation of this event.

[231] On the LXX side, a number of texts add the phrase καὶ τέρπου, "and rejoice," after βόησαν in an obvious attempt to render the Masoretic רנּי, which has no equivalent in the LXX text. Paul follows the primary LXX reading here. On the Pauline side, the uncials D E F G (and no others) contain the more grammatically correct μή in place of οὐ before the participle τίκτουσα, another obvious scribal "correction."

V   Adding μή.   The LXX manuscript tradition is divided between the simple οὐ and the more emphatic οὐ μή in its rendering of Gen 21.10.[232] The Pauline tradition, on the other hand, is almost completely united.[233] Though the intensification is well suited to the present context, Paul appears to have passed over a similar opportunity to add stress to his quotation in Rom 9.33/10.11, while allowing a contextually useless οὐ μή construction to stand in Rom 4.8.[234] Apparently Paul was content to reproduce whatever form of the negative he found in his own biblical text. This observation, combined with the solid evidence for a LXX reading with μή, makes it highly probable that Paul has simply reproduced the wording of his biblical *Vorlage* at this point.[235]

V   Reading κληρονομήσει (Indicative) instead of κληρονομήσῃ (Subjunctive).   A number of manuscripts in both traditions cast the verb in the Subjunctive rather than the Indicative mood in Gen 21.10 and Gal 4.30 respectively.[236] The variation is common in the manuscript tradition, and the meaning is the same in either case.[237] Kautzsch, noting that the uncial A never shows Paul using the Indicative with οὐ μή and ℵ B do so only here, suggests that the Subjunctive might actually be original in Gal 4.30.[238] Even if this were true, however, a Pauline motive for the change is nowhere to be found, while the LXX evidence is adequate to support either reading. A pre-Pauline origin for the present reading seems assured.

B   Omitting ταύτην and ταύτης.   While a number of LXX texts drop one or the other of the demonstratives in Gen 21.10, none

---

[232] The Göttingen LXX follows D⁽ᵛⁱᵈ⁾ M 961⁽ᵛⁱᵈ⁾ 72' 413 d n 318' 120' 54 59 in reading οὐ rather than οὐ μή in Gen 21.10. Still, the evidence for the latter reading is quite strong: the uncial A, the entire Hexaplaric and Catena groups, and the b f n s t y families of minuscules, among others.

[233] Only the frequently divergent texts F G 37 omit μή here.

[234] See above at these entries.

[235] So also Koch, *Schrift*, 52 n. 19, though for somewhat different reasons.

[236] On the LXX side, the Subjunctive is found in 135'–400–618 C'ˢ⁻¹⁶ 131* 413 422 500 569 761* 19-314-537ᶜ 610 f 74'-370 424 55 630 730 Chr. For the Pauline text, the evidence is more divided: the uncials A C F G Ψ and the bulk of the minuscules contain the Subjunctive, while 𝔭⁴⁶ ℵ B D H P 0261ᵛⁱᵈ 6 33 81 326 1175 1241ˢ 2464 2495 *pc* Euthal Thphyl have the Indicative.

[237] BDF § 365. Note the similar variation in Rom 9.33 above.

[238] Kautzsch, 62–3. The verses concerned are Rom 4.8, 1 Cor 8.13, Gal 5.16, and 1 Thess 4.15, 5.3.

but the b family of minuscules (five manuscripts) agrees with Paul in eliminating both.[239] Apparently certain scribes felt the redundancy of the repeated demonstratives and sought to eliminate one or the other of them as a corruption.[240] Whether Paul knew the text with both or only one of these demonstratives can no longer be determined. In light of the way the verse is used in Gal 4, however, a reasonable case can be made for viewing the present form of the text as a Pauline creation. The quotation occurs at the end of an extended allegory (Gal 4.21–31) in which Hagar and Sarah are interpreted as two "covenants," one characterized by "flesh" (vv. 23, 29) and "slavery" (vv. 24–5), the other by "promise" (vv. 23, 28) and "Spirit" (v. 29). By the time Paul reaches v. 30, the historical particularities of the narrative have long since given way to what he regards as the typical features of each character. As a result, the "servant-girl," the "free woman," and their respective "sons" in v. 30 are no longer specific historical individuals, but rather broad classes of people with certain attendant behaviors. The quotation from Gen 21.10 now takes the place of a direct injunction to Paul's Christian hearers: the Galatians are urged to "cast out the servant-girl and her son," i.e. to leave behind once for all the covenant of "flesh" and "slavery" with all its trappings and order their lives as truly free "sons" of God (cf. 4.5–7, 5.1). In such an application, the original references to "this" servant-girl lose their significance, and might even distract the hearer from the point that Paul is trying to make. It comes as no surprise, then, to see Paul dropping them entirely from his citation.

---

[239] The evidence is stronger for omitting ταύτην than ταύτης. Outside of Christian sources, the first demonstrative (ταύτην) is missing in all the Catena texts, the b f z families of minuscules (except for MS 122 in the z family), the miscellaneous minuscules 82 370 346–424 59, and a quote by Philo. The second (ταύτης) is lacking only in the uncial A, the b family, and a handful of assorted minuscules (17' 121 122). Interestingly, the uncial A also adds the word ταύτην to the text of Gal 4.30 (as also the Coptic version), which is thereby assimilated to this manuscript's version of Gen 21.10 (including the first demonstrative but not the second).

[240] Though it is probably inadequate to ground a pre-Pauline reading here, it is interesting to note that the b family supplies the only witness for the likely pre-Pauline variant δέ in Rom 4.3, a quotation from Gen 15.6. The b family stands independent of Paul in the Deuteronomy texts cited in Gal 3.10 (ὅς instead of ὅστις, ποιεῖν instead of ποιῆσαι) and 3.13 (omitting the article).

A   Substituting τῆς ἐλευθέρας for μου Ἰσαακ. As might be
expected, the substitution of τῆς ἐλευθέρας for μου Ἰσαακ in
Gal 4.30 finds no support in the LXX tradition. Moreover, the
sheer awkwardness of having Sarah refer to herself as "the free
woman" in the Genesis context (in place of a direct first-person
reference) renders a textual origin for the substitution highly
unlikely. The fit with the Pauline context, on the other hand,
could hardly be better: note especially the repeated use of
ἐλευθέρα/ἐλευθερία in 4.22, 23, 26, 31, 5.1, and 5.13. While
many of the ideas with which Paul works in Gal 4.21–31 are no
doubt traditional,[241] there is nothing to suggest that the precise
formulation of Gen 21.10 encountered here arose within the
pre-Pauline Jewish or Christian communities. Taken together,
the evidence points overwhelmingly toward a Pauline origin for
the present reading.

(74)   **Gal 5.14** (= Lev 19.18)

U⁻ As with the identical citation in Rom 13.9b, the LXX and
Pauline traditions show a measure of fluctuation between
σεαυτόν and ἑαυτόν here.[242] In both instances, the external
evidence strongly favors the second-person form of the
pronoun. In this case, the Pauline text would represent an exact
reproduction of the wording of the LXX.

---

[241] See especially Mary C. Callaway, "Mistress and the Maid: Midrashic Traditions Behind Galatians 4.21–31," *Radical Religion* 2 (1975), 94–101. Though she sees
Paul interacting with traditional materials throughout Gal 4.21–31, Callaway's
understanding of the altered language of v. 30 is identical to that presented here: "By
this accommodation of the text he broadened its application to his own needs and
subtly changed the speaker from Sarah to Yahweh. Hence Sarah's request that
Abraham cast out Hagar and Ishmael because she did not want Ishmael to share
Abraham's inheritance becomes a divine command to cast out the slave woman (the
Law) because her son (the Jews) will not share Abraham's inheritance with God's son
(the Christians)" (99).

[242] For the LXX evidence, see note 316 under Rom 13.9b in chap. 4. On the
Pauline side, the evidence is so similar to that already cited for Rom 13.9b that no
separate listing is needed.

6

PAUL AND THE TEXT OF SCRIPTURE

The last two chapters have produced a massive amount of data on the way Paul handled the text of Scripture in his explicit biblical citations. In accordance with the procedures outlined in chapter 2, only the most secure evidence (A and B ratings) will be used in constructing a portrait of Paul's normal citation technique. In view of the generally conservative method applied throughout the present study, the following conclusions can be affirmed with a reasonable degree of confidence:

(1) Counting the individual verses that make up the so-called "combined citations" (Rom 3.10–18, 9.25–6, 1 Cor 15.54–5, 2 Cor 6.16–18), the present study has examined eighty-three explicit quotations at seventy-four different sites within the assured letters of Paul. Of this number, seventy-six could be identified by the presence of an explicit introductory formula, three by the appearance of specific interpretive comments in the surrounding verses, and four by grammatical incongruities with the new Pauline context.[1] Of the seventy-six verses marked by formal introductions, fifty-eight (76 percent) quote individual biblical texts, five (7 percent) conflate verses from more than one passage, and thirteen (17 percent) appear in one or another of Paul's "combined citations."[2]

---

[1] On the use of these three categories to identify assured citations, see the discussion in chap. 2. The three places where interpretive comments play a key role are Rom 4.22, 13.9a, and 1 Cor 15.27. The four verses that stand in grammatical discontinuity with their present Pauline contexts are Rom 9.7, 10.18, and Gal 3.8, 3.12. In Rom 10.6–8, a vague introductory formula (ἡ δὲ ἐκ πίστεως δικαιοσύνη οὕτως λέγει, v. 6a) is reinforced by repeated interpretive comments (τοῦτ᾽ ἔστιν, vv. 6–7) and a subsequent formula (ἀλλὰ τί λέγει, v. 8). The whole passage is counted among those with an introductory formula. Two questionable verses have also been included here: 2 Cor 10.17, admitted on the presumption that it would be recognized as a quotation from its appearance in Paul's earlier letter to the Corinthians (1 Cor 1.31), and Gal 3.6, where καθώς may or may not signify the presence of a citation.

[2] The conflated passages are Rom 9.27, 9.33, 10.6–8, 11.8, and Gal 3.10, each of which has been counted as a single quotation for the purposes of tallying up the Pauline citations. Additional conflations in 2 Cor 6.17 and 6.18 have been included in

(2) It has become common to use the term "introductory formulae" to describe the various phrases that Paul and other New Testament writers use to identify their explicit quotations. In Paul's case, however, such terminology can be rather misleading, since Paul is by no means "formulaic" in the way he incorporates biblical materials into his own compositions. The phrase καθὼς γέγραπται (ὅτι) is the only fixed expression used for this purpose in the Pauline epistles, and even it appears only eighteen times (27 percent) out of the sixty-six places where such formal introductions occur.[3] Indeed, Paul can be quite creative in his formulations: note "for this is the word of promise" (Rom 9.9); "but Isaiah cries out concerning Israel" (Rom 9.27); "but what does the (divine) decree say?" (Rom 11.4); "if (there be) any other commandment, it is summed up in this word" (Rom 13.9b); "but Scripture ... announced beforehand to Abraham" (Gal 3.8); etc. At the same time, certain patterns are evident in Paul's practice. The words γράφειν or λέγειν appear at some point in almost every introduction, and many of the non-"formulaic" introductions exhibit "formula-like" qualities as well.[4]

(3) More important for the present study is the fact that there appears to be no correlation between the way a citation is introduced and the degree to which it adheres to the biblical wording. "Formulaic" expressions appear with both verbatim and highly adapted quotations; "semi-formulaic" and "free" introductions

the verse count for "combined citations." The conflation in Rom 11.26–7 has been classed with the simple citations here, since there are reasons for thinking that Paul himself was unaware that the passage brought together verses from different sources (note the D rating in the earlier discussion). The possible conflation in 1 Cor 14.21 has been omitted from the count due to its uncertain status (note the C rating above). Among the combined citations, Rom 3.10–18 contains six distinct biblical verses, 2 Cor 6.16–18 has three (counting the conflated texts in v. 17 and v. 18 as one verse each), and Rom 9.25–6 and 1 Cor 15.54–5, two each. On the difference between "conflated" and "combined" citations, see under (7) below.

[3] The variant γὰρ γέγραπται appears in six other places (Rom 12.19, 14.11, 1 Cor 1.19, 3.19, Gal 3.10, 4.27; cf. 1 Cor 10.7 (ὥσπερ) and Gal 3.13 (ὅτι)). The total of sixty-six locations represents fifty-six individual quotations plus six conflated texts plus four combined citations.

[4] Besides καθὼς γέγραπται, expressions with γράφειν are found in fourteen other introductions (21 percent), while forms of λέγειν appear in twenty-five passages (38 percent). In two other places (Rom 15.11 and 1 Cor 3.20) one of these words is implied by the context. Only seven quotations (11 percent of the total) contain neither word (Rom 9.9, 9.28, 13.9b, 1 Cor 6.16, 2 Cor 10.17, Gal 3.6, 5.14), and two of these are questionable (2 Cor 10.17 and Gal 3.6 – see note 1). The more "formula-like" introductions are those in which a form of γράφειν or λέγειν is accompanied by a simple conjunction and/or identifying reference, as in "first Moses says" (Rom 10.19), "and David says" (Rom 11.9), "for it is written in the law of Moses" (1 Cor 9.9), etc.

show a similar pattern.[5] On several occasions Paul offers a verbatim quotation with no explicit sign that an outside text is even present (e.g. Rom 10.13, 12.20, 1 Cor 10.26, 15.32).[6] Especially interesting are those places where Paul uses a formal introductory expression to adduce a text that has no specific biblical antecedent (1 Cor 2.9, 9.10, 2 Cor 4.6).[7] Clearly the type of introductory expression used (or omitted) can offer no clue as to Paul's attitude toward the wording of a particular biblical citation.[8]

(4) The quotations studied here present a complex and diverse portrait of Paul's biblical *Vorlage*. A careful study of the textual affinities of Paul's assured quotations shows agreements with a wide variety of manuscripts and text-types of the Greek Jewish Scriptures. Though his primary text is clearly that Greek translation known today as the "Septuagint" (LXX),[9] a number of Paul's quotations agree with readings preserved in only a minority tradition within the text-history of the LXX.[10] In other places, Paul

---

[5] (1) Among the καθὼς γέγραπται texts, verbatim quotations appear in such passages as Rom 4.17, 8.36, 15.3, and 15.21, while clearly adapted texts can be seen in Rom 1.17, 2.24, 10.15, and 2 Cor 8.15. Conflated texts (Rom 9.33, 11.8, 11.26–7; cf. Gal 3.10) and combined citations (Rom 3.10–18) are also introduced by this standardized expression. (2) Among the passages with "semi-formulaic" introductions (see previous note), verbatim quotations appear in Rom 4.3, 4.18, 9.15, 10.16, etc., while freely adapted texts can be seen in Rom 10.11, 1 Cor 3.20, 15.45, and Gal 4.30. The combined quotations in Rom 9.25–6 and 2 Cor 6.16–18 are also introduced by such "semi-formulaic" expressions. (3) Even quite "free" formulations can be used with both verbatim (Rom 4.7–8, 9.12, 13.9b, Gal 5.14) and adapted citations (Rom 9.9, 11.3, 2 Cor 4.13), while combined (1 Cor 15.54–5) and conflated texts (Rom 9.27, 10.6–8) are also found under this heading.

[6] Clearly adapted quotations are presented in the same unannounced fashion: see Rom 11.34–5, 1 Cor 2.16, 5.13, 2 Cor 13.1, Gal 3.11.

[7] A similar phenomenon can be seen in Eph 5.14 , 1 Tim 5.18b, and 2 Tim 2.19a within the Pauline corpus.

[8] Though it goes beyond the parameters of the present study, it might be noted in passing that Paul's fidelity to the wording of the biblical text is likewise unrelated to how closely he adheres to the "original meaning" of a given quotation. As with his introductory expressions, Paul can employ a highly adapted text in a manner quite close to its "literal" biblical sense (e.g. Rom 9.9, 11.3, 1 Cor 1.31, 15.45), while elsewhere he can adduce a verbatim citation in a manner that is only tangentially related to any such "literal" interpretation (e.g. Rom 10.18, 15.3, 15.21, 2 Cor 4.13). A fuller demonstration of this thesis will have to await a separate study.

[9] As seen from his consistent agreement with the wording of the LXX even when he adapts its language to suit his own purposes and even when it diverges from the MT. See the discussion in chap. 3.

[10] Omitting instances where the LXX shows clear signs of having been assimilated to the Pauline text, Paul follows a minority reading against the majority text in Rom 9.25, 9.27, 9.28 (*bis*), and Gal 4.30 (*bis*). Less certain instances include Rom 3.4, 3.17 (ἔγνωσαν), 4.3, 9.17 (δύναμις), 10.8 (σφόδρα), 10.20, 1 Cor 15.55 (νίκη), 2 Cor 8.15 (ὀλίγον), Gal 3.10 (ἐν), and 3.13 (ὁ).

agrees with the majority tradition against a significant minority reading, or follows one strand of a strongly divided LXX tradition.[11] Most interesting are those places where Paul's quotations appear to have come from a biblical text that is only weakly attested (if at all) in the extant LXX manuscripts. Included here are not only isolated divergences from the known LXX tradition (Rom 2.24 (?), 9.26 (?), 11.9–10, 11.26, 1 Cor 9.9, 15.45, 2 Cor 9.9 (?)), but also places where Paul follows a version of the Old Greek text that has been systematically revised in pre-Christian times toward a different (usually "proto-Masoretic") Hebrew text (Rom 9.17 (?), 9.33, 10.15, 12.19, 1 Cor 15.54). In one passage (Rom 11.3–4), it appears that Paul's text actually reflects an earlier stage in the tradition than the present "LXX," while in two other places the possibility exists that Paul's quotation comes from an entirely different translation, one wholly outside the scope of the "LXX" tradition (1 Cor 3.19 (cf. Rom 11.35), 1 Cor 14.21). Two places where Paul's *Vorlage* may already have suffered from haplography were also noted (Rom 10.15, 9.28). In a handful of cases, the nature of Paul's *Vorlage* remains entirely uncertain (1 Cor 2.9, 9.10, 2 Cor 4.6). The same diffuse textual situation can be documented for every one of Paul's letters, and even for quotations from the same book of Scripture within a single letter.[12]

(5) This diversified portrait of Paul's biblical *Vorlage* agrees well with the contention of the present study that Paul drew the bulk of his quotations from some sort of written collection.[13] Had Paul relied on a version of the Greek text that he had (presumably) memorized in childhood, one would expect to see at least a measure of consistency in the textual affinities of his various quotations, at least among those that come from the same book of Scripture. The present study, in agreement with earlier investigations of Paul's

[11] Paul supports the majority tradition against a significant minority reading in Rom 2.24, 3.12, 3.15, 10.21 (*bis*), and Gal 3.8. Agreements with one strand of a strongly divided tradition can be seen in Rom 8.36, 9.26, 9.33, 10.5, 10.11, 10.20, 13.9a, 14.11, 15.11 (*bis*), Gal 3.10 (*bis*), and 3.12.

[12] For example, Paul's quotations from Isaiah in Romans run the gamut from verbatim (or adapted) reproduction of a unified LXX tradition (9.29, 10.16, 15.12, 15.21), to agreement with diverse strands of a divided LXX tradition (2.24 (A Q S B L C vs. V), 3.15 (A Q S B C vs. V L Qᵐᵍ), 3.17 (A Qᵐᵍ vs. Q S B V L C), 9.27 (A Q vs. S Qᵐᵍ O L C), 9.28 (B V Qᵐᵍ O vs. A Q S L C), 9.33/10.11 (A Q S L C vs. B V α' θ' σ'), 10.20 (A S L vs. Sᶜ Q O C), 11.8 (S α' θ' σ' vs. A Q B V O L C), 11.14 (A Q Sᵐᵍ O vs. S B V L C)), to reliance on a "Hebraizing" revision of the Old Greek text (9.33, 10.15), to appropriation of an earlier "Christianized" version of the biblical text (9.33), to wholly uncertain cases (1.17, 10.20).

[13] See the discussion in chap. 3.

biblical *Vorlage*, has found no such pattern.[14] Especially trouble-some for the "memory quotation" view are those places where Paul seems to have taken his quotations from an early Jewish revision of the Old Greek text. Only if one assumes that Paul has allowed these revised versions to displace the form of the text that he had known since childhood can it be maintained that these quotations, too, arose out of the apostle's memory in the moment of composition. The question becomes especially poignant when the same biblical context yields quotations that agree with the LXX against the MT along with others that come from a "Hebraizing" revision.[15]

Careful examination of Paul's "combined" and "conflated" cit-ations has demonstrated further that far from upholding the "memory quotation" explanation, the passages in question actually support the opposing view. The skill with which these composite units have been knit together and adapted for their present use shows that it was no careless lapse of memory, but rather a conscious editorial hand that produced such sophisticated pieces of literary and rhetorical artistry.[16] A similar phenomenon is attested in several instances where the wording of adjacent quotations appears to have been molded to create a closer verbal bond between the two texts.[17] Only a handful of readings in Paul's quo-tations diverge from their presumed *Vorlagen* in such a way that a memory lapse might be posited as one possible explanation for the deviation.[18] Reliance on oral tradition likewise explains only a very few readings.[19] All in all, the evidence seems to require the use of

---

[14] See Vollmer, 9–48; Michel, 55–68; Koch, *Schrift*, 48–83.

[15] Isa 52 is a case in point: whereas Paul quotes v. 7 (Rom 10.15) in a version that has been revised to conform to a "proto-Masoretic" Hebrew text, his quotations from verses 5 (Rom 2.24), 11 (2 Cor 6.16), and 15 (Rom 15.21) of the same passage follow the LXX, even where it diverges significantly from a literal rendering of the "Masoretic" tradition.

[16] See the discussions of the individual passages, along with the summary at number (7) below.

[17] See above at Rom 9.25–6, 11.8, 10, 1 Cor 3.19–20, 1 Cor 15.54–5, and Gal 3.10, 13.

[18] Of the 112 deviations that cannot be explained by reference to a written *Vorlage* (see (8) below), only ten show the kind of arbitrariness that might be attributed to a lapse of memory (Rom 9.9 (κατά), 9.27 (conflation with Hos 2.1 and use of ὑπόλειμμα), 11.9 (αὐτοῖς, καὶ εἰς θήραν, and ἀνταπόδομα), 14.11 (ζῶ ἐγώ λέγει κύριος), 1 Cor 9.9 (κημώσεις), 15.27 (ὑποκάτω τῶν ποδῶν), Gal 3.8 (πάντα τὰ ἔθνη)), and even these are by no means certain. See the discussions of the individual verses in chaps. 4 and 5.

[19] The places where oral tradition appears to have had an effect on the way Paul quotes a particular biblical text are Rom 7.7, 9.33 (*bis*), 11.8 (?), 11.26–7, 13.9a, 14.11

some sort of written *Vorlage* for the bulk of Paul's biblical citations.[20]

(6) This leads to an obvious question: how can Paul have relied on written sources in a day when access to biblical scrolls was limited and chapter and verse references unknown? The best explanation seems to be that Paul compiled his own anthology of potentially useful verses in the course of his own personal study of Scripture.[21] Several factors could have led Paul to make such a collection: the burden of answering the "Judaizing" views that he encountered repeatedly in his churches;[22] the need to offer authoritative guidance to his churches on matters of personal conduct; even a concern to clarify his developing "Christian" understanding of existence in light of the authoritative Jewish Scriptures. The practice of excerpting useful passages from written documents for later study and use was common throughout Antiquity.[23] Such a picture of Paul's activities helps to explain a number of otherwise problematic aspects of Paul's handling of the biblical text: the extensive evidence for a written *Vorlage* for the bulk of his quotations; the diversity of LXX text-types encountered in his citations; the close integration of the majority of his biblical quotations into their present argumentative contexts; the intrusion of interpretive elements into the wording of many of his quotations; and even the tenuous link with the original context that characterizes his appropriation of certain texts. Of course, no explanation can ever qualify as "proven" in the

---

(?), 1 Cor 2.9 (?), 9.10 (?), and 2 Cor 4.6 (?). See the discussions of the individual verses in chaps. 4 and 5.

[20] See the discussion in chap. 3. Other evidence set forth there includes Paul's general adherence to the wording of the LXX for both well-known and obscure passages, even where the LXX diverges from the MT and even when he adapts its language to suit his own purpose; his close reproduction of the form of the divine name (ὁ θεός or ὁ κύριος) as it appears in the LXX (an easy matter to confuse in memory citation); the consistently close link between divergences from the LXX (or another presumed *Vorlage*) and the role a particular quotation plays in Paul's own argument (as opposed to the random deviations one would expect from a faulty memory); and two instances where his quotations appear to have been taken from manuscripts that had already lost several words due to haplography (Rom 9.28, 10.15).

[21] See the discussion in chap. 3.

[22] In a lengthy review of the various thematic contexts in which Paul makes explicit appeal to Scripture (*Schrift*, 285–302), Dietrich-Alex Koch finds that the great majority of the citations revolve around two related foci: (1) the righteousness of God vs. observance of the Law, and (2) the calling of the Gentiles vs. the election of Israel. In both cases Paul is clearly offering alternatives to the "received wisdom" of Jewish exegetical tradition.

[23] See the extensive listings of Greco–Roman and Jewish evidence in chap. 3.

absence of direct manuscript evidence or a contemporaneous account of Paul's activities. Nevertheless, the evidence at hand would appear to be more than sufficient to shift the burden of proof to those who would argue that Paul did not have a written text before him (or ready at hand) when he introduced a particular biblical quotation into his own developing argument.

(7) A variety of patterns can be observed in the way the quotations relate to one another within their new epistolary context. At one end of the spectrum are numerous places where Paul adduces an isolated biblical text to undergird or demonstrate a point that he has just made more prosaically in his own language.[24] At other times, quotations from Scripture play a more pivotal role in the development of a broader argument, so that a number of them appear together in a relatively short space, linked only by the overarching prose of the primary composition.[25] A measure of physical coherence between individual citations appears for the first time in those places where a string of quotations is introduced *seriatim* to support a single point within a broader argument (Rom 10.19–21, 15.9–12). More intimate linkages can be observed in a number of instances where the wording of one citation appears to have affected the phrasing of a neighboring text. Quotations of this type usually occur in pairs (cf. Rom 11.8, 10, 1 Cor 3.19, 20), though chiastic relationships are also encountered (Gal 3.10–13).[26] A higher level of mutual influence can be seen in the so-called "combined citations" (Rom 3.10–18, 9.25–6, 1 Cor 15.54–5, 2 Cor 6.16–18). Here again several verses are adduced in support of a single proposition, but now the individual verses have been melded together into a tightly knit, coherent unit with its own internal logic and carefully balanced rhetorical structure. Grammatical and other types of adaptations are common. Finally, in several places the wording of two verses has actually been merged together to create a new text (the so-called "conflated" citations: Rom 9.27, 9.33, 10.6–8, 11.8, 2 Cor 6.17, 2 Cor 6.18, and Gal 3.10). One of the verses is generally primary and

---

[24] Twenty-three of the seventy-four different citation units (see under (1) above) are introduced in this way.

[25] Romans 9–11 and Gal 3.6–16 are the most obvious examples. All in all, twenty-seven different verses are quoted in such contexts.

[26] The same pattern can be observed within some of the combined citations: see Rom 3.11 (οὐκ ἔστιν), 9.26 (κληθήσονται), and 1 Cor 15.55 (θάνατε, νίκος). The pairing of verses in Rom 11.3–4 and Rom 13.9 arises out of the original context, and should not be included under this heading.

the other secondary in such cases.[27] In most such instances, elements of the secondary verse have been grafted into the primary verse in a manner that significantly alters the meaning of the original text. Here, too, adaptations are often required to complete the merger. In both "combined" and "conflated" citations, the component parts have so lost their individuality that an uninformed reader would have no way of knowing that the resulting "quotation" did not come from a single biblical context.[28]

(8) This leads directly to the question of how Paul normally handled the wording of his biblical quotations. After every textual explanation has been exhausted, there remain a great number of places where Paul diverges from his presumed *Vorlage* in a manner that accords well with his own use of the passage in question. Using clear and relatively strict criteria for determining the origins of each reading, the present study has isolated 112 different readings (in fifty separate verses) where it can be affirmed with reasonable confidence that Paul has indeed adapted the wording of the biblical text.[29] This compares with twenty-six places (in eighteen verses) where Paul's wording agrees with one strand of the LXX tradition against various others; fifteen places (nine verses) where he has apparently relied on a revised or independent Greek text; ten places (nine verses) where oral tradition appears to lie behind an unattested reading; and fifty-six instances (in thirty-four verses) where the origins of a particular reading cannot be determined with confidence.[30] In other words, roughly half the deviations from the

---

[27] This would appear to be the best way of distinguishing between "combined" citations and "conflated" texts. In the former, the individual verses stand on a relatively equal footing and retain a measure of their original independence; in the latter, one verse is clearly dominant and the other subordinate.

[28] The impression of a unified context is heightened by the fact that these combined units are introduced with the same language used elsewhere for individual quotations (see note 5).

[29] The total includes only readings that could qualify for an A or B rating under the guidelines of the present study (see chap. 2). Included in this figure are seven verses where the only assured adaptation is the omission of an initial particle (Rom 9.17, 11.26, 15.3, 15.12, 15.21) or the use of "limited selection" (Rom 3.4, 4.7–8). Of the remaining thirty-three verses examined in the present study, twenty-one reproduce the wording of the LXX verbatim, while two follow one strand of a clearly divided tradition. In six more cases (Rom 4.3, 10.20, 11.9–10, 1 Cor 3.19, 9.9, 2 Cor 9.9), it seems likely that Paul has reproduced the wording of a divergent Greek *Vorlage* unaltered, while in the remaining four places (Rom 9.26, 1 Cor 2.9, 9.10, 2 Cor 4.6) the textual situation remains unclear.

[30] The various readings that can be traced to the use of different textual or oral traditions are set forth under heading (4) above (including notes). Those whose

primary LXX tradition within the letters of Paul can be attributed with confidence to the apostle himself.[31]

(9) From a grammatical standpoint, the various Pauline adaptations can be broken down into six distinct categories:[32]

(a) Changes in word order: Rom 2.24, 3.14 (*bis*), 3.15, 9.15, 9.25, 10.21, 11.3, 11.8, 14.11, 15.11, 1 Cor 1.31, 15.55, 2 Cor 6.17, 8.15, 10.17, Gal 3.6;[33]

(b) Alterations in grammar (person, number, gender, case, tense, mood): Rom 3.14, 3.18, 9.25 (*bis*), 10.5, 10.15, 10.19, 11.8, 1 Cor 14.21, 15.27, 2 Cor 6.16 (*bis*), 6.18 (*bis*), Gal 3.10, 3.12;[34]

(c) Omissions (words, phrases, clauses, etc.): Rom 1.17, 3.10, 3.14, 3.15 (*ter*), 9.9, 9.13, 9.17, 9.25 (*bis*), 9.27, 9.33, 10.6, 10.7, 10.15, 10.19, 11.3 (*ter*), 11.4, 11.8 (*ter*), 11.26, 13.9a, 15.3, 15.9, 15.12, 15.21, 1 Cor 1.19, 14.21, 15.45, 2 Cor 6.16 (*ter*), 10.17, Gal 3.6, 3.8 (*bis*), 3.10 (*bis*), 3.12, 3.13 (*bis*), 4.30;[35]

(d) Additions to the text: Rom 3.11 (*bis*), 9.25 (*bis*), 10.11, 10.15, 11.8, 12.19, 1 Cor 14.21, 15.45, 2 Cor 6.18;[36]

(e) Substitutions (words, phrases, clauses, etc.): Rom 2.24, 3.10 (*bis*), 3.11, 9.9, 9.25, 9.27, 9.28, 10.7, 14.11, 1 Cor 1.19, 1.31,

origins remain unclear (i.e. those rated C, D, or E in the present study) will be listed separately below, along with the more certain readings of the same type.

[31] Based on 112 out of 219 questionable readings that can be identified as adaptations. The figure is higher when the verses alone are counted – fully 60 percent (fifty out of eighty-three) of Paul's quotations show signs of adaptation. The question of whether these adapted readings should be described as *intentional* adaptations of the biblical text has been reserved for the final chapter.

[32] Except for the verses listed under "limited selection," these are the same categories that Dietrich-Alex Koch uses to set forth his conclusions (*Schrift*, 103–60). The list of verses included under each heading is generally narrower than that of Koch, however, due to the stricter criteria employed in the present study. For more details, see the discussions of the individual verses in chaps. 4 and 5.

[33] Other deviations from the word order of the LXX whose origins remain uncertain can be seen in Rom 10.8, 10.20, 11.8, 11.9, and 11.27.

[34] Additional variations of uncertain origin occur in Rom 3.4, 11.27 (*bis*), 1 Cor 14.21, 2 Cor 6.17, and Gal 3.10.

[35] Other places where omissions remain unexplained include Rom 2.24, 3.14, 9.26, 9.28, 10.8, 11.4, 11.26, 15.12, 2 Cor 9.9, and Gal 3.10.

[36] "Extra" words that cannot be counted with confidence as Pauline additions are found in Rom 9.26, 10.15 (*bis*), 10.20, 11.3, 11.4, 11.9, 1 Cor 3.19, 15.45, 2 Cor 6.17 (*ter*), 6.18, and Gal 3.13.

3.20, 14.21, 15.27, 15.55 (*bis*), 2 Cor 6.16, 10.17, Gal 3.8, 3.13, 4.30;[37] and

(f) Limited selection: Rom 3.4, 3.10, 3.11, 3.18, 4.8, 9.33, 10.6–8, 15.21, 2 Cor 8.15.[38]

(10) A number of patterns emerge from this study of the way Paul handles the wording of his quotations. In the first place, it is interesting to note the relative frequency with which various types of adaptations appear in the Pauline corpus. Simply omitting problematic or irrelevant materials is by far the most common method of adapting the biblical text to its new literary environment (forty-seven times).[39] Replacing troublesome words or phrases with more serviceable terminology is also standard procedure (twenty-two times). Less frequent though still common are reversals in word order, typically designed to accentuate one particular element within a verse (seventeen times), and minor changes in grammar, often required to bring a text into agreement with its new linguistic context (sixteen times). Adding one or more words to the biblical text (eleven times) is another technique used occasionally to highlight a particular interpretation of a given verse.

Differences can also be noted in the level of confidence with which the origins of various types of divergent readings can be established. Roughly three-quarters of the omissions, shifts in word order, and changes in grammar (compared to what can be known of Paul's *Vorlage*) can be traced with reasonable confidence (A or B rating) to

[37] The inevitable substitutions that characterize so-called "conflated texts" have not been counted in these listings, since they have been treated elsewhere (see under (7) above). Other places where the language of the Pauline quotations differs inexplicably from that of the LXX include Rom 3.15 (*bis*), 4.3, 9.9, 9.17 (*quater*), 9.27, 9.33, 10.5, 10.11, 11.8, 11.9 (*bis*), 14.11, 1 Cor 9.9, 2 Cor 6.17, and 8.15.

[38] The term "limited selection" refers to those places where a citation begins or ends at precisely that point where the wording of the original text would have caused problems for the interpretation/application offered in the Pauline context. Extensive omissions in the middle of a verse (e.g. Rom 3.16, 9.28, 1 Cor 14.21, 2 Cor 6.16) have not been counted here unless the omission reflects an obvious concern to avoid problematic materials (e.g. Rom 10.6–8). Only the clearest instances have been included in the listings above (see the comments on the individual verses in chaps. 4 and 5). Other places where the same procedure might conceivably be at work include Rom 3.14 (parallel line), 10.16 (*idem*), 10.20 (*idem*), 11.4 (last clause), 14.11 (introductory clauses), 15.10 (parallel line), 15.12 (last clause), 1 Cor 1.19 (introductory clauses), 3.19 (parallel line), 1 Cor 15.27 (*idem*), 2 Cor 4.13 (last clause), and 9.9 (*idem*).

[39] The verses included under "limited selection" (nine instances cited) should probably also be included here, since the underlying purpose is the same in both categories.

the editorial activity of Paul himself.[40] The figure is notably lower in the case of substitutions (54 percent), and even less for additions (44 percent). Setting these findings alongside earlier observations about the frequency of adaptations in the Pauline corpus produces certain guidelines that might prove helpful in evaluating whether a particular reading might be original with Paul. Specifically, the data suggest that an omission is more likely to represent a genuine adaptation than either a substitution, a shift in word order, or a change in grammar, while additions to the biblical text have the least chance of going back to the apostle Paul.[41]

(11) A variety of reasons have been noted as to why Paul sometimes chooses to adapt the wording of the biblical text:

(a) In some cases, the answer is as simple as the need to conform the biblical wording to the grammar of its new context. Instead of shaping his own language to coincide with the linguistic parameters of the original passage (a practice he employs only occasionally: see Rom 4.6, 4.18, 10.5, 11.3–4), Paul's normal technique is to adjust the wording of the biblical text to fit the structure of his own argument. At the same time, he is by no means wedded to this practice: grammatical inconsistencies are allowed to stand on a number of occasions (Rom 3.4, 9.7, 10.18, Gal 3.8), and in at least one instance it appears that Paul has actually created such an incongruity for rhetorical effect (Rom 10.19). Adaptations of this type are especially common in combined and conflated texts, where verses from several different contexts have been melded together to form a single coherent unit. In addition, Paul regularly eliminates introductory particles from his quotations to create a smoother transition from his own language to that of the biblical text.[42]

(b) More common are places where the biblical wording has

---

[40] Excluding those that can be traced to Paul's presumed *Vorlage*, 82 percent of the omissions (forty-six of fifty-six), 77 percent of the shifts in word order (seventeen of twenty-two), and 73 percent of the grammatical changes (sixteen of twenty-two) received an A or B rating in the present study.

[41] The probabilities can be expressed in terms of weighted averages, where the percentage of each type of divergent reading that can be attributed to the apostle Paul is multiplied by the frequency of each type of adaptation as it appears in the Pauline corpus (expressed as a percentage of the total adaptations) to produce a relative confidence factor. The resultant calculations show omissions to be three times more common among the genuine Pauline adaptations than substitutions, shifts in word order, or changes in grammar, and eight times more frequent than additions.

[42] See Rom 3.15, 9.13, 9.17, 9.27, 10.19, 11.8, 11.26, 15.3, 15.12, 15.21, 1 Cor 1.19, 15.45, 2 Cor 6.16 , and Gal 3.6, 3.8, 3.13, all of which are included in the omissions total above.

been abridged or modified to eliminate irrelevant, redundant, or potentially troublesome language. Here again, Paul could just as easily have quoted the passage *in toto* in the great majority of cases, but then additional clarification would have been required to explain how the quotation related to whatever point it was meant to support. By paring down the verse to its essentials (i.e. those parts deemed relevant to the issue at hand), Paul is able to make his point quickly and then continue with his primary argument. In a number of places, the aim is simply to create a smoother rhetorical unit (Rom 3.10–12, 11.3, 1 Cor 1.31); in others, a clear interpretive motive is evident (Rom 9.25, 9.33, 10.6–8, 1 Cor 14.21). In either case, the result is typically a more concise "quotation" in which every word speaks directly to the need at hand.

(c) Rhetorical concerns would appear to be the driving force behind another whole series of adaptations. Most of the shifts in word order that can be identified in the Pauline quotations have the effect of accentuating and thereby calling attention to that portion of the biblical text that seemed relevant to the matter at hand.[43] Other adaptations help to create a balanced and sometimes repetitive structure that serves to knit the quotation more closely to the surrounding verses (especially in the "combined" citations) or drive a point home (see 1 Cor 1.19, 2 Cor 8.15, Gal 3.10–13). Still other changes seem designed to signal to the hearer that a transition of some sort is at hand (Rom 10.19, 1 Cor 15.55, 2 Cor 6.16). Though such cues to meaning and development of thought can appear overly subtle to modern readers, their value to ancient audiences accustomed to such conventions should not be underestimated.[44]

(d) Perhaps most interesting are those places where interpretive comments are incorporated into the very wording of the text itself. Here again Paul avoids the necessity of detouring into what could well become an exegetical morass by simply recasting the wording of the biblical text to show his own understanding of the passage in question. In some cases the aim is to insure that the hearers will see how the quotation relates to the surrounding argument;[45] in others,

---

[43] See the listings under (9)(b) above.

[44] On the value of such verbal cues in a predominantly oral society, see Achtemeier, 17–25.

[45] As in the substitutions of ἀθετήσω for κρύψω in 1 Cor 1.19, the replacement of ἀνθρώπων by σοφῶν in 1 Cor 3.19, and the conflation of Deut 27.26 and 28.58 in Gal 3.10.

to avoid potential misunderstandings.[46] In several instances, the biblical text becomes a mere vehicle for advancing a particular Pauline theme.[47] In every case, the pastoral and rhetorical interests of the letter remain paramount; quotations are important only insofar as they help to advance those interests.

(12) This leads to one final observation: Paul takes no pains to conceal from his audience the fact that he has incorporated interpretive elements into the wording of his quotations. Not just obscure texts, but verses that anyone with even a rudimentary acquaintance with the Jewish Scriptures would know have undergone significant adaptation at Paul's hands (e.g. Gen 2.7 in 1 Cor 15.45, Lev 18.5 in Rom 10.5, Ps 8.6 in 1 Cor 15.27). Other adaptations are so obvious that no one could possibly mistake them for the original biblical wording (see Rom 10.6–8, 11.26–7, Gal 4.30). Two other passages are particularly revealing. In Rom 10.11, Paul quotes Isa 28.16 in a form different from that which he had used only twelve verses earlier in Rom 9.33. In 1 Cor 15.27, the shift is even more explicit: the verb is changed from Aorist to Perfect tense within the very same verse.[48] Evidently Paul felt confident that his hearers would be unperturbed by such "interpretive renderings" of the authoritative biblical text. Had such a practice been unique to Paul, or even to the early Christian community, one would expect to see more circumspection in the use of the technique. On what basis could Paul presume that his audiences would understand and accept such cavalier handling of the Jewish Scriptures? Are there common social and/or literary patterns that might help to explain this practice? The next two chapters will examine the evidence for such patterns in the quotations of selected Greco–Roman and Jewish authors.

[46] As with the substitution of δίκαιος for ποιῶν χρηστότητα in Rom 3.10 and the replacement of κεκατηραμένος by ἐπικατάρατος and the omission of ὑπὸ θεοῦ in Gal 3.13.

[47] As in the shift to the plural τῶν εὐαγγελιζομένων in Rom 10.15; the omission of both demonstratives and the substitution of τῆς ἐλευθέρας for μου Ἰσαακ in Gal 4.30; the massive reworking of Hos 2.25 in Rom 9.25; and the shift to plural forms and the addition of καὶ θυγατέρας in 2 Cor 6.18.

[48] A similar phenomenon can be observed in Rom 4.9, where the words ἡ πίστις are added to the recapitulation of Gen 15.6 (cf. Rom 4.3). The same procedure can be seen in *1QpHab* 12.6–7 (cf. 12.1) and at numerous points in Philo's writings (see chap. 8).

PART III

Comparative studies

7

CITATION TECHNIQUE IN GRECO–ROMAN LITERATURE

1. Introduction[1]

In his recent study of Paul's use of the Jewish Scriptures, Dietrich-Alex Koch devotes one full chapter and part of another to comparing Paul's exegetical techniques with those of other first-century authors.[2] Following the normal pattern for such studies, Koch's investigation focuses almost entirely on Jewish materials. The possibility that Paul's handling of the biblical text might find parallels in contemporary Greco–Roman literature is dismissed in a few brief sentences: the "notoriously free citation practice of antiquity" can shed no light on the citation technique of the apostle Paul. As Koch sees it, both the highly fluid manuscript tradition on which Greco–Roman quotations are based and the wholly different relation of the author to the literature cited – i.e. its lack of normative value as "Scripture" to him – render all such comparisons useless.[3] In his investigation of contemporary Jewish literature, on the other hand, Koch finds almost no traces of the characteristically Pauline

---

[1] A somewhat expanded version of the present chapter appears under the title "Paul and Homer: Greco–Roman Citation Practice in the First Century C.E.," in *NovT* 32 (1990), 48–78.

[2] The bulk of chap. 4 (*Schrift*, 199–256) compares Paul's practices with those of early Judaism; the remainder (232–56) examines pre-Pauline Christian uses of Scripture. At the end of chap. 3 (190–6), Koch searches for parallels to Paul's relative "freedom" with the wording of the biblical text. In the end, he finds little basis for comparison.

[3] *Schrift*, 190. W. D. Davies stakes out a similar position in his recent article, "Reflections About the Use of the Old Testament in the New in Its Historical Context," *JQR* 74 (1983), 105–36. In Davies's view, "The differences [between Jewish attitudes toward the TaNaK and Greek views of the poets and philosophers] can be summed up in the one word 'canon'" (120), a concept that included "the necessity to reproduce those texts without distortion" (*ibid.*). Like Koch, Davies relies overly much on the declamations of theorists (both Jewish and Greek) without examining the way quotations were actually handled in the two spheres. As will appear below, the similarity is much closer than either Koch or Davies would lead one to believe.

"freedom" with the wording of the biblical text. According to Koch, unaltered citation is the rule, even in the more "Hellenized" circles of Judaism.[4] While acknowledging that most of Paul's specific exegetical techniques stem from the Diaspora synagogue,[5] Koch insists that Paul's relatively "free" approach to the biblical text can only be understood as the fruit of a totally new view of Scripture that he received as a Christian. The *locus classicus* for this new view is 2 Cor 3.12–18: Paul sees in the Jewish Scriptures a "witness to the gospel" whose true meaning is visible only to the believer, through the testimony of the Spirit.[6]

Setting aside for the moment the problems surrounding his treatment of the Jewish sources, it is difficult not to question Koch's summary dismissal of the whole of Greco–Roman literature as a resource for understanding Paul's technique of quoting from Scripture. One need not posit a full-scale Greek education for Paul (though this cannot be ruled out in advance) to credit him with a certain familiarity with Greco–Roman citation practices. Either direct exposure through daily contact with Greek society or indirect absorption via "Hellenistic" influences on Judaism could easily account for any similarities in practice.[7] Koch's questions concerning the fluidity of the manuscript tradition and alleged differences in attitude toward the primary sources will be addressed below. For now it is sufficient to note that one cannot legitimately deny in advance the possibility that Paul might have been influenced either directly or indirectly by Greco–Roman practices in the way he handles the biblical text.

The purpose of the present chapter is not to put forward a particular theory regarding Paul's relation to Greco–Roman citation practice, but rather to explore a portion of the evidence that has been largely overlooked in previous attempts to understand the citation technique of the apostle Paul.[8] Once all the relevant mater-

---

4   *Schrift*, 190–6.
5   *Schrift*, 199–231 (conclusions on pp. 230–1).
6   *Schrift*, 197–8, 231–2, 322–52.
7   The pervasive influence of Hellenistic thought and practice on Judaism from an early period, in Palestine as well as the Diaspora, has been thoroughly documented by Saul Lieberman, *Hellenism* and *Greek in Jewish Palestine* (New York: Jewish Theological Seminary, 1942), and especially Martin Hengel, *Judaism and Hellenism*, trans. John Bowden (Philadelphia: Fortress, 1974).
8   The only studies of which I am aware that compare the New Testament quotations with Greco–Roman literature are those of James Scott (1877) and Franklin Johnson (1895) (see chap. 1). From the dearth of recent studies on the subject, it

ials have been taken into consideration, it will be seen that Paul employs no citation technique that cannot be traced directly to Jewish or Greco–Roman antecedents. In fact, much of what is generally regarded as "unique" in Paul's handling of Scripture will be shown to have clear parallels in the Greco–Roman literature of his day. It is his conclusions, not his practice, that marks Paul as a "Christian" expositor of Scripture.

2. Comparability of materials

First, however, Koch's objections concerning the fundamental incomparability of the underlying materials must be addressed. Of course, Koch is quite right in his observation that the textual tradition of even the "classics" remained somewhat fluid through-out much of antiquity. This was especially true in the case of materials designed for public presentation (epics and dramas), since rhapsodes and actors then as now had a marked penchant for "improving" the traditional texts to suit their own tastes.[9] Similarly, comparisons between the quotations put forward by classical authors and the known texts of their sources show a consistent lack of concern for the precise wording of the text, apparently reflecting a practice of citing "loosely" from memory.[10]

With the founding of the Museum at Alexandria toward the end of the fourth century B.C.E, however, the stage was set for the rise of a succession of scholars whose primary concern was to collect and standardize the significant texts of antiquity. Collation and editing continued at the Museum for nearly two centuries, into the late second century B.C.E.[11] Though all the works deemed "classics" were eventually affected by this massive scholarly effort, the primary beneficiaries were the "classical" texts *par excellence*,

would appear that the broader perspective of Scott and Johnson has been lost from view.

[9] On rhapsodes, actors, and the Homeric text, see Rudolph Pfeiffer, *History of Classical Scholarship* (Oxford: Clarendon, 1968), chap. 1, and J. A. Davison, "The Transmission of the Text," in *A Companion to Homer*, ed. A. J. B. Wace and Frank H. Stubbings (London: Macmillan, 1962; New York: St. Martin's Press, 1962). L. D. Reynolds and Nigel Wilson, *Scribes and Scholars: A Guide to the Transmission of Greek and Latin Literature*, 2nd edn, rev. and enl. (Oxford: Clarendon, 1974), 14–15, give examples of similar additions in the manuscripts of Euripides' plays.

[10] See Pfeiffer, 22–3 (on Plato), and 109 (in general).

[11] The Museum was founded by Ptolemy I Soter, ruler of Egypt from 323 to 285 B.C.E, probably toward the earlier years of his reign. The standard study of Alexandrian scholarship is that of Pfeiffer (note 9). For a good summary treatment, see Reynolds and Wilson, 5–15.

the *Iliad* and *Odyssey* of Homer. By the late second century B.C.E,
the critically revised "vulgate" of Homer, the result of painstaking
labors by the Alexandrian scholars Zenodotus, Aristophanes, and
especially Aristarchus, had carried the day. Practically all Homeric
manuscripts from that time forward (including early papyri)
conform to its standards.[12] The evidence seems clear that in the case
of the Homeric text, at any rate, it is incorrect to think of a highly
fluid textual tradition lying behind the quotations brought forward
by Greco–Roman writers contemporary with Paul.

As for Koch's view that the first-century Greco–Roman author
stood in a fundamentally different relationship to the text than did
his Jewish or Christian contemporaries, the issue is not nearly so
simple as Koch contends. Not only is it unclear why an ancient
author would necessarily have employed different techniques when
citing "normative" texts than with any other kind of text, but it is
also something of an exaggeration to think that the Greco–Roman
world attributed no such "normative" status to any of its literary
monuments. While it is undoubtedly true that no single text played
the determinative role in the Greco–Roman world that the Bible did
for Jews and Christians, there was nonetheless one text (or set of
texts) that could claim at least a relatively comparable position in
society: the *Iliad* and *Odyssey* of Homer. A number of similarities
invite comparison:

(1) Both the Homeric epics and the Hebrew Scriptures func-
     tioned as the "primordial texts" of their respective societies,
     exercising a formative influence on community life and
     thought from earliest recorded history;

(2) Both were widely regarded as unique "revelations" of
     divine truth, whose full and correct meaning was available
     only to those attuned to the proper way of reading them
     (often requiring the use of allegorical exegesis);[13]

---

[12] The precise relation between the labors of Aristarchus and the emergence of the
Homeric vulgate remains shrouded in mystery. See Knox and Easterling, 1:34;
Reynolds and Wilson, 8; and especially Stephanie West, *Ptolemaic Papyri of Homer*,
Papyrologica Coloniensis 3 (Cologne: Westdeutscher Verlag, 1967). The principles
and methods employed by the Alexandrian scholars are admirably summarized in
John David Dawson's 1988 Yale dissertation, "Ancient Alexandrian Interpretation
of Scripture," chap. 1.

[13] See Felix Buffière, *Les mythes d'Homère et la pensée grecque* (Paris: Les belles
lettres, 1956) for an extensive discussion of this attitude toward Homer throughout
much of Greek Antiquity.

(3) Both served as fundamental source books for their society's views concerning the divine order, the nature of the universe, and the proper behavior of individuals and society;

(4) Both were thoroughly etched into the memories and lives of their peoples from earliest childhood through their central role in education;[14]

(5) Both were frequently cited in argumentation as possessing authoritative value for both author and audience; and

(6) Both appear to have become established in a relatively standard text-form by the turn of the era, though scattered manuscripts representing earlier text-types continued to be available in both traditions.[15]

Thus, while the equation is not perfect, it appears that a study of the way contemporary authors cited the Homeric texts might provide an interesting and useful counterpoint to Paul's method of quoting the Jewish Scriptures. The remainder of this chapter presents the results of one such investigation.

3. General observations

The following works were examined for the present study:

(1) The *Geography* of Strabo (turn of the era),[16] Books 1.1–1.2;[17]

---

[14] See H. I. Marrou, *History*, for a thorough exposition of the central place of Homer in Greco–Roman elementary education, including the important role of his works in moral instruction.

[15] The Greek biblical text was actually more fluid than the Homeric text during this time – see the discussion in chap. 2. Elias Bickermann, "Notes," 154–5, 157, 165, draws a similar comparison between the Homeric and LXX manuscript traditions.

[16] Most readily available in the Loeb Classical Library series, 8 vols., trans. H. L. Jones (London: William Heinemann, 1917; New York: G. P. Putnam's Sons, 1917). More reliable critical texts (used in this study) have been published in recent years by Wolfgang Aly (Bonn: Rudolf Habelt, 1968) and by Germaine Aujac in the Budé series (Paris: Les belles lettres, 1969). Opinions concerning the date and provenance of this work are divided. Noting the long-accepted opinion of Niese that the work was written in Rome around 18–19 C.E., Jones opted for the more recent view (in his day) of an origin in Asia Minor around 7 B.C.E. Aujac, summarizing the subsequent discussion, argues for an early date for the commencement of the study, but agrees with Aly in viewing the finished work as a posthumous publication. Strabo died around 21 C.E.

[17] This particular section was selected out of Strabo's massive study (eight volumes in the Loeb series, seventeen in Aly's edition) not only because it is foundational to the entire work, but also because it is replete with citations from Homer, far more than in any other part of the study.

(2) *On the Sublime*, by "Longinus" (first century C.E.);[18]
(3) The *Homeric Allegories* of Heraclitus (first century C.E.);[19] and
(4) Two of Plutarch's essays, *How the Young Man Should Read Poetry*[20] and *A Letter of Condolence to Apollonius* (late first century C.E.).[21]

These works were selected over others for a variety of reasons. All the authors are relative contemporaries of Paul, spanning the period from just before to just after his time. Each represents a different type of literature: Strabo writes a semi-scholarly treatise on a "scientific" subject; "Longinus" offers an exercise in literary criticism designed to promote a particular style of writing; Heraclitus puts forward a passionately rhetorical defense of Homer against the accusations of certain detractors; and Plutarch's two essays represent first, a moral critique of poetry in general (and Homer in particular), and secondly, a personal letter of condolence to a friend grieving over a lost child. Finally, each author employs the Homeric materials in a somewhat different fashion, permitting the study of a reasonable variety of citation techniques within a narrow range of texts.[22]

[18] Critical Greek text (entitled *On Sublimity*) edited by D. A. Russell (Oxford: Clarendon, 1964); English translation published separately, also by D. A. Russell, *On Sublimity* (Oxford: Clarendon, 1965). Long attributed to the third-century C.E. literary scholar Cassius Longinus, the actual author of this work remains unknown. The commonly accepted first-century date is based on internal evidence from the final chapter.

[19] Critical text published in the Budé series with a French translation under the title *Allégories d'Homère*, trans. Felix Buffière (Paris: Les belles lettres, 1962). Nothing is known of this author outside the manuscript testimony regarding his name and place of residence (Pontus). A date earlier than Plutarch is generally assumed due to the complete absence of the type of "mystical" allegorical exegesis developed by the neo-Pythagoreans and neo-Platonists from the second century C.E. onwards.

[20] Readily available in volume one of *Plutarch's Moralia* in the Loeb Classical Library series, trans. F. C. Babbitt (London: William Heinemann, 1927; New York: G. P. Putnam's Sons, 1927), 72–197. A recent critical edition is Ernesto Valgiglio's *De Audiendus Poetis* (Torino: Loescher Editore, 1973).

[21] In volume two of the Loeb edition of *Plutarch's Moralia*, 105–211. The most recent critical edition (with French translation) is that of Jean Hani, *Consolation à Apollonius* (Paris: Klincksieck, 1972). Questions concerning the authorship of this work will be discussed later (see note 71).

[22] Others considered for inclusion but rejected for one reason or another include Diodorus Siculus, whose chapters on the Trojan War (where citations from Homer might have been expected) have survived only in fragments; Cornutus, whose *Theologia Graeca* is unavailable in translation; Epictetus, whose work is known only through the notes of his pupil Arrian (hence unreliable for careful study of citations);

Before turning to the individual authors, it might be helpful to note a few findings of a more general nature. The first concerns the reputation of Greco–Roman authors for being rather careless and "loose" with the wording of their citations. While this may indeed be true for Greek writers of the "classical" period, the present study suggests that it is totally unjustified to extend such generalizations to the literature of late Hellenistic and early Roman times. When one takes into account the difficulties associated with unraveling a bulky scroll to find and check references (hence the frequent reliance on memory in the ancient world), it is rather the *faithfulness* of the authors of this period to the wording of their sources that appears remarkable. Not only is the frequency of textual variation in the authors studied here much less than one finds in, say, Paul or the Qumran materials, but those that do exist can usually be traced with confidence to the intentional editorial activity of the author himself.[23] Differences that cannot be attributed to intentional adaptation or the use of a different text are very few in number. Clearly one sees here the tangible results of the emphasis on rote memorization that lay at the heart of the ancient Greek educational system.[24]

A second point of note concerns the manner in which various authors incorporate citations into the body of their texts. Even more than Paul, the Greco–Roman writers examined here exhibit a high degree of flexibility and originality in the way they merge quotations into the developing flow of their own compositions. To be sure, certain more or less formulaic expressions do appear on occasion, usually in combinations that include the words φησί, λέγει, and ἑτέρωθι (e.g. φησὶν ὁ ποιητής, ἐν οἶς φησίν, ἀμέλει φησίν, λέγει γοῦν ἑτέρωθι που, etc.).[25] Linking back-to-back citations by καί, καὶ πάλιν, or some similar short phrase is also a common practice.[26] Far more common, however, are those instances where the author

and Dionysius of Halicarnassus and Dio Chrysostom, both of whom quote Homer only infrequently. Philo and Josephus were left out to avoid any confusion between Greco–Roman and Jewish citation practices. Latin authors were omitted due to the notoriously difficult textual tradition of their Greek citations, the result of a general ignorance of Greek on the part of the medieval scribes who passed their works on to us.

[23] See below under individual authors.

[24] See Marrou, *History*.

[25] Not one of these expressions is used regularly in the New Testament, though forms of λέγειν are common with quotations.

[26] Within the Pauline corpus, cf. Rom 10.19–21, 15.9–12, 1 Cor 3.19–20, 1 Tim 5.18, 2 Tim 2.19.

uses his own words to integrate the citation in a creative manner into its new literary context. Often this means omitting every explicit indication that a quotation is even being offered: the reader is expected to recognize the verse as a quotation by its metrical qualities, its familiar content, or both. In many cases the author assumes that the reader will be familiar enough with the original text to supply its precise context – yet another indication of just how deeply the Homeric texts had become engraved upon the corporate psyche.

Finally, at least brief mention should be made of a few scattered places where the texts under investigation make explicit mention of the ancient practice of "correcting" the wording of a text to bring it into line with later sensibilities. In his discussion of Homer's geography, Strabo refers three times in the first two chapters to emendations introduced by Zeno or Crates to excuse Homer from the possibility of having made a mistake on a geographical matter.[27] Plutarch's discussion of such "corrections" is more subtle. Where Homer (or any other poet) appears to teach something contrary to accepted morality, it is the duty of the poetry instructor to use every means at his disposal (attention to context, word usage, authorial judgments, etc.) to "convert" the text to the common view, even if it means offering the pupil a revised text to counterbalance the troublesome original.[28] Though in Plutarch's case this "revised" reading is to be set alongside the original, not replace it, it requires no great leap of imagination (especially given Strabo's examples from Crates and Zeno) to see how another scholar might have introduced the necessary modifications into the text itself to eliminate potential misunderstandings. Modern notions of the inviolability of an author's original text simply cannot be transferred to the ancient world.

4. Specific examples

For the remainder of the chapter, attention will be centered on the citation techniques of the four authors noted above. The intention is not to present an exhaustive study of how each author handles the Homeric text, but rather to examine certain specific issues that might prove relevant to the citation practice of the apostle Paul.

[27] In 1.1.6 (Crates), 1.2.24 (Crates), and 1.2.34 (Zeno). For Crates as a defender of Homeric infallibility, see Buffière, chap. 9.
[28] *Poetry* 33C–34A. A further example can be found in *Condolence* 110B.

Each survey begins with a brief discussion of the apparent source of the author's Homeric citations (memory, "vulgate," or some other text). The concern here is to avoid labelling as an intentional adaptation a reading that actually reflects the use of a non-standard text. Following this is a summary description of the author's citation technique, with primary emphasis on the role of authorial adaptations (from minor smoothing of grammar to elimination of problematic references) and the use of unusual formats (combined citations, conflated texts, etc.). Once all four authors have been considered individually, a final section will sum up the overall findings.

Strabo

As the title indicates, Strabo's *Geography* is fundamentally "an encyclopedia of information concerning the Inhabited World as known at the beginning of the Christian era."[29] It would be a mistake, however, to think of Strabo's work as a dry compilation of dusty facts about cities, mountains, rivers, and seas. As was customary in his day, Strabo's work on "geography" includes a veritable cornucopia of observations on anthropological, sociological, historical, and philosophical matters that make his work an invaluable resource for modern scholars seeking to understand the ancient world.

For the most part, Strabo's interest in Homer is limited to questions concerning the latter's familiarity with geography. The reasons for this concern are obvious. In the first place, the pre-eminence of Homer in the ancient world and the tendency to look to him for answers on every issue made it only natural that Strabo would examine Homer's views on matters of geography. In addition, the Homeric writings (especially the *Odyssey*) are replete with geographical references. Thus it became doubly necessary for Strabo to evaluate the reliability of Homer's picture of the world, a picture that he appears generally willing to defend, though not without criticism.

Reliance on a non-"vulgate" written text of Homer (or excerpts from such a text) seems relatively assured for Strabo. Indeed, one might anticipate the use of a written text in a study such as Strabo's, where the focus is not on important events and speeches from the

---

[29] H. L. Jones in the Introduction to the Loeb edition of Strabo, xxviii.

Homeric narrative, but on a variety of obscure geographical details mentioned in passing at diverse points throughout the text. Strabo's common practice of omitting precisely those words, phrases, or even whole lines of the Homeric text that seemed irrelevant to his geographical interests (see below) would also be easier to comprehend if he had worked with a written text at some point in his studies. Confirmation of these presumptions can be found in a careful examination of the divergent wording of Strabo's quotations, which follow deviant Homeric manuscripts at least five times in the opening two chapters.[30] This implies that one can largely rule out memory lapses as an explanation for those places where the wording of Strabo's quotations diverges from that of the Homeric vulgate.

In all, Strabo cites Homer 105 times in the opening two chapters of his work (roughly 85 printed pages of Greek text), against only ten citations from sources other than Homer. When these quotations are set alongside the standard readings of the *Iliad* and *Odyssey*, the pattern that emerges is one of general faithfulness to the Homeric wording, though without rigidity. In six cases Strabo clearly introduces minor adaptations to conform the wording of a quotation to the grammar of his own sentence. Techniques employed include altering cases of nouns and tenses of verbs, adding connective links, and in one case substituting the name of a particular locale (Ὠγυγίη) for a descriptive adjective (ἀμφιρύτη) to make the original reference of the passage clear in its new context.[31] "Limited selection" is also encountered on occasion, though Strabo's focus on the hard geographical data of the Homeric literature keeps him close to a "literal" reading of the texts in most cases.[32] More typical of Strabo's citation technique, however, are

[30] At 1.1.10, 1.1.16 (6th citation), 1.2.20 (11th), 1.2.21, and 1.2.33 (7th). Two other readings that appear to reflect the use of a different text may be seen at 1.2.20 (10th citation) and 1.2.36 (7th). The Greek texts of Homer used for this and all subsequent comparisons are Thomas W. Allen (ed.), *Homeri Ilias*, 3 vols. (Oxford: Clarendon, 1931); W. Walter Merry and James Riddell (eds.), *Homer's Odyssey, Books I-XII*, 2nd edn rev. (Oxford: Clarendon, 1886); and D. B. Monro, *Homer's Odyssey, Books XIII-XXIV* (Oxford: Clarendon, 1901). Victor Berard's three-volume *L'Odyssey* in the Budé series (Paris: Les belles lettres, 1924) was also consulted for its critical apparatus. English translations are normally taken from *The Odyssey*, trans. Robert Fitzgerald (Garden City, NY: Doubleday, 1961; Anchor Books, 1963) and *The Iliad of Homer*, trans. Richmond Lattimore (Chicago, London: University of Chicago Press, 1951).

[31] The last-named modification occurs in 1.2.18. The others are found at 1.1.6 (6th citation), 1.1.16 (1st), 1.2.33 (3rd, 4th), and 1.2.38 (1st).

[32] At least three instances can be noted: in 1.2.7 (quoting *Od* 19.203), a line that describes the disguised Odysseus as telling "lies in the likeness of truth" is extracted

his repeated omissions of materials that no doubt seemed irrelevant to his own narrow geographical interests. At least three types of omissions can be noted in Strabo's citations from the Homeric text:

(1) Omissions designed to condense the wording by eliminating apparent redundancies, irrelevant words or phrases, and flowery poetic descriptions. A good example is the dropping of the words οὔτε ποτ' ὄμβρος, "nor ever a thunderstorm," just after the words "no great storm" in a description of the joys of the Elysian Plain.[33] In most cases the sense is unaffected by such omissions.

(2) Omissions of narrative details that have no bearing on the geographical elements of the passage. In most cases this means subordinating the story-line to any incidental geographical references that the verse may contain. For instance, in a passage describing the lands traversed by Hera in her flight from Olympus to Lemnos, Strabo eliminates a line that says of her that she "never touched the ground with her feet."[34] Presumably this was because such poetic details added nothing to his argument that Homer knew the proper locations of many of the sites that he named in his depiction of Hera's journey. In another place, where Homer's familiarity with the Sidonians is at issue, Strabo recalls Homer's mention of certain Sidonian women that Alexander had brought back with him on the trip that carried Helen to Troy. In the process, he drops out a line that refers to Alexander as "having sailed over the wide sea," along with a characterization of Helen as "high-born" (εὐπατέρειαν).[35] One can only assume that both phrases were felt to be irrelevant and even to distract from the primary purpose of the citation.

(3) Omissions intended to suppress problematic data. An apparent example of this technique appears in Strabo's discussion of Homer's view of the river Oceanus. Here he drops the words Ὠκεανοῖο/νηῦς from the text in order to guard Homer against the possibility of saying redundantly, "After Odysseus had gone out of

and generalized to support the view that there is an element of truth in every lie; in 1.2.9, two different lines describing the activities of metalworkers (*Il* 18.541 and *Od* 6.232) are applied metaphorically to the work of Homer himself (he "mingles in" a false element with the true, he "overlays" history with myth). Only by a careful delimitation of the content of the quotation could any of these passages have been used for their present purposes.

[33] *Ibid.*, 1.1.4, citing *Od* 4.563. Other examples can be seen at 1.1.10 and 1.2.33 (3rd).

[34] *Ibid.*, 1.2.20 (2nd), citing *Il* 14.225–9.

[35] *Ibid.*, 1.2.33 (7th), citing *Il* 23.742. Other omissions of this type may be seen at 1.2.3 (2nd), 1.2.20 (6th, 7th, 8th), 1.2.28, and 1.2.31.

Oceanus, he came into Oceanus."[36] More subtle are a number of instances where Strabo leaves out certain words or phrases that associate the gods with specific geographical phenomena. For example, while recounting Homer's description of the "cave of the nymphs," Strabo passes over Homer's mention of two doors, the one open to mortals and another by which only "immortals" can enter.[37] A similar concern would appear to lie behind his suppression of the epithet αἰθρηγενέτης ("heaven-born") for Boreas, the north wind, in a passage where he retains the more prosaic adjective δυσάης ("stormy") used to describe Zephyr, the west wind.[38] Omissions of this sort agree well with Strabo's express judgment that all such references to the "ancient theology" are pure "myths," suitable only for women, children, and the illiterate, and utterly beneath the dignity of the philosophical mind.[39]

One notable result of this method of handling irrelevant or problematic data is that once the offending materials have been removed, the resultant "quotation" gives every appearance of being a continuous excerpt from the Homeric text. In fact, most of Strabo's omissions are carried out so smoothly that only a careful reader would ever notice that anything was amiss. Certainly nothing in the quotation itself would indicate to the reader that he or she might be looking at a form of the text that reflects the specific interests and concerns (and even prejudices) of a later author.

In sum, Strabo is for the most part quite faithful to the language of the Homeric text, citing it according to its original wording in 83 out of 105 instances. Nevertheless, Strabo's primary interest is geography, not Homer *per se*. As a result, he does not hesitate to introduce minor alterations into the text to create a better fit with his own sentence structure, nor to omit words, phrases, or even whole lines that appear irrelevant to his purposes or disconsonant with his own personal views.

"Longinus"

The primary aim of the first-century text *On the Sublime* is to inculcate and exemplify a particular style of writing that the author calls "sublimity" (ὕψος). "Sublimity," says the author,

---

[36] *Ibid.*, 1.1.7, citing *Od* 12.1.
[37] *Ibid.*, 1.2.20 (6th), citing *Od* 13.109.
[38] *Ibid.*, 1.2.20 (10th), citing *Od* 5.295.
[39] *Ibid.*, 1.2.8–10.

is a kind of eminence or excellence of discourse. It is the source of the distinction of the very greatest poets and prose writers and the means by which they have given eternal life to their own fame. For grandeur [τὰ ὑπερφυᾶ, a synonym of ὕψος] produces ecstasy rather than persuasion in the hearer; ... produced at the right moment, [it] tears everything up like a whirlwind, and exhibits the orator's whole power at a single blow.[40]

The author is clearly of the opinion that there is an "art" of "sublimity" that can be reduced to a few rules and taught to others,[41] but he also finds it useful to present examples from the great poets and orators to illustrate the various principles involved. It is in this context that he brings forward his quotations from Homer.

Though the author clearly holds Homer in the highest regard (the *Iliad* more so than the *Odyssey*),[42] excerpts from the Homeric epics make up only a small percentage of his examples of "sublime" style (16 out of 115 citations). Others cited frequently include Demosthenes, Sophocles, Euripides, Hesiod, and Plato. The sheer number of authors cited (over 30 different individuals in 55 pages of Greek text) and the fact that he is citing well-known passages from most of them would seem to point toward memory as the most likely source for the author's citations. Yet the evidence from the text itself is somewhat ambiguous. On the one hand, an argument for memory quotation might be made from three different instances where words are changed or omitted with no apparent link to the author's specific concerns and no Homeric manuscript support.[43] On the other side stands at least one variant reading that finds support in a minority textual tradition, and another in which the use of a deviant text is highly likely.[44] Perhaps the best explanation for such ambivalent evidence is to suppose that the author drew his quotations from a written anthology containing examples of "sublime" writing style, a collection compiled by the author for use in instructing

[40] Russell (English), 1–2.
[41] *Ibid.*, 2.
[42] *Ibid.*, 12–14.
[43] See Russell (Greek), 19.2, 26.1, and 44.5.
[44] The first is found in 27.1 (ἐθέλοντα for ἑτέρωθι), the second in 15.3. In the latter case, the difference is between singular and plural forms of a word that can be used in either form with similar meaning (ἰσχίον in "Longinus," ἰσχία in Homer), a likely point for textual corruption.

others and eventually incorporated into the present work.[45] The passages noted above as favoring memory citation could then be understood either as authorial adaptations whose purpose is unclear, or else as quotations from memory of passages not included in the original collection.

Apart from the questionable examples cited above, modification of the actual wording of the text plays a very small role in *On the Sublime*. In one clear instance, the author converts the tenses of two verbs from past to present to suit his re-application of a Homeric metaphor to Homer himself.[46] Omissions are more common. In some cases the concern appears to be to eliminate elements that might be viewed as detracting from the "sublimity" of the text at hand. In one such instance, drawn from Penelope's scathing indictment of her suitors' conduct, the phrase "the possession of fiery [?] Telemachus" is omitted after a reference to the "wealth" that her suitors have squandered, most likely because it appeared to detract from the unified focus of the speech.[47] In other places the motive seems more theological. For example, in one place the author omits several words from the middle and end of a verse to eliminate all reference to Zeus bringing troubles upon men, in the process "secularizing" it into a timeless maxim.[48] Whatever the case, it seems clear that omissions have played a prominent role in this author's attempts to accommodate the Homeric text to his own didactic purposes.

When it comes to format, the author offers two instances of unusual and highly creative formulations that serve his purposes well. Both are examples of what are commonly called "combined citations," the placing of two or more quotations back-to-back to

[45] Jean Hani, commenting on the text used by Plutarch in his *Condolence* (30, 49–50), notes the frequent use of such florilegia in contemporary schools of rhetoric. References to individuals compiling written excerpts while engaged in personal study abound in the literature: see the evidence in chap. 3.

[46] Russell (Greek), 9.11. In a re-application of a passage that originally referred to Hector (*Il* 15.605–6), Homer is said to "foam at the mouth" as he "rages like Ares" through his text. The same passage could also be cited as an instance of "limited selection," as could a similar description of Euripides in 15.3 (citing *Il* 20.170).

[47] *Ibid.*, 27.4 (the Greek adjective is δαΐφρονος). A similar example may be found at 26.1.

[48] *Ibid.*, 44.5. After modifications, the original reading, "For thundering Zeus takes away half (a man's) manhood whenever the day of slavery takes him" (*Od* 17.322–3), becomes "The day of slavery takes away half (a man's) manhood." Of course, such a "secularization" of the text could well have occurred prior to its appropriation by "Longinus," but there is no textual evidence to support such a conclusion.

create a unified whole. In the first case, two different passages from
the *Iliad*'s "Combat of the Gods" are joined together in a format
clearly calculated to increase the "sublime" effects of the original
passage. Adding further weight to the combination is the conflation
of two verses from different sources into a single sentence in the first
line of the citation. The supreme artistry of the resultant "quotation" can be seen in the following reproduction of the text as it
appears in *On the Sublime*, with additions to the primary passage
noted by underlines and italics:

> *And the great heavens* <u>and Olympus</u> *trumpeted around*
>   *them,*
> Aîdoneus, lord of the dead was frightened in his depths;
> For fear the earth-shaker Poseidon might break through
>   the ground,
> And gods and men might see
> The foul and terrible halls, which even the gods detest.[49]

A similar instance combines three passages dramatizing the seismic
effects of Poseidon's travels over land and sea to produce a more
"awesome" effect.[50]

Although the percentage of adapted texts is higher in *On the
Sublime* than in Strabo (six out of sixteen passages), it is difficult to
say whether this reflects a "freer" attitude toward the Homeric text
or simply the smaller size of the sample. Whichever is the case, the
characteristic features of this author's citation technique (apart
from simple verbatim quotations) can be identified with a reasonable degree of confidence as (1) omitting words or phrases that
could be viewed as detracting from the "sublimity" of the text at
hand, and (2) combining texts from different sources to increase
their "sublime" effect. Here again the literary concerns of the author
have clearly served to shape the way he makes use of the Homeric
text.

Heraclitus

As its title shows, the *Homeric Allegories* of Heraclitus of Pontus
(first century C.E.) is a work specifically about Homer. At no point,

---

[49] *Ibid.*, 9.6, conflating *Il* 21.388 with 5.750 (note the overlapping words μέγας
οὐρανός) and combining this with *Il* 20.61–5. The translation is Russell's.

[50] *Ibid.*, 9.8, where the author inserts a line from *Il* 20.60 between *Il* 13.18 and
13.19 and then skips to 13.27–9 for the finale.

however, does its author pretend to any modern "scholarly object-ivity" toward his subject matter. From first to last, Heraclitus makes it clear that his book is meant to defend Homer from his many detractors, especially those who accuse him of "impiety" for his overly human portraits of the gods. His primary line of defense is the repeated affirmation that much of what Homer wrote about the gods reflects intentional allegorization, by which he sought to conceal the great truths about the cosmos from those unprepared to take them to heart. The bulk of Heraclitus' work is devoted to exposing the "true sense" of these allegorical pronouncements in order to justify Homer against his critics.[51]

Since his general approach is to proceed first through the *Iliad* and then the *Odyssey* selecting specific episodes about the gods for extended allegorical treatment, it seems reasonable to presume that Heraclitus made use of a written text of Homer in the composition of his work. Support for this view appears in one place where a divergent reading finds support in a minority textual tradition, and in another where two lines traditionally marked with a dotted *diple* (a sign of early disputes concerning the proper Homeric text) are absent from Heraclitus' quotation when their inclusion would have materially strengthened the author's case.[52] The only evidence for memory quotation is one instance where the author substitutes a γάρ for a δέ in his second quotation of the same passage in a brief span.[53] It is probably best to assume that the latter is an isolated careless oversight in a work composed with a written manuscript of Homer close at hand.

As might be anticipated from the nature of the study, adaptations of the Homeric text are common in Heraclitus' work, though their overall extent is less than might be expected (19 out of 136 total citations, covering 87 pages of printed text). Modifications designed to conform the text to the grammar of its new context (altering cases of nouns, persons of pronouns, tense, aspect and number of verbs,

---

[51] The hermeneutical dimensions of Heraclitus' interpretation of the Homeric text are discussed in Dawson, 53–61.

[52] In *Allégories d'Homère* at 73.8 (τίφθ' for πη δ') and 77.2 (citing *Il* 2.484, 487). The dotted *diple* or *diple periestigmene* (⸖) was used by Aristarchus to indicate places where his readings differed from those of his Alexandrian predecessor Zenodotus. See Reynolds and Wilson, 10.

[53] *Ibid.*, 26.2 and 27.3. Even here an unattested corruption might lie at the root of the difference. Dr. John Herington of Yale University informs me that the phrase τό δὲ ἀντὶ τοῦ γάρ, "the δέ means γάρ," occurs again and again in medieval scholia and marginalia, reflecting the frequent interchange between these two particles throughout the entire Greek manuscript tradition.

etc.) are standard procedure. Insertions meant to preserve the identity of the original referent in the new context or to clarify an obscure text are also found.[54] Most interesting are those instances where the adaptation renders the wording of the quotation more germane to the author's point. In a section where the author seeks to demonstrate the supreme piety of Homer by adducing several passages that exhibit a lofty view of the gods, a simple substitution of one word (ἰσοφαρίζειν for ἀφρονέοντες) subtly highlights the supremacy of Zeus over all the other gods: the "foolishness" of the others is seen now not in their "raging foolishly" against Zeus, but rather in their "desiring to be equal to" him.[55] In another place, an omission of one word and a minor change in another converts the "three-barbed arrow" with which Heracles once struck Hera into a "three-barbed thing," which is subsequently interpreted allegorically as a reference to the three branches of philosophy whereby one seeks to attain true knowledge of the divine.[56] While adaptations of this sort are no doubt subtle, they do help to bring text and interpretation into closer alignment and thus create a more convincing argument. A similar pattern can be discerned with regard to omissions. In a number of places where he is moving through a passage line by line to explicate its underlying "allegorical" sense, Heraclitus skips over one or more lines that cannot be forced into his allegorical schema.[57] More to the point are several instances where he leaves out personalizing epithets of the gods that might appear to conflict with his "allegorical" emphasis.[58] One could guess that only the familiarity of his intended audience with the Homeric text hindered Heraclitus from making even greater use of these techniques.

As for the format of his citations, Heraclitus like others can quote

[54] *Modifications*: 22.6, 37.4 (2nd), 47.2, 54.3 (1st, 2nd), 62.7, 73.2, and 79.4. *Insertions*: 10.6 (adding καί to clarify), 26.2, 27.3 (inserting Ἥφαιστος as subject), and 52.5.

[55] *Ibid.*, 2.1, citing *Il* 15.104.

[56] *Ibid.*, 34.4, citing *Il* 5.393. Similar modifications appear at 3.1 (substituting a stronger line for a weaker one), 37.4 (changing the gender of certain adjectives to suit their application to humanity rather than minor female deities), 41.10 (altering one word to "universalize" the text and thus create a better fit with an allegorical interpretation), and possibly 2.5 (stressing "possession" over against mere "awareness" of divine knowledge).

[57] See chaps. 14 (two lines omitted), 15 (one line), 16.1 (two lines), 57 (one line), 75.1–4 (two lines), and 79.4 (three lines). Heraclitus' allegorical approach to the text produces numerous other instances of "limited selection," where only that part of a line or passage that coincides with a given interpretation is actually quoted.

[58] See 56.1 ("holding feathered arrows") and 57.1 ("sister of the far-striker").

two or more verses back-to-back with no indication of their diverse origins. In every case the materials thus combined deal with similar topics, producing a single "quotation" that better supports or exemplifies the author's point.[59] One peculiarity worth noting is a single instance in which an introductory formula that anticipates a quotation concerning Athena (in a list of citations showing Homer's favorable attitudes toward different gods) is actually followed by a "quotation" that combines one passage on Athena with another that originally referred to Artemis.[60] Though a memory lapse is always possible, it may be that here again one sees a certain willingness on the part of the author to adapt the Homeric text to his own purposes.

In sum, it seems clear that Heraclitus' overarching program of setting forth a thorough defense of Homer has influenced the way he quotes the Homeric text. In addition to the rather standard practices of modifying the text to fit his own grammar and combining verses from different sources without specific indication, Heraclitus can also be seen changing words, omitting unnecessary or problematic language, and otherwise molding the text of his quotations to bring them into agreement with his fundamental thesis of a hidden allegorical meaning behind Homer's depictions of the gods.

Plutarch

Two essays by Plutarch will be examined here, *How the Young Man Should Read Poetry* and *A Letter of Condolence to Apollonius*. Since questions have been raised about the authorship of the second essay, the two will be treated separately in the following discussion.

The first text, *How the Young Man Should Read Poetry*, is essentially a study in the moral aspects of literary criticism. The essay is structured as a letter offering guidance to a friend on the proper use of poetry for training young men prior to their later, more valuable studies in philosophy. Highly conscious of the questionable morality of some of the poets, Plutarch nonetheless believes that there is much to be learned from reading them through a proper moral framework, in preparation for the more rigorous requirements of philosophical reasoning. It is with this in mind that he offers a

---

[59] *Ibid.*, 2.1, 2.4, 2.5 (4th), 3.1, and 23.4.
[60] *Ibid.*, 2.4, citing *Il* 1.199–201 and *Od* 6.102–4.

wide-ranging series of observations concerning how even the most troublesome poets might be read with advantage.[61]

As might be expected, the text of this first essay is filled with excerpts from the Greek poets, which are then used to demonstrate the critical principles set forth in the essay proper. Of the 193 total citations in the essay (in 62 printed pages of Greek text), 103 come from the *Iliad* or *Odyssey*.[62] Though in general he thinks quite highly of Homer, Plutarch does not hesitate to criticize even the great bard himself when he has questions about the morality of some of his statements, particularly his portraits of the gods. In this, of course, he stands light-years away from a man like Heraclitus.

The evidence seems conclusive that Plutarch drew his quotations from a different text of Homer than that represented in the "vulgate." At least five examples can be cited of Plutarchian readings that agree with Homeric texts other than the "vulgate,"[63] and in one instance Plutarch actually states his preference for a non-Aristarchian text ("Now Aristarchus removed these lines from the text through fear ...").[64] In another case he omits a line found in the "vulgate" and adds another that appears in none of the Homeric manuscripts. Here, too, a different *Vorlage* must be presumed, since the whole point of adducing the passage is to object to the content of the "extra" line.[65] Several other readings that might conceivably have arisen from a faulty memory could just as easily be understood as variant readings derived from a non-"standard" text.[66] On the other hand, the question of whether Plutarch actually consulted such a text while writing his essay or simply learned Homer from a non-vulgate text as a child cannot be resolved from the present essay.

Fortunately, what might have been a major problem for the

---

[61] Dawson describes how this notion of what was "fitting" (τὸ πρέπον) was used as a critical tool by both the Alexandrians (chap. 1) and the Stoics (chap. 2) in their study of the Homeric epics.

[62] The high number of citations in this text from all sources sets it apart from almost all of Plutarch's other works. Elsewhere he seems to use quotations neither more nor less than his contemporaries. On the whole, Plutarch appears to cite the *Iliad* and *Odyssey* less often than many of his contemporaries, perhaps because he does not attribute to them the same degree of authority that many others do. At any rate, the number and breadth of citations in the present essay is highly unusual for Plutarch.

[63] In *Poetry* 23D, 24C, 30A, 32B, and 36A. See also 27B and 35B, where minor divergences also seem to reflect a different text.

[64] *Ibid.*, 26F, citing four lines not found in the vulgate.

[65] *Ibid.*, 24C. The same combination also occurs in 36A.

[66] *Ibid.*, 22E, 27B, 27D, 28F, and 35B.

analysis of certain other authors (i.e. whether differences in wording represent purposeful changes or merely the use of a divergent text) never becomes an issue in the case of Plutarch, since the essay on *Poetry* contains almost no variations that might be regarded as intentional adaptations of the text. In two places minor changes are introduced to conform the citation to the grammar of its new context,[67] and in another case a difference in wording might possibly reflect an intentional alteration of the text to suit the purposes of the author.[68] All in all, however, adapting the wording of the text appears to have played only a minor role in Plutarch's citation practice in this essay.

More typical is the omission of narrative details that have no bearing on the point the author is trying to make.[69] In Plutarch's case, such omissions always involve entire lines of text, never individual words or phrases. The care with which the omissions were selected is evident: none but an observant reader would ever know that the original texts had undergone abbreviation. In every case the resultant "quotation" reads as an integrated, free-standing whole, while the basic sense of the original passage comes through clearly in every case. Though it is still correct to speak of the author's purposes influencing his citation technique in such instances, it seems that it was a desire to eliminate irrelevant materials rather than any concern to reinterpret the text that motivated these adaptations.[70] Beyond this, the format of Plutarch's citations is quite straightforward.

---

[67] *Ibid.*, 29A (4th, addition of φησί), and 30D (omitting the first word, Ἕκτωρ, as redundant).

[68] *Ibid.*, 22B (citing *Od* 4.197–8). The coordinated substitution of που for καί and ἐστίν for οἷον reflects Plutarch's concern (seen in the subsequent interpretation) to tone down the "absoluteness" of Homer's depiction of the miseries of the present life.

[69] *Ibid.*, 29D, citing *Il* 9.70, 74–5 (omitting three lines that relate to the availability of victuals for a proposed feast); 31A, citing *Il* 24.560–1, 569–70 (leaving out seven lines that speak of the divine assistance granted Priam on his supplicatory visit to Achilles); and 35C (2nd), citing *Il* 23.474, 478 (skipping three lines relating to the contest scene at which the quoted words were spoken). The frequency of omissions in Plutarch's Homeric quotations is also noted by M. van der Valk, *Textual Criticism of the Odyssey* (Leiden: A. W. Sijthoff, 1949), 280–1.

[70] This is not to say, however, that Plutarch always interprets the text in a "literal" manner. In accordance with a principle from Chrysippus to the effect that "what is serviceable should be taken over and made to apply to like situations" (34B), Plutarch several times quotes only as much of the original text as was required to support the point that he wanted to make (= "limited selection"). In this way Homer's poetry can be compared to the drugs of Egypt (*Od* 4.230) or the love-philter of Aphrodite (*Il* 14.216) – both contain a potentially deceptive mixture of good and ill (15C). In a similar manner, the young readers of Homer can be encouraged to

Interestingly, most of the questions that have been raised about the authorship of the second essay, *A Letter of Condolence to Apollonius*, revolve around the way this text handles quotations. As one author puts it, it appears that "quotations from earlier authors have been emptied by the sack rather than scattered by hand."[71] In content, the essay takes the form of a letter of condolence to a friend who is still grieving over the loss of his young son. In an effort to console his friend, the author sets forth a variety of reasons why lingering grief is both inappropriate and unnecessary. Each point is backed up by a series of often lengthy quotations culled from a plethora of ancient authors who affirmed the same views. The result is a nearly exhaustive catalogue of ancient and contemporary views on the nature of human life and death.

Surprisingly, quotations from Homer make up only a small percentage of the materials called into service by this author. Out of 99 total citations (in 52 printed pages of Greek text), only 19 come from the *Iliad* or the *Odyssey*. Other authors quoted frequently include Euripides, Pindar, Aeschylus, Sophocles, and Hesiod. The sheer number of different authors cited in the essay would lead one to presume that the author did not consult the original texts in making his citations, though the extreme length of some of them (up to 18 lines in one case) makes memory quotation unlikely as well. The

---

"hasten to the light" (*Od* 11.233, quoted in 16E-F) or "think of a better saying than this one" (*Il* 7.358, quoted in 20E), whenever they feel themselves succumbing to the "base beliefs" that Homer sometimes sets forth about gods and men. Such non-"literal" applications become possible only through a severe delimitation of the materials selected for quotation.

[71] F. C. Babbitt in his introduction to the essay in the Loeb series, 105. Other arguments that have been brought forward against Plutarchian authorship include the omission of Plutarch's characteristic address to the dedicant during the course of the essay; the omission of the work from the Catalogue of Lamprias, an early (second-century?) listing of the titles of Plutarch's works; differences in the treatment of certain anecdotes that occur both here and in other Plutarchian essays; the preference for literary citations over historical examples as a means of instilling a desired behavior; the general lack of emotion with which so serious a subject is treated; the uncharacteristically loose integration of citations into the body of the text; and certain arguable differences in language and style (examples in Hani, 27–39). Jean Hani (28–50) offers a variety of arguments to explain or counter these objections: our lack of the full Plutarchian corpus; the possibility that the *Condolence* represents an early work, a school exercise, or a rough draft; the probability that the author used florilegia rather than original texts in formulating his citations; and especially the author's apparent efforts to conform his text to an ancient "consolation" genre. Critics of authenticity see the real author as, in Hani's words, "un écrivain mineur, et inexpert d'ailleurs, de l'âge sophistique, comme Dion Chrysostome ou Favorinos" (*ibid.*, 28). Hani offers no firm date for the work, though he declares it authentic. Plutarch died around 120 C.E.

handful of divergences from the standard Homeric text offer no real guidance on the matter: most are mere spelling differences, and the one instance of a clearly variant reading finds no support in the manuscript tradition.[72] The most likely solution would see the author relying here on a florilegium of "consolation" texts compiled for use in the rhetorical schools of his day.[73]

Modifications designed to integrate the quotation into the grammatical context of the new document are more frequent in this essay than in the last. Four of the essay's nineteen Homeric citations have been adapted in this way.[74] At the same time, not one of these changes affects the basic sense of the passage cited. Omissions of extraneous or redundant narrative materials to create a smooth-flowing whole can be seen in three instances, but here again the original sense comes through unimpaired in every case.[75] One instance of an addition to the text is also found: the insertion of the words οὐδέ τις ἀλκή ("nor any help") at the end of a line seems designed to increase the pathos of a passage describing the fleeting nature of human existence.[76]

In addition to occasionally leaving out whole lines of text to create a new free-standing "citation," the present essay echoes two other aspects of unusual citation format encountered in earlier authors. In one case, the author combines passages from different books of the *Iliad* on the same topic to form a single artificial "quotation" that better supports his point.[77] In another instance, two verses from different contexts (one from the *Iliad*, the other from the *Odyssey*) that contain an overlapping element (the Greek word τοῖσι) are conflated in a way that adds a somber tone to the primary passage, in accordance with the author's stated purpose throughout the essay.[78] Though it is by no means a long step from

[72] Spelling differences/common variants in *ibid.*, 104D, 105C–D, 113F–114B, and 118B; clearly divergent reading in 117B.

[73] See Hani, 30, 49–50, in addition to the evidence in chap. 3 of the present study. At the same time, the possibility that the author compiled such an anthology himself cannot be ruled out: see *Peri Euthumias* 464F, quoted in chap. 3, note 32.

[74] *Ibid.*, 104F (converting an Indicative to an Infinitive), 117B (turning second-person address into third-person description), 117C (*idem*), and 118F (changing a participle from Nominative to Accusative).

[75] *Ibid.*, 104D, citing *Od* 18.130–5 (omits one line); 104F, citing *Il* 21.463–6 (omits beginning of one line); and 113F–114B, citing *Il* 22.56–68, 74–8 (omits five lines).

[76] *Ibid.*, 104F, citing *Il* 21.463–6.

[77] *Ibid.*, 117C, combining *Il* 23.222 and 17.37.

[78] *Ibid.*, 114E, conflating *Il* 23.109 (μυρομένοισι δὲ τοῖσι φάνη ῥοδοδάκτυλος Ἠώς) with *Od* 1.423 (τοῖσι δὲ τερπομένοισι μέλας ἐπὶ ἕσπερος ἦλθε). Underlines indicate words taken up into the conflated citation. The former passage spoke

the simple procedure of omitting "extraneous" lines to the more complex techniques of combining and conflating verses from different sources into a distinctive literary unit, the fact remains that the more creative procedures are found nowhere in the more than one hundred citations from Homer in the previous essay.

All in all, a study of the citation practices of the *Letter of Condolence* reveals a marked development beyond the more conservative techniques witnessed in the essay on *Poetry*. Not only does the *Letter of Condolence* adapt the wording of its quotations much more frequently within its admittedly limited purview (10 out of 19 passages vs. 8 out of 103), but it also exhibits a significantly greater variety of treatments and a generally higher degree of literary artistry in its handling of the texts it does cite. The earlier noted fact of the unusual density and length of the quotations in the *Letter of Condolence* should also be recalled at this point. Of course, such differences in literary technique cannot on their own prove that the two works were produced by different authors – the uniqueness of the clearly Plutarchian *How the Young Man Should Read Poetry* compared to Plutarch's other works should counsel against such premature conclusions. But when the evidence is expanded to include the positive attitude in the *Letter of Condolence* toward a Homeric passage whose sentiments were expressly rejected in the essay on *Poetry* (attributing human troubles to the designs of Zeus), along with several others like it,[79] the evidence of the quotations would seem to tell strongly against the Plutarchian authorship of the former essay. If this is so, then the essays studied here would offer two distinct examples of Greco–Roman citation technique instead of one.

5. Summary of findings

In conclusion, it might be useful to sum up the findings of the present study regarding the citation techniques of four (or five) authors from the Greco–Roman world of the first century C.E.

originally of the weeping of the Greeks over the death of Patroclus; the latter described the end of a day of feasting by the suitors ensconced at Penelope's house. The conflated form ("While they were weeping and wailing, black darkness descended upon them") is applied in the *Condolence* to mourners who refuse to cease their mourning after an appropriate period.

[79] The passage in question is *Il* 24.528–9, cited as a source of comfort in *Condolence* 105C–D and explicitly rejected in *Poetry* 24B. Other passages in the *Condolence* that express the same sentiments include 104D–E (citing *Od* 18.130), 107B

(1) All of the writers examined here exhibit a high degree of flexibility and originality in the way they incorporate quotations into their own developing compositions. While certain more or less formulaic expressions could be called in from time to time to help ease the transition, in most cases the author simply used his own words to integrate the quotation in a creative manner into its new literary context.

(2) No pattern can be discerned in the various types of materials used by the authors in adducing their quotations. Though the evidence is limited, a case can be made for the use of both "standard" and non-"standard" texts of Homer, while written texts, anthologies, and memory quotation are all attested as proximate sources.

(3) The great majority of the quotations studied here agree precisely with the "vulgate" tradition of the Homeric epics. Where the wording of that text has experienced modification, the extent of the changes varies widely from author to author. The proportion of adapted texts in the authors studied here ranges from 6 percent in Plutarch's *Poetry* essay to 15 percent for Heraclitus, 24 percent for Strabo, 50 percent for the *Sublime*, and 52 percent for the *Letter of Condolence*.[80]

(4) A variety of adaptive techniques can be seen in the works examined here. Omitting words, lines, or phrases that seemed redundant or otherwise irrelevant to the later author's interests is by far the most common technique. In almost every case the result is a smooth-flowing literary unit that takes the place of a genuine "quotation" in the later author's text. Grammatical alterations intended to conform a quotation to its new linguistic environment are also quite common. Additions and substitutions appear less often in the texts studied here, while changes in word order are almost unknown. "Limited selection" is employed on a number of occasions when an author wants to apply a passage in a sense quite different from the original.

(5) Though not as common as the other modes of adaptation, combined citations and (to a lesser extent) conflated texts were also encountered in the materials under study. Far from reflecting occasional lapses in memory, the passages examined here showed a high

(citing Pindar), and 116E–F (citing "the Pythagoreans"). For other arguments against Plutarchian authorship, see note 71.

[80] By way of comparison, adaptations of one type or another were counted in fifty of the eighty-three Pauline texts examined in chaps. 4 and 5 (60 percent).

degree of literary artistry and appeared to function in direct subservience to the later author's rhetorical purposes.

(6) A variety of motives can be discerned behind the textual adaptations noted above. From the conduct of the authors surveyed here, one could reasonably infer that the technique of adapting the language of a quotation to suit the grammatical requirements of the new context was standard fare in the Greco–Roman world. The same can be said for modifications designed to clarify the original reference of an otherwise obscure quotation. In the case of omissions, the primary purpose seems to have been to eliminate extraneous materials (especially narrative details) that might have drawn attention away from the point the author wanted to make in adducing the text. In a few instances, however, the same technique appears to have been used to excise potentially troublesome references or otherwise to bring a text into closer alignment with the author's own literary agenda.[81] Adaptations designed to conform the text to the later author's beliefs seem limited to writings with a strong apologetic interest, such as those of Heraclitus, Crates, Zeno, and on occasion ("for the good of the reader"), Plutarch. Combined and conflated citations arise for the most part out of rhetorical concerns.

On the whole, the similarities between this list and the conclusions of the previous chapter are too close to be coincidental. Despite Koch's summary dismissal of the possibility of Greco–Roman parallels, a careful sifting of the evidence reveals a near-identity of conceptions between Paul and his Greco–Roman counterparts as to the acceptable parameters for citing literary texts. The question of whether Paul absorbed these techniques directly from his Greco–Roman environment or whether they might have been mediated to him via his Jewish upbringing must remain open pending an inquiry into the citation techniques of contemporary Judaism. Whatever the outcome, however, it can be affirmed with confidence that in the way he handled the wording of his biblical quotations, Paul was in every respect a man of his world.

[81] M. van der Valk, 280, reaches a similar conclusion after a much more cursory examination of the evidence: "First of all these authors did not quote Homer with scrupulous care, and secondly they quoted only those lines from a Homeric passage, which were relevant for their purpose, whereas they omitted the irrelevant lines."

8

CITATION TECHNIQUE IN EARLY JUDAISM

1. Introduction

Countless studies have sought to correlate the apostle Paul's handling of Scripture with the methods of his Jewish contemporaries. In addition to the summary treatments that accompany most investigations of Paul's use of the "Old Testament," a variety of monographs have compared Paul's mode of interpretation with those of Philo, the rabbinic literature, and the Qumran community.[1] Similar investigations have been carried out for every book of the New Testament where biblical quotations can be identified.[2] Additional studies have examined the interpretational techniques of the Jewish materials themselves.[3] After so much scholarly effort, one would expect to find a wealth of data on the way early Jewish writers handled the wording of their quotations. In reality, very few

---

[1] Comparisons with rabbinic literature go back at least to Surenhusius (see chap. 1), who laid the groundwork for subsequent studies in this area. More recent investigations include J. Bonsirven, *Exégèse*; Birger Gerhardsson, *Memory*; and Daniel Cohn-Sherbock, "Paul and Rabbinic Exegesis," *SJT* 35 (1982), 117–32. The discovery of the "sectarian" literature of the Qumran community stimulated a whole new round of comparative studies, including E. E. Ellis, *Use*, and "*Midrash Pesher* in Pauline Hermeneutics," in *Prophecy and Hermeneutics in Early Christianity: New Testament Essays*, WUNT 18 (Tübingen: Mohr, 1978), 173–81; J. Murphy-O'Connor, *Paul and Qumran: Studies in New Testament Exegesis* (London: G. Chapman, 1968; Chicago: Priory Press, 1968); and J. A. Sanders, "Habakkuk in Qumran, Paul, and the Old Testament," *JR* 39 (1959), 232–44. Comparisons with Philo have normally focused on the authors' respective hermeneutical techniques, though see Peder Borgen, *Philo, John, and Paul*, Brown Judaic Studies 131 (Atlanta: Scholars, 1987). Investigations comparing Paul's use of Scripture with that of Josephus, the Targumin, and the so-called "pseudepigrapha" are almost non-existent. For more generalized studies, see the bibliography.

[2] An extensive list of recent titles can be found in the author's 1990 Duke Ph.D. dissertation, "Citation Technique in the Pauline Epistles and Contemporary Literature," 330 n. 2.

[3] See any of the numerous works listed in the bibliography.

researchers have concerned themselves with this problem.[4] Several explanations can be posited for this comparative neglect: the complex and uncertain text-history of the biblical materials themselves; the difficulty of fixing an individual author's biblical *Vorlage*; the loss of original language versions of many of the works in question; a notable lack of comparative studies on other documents; and especially the higher visibility and relative accessibility of an author's exegetical techniques as compared to the way he handled the wording of Scripture. Comparing hermeneutical models is certainly a more promising enterprise than entering into a labyrinthine discussion of the relationship between a series of quotations and their presumed biblical *Vorlage*. In the long run, however, there is no escaping the close analysis that is required to render an adequate portrait of an author's approach to the biblical text.

The general lack of data in this area has several implications for the present study. On the one hand, the structure of the study requires that the same methods be applied to every document studied in order to insure consistency and comparability among the results. On the other hand, a close analysis of every quotation in the entire corpus of early Jewish literature is clearly impractical. Without compromising the methods of the investigation, the only way to obtain a reliable data base is to follow the example of the previous chapter and limit the study to a representative sampling of Jewish materials from around the turn of the era. No doubt Judaism was a variegated phenomenon during this period, and caution must be exercised in drawing far-ranging conclusions from a limited selection of materials. But the world of Judaism was no more diverse than Greco–Roman society in general. If certain patterns can be discerned in the way various non-Jewish authors handled the wording of their quotations during this period, there is no reason to think that the same might not be true for Jewish literature. Only a careful study of the materials themselves can show whether a similar literary ethos informed the way Jewish authors approached the biblical text at the time of Paul.

---

[4] The studies of Stendahl, Ellis, and Bonsirven are notable exceptions on the New Testament side. On the Jewish side, the biblical texts of Philo and Josephus have attracted a certain amount of scrutiny, and much has been written about the *Vorlage* of the Qumran *pesharim*. Quotations in the non-*pesher* materials from Qumran and the "pseudepigrapha," on the other hand, have been largely neglected.

2. Materials

Problems plague every attempt to select a representative sampling of early Jewish materials for inclusion in the present study. Alongside the sheer breadth of the options stands the fact that biblical quotations abound throughout the literature. In some cases (particularly Philo and Josephus), a single author's literary output is so prodigious as to render a thorough investigation impracticable within the constraints of the present study. In others (primarily the rabbinic literature), the materials have experienced such wholesale revision and editing over the centuries that the original wording of their quotations can no longer be fixed with any level of certainty. Moreover, questions persist concerning the literary integrity and even the original language of many of the documents in question. Materials that are extant only in translation simply cannot be subjected to the same degree of scrutiny as those that remain available in their original languages.

To insure adequate diversity within the sample, three different types of literature have been selected for investigation. First to be examined will be the community documents from Qumran. The materials to be canvassed here are not the so-called *pesher* texts, whose textual and hermeneutical problems have attracted the attention of numerous investigators, but the quotations that appear in such non-*pesher* texts as the *Manual of Discipline*, the *War Scroll*, the *Damascus Document*, and the Melchizedek fragments. It is these documents, not the *pesharim*, that offer the closest parallel to Paul's practice of adducing quotations from various parts of Scripture to support and further his own free-standing argument.

Next to be considered is that amorphous body of literature termed somewhat unhappily the "apocrypha" and "pseudepigrapha." Whereas the former term is normally reserved for a fixed group of early Jewish writings that eventually found a place in Christian codices of the "Septuagint," the latter has come to be applied loosely to any Jewish composition of the Second Temple period (or beyond) that cannot be conveniently subsumed under any other broad heading. As such, it is not only a misnomer (false ascriptions of authorship characterize only certain parts of the literature), but also an increasingly useless category for serious analysis. The distinction between the two categories is in fact quite artificial from a literary perspective, as any survey of their contents will show. As no other label has succeeded in replacing the traditional terminology in current usage, however, the usual designations have been retained for the present study, with the proviso that each document will be examined in its integrity and not forced to fit some Procrustean bed called the "apocrypha" or "pseudepigrapha."[5] The materials have been divided into three groups according to their likely period of origin: pre-Hasmonean, Hasmonean, or Roman. Most of the documents appear to have arisen (like the letters of Paul) in the Jewish Diaspora, though in some cases the evidence is too scanty to form reliable conclusions. A list of the texts to be examined appears at the head of the appropriate section.

Finally, a few remarks must be made about the citation technique of the Alexandrian Jew Philo. While many have seen in his writings an acute "Hellenization" of Judaism, contemporary scholarship has moved toward a fuller appreciation of the deep "Jewishness" of Philo's own faith and literary mission. Though his aristocratic background undoubtedly placed him on a higher social level than the apostle Paul, the cultural gap between the two is probably not as great as some have thought.[6] Since the two were also relative contemporaries, a comparison of their respective ways of handling biblical quotations should prove enlightening.[7] Of course, the sheer bulk of Philo's voluminous literary output requires that the present study be limited to one corner of the Philonic corpus. For reasons

[5] Even the otherwise attractive label "Jewish Literature of the Second Temple Period" (the title used in the series Compendia Rerum Iudaicarum) cannot encompass the numerous post-70 works included in James H. Charlesworth's *OT Pseudepigrapha*.

[6] On the social level of Paul and his congregations, see John Gager, *Kingdom and Community* (Englewood Cliffs, NJ: Prentice-Hall, 1975); Ronald F. Hock, *The Social Context of Paul's Ministry* (Philadelphia: Fortress, 1980); E. A. Judge, *The Social Pattern of Christian Groups in the First Century* (London: Tyndale, 1960); *Rank and Status in the World of the Caesars and St. Paul* (Christchurch: University of Canterbury, 1982); and the studies of Malherbe, Meeks, and Theissen cited in chap. 3, note 27.

[7] As a younger contemporary of Paul, one might think that Josephus, too, would offer a wealth of materials for comparative study. In this case, however, the expected parallels fail to materialize. Though he draws heavily on the biblical record (especially its narrative sections), Josephus almost never offers the sort of explicit quotations that form the focus of the present study (see definitions in chap. 2). Instead, his appropriation of Scripture is limited almost exclusively to running paraphrases of the biblical narrative. Moreover, Josephus is renowned for being, as Louis Feldman puts it, "almost pathological about avoiding the usage of the same word as that found in his source," as can be seen from his handling of *1 Maccabees* and the *Letter of Aristeas* ("Use, Authority and Exegesis of Mikra in the Writings of Josephus," in Mulder (ed.), *Mikra*, 461, 479; similarly Sidney Jellicoe, *The Septuagint and Modern Study* (Oxford: Clarendon, 1968), 288). For these reasons the works of Josephus have been excluded from the present study.

that will be explained below, two treatises have been chosen for study here, the *Legum Allegoria* (*Allegorical Interpretation of Genesis II and III*) and the *De Ebrietate* (*On Drunkenness*). While it is no doubt risky to generalize from such a limited compass of materials, the possibility of unearthing a consistent citation technique within these two highly disparate treatises make such a study valuable in its own right.

As with the previous chapter, only the broad outlines of each author's citation technique can be set forth in the pages below. Though no sample can claim absolute reliability, the discovery of a consistent approach to the biblical text within this diverse body of literature could be taken as strong evidence for the presence of a common attitude toward the wording of biblical quotations in early Judaism.

3. Qumran[8]

Much has been written over the years about the use of Scripture in the Qumran community. Most of the attention has centered on the interpretational techniques of the so-called "*pesher*" texts (*1QpHab*, *4QpNah*, etc.), whose unique literary form has piqued scholarly interest from their first discovery.[9] The "Messianic" quotations of *4QTestimonia* and *4QFlorilegium* have also been examined for their possible relevance to the Messianism of the New Testament.[10] Otherwise only isolated passages such as the expanded Aaronic benediction in *1QS* 2.2–4 and the Amos–Numbers midrash in *CD* 7.13–8.1 have received significant scholarly comment. Little has

---

[8] An earlier version of the section on Qumran was presented at the Annual Meeting of the Society of Biblical Literature, Anaheim, California, November 1989.

[9] More recent studies include William Brownlee, *The Midrash Pesher of Habakkuk* (Missoula, MT: Scholars, 1979); Bruce D. Chilton, "Commenting on the Old Testament," in Carson and Williamson (eds.), *It is Written*, 122–7; Devorah Dimant, "Qumran Sectarian Literature," in *Jewish Writings of the Second Temple Period*, Compendia Rerum Iudaicarum ad Novum Testamentum II/2, ed. Michael E. Stone (Assen: Van Gorcum, 1984; Philadelphia: Fortress, 1984), 483–550; Michael Fishbane, "The Qumran-*Pesher* and Traits of Ancient Hermeneutics," in *Proceedings of the Sixth World Congress of Jewish Studies*, ed. Avigdor Shinan (Jerusalem: World Union of Jewish Studies, 1977), 1:97–114; Maurya Horgan, *Pesharim: Qumran Interpretation of Biblical Books*, CBQMS 8 (Washington, DC: Catholic Biblical Assoc., 1979); and I. Rabinowitz, "*Pesher/Pittaron*: Its Biblical Meaning and Its Significance in the Qumran Literature," *RevQ* 8 (1972–4), 219–32.

[10] E.g. J. A. Fitzmyer, "*4QTestimonia* and the New Testament,", *TS* 18 (1957), 513–37, and George J. Brooke, *Exegesis at Qumran: 4QFlor in its Jewish Context* (Sheffield: JSOT Press, 1985).

been done to this point to characterize the citation technique of the non-*pesher* materials as a whole.[11]

Nonetheless, it is precisely these non-*pesher* texts that offer the greatest potential for comparison with the citation technique of the apostle Paul. In the *pesharim*, the bulk of the biblical material appears in the *lemma* that stands at the head of each new section as the interpretation moves piecemeal through a particular portion of Scripture.[12] In the non-*pesher* materials (*1QS*, *1QM*, *4QFlor*, etc.), on the other hand, biblical quotations are scattered strategically throughout the document according to the needs of the argument, as in the Pauline epistles. Of course, nothing in these differing uses of Scripture requires a different approach to the wording of the biblical text. In practice, however, a marked distinction can indeed be discerned. In the *pesharim*, verbatim citation is the norm, though at times one has to look to the Samaritan Pentateuch, the Septuagint, or other early versions to find evidence for the Hebrew *Vorlage* employed by the Qumran interpreter.[13] Outside the *pesharim*, on the

---

[11] Among the few studies that deal with biblical interpretation in individual documents outside the *pesharim*, see (in adition to the previous note) G. Brin, "Concerning Some of the Uses of the Bible in the *Temple Scroll*," *RevQ* 12 (1987), 519–28; J. Carmignac, "Les citations de l'Ancien Testament dans 'La guerre des fils de lumière contre les fils de ténèbres,'" *RB* 63 (1956), 234–60, 375–90; "Les citations de l'Ancien Testament, et spécialement des Poèmes du Servitur, dans les Hymnes de Qumran," *RevQ* 2 (1960), 357–94; Andrew Chester, "Citing the Old Testament," in Carson and Williamson (eds.), *It is Written*, 141–50; Hans A. Mink, "The Use of Scripture in the *Temple Scroll* and the Status of the Scroll as Law," *SJOT* 1 (1987), 20–50; B. J. Roberts, "Some Observations on the *Damascus Document* and the Dead Sea Scrolls," *BJRL* 34 (1951–2), 366–87; J. A. Sanders, "The Old Testament in *11QMelchizedek*," *JANESCU* 5 (1973), 373–82; Ottilie Schwarz, *Der erste Teil der Damaskusschrift und das Alte Testament* (Diest: Lichtland, 1965); and P. Wernberg-Møller, "Some Reflections on the Biblical Material in the *Manual of Discipline*," *ST* 1 (1955), 40–66. More general studies are even harder to come by: see Herbert Braun, *Qumran und das Neue Testament* (Tübingen: Mohr, 1966); J. A. Fitzmyer, "The Use of Explicit Old Testament Quotations in the Qumran Literature and in the New Testament," *NTS* 7 (1961), 297–333; Moshe Goshen-Gottstein, "Bible Quotations in the Sectarian Dead Sea Scrolls," *VT* 3 (1953), 79–82; E. Slomovic, "Toward an Understanding of the Exegesis in the Dead Sea Scrolls," *RevQ* 7 (1969–71), 3–15; and Jan de Waard, *Study*.

[12] On this use of the term *pesher* to refer to a literary genre rather than a particular mode of interpretation, see the works by Brooke, Horgan, and Rabinowitz cited in the previous notes.

[13] Applying the rigid methods of the present study to the *pesharim* yields only a handful of instances where it can be affirmed with reasonable confidence that the wording of the biblical text has indeed been adapted for its present use. Of fifty-nine deviations from the MT in the quotations of *1QpHab*, fourteen appear to reflect the use a different Hebrew text, while only two to four (4.9?, 5.1?, 5.8, 12.1) could qualify for an A or B rating as authorial adaptations. (Six others received a C rating; the majority were left undetermined.) In *4QpNah*, only three of thirty-two divergent

other hand, biblical passages are quoted with a mixture of slavish reproduction and free adaptation that defies any easy categorization. A careful examination of the types of adaptations that appear in these texts could prove useful in a comparison with the citation technique of the apostle Paul.

What follows is a summary of the results of one such examination. The study is necessarily limited to those documents where biblical quotations have been sufficiently preserved to allow for an evaluation of their relation to the Masoretic Hebrew text.[14] As with the Pauline texts, orthographic and spelling differences have been ignored. Except where common patterns can be discerned, the results are presented separately for each document so as to avoid any hasty generalizations about "the" citation practice of the Qumran community.[15] A concluding section will sum up what can be learned from the materials as a whole.

4QTestimonia, 11QMelchizedek and 4QPatriarchal Blessings

The document known as *4QTestimonia* consists entirely of four lengthy quotations from various parts of the Pentateuch plus one from Joshua, of which only the last receives any sort of interpretive comment.[16] None of these quotations shows any sign of having been adapted for its present use. Of the nineteen divergences from the

readings were deemed worthy of an A or B rating (frag. 1–2, lines 5 and 9, plus one in 3.2), while six others show signs of a textual basis. (Here again, the origins of most remain unclear.) The picture is similar in the case of *4QpPs 37*: eight out of twenty-three deviations seem to reflect the use of a non-MT *Vorlage*, while not one could be regarded as a clear adaptation. The pattern is exactly what one would expect of a genre in which a continuous portion of the biblical text is reproduced in discrete segments throughout the body of the composition. From all appearances, the biblical excerpts in the *pesharim* were copied directly from a written *Vorlage*.

[14] Only texts published in the first seven volumes of DJD were considered for inclusion. The *Hodayoth* and the *Temple Scroll* have been left out of the discussion entirely, since neither contains the kind of explicit citations that serve as the basis for the present study.

[15] Continuing uncertainty as to the dating and origins of certain documents (i.e. whether they were composed within the Qumran community or brought in from outside) is the primary reason for such caution. For a recent attempt to sort out the materials from an orthographic point of view, see Emanuel Tov, "The Orthography and Language of the Hebrew Scrolls Found at Qumran and the Origin of These Scrolls," *Textus 13* (1986), 31–57.

[16] The same quotation from Josh 6.26 (agreeing with the LXX vs. the MT) accompanied by the same interpretive comment appears in the so-called "*Psalms of Joshua*" (*4Q379*, frag. 22, 2.8–14). See Carol A. Newsome, "The '*Psalms of Joshua*' from Qumran Cave 4," *JJS 39* (1988), 56–73.

Masoretic Hebrew tradition in this document, fully half have a clearly identifiable textual basis (LXX, Samaritan Pentateuch, etc.). Most of the others can probably be traced to a similar background.

A comparable approach can be seen in the fragmentary texts *11QMelchizedek* and *4QPatriarchal Blessings*. Of the eight explicit biblical quotations in *11QMelch*, six agree precisely with the Masoretic tradition, while the other two contain only minor variants that show no relation to their present contexts. The single brief citation that introduces *4QPBless* diverges at two points from the later Masoretic Hebrew text, but the background of both readings remains highly uncertain.

In sum, unaltered quotation would appear to be the rule in all three of these texts. The only clear deviation from a simple verbatim reproduction of the original passage is the replacement of the Tetragrammaton with four dots in the quotation from Deut 33.11 in *4QTestim* 19.[17] Such a practice is typical of the consistent displacement of the divine name in all the biblical quotations from Qumran outside the *pesharim* and *4QFlorilegium*.[18]

4QFlorilegium

The text of *4QFlorilegium* testifies to a more diverse citation technique than was displayed in the previous documents. Of the twelve explicit biblical quotations in this text, five agree precisely with the Masoretic textual tradition, while the other seven show substantial differences. Fully ten divergent readings can be identified in these seven texts, of which only one can be traced with certainty to the use of a different *Vorlage*. Two of these passages show clear evidence of an editorial hand at work. In one instance (1.10–11a), the author has eliminated the historical parameters of the Davidic covenant narrated in 2 Sam 7.11–14 so as to render the text more amenable to an eschatological interpretation.[19] In the other place (1.15), an additional verb (וְיִהִי) has been affixed to the beginning of the citation to maintain the temporal reference of the original passage in

[17] The "combined citation" in *4QTestim* 1–7 (citing Deut 5.28–9 and Deut 18.18–19 back-to-back under a single introductory formula) is found already at Exod 20.21 in the Samaritan Pentateuch, and thus cannot be attributed to the author of *4QTestimonia*.

[18] Additional evidence is cited in the discussions of other texts below.

[19] Omitted are v. 12a ("when your days are full and you lie down with your fathers"), v. 12c ("who will come out from your belly"), and vv. 12e–13a ("and I will establish his kingdom; he will build a house for my name").

its new grammatical context. The origins of the other deviations remain entirely unclear. Other noteworthy features include the presence of a "combined citation" (Dan 12.10 plus Dan 11.32) in 2.4, as well as a single instance of "limited selection" in 1.16–17, where a useful phrase from Ezek 37.23 (or 44.10) is applied in a manner quite foreign to its original context.[20]

Manual of Discipline (1QS)

Every reader of the *Manual of Discipline* is impressed with the wealth of biblical language that permeates every quarter of this important text.[21] It thus comes as something of a surprise to discover only three explicit quotations within the eleven columns of this diverse work. Clearly the direct citation of biblical texts played almost no role in the literary and rhetorical aims of the author(s) of this document. The few quotations that do occur bear out this conclusion: one agrees fully with the Masoretic text (5.17), another diverges from it only in the characteristic Qumran elimination of the divine name (8.14), and the third shows only one minor deviation that can be seen also in the Septuagint (the addition of כּוֹל in 5.15). The only feature of note is a further instance of "limited selection" in 5.15.[22]

War Scroll (1QM)

Like the *Manual of Discipline*, the *War Scroll* resounds with biblical language.[23] Nevertheless, explicit quotation remains the exception rather than the rule in *1QM* as in *1QS*. Only four times in the entire document (all in the hortatory sections of columns ten and eleven) is a specific biblical text adduced with an introductory formula, and

---

[20] The text of *4QFlor* is damaged at this point, making it impossible to be certain which of the two passages from Ezekiel was intended. In either case, a brief phrase was selected out of a larger passage for its verbal usefulness and not for its original meaning. A fuller quotation of either verse would have been impossible in the present context.

[21] In a valuable 1955 article, Preben Wernberg-Møller listed scores of biblical references that he had identified in the body of *1QS* (see note 11).

[22] In order to use Exod 23.7 as an injunction against sharing in the possessions of the ungodly (read here as "keep away from every thing [דְּבַר] of falsehood"), the Qumran interpreter is forced to omit the latter half of the verse (וְצַדִּיק אַל־תַּהֲרֹג כִּי לֹא־אַצְדִּיק רָשָׁע) where the original judicial context of the passage comes into view.

[23] Jean Carmignac listed and analyzed several dozen of what he called biblical "citations" in two 1956 articles in *Revue Biblique* (see note 11).

this always with the stereotyped לֵאמוֹר. Within these few verses, however, a wide variety of citation techniques can be observed. Of the fourteen identifiable divergences from the Masoretic tradition, six can be ascribed with confidence to the editorial activity of the author. The reasons for these adaptations are diverse. Two are simple omissions of the divine name (10.4, 10.7), a practice common in the Qumran materials. One seems designed to conform the text to the author's own literary style (10.3).[24] Especially interesting is the treatment of the important "Star" prophecy of Num 24.17–19. While "Moab" and the elusive "sons of Sheth" remain in *1QM* 11.6–7 as enemies to be crushed by the "Star" who is to arise "out of Jacob" (v. 17c), the parallel references to "Edom" and "Seir" (v. 18) have been removed entirely.[25] Could this reflect the relatively favorable treatment that the Essenes are reported to have received (per Josephus, *Ant.* 15.371–9) at the hands of the Idumean king Herod? The reversal of vv. 18 and 19 in the same passage, by contrast, seems designed to create a more effective rhetorical unit by grouping all the references to the activity of the "Star" in one place, while also making it clear that it is the "Star" and not "Israel" who is viewed as the subject of v. 19.[26] Elsewhere in *1QM*, at least one and possibly three instances can be identified where an initial phrase or particle has been omitted in order to produce a smoother literary product (10.2, 10.6?, 11.6?).[27] Proportionately speaking, the *War Scroll* shows a greater degree of freedom with the biblical text than any document examined thus far.

Damascus Document (CD)

In both the number of its citations and the diversity of its technique, the so-called *Damascus Document* dwarfs all the other Qumran

---

[24] In the latter case, the Masoretic phrase וְאָמַר אֱלֹהִם is replaced by the same stereotypical לֵאמוֹר with which the author introduces all of his own quotations.

[25] Josephus describes Moab as "still today a mighty nation [ὁ μὲν Μωαβίτας μέγιστον ὄντας καὶ νῦν ἔθνος] in *Ant.* 1.206 (Thackeray's translation in the Loeb series). The proper name אֱדוֹם has been replaced by the generic term אוֹיֵב ("enemy") in v. 18a, while the clause that pertains to "Seir" in v. 18b (שֵׂעִיר וְהָיָה יְרֵשָׁה אֹיְבָיו) has been removed from the text.

[26] Verse 17 is identical to the MT, but v. 19 stands ahead of v. 18 in the Qumran version. In the original, the closest grammatical antecedent for the verbs of v. 19 (וְיֵרְדְּ ... וְהַאֲבִיד) is the proper noun יִשְׂרָאֵל in v. 18c.

[27] In 10.2, the word וְהָיָה has been omitted at the beginning of the quotation, presumably to create a smoother transition after the author's own introductory לֵאמוֹר. In both 10.6 and 11.6, an initial ו has dropped out under similar circum-

materials as a witness to ancient Jewish citation practice.[28] The precise relation of this text to the Qumran community is not at issue here – whether it originated in circles associated with Qumran or merely received a sympathetic hearing among its members, its importance as an exemplar of early Jewish citation technique remains unparalleled. Fully thirty-two explicit biblical quotations can be identified in the A text of the *Damascus Document*; the B text repeats two of the same passages while adding six more of its own. Despite their divergent text-histories and content, the two recensions are similar enough in their handling of biblical quotations to allow them to be treated together in the discussion that follows.

Of the thirty-eight citations encountered in the *Damascus Document*, only nine agree verbatim with the wording of the Masoretic text. Five others appear to reproduce a different *Vorlage* without evident adaptation.[29] The remaining twenty-four citations show a total of sixty-one divergences from the Masoretic tradition (nearly two and a half per citation), of which only seven can be traced with reasonable certainty to the use of a different *Vorlage*. Fully thirty-three of these readings (60 percent of the total) can be attributed with reasonable confidence to the hand of the person who penned the citation, if the criteria outlined in chapter 2 are to be trusted.[30]

Two procedures clearly dominate the handling of the biblical text in the *Damascus Document*. In nineteen places an infelicitous word or phrase is replaced by one judged more consistent with the new application; on seven occasions, problematic or irrelevant materials are simply omitted from the biblical record.[31] Less common means of adaptation include adding words to the text (three times) and altering grammatical details of the passage

stances, though a textual basis cannot be ruled out for such a common variant. For 11.6, the ו is present in the parallel citation in *CD* 7.19.

[28] Chaim Rabin identified scores of biblical references in the footnotes to his classic commentary on what was once known as *The Zadokite Documents* (Oxford: Clarendon, 1954). Rabin even goes so far as to characterize the Admonitions section as "a mosaic of quotations ... a clever presentation of *testimonia*, not a history of the sect" (ix).

[29] In 6.8, 7.16, 7.19–21, 14.1, and 16.15.

[30] Ottilie Schwartz (90–135) draws similar conclusions from her careful study of the quotations in columns I–VII and XIX–XX. Some of the lesser deviations she attributes to the vagaries of memory quotation (97), but numerous others can be understood only as adaptations designed to coincide with the author's use of the text (98, 102–3, 119).

[31] *Substitutions*: 4.2, 7.8, 7.11, 7.14. 7.15, 8.14 (*ter*), 9.5, 9.9, 11.18, 16.7, 16.10, 19.8, 20.16, 20.19 (*bis*), 20.21, 20.22. *Omissions*: 4.20, 5.1, 7.11, 7.15, 7.20, 11.21 (*bis*).

(person, number, aspect, etc., also three times) to conform the passage to its new context.[32]

When it comes to explaining what caused these adaptations, the reasons again vary from passage to passage. In nine cases, the purpose is simply to avoid mentioning the divine name or attributing certain activities directly to the deity (7.11–12, 8.14, 9.5, 11.18, 11.20–1, 19.7–9, 20.19 (*bis*), and 20.21). Two other changes appear to reflect the general ideology or practice of the community, the one (8.14) stressing Yahweh's special covenant with the "fathers" of the community, the other reflecting the group's ambivalent attitude toward the Jerusalem Temple (11.20–1).[33] In thirteen instances the adaptation serves to render the wording more suitable to the interpretation/ application put forward in the present context (3.21–4.2 (*bis*), 4.19, 4.20 (*bis*), 7.8, 7.11–12, 7.14–15 (*ter*), 9.9, 20.16, 20.19).[34] In two places, on the other hand, the concern is just the opposite – to clarify the original referent of a passage for the sake of the later reader (8.14, 16.10).[35] Other adaptations appear to have arisen out of linguistic interests, either to create a smoother flow of thought within the new context (1.13–14, 5.13, 11.20–1) or else to conform the text to the idiom of the community or of other biblical passages (16.6–7, 16.10, 20.22).

Other noteworthy aspects of the citation practice of *CD* include two more occurrences of "combined citations"[36] and one of a

---

[32] *Additions*: 3.21, 11.21, 20.19. *Grammatical changes*: 4.19, 4.20, 16.10.

[33] In 8.14, it is "your fathers" (אֲבוֹתֶיךָ), not "you" (אֶתְכֶם), who are portrayed as the objects of Yahweh's covenant love. In 11.20–1, the insertion of the phrase כְּמִנְחַת (and the corresponding removal of the suffix from רְצוֹנוֹ) coincides with the valuation of prayer as a (substitute for?) sacrifice that appears elsewhere in the Qumran texts (*1QS* 10.5–6, 8–9, 14; *1QH passim*).

[34] A few brief examples should suffice to demonstrate the kinds of changes included here. In 3.21–4.2, the addition of an extra ו before the words הַלְוִיִּם and בְּנֵי צָדוֹק coincides with the application of the verse to three different classes of people within the community. In 7.8, the change from לְבִתּוֹ ("his daughter") to לִבְנוֹ ("his son") was necessary to bring the verse into line with the reference to bearing "sons" in 7.7. In 7.14–15, the heavily adapted form of Amos 5.26–7 show the effects of the allegorical interpretation offered in 7.15–8.1. In 20.19, the addition of the phrase אֶל דִּבְרֵיהֶם ("to their words") offers a clear backward glance at the things that the members of the community are portrayed as saying to one another in 20.17–18.

[35] In 8.14, the apparent shift from "their land" (אַרְצָם) to "these nations" (הַגּוֹיִם הָאֵלֶּה, from the next clause of Deut 9.5) brings clarity to what would have been an obscure reference in the new text, as does the use of the word שְׁבוּעָתָהּ ("her oath") in 16.10 in place of the simple suffix of the MT.

[36] In 8.14, where Deut 9.5 and 7.8 are quoted back-to-back under a single introductory formula, and 20.22, where portions of Mal 3.16, 3.18, and Exod 20.6 are combined into a single text.

"conflated citation" (an amalgamation of Exod 20.6 and Deut 7.9 in *CD* 20.21–2). Finally, up to seven instances of "limited selection" help the author either avoid problematic data in the original context or create a smoother rendering in the new one (4.20, 6.8, 7.12, 7.16, 9.9, 11.18, 20.18).[37]

Conclusions

A number of conclusions emerge from this brief survey of the citation techniques of the non-*pesher* materials from Qumran.

(1) Biblical quotations are introduced by a relatively narrow range of formulae in the community documents from Qumran, with most showing variations on the expressions "it is written" (כָּתוּב) or "it says" (אָמַר). The dearth of comments on the subject in the foregoing investigation is fully reflective of this situation.[38]

(2) As might be expected from the diversity of biblical manuscripts found at Qumran, the quotations studied here follow no single strand within the Hebrew textual tradition. While many passages follow the Masoretic text, agreements with the LXX and even the Samaritan Pentateuch are common.[39] In many cases it remains unclear whether non-Masoretic wording should be attributed to authorial adaptation or the use of a different *Vorlage*.[40]

(3) Little can be learned from the citations themselves about whether their authors worked from written texts or quoted from memory. Manuscript discoveries have shown that written anthologies of biblical texts were in use at Qumran,[41] but memory quotation must also have played a role in such a "Bible-centered" community as Qumran.

(4) The degree of "freedom" with which the biblical text is quoted

---

[37] Brief phrases are selected out of a passage that could not be quoted in its entirety in 4.20, 6.8, 9.9, and 11.18; an initial or final phrase that would have conflicted with the present application is dropped in 7.12 and 7.16; duplication of thought is avoided by the omission of Mal 3.16a in 20.18.

[38] The various patterns that appear in the Qumran citation formula are examined by Fred L. Horton, Jr., "Formulas of Introduction in the Qumran Literature," *RevQ* 7 (1971), 505–14. See also the article by J. A. Fitzmyer cited in note 11.

[39] In all, 21 of the 71 quotations examined here agree fully with the Masoretic tradition (30 percent). Of 110 divergences from the MT, 24 could be traced to the use of a different text (22 percent). Emanuel Tov finds a similar diversity in the *Temple Scroll*: see "The '*Temple Scroll*' and Old Testament Textual Criticism," *Eretz Israel* 16 (1982), 100–11 (Eng. summary, 255*).

[40] Of 110 divergences from the Masoretic tradition in the texts under study, the origins of 44 were left undetermined.

[41] The evidence is discussed in chap. 3.

seems unrelated to either the type of literature in which the citation occurs or the frequency of explicit citations within a given document. The close adherence to the biblical wording in the eschatological *11QMelchizedek* must be considered alongside the looser approach found in the similarly oriented *4QFlorilegium* and especially the *War Scroll*. The faithful renditions in the "community-centered" *Manual of Discipline* cannot be examined apart from the adapted citations in the halakhic section of the *Damascus Document*. Within individual documents, verses given a prophetic turn are quoted both literally and freely in *4QFlorilegium*, while adapted citations can be found in both the hortatory and legal sections of the *Damascus Document*. A unified approach is evident only in those texts where lengthy excerpts from Scripture form the backbone of the entire composition, as in the *pesharim* and *4QTestimonia*. Here verbatim citation appears to be the norm.[42]

(5) Careful study reveals no monolithic attitude toward the wording of the biblical text at Qumran. Treatments range from a close adherence to the precise wording of the text in *4QTestimonia*, *11QMelchizedek*, the *Manual of Discipline*, and the *pesharim*, to a less constrained mode of citation in *4QFlorilegium* and the *War Scroll*, to the free adaptation witnessed on numerous occasions in the *Damascus Document*.[43] In those documents where adapted citations appear, a variety of techniques help to conform the biblical text to its new context. Replacing one word or phrase with another or simply omitting those portions deemed problematic are by far the most common practices. Careful selection of the beginning- and ending-points of a citation is another technique employed for the same end. Adding explanatory words to a text and altering gram-

[42] See note 13. In view of this evidence, the continued use of the term *midrash pesher* to describe the way New Testament authors adapt the wording of their *Vorlagen* (so Stendahl, Ellis *et al.*) is clearly without warrant. Used in this way, the term is positively misleading – the phenomenon of interpretive adaptation of the biblical text is far broader than the Qumran materials, as the present study shows. Properly speaking, the term *pesher* refers to a unique literary genre found only at Qumran (cf. Brooke, Horgan), though its more generalized use to describe any "contemporizing" mode of biblical interpretation is probably here to stay.

[43] Adapted wording was founded in one of two citations in *1QS*, two of five in *4QFlor*, four of four in *1QM*, and twenty-two of thirty-eight (58 percent) in *CD*. Of the eighty-seven deviations from the MT that can be identified in these four documents, forty-two (48 percent) could be traced with reasonable confidence (A or B rating) to the editorial activity of the author. For specific documents, the rates range from 20 percent for *4QFlor* (two of ten deviations) to 43 percent for *1QM* (six to fourteen), 50 percent for *1QS* (one of two), and 54 percent for *CD* (thirty-three of sixty-one).

matical forms to suit the new context occur less often. Several instances of "combined citations" and one "conflated citation" were also noted.

(6) Reasons for adapting the wording of the text vary from passage to passage. The most common concern seems to be to insure conformity between the language of the biblical text and the interpretation/application given to it in its new literary context. In these cases, the biblical wording has been adapted to reflect the sense in which the author wishes his readers to understand the verse in question, i.e. the interpretation is embedded in the very wording of the quotation. In other places, the community's broader ideology and practice has led to a molding of the biblical text, as in the various attempts to avoid mentioning the divine name or ascribing certain activities to the deity. Adjustments intended to fit the citation to the grammar of its new context or to create a smoother literary product are also encountered. Other reasons for altering the wording of a text include clarifying the original referent of a term rendered vague by its transfer to a new context; creating a more idiomatic rendering of a particular biblical verse; and improving the rhetorical impact of a given passage.

Once again the resemblance to the citation technique of the apostle Paul is too close to be overlooked. At the same time, the results are by no means uniform. In documents such as *4QTestimonia*, *11QMelchizedek*, and *1QS*, verbatim citation appears to be the norm. In other texts – *4QFlorilegium*, *1QM*, and especially *CD* – a wide range of adaptations can be found. Clearly it is this latter group of texts that stands closest to the way citations are handled in the Pauline epistles. Whether the different approaches encountered in the Qumran corpus are purely coincidental, or whether they reflect the divergent attitudes of different authors or communities, can no longer be determined. In either case, the results of the present study make it difficult to argue that the relatively "free" approach of *4QFlorilegium*, *1QM*, and *CD* is in any way typical of the Qumran community *per se*. The same can be said of attempts to trace the similar attitudes of Qumran and the New Testament to their common eschatological consciousness or even to the shared Jewish backgrounds of the two communities. Taken together with the conclusions of the previous chapter, the Qumran materials offer strong evidence that the practices observed thus far are part of a broader cultural phenomenon that understood and made allowance for such "interpretive renderings" of well-known and/or authoritative texts.

4. Apocrypha and pseudepigrapha

Whereas the materials from Qumran reflect the views and practices of a relatively self-contained segment of Palestinian Judaism, the documents included in the so-called "apocrypha" and "pseudepigrapha" reveal the truly diverse character of Judaism as it appeared from roughly 300 B.C.E. to 100 C.E. Even after their differing dates of composition have been taken into account, many of the documents to be examined here agree on little more than the basic tenets of Jewish monotheism. Apologies and romances, paeans and propaganda, historical narratives and philosophical treatises all find their place in the literary output of post-biblical Judaism. Though the precise provenance of many of these texts remains obscure, both Palestine and the Diaspora (especially Alexandria in Egypt) appear to be well-represented. The sheer breadth of the materials included in the so-called "apocrypha" and "pseudepigrapha" makes these documents a valuable counterpoint to the more homogeneous outlook of the Qumran community examined above.

When it comes to analyzing the way biblical quotations are handled in these documents, however, a problem arises. While many of them remain available in their original languages (most often Greek), many others (perhaps the majority) have been preserved only in translation (Greek, Latin, Syriac, Ethiopic, Slavonic, etc.). In these cases it becomes difficult to carry on the sort of close textual analysis that is required for the present study. One way around this obstacle would be to restrict the study to documents that can be studied in their original languages. But with biblical quotations so scarce in most of the literature (see below), such an approach would yield only a very limited amount of data from which to draw conclusions.[44] An alternative would be to subject the translated materials to a somewhat lesser degree of scrutiny, laying aside the goal of rendering a holistic portrait of an author's citation technique in favor of pointing out particularly egregious examples of the kinds of adaptations found already in other texts. Though the results in such cases could hardly be considered conclusive, the illustrative value of the materials thus isolated would appear to be sufficient to justify the effort. This at any rate is the approach that will be followed here.

---

[44] The greatest number of explicit quotations appear in the *Biblical Antiquities* of Pseudo-Philo (available only in Latin), *4 Maccabees* (present in its original Greek) and the book of *Jubilees* (extant in full in Ethiopic and partially in Latin, with Greek, Syriac, and Hebrew fragments).

In addition to the standard list of "apocryphal" books, all of the texts in James H. Charlesworth's *Old Testament Pseudepigrapha* were surveyed for possible relevance to the present study. To qualify for inclusion, a document had to contain at least one explicit quotation and date from no later than the first century C.E. It is rather remarkable how few works met even these modest requirements.[45] To aid in analysis, materials have been grouped according to their likely period of origin rather than by such artificial categories as "apocrypha" or "pseudepigrapha."[46] Documents to be examined in the present study include (asterisks indicate works available only or primarily in translation):

Pre-Hasmonean	Hasmonean	Roman
*1 Esdras**	*Jubilees**	*3 Maccabees*
*Tobit**	*1 Maccabees**	*4 Maccabees*
*Judith**	*2 Maccabees*	*Sibylline Oracles 1*
Sirach	*Aristeas*	*Biblical Antiquities**
*Baruch**		*Testament of Abraham*
		Testament of Solomon
		4 Ezra

Though this might appear to be a rather extensive list of sources for such a limited study, many of the documents contain only one or two explicit quotations. In only a few cases is the sample of quotations large enough to justify broad comments about the "citation technique" of this or that author or document. Properly speaking, of course, only materials from the Roman period can be adduced as witnesses to the way Jewish authors handled biblical quotations in the first century C.E. Earlier materials have been included on the assumption that there may have been a measure of continuity between the practices of earlier periods and those that prevailed in Paul's own day.

---

[45] Devorah Dimant ("Use and Interpretation of Mikra in the Apocrypha and Pseudepigrapha," in Mulder (ed.), *Mikra*, 400) likewise notes the rarity of explicit quotations in the materials under investigation. Other broad treatments of the use of Scripture in the apocryphal literature include James K. Zink, "The Use of the Old Testament in the Apocrypha," (Ph.D. diss., Duke University, 1963) and the article by Andrew Chester in Carson and Williamson (eds.), *It is Written*, 150–64.

[46] The dates advocated in the various articles in Charlesworth's *OT Pseudepigrapha* have been followed in the texts that appear in that collection.

Pre-Hasmonean period

One fact that stands out in any study of Jewish literature from the pre-Hasmonean era is the scarcity of explicit quotations in the texts of that period. While echoes of biblical language abound, not one of the texts that has survived contains more than one or two explicit quotations from Scripture. No doubt the continued flux of the textual tradition and the fluid state of the "canon" (to use an anachronistic term) of Scripture throughout this period had much to do with this shortage of appeals to the authoritative biblical text.[47] Whatever the reasons, the scanty nature of the evidence makes it difficult to generalize about the way any particular author handled the wording of his biblical quotations. A few summary comments will suffice to detail what little can be learned about each author's citation technique.

(1) In *1 Esdras* 1.58 (55), a verse that was framed as an indirect statement in 2 Chr 36.21 (a midrashic conflation of Jer 25.12 and Lev 26.34) appears as a direct quotation and is attributed in its entirety to the prophet Jeremiah (εἰς ἀναπλήρωσιν τοῦ ῥήματος τοῦ κυρίου ἐν στόματι Ἰερεμιου, Ἕως τοῦ εὐδοκῆσαι κτλ.). But whereas in 2 Chr the language of the Leviticus and Jeremiah passages has been adapted to reflect the shift from future prediction to realized event, the original futuristic orientation has been restored (or retained) in the parallel passage in *1 Esdras*. The origins of this conflation and adaptation remain obscure, though the presence of different translation equivalents for certain words in the Greek versions of both passages seems to point to a common Hebrew source.[48] Whatever its background, the verse offers early testimony to the technique of conflating texts from various sources to form a single quotation, in addition to adapting the biblical wording to reflect a later interpretation.

(2) A similar technique can be seen in the two citations that appear in the book of *Baruch*.[49] Twice in the penitential prayer that

---

[47] On the continued development of the biblical text and traditions during this period, see Fishbane, *Interpretation*.

[48] Michael Fishbane (*Interpretation*, 480–1) traces the combination to the Chronicler himself, without apparently considering the possibility that both passages might go back to a common source. The parallel with *1 Esdras* is never even mentioned in Fishbane's discussion.

[49] A third verse that might be viewed as a quotation is *Bar* 2.2, where the words κατὰ τὰ γεγραμμένα ἐν τῷ νόμῳ Μωυσῆ give the appearance of introducing a specific quotation. In the context, however, the same words could be read equally well as a generalized allusion (cf. *2 Macc* 1.29, 10.26), and the loose biblical moorings of the

occupies *Bar* 1.15–3.8, quotations from Scripture are introduced with the help of explicit citation formulae ("just as you spoke by the hand of your servants the prophets, saying ..." (2.20); "just as you spoke by the hand of your servant Moses on the day when you commanded him to write your law before the sons of Israel, saying ..." (2.28)). What follows in both cases is a polyglot of verses from different sources that have been condensed, adapted, and otherwise conflated to form a single "quotation" that is then attributed in its entirety to "your servants the prophets" (2.21–3) and "Moses your servant" (in a specific setting no less!) (2.29–35).[50] In both cases the language of the original verses has been so thoroughly assimilated to the later author's literary agenda that even identifying the sources behind the quotation proves difficult.[51] Here again the technique of conflating and adapting a series of verses to suit a later author's interpretive agenda finds a ready witness.

(3) In the only explicit quotation in the book of *Sirach* (46.19b), a statement offered by Samuel in 1 Sam 12.3 is condensed and paraphrased to fit the poetic structure of the book in which it now appears. Though the sense of the verse is unaffected by the change, its reformulation in *Sirach* shows just how thoroughly a biblical passage could be molded to fit the literary style of a later author's composition.

(4) The remaining quotations from the pre-Hasmonean period stand closer to a verbatim citation technique. In *Judith* 9.2 and *Susanna* 53, quotations from Gen 34.7c and Exod 23.7 respectively follow the wording of the Septuagint precisely.[52] Another apparent

---

words that follow (cf. Deut 28.58, Isa 9.20, Jer 19.9) show that this is exactly what was intended. The introductory formulae in 2.20 and 2.28 are more explicit, and both conclude with the stereotyped λέγων (= לֵאמֹר).

[50] Omissions of irrelevant material, condensing summaries, and additions designed to link the various selections into a coherent whole are the most visible forms of adaptation.

[51] Zink (109–13) finds in *Bar* 2.21–3 a combination of Jer 27.11–14 and 7.34, while in 2.29–35 he discovers the influence of Lev 26.12, 1 Kgs 8.47, Jer 16.15b, Gen 50.24b, and Jer 31.31, 33. While the identification of Jer 27.11–14 in the first passage appears secure, several of the other verses adduced by Zink are open to question. In place of Jer 7.34 for the first passage one could point to Jer 33.10–11 and 34.22b, while the narrative of Deut 27.2–3, 8, would seem to imply that it was the "curses" of Deut 28.58–64 that the author had in mind when he referred to "the day when you commanded him to write your law before the sons of Israel." Other verses whose influence might be detected in the second passage include Jer 32.37–41, 29.6, and Deut 30.20.

[52] The *Susanna* passage also agrees with the MT, but the quotation in *Judith* diverges somewhat (οὐχ οὕτως ἔσται vs. כֵּן לֹא יֵעָשֶׂה). If the consensus is correct in seeing a Hebrew original behind the present Greek text of *Judith* (see e.g. Robert

quotation appears in *Sus* 5 (περὶ ὧν ἐλάλησεν ὁ δεσπότης ὅτι . . .), but its source remains unknown.[53] The two quotations in *Tobit* (2.6 and 8.6) diverge somewhat from the Septuagint, but for the most part represent faithful renderings of the same Hebrew text found in the later Masoretic tradition.[54] Only the shift from first-person speech to the "divine Passive" in *Tob* 2.6 would appear to represent an authorial adaptation.[55]

In sum, the few biblical quotations that can be identified in pre-Hasmonean Jewish literature appear to follow one of two patterns. Either a specific biblical text is quoted verbatim (or slightly adapted), or else a number of texts from different sources are adapted and conflated together to coincide with the literary aims of the later author.

Hasmonean period

The Maccabean revolt inspired a wealth of Jewish literary activity, from the canonical book of Daniel to the "sectarian" literature of Qumran. Fewer documents have been preserved from later in the Hasmonean period, and those that do exist are almost devoid of quotations.[56] Since the Qumran literature has already been dis-

Doran, "Narrative Literature," in Kraft and Nickelsburg (eds.), *Early Judaism*, 302–3), one must assume either that the quotation was assimilated to the LXX in the process of translation or else that the author had access to a Hebrew text of Genesis that resembled the *Vorlage* of the LXX. Given the obscurity of the quotation, however, one could question the adequacy of both explanations.

[53] Cf. the similarly unknown (non-biblical?) quotations in 1 Cor 2.9, 9.10, Eph 5.14, and 2 Tim 2.19. The use of ὁ δεσπότης here is unusual: everywhere else in the book Yahweh is identified as ὁ κύριος, including the introduction to the quotation in v. 53. Could this be a shorthand reference to some non-biblical source, like the designation of Homer as ὁ ποιητής in Greek literature? The quotation itself ("Lawlessness came out of Babylon, from elder judges who were supposed to be governing the people") has no identifiable "religious" content, and seems to reflect an exilic point of view. In any event, the quotation is useless for the present study so long as its source remains unknown.

[54] The only sign of a different text appears in 8.6 (= Gen 2.18), where the translation presupposes a first-person plural verb as in the LXX.

[55] Without the shift, it might have appeared that Tobit himself was the speaker in the quotation. The introduction reads, "And I remembered the prophecy of Amos, as he said, 'I will turn . . .'" (AB version; similar in S). Another explanation would see the author "removing the activity of causing woe from God and giving it a more impersonal connection" (Zink 44; so also Chester, 154). While this is always a possibility in cases such as this, the author does not hesitate to attribute ill circumstances to Yahweh in 3.3–6, 13.5, and 14.4.

[56] The sole apparent exception is the single quotation in the *Letter of Aristeas* discussed below.

cussed above, the present section will focus almost exclusively on documents from the early Maccabean period.

The book of *Jubilees* is extant in its entirety only in an Ethiopic version, so that any comments concerning the way it handles biblical quotations will necessarily remain quite general.[57] The fact that the book contains several explicit quotations, however, makes the matter worthy of pursuit. One of the more unusual aspects of the citation technique of *Jubilees* is the way certain quotations are said to come from the "heavenly tablets" (3.10, 4.5, 4.32, 30.9).[58] The fact that these "quotations" are introduced by the same sorts of formulaic expressions used elsewhere with biblical materials ("therefore it is written/ordained in the heavenly tablets") shows that the author expected his readers to regard these passages as extracts from a specific written document. Since it seems unlikely that such a document ever existed outside the literary world of *Jubilees* and related compositions, however, it would be fruitless to talk about the way the author handled the wording of his *Vorlage* in these instances. Two other citations whose origins remain unknown (5.17 and 5.18) are introduced by expressions similar to those used for quotations from the "heavenly tablets" ("it has been written and ordained"), so that these, too, are probably best regarded as free formulations created by the author.[59] In several other places, excerpts from the biblical narrative are placed in the mouths of

[57] The problem is not as great as it might seem. After a careful and thorough examination of the various manuscripts and textual traditions of *Jubilees*, James VanderKam concludes, "The text of *Jub.* which the Ethiopic manuscripts provide is very accurate and reliable. It reproduces the Hebrew text (*via* a Greek intermediate stage) literally and precisely in nearly all cases [where Hebrew fragments exist for comparison]." See *Textual and Historical Studies in the Book of Jubilees*, HSM 14 (Missoula, MT: Scholars, 1977), 94.

[58] The "heavenly tablets" are not themselves unique to *Jubilees* – they appear also in *1 Enoch* 81.1–2, 93.2, 103.2, 106.19, *TLevi* 5.4, *TAsher* 2.10, 7.5 (list by Devorah Dimant, "Use," 398 n. 78). But *Jubilees* is the only book that actually claims to quote from what is written in those tablets. The "heavenly tablets" are also adduced in conjunction with indirect quotations in 3.31, 6.17, 16.29, 18.19, 28.6, and 33.10. According to John Endres (*Biblical Interpretation in the Book of Jubilees* (Washington, DC: Catholic Biblical Association, 1977), 221), quotations from the "heavenly tablets" are introduced for the most part when the author "seemed vexed by the absence of biblical warrants for some *Halakot* which appeared in the [biblical] story." Similar "pseudo-citations" can be seen at several points in the biblical record itself (examples in Fishbane, *Interpretation*, 125, 133–4, 533–4). Additional references to these "tablets" can be found in *Jub* 1.29, 5.13, 6.29, 6.31, 6.35, 15.25, 16.3, 16.9, 23.32, 24.33, 30.20, 31.32, 32.15, and 50.13 (list from R. H. Charles, *The Book of Jubilees* (London: Adam and Charles Black, 1902), 24–5).

[59] The latter part of the first quotation bears a loose resemblance to Jer 36.3, while the second passage shows no clear biblical foundation.

characters in the story (1.7, 2.25, 3.4, 3.6, 3.17–19, 3.24–5, 4.7, 7.10, 7.11–12, etc.), but the reader is given no indication that these instances represent quotations from the biblical record and not just the free literary creations of the author.

This leaves only three instances in *Jubilees* (4.30, 30.12, 33.12) where the wording of an explicit biblical quotation can be checked against its presumed *Vorlage*. Though a handful of variations from the Masoretic tradition can be identified in these three passages, in only one case does it appear that the author has adapted the text to suit his own use of the verse.[60] Apparently the author of *Jubilees* felt constrained to adhere closely to the biblical wording when adducing a specific verse as "Scripture," though he shows no such hesitation in situations where biblical language is placed on the lips of his characters without attribution.[61] Where a major reinterpretation or reapplication is desired, the author commonly resorts to the literary device of quoting from the "heavenly tablets" rather than introducing major changes into the wording of the text itself. In this way he is able to preserve both the "historicity" of his story-line (by avoiding anachronistic quotations from the prophetic or historical books) and the relative sanctity of the biblical text.

The sole explicit quotation in *1 Maccabees* reveals what might be

---

[60] In 4.30 (= Gen 2.17), the shift to second-person plural verbs in the Hebrew fragment *11QJub2* (see VanderKam, *Studies*, 31–5) agrees with the majority LXX reading, while the omission of the redundant word מוֹת is paralleled in the Ethiopic manuscripts of *Jubilees* and the Ethiopic version of Genesis. The quotation in 33.12 appears to follow the MT of Deut 27.20. The sole adaptation is found in 30.12 (quoting Gen 34.14), where the word "daughter" replaces the original "sister." Though he identifies the quotation as the words of "the sons of Jacob" to the Shechemites, the author renders the verse, "We will not give our daughter [MT "sister," referring to Dinah] to a man who is uncircumcised because that is a reproach to us." The author of *Jubilees* is of course quite aware that Dinah was Jacob's daughter and not his granddaughter, as can be seen from 30.3–4, where she is described as the "sister" of Jacob's sons. The change is thoroughly consistent, however, with the moralizing application that follows: "Let nothing like this be done henceforth to defile a *daughter* of Israel ... " (v.5); "if there is any man in Israel who wishes to give his *daughter* or his sister to any man who is from the seed of the gentiles ..." (v.7); "the man who caused defilement of his *daughter* ..." (v.10; cf. also vv. 11, 14). Though it is always possible that the change could have entered the text of *Jubilees* in the course of transmission, the emphatic stance of the surrounding verses makes it highly likely that the reading is original (so also Endres, *Interpretation*, 125 n. 44). In the same verse, the shift from "we will not be able to do this thing, to give ..." to the simpler "we will not be able to give ..." is clearly a more idiomatic rendering, but whether it entered the tradition at the level of the original text or in the Ethiopic translation is impossible to judge at this point.

[61] See the examples listed above in the text. In most such cases the wording stands close to the MT, but with minor variations designed to conform the text to its new setting.

called a more "liberal" attitude toward the biblical text.[62] In 7.17, a reference to the high priest Alcimus' execution of sixty men from the "Hasidim" reminds the author of Ps 79.2–3, which speaks of "the flesh of your *hasidîm*" being left as carrion for wild scavengers. Instead of reproducing the full biblical wording, however, the author abridges and adapts the text to form a new three-membered "quotation" that emphasizes precisely those aspects of the passage that accord with the situation to which the verse is applied.[63] Omissions, additions, and changes in word order all have a role to play in the formation of this reconstructed text.[64] As Devorah Dimant remarks on this passage, "This shows that a precise reproduction of the text cited was not imperative; it was enough to quote the essentials, and sometimes it was deemed necessary to alter some details in accordance with the context."[65] The final form of the text reflects a high degree of literary artistry.

The citation technique of *2 Maccabees* follows no consistent pattern. On the one hand, the author reproduces the wording of Deut 32.36 verbatim (LXX = MT) in a single brief quotation in 7.6. In 2.11, on the other hand, a verse attributed to Moses (καὶ εἶπεν Μωυσῆς) has been so thoroughly reworked that even its precise source remains open to question.[66] A similar situation prevails in

---

[62] Biblical passages are echoed in *1 Macc* 4.24 (= Ps 135 *passim*) and 9.21 (cf. 2 Sam 1.19, 25, 27), but in neither place is there an explicit quotation.

[63] Retroverted from Greek to Hebrew, the quotation reads as follows:

בְּשַׂר חֲסִידֶיךָ וּדְמָם

שָׁפְכוּ סְבִיבוֹת יְרוּשָׁלָם

וְאֵין לָהֶם קוֹבֵר

[64] The changes include omitting the words לְחַיְתוֹ־אָרֶץ at the end of v. 2, so that בְּשַׂר חֲסִידֶיךָ becomes the object of שָׁפְכוּ in v.3 rather than נָתְנוּ in v. 2a; advancing דְּמָם and prefixing a ו to create a compound object בְּשַׂר ... וּדְמָם; omitting the word כַּמַּיִם in v.3a, either for rhetorical condensation or because it seemed inappropriate to the new compound object *"flesh and blood"*; and adding לָהֶם to the last line to create a three-word parallel to the first two cola. None of these changes finds any support in either the Hebrew or Greek textual traditions.

[65] "Use," 391.

[66] The wording of the text, διὰ τὸ μὴ βεβρῶσαι τὸ περὶ τῆς ἁμαρτίας ἀνηλώθη, is close to such LXX passages as Exod 29.34, Lev 6.23 (16), and Lev 6.30 (23), but notable differences remain in every case. The parallel is no better in Lev 10.16–20, the passage that Zink (145–6) sees as the background for the quotation. The phrase τὸ περὶ τῆς ἁμαρτίας (Heb. הַחַטָּאת) appears often in the Greek Pentateuch (25x in Leviticus, plus Num 6.16 and 29.11), but the verb ἀναλίσκειν appears only in Gen 41.30 and Num 14.33, neither of which is relevant here. The presence of the same form in *2 Macc* 1.31 suggests that the present "quotation" may have been translated directly from the Hebrew of Jason's original work by the epitomizer of *2 Maccabees*. If this is so, then Lev 6.30 (23), where the sin-offering forms the focus of the discourse, is the most likely source. At the end of this verse appear the following words: לֹא תֵאָכֵל בָּאֵשׁ תִּשָּׂרֵף. Only minor modifications would be needed to produce from this text a suitable Hebrew *Vorlage* for the Greek quotation in *2 Macc*

two other passages where it is not entirely clear whether a quotation or an allusion was intended (1.29 and 10.26).[67] Perhaps the fact that it was prepared as an epitome of a much longer work (see 2.19–31) might explain the unevenness of the citation technique in the final composition.

The only other explicit quotation from the Hasmonean period comes from a very different venue, Alexandria in Egypt. In the *Letter of Aristeas* 155, there appears under an obvious introductory formula (διὰ τῆς γραφῆς ὁ λέγων οὕτως) a conflation of texts from Deut 7.18 and 10.21. Both verses appear to follow the Septuagint version, but the two texts have been so thoroughly adapted and commingled that neither can be said to occupy the dominant position.[68] In this respect the resultant "quotation" is similar to those encountered already in the books of *Baruch* and *2 Maccabees*, though neither of these employs the sort of key-word linkage that appears in *Aristeas*.[69] The adaptations encountered in *Aristeas* are

2.11: adding an explanatory "because" at the beginning of the verse; converting the verbs from Imperfects to an Infinitive and a Perfect, respectively; inserting הִתְהַלֵּךְ from earlier in the verse to make the subject clear in its new context; and omitting the word בָּאֵשׁ as redundant. The effect is to convert the verse from prescription to description, thus improving the parallel with the description of Solomon's activities that follows in v. 12. The reconstruction suggested here is by no means certain, but it does at least supply a workable explanation of how the author may have derived the present "citation" from his biblical text.

[67] In 1.29, the words "Plant your people in your holy place" are followed by the phrase καθὼς εἶπεν Μωυσῆς, normally a sure sign of a quotation. But since the words stand alongside several other petitions in a prayer that fills vv. 24–9, it is possible to view the words in question as a generalized allusion rather than a specific quotation (i.e. "just as Moses said you would"). The fact that no clear biblical antecedent can be found for the words in question reinforces the latter interpretation. Zink (145) points to Exod 15.17, which may well be the passage the author had in mind, but the actual verbal similarity is limited to a single word καταφύτευσον. Cf. also 2 Kgdms 7.10, Amos 9.15, Jer 24.6, Ezek 17.22–3. The situation is similar in 10.26. There several words from Exod 23.22, adapted to fit the grammar of the new context, are incorporated into a report of a prayer cast in indirect speech, the whole unit concluding with the phrase καθὼς ὁ νόμος διασαφεῖ. Despite the similarity to a standard citation formula, the fact that the transition from narrative to quotation remains entirely unmarked makes it difficult to regard the present verse as a true citation.

[68] The adaptations can best be seen by setting the relevant parts of each verse alongside the version found in *Aristeas* (underlines show direct appropriations; adaptations in italics):

Deut 7.18: μνεία μνησθήσῃ ὅσα *ἐποίησεν* κύριος ὁ θεός σου τῷ Φαραῳ ...
Deut 10.21: οὗτος καύχημά σου καὶ οὗτος θεός σου, *ὅστις ἐποίησεν ἐν σοὶ τὰ μεγάλα καὶ τὰ ἔνδοξα ταῦτα* ...
Arist 155: μνείᾳ μνησθήσῃ κυρίου τοῦ *ποιήσαντος* ἐν σοὶ τὰ μεγάλα καὶ θαυμαστά.

[69] The verbal overlap between the two verses reaches farther than the obvious duplication of ἐποίησεν (converted to a participle in *Aristeas*). Deut 7.19 goes on to

clearly intentional: all references to the Exodus event have been thoroughly excised, producing a generalized statement that is then applied to the human body (as a "great and glorious" work of Yahweh) in the succeeding verses. Whether the author would have treated other biblical texts with a similarly free hand is impossible to judge from this single instance.[70]

All in all, the picture that emerges from this period is little different from the previous era. Relatively few direct appeals to Scripture can be found in any of the literature, and those that do appear follow no consistent pattern. Verbatim citations appear side-by-side with highly adapted formulations, while conflating verses from different sources to form a single "quotation" remains a common practice. In both adapted and conflated texts, the changes that can be identified are by no means random, but rather provide immediate support for the author's use of a particular passage.

Roman period

Though Roman rule overtook the various segments of the Jewish Diaspora at different times, it is convenient to use Pompey's conquest of Jerusalem in 63 B.C.E. as the starting point for the "Roman Period" in the study of early Judaism. The great majority of extant Jewish works normally classed as "pseudepigrapha" date from this period. While the leveling of Jerusalem in 70 C.E. marks a turning

---

speak of τοὺς πειρασμοὺς τοὺς μεγάλους, <u>οὓς εἴδοσαν οἱ ὀφθαλμοί σου</u>, τὰ σημεῖα καὶ τὰ τέρατα τὰ <u>μεγάλα</u> ἐκεῖνα, while Deut 10.21 continues with <u>ἃ εἴδοσαν οἱ ὀφθαλμοί σου</u>.

[70] A slightly earlier Alexandrian author whose citation technique might be compared with that of the *Letter of Aristeas* is Aristobulus, whose writings were not included in this part of the study because they do not technically qualify as "pseudepigrapha," despite their inclusion in Charlesworth's *OT Pseudepigrapha*. Of the five biblical quotations that appear in the extant fragments of Aristobulus' writings (2.8a, 2.8b, 2.8c, 2.13, 4.3), all follow the LXX version with only minor differences. In two cases, initial particles are omitted (2.8a, 2.8b; cf. Paul), while in four other places redundant or otherwise unnecessary language is simply left to the side (σφόδρα in 2.8c and οὕτως in 4.3, plus the long clause ἔν τε τοῖς ἵπποις καὶ ἐν τοῖς ὑποζυγίοις καὶ ταῖς καμήλοις καὶ βουσὶν καὶ προβάτοις in 2.8c (= Exod 9.3) and the various divine pronouncements in 4.3 (= Gen 1 *passim*)). In addition, a summarizing addition (καὶ ἐν πᾶσι) replaces the lengthy phrase omitted in 2.8c, and a grammatical adaptation (a first-person Indicative replacing a participle) is introduced in 2.8a to conform the excerpt to its new context. In only one instance (2.3) is the wording of the LXX reproduced verbatim. None of the changes has any real effect on the meaning of the verse quoted, but taken together they show a marked tendency toward rhetorical stylization of the biblical text. A similar concern is apparent in the citation technique of *3 Maccabees* (see below). On the broader interpretational agenda of Aristobulus and *Aristeas*, see Dawson, 73–88.

point for Palestinian Judaism, the literature of the Diaspora seems to have been little affected by this event. Since most of the texts to be considered here stem from Diaspora sources, no attempt has been made to distinguish between pre- and post-70 citation practices. All of the materials discussed below should be regarded as primary witnesses for the way Jewish authors handled biblical quotations in the time of Paul.

Direct appeals to specific biblical texts are more abundant in this period, though the proportions vary widely from author to author. In several texts, the earlier reticence toward explicit citations continues in force. Solitary verbatim citations can be seen in *Testament of Solomon* 23.4 (Ps 117.22) and *4 Ezra* 7.59 (129) (Deut 30.19), both from near the end of the period under examination.[71] Both of the quotations in the B recension of the *Testament of Abraham* (2.8 and 2.9) diverge from the majority reading of the LXX for Gen 12.1 and 17.5 respectively, but the differences have no effect on the meaning of either verse. Minority witnesses supply a textual basis for all but a small part of the evidence.[72] In *3 Maccabees*, the lone direct citation (6.15) shows several minor deviations from the LXX of Lev 26.44, none of which appears to bring the wording any closer to the Masoretic or any other Hebrew text.[73] All of the variations are stylistic in nature, which accords well with the high degree of rhetorical stylization that characterizes *3 Maccabees* as a whole.[74]

[71] The addition of the word *tibi* in the Latin text of *4 Ezra* coincides with the individualistic emphasis of the broader context (i.e. "choose *for yourself* ..."; note also the omission of "you and your seed" at the end of the verse), but a clarification in the course of translation is equally possible. The quotation in *TSol* appears only four verses after an explicit (redactional) reference to the coming of Jesus, while the same verse was in common use in early Christian proclamation (cf. Mark 12.10/Matt 21.42/Luke 20.17, Acts 4.11, 1 Pet 2.7). Since this is the only explicit citation in the entire text, a Christian origin (third century C.E.) seems likely.

[72] Only the double Imperative at the beginning of 2.8 (ἀνάστηθι καὶ πορεύου) and the substitution of ἐκ τοῦ οἴκου (from later in the verse) for ἐκ τῆς γῆς are without parallel in the manuscript tradition, and the former could well reflect a Hebrew tradition that contained the word קֻם at the beginning of the verse.

[73] The divergences include omitting initial καί, dropping the unnecessary ὡς after οὐδ᾽, shifting the participle ὄντων to a place after the second αὐτῶν (and dropping the now redundant first αὐτῶν), and omitting the duplicative οὐχ. Only the omission of ὡς and the first αὐτῶν find any support in the LXX manuscript tradition, and the evidence for these is weak (the minuscules 761 and 318 for the former, the d and t families and the minuscules 343 and 392 for the latter). While a textual basis cannot be ruled out for any of the changes, rhetorical stylization seems a more likely explanation in a text like *3 Maccabees*.

[74] See the comments by Hugh Anderson in Charlesworth (ed.), *OT Pseudepigrapha*, 2:510, and Moses Hadas, *The Third and Fourth Books of Maccabees* (New York: Harper and Bros., 1953), 22.

An even more stylized quotation appears in *Sibylline Oracles* 1.57–8, where the wording of Gen 1.28 and 3.19 (a combined citation) has been adapted to fit the epic hexameters in which the entire work is composed. In the process, a subtle shift in meaning occurs: here the command to "be fruitful and multiply" comes *after* the "Fall," while the command to work the earth is likewise cast in a more favorable light by the addition of the word ἐντέχνως and the omission of all references to the "curse" that affects the ground.[75] In this case a clearly "stylistic" adaptation cloaks a deeper reinterpretation of the entire creation account.

The bulk of the citations in *4 Maccabees* appear in the closing chapter, as part of the mother's *post hoc* address to her seven martyred sons.[76] Three of the eight quotations in the treatise (2.19, 17.19, 18.15) follow the wording of the LXX precisely, while four of the remaining five verses show contextual or stylistic adaptations of some sort.[77] Minor changes include advancing the position of the phrase διὰ πυρός in 18.14 (note that the mother and at least two of her sons died by fire, in 12.19, 15.15, and 17.1); omitting the words οὐ μὴ κατακαυθῇς from the same verse (redundant with the clause that follows); and adding the words τὰ ξήρα (from the previous verse) to the quotation of Ezek 37.3 in 18.17 (for emphasis). More significant adaptations appear in 18.16, where the substitution of the words ποιοῦσιν αὐτοῦ τὸ θέλημα for the ἀντεχομένοις αὐτῆς of Prov 3.18 shifts the focus from the importance of wisdom to the need for faithfulness to Yahweh, and in 18.19, where grammatical changes conform the wording of Deut 30.20 to the plural address of the present passage.[78] The final quotation (18.19) also

---

[75] The wording of the quotation as it appears in *Sib Or* is as follows:
αὔξετε, πληθύνεσθε καὶ ἐργάζεσθ' ἐπὶ γαίης
ἐντέχνως, ἵν' ἔχητε τροφῆς κόρον ἱδρώοντες.

[76] The integrity of this section has been challenged by some on the basis of its loose integration with the main story-line and its inferior Greek style. Hugh Anderson offers a well-reasoned argument for the unity of the document in his article "*4 Maccabees*" in Charlesworth (ed.), *OT Pseudepigrapha*, 2:532. As nothing in this section adds anything new to the evidence collected thus far, the originality of the section will be allowed to stand.

[77] The exception is 2.5, where the abbreviation of Exod 20.17b (οὐδὲ ὅσα τῷ πλησίον σού ἐστιν) reflects common Diaspora practice (see note on Rom 7.7 in chap. 4). Though it adheres verbally to the wording of the biblical text, the omission of the second colon of Ps 33.20 in *4 Macc* 18.15 is by no means accidental. The confession καὶ ἐκ πασῶν αὐτῶν ῥύσεται αὐτούς would have rung rather hollow in a text where οἱ δίκαιοι were by no means "rescued," but rather met the fate of martyrs.

[78] The changes involve two occurrences of the possessive pronoun σου, one of which is converted to the plural ὑμῶν and the other dropped out.

presents a textbook example of a combined (back-to-back) citation.[79]

The *Biblical Antiquities* of Pseudo-Philo contains more explicit quotations than any work normally classed among the "pseudepigrapha." Since its text is extant only in Latin, however, any examination of the way the author handles the wording of his quotations will necessarily remain rather superficial. After a painstaking analysis of both the explicit quotations and the use of biblical language throughout the document, Daniel Harrington concluded that the quotations had been translated directly from the Hebrew without being assimilated to the Septuagint in the Greek translation that formed the basis for the present Latin version. He also judged that the author had used a Hebrew text from the "Palestinian" family (i.e. an "expansionist" text) rather than a prototype of the later Masoretic Hebrew text.[80] Whether or not one accepts the classification of the text as "Palestinian,"[81] the fact that the author seems to have used a Hebrew *Vorlage* that diverged at points from the standard Masoretic tradition is reason for added caution in attributing non-Masoretic readings to the editorial activity of the author.

Of the twenty-four explicit quotations in the *Biblical Antiquities*, seven appear to follow the wording of the later Masoretic text with no evident adaptation (15.6, 18.5a, 21.5, 23.5, 23.6, 49.6, 59.2).[82] In a handful of cases, a non-Masoretic reading appears to lie behind the present text.[83] In the majority of places where a quotation

[79] The passages combined here are Deut 32.39 and Deut 30.20. The link was probably dictated by the recurrence of the phrase "life and death" in Deut 30.19–20. Aside from the changes listed in the previous note, the only other possible adaptation is a shift from the neuter pronoun τοῦτο to the feminine αὕτη, a grammatical "correction" necessitated by the removal of the latter verse from its original context. There an entire clause stood as the antecedent.

[80] "The Biblical Text of Pseudo-Philo's *Liber Antiquitatum Biblicarum*," *CBQ* 33 (1971), 1–11. Though he says that he intends to confine himself to "clear biblical quotations" (3), Harrington actually comments on only two or three of the explicit quotations included in the present study. Most of his examples are instances where biblical language is taken up into the narrative itself. The ambiguity that surrounds the term "quotation" (see chap. 2) is apparent in this case.

[81] See chap. 2 for a summary of Frank M. Cross's "local texts" theory and the criticisms of it.

[82] The other quotations appear at 9.3, 9.8, 10.2, 12.3, 12.4, 14.2, 15.4, 15.5, 15.6, 19.4, 19.11, 21.9, 38.2, 51.6, 53.10, 56.1, and 58.1. Less explicit appropriations of biblical language abound throughout the document. Only those places where one of the characters adduces a specific text through the use of an introductory formula have been included in the present study.

[83] E.g. in the rendering "eo quod" ("because") (MT בְּשֶׁם) in 9.8, supported by the LXX (and apparently by the Syriac, Vulgate, and Targum, per BHS), and the presence of "God" for "Yahweh our God" and the reversal of the verbs "hear" and

departs from the Masoretic tradition, however, a reason for the change can be discerned in the immediate context. In 10.2, 12.4, and 21.9, for example, the author reproduces Gen 12.7 in a form that diverges at two points from the Masoretic text: omitting the word "this" before "land" and adding the words "in which you [plural] dwell" at the end of the verse. Both changes appear innocuous enough until it is noticed that the same verse is quoted in 23.5 without these variations. The reason for the difference lies in the context: in the latter instance, the quotation occurs as part of a general recapitulation of the divine epiphany to Abraham, while in the other places Yahweh's faithfulness to "our fathers" [plural] has somehow been called into question.[84] A similar motive is apparent in the omission of two separate references to Yahweh's "covenant" with his creation in Moses' retelling of the Flood story in 19.11. In this book, the term "covenant" is reserved almost exclusively for Yahweh's promises to Abraham.[85] In several places grammatical adjustments have been introduced to construct a free-standing "quotation" out of an excerpt from a larger verse.[86] Omissions designed to condense the text or eliminate irrelevant or redundant materials are also encountered on a number of occasions.[87] Numerous other minor adaptations (additions, omissions, substitutions, and grammatical changes) help to produce a closer alignment between the wording of the biblical text and its new context.[88]

"do" in 19.4. A pre-existing text should probably also be posited for the conflated citation in 21.9 (Gen 12.7 plus Exod 3.8), as the same conflation (though in a more condensed form) appears in *Jub* 1.7.

[84] A similar instance appears in 14.2, where the pronoun "your" is converted from singular to plural to suit the application of the verse to "their fathers" (cf. 18.5a, where the same verse is quoted with a singular pronoun).

[85] Excerpts from these promises are quoted explicitly in 9.3, 10.2, 12.4, 14.2, 15.5, 18.5, 21.9, and 23.5, while glowing descriptions appear in 4.11, 7.4, 8.3, 9.7, 19.2, 23.6–7, 11, 30.7, and 32.13–14 (sometimes cast more generally as Yahweh's covenant with "our fathers"). The sole exceptions appear in 11.1–2, 21.10, and 32.8, where the reference is to the covenant at Sinai.

[86] Additions are used to convert a brief excerpt into a free-standing "quotation" in 12.3 ("and now unless I stop them") and 14.2 ("they will be"); an Infinitive is converted to an Indicative to the same end in 15.4 ("I will bring").

[87] In 15.4, where the words "out of that land to a good and broad land" have been dropped from Exod 3.8; in 15.5, where the omitted words "they will enslave them and oppress them for four hundred years" had just been quoted in 9.3; in 38.2, eliminating Josh 1.7b–8a in the middle of a quotation; and 53.10, where the details of a halakhic injunction have been left out of Deut 22.6.

[88] E.g. the addition of the words "and they will dare worse," referring no doubt to the Golden Calf episode in which the quotation appears, in 12.3 (Gen 11.6); the addition of the words "in multitude" at the end of Gen 22.17 in 14.2, where the numerical growth of Abraham's "seed" is in view; the shift from "them" to "you" in

All in all, the texts of this period display at least as much diversity in their handling of explicit quotations as was seen in either of the earlier periods. As with the older writings, certain authors appear to prefer a verbatim citation technique. Others, however, consistently adapt the wording of their biblical quotations to bring them into closer verbal or conceptual alignment with their new context. Every type of adaptation encountered in the earlier materials appears in abundance in the texts of this period, and combined and conflated citations are also in evidence. Broadly speaking, the level of literary artistry with which some of the authors of this period handle the wording of their quotations appears more complex than in the earlier periods, but the difference could well be due to the selectivity of the preservation process. In any event, the general pattern of adapting the wording of the text to reflect a later interpretation seems to hold here as well.

Conclusions

Any attempt to catalogue the practices of such a diverse collection of writings is bound to sacrifice some of the specificity of the individual texts. Nevertheless, some sort of summary is clearly needed to bring a measure of order out of the wealth of data that has been uncovered thus far. The very fact that common patterns can be discovered within such a disparate array of documents is itself strong evidence for the existence of a general literary ethos that shaped the way quotations were handled throughout Jewish literature.

(1) Explicit quotations are quite scarce in the earlier (pre-Hasmonean) literature. The frequency and diversity of appeals to Scripture seem to increase somewhat with the passage of time, but texts with few or no citations remain common even in the latest

---

15.4 (Exod 3.8) (cf. "God spoke to *us*"); the substitution of "men" for "the land" in 19.11 (Gen 9.15), improving the parallel between the rainbow and Moses' staff as reminders to Yahweh to be merciful toward humanity; the omission of the words "from it" in 38.2 (Josh 1.7), where the singular pronoun conflicts with the reference to "the commandments" in the same verse; the addition of "your heart" and "the law of the Lord" (replacing the simple "it") in 28.1, where the issue is whether to serve Yahweh or Baal; and the substitution of the words "there among them [i.e. with Moses and Aaron]" (Ps 99.6) for "among those who called his name," to increase the stature of Samuel in a passage where his coming is extolled (51.6).

period.[89] The presence or absence of quotations bears little relation to the type of literature under investigation.[90]

(2) Compared to the Qumran writings, the introductory formulae used in the "apocrypha" and "pseudepigrapha" display a higher degree of originality, but hardly the creativity that one encounters in the broader Greco–Roman milieu. The great majority employ the words "written" or "says/said" at some point in their phrasing. Similar expressions appear with both verbatim and highly adapted quotations. The same forms are used with conflated and combined citations, texts drawn from unknown (non-biblical?) sources, and even (in the book of *Jubilees*) free authorial formulations (citing the "heavenly tablets").

(3) The awkwardness of working with translations makes it difficult to say anything meaningful about the biblical texts employed by the authors in question. Most appear to base their quotations on a proto-Masoretic Hebrew or standard "Septuagintal" text-type, though examples can be cited where the use of a different text appears likely. Very few instances were noted where a divergent reading agreed with a known minority tradition for either text.

(4) Given the scarcity of quotations throughout the literature, it would be natural to assume that the few texts that are mentioned were drawn from memory, though there is no way to prove or disprove this hypothesis. Only in the case of the *Biblical Antiquities*, where biblical language has been appropriated *en masse*, is there reason to think that perhaps the author might have worked from a written text.[91]

(5) As with the Qumran literature, no monolithic attitude toward the wording of the biblical text can be discerned in the documents under investigation. Verbatim citations and highly adapted formulations appear side-by-side in every period, even within the same document. Conflated texts also appear throughout the literature, though they are proportionately more common in the earlier texts. Only one instance of a combined (back-to-back) citation was noted (*4 Macc* 18.19).

[89] The best way to see this is to compare the brief lists of texts included in the present study with the extensive lists of contents in the two volumes of Charlesworth's *OT Pseudepigrapha*.

[90] For every type of literature represented in the present study, several examples could be cited of similar texts that contain no quotations at all.

[91] Support for this view might be found in Harrington's conclusion ("Text of Pseudo-Philo") that the author follows a non-Masoretic text-type throughout, but

(6) In texts where an adaptation of some sort could be demonstrated, the range of adaptations was quite similar to that found in the other materials examined to this point. Omissions and grammatical adjustments are common throughout the literature. Additions occur somewhat more often and substitutions less frequently in the texts studied here than in, say, the Qumran literature or the Pauline epistles. Changes in word order were harder to detect in the translated literature, but their appearance in original language documents was noted on occasion. Clear instances of "limited selection" are rare.

(7) A variety of explanations can be noted for those adaptations that do appear. For the most part the reasons are similar to those adduced for other texts studied thus far. Adjusting the wording to suit the linguistic requirements of the new context is standard practice. Condensing a lengthy quotation to call attention to the part deemed most important by the later author is another common technique. Rhetorical and stylistic concerns appear to have molded the language of the biblical text on several occasions. In still other cases, the biblical wording has been adapted to reflect the interpretation/application put forward by the later author in his own composition.

Thus it appears that despite the diversity of materials included under the headings "apocrypha" and "pseudepigrapha," the same basic approach to quotations can be seen here as has been noted already in the case of the Qumran literature, the quotations of non-Jewish Greco–Roman authors, and the various Pauline epistles. Taken together, the materials examined thus far offer strong evidence for a common societal attitude on the way primary sources should be handled in a secondary literary composition.

5. Philo

The importance of explicit biblical quotations in the writings of Philo Judaeus is well-known, and need not be rehearsed here. F. H. Colson, one of the editors of the Loeb edition of Philo's works, counted some 2,000 citations in Cohn and Wendland's standard critical text, of which all but fifty stem from the Pentateuch.[92]

even here it seems likely that the author simply quoted the biblical text in the form in which he himself had learned it.

[92] F. H. Colson, "Philo's Quotations from the Old Testament," *JTS* 41 (1940), 238; similarly W. L. Knox, "Notes on Philo's Use of the Old Testament," *JTS* 41

Roughly 40 percent of Philo's quotations serve as *lemmata* for his various "commentaries" on the biblical text. The remainder are used in what Colson calls an "illustrative" sense, i.e. to lend support to a point made in the same context in the author's own words.[93] The sheer diversity of these "illustrative" quotations offers vivid testimony to Philo's thorough familiarity with the biblical text.

Given the breadth of Philo's engagement with the biblical text, the most that the present study can offer is a representative inquiry into the way Philo handles explicit quotations in certain selected treatises. The two essays chosen for examination here, the *Legum Allegoria* (*Allegorical Interpretation of Genesis II and III*) and the *De Ebrietate* (*On Drunkenness*), offer two very different approaches to the biblical text. The first is an extended allegorical exposition of Gen 2.1–3.19 in which Philo's standard religio–philosophical interpretation of the biblical narrative comes to full expression. The second is a topical study that adduces a variety of biblical passages as part of a general treatise on drinking and drunkenness.[94] The first moves verse by verse through a single portion of Scripture that serves as the backbone for the entire study. The second ranges throughout the Pentateuch and even into Proverbs and 1 Kingdoms in search of relevant materials. The first is "allegorical" from start to finish. The second mixes allegory with a more "literal" approach. If a common citation technique can be identified within these two distinctive compositions, then the limitations of the present selective examination will have been at least partially overcome.

The procedure to be followed here is basically the same as with the other materials examined thus far. Nonetheless, a few preliminary comments would appear to be in order. (1) Philo has a habit of repeating portions of an earlier citation within the body of his exposition in order to derive further meanings from the individual parts (e.g. *Eb* 123, *LA* 2.97–104, 3.157, 167, 192). In the process, he sometimes modifies the wording of the excerpt so as to highlight the sense in which he meant the verse to be understood. Though important as a class for understanding Philo's attitude toward the

(1940), 30–4. The standard critical edition of Philo's works is L. Cohn and P. Wendland (eds.), *Philonis Alexandrini opera quae supersunt*, 7 vols. (Berlin: Georgii Reimeri, 1896–1915). Verse references follow this edition throughout.

[93] Colson, "Quotations," 239.

[94] The treatise begins, "The views expressed by the other philosophers on drunkenness have been stated by me to the best of my abilities in the preceding book [*De Plantatione*]. Let us now consider what the great lawgiver [Moses] in his never-failing wisdom holds on this subject" (trans. F. H. Colson, Loeb Classical Library edition).

wording of his quotations, the inclusion of all these repeated excerpts would have burdened the presentation unnecessarily. Accordingly, all such partial repetitions have been left to the side for the time being, to be reintroduced as evidence in the closing section. (2) The study of the *Legum Allegoria* has been restricted to those passages that Colson calls "illustrative," i.e. the *lemma* texts have been left out of consideration. Two facts have argued in favor of this procedure: (a) the "illustrative" quotations stand closer to Paul's method of adducing biblical quotations in the midst of his own compositions;[95] and (b) the original text of Philo's biblical *lemmata* remains highly uncertain due to problems within the various manuscript traditions.[96] (3) A high percentage of Philo's divergences from the Septuagint (his primary text) have been relegated to the "uncertain" category due to the difficulty of fixing the origins of a series of stylistic changes that appear throughout Philo's biblical quotations. While the frequency of the changes (combined with their lack of support in the LXX tradition) makes it tempting to attribute them all to Philo, the possibility that Philo might have worked with a biblical text that had been revised here and there to improve its Greek style (a common practice of Alexandrian copyists) cannot be ruled out. For this reason purely stylistic variants have been relegated to the lower probability categories throughout the present study.

Philo and Homer

Before turning to the two treatises that form the nucleus of the present study, a few comments about the way Philo handles the wording of his Homeric quotations might offer a useful benchmark.

---

[95] Note the similar omission of the *pesher* materials in the section on Qumran.

[96] The manuscripts testify to two distinct traditions regarding the wording of Philo's biblical *lemmata*. One stands quite close to the standard text of the "Septuagint," while the other reflects a more "Hebraizing" Greek text. For a survey of the history of the problem, see Peter Katz, *Philo's Bible* (Cambridge University Press, 1950), 125–38. After a thorough and painstaking analysis, Katz concluded that the "Hebraizing" biblical text had been inserted into the manuscripts at a time when the original *lemma* texts were no longer being copied. Katz's findings were endorsed by no less a scholar than John William Wevers in "Proto-Septuagint Studies," 66–8. The issue was re-opened by George Howard ("The 'Aberrant' Text of Philo's Quotations Reconsidered," *HUCA* 44 (1973), 197–207), who argued that the matter is not so simple as Katz supposed. In fact, as Howard demonstrates, the "Hebraizing" text coincides better with Philo's exposition in a number of cases. Like Paul, Philo appears to have relied primarily on the "Septuagint," but he may have consulted other Greek texts (or simply used a mixed text) on certain occasions.

Of the various Jewish writings that have survived from the Second Temple period, only Philo quotes Homer often enough to allow for a reasonable judgment as to the way he handled the Homeric text. At least sixteen explicit quotations from Homer can be identified in the Philonic corpus.[97] Of these, fully thirteen reproduce the "vulgate" text verbatim, while two others show only minor deviations that have no effect on the sense of the verse.[98] In only one instance would it be proper to speak of a verse being adapted for a later use, and in this case the adapted version is attributed to another speaker, Chaereas of Alexandria.[99] The unavoidable conclusion is that Philo habitually quoted the Homeric epics verbatim according to the vulgate text.

De Ebrietate

The treatise *De Ebrietate* (*On Drunkenness*) offers thirty-seven explicit biblical quotations in forty-four pages of printed Greek text, or nearly one per page.[100] Of this total, only nine (24 percent) reproduce the wording of the LXX without deviation. In thirteen other verses, the few minor divergences that do appear show no evident link to the immediate context. Though support is lacking in the LXX tradition, these passages, too, may well follow the wording of Philo's Greek *Vorlage*.[101] The same is true in five other places (*Eb* 37, 96, 127, 143, 166) where the only assured adaptation is the omission of an initial particle, a practice as common in Philo as it is in Paul.[102] With the textual status of two quotations entirely uncertain (*Eb* 31, 120), this leaves only nine passages (24 percent)

---

[97] The Index to the Loeb edition gives some sixty references to the Homeric epics in its notes, but some of these represent duplicate entries, while others refer to passing allusions or the comments of the later editors.

[98] The divergences appear in *De Providentia* 2.7 (substituting ὅν for τόν to suit the grammar of the new context) and *De Aeternitate Mundi* 37 (omitting δ').

[99] In *De Migratione Abrahami* 156, where a verse originally addressed to Agamemnon (*Il* 1.180–1) is applied to Ptolemy, yielding a corresponding change in the nationality of the addressed (Μυρμιδόνεσσιν converted to Αἰγυπτίουσιν).

[100] In the critical edition prepared by Cohn and Wendland.

[101] The latter group comprises quotations in *Eb* 14, 19, 31, 39, 40, 52, 67 (*bis*), 82, 101, 114, 210, and 222. The various unattested deviations include changes in word order, minor differences in grammar, exchanges of synonyms, and occasional omissions of possessive pronouns.

[102] Initial particles are dropped from quotations eight times in *Eb* and seventeen times in *LA*, almost always in conjunction with an intruded or immediately preceding introductory formula.

where significant adaptations can be linked to the role of the verse in its new Philonic context.[103]

Under further scrutiny, the proportion of meaningful adaptations can be reduced even further. Of seventy-eight total deviations from the standard critical text of the LXX (an average of three per verse), only eighteen (23 percent) could qualify as probable adaptations (A or B rating) under the criteria of the present study. In eight of these the only change is the omission of an initial particle.[104] The remaining ten instances offer a narrow base indeed for any broader discussion of the way Philo handled the wording of his quotations.

Still, the evidence that remains is worth noting. Included in the total are examples of virtually every type of adaptation encountered thus far. In three places, a portion of a verse is omitted to create a better fit with the interpretation offered in the main body of the treatise. In two of these passages (both in *Eb* 210), the name of Joseph's Egyptian owner (Πετεφρης in the LXX) is left out (along with a reference to "Egypt" in the second verse) so as to clear away narrative details that find no place in Philo's "spiritualizing" interpretation of the Joseph story (*Eb* 206–24). The same explanation holds for the omission of the words ἀπὸ προσώπου Ἰσαακ τοῦ πατρὸς αὐτοῦ in the allegorizing treatment of Gen 27.30 in *Eb* 9–10. Though only one instance of adding words to the text can be documented, that insertion (a gloss on the quotation of Exod 33.7 in *Eb* 100) is entirely consistent with Philo's practice as seen in the *Legum Allegoria*.[105] In another instance, the advancement of the words θλαδίας καὶ ἀποκεκκομένος to primary position accords well with the emphatic phrasing of the preceding comment.[106] In three other places, minor adjustments in grammar help to conform a

---

[103] The verses are *Eb* 9, 84, 100, 111, 113, 203, 210b, 210c, and 213. The figure rises to 38 percent when verses that drop only an initial particle are included in the total.

[104] Fourteen others would appear to have a textual basis, while the origins of forty-six (59 percent) remain uncertain. Most of the latter group are stylistic in nature.

[105] The addition is apparent even in translation: "'Moses,' we read, 'took his tent and pitched it outside the camp, *not near, but very far*, at a distance from the camp'" (Colson's translation; emphasis mine). The significance of the insertion becomes clear when one notes the interpretive comment that precedes it: "That camp [= "the body," *Eb* 99] the mind is wont to leave, when, filled with the divine, it finds itself in the presence of the existent Himself and contemplates the eternal ideas" [trans. Colson, Loeb series].

[106] The emphatic parallelism is obvious in the Greek: τῶν τοιούτων οὐδενὶ ἐπιτρέπει Μωυσῆς εἰς ἐκκλησίαν ἀφικνεῖσθαι θεοῦ. λέγει γὰρ ὅτι θλαδίας καὶ ἀποκεκκομένος οὐκ εἰσελεύσεται εἰς ἐκκλησίαν κυρίου (emphasis mine). The shift in word order finds no support in either the LXX or Hebrew manuscript traditions.

citation to its new linguistic environment.[107] Two cases of "limited selection" can also be identified.[108]

Though the evidence is limited, the treatise *De Ebrietate* seems to indicate that Philo handled the wording of Scripture much more freely than he did the epics of Homer. In addition to minor grammatical and stylistic adjustments,[109] a number of places can be noted where Philo clearly adapts the wording of a quotation to accord with his own interpretation. The bulk of these adaptations occur in conjunction with an allegorical or "spiritualizing" exposition of the verse in question.[110] The fact that the present treatise interprets the bulk of its citations in a relatively "literal" fashion might help to explain the relative paucity of adapted texts.

Legum Allegoria

Even after the biblical lemmata have been excluded, Philo's *Allegorical Interpretation of Genesis II–III* contains nearly twice the density of explicit quotations as his treatise *On Drunkenness*.[111] Of the 111 quotations listed in the standard critical edition of Philo's works, thirty-one reproduce the wording of the LXX verbatim, while another fifteen contain only minor deviations that appear to have a textual basis. Sixteen others show more significant divergences that may nonetheless go back to an unattested Greek tradition, while the textual background of seven others (*LA* 2.27, 2.105, 3.102, 3.105, 3.118, 3.133, and 3.177) remains unclear.[112] This leaves

---

[107] In *Eb* 84 (converting a particle from singular to plural to suit the application to a particular class of people (cf. 80–1)); 111 (shifting from a finite verb to a participle to subordinate the quotation to the comment that follows); and 203 (changing a pronoun from singular to plural to accord with a new plural antecedent). The five places where initial particles are dropped from a quotation (*Eb* 37, 96, 127, 143, 166) reflect a similar concern.

[108] In *Eb* 9, where the words ἀπὸ τῆς θήρας are left off the end of Gen 27.30 as part of a programmatic effort to eliminate all "historical" references in favor of a wholly allegorical treatment, and 113, where the word ἐθνῶν at the end of Num 21.18 causes problems for the interpretation offered.

[109] As noted above, these sorts of adjustments may be more common than the present study can show – the number of divergent readings whose origin remains uncertain (59 percent) is quite high.

[110] The same was seen for Heraclitus in the previous chapter.

[111] The total of 111 quotations in 56 pages of Greek text (per Cohn and Wendland), or two per page, compares with 37 quotations in 44 pages in the *De Ebrietate*. On the omission of the *lemmata*, see the introduction above.

[112] Passages where an unattested tradition might lie behind the present wording include *LA* 2.11, 2.34, 2.51, 2.78, 2.88, 2.94, 3.1, 3.16, 3.148, 3.180b, 3.191, 3.212, 3.225 (*bis*), 3.228b, and 3.248. As with the previous treatise, the minor deviations

forty-two verses (38 percent) where the wording of the biblical text has been adapted in some way to conform to its new literary environment. In eleven cases the adaptation extends only to the omission of an initial particle (*LA* 3.20b, 3.39, 3.43a, 3.129, 3.151, 3.152, 3.186, 3.214a, 3.217a) or an instance of "limited selection" (*LA* 3.9, 3.42). Omitting these verses leaves thirty-one passages (28 percent) where the wording of a quotation has experienced significant adaptation.

The picture is the same when the incidence of divergent readings is taken into account. Of 181 identifiable deviations from the standard text of the LXX, fully sixty-nine (38 percent) can be explained as adaptations designed to conform the text to its new environment. Disregarding for the moment those places where the only adaptation is the omission of an initial particle or an occurrence of "limited selection," the number of adaptations per verse is still significantly higher in this treatise than in the *De Ebrietate*.[113] Thirty-four of the remaining divergences find at least minimal support in the Greek or Hebrew manuscript traditions, while the origins of seventy-eight (43 percent) cannot be settled with confidence within the parameters of the present study.

In contrast to the *De Ebrietate*, the sixty-nine adaptations identified in the *Legum Allegoria* offer a sizeable data base for an analysis of Philo's citation technique. As with most of the other authors examined thus far, simply leaving out unnecessary or problematic words or phrases is by far the most common method by which Philo adapts the wording of a quotation to its new literary setting. Fully half of his adaptations can be classed under this heading. In many cases the omission is purely stylistic, as in the seventeen cases where he leaves off an initial particle (καί, δέ, γάρ, etc.) after an introductory formula so as to smooth the transition from text to citation. In other cases, the omission is fairly required by the grammar of the new context.[114] In a few places, the omitted words are merely

---

encountered here include changes in word order, minor differences in grammatical forms, exchanges of synonyms, and occasional omissions of possessive pronouns that show no obvious relation to the new context. Whether these minor differences reflect Philo's own literary sensitivities or earlier Alexandrian attempts to improve on the style of the LXX remains unclear.

[113] Subtracting out the items noted yields 59 A or B rated adaptations in 31 verses in *LA* (two per verse) versus 13 adaptations in 9 verses for *Eb* (1.5 per verse), an increase of 33 percent.

[114] As in *LA* 2.59, where the words ὁ ἀδελφός μου conflict with a shift to third-person speech, or 2.81, where the word ἄνθρωπον becomes unnecessary after

redundant, and can be set aside with no visible effect on the meaning of the verse.[115] This said, there remain a number of instances in which the omission is clearly meant to facilitate the interpretation offered by Philo in his own composition. More often than not the concern is to eliminate certain "historical" and "physical" elements from the citation so as to make room for a more "spiritual" and "allegorical" reading.[116] In other cases the effect is more subtle, as when the omission of the words ἡ γυνή in *LA* 3.150 allows the feminine adjectives of Num 5.28 to be read as referring to ἡ ψυχή, the next preceding feminine noun in the Philonic context.[117] In every instance it is the interests of the later author (Philo) that determine the form in which the verse is quoted in the new context.

The same can be said for the other types of adaptations that appear in the *Legum Allegoria*. The role of insertions is especially noteworthy, as they occur with unusual frequency in this treatise (twelve times). The most striking aspect of these interpretive additions is their sheer obviousness. In three places glosses help to explain how the wording of the verse comports with the allegorical interpretation offered in the context. In 3.12, for example, the interjected words τῇ κρίσει τῶν φύσεως πραγμάτων give the allegorical meaning of the statement in Exod 2.15 that Moses "settled in the land of Midian" (i.e. "in the examination of the things of nature"), while in 3.43b, a similar insertion explains that the "city" referred to in the quotation of Exod 9.29 is the human soul.[118] The same effect is achieved with less disruption in 3.175, where the words τὸ πάθος explain the noun Αἴγυπτον; 3.212, where the

the relative pronoun ὅν (ἄν) that is used to incorporate the citation into its new context.

[115] As in *LA* 2.48 (omitting the repetitious words ἡ ἠγαπημένη καὶ ἡ μισουμένη and the redundant clause καὶ ἔσται ᾗ ἂν ἡμέρᾳ κατακληροδοτῇ τοῖς υἱοῖς αὐτοῦ τὰ ὑπάρξοντα αὐτοῦ from Deut 21.15–16), 3.81 (eliminating the words Ἀμμανίτης καὶ Μωαβίτης from Deut 23.3–4 after incorporating them in the introduction to the quotation), and 3.142 (leaving out the words καὶ τεσσαράκοντα νύκτας after τεσσαράκοντα ἡμέρας in Exod 34.28).

[116] E.g. *LA* 3.8, omitting the words πρόσταξον τοῖς υἱοῖς Ἰσραηλ καί from the beginning of Num 5.2; 3.21, eliminating the word μαχαίρα from the end of Gen 31.26; 3.71, leaving out the words πρωτότοκος Ἰουδα used to describe Er in Gen 38.7; and 3.196, omitting the words εἰς ὀσμὴν εὐωδίας so as to dissociate Num 28.2 from its sacrificial context.

[117] An equally subtle instance appears in *LA* 3.4, where the omission of the pronoun οὗτος allows Philo to read Deut 4.39 as a prooftext for the omnipresence of God rather than as one element of a general theolegoumenon.

[118] The other example appears in *LA* 1.81, where the names Ῥουβὴν Συμεών Λευί are added to Exod 28.17 to correlate the stones on the high priest's breastplate with their respective tribes.

adjectives σωματικῶν καὶ Αἰγυπτιακῶν give an allegorical turn to the noun ἔργων; and 3.218, where Sarah's κύριος is said to be none other than the θεῖος λόγος. The introductory formulae that accompany these obviously reworked citations differ in no way from those used with verbatim citations. In other places, insertions are employed to create new links between citations (3.108 *bis*), to emphasize a point (3.32), and to smooth the grammar of a citation in connection with other changes (3.103 *bis*).

Substitutions likewise serve the interpretive aims of the author on numerous occasions. In *LA* 3.8, a simple shift from the word παρεμβολῆς ("camp") (Num 5.2) to the phrse ἁγίου ψυχῆς yields the typically Philonic reading, "Let them send forth *out of the holy soul* every leper ... " A similar move can be seen in 3.15, where the phrase "sons of Israel" (so Lev 15.31) becomes "sons of the Seeing One [τοῦ ὁρῶντος]" in accordance with Philo's insistence that the human soul must remain open before God in order to make progress in its spiritual quest (cf. 3.11–13). Likewise in 3.103 the substitution of the words καὶ ἐν σκιᾷ ... οὐκ ἐναργῶς ("indeed in a shadow ... not openly") for the original καὶ ἐν ὕπνῳ λαλήσω αὐτῷ ("and in a dream I will speak to him") of Num 12.6 fits Philo's broader distinction between those who know God only through his creation (called his "shadow" [σκιά] in 3.99–102) and those who (like Moses) see God face to face.[119] As with the additions, nothing in the introductory formulae would distinguish any of these quotations from the more "literal" renderings found in other places. Elsewhere substitutions are used to condense a more lengthy text (3.103, 3.139, 3.141) or to conform a quotation to the grammar of its new context (2.59).

Even changes in word order and grammatical adjustments can serve an interpretive purpose on occasion. In *LA* 3.71 and 3.141, the very part of the citation that offers a point of contact with the surrounding argument is advanced to primary position in the verse.[120] The interpretive effect of a simple change in grammar can

---

[119] A further example appears in 3.193, where the clause ἔσται δὲ ἡνίκα ἐὰν καθέλῃς is replaced by the interpretive comment ἀλλ᾽ οὐχὶ νῦν – οὐ γὰρ ἀνέξεταί σε ἀφηϊάζοντα – ἀλλ᾽ ὅταν, in line with Philo's allegorical reading that regards the slavery of Esau (the soul ruled by passions) to Jacob (the soul that has come to know God) as something to be desired (3.189–94).

[120] In 3.71 (Gen 38.7), the advancement of ἐναντίον κυρίου accords with the preceding affirmation that the wickedness of the human soul "is not evident to all ... but to God alone and to anyone who is dear to God." In 3.141 (Lev 9.14), the primary position of καὶ τὴν κοιλίαν (καὶ τοὺς πόδας) comports well with the emphasis

be seen in 3.103, where a shift from first-person divine speech ("I will reveal myself") to third-person narrative ("God will make himself known") accords with Philo's distinction between those who know God directly and those who see him only in his creation (3.99–102). A similar shift to a second-person singular verb in 3.196 allows Philo to read a corporate injunction as a direct address to the soul.[121] "Limited selection" is also used on occasion to eliminate potentially troublesome materials, as when Philo ends his citation of Exod 17.6 in *LA* 3.4 before the words (ἐκεῖ) ἐπὶ τῆς πέτρας ἐν Χωρηβ so that he can read the phrase πρὸ τοῦ σε in a temporal rather than a spatial sense. A similar instance can be seen in *LA* 3.15, where he drops the cultic phrase ἀπὸ τῶν ἀκαθαρσιῶν αὐτῶν from the end of Lev 15.31 in order to make room for a moralizing interpretation of the word εὐλαβεῖς as οὐ θρασεῖς καὶ τῶν μὴ καθ' αὑτοὺς ἐρῶντας ("not bold and yearning for things that are beyond them").[122] Indeed, it would not be going too far to say that nearly all of Philo's adaptations coincide precisely with the needs of the surrounding argument.

Certain aspects of the way citations are grouped in their Philonic context are also worth noting. Though most of Philo's biblical quotations are interspersed with a greater or lesser amount of interpretive or argumentative material, in several cases a closer relationship can be observed. The simplest and most common pattern appears when the various parts of a narrative unit are broken apart for separate exposition. In these cases the gap between the verses is filled sometimes with interpretive comments (2.46, 2.77–9, 3.1–2, 3.20–1, 3.151–3, 3.212–14), sometimes with a simple phrase of continuation such as καὶ ἐπιλέγει (3.74, 3.85, 3.179,

---

throughout the passage (3.138–50) on the need for special effort in reigning in the passions of the "belly"

[121] Less obvious examples appear in 2.59, where the shift from ἔστιν to ἦν helps to convert a statement made by Jacob into a statement about Jacob, and 3.81, where a plural verb is required to conform to an allegorical interpretation that reads the accompanying nouns as plurals. The shift from λαλήσει to λαλήσω in 3.103 is required by the conversion of the entire passage to third-person speech.

[122] At least five other instances of the same technique can be identified in *LA*. In 1.81, 3.42, and 3.153, words that were integral to the original passage are simply omitted at the end of the citation unit as being irrelevant to the interpretation offered. In 3.9, breaking off the quotation of Gen 18.23 before the words καὶ ἔσται ὁ δίκαιος ὡς ὁ ἀσεβής allows Philo to take the verse as an imperative rather than a question, a reading that coincides with his subsequent use of the verse. A similar situation prevails in 3.169, where the first words of Exod 16.16 are appended to the previous verse in full violation of the original grammar so as to create an artificial link between the manna in the desert and the word of God.

3.217). A more complex situation arises when two disparate verses are quoted *seriatim* in support of a single point. Here the verses are typically linked by some brief expression such as καὶ πάλιν (3.4; cf. *Eb* 19, 210) or παρὰ καί (3.2–3), though a separate introductory formula can be used on occasion (3.43). An even closer relationship becomes apparent when the wording of one quotation begins to influence the text of another, as when the words αἱ μαῖαι are advanced to primary position in 3.3 (Exod 1.21) to parallel the word order of the previous two citations, or when the phrase πρωτότο-κος Ἰουδα is dropped from a quotation of Gen 38.7 in 3.74 to avoid redundancy with the just-cited Gen 38.6.[123] The bond between quotations reaches its height when two verses merge together under a single citation formula (a so-called "conflated citation"), as in 3.8 (Num 5.2 + Deut 23.2) and 3.108 (Deut 27.18 + Deut 27.24). In these cases the verbal integrity of the individual verses is dissolved in favor of the rhetorical and interpretive aims of the later author.

To sum up, the citation technique encountered in the *Legum Allegoria* is notably more diverse and creative than that witnessed in the *De Ebrietate*. Omissions, additions, substitutions, changes in word order, adjustments in grammar, "limited selection," and even conflated citations work together to bring out the "spiritual" sense of the verses cited. Most remarkable is the openness with which many of these adaptations were carried out – few of Philo's readers could have mistaken some of his more obvious interpretive addi-tions for the original language of the biblical narrative. Apparently Philo had reason to think that no one would be disturbed by this method of incorporating interpretive elements into the text of his biblical quotations.

Conclusions

The present study has examined two treatises that represent less than five percent of the extant literary output of Philo Judaeus. Strictly speaking, any generalizations about Philo's citation tech-nique will apply to these two essays alone. If common patterns can be identified within these disparate materials, however, it would be reasonable to think that similar results could be obtained from a

---

[123] Another likely example appears in 3.108, where the addition of the words μεντοί καί ("and all the more") to Deut 17.18 seems designed to create a closer bond with the indirect quotation of Deut 17.18 in the previous section (note the repetition of ἐπικατάρατος in both verses).

study of the Philonic corpus as a whole. Even without this presumption, however, the two treatises examined here offer valuable evidence for the way a well-educated Diaspora Jew could handle biblical quotations in the first century C.E.

(1) Like the other Jewish writers examined thus far, Philo works with a relatively limited but still flexible stock of introductory formulae that help to smooth the transition from his own language to that of his quotations. Phrases with the word φησί (especially the stereotyped γὰρ φησί) are particularly common, while expressions with γράφειν are almost unknown. At the same time, Philo can match any other Greco-Roman author for creativity when he has reason to do so. On the whole, Philo's method of introducing explicit quotations places him somewhere between the relative freedom of the non-Jewish authors examined in chapter 7 and the rather limited options witnessed in the Qumran materials.

(2) In most cases it seems clear that Philo drew his biblical quotations from the Greek text known as the "Septuagint." Assimilations to the Masoretic Hebrew text are rare. A large percentage of Philo's deviations from the attested readings of the LXX can be traced to the editorial activity of the author himself. Numerous places remain, however, where a Philonic reading represents a purely stylistic improvement over the wording of the LXX. In these cases it can no longer be determined whether the improvement goes back to Philo himself or to an earlier Alexandrian revision.

(3) Nothing in the passages studied here sheds any real light on the question of whether Philo drew his quotations entirely from memory or used written sources on occasion. The fact that he quotes almost exclusively from the Pentateuch could be taken as *prima facie* evidence for memory quotation, as could the sheer diversity and relative commonness of the texts employed. The topical nature of the treatise *De Ebrietate* makes it at least plausible that Philo may have compiled a written list of passages that dealt with the issue under discussion, but any such suggestion must remain entirely conjectural.

(4) As with the other authors examined thus far, the writings of Philo reveal no monolithic attitude towards the wording of the biblical text. Verses are quoted verbatim when it suits the purposes of the author, but Philo shows no scruples about conforming the language of a quotation to its new context where the change would help his argument. At the same time, the approach observed in the *De Ebrietate* is clearly more conservative than that of the *Legum*

Allegoria. The fact that Philo grounds his interpretations more often on the "literal" meaning of the biblical narrative in the former treatise might help to explain this difference.

(5) The bulk of Philo's quotations are presented as free-standing units in the midst of the author's own composition. In several instances, however, a longer passage is broken up into smaller units for more extended treatment of the individual parts. In other cases, verses from two disparate contexts are quoted *seriatim* in support of a particular point, linked in most cases by a brief phrase such as καὶ πάλιν. In a few places, the physical proximity of two consecutive quotations has caused one or both of the texts to be reshaped in a way that highlights the relationship between them. On two occasions this molding extends to a physical merger of the two passages into one (i.e. a conflated citation).

(6) A sizeable proportion of Philo's biblical quotations show definite signs of authorial adaptation. The percentage of verses affected in both treatises is roughly the same (38 percent), though the frequency of adaptations is somewhat higher in the *Legum Allegoria* (two per verse) than the *De Ebrietate* (one and a half per verse). The same categories used to classify the adaptations of other authors apply here as well. Simply omitting unnecessary or problematic words or phrases is by far the most common means of conforming a quotation to its new context. Included here are numerous places where the author drops initial particles (καί, δέ, γάρ, etc.) to create a smoother transition from text to citation. Adding interpretive comments to the text is another very common (and highly visible) practice. Substitutions are employed from time to time to introduce interpretive elements into the text, while minor grammatical adjustments and changes in word order sometimes serve a similar purpose. In a number of places the method of "limited selection" helps to insure that the wording of a verse does not conflict with the interpretation/application put forward in the new context.

(7) Specific reasons for the adaptations that do appear in Philo's writings are not hard to find. In the overwhelming majority of instances, the aim is clearly to highlight the way a particular passage relates to the subject under discussion. Apart from the *lemmata*, Philo adduces biblical quotations primarily to illustrate his own religio-philosophical beliefs and to exhort his hearers to appropriate action. Where the precise wording of the biblical text is less than congenial to the point he wants to make – whether due to excessive

wordiness, lack of clarity, or potentially troublesome language – or where the relevance of the verse can be sharpened by highlighting one or another aspect of its content, Philo does not hesitate to adapt the wording of his quotation to bring out the sense in which he means the verse to be understood.[124] Purely rhetorical stylization plays almost no role in Philo's citation technique, though a concern for more fluid Greek expression may be reflected in some of the stylistic improvements whose origins could not be fixed under the terms of the present study. Adaptations designed to conform a quotation to the linguistic demands of its new context were also noted on several occasions, though perhaps less often than in some of the other authors examined thus far.

(8) Perhaps the most striking aspect of Philo's frequent adaptation of the biblical text is the sheer obviousness of many of his changes. On a number of occasions Philo introduces an unmistakable interpretive gloss into the middle of one of his quotations (*LA* 1.81, 3.12, 3.43b, 3.175, 3.212b, 3.218), while in other places he simple replaces what was originally a "literal" expression with his own "spiritual" equivalent (e.g. replacing "camp" with "holy soul" in *LA* 3.8; cf. 3.15, 3.103, 3.193). In none of these cases does the introductory formula tell the reader that anything other than a normal citation is present. A similar phenomenon can be seen in those places where Philo repeats a portion of a verse he has already quoted using words that differ somewhat from the version just given (e.g. *Eb* 118, cf. 114; *LA* 3.157, cf. 3.153; 3.192, cf. 3.191). The changes are minor, but visible nonetheless. Presupposed in such instances is a reader who will not be disturbed by even the most obvious intrusions into the language of the biblical text. One can only assume that Philo knew and took into account the literary expectations of his intended audience.

6. Summary

The present chapter has examined the citation techniques of a variety of Jewish writings composed over some three centuries at cites throughout the eastern Mediterranean world. The diversity of

---

[124] Similar observations have been made by other investigators. See Carl Siegfried, "Philo und der überlieferte Text der Septuaginta," *ZWT* 16 (1873), 217–38, 411–28, 522–40; Peter Katz, *Philo's Bible*, 46, 69, 71, 79, 82, 85, 112, 134 (on specific passages); and most recently Marguerite Harl in Dorival, Harl, and Munnich, *Septante*, 273.

ideas and literary genres represented in these texts is fully reflective of the multiform character of Judaism in the centuries around the turn of the era. Any agreements that might be noted against such a variegated backdrop would surely have to be regarded as significant.

Such a pattern of agreements has indeed been uncovered in the way these texts handle the wording of their explicit quotations from Scripture. Without overlooking the differences in emphasis within individual documents, it can be affirmed with confidence that the methods followed by the authors examined here differ little from those documented already for Greco–Roman writers working outside the Jewish sphere. Passages are either quoted verbatim or altered according to the needs of the immediate context and the inclinations of the individual author. Methods of adapting the text include omitting unnecessary or problematic materials (usually the most common approach), adding words to the text to clarify its intended meaning, substituting more appropriate expressions for words or phrases considered unclear or troublesome in some way, adjusting the grammar of the quotation to suit the linguistic requirements of the new context, and altering the word order to highlight a particular element within the verse. Quotations are normally introduced one at a time as needed, each with its own citation formula, but occasionally two or more verses will be adduced *seriatim* in support of a single point. In a few instances verses have been combined back-to-back or even merged together under a single citation formula in pursuit of the same end. In the great majority of cases, it can be demonstrated with confidence that this adapting and combining of texts took place under the influence of the author's own literary or rhetorical agenda. Such broad-based agreement on such a common matter must be regarded as strong evidence for a general cultural and literary ethos in which incorporating interpretive elements into the wording of a quotation was considered a normal and acceptable means of advancing one's argument.

9

CONCLUSIONS

1. Paul and his contemporaries

Literary techniques are part of the shared cultural heritage of a given society at a particular time in its history. Apart from a few brave souls who are constantly testing the limits of the established conventions, the great majority of writers in any society will consciously or unconsciously model their compositions on the prevailing cultural norms. As a Jewish writer of the first century C.E. who traveled extensively throughout the eastern Mediterranean world, Paul was nurtured in the values and practices of both Jewish and Greco–Roman culture from his infancy.[1] It therefore comes as no surprise to discover a close correlation between the citation technique of the apostle Paul and that of his Jewish and Greco–Roman contemporaries.

(1) Though he quotes his ancestral Scriptures for a variety of purposes,[2] there is no questioning the fact that Paul regarded the words of Scripture as having absolute authority for his predominantly Gentile congregations. How this is to be reconciled with his insistence that the Jewish Torah is no longer in force for these same Gentile Christians has perplexed numerous investigators, and cannot be resolved here.[3] The important point for now is that,

[1] Whether Paul was educated in the Greek rhetorical tradition makes little difference at this point, since he was obviously literate and thus aware of contemporary norms for literary compositions.

[2] Dietrich-Alex Koch has catalogued the various ways in which quotations function in the letters of Paul in *Schrift*, 257–85. See also Bonsirven, 294–324.

[3] A number of recent studies have provoked a reappraisal of traditional views concerning Paul and the law. See E. P. Sanders, *Paul and Palestinian Judaism* (Philadelphia: Fortress, 1977) and *Paul, the Law, and the Jewish People* (Philadelphia: Fortress, 1983); Heikki Räisänen, *Paul and the Law* (Tübingen: Mohr, 1983); Hans Hübner, *Law in Paul's Thought*, trans. James C. G. Greig (Edinburgh: T. and T. Clark, 1984); Stephen Westerholm, *Israel's Law and the Church's Faith* (Grand Rapids: Eerdmans, 1988).

however his theological pronouncements are to be understood, Paul's reliance on the authority of Scripture is wholly in line with contemporary Jewish practice. While most Greco–Roman authors appear to have held the words of Homer in high regard, their tendency to subject the Homeric epics to "scientific" or moral criticism finds little parallel in the Jewish sources. The closest approximation to the Jewish attitude toward Scripture appears in such authors as Crates or Heraclitus of Pontus, to whom Homer stands as an infallible revealer of divine truth.

(2) The frequency and diffusion of quotations within the Pauline epistles is by no means unusual among contemporary authors. The same variation from high density in one treatise (Romans, Galatians) to total void in another (Philippians, 1 and 2 Thessalonians) can be seen in the writings of Plutarch or Philo, while a similar clustering of quotations within a single composition (cf. Rom 9–11, Gal 3.6–14) can be observed in Strabo, Plutarch, the Qumran materials (*1QM* 10–11, *CD* 4.12–5.15, 7.9–8.2), and portions of Philo's writings. In general it seems that the more argumentative and/or apologetic the writing, the more likely the author will trade on the authority of outside sources. But quotations with a more illustrative or rhetorical purpose appear throughout the literature.

(3) In his method of indicating the presence of an explicit quotation, Paul stands midway between the rather formulaic expressions encountered in the Qumran materials and the highly stylized approach favored by most of the Greco–Roman authors surveyed above. A similar mediating stance appears in the writings of Philo, though there is little overlap in the actual language used by the two authors.[4] In fact, Paul's frequent use of forms of γράφειν to introduce his quotations is without parallel in any of the materials examined here. Even in Qumran, expressions using forms of אמר far outnumber those with כתב.[5] The practice is by no means peculiar to Paul, however, as similar language appears with quotations throughout the New Testament. Whether the difference in terminology reflects a fundamental difference in the way the Scriptures were viewed in Jewish and Christian circles lies beyond the scope of the present study.[6]

---

[4] The word φησί, ubiquitous in Philo's introductions, appears only seven times (in varying forms) in the writings of Paul, only once in connection with a quotation (1 Cor 6.16).

[5] Noted also by Koch, *Schrift*, 29–30.

[6] Koch cites numerous examples of the use of γράφειν in contemporary literature (*Schrift*, 28–30), but takes surprisingly little note of the practice of other NT authors.

(4) In none of the materials surveyed does there appear to be any correlation between the way a quotation is introduced and the degree to which it adheres to the wording of the source text. The same expressions appear with verbatim quotations as with highly adapted formulations, not only in similar materials but even within a single document. Among the Jewish writers surveyed, quotations from non-biblical sources (Homer and other Greek authors in Philo and Aristobulus) and verses whose origins remain entirely obscure (*Susanna* 5, 1 Cor 2.9, 9.10, 2 Cor 4.6) follow the same pattern. Even an author's own literary creations can be introduced by one of the standard introductory formulae (*Jubilees*). In this environment it becomes impossible to think that the presence of a particular introductory expression offers any clue as to how Paul or any other author has handled the wording of the accompanying citation.

(5) In his dependence on the primary Greek translation of the Jewish Scriptures (the "Septuagint") as well as his occasional resort to other versions (most often a revision of the LXX), Paul mirrors the practice of other Diaspora Jewish authors of his time. For the most part, the evidence of the quotations seems to support the emerging consensus that sees (a) a single primary Greek translation for each book of the Jewish Scriptures circulating alongside (b) one or more thorough revisions of that primary version,[7] accompanied by (c) an indeterminate number of manuscripts that had experienced more sporadic "corrections" designed either to bring the wording of the text into line with a particular Hebrew *Vorlage* or to improve the Greek style of the original. The Hebrew text itself remained in a similar state of flux during this time, with at least three and possibly several versions in current use around the turn of the era.[8] The wording of the Homeric texts appears to have been largely fixed by this time, but the evidence of the authors studied

---

As a result, he places too much stress on the individuality of Paul at this point: "Anderseits weisen die paulinischen Zitateinleitungen durch die Bevorzugung von γράφειν, vor allem durch die formelhafte Verwendung von γέγραπται, auch ein eigenständiges Profil auf. Die besondere Betonung des schriftlichen Charakters der zitierten Texte ist wohl kaum als Zufall zu bewerten und am ehesten verständlich, wenn man für Paulus einen eigenen Umgang mit der 'Schrift' auch in schriftlicher Gestalt voraussetzt" (32).

[7] Whether such revisions would have been available for every book or only for certain ones remains unclear at this point.

[8] How far one can generalize from the situation at Qumran to the broader society (i.e. whether more than one text would have been available to a given writer in a particular locale) remains a subject of debate. See the discussion and notes in chap. 2.

here shows that they, too, had access to non-"standard" *Vorlagen* for at least some of their quotations.

(6) Though the picture is far from clear, the sparse evidence uncovered here suggests that ancient writers drew their quotations from a wide variety of sources. No one would question the importance of memory quotation in the ancient world, though the growing standardization of written texts (both the Jewish Scriptures and the Greek classics) toward the turn of the era can only be understood in the context of an increasingly text-oriented culture. Direct resort to written sources at the moment of composition can be posited only for those documents where running excerpts from a specific text form the backbone of the entire work, as in the Qumran *pesharim*, the commentaries of Philo, or the *Homeric Allegories* of Heraclitus. Even in these instances quotation from memory cannot be ruled out. The use of a pre-existing *florilegium* is likely only in the case of Plutarch's *A Letter of Condolence to Apollonius*, where a host of lengthy quotations are adduced on a topic of common societal interest, the passing of a loved one. In several instances it seems likely that the author has drawn his quotations from written notes compiled in the course of his own personal studies.[9] Factors that might suggest the use of such a collection include a clustering of quotations around one or more topics known to be central to an author's interests; the presence of a high volume of minute and/or obscure data in the verses cited; and specific evidence for a textual basis for at least some of the materials quoted. Of the authors studied here, the quotations of Strabo, "Longinus," Philo (for the *De Ebrietate*), and Paul show the greatest likelihood of having been drawn in whole or in part from such a personal collection of excerpts.

(7) For nearly all the writers surveyed here, the normal mode of citation is to reproduce (with varying degrees of accuracy) the wording of a single excerpt from a clearly identifiable source text. At times one of these free-standing excerpts will be used to support or illustrate a point made by the author in his own language, while in other places the quotations appear in clusters and form a more integral part of the author's argument. Occasionally an author will break up a longer text into smaller units for individualized comment (Heraclitus, Plutarch, *CD*, Philo; cf. Rom 10.20–1), while in other places the process is more selective, so that only the relevant parts of

---

[9] For contemporary parallels, see the evidence cited in chap. 3.

a broader passage come in for explicit quotation (*ibid.*; cf. Rom 11.3–4). In a few places, two or more verses from different sources are quoted *seriatim* in support of a single point, linked only by a short phrase like καὶ πάλιν (Heraclitus, Philo; cf. Rom 10.19–21, 15.9–12). A closer bond (on the literary level) appears in the handful of cases where the wording of one quotation has influenced the language of another passage nearby (Philo; cf. Rom 11.8, 10, 1 Cor 3.19, 20). More common are instances where two originally distinct verses have been joined back-to-back under a single citation formula to form what is commonly called a "combined citation."[10] In a few places the bonding has progressed to the point of an actual commingling of the language of two or more verses into a single "quotation," a so-called "conflated citation."[11] In every case the choice of a more "bonded" citation technique appears to have been dictated by the special literary and rhetorical concerns of the later author.

(8) No unifying schema can be identified that would explain why a particular author adopts the attitude that he does toward the wording of his source text. While certain authors reproduce the wording of their *Vorlagen* verbatim in virtually all of their quotations, others exhibit a high proportion of adapted texts.[12] More importantly, a single author will often employ verbatim and adapted citations side-by-side in the same passage, or quote from the same context using differing methods. In these cases, it seems that the choice of one approach over the other was based solely on how well the original wording coincided with the point that the later author wanted to make in adducing the passage. While some authors may well have opted for a more verbatim citation technique as a rule, there is nothing to indicate that this was the preferred approach in either Greco–Roman or Jewish society around the turn of the era. If anything, the evidence says just the opposite: incorporating interpretive elements into the wording of a quotation was a

[10] Examples of this type of treatment were identified in "Longinus," Heraclitus, Plutarch, the Qumran materials, *Sibylline Oracles*, *4 Maccabees*, and of course Paul (Rom 3.10–18, 9.25–6, 1 Cor 15.54–5, 2 Cor 6.16–18).

[11] Instances were noted in Plutarch, CD, *1 Esdras*, *Baruch*, *2 Maccabees*, *Aristeas*, Philo, and again Paul (Rom 9.27, 9.33, 10.6–8, 11.8, 2 Cor 6.17, 2 Cor 6.18, Gal 3.10).

[12] Verbatim or near-verbatim citation techniques were seen in Plutarch (the *Poetry* essay), several of the documents from Qumran (*4QTestim*, *11QMelch*, *4QPBless*, *1QS*), and the books of *Judith*, *Susanna*, *Jubilees*, *TSol*, and *4 Ezra*. In several of these texts the number of quotations is too small for the results to be considered significant. The highest rates of adaptations were found in Plutarch (the *Letter of Condolence*), "Longinus," CD, *1QM*, *Baruch*, *2 Maccabees*, Pseudo-Philo, and Paul.

common and apparently well-accepted practice throughout the ancient Mediterranean world. In other words, there is no reason to think that either Jewish or non-Jewish readers would have been disturbed by the relative freedom with which Paul reproduces the wording of the Jewish Scriptures throughout his writings.[13]

(9) Though authors will differ in their preference for one technique over another, the types of adaptations encountered in the present study can be summed up under a few broad headings.

(a) The most common technique for virtually every author is simply to omit words, phrases, or even whole clauses deemed irrelevant to the author's purpose in adducing the citation. In some cases, the aim is purely rhetorical: removing extraneous elements from the original wording allows the central point of the verse (as understood by the later author) to shine through unobscured. In other instances, a concern for style predominates, as when initial particles are repeatedly dropped to create a smoother transition from text to citation.[14] In still other places, the omitted materials might be viewed as running contrary to the interpretation/application offered in the new context, so that removing them helps to clear away a possible source of "misunderstanding" on the part of the reader. In each case, any interest that the author might have had in preserving the precise wording of his *Vorlage* has been subordinated to his concern that the verse properly reflect the sense in which he wanted the quotation to be understood.

(b) Adjusting the grammar of the source text (person, number, case, tense, mood, etc.) to suit the new context is another technique that appears widely throughout the literature. Most often the change is required to bring the text into line with the linguistic demands of its new environment, though examples can be cited where ideological concerns have produced similar revisions in the grammar of the text.[15] Had the later authors been concerned to preserve the verbal integrity of the original text, it would have required little effort in most cases to shape the grammar of the author's own composition to suit the phrasing of his presumed *Vorlage*. The fact that the opposite adjustment occurs regularly in nearly all the materials surveyed here speaks volumes about con-

---

[13] The same cannot be said for the explanations that Paul gives for the passages that he cites, which presumably left at least some of his readers confused and even outraged on occasion.

[14] The practice of omitting initial particles is almost standard for Philo and Paul.

[15] As when a desire to avoid mentioning the divine name causes several verbs to be recast as "divine Passives" in the Qumran literature.

temporary attitudes toward reproducing the original wording of a quoted text.

(c) Less frequent but still common are cases where a word or phrase has been replaced by another that seemed somehow more appropriate to the point the later author was wanting to make. As with omissions, the reasons for verbal substitutions range from rhetorical or stylistic concerns (e.g. a preference for a special vocabulary or a particular form of expression), to creating a closer verbal link between text and interpretation, to removing a potentially troublesome reference from an otherwise useful passage. Substitutions appear more often in quotations from the Jewish Scriptures than in Greco–Roman citations of Homer, perhaps because metrical constraints made substitutions more difficult in the Homeric texts.[16]

(d) Adding interpretive words or phrases to the original text is a technique whose general acceptability is harder to evaluate. Common in Philo and vital to most "conflated" texts, simple additions appear less often in *CD* and Paul and only sporadically elsewhere.[17] The contrast with the attitude toward omitting words from the text is striking. Perhaps ancient readers sensed a difference between clarifying the meaning of a passage and intruding new elements into the time-honored texts,[18] or perhaps the other techniques were simply viewed as less intrusive and therefore in better style. Whatever the reason, adding interpretive elements to the text does not appear to have gained the same currency in the ancient world as the other techniques examined thus far.

(e) Changes in word order are often difficult to ascribe to their proper source due to the high possibility of transcriptional errors in changes of this sort. Nevertheless, a number of instances have been

[16] Substitutions are the most common mode of adaptation in *CD*, while they rank second only to omissions in Paul and just behind omissions and additions in Philo's *Legum Allegoria*.

[17] Further examples can be seen in Plutarch (the *Letter of Condolence*), *4QFlor*, *1 Maccabees*, and Pseudo-Philo.

[18] Cf. Josephus's insistence (belied by his actual practice) that he has neither added to nor taken away from the biblical narrative while composing his own record of the biblical events (*Ant.* 1.17; the passage is discussed by Louis H. Feldman in "Use," 466–70, and in *Josephus and Modern Scholarship (1937–1980)* (Berlin, New York: de Gruyter, 1984), 121–4). Though assurances such as this are commonplace among ancient historians (so Shaye Cohen, *Josephus in Galilee and Rome* (Leiden: Brill, 1979), 24–33), they presuppose an ethos in which adding to the content of one's sources is regarded with suspicion. Removing added lines from the Homeric texts was one of the primary occupations of the *grammatikoi* of Alexandria: see Pfeiffer, 109–11, 230–1; West, 12–16.

identified where shifts in word order can be attributed with a high degree of probability to the author who penned the quotation.[19] In almost every case the aim seems to be to call attention to a particular word or phrase that plays an important role in the author's own interpretation/application of the verse in question. The Greek language is renowned for its facility in communicating such subtleties of emphasis.[20] As with additions, the popularity of this technique appears to vary from author to author. The metrical constraints of the Homeric epics make such shifts highly unusual among the Greco–Roman writers studied here. The same is true of the Qumran materials, where the vagaries of Hebrew syntax leave little room for such techniques outside the poetic passages of Scripture. The frequency of shifts in word order in texts extant only in translation is nearly impossible to verify. Changes in word order are common in conflated texts, but this is more often a product of the conflation itself than an independent preference of the author. In fact, almost every certain instance of an interpretive shift in word order occurs in the writings of Philo or Paul.[21] Whether this means that this technique was used less often than some of the others or whether the results simply reflect the limitations of the present study is impossible to assess.

(f) "Limited selection" – the careful extraction of a useful passage from an otherwise problematic original context – lies on the boundary between verbal adaptation and hermeneutical transformation of a given text. As such, its presence depends not so much on an author's attitude toward the wording of his *Vorlage* as on the degree of exegetical license that he (and his society) is willing to accept in the handling of a text. Where faithfulness to the original context is valued (as in modern Western societies), an approach that defines the beginning and ending points of a citation according to what the later author finds useful for advancing his own argument will normally be viewed with deep suspicion. In the ancient world, on the other hand, where consulting the original context was an infinitely more difficult procedure, it appears that authors were allowed a greater measure of leeway in selecting their quotations

[19] The combination of a lack of manuscript support and an obvious link to the new context is normally sufficient to link a shift in word order to the later author, but a B rating is the best that can be hoped for in such a situation.

[20] The emphatic significance of various changes in Greek word order is treated in BDF § 472–5.

[21] Other isolated instances can be seen in *1 Maccabees*, *3 Maccabees*, and *4 Maccabees*.

than modern readers would find acceptable. Both Greco–Roman and Jewish writers repeatedly use this technique. Its similarity to the widely accepted practice of omitting extraneous or problematic elements from the original text probably helps to explain the acceptability of this procedure.

(10) Reasons for adapting the wording of the text vary from author to author and from situation to situation. Nevertheless, a number of concerns recur throughout most of the texts studied here.

(a) Perhaps the simplest reason for changing certain elements of a text is to conform the grammar of the citation to its new linguistic environment. Ancient writers were clearly interested in minimizing the disruption that results from injecting a foreign linguistic unit into an otherwise free-flowing composition. This concern led them to adopt a variety of techniques for smoothing the transition from text to citation. One approach followed more often by Greco–Roman writers than their Jewish counterparts is to frame the surrounding verses in such a way as to produce a natural receptacle for the original text. More common among Jewish authors is the practice of adapting the case, number, tense, etc., of certain words to bring the quotation into alignment with the author's own developing composition. Eliminating initial particles and/or changing the order of words can also help to create a smoother transition from text to citation. Omitting words that might seem redundant alongside the author's own statements is another technique that comes under this heading. Even substitutions can sometimes be used to integrate a text more closely into its new literary context.

(b) In other places, the wording of a quotation is adapted to improve the rhetorical impact of the original text. Though modern readers are often insensitive to such subtleties of expression, the question of *how* something was said was as crucial to the effectiveness of a public statement in the ancient world as the actual content of what was communicated. Jewish writers arguing from the sometimes awkward Greek of the Septuagint could be expected to be especially sensitive to such matters. Since the present study was designed to identify only the most egregious adaptations, the extent of such rhetorical and stylistic molding of the biblical text has probably been understated here.[22] Omitting words, phrases, or even whole clauses deemed irrelevant to the author's purpose is a

---

[22] The countless unattested variations that recur throughout Philo's quotations offer numerous examples of unattributable stylistic improvements.

common mechanism for creating a rhetorically concise and relevant "citation" out of a rather diffuse original text. Displacing certain parts of a verse from their normal positions for emphasis is another way to improve the rhetorical effectiveness of a passage. Omissions, additions, and substitutions can be used in tandem to inject a parallel or chiastic structure into a rather prosaic original text. The same tools are often employed to improve the verbal and/or thematic unity of a combined or conflated citation. Occasionally the structure of a quotation will be adapted to signal to the reader that a transition of some sort is at hand. Though such verbal cues to meaning and progress of thought can appear overly subtle to modern ears, their value to ancient audiences accustomed to such conventions can hardly be overestimated.

(c) By far the most common motive for adapting the wording of a quotation is to insure that it communicates the precise point that the later author wanted to make in adducing the text. Every adaptive technique encountered thus far is pressed into service at one time or another to help draw out the "correct" meaning of a given quotation. Omissions remove materials that might cause problems for a later interpretation or that otherwise fail to advance the author's argument. "Limited selection" insures that the excerpt is tailored to the needs of the new context. Substitutions replace troublesome or unnecessary verbiage with terminology expressly suited to the later author's interests. Additions offer a more explicit means of injecting interpretive elements into the wording of a quotation. Shifts in word order help to highlight those parts of a verse that link the quotation to its new argumentative context. Even minor adjustments in grammar can be used to advance the interpretational or ideological interests of the later author. Combined and conflated quotations employ all of these techniques to create a new literary unit that is uniquely suited to the rhetorical needs of the new context. In every case it is the interpretational and rhetorical interests of the later author that determine whether a particular verse will be quoted verbatim or in an adapted format. The original wording of the verse is preserved only insofar as it proves useful in furthering these interests.

(11) Perhaps the most noteworthy point about the adaptations noted here is the sheer obviousness and even naïveté with which many of them are carried out. Any Greco–Roman reader with enough education to be reading contemporary literature would be familiar enough with the text of Homer to recognize at least some of

the changes introduced by the authors examined here.[23] The same goes for Jewish readers nurtured on the language of Scripture in the synagogue and its schools.[24] In a few places the changes coincide so thoroughly with the later author's language and interests that even an untrained reader could trace their origins.[25] Especially significant are those places where an author actually lets his readers see him shaping the wording of his *Vorlage*, as when he quotes a verse in two different forms within a brief span of text.[26] Clearly the authors studied here felt no concern that their readers might accuse them of dishonesty or impugn their integrity as a result of their relatively "free" approach to the wording of their respective *Vorlagen*. Nothing could show more clearly the social acceptability of the various adaptive techniques identified in the present study.

(12) From this survey it should be clear that there is nothing particularly unique or even out of the ordinary about the way Paul handles the wording of his biblical quotations. In adapting the language of Scripture to reflect his own interpretation of a given passage, Paul was simply following the normal literary conventions of his day. Nevertheless, there remain certain areas where Paul has left his own personal stamp on the way he employs these techniques in his letters.

(a) The unusual frequency of forms of γράφειν in Paul's introductory formulae has already been noted.[27] The use of such expressions is by no means unique to Paul, but the concentration of similar language throughout the New Testament is surely noteworthy. However it is to be explained, the commonness of γράφειν formulae in Paul's quotations locates him squarely in the mainstream of early Christian biblical interpretation.

(b) The percentage of adapted citations identified in Paul's letters (60 percent) places him at the high end of the spectrum among the authors surveyed here. Comparable figures were obtained for Plutarch's *Letter of Condolence* (52 percent), "Longinus'" *On the Sublime* (50 percent), the *Damascus Document* (58 percent), and the

---

[23] On the central role of Homer in the educational systems of Antiquity, see Marrou, *History*.

[24] Whether Paul's Gentile readers would have been aware of his free approach to the wording of the Jewish Scriptures is a different question, one that cannot begin to be answered here.

[25] Many of Philo's interpretive additions and substitutions fit this category.

[26] Often in Philo, occasionally in the Qumran *pesharim* (e.g. *1QpHab* 12.1/12.6–7) and Paul (Rom 4.3/4.9, 9.33/10.11, 1 Cor 15.27).

[27] See heading (3) above.

Biblical Antiquities of Pseudo-Philo (48 percent). Comparisons of this sort are of limited significance, of course, since they overlook differences in the manner and frequency of adaptations in the various documents. Moreover, many of the materials examined here contained too few quotations to allow for reliable conclusions about their attitude toward the wording of their source text. Nevertheless, the extreme frequency with which Paul adapted the wording of the biblical text surely says something about how important it was to him that his quotations communicate exactly what he intended in adducing a particular passage. Such close attention to the implications of every word is at least consistent with the suggestion that Paul drew his quotations from a personal collection of excerpts to which he resorted for meditation and study when he was traveling or otherwise denied access to a written copy of the Scriptures.

(c) The prominent role of omissions and grammatical adjustments in Paul's citation technique is wholly consistent with the practices of the other authors surveyed here. The relative frequency of some of the other types of adaptations, on the other hand, calls for comment. Substitutions are used more often by Paul than by most of the other authors studied here, but the practice is still common enough that no definite significance can be read into Paul's usage. Additions are likewise more numerous in Paul's letters than in the bulk of the literature, but there is nothing in Paul to compare with the blatant insertions that recur in Philo's allegorical rendering of Genesis. In fact, most of Paul's additions appear in combined and conflated citations, a thoroughly normal procedure, and the few interpretive additions that can be identified (Rom 10.11, 10.15, 1 Cor 15.45, 2 Cor 6.18) are all quite minor in significance. Shifts in word order, on the other hand, occur far more often in Paul's quotations than in any of the other materials examined here. The most common reason for such a change is to highlight a particular point of contact between the quotation and its new context. The unusual frequency of this technique in Paul agrees well with the close integration between quotation and interpretation/application that can be seen throughout his letters, a closeness that is unlikely to have arisen with such consistency in the moment of dictation.

(d) Though a number of examples of combined and conflated citations were noted in the documents studied here, nothing in them could even begin to compare with the elaborate constructions encountered in Rom 3.10–18 and 2 Cor 6.16–18. In the other materials, combinations are limited for the most part to two verses (as in Rom 9.25–6 and 1 Cor 15.54–5), or else the wording of several passages has been so commingled that even identifying their sources becomes problematic.[28] The closest parallels to Paul's practice would seem to be a single instance in *On the Sublime* 9.6 and another in *CD* 20.22, but even these pale beside the verbal complexity and rhetorical sophistication of the Pauline combinations. The common impression that these passages represent genuine works of art is thus reinforced by the comparative materials. This in turn agrees well with other evidence that highlights the importance of literary and rhetorical concerns in the way Paul handles the wording of his quotations.

2. Form and freedom

Up to now the focus of the present investigation has been entirely descriptive. The aim has been to discover to what extent the apostle Paul followed the methods of his Greco–Roman contemporaries in the way he framed his quotations from the Jewish Scriptures, with special emphasis on the way he handled the wording of his biblical *Vorlage*. Careful study has shown that for the most part Paul adhered to the normal literary practices of his day. This conclusion leads to another more difficult question: why do Paul and his contemporaries diverge so sharply from modern concerns to reproduce the precise wording of an outside text? What made Greco–Roman society (including its Jewish component) so tolerant of even the most obvious "interpretive renderings" of its archetypal texts? What literary and/or social factors contributed to the continuance of what modern readers would regard as an intolerably permissive state of affairs?

The most common explanation begins with the observation that Greco–Roman society around the turn of the era remained a fundamentally oral culture in which genuine literacy was uncommon and memory quotation the rule. In such an environment (so the argument goes) mistakes and interpretive elements were bound to creep into the text of any quotation, no matter how familiar the source. But while there is certainly no denying the oral dimensions of ancient society, the evidence that several of the writers surveyed here (including the apostle Paul) derived their quotations from some sort of written text argues against such an oversimplified under-

---

[28] On the latter point, see especially *Bar* 2.21–3 and 2.29–35.

standing of citation technique in the ancient world. While it would certainly be anachronistic to think of ancient writers checking the wording of their references in the moment of dictation, the evidence that at least some ancient readers took extensive notes while reading and then referred back to these notes when preparing a later composition is widespread, and cannot be ignored.[29] Paul Achtemeier's depiction of Greco–Roman society as "a culture of high residual orality which nevertheless communicated significantly by means of literary creations"[30] is quite apt, and to overemphasize either the oral or the literary dimensions of that culture is to court misunderstanding.

More helpful than broad generalizations about the oral nature of ancient society and the importance of quotation from memory are specific observations about the various ways in which citizens of the ancient world would have encountered the "text" of an original composition. Though the level of literacy in the Greco–Roman world remains a subject of debate,[31] it seems likely that for the bulk of the population the most common means of experiencing a "text" was in the form of an oral recitation or performance. Episodes from the Homeric epics were recited regularly at public festivals and private parties. Performances of classical and contemporary plays drew huge and enthusiastic crowds to the local theaters. Reciting and listening to artfully prepared speeches was a highly popular form of entertainment. For the Jewish community, one could add here the regular public readings and translations of the Scriptures that took place in the synagogue every Sabbath and at festivals. Except where individual listeners may have committed a passage to memory, the audience in these situations had no way to check the oral performance of a text against its original written form. In such a context, the wording of the recitation actually supersedes the written text; cloaked in the authority of the original, it retains its own inherent power to move its hearers regardless of how closely it adheres to the original composition. For the ancients, moving the

[29] The evidence is laid out in chap. 3. See also the helpful discussion of composition techniques and the related notes in Achtemeier, 12–15. Achtemeier's otherwise helpful and illuminating article is at its weakest when he adopts the common expedient of assuming that memory quotation is the necessary alternative to looking up a reference in the moment of composition (26–7).

[30] *Ibid.*, 3. A lengthy discussion of the dynamic interplay between oral and written culture in the ancient world can be seen in Harris, *Literacy*, chap. 2.

[31] A thorough and judicious review of the evidence appears in William Harris's recent book, *Ancient Literacy*.

audience was the chief aim of any oral recitation, whether that movement involved only the hearers' emotions or their beliefs and wills as well. In this sense, the same power is at work in the rhapsode's interpretation of Homer as in the meturgeman's translation of the Torah.[32] "Interpretive renderings" are thus an integral part of every public presentation of a written text, a reality well understood and perhaps even anticipated by ancient audiences.

Within the Jewish sphere, moreover, a long-standing tradition allowed for repeated reinterpretation and even rewriting of certain parts of the biblical record so as to draw out its significance for a later time. Already within the canonical text, the book of Deuteronomy covers much the same ground as the books of Exodus, Numbers, and Leviticus, while the books of Chronicles offer an even closer rewriting of the books of Kings. In several places narrative sections in the prophetic books overlap the versions found in the historical books. Numerous instances of the reuse of biblical traditions, motifs, and even specific language recur throughout the literature.[33] While it is doubtful whether Jewish readers around the turn of the era would have understood the notion of "inner-biblical exegesis," their constant exposure to such "interpretive renderings" within the pages of Scripture itself would have shaped the expectations of even the most illiterate attendees at the regular readings in the Jewish synagogues. The growth of the so-called "oral Torah," that body of interpretive traditions and legal rulings that circulated orally alongside the written text, no doubt reinforced this blurring of the lines between text and interpretation in early Judaism.

Among the more literate members of society, a category that includes all of the writers surveyed here, the opportunities for exposure to written texts were of course much broader. In addition to studying physical copies of the work itself, an educated reader would have had access to numerous "rewritten" or adapted versions of the same base text, not to mention the influence of an endless stream of quotations scattered throughout the writings of ancient and contemporary authors. On the Greco–Roman side, the most obvious examples of such "rewritten" texts are the various expansions of the Homeric epics that were incorporated into the so-called

---

[32] For this reason one should not overly stress the "targumic" quality of the New Testament quotations. Apart from the fact that there is no actual translation involved, the "targumizing" process itself is only one manifestation of a larger cultural and literary reality.

[33] See especially Fishbane, *Interpretation*.

"Homeric cycle" from classical times onward. In a similar manner, countless plays were framed around familiar episodes from the *Iliad* or *Odyssey* in order to drive a point home to a later audience. A similar approach can be seen in those Jewish materials that modern investigators call "rewritten Bible." Included here are such diverse works as the book of *Jubilees*, the *Temple Scroll* and *Genesis Apocryphon* from Qumran, Pseudo-Philo's *Biblical Antiquities*, and Josephus' *Jewish Antiquities*.[34] Similar reworkings of the biblical text to serve a later interest can be seen in the testamentary literature of early Judaism (e.g. the *Testament of Abraham*, *Testaments of the Twelve Patriarchs*, etc.) and in such documents as the *Life of Adam and Eve* and *Joseph and Aseneth*. Although little is known about how widely some of these texts circulated in the Jewish community, the sheer number of documents extant makes it unlikely that any educated Jew could have been ignorant of the entire genre. Since works of this sort were being composed throughout the period in question, there is ample reason to suppose that they reflect the same "free" attitude toward the use of the biblical (and Homeric) text that comes to expression in the citation technique of Paul and his contemporaries.

Indirect contacts such as these – oral recitation, "inner-biblical exegesis," literary citations, and "rewritten" texts – played a vital role in shaping the way even the more literate members of Greco–Roman (and Jewish) society related to the archetypal texts of their culture. Nonetheless, many of these same people also carried on a regular program of studies in the texts themselves. From infancy the epics of Homer (and/or the Jewish Scriptures, as the case may be) served as the cornerstone of the ancient educational system, so much so that one occasionally sees references to a person who has learned the entire corpus by heart.[35] The sheer breadth of quotations from these sources in the literary product of antiquity, combined with the close integration of the quoted texts into their new argumentative contexts, is sufficient to show that ancient authors did not cease their readings in the Homeric epics (or the Jewish Scriptures) once they had completed their formal educations.

[34] See the discussions by Harrington, "Narratives," in Kraft and Nickelsburg (eds.), *Early Judaism*, 239–46, and Philip S. Alexander, "Retelling the Old Testament," in Carson and Williamson (eds.), *It is Written*, 99–121.

[35] On the central place of Homer in the Greco–Roman educational system, see Marrou, *History*. Comments concerning students who had memorized the entire Torah recur throughout the rabbinic literature, but it is difficult to know how much of the rabbinic educational system can be read back into the Second Temple period.

Surely these direct and repeated encounters with the primary text would have more than offset any broader societal tendencies toward a looser, more "interpretive" rendering of the ancient classics.

Or would it? In an era when books are published and printed in thousands or even millions of standardized copies, it is easy to forget that for the ancient reader, no two manuscripts of the same work were exactly alike. In fact, one of the first tasks of every schoolmaster was to collate the readings of his students' manuscripts to insure that everyone in the class was working from the same text.[36] While many of the differences between manuscripts were clearly accidental, recent studies suggest that intentional interpolations and interpretive renderings played a greater role in the scribal practices of antiquity than has been recognized heretofore. Stephanie West has examined the wealth of papyrus fragments from the Ptolemaic period that have turned up in the sands of Egypt. Her studies show that the manuscript tradition for the Homeric epics remained highly fluid until the text was finally standardized in the mid-second century B.C.E., with additional lines, transpositions, and a variety of unattested secondary variants appearing throughout the period. In her view, such variations can only be attributed to the activities of rhapsodes and/or scribes seeking to update or "improve" the traditional texts.[37] Even more revealing is the evidence from the caves of Qumran, where ancient biblical manuscripts have yielded a wealth of clearly interpretive variants.[38] A careful analysis of the evidence leads Shemaryahu Talmon to speak of a "controlled freedom of textual variation" that arose out

[36] Marrou, *History*, 165; cf. *Saint Augustin et la Fin de la Culture Antique* (Paris: E. de Boccard, 1938), 22.

[37] West, 5–14. On the influence of rhapsodes on the language of ancient manuscripts, see Reynolds and Wilson, 23–7, and D. L. Page, *Actors' Interpolations in Greek Tragedy* (Oxford: Clarendon, 1934). On the commonness of scribal emendations and interpolations, see Marrou, *Augustin*, 22–3; G. M. Bolling, *External Evidence of Interpolation in Homer* (Oxford: Clarendon, 1925); M. van der Valk, *Criticism*; R. Renehan, *Greek Textual Criticism: A Reader* (Cambridge: Harvard University Press, 1969); M. J. Apthorp, *The Manuscript Evidence for Interpolation in Homer* (Heidelberg: Carl Winter and Universitätsverlag, 1980).

[38] See especially Talmon, "Textual Study," 338–78, and the numerous examples cited in Talmon's earlier articles, "Aspects" and "*DSIa*." Patrick Skehan ("Qumran," 151), discussing the variant readings in *1QIsᵃ*, speaks similarly of "an exegetical process at work within the transmission of the text itself." See also Fishbane, *Interpretation*; M. J. Mulder, "The Transmission of the Biblical Text," in *Mikra*, 90–5; I. L. Seeligmann, "Indications of Editorial Alteration and Adaptation in the Massoretic Text and the Septuagint," *VT* 11 (1961), 201–21; J. König, "L'existence et l'influence d'une herméneutique sur la transmission du texte hébreu de la Bible," *RHR* 187 (1975), 122–5.

of the scribe's role as not only a copyist but also an interpreter of the sacred text. According to Talmon, "The limited flux of the textual transmission of the Bible appears to be a legitimate and accepted phenomenon of ancient scribal tradition and not a matter which resulted from sheer incompetence or professional laxity."[39] A similar scribal ethos can be traced in the various tendentious adaptations and interpretive renderings that made their way into the biblical text in both the Samaritan Pentateuch and the Greek version of the Jewish Scriptures.[40]

Thus it appears that even regular scholarly study in the "original text" would have offered no true counterbalance to the broader societal tendency toward "interpretive renderings" of both the Homeric epics and the Jewish Scriptures. In fact, one could even argue that the social realities of the transmission process actually reinforced this more "liberal" attitude toward the written text. The issue can be approached from two different angles. In the first place, the very fact that no two manuscripts were exactly alike would have fostered a wholly different view of the "fixedness" of the original text than that which prevails in modern print-oriented societies. While the basic parameters of the text were no doubt regarded as fixed, no single manuscript could ever claim to have preserved the precise and unalterable wording of the original composition. In fact, the application of a rudimentary form of "textual criticism" (albeit of a highly subjective nature) was a *sine qua non* for the use of any ancient manuscript, especially where a reader had been exposed to differing copies of the same work over the course of a lifetime. In other words, the physical realia of the manuscripts would have encouraged not a reverence for the wording of this or that exemplar, but rather a critical attitude toward the text of every individual manuscript.

More important for the present study are a variety of insights that

[39] Talmon, "Textual Study," 326. Michael Fishbane paints a similar picture of scribal practices in ancient Israelite society in *Interpretation*, Part I.

[40] On the Samaritan Pentateuch, see most recently Abraham Tal, "The Samaritan Targum of the Pentateuch," in Mulder (ed.), *Mikra*, 200–16. Good recent summaries of LXX translation technique include S. P. Brock, "Translating the Old Testament," in Carson and Williamson (eds.), *It is Written*, 87–98, and Emanuel Tov, "The Septuagint," in Mulder (ed.), *Mikra*, 168–78. The latter article includes a list of similar studies on individual books (168 n. 22). The extent to which the LXX represents an "interpretive rendering" of the Hebrew original would of course have been much more evident to a reader versed in both Greek and Hebrew (as is normally assumed for Paul) than to one whose knowledge of Hebrew was limited to an occasional reference in a synagogue sermon.

have been emerging recently concerning the role and function of the scribe in antiquity. Shemaryahu Talmon's conclusions about scribal practices at Qumran can be applied *mutatis mutandis* to the activities of scribes throughout the ancient world. As an acknowledged expert in both copying and interpreting the written text, the scribe (סופר/ γραμματικός) occupied a prestigious position in ancient society, "a comprehensive literate who could be author, editor, transmitter, scribe, or copyist when performing different aspects of his profession."[41] With such a multifaceted role, says Talmon, "it surely must be agreed that [the scribe's] literary techniques would not automatically change whenever he turned from one task to another. Quite to the contrary, it may be taken for granted that some basic canon of literary conventions would be followed by him in all the variegated performances of his craft."[42] The result was that "controlled freedom of textual variation" that can be seen even now in the manuscript tradition of antiquity.[43] In view of the prominent place of scribes as the authorized guardians and interpreters of the ancestral texts, it can be presumed that their approach to the written word would have exercised a decisive influence on the way documents were viewed and handled in the society at large, especially among the literati. When this dominant scribal ethos is set alongside the interpretive freedom exhibited in oral recitations and literary citations from the period and the continued production of "rewritten" texts of various sorts, one arrives at a coherent and holistic explanation for the relatively "free" approach to the written text that can be seen throughout Greco–Roman antiquity.[44] Only where

---

[41] Talmon, "Textual Study," 336. The *grammatikoi* of Alexandria were merely the upper echelon of such scholars, especially after the persecutions of Ptolemy VIII Euergetes II (mid-second century B.C.E.) scattered the *grammatikoi* and their students all across the Greek world (so Pfeiffer, 1:157–8, 252–3). On the activities of scribes and textual scholars in the ancient world, see the studies cited in note 37.

[42] *Ibid.*, 337.

[43] *Ibid.*, 326. Stendahl, 127, makes brief reference to the same reality in his analysis of the free handling of the "formula quotations" in Matthew.

[44] Talmon overlooks the possibility of such a broader sphere of reference when he links the scribal practices of Qumran to a continuation of the creative milieu of the biblical period within the Qumran community. In his view, "the Covenanters [of Qumran] perceived themselves as standing within the framework of the biblical period, not less so than, e.g. the author of the book of Daniel ... The Qumran Covenanters did not subscribe to the idea that the biblical era had been terminated, nor did they accept the concomitant notion that 'biblical' literature and literary standards had been superseded or replaced by new conceptions. ... [The] Qumran literati considered biblical literature a living matter, and participated in the ongoing process of its creation" ("Textual Study," 378–9). Even if these observations are true,

a single text-type comes to be regarded as "canonical" and the dominant authority structures wield sufficient power to procure widespread adherence to this text does the fluid approach of this earlier period come to be replaced by a concern for reproducing the precise wording of a single fixed text. The only place in the ancient world where a single text-type appears to have obtained such authoritative backing is in the sphere of rabbinic Judaism.[45]

In the final analysis, of course, there is nothing particularly "first-century" or "Greco–Roman" about the practice of introducing interpretive elements into the wording of a quotation. Similar "interpretive renderings" of significant texts can be seen in nearly every literate culture in Western history, except where formal power structures or informal conventions have placed curbs on the prac-

---

they do not begin to explain the similarities between scribal practices at Qumran and those outside the community. The peculiar Qumran self-understanding may well have reinforced the traditional scribal mindset within the community, but the practices of the Qumran scribes cannot be viewed in isolation. The similarities between Talmon's view and the various theological explanations examined in chap. 1 are too close to ignore.

[45] Present evidence suggests that by the early second century C.E. the rabbis had set their stamp of approval on a single text of the Hebrew Bible, the so-called "proto-Masoretic" text, which was then preserved according to rigid standards of copying and use (see the references in chap. 2, note 23). Even after the language of other compositions (the Homeric epics, the New Testament writings) had become substantially fixed, no social institutions ever arose to insure that these texts would be reproduced according to a common wording and format. The difference is evident in the way the respective texts are quoted in the first few centuries of the common era. While Greco–Roman authors continue in their earlier patterns (Johnson offers examples from Lucian, Julian, Gallus, Porphyry, Maximus *et al.*; Achtemeier (27) adds several passages from Dio Chrysostom) and the looseness of early Christian quotations is legendary, biblical citations in the rabbinic literature seem for the most part to follow the wording of the "Masoretic" Hebrew text (see Bonsirven, 336; Victor Aptowitzer discovered numerous textual variants in the rabbinic quotations from the books of Samuel and Joshua, but few true adaptations). Of course, conclusions about rabbinic practices must remain tentative in view of the lack of a critical text for the rabbinic materials and the possibility that later copyists systematically "corrected" the wording of rabbinic quotations toward the Masoretic text. Nevertheless, the apparent differences in citation technique coincide well with the social realities of rabbinic Judaism *vis-à-vis* the broader Greco–Roman world. Talmon, "Textual Study," comes to a similar conclusion as a result of his investigation of scribal practices at Qumran: "The right to introduce variations into the biblical text, within limits, had come to be Bible-oriented copyists and quoting authors of post-biblical works, together with the transmitted writings. Mechanical faithfulness to the letter of the sanctified traditional literature is to become the rule only after the undirected and intuitive process of canonisation had completed its course, i.e. not earlier than the first century B.C.E. and not later than the second century C.E."

tice.[46] The process is more complicated, however, in cases where the text in question (Hebrew Bible, New Testament, Koran, etc.) is held to be authoritative within a particular community. Here the normative text becomes an object of study in its own right, while the ongoing necessity of applying its fixed wording to changing social or intellectual conditions or to situations of conflict produces a further stock of exegetical traditions.[47] Explicit citations invariably play a vital role in attempts to mediate between the fixed language of the written text and the living needs of the community. Where the technology of writing is not sufficiently developed to allow for an easy verification of references, it is only natural that the interpretational needs that called forth a particular quotation would find expression in the way the verse is quoted.[48] The resultant tension between the wording of the quotation and the language of the underlying text becomes apparent only when these "interpretive renderings" are themselves set down in writing. Even then, there is no basis for assuming that a community accustomed to such practices would conclude that the wording of the sacred text had somehow been violated in these instances. The fact that faithful copies of the authoritative text remained available in the local repository for consultation and use by members of the community (or their authorized representatives) would presumably have served as a subliminal corrective to any concerns that an individual reader might have felt on this score.[49] In an environment such as this, it

[46] More recent parallels include the formal protection accorded the text of the Koran in Muslim tradition and the informal dominance of the King James Version of the Bible in English-speaking Christianity well into the present century.

[47] Geza Vermes terms these two parallel processes "pure exegesis" and "applied exegesis": see "Bible and Midrash: Early Old Testament Exegesis," in *Studies*, 59–91.

[48] In the famous words of T. W. Manson, 135: "We tend to think of the text as objective fact and interpretation as subjective opinion. It may be doubted whether the early Jewish and Christian translators and expositors of Scripture made any such sharp distinction. For them the meaning of the text was of primary importance; and they seem to have had greater confidence than we moderns in their ability to find it. Once found it became a clear duty to express it; and accurate reproduction of the traditional wording of the Divine oracles took second place to publication of what was held to be their essential meaning and immediate application."

[49] Alternatively, one could speak with Michael Fishbane of the social acceptability of incorporating interpretive elements into the language of the authoritative text itself, as a means of insuring its continued relevance and validity for the life of the community. To use Fishbane's words, "The insertion of a human teaching and correcting voice into the context of a divine teaching and prescribing voice serves to highlight the fact that the divine *traditum* survives only in so far as it is transmitted, only in so far as its meanings are understood, and often only to the extent that its meanings are altered or transformed" (*Interpretation*, 272).

requires little imagination to see how the use of "interpretive renderings" as a technique for advancing a particular reading of the authoritative text could be regarded as an entirely acceptable phenomenon.

3. Intentional adaptations?

With this understanding of the way literary and cultural factors shaped the handling of quotations in antiquity, the question naturally arises as to how appropriate it would be to describe the editorial intrusions of ancient authors as "intentional adaptations." Two possible answers to this question can be immediately set aside. On the one hand, the evidence of the present study makes it impossible to argue that the authors were simply unaware that they were not always following the precise wording of their *Vorlagen*. Neither the close and repeated links between the revised wording of a citation and its later context nor the sophisticated literary artistry seen in certain "combined citations" can be explained by a theory of arbitrary lapses in memory. On the other hand, it would be equally inappropriate to think of the New Testament authors as consciously manipulating the wording of the biblical text to create artificial prooftexts to support their own tendentious arguments. The bulk of the adaptations uncovered in the present study have little effect on the meaning of the original text, and those that do can normally be explained as the result of a sincere attempt to understand the meaning of a particular passage within the context of the author's own culture and/or community.

A more adequate explanation would view the authors studied here as working consciously but unreflectively within the bounds of contemporary literary conventions that governed the way quotations could be handled. In the case of the apostle Paul, such a view of his activities finds support in his often-noted lack of reflection on the broader hermeneutical issues implied in his own use of Scripture. Only in 2 Cor 3.7–18 and such isolated verses as Rom 4.23–4, 15.4 and 1 Cor 9.10, 10.11 does Paul offer any hint as to the principles that guided his "Christian" reading of the Jewish Scriptures, and even these statements illuminate only a fraction of his explicit appeals to Scripture. A thorough examination of Paul's hermeneutic would have to take into account both the way Paul *reads* individual passages from the Jewish Scriptures, i.e. how his Jewish and Christian presuppositions and his own existential concerns shape the way he understands and appropriates the wording of the biblical text, and his method of *applying* these same texts to the concrete circumstances of his readers in order to bring about changes in their understanding and/or behavior. As with the translation of a document from one language to another, the intrusion of interpretational elements at both stages of the process (i.e. in understanding the text and in applying it) is unavoidable.[50] In some cases the hermeneutical process leads Paul to reshape the wording of a biblical quotation, while in others the original text is deemed suitable to express what Paul himself understands and wants his readers to glean from a given verse. In both instances the result might still be called an "interpretive rendering" of the original text, a contextual application in which introductory expressions, interpretive comments, explicit deductions, and (in many cases) changes in the wording of the text work together to bring the authoritative biblical text to bear on the pastoral needs of the people being addressed.

[50] The question of how far it is possible to distinguish "Paul the reader" from "Paul the rhetor" must be left for a separate study.

SELECT BIBLIOGRAPHY

1. Primary sources

(1) Hebrew Bible

Elliger, K., and W. Rudolph, eds. *Biblia Hebraica Stuttgartensia*. Stuttgart: Deutsche Bibelstiftung, 1977.

(2) New Testament

Aland, Kurt, Matthew Black, Carlo M. Martini, Bruce M. Metzger, and Allen Wikgren, eds. *The Greek New Testament*. 3rd edn. New York: United Bible Societies, 1975.
Novum Testamentum Graece. 26th edn. Stuttgart: Deutsche Bibelgesellschaft, 1979.
Tischendorf, Constantinus, ed. *Novum Testamentum Graece*. 2 vols. Leipzig: Giesecke und Devrient, 1869–72.

(3) Septuagint

Academia Litterarum Gottingensis. *Septuaginta: Vetus Testamentum Graecum*. Göttingen: Vandenhoeck und Ruprecht, 1931– .
   Vol. I: Wevers, John William, ed. *Genesis* (1974).
   Vol. II/2: Wevers, John William, ed. *Leviticus* (1986).
   Vol. III/1: Wevers, John William, ed. *Numeri* (1982).
   Vol. III/2: Wevers, John William, ed. *Deuteronomium* (1977).
   Vol. X: Rahlfs, A., ed. *Psalmi cum Odis* (1931).
   Vol. XI/4: Ziegler, Joseph, ed. *Iob* (1982).
   Vol. XIII: Ziegler, Joseph, ed. *Duodecim prophetae* (1943).
   Vol. XIV: Ziegler, Joseph, ed. *Isaias* (1939).
   Vol. XVI/1: Ziegler, Joseph, ed. *Ezechiel* (1952).
Brooke, Alan England, Norman McLean, and Henry St. J. Thackeray, eds. *The Old Testament in Greek*. Cambridge University Press, 1906–40.
Field, F., ed. *Origenis Hexaplorum quae supersunt*. 2 vols. Oxford: Clarendon, 1867, 1875; repr., Hildesheim: G. Olms, 1964.
Holmes, A. Roberto, and Jacobus Parsons, eds. *Vetus Testamentum Graecum cum variis lectionibus*. 5 vols. Oxford: Clarendon, 1798–1827.
Rahlfs, Alfred. *Septuaginta*. Stuttgart: Deutsche Bibelstiftung, 1935.

(4) Qumran

Discoveries in the Judean Desert. Oxford: Clarendon, 1955– .
  Vol. I: Barthélemy, D., and J. T. Milik, eds. Qumran Cave I (1955).
  Vol. III: Baillet, M., J. T. Milik, and R. de Vaux, eds. *Les 'Petites
    Grottes' de Qumrân* (1962).
  Vol. V: Allegro, John M., ed. *Qumrân Cave 4: I. (4Q158–4Q186)*
    (1968).
  Vol. VII: Baillet, M., ed. *Qumrân Grotte 4: III. 4Q482–4Q520* (1982).
  Vol. VIII: Tov, Emanuel, with Robert A. Kraft, ed. *The Greek Minor
    Prophets Scroll from Naḥal Ḥever (8ḤevXIIgr)* (1989).
Kobelski, Paul J. *Melchizedek and Melchiresha: The Heavenly Prince of
  Light and the Prince of Darkness in Qumran Literature.* CBQMS 10.
  Washington, DC: Catholic Biblical Association, 1981.
Lohse, Eduard, ed. *Die Texte aus Qumran: Hebräisch und Deutsch.* 2nd edn,
  revised and enlarged. Münich: Kösel-Verlag, 1971.
Sukenik, E. L., ed. *Otsar ha-megiloth ha-genuzoth she-beyadei ha-universitah
  ha-ivrit.* Jerusalem: Magnes, 1954.

(5) Philo

Cohn, Leopold, and Paul Wendland, ed. *Philonis Alexandri opera quae
  supersunt.* 7 vols. Berlin: Georgii Reimeri, 1896–1915.
Colson, F. H., and G. H. Whittaker, eds. *Philo*, vols. 1, 3. Loeb Classical
  Library. London: William Heinemann, 1929, 1930; New York: G. P.
  Putnam's Sons, 1929, 1930; repr., Cambridge: Harvard University
  Press, 1962, 1968; London: William Heinemann, 1962, 1968.

(6) Apocrypha and pseudepigrapha

Academia Litterarum Gottingensis. *Septuaginta: Vetus Testamentum
  Graecum.* Göttingen: Vandenhoeck and Ruprecht, 1931– .
  Vol. VIII/1: Hanhart, Robert, ed. *Esdrae liber I* (1974).
  Vol. VIII/4: Hanhart, Robert, ed. *Iudith* (1983).
  Vol. VIII/5: Hanhart, Robert, ed. *Tobit* (1983).
  Vol. IX/1: Kappler, Werner, ed. *Maccabaeorum liber I* (1936).
  Vol. IX/2: Hanhart, Robert, ed. *Maccabaeorum liber II* (1959).
  Vol. IX/3: Hanhart, Robert, ed. *Maccabaeorum liber III* (1960).
  Vol. XII/2: Ziegler, Joseph, ed. *Sapientia Iesu Filii Sirach* (1965).
  Vol. XVI/4: Ziegler, Joseph, ed. *Susanna, Daniel, Bel et Draco* (1954).
Geffcken, J. *Die Oracula Sibyllina.* GCS 8. Leipzig: Hinrich, 1902.
Harrington, D. J., J. Cazeaux, C. Perrot, and P.-M. Bogaert. *Pseudo-
  Philon, Les Antiquités Bibliques.* 2 vols. Sources chrétienne 229–30.
  Paris: Cerf, 1976.
James, M. R. *The Testament of Abraham.* Cambridge University Press,
  1892.
McCown, C. C. *The Testament of Solomon.* Leipzig: Hinrich, 1922.
Odeberg, H. *3 Enoch.* Cambridge University Press, 1928; reprinted with
  Prolegomenon by J. Greenfield, New York: Ktav, 1973.

Rahlfs, Alfred, ed. *Septuaginta*. Stuttgart: Deutsche Bibelstiftung, 1935.

Schmidt, F. *Le Testament d'Abraham: Introduction, édition de la recension courte, traduction et notes.* 2 vols. Ph.D. dissertation, University of Strasbourg, 1971.

Thackeray, H. St J., ed. "The Letter of Aristeas." In *Introduction to the Old Testament in Greek*, ed. H. B. Swete, 501–74. Cambridge University Press, 1900.

VanderKam, J. C. *Textual and Historical Studies in the Book of Jubilees.* HSM 14. Missoula, MT: Scholars, 1977.

(7) Homer

Allen, Thomas W., ed. *Homeri Ilias*. 3 vols. Oxford: Clarendon, 1931.

Bérard, Victor. *L'Odyssey*. Paris: Les belles lettres, 1924.

Merry, W. Walter, and James Riddell, eds. *Homer's Odyssey, Books I-XII*, 2nd edn rev. Oxford: Clarendon, 1886.

Monro, D. B., ed. *Homer's Odyssey, Books XIII-XXIV*. Oxford: Clarendon, 1901.

(8) Greco–Roman authors

Aly, Wolfgang, ed. *Strabonis Geographica*, vol. 1. Bonn: Rudolf Habelt, 1968.

Aujac, Germaine, ed. *Géographie: Strabon*, vol. 1. Budé Series. Paris: Les belles lettres, 1969.

Babbitt, F. C., ed. *Plutarch's Moralia*, vol. 1–2. Loeb Classical Library. London: William Heinemann, 1927, 1928; New York: G. P. Putnam's Sons, 1927, 1928; repr., Cambridge: Harvard University Press, 1969, 1962; London: William Heinemann, 1969, 1962.

Buffière, Felix, ed. *Allégories d'Homère*. Budé Series. Paris: Les belles lettres, 1962.

Hani, Jean. *Consolation à Apollonius*. Paris: Klincksieck, 1972.

Jones, H. L., ed. *The Geography of Strabo*, vol. 1. Loeb Classical Library. London: William Heinemann, 1917; New York: G. P. Putnam's Sons, 1917; repr., Cambridge: Harvard University Press, 1960; London: William Heinemann, 1960.

Russell, D. A., ed. *On Sublimity*. Oxford: Clarendon, 1964.

Valgiglio, Ernesto. *De Audiendus Poetis*. Turin: Loescher Editore, 1973.

2. Secondary sources

Aageson, James. "Paul's Use Of Scripture: A Comparative Study of Biblical Interpretation in Early Palestinian Judaism and the New Testament with Special Reference to Romans 9–11." Ph. D. dissertation, University of Oxford, 1984.

Achtemeier, Paul. "*Omne verbum sonat*: The New Testament and the Oral Environment of Late Antiquity." *JBL* 109 (1990), 3–27.

Aejmelaeus, Anneli. "What Can We Know About the Hebrew *Vorlage* of the Septuagint?" *ZAW* 99 (1987), 58–89.

Aicher, Georg. *Das Alte Testament in der Mischna*. Freiburg: Herder, 1906.

Albrektson, B. "Reflections on the Emergence of Standard Text of the Hebrew Bible." In *[9th IOSOT] Congress Volume, Göttingen, 1977*, ed. J. A. Emerton, 49–65. VTSup 29. Leiden: Brill, 1978.

Allen, T. W. *Homer: The Origins and the Transmission*. Oxford: Clarendon, 1924.

Aly, Z., and L. Koenen. *Three Rolls of the Early Septuagint: Genesis and Deuteronomy*. Bonn: R. Habelt, 1980.

Amir, Y. "Philo and the Bible." *Studia Philonica* 2 (1973), 1–8.

Apthorp, M. J. *The Manuscript Evidence for Interpolation in Homer*. Heidelberg: Carl Winter and Universitätsverlag, 1980.

Aptowitzer, V. *Das Schriftwort in der rabbinischen Literatur*. 5 vols. Vienna: Kais. Akademie der Wissenschaften, 1906–15. Reprinted with Prolegomenon by Samuel Loewinger in Library of Biblical Studies, ed. H. M. Orlinsky, New York: Ktav, 1970.

Archer, G. L., and G. C. Chirichigno, *Old Testament Quotations in the New Testament: A Complete Survey*. Chicago: Moody, 1983.

Barrett, C. K. *The First Epistle to the Corinthians*. Harper's New Testament Commentaries. New York: Harper and Row, 1968.

"The Interpretation of the Old Testament in the New." In *Cambridge History of the Bible*, ed. P. R. Ackroyd and C. F. Evans, 1:377–411. Cambridge University Press, 1963.

The Second Epistle to the Corinthians. Harper's New Testament Commentaries. New York: Harper and Row, 1973.

Barthélemy, D. "A Reexamination of the Textual Problems in 2 Sam 11.2–1 Kings 2.11 in the Light of Certain Criticisms of *Les devanciers d'Aquila*." In *[1972] Proceedings of IOISCS: Pseudepigrapha Seminar*, ed. Robert Kraft, 16–89. SBLSCS 2. Missoula, MT: Scholars, 1972.

Les devanciers d'Aquila. VTSup 10. Leiden: Brill, 1963.

"Text, Hebrew, History of." In *Interpreter's Dictionary of the Bible, Supplementary Volume*, ed. Keith Crim, 878–84. Nashville: Abingdon, 1976.

Beker, J. C. *Paul the Apostle*. Philadelphia: Fortress, 1980.

Betz, Hans Dieter. *Galatians: A Commentary on Paul's Letter to the Churches in Galatia*. Hermeneia Series. Philadelphia: Fortress, 1979.

Betz, O. *Offenbarung und Schriftforschung in der Qumransekte*. Tübingen: Mohr, 1960.

Bickermann, Elias J. "Some Notes on the Transmission of the Septuagint." In *Studies in Jewish and Christian History*, 1:137–66. Leiden: Brill, 1976.

"The Septuagint As a Translation." *PAAJR* 28 (1959), 1–39.

Bock, Darrell L. "Evangelicals and the Use of the Old Testament in the New." *BSac* 142 (1985), 209–23, 306–19.

Böhl, E. *Die alttestamentlichen Citaten im Neuen Testament*. Vienna: W. Braumüller, 1878.

Forschungen nach einer Volksbibel zur Zeit Jesu, und deren Zusammenhang mit der Septuaginta Übersetzung. Vienna: W. Braumüller, 1873.

Bolling, G. M. *External Evidence of Interpolation in Homer*. Oxford: Clarendon, 1925.

Bonsirven, Joseph. *Exégèse rabbinique et exégèse paulinienne*. Paris: Beauchesne et ses fils, 1939.

Borgen, Peder. *Philo, John and Paul*. Brown Judaic Studies 131. Atlanta: Scholars, 1987.

"Philo of Alexandria." In *Jewish Writings of the Second Temple Period*, ed. Michael E. Stone, 233–82. Compendia Rerum Iudaicarum ad Novum Testamentum II/2. Assen: van Gorcum, 1984; Philadelphia: Fortress, 1984.

Braun, H. "Das Alte Testament im Neuen Testament." *ZTK* 59 (1962), 16–31.

Qumran und das Neue Testament. 2 vols. Tübingen: Mohr, 1966.

Brin, G. "Concerning Some of the Uses of the Bible in the *Temple Scroll*." *RevQ* 12 (1987), 519–28.

Brock, Sebastian P. "Bibelübersetzungen: Die Übersetzungen des Alten Testaments ins Griechische." In *Theologische Realenzyklopädie*, ed. Gerhard Krause and Gerhard Müller, 6:163–72. Berlin, New York: de Gruyter, 1976.

"Lucian *redivivus*: Some Reflections on Barthélemy's *Les devanciers d'Aquila*." In *Studia Evangelica 5*, ed. F. L. Cross, 176–81. TU 103. Berlin: Akademie Verlag, 1968.

Brooke, George J. *Exegesis at Qumran. 4QFlor in its Jewish Context*. Sheffield: JSOT Press, 1985.

"Qumran *Pesher*: Towards the Redefinition of a Genre." *RevQ* 10 (1981), 483–503.

"The Amos–Numbers Midrash (*CD* 7.13b–8.1a) and Messianic Expectation." *ZAW* 92 (1980), 397–404.

Brownlee, William. "Biblical Interpretation Among the Sectaries of the Dead Sea." *BA* 14 (1951), 54–76.

"The Background of Biblical Interpretation at Qumran." In *Qumrân, sa piété, sa théologie et son milieu*, ed. M. Delcor, 183–93. BETL 46. Paris: Duculot, 1978.

The Meaning of the Qumran Scrolls for the Bible. New York: Oxford University Press, 1964.

The Midrash Pesher of Habakkuk. Missoula, MT: Scholars, 1979.

The Text of Habakkuk in the Ancient Commentary From Qumran. Philadelphia: Society for Biblical Literature and Exegesis, 1959.

Bruce, F. F. *Biblical Exegesis in the Qumran Texts*. Grand Rapids: Eerdmans, 1959.

Buffière, Felix. *Les mythes d'Homère et la pensée grecque*. Paris: Les belles lettres, 1956.

Burton, Ernest deWitt. *A Critical and Exegetical Commentary on the Epistle to the Galatians*. ICC Series. Edinburgh: T. and T. Clark, 1921.

Callaway, Mary C. "Mistress and the Maid: Midrashic Traditions Behind Galatians 4.21–31." *Radical Religion* 2 (1975), 94–101.

Capellus, L. "Quaestio de locis parallelis Veteris et Novi Testamenti." In *Critica sacra*, 443–557. Paris: S. et G. Cramoisy, 1650.

Carmignac, J. "Les citations de l'Ancien Testament dans 'La guerre des fils de lumière contre les fils de ténèbres.'" *RB* 63 (1956), 234–60.

"Les citations de l'Ancien Testament, et specialement des Poèmes du Serviteur, dans les Hymnes de Qumran." *RevQ* 2 (1960), 357–94.

Carpzov, Johann G. *A Defense of the Hebrew Bible*. Translated by Moses Marcus. London: Bernard Lintot, 1729.

Carson, D. A., and H. G. M. Williamson, eds. *It is Written: Scripture Citing Scripture: Essays in Honour of Barnabas Lindars*. Cambridge University Press, 1988.

Charles, R. H. *The Book of Jubilees*. London: A. and C. Black, 1902; repr., Jerusalem: Makor, 1972.

"The Fragments of a Zadokite Work." In *The Apocrypha and Pseudepigrapha of the Old Testament*, 2:785–834. Oxford: Clarendon, 1913.

ed. *The Apocrypha and Pseudepigrapha of the Old Testament*. 2 vols. Oxford: Clarendon, 1913.

Charlesworth, James H. "Biblical Interpretation: The Crucible of the Pseudepigrapha." In *Text and Testimonies: Essays in Honour of A. F. J. Klijn*, ed. T. Baarda, A. Hilhorst, G. P. Luttikhuisen, and A. S. van der Woude. Kampen: Kok, 1988.

ed. *The Old Testament Pseudepigrapha*. 2 vols. Garden City, NY: Doubleday, 1983–5.

Clemen, August. *Der Gebrauch des Alten Testaments in den neutestamentlichen Schriften*. Gütersloh: C. Bertelsmann, 1895.

Cohn-Sherbock, Daniel. "Paul and Rabbinic Exegesis." *SJT* 35 (1982), 117–32.

Collins, Anthony. *A Discourse on the Grounds and Reasons of the Christian Religion*. London, n.p., 1724.

Colson, F. H. "Philo's Quotations From the Old Testament." *JTS* 41 (1940), 237–51.

Cox, Claude, ed. *VI Congress of IOSCS*. SBLSCS 23. Atlanta: Scholars, 1987.

Cranfield, C. E. B. *A Critical and Exegetical Commentary on the Epistle to the Romans*. ICC Series. Edinburgh: T. & T. Clark, 1979.

Cross, Frank M. *The Ancient Library of Qumran and Modern Biblical Studies*. Garden City, NY: Doubleday, 1958.

"The Contribution of the Qumran Discoveries to the Study of the Biblical Text." *IEJ* 16 (1966), 81–95.

"The History of the Biblical Text in Light of Discoveries in the Judaean Desert." *HTR* 57 (1964), 281–99.

"The Text Behind the Text of the Hebrew Bible." *Bible Review* 1 (1985), 13–25.

and Shemaryahu Talmon, eds. *Qumran and the History of the Biblical Text*. Cambridge: Harvard University Press, 1975.

Daube, David. "Alexandrian Methods of Interpretation and the Rabbis." In *Festschrift Hans Lewald*. Basel: Helbing and Lichtenhahn, 1953; repr., Vaduz, Lich.: Topos-Verlag, 1978.

Davies, W. D. "Reflections About the Use of the Old Testament in the New in its Historical Context." *JQR* 74 (1983), 105–36.

Davison, J. A. "The Transmission of the Text." In *A Companion to Homer*, ed. A. J. B. Wace and Frank H. Stubbings, 215–33. London: Macmillan, 1962; New York: St. Martin's Press, 1962.

Dawson, John David. "Ancient Alexandrian Interpretation of Scripture." Ph.D. dissertation, Yale University, 1988.

Deissmann, Adolf. *Die Septuaginta-Papyri und andere altchristliche Texte der Heidelberger Papyrussammlung.* Heidelberg: C. Winter, 1905.

Dimant, Devorah. "Qumran Sectarian Literature." In *Jewish Writings of the Second Temple Period*, ed. Michael E. Stone, 483–550. Compendia Rerum Iudaicarum ad Novum Testamentum II/2. Assen: Van Gorcum, 1984; Philadelphia: Fortress, 1984.

Dittmar, W. *Vetus Testamentum in Novo: Die alttestamentlichen Paralleles des Neuen Testaments im Wortlaut der Urtexte und der Septuaginta.* Göttingen: Vandenhoeck, 1903.

Dodd, C. H. *According to the Scriptures.* London: Nisbet, 1952.
The Old Testament in the New. London: University of London Press, Athlone Press, 1952.

Doeve, J.W. *Jewish Hermeneutics in the Synoptic Gospels and Acts.* Translated by Mrs. G. E. van Baaren-Pape. Assen: Van Gorcum, 1954.

Döpke, J. C. C. *Hermeneutik der neutestamentlichen Schriftsteller.* Leipzig: Vogel, 1829.

Dorival, Gilles, Marguerite Harl, and Olivier Munnich. *La Bible grecque des Septante. Du judaïsme hellénistique au christianisme ancien.* Paris: Cerf and CNRS, 1988.

Drusius, Joannes. *Parallela sacra.* Frankfurt: Aegidium Radacum, 1594.

Edersheim, Alfred. *The Life and Times of Jesus the Messiah.* 8th rev. edn. New York: Longmans, Green and Co., 1896–8; repr., Grand Rapids: Eerdmans, 1971.

Ellis, E. Earle. "*Midrash Pesher* in Pauline Hermeneutics." In *Prophecy and Hermeneutics in Early Christianity: New Testament Essays*, 173–81. WUNT 18. Tübingen: Mohr, 1978.
"Midrash, Targum, and New Testament Quotations." In *Neotestimentica et Semitica: Studies in Honour of Matthew Black*, ed. E. Earle Ellis and Max Wilcox, 61–69. Edinburgh: T. and T. Clark, 1969.
Paul's Use of the Old Testament. Edinburgh: Oliver and Boyd, 1957; repr., Grand Rapids: Baker, 1981.
Prophecy and Hermeneutics in Early Christianity: New Testament Essays. WUNT 18. Tübingen: Mohr, 1978.

Endres, John C. *Biblical Interpretation in the Book of Jubilees.* CBQMS 18. Washington, DC: Catholic Biblical Association, 1987.

Feldman, Louis H. "Hellenizations in Josephus' Portrayal of Man's Decline." In *Religions in Antiquity: Essays in Memory of Edwin Ramsdell Goodenough*, ed. Jacob Neusner, 336–53. Studies in the History of Religions 14. Leiden: Brill, 1968.
Josephus and Modern Scholarship (1937–1980). Berlin, New York: de Gruyter, 1984.

Fernández Marcos, Natalio. "The Lucianic Text in the Books of Kingdoms: From Lagarde to the Textual Pluralism." In *De Septuaginta: Studies in Honour of John William Wevers on his Sixty-Fifth Birthday,* ed. Albert Pietersma and Claude Cox. Mississauga, Ont.: Benben Publications, 1984.

Fishbane, Michael. *Biblical Interpretation in Ancient Israel*. Oxford: Clarendon, 1985; New York: Oxford University Press, 1985.

"The Qumran-*Pesher* and Traits of Ancient Hermeneutics." In *Proceedings of the Sixth World Congress of Jewish Studies*, ed. Avigdor Shinan, 1:97–114. Jerusalem: World Union of Jewish Studies, 1977.

Fitzmyer, J. A. "*4QTestimonia* and the New Testament." *TS* 18 (1957), 513–37.

"The Use of Explicit Old Testament Quotations in the Qumran Literature and in the New Testament." *NTS* 7 (1961), 297–333.

Fox, Michael V. "The Identification of Quotations in Biblical Literature." *ZAW* 92 (1980), 416–31.

Freund, Richard. "Murder, Adultery, or Theft?" *SJOT* 2 (1989), 72–80.

Furnish, Victor Paul. *II Corinthians*. Anchor Bible Series. Garden City, NY: Doubleday, 1984.

Gerhardsson, Birger. *Memory and Manuscript*. Translated by Eric J. Sharpe. Lund: Gleerup, 1961; Copenhagen: Munksgaard, 1961.

Gooding, D. W. "A Sketch of Current Septuagint Studies." *Proceedings of the Irish Biblical Association* 5 (1981), 1–13.

"Pedantic Timetabling in 3rd Book of Reigns." *VT* 15 (1965), 153–66.

"Problems of Text and Midrash in the Book of Reigns." *Textus* 7 (1969), 1–29.

Gordis , Robert. "Quotations as a Literary Usage in Biblical, Oriental, and Rabbinic Literature." *HUCA* 22 (1949), 157–219.

"The Origin of the Masoretic Text in the Light of Rabbinic Literature and the Qumran Scrolls." In *The Word and the Bible: Studies in Biblical Language and Literature*, 29–74. New York: Ktav, 1976.

Goshen-Gottstein, Moshe. "Bible Quotations in the Sectarian Dead Sea Scrolls." *VT* 3 (1953), 79–82.

"Hebrew Biblical Manuscripts: Their History and Their Place in the HUBP Edition." *Bib* 48 (1967), 243–90.

"Linguistic Structure and Tradition in the Qumran Documents." In *Aspects of the Dead Sea Scrolls*, ed. Chaim Rabin and Yigael Yadin, 101–37. Scripta Hierosolymitana 4. Jerusalem: Magnes, 1958.

"The Hebrew Bible in the Light of the Qumran Scrolls and the Hebrew University Bible." In *[12th IOSOT] Congress Volume, Jerusalem, 1986*, ed. J. A. Emerton, 42–53. VTSup 40. Leiden: Brill, 1988.

Gough, H. *The New Testament Quotations*. London: Walton and Maberly, 1855.

Greenburg, Moshe. "The Stabilization of the Text of the Hebrew Bible." *JAOS* 76 (1956), 157–67.

Greenspoon, Leonard. "The Use and Misuse of the Term 'LXX' and Related Terminology in Recent Scholarship." *BIOSCS* 20 (1987), 21–9.

Gwynn, Aubrey O. *Roman Education From Cicero to Quintilian*. Oxford: Clarendon, 1926.

Hadas, Moses. *The Third and Fourth Books of Maccabees*. New York: Harper and Bros., 1953.

Hanhart, R. "Das Neue Testament und die grieschiche Überlieferung des Judentums." In *Überlieferungsgeschichtliche Untersuchungen*, ed. F. Paschke, 293–303. TU 125. Berlin: Akademie, 1981.

"Die Bedeutung der Septuaginta in neutestamentliche Zeit." *ZTK* 81 (1984), 395–416.

Hanson, A. T. *Jesus Christ in the Old Testament*. London: SPCK, 1965.

Studies in Paul's Technique and Theology. Grand Rapids: Eerdmans, 1974; London: SPCK, 1974.

The Living Utterances of God. London: Darton, Longman, and Todd, 1983.

The New Testament Interpretation of Scripture. London: SPCK, 1980.

Harrington, Daniel J. "The Bible Rewritten (Narratives)." In *Early Judaism and Its Modern Interpreters*, ed. Robert A. Kraft and George W. E. Nickelsburg, 239–47. Atlanta: Scholars, 1986.

"The Biblical Text of Pseudo-Philo's *Liber Antiquitatum Biblicarum*." *CBQ* 33 (1971), 1–11.

Harris, J. Rendel. "St. Paul's Use of Testimonies in the Epistle to the Romans." *Exp*, 8th ser., 17 (1919), 401–14.

Testimonies. 2 vols. Cambridge University Press, 1916–20.

Harris, William V. *Ancient Literacy*. Cambridge: Harvard University Press, 1989.

Hatch, Edwin. *Essays in Biblical Greek*. Oxford: Clarendon, 1889.

Hays, Richard B. *Echoes of Scripture in the Letters of Paul*. New Haven, London: Yale University Press, 1989.

Helmbold, William C., and Edward O'Neill, eds. *Plutarch's Quotations*. American Philological Association Monographs 19. Oxford: B. H. Blackwell, 1959.

Hodgson, Robert. "The Testimony Hypothesis." *JBL* 98 (1979), 361–78.

Horgan, Maurya. *Pesharim: Qumran Interpretation of Biblical Books*. CBQMS 8. Washington, DC: Catholic Biblical Association, 1979.

Horton, F. L., Jr. "Formulas of Introduction in the Qumran Literature." *RevQ* 7 (1971), 505–14.

Howard, George. "Frank Cross and Recensional Criticism." *VT* 21 (1971), 440–50.

"*Kaige* Readings in Josephus." *Textus* 8 (1973), 45–54.

"Lucianic Readings in a Greek Twelve Prophets Scroll from the Judean Desert." *JQR* 62 (1971), 51–60.

"The 'Aberrant' Text of Philo's Quotations Reconsidered." *HUCA* 44 (1973), 197–207.

"The Quinta of the Minor Prophets: A First Century Septuagint Text?" *Bib* 55 (1974), 15–22.

Hühn, Eugen. *Die alttestamentlichen Citate und Reminiscenzen im Neuen Testamente*. 2 vols. Freiburg: Mohr, 1899–1900.

Jachmann, G. "Vom früh alexandrinischen Homertext." In *Nachrichten von der Akademie der Wissenschaften in Göttingen aus dem Jahre 1949: Philologische-Historische Klasse*, 167–224. Göttingen: Vandenhoeck und Ruprecht, 1949.

Jellicoe, Sidney. *Studies in the LXX: Origins, Recensions, and Interpretations*. New York: Ktav, 1974.

Jellicoe, Sidney, ed. *The Septuagint and Modern Study.* Oxford: Clarendon, 1968.

Johnson, Franklin. *The Quotations in the New Testament From the Old.* London: Baptist Tract and Book Society, 1895.

Juel, Donald. *Messianic Exegesis: Christological Interpretation of the Old Testament in Early Christianity.* Philadelphia: Fortress, 1988.

Junius, Franciscus. *Sacrorum parallelorum libri tres.* London: G. Bishop, 1590.

Kahle, Paul. "Der gegenwartige Stand der Erforschung der in Palästina neu gefundenen hebräischen Handschriften: 27. Die in August 1952 entdeckte Lederrolle mit dem griechischen Text der kleinen Propheten und das Problem der Septuaginta." *TLZ* 79 (1954), 81–94.

The Cairo Genizah. London: Oxford University Press, 1947.

Kaiser, Walter C. *The Uses of the Old Testament in the New.* Chicago: Moody, 1985.

Käsemann, Ernst. *Commentary on Romans.* Grand Rapids: Eerdmans, 1980.

Katz, P. *Philo's Bible.* Cambridge University Press, 1950.

"Septuagintal Studies in Mid-Century." In *The Background of the New Testament and Its Eschatology,* ed. W. D. Davies and David Daube, 176–208. Cambridge University Press, 1956.

Kautzsch, Emil. *De Veteris Testamenti locis a Paulo Apostolo allegatis.* Leipzig: Metzger und Wittig, 1869.

Kenyon, Frederic. *Books and Readers in Ancient Greece and Rome.* Oxford: Clarendon, 1932.

Our Bible and the Ancient Manuscripts. 5th edn. revised by A. W. Adams. London: Eyre and Spottiswoode, 1958.

Klauser, Theodor, ed. *Reallexicon für Antike und Christentum.* Stuttgart: Heirsemann, 1954. S. v. "Buch I (technische)," by L. Koep; "Buch II (heilig, kultisch)," by S. Morenz and J. Leipoldt; "Florilegium," by Henry Chadwick.

Klein, Ralph. *Textual Criticism of the Old Testament: From the Septuagint to Qumran.* Guides to Biblical Scholarship. Philadelphia: Fortress, 1974.

Knox, B. M. W., and P. E. Easterling. "Books and Readers in the Ancient World." In *Cambridge History of Ancient Literature,* ed. P. E. Easterling and B. M. W. Knox, 1:1–41. Cambridge University Press, 1985.

Knox, W. L. "Notes on Philo's Use of the Old Testament." *JTS* 41 (1940), 30–4.

Koch, Dietrich-Alex. "Beobachtungen zum christologischen Schriftgebrauch in den vorpaulinischen Gemeinden." *ZNW* 71 (1980), 174–91.

"Der Text von Hab. 2.4b in der Septuaginta und im Neuen Testament." *ZNW* 76 (1985), 68–85.

Die Schrift als Zeuge des Evangeliums. Tübingen: Mohr, 1986.

König, J. "L'existence et l'influence d'une herméneutique sur la transmission du texte hébreu de la Bible." *RHR* 187 (1975), 122–5.

Kraft, Robert A. "Barnabas' Isaiah-Text and the 'Testimony Book' Hypothesis." *JBL* 79 (1960), 336–50.

and George W. E. Nickelsburg, eds. *Early Judaism and Its Modern Interpreters*. Atlanta: Scholars, 1986.

Kugel, James L., and Rowan Greer. *Early Biblical Interpretation*. Library of Early Christianity 3. Philadelphia: Westminster, 1986.

Lagarde, Paul Anton de. *Ankündigung einer neuen Ausgabe der grieschischen Übersetzung des Alten Testaments*. Göttingen: Dieterischen Univ.-Buchdruckerei, 1882.

Lamberton, Robert. *Homer the Theologian*. Berkeley: University of California Press, 1986.

Le Déaut, R. "Targumic Literature and New Testament Interpretation." *BTB* 4 (1974), 243–89.

Lieberman, Saul. *Greek in Jewish Palestine*. New York: Jewish Theological Seminary, 1942.

Hellenism in Jewish Palestine. New York: Jewish Theological Seminary, 1950.

Lindars, Barnabas. *New Testament Apologetic*. Philadelphia: Westminster, 1961.

"Second Thoughts – IV. Books of Testimonies." *ExpTim* 75 (1964), 173–5.

Loewinger, Samuel. "The Variants in *DSI II*." *VT* 4 (1954), 155–64.

Longenecker, Richard. *Biblical Exegesis in the Apostolic Period*. Grand Rapids: Eerdmans, 1974.

McNamara, Martin. "Half A Century of Targum Study." *IBS* 1 (1979), 157–68.

Targum and Testament. Shannon, New York: Irish University Press, 1972.

The New Testament and the Palestinian Targum to the Pentateuch. Rome: Pontifical Biblical Institute, 1966.

Malan, F. S. "The Use of the Old Testament in I Corinthians." In *The Relationship Between the Old and New Testament: Proceedings of the Sixteenth Annual Meeting of the New Testament Society of South Africa, July 1–3, 1980*, 134–70. Neotestamentica 14. Bloemfontaine, S. A.: N. T. Society of South Africa, 1981.

Malherbe, A. *Social Aspects of Early Christianity*. 2nd edn, enlarged. Philadelphia: Fortress, 1983.

Manson, T.W. "The Argument From Prophecy." *JTS* 46 (1945), 129–36.

Marrou, H. I. *History of Education in Antiquity*. 3rd edn. translated by George Lamb. New York: Sheed and Ward, 1956.

Mánek, J. "Composite Quotations in the New Testament and their Purpose." *Communio Viatorum* 13 (1970), 181–8.

Metzger, Bruce M. *A Textual Commentary on the Greek New Testament*. Corrected edition. London, New York: United Bible Societies, 1975.

"The Formulas Introducing Quotations of Scripture in the New Testament and in the Mishnah." In *Historical and Literary Studies: Pagan, Jewish, Christian*, 52–63. Grand Rapids: Eerdmans, 1968.

Mez, A. *Die Bibel des Josephus*. Basel: Jaeger und Kober, 1895.

Michel, O. *Paulus und seine Bibel*. Gütersloh: C. Bertelsmann, 1929; repr., Darmstadt: Wissenschaftliche Buchgesellschaft, 1972.

Miller, Merrill. "Targum, Midrash, and the Use of the Old Testament in the New Testament." *JSJ* 2 (1971), 29–82.

Mink, Hans A. "The Use of Scripture in the *Temple Scroll* and the Status of the Scroll as Law." *SJOT* 1 (1987), 20–50.

Mulder, M. J., ed. *Mikra: Text, Translation, Reading and Interpretation of the Hebrew Bible in Ancient Judaism and Early Christianity.* Compendia Rerum Iudaicarum ad Novum Testamentum II/1. Assen: Van Gorcum, 1988; Philadelphia: Fortress, 1989.

Müller, Morgens. "*Hebraica sive graeca veritas*: The Jewish Bible at the Time of the New Testament and the Christian Bible." *SJOT* 2 (1989), 55–71.

Muraoka, T. "The Greek Texts of Samuel-Kings: Incomplete Translations or Recensional Activity?" In *1972 Proceedings of IOSCS: Pseudepigrapha Seminar*, ed. Robert A. Kraft, 90–107. SBLSCS 2. Missoula, MT: Scholars, 1972.

Newsome, Carol A. "The *Psalms of Joshua* from Qumran Cave 4." *JJS* 39 (1988), 56–73.

Nickelsburg, George W. E. "Reading the Hebrew Scriptures in the First Century: Christian Interpretations in Their Jewish Context." *Word and World* 3 (1983), 38–50.

Nicole, R. "The New Testament Use of the Old Testament." In *Revelation and the Bible*, ed. Carl F. H. Henry, 137–51. Grand Rapids: Baker, 1958.

O'Connell, Kevin G. "Greek Versions (Minor)." In *Interpreter's Dictionary of the Bible: Supplementary Volume*, ed. Keith Crim, 377–81. Nashville: Abingdon, 1976.

Orlinsky, H. M. "Current Progress and Problems in Septuagint Research." In *The Study of the Bible Today and Tomorrow*, ed. H. R.Willoughby, 144–61. University of Chicago Press, 1947.

"On the Present State of Proto-Septuagint Studies." *JAOS* 61 (1941), 81–91.

"The Septuagint as Holy Writ and the Philosophy of the Translators." *HUCA* 46 (1975), 89–114.

Owen, H. *The Modes of Quotation Used by the Evangelical Writers Explained and Vindicated.* London: J. Nichols, 1789.

Patte, Daniel. *Early Jewish Hermeneutics in Palestine.* SBLDS 22. Missoula, MT: Scholars, 1975.

Pfeiffer, Rudolf. *History of Classical Scholarship.* Vol. 1, *From the Beginning to the End of the Hellenistic Age.* Oxford: Clarendon, 1968.

Pick, P. "Philo's Canon of the Old Testament and His Manner of Quoting the Alexandrian Version." *Journal of the Society of Biblical Literature and Exegesis* (1884), 126–43.

Pietersma, Albert, and Claude Cox, eds. *De Septuaginta: Studies in Honour of John William Wevers on his Sixty-Fifth Birthday.* Mississauga, Ont.: Benben Publications, 1984.

Pinner, H. L. *The World of Books in Classical Antiquity.* Leiden: A. W. Sijthoff, 1948.

Rabin, Chaim. "The Dead Sea Scrolls and the History of the Old Testament Text." *JTS* 6 (1955), 174–82.

The Zadokite Documents. Oxford: Clarendon, 1954.

Rabinowitz, I. "*Pesher/Pittaron*: Its Biblical Meaning and Its Significance in the Qumran Literature." *RevQ* 8 (1972–74), 219–32.

Rahlfs, A. "Über Theodotion–Lesarten im Neuen Testament und Aquila–Lesarten bei Justin." *ZNW* 20 (1921), 182–99.

Randolph, T. *The Prophecies and Other Texts Cited in the New Testament.* Oxford: J. and J. Fletcher, 1782.

Reynolds, L. D, and Nigel Wilson. *Scribes and Scholars: A Guide to the Transmission of Greek and Latin Literature.* 2nd edn, revised and enlarged. Oxford: Clarendon, 1974.

Roberts, B. J. "Some Observations on the Damascus Document and the Dead Sea Scrolls." *BJRL* 34 (1951–2), 366–87.

"Text: Old Testament." In *Interpreter's Dictionary of the Bible*, ed. G. A. Buttrick. Nashville: Abingdon, 1962.

"The Dead Sea Scrolls and the Old Testament Scriptures." *BJRL* 36 (1953–4), 75–96.

The Old Testament Text and Versions. Cardiff: University of Wales Press, 1951.

"The Second Isaiah Scroll From Qumran." *BJRL* 42 (1959), 132–44.

"The Textual Transmission of the Old Testament." In *Tradition and Interpretation : Essays by Members of the Society for Old Testament Studies*, ed. G. W. Anderson, 1–30. Oxford: Clarendon, 1979; New York: Oxford University Press, 1979.

Roberts, C. H. "Books in the Greco–Roman World and in the New Testament." In *Cambridge History of the Bible*, ed. P. R. Ackroyd and G. F. Evans, 1:48–66. Cambridge University Press, 1963–70.

and T. C. Skeat. *The Birth of the Codex.* Oxford University Press for the British Academy, 1983.

Roepe, G. *De Veteris Testamenti locrum in apostolorum libris allegatione.* n.p., 1827.

Rosenblatt, S. *The Interpretation of the Bible in the Mishnah.* Baltimore: Johns Hopkins Press, 1935.

Ryle, H. E. *Philo and Holy Scripture.* London: Macmillan, 1895.

Sanders, J. A. "Habakkuk in Qumran, Paul, and the Old Testament." *JR* 39 (1959), 232–44.

"The Old Testament in *11QMelchizedek*." *JANESCU* 5 (1973), 373–82.

Schaller, Berndt. "ΗΞΕΙ ΕΚ ΣΙΩΝ ΗΟ ΡΥΟΜΕΝΟΣ: Zur Textgestalt von Jes 59.20f in Rom 11.26f." In *De Septuaginta: Studies in Honour of John William Wevers on his Sixty-Fifth Birthday*, ed. Albert Pietersma and Claude Cox, 201–6. Mississauga, Ont.: Benben Publications, 1984.

"Zum Textcharakter der Hiobzitate im paulinischen Schrifttum." *ZNW* 71 (1980), 21–6.

Schubart, W. *Die Buch bei den Grieschen und Römern.* Berlin: G. Reimer, 1907; repr., Heidelberg: L. Schneider, 1962.

Schwarz, Ottilie. *Der erste Teil der Damaskusschrift und das Alte Testament.* Diest: Lichtland, 1965.

Scott, James. *Principles of New Testament Quotation: Established and Applied to Biblical Science.* 2nd edn. Edinburgh: T. and T. Clark, 1877.

Seeligmann, I. L. "Indications of Editorial Alteration and Adaptation in the Massoretic Text and the Septuagint." *VT* 11 (1961), 201–21.

Segal, M. H. "The Promulgation of the Authoritative Text of the Hebrew Bible." *JBL* 72 (1953), 35–47.

Siegfried, Carl. "Philo und der überlieferte Text der Septuaginta." *ZWT* 16 (1873), 217–38, 411–28, 522–40.

Silberman, Lou H. "Unriddling the Riddle: A Study in the Structure and Language of the Habakkuk Pesher." *RevQ* 3 (1961–2), 323–64.

Silva, Moises. "The New Testament Use of the Old: Text-Form and Authority." In *Scripture and Truth*, ed. D. A. Carson and John D. Woodbridge. Leicester: Inter-Varsity, 1983; Grand Rapids: Zondervan, 1983.

Skehan, Patrick W. "*4QLXXNum*: A Pre-Christian Reworking of the Septuagint." *HTR* 70 (1977), 39–50.

"Qumran and Old Testament Criticism." In *Qumrân, sa piété, sa théologie et son milieu*, ed. M. Delcor, 163–82. BETL 46. Paris: Duculot, 1978.

"Scrolls and the Old Testament Text." *McCQ* 21 (1968), 273–83.

"The Biblical Scrolls From Qumran and the Text of the Old Testament." *BA* 28 (1965), 87–100.

"The Qumran Manuscripts and Textual Criticism." In *Volume de [IOSOT 2nd] Congrès, Strasbourg, 1956*, ed. G. W. Anderson, 148–58. VTSup 4. Leiden: Brill, 1957.

Slomovic, E. "Toward an Understanding of the Exegesis in the Dead Sea Scrolls." *RevQ* 7 (1969–71), 3–15.

Smith, D. Moody. "The Pauline Literature." In *It is Written: Scripture Citing Scripture: Essays in Honour of Barnabas Lindars*, ed. D. A. Carson and H. G. M. Williamson, 265–91. Cambridge University Press, 1988.

"The Use of the Old Testament in the New." In *The Use of the Old Testament in the New and Other Essays*, ed. James B. Efird, 3–65. Durham: Duke University Press, 1972.

Sperber, A. "New Testament and Septuagint." *JBL* 59 (1940), 193–293.

Staerk, W. "Die alttestamentlichen Citate bei den Schriftstellen des Neuen Testaments." *ZWT* 35 (1892), 464–85; 36 (1893), 70–98; 38 (1895), 218–30; 40 (1897), 211–68.

Stendahl, Krister. *The School of St. Matthew*. Acta Seminarii Neotestamentica Upsaliensis 20. Lund: Gleerup, 1954; Copenhagen: Munksgaard, 1954; 1st American edn, Philadelphia: Fortress, 1968.

Sundberg, A. C. "On Testimonies." *NovT* 3 (1959), 268–81.

Surenhusius, Guilielmus. ספר המשוה *sive βιβλος καταλλαγης in quo secundum veterum Theologorum Hebraeorum*. Amsterdam: Johannes Boom, 1713.

Swete, H. B. *Introduction to the Old Testament in Greek*. Cambridge University Press, 1900.

Talmon, Shemaryahu. "Aspects of the Textual Transmission of the Bible in the Light of the Qumran Manuscripts." *Textus* 4 (1964), 95–132.

"*DSIa* as a Witness to Ancient Exegesis of the Book of Isaiah." *Annual of the Swedish Theological Institute* 1 (1962), 62–72.

"The Old Testament Text." In *The Cambridge History of the Bible*, vol. 1: *From the Beginnings to Jerome*, ed. P. R. Ackroyd and C. F. Evans, 159–99. Cambridge University Press, 1970.

"The Textual Study of the Bible – A New Outlook." In *Qumran and the History of the Biblical Text*, ed. Frank M. Cross and Shemaryahu Talmon, 321–400. Cambridge: Harvard University Press, 1975.

Thackeray, H. St. J. *The Septuagint and Jewish Worship*. 2nd edn. London: H. Milford, 1923.

Tholuck, F. A. G. *Das Alte Testament im Neuen Testament*. 6th edn. Gotha: F. A. Perthes, 1877.

"The Citations of the Old Testament in the New." Translated by Charles A. Aiken. *BSac* 11 (1854), 568–616.

Tov, Emanuel. "A Modern Textual Outlook Based on the Qumran Scrolls." *HUCA* 53 (1982), 11–27.

"Hebrew Biblical Manuscripts From the Judean Desert: Their Contribution to Textual Criticism." *JJS* 39 (1988), 5–37.

"Lucian and Proto-Lucian: Toward a New Solution of the Problem." *RBib* 79 (1972), 101–113.

"The Nature of the Hebrew Text Underlying the LXX: A Survey of the Problems." *JSOT* 7 (1978), 53–68.

"The Orthography and Language of the Hebrew Scrolls Found at Qumran and the Origin of These Scrolls." *Textus* 13 (1986), 31–57.

"The Rabbinic Tradition Concerning the 'Alterations' Inserted into the Greek Pentateuch and their Relation to the Original Text of the LXX." *JSJ* 15 (1984), 65–89.

"The State of the Question: Problems and Proposed Solutions." In *1972 Proceedings of IOSCS: Pseudepigrapha Seminar*, ed. Robert A. Kraft, 3–15. SBLSCS 2. Missoula, MT: Scholars, 1972.

The Text-Critical Use Of the Septuagint in Biblical Research. Jerusalem: Simor, 1981.

"The Textual Affiliations of 4QSam^a." *JSOT* 14 (1979), 37–53.

ed. *The Greek Minor Prophets Scroll from Naḥal Ḥever (8ḤevXIIgr)*. DJD VIII. Oxford: Clarendon, 1990.

Toy, C. H. *Quotations in the New Testament*. New York: Scribner, 1884.

Turner, Eric Gardiner. *Greek Manuscripts of the Ancient World*. Princeton University Press, 1971.

Greek Papyri: An Introduction. Oxford: Clarendon, 1968.

The Typology of the Early Codex. Philadelphia: University of Pennsylvania Press, 1977.

Turpie, David M. *The New Testament View of the Old*. London: Hodder and Stoughton, 1872.

The Old Testament in the New. London: Williams and Norgate, 1868.

Ulrich, Eugene. "Horizons of Old Testament Textual Research at the Thirtieth Anniversary of Qumran Cave 4." *CBQ* 46 (1984), 613–36.

Valk, M. van der. *Textual Criticism of the Odyssey*. Leiden: A. W. Sijthoff, 1949.

VanderKam, J. C. *Textual and Historical Studies in the Book of Jubilees*. HSM 14. Missoula, MT: Scholars, 1977.

"The Textual Affinities of the Biblical Citations in the *Genesis Apocryphon*." *JBL* 97 (1978), 45–55.

Venard, L. "Citations de l'Ancien Testament dans le Nouveau Testament." In *Supplément au Dictionnaire de la Bible*, ed. Louis Pirot, 2:23–51. Paris: Letouzey et Ané, 1934.

Vermes, Geza. "Apropos des Commentaires bibliques découvertes à Qumrân." *RHPR* 35 (1955), 95–102.

"Bible and Midrash: Early Old Testament Exegesis." In *Cambridge History of the Bible*, ed. P. R. Ackroyd and G. F. Evans, 1:198–231. Cambridge University Press, 1963.

"Interpretation, History of: At Qumran and in the Targums." In *Interpreter's Dictionary of the Bible, Supplementary Volume*, ed. Keith Crim, 438–43. Nashville: Abingdon, 1976.

Post-Biblical Jewish Studies. Leiden: Brill, 1975.

"The Qumran Interpretation of Scripture in its Historical Setting." In *Post-Biblical Jewish Studies*, 37–49. Studies in Judaism in Late Antiquity 8. Leiden: Brill, 1975.

Vollmer, Hans A. *Die alttestamentlichen Citate bei Paulus*. Freiburg: Mohr, 1895.

Waard, Jan de. *A Comparative Study of the Old Testament Text in the Dead Sea Scrolls and in the New Testament*. Leiden: Brill, 1965.

Weingreen, J. *Introduction to the Critical Study of the Text of the Hebrew Bible*. Oxford: Clarendon, 1982; New York: Oxford University Press, 1982.

Wernberg-Møller, P. "Some Reflections on the Biblical Material in the *Manual of Discipline*." *ST* 1 (1955), 40–66.

West, Stephanie. *Ptolemaic Papyri of Homer*. Papyrologica Coloniensis 3. Cologne: Westdeutscher Verlag, 1967.

Wevers, John William. "Barthélemy and Proto-Septuagint Studies." *BIOSCS* 21 (1988), 23–34.

"Proto-Septuagint Studies." In *The Seed of Wisdom: Essays in Honour of Theophile J. Meek*, ed. William S. Mc Cullough, 58–77. University of Toronto Press, 1964.

"Septuaginta-Forschungen." *TRu* 22 (1954), 85–138, 171–90.

"Septuaginta: Forschungen seit 1954." *TRu* 33 (1968), 18–76.

"Text History and Text Criticism of the Septuagint." In *[9th IOSOT] Congress Volume, Göttingen, 1977*, ed. J. A. Emerton, 392–402. VTSup 29. Leiden: Brill, 1978.

Text History of the Greek Deuteronomy. MSU 13. Göttingen: Vandenhoeck und Ruprecht, 1978.

"The Earliest Witness to the LXX Deuteronomy." *CBQ* 39 (1977), 240–44.

Whiston, William. *An Essay Toward Restoring the True Text of the Old Testament*. London: J. Senex, 1722.

Wilcox, Max. "On Investigating the Use of the Old Testament in the New Testament." In *Text and Interpretation: Studies in the New Testament Presented to Matthew Black*, ed. Ernest Best and R. McL. Wilson, 231–43. New York: Cambridge University Press, 1979.

Ziegler, J. "Die Vorlage der Isaias-Septuaginta (LXX) und die erste Isaias-Rolle von Qumran." *JBL* 78 (1959), 34–59.

Zink, J. L. "Use of the Old Testament in the Apocrypha." Ph.D. dissertation, Duke University, 1963.

INDEX OF PASSAGES CITED

*Books are listed as they appear in the Greek version ("Septuagint"). Passages where Hebrew nomenclature or versification is significant are noted by the symbol (H) (= "Hebrew text").

AUTHOR INDEX